# THE ESSAY

# The Essay

## *Old and New*

Edited By

Edward P. J. Corbett
*Ohio State University*

Sheryl L. Finkle
*Northern Illinois University*

A Blair Press Book

Prentice Hall, Englewood Cliffs, NJ 07632

Library of Congress Cataloging-in-Publication Data

The Essay, old and new / edited by Edward P.J. Corbett, Sheryl L.
Finkle.
p. cm.
Rev. ed. of: The Essay, subjects and stances. 1974.
"A Blair Press book."
Includes bibliographical references and index.
ISBN 0-13-284621-7
1. English essays. 2. American essays. 3. College readers.
I. Corbett, Edward P. J. II. Finkle, Sheryl L. III. Essay,
subjects and stances.
PR1362.E67 1993
824.008--dc20 92-34201
CIP

Editorial/production supervision and interior design: Sally Steele
Copy editor: Roberta Winston
Cover designer: Mark Berghash, 20/20 Services Inc.
Prepress buyer: Herb Klein
Manufacturing buyer: Robert Anderson
Cover art: Juan Gris, *The Open Book*, 1925. Oil on canvas, 73 x 92 cm. ($28^{1/4}$ x $36^{1/4}$ in.) Kunstmuseum Bern, Hermann and Margrit Rupf Foundation.
Acknowledgments appear on pages 415–417, which constitute a continuation of the copyright page.

Blair Press
The Statler Building
20 Park Plaza, Suite 1113
Boston, MA 02116-4399

Printed in the United States of America
10 9 8 7 6 5 4 3 2 1

ISBN 0-13-284621-7

Prentice-Hall International (UK) Limited, *London*
Prentice-Hall of Australia Pty. Limited, *Sydney*
Prentice-Hall Canada Inc., *Toronto*
Prentice-Hall Hispanoamericana, S.A., *Mexico*
Prentice-Hall of India Private Limited, *New Delhi*
Prentice-Hall of Japan, Inc., *Tokyo*
Simon & Schuster Asia Pte. Ltd., *Singapore*
Editora Prentice-Hall do Brasil, Ltda., *Rio de Janeiro*

To our parents and
To our brothers and sisters

# PREFACE

*The Essay, Old and New* presents a collection of essays written during the period ranging from the sixteenth century to the present day. It is, in essence, the second edition of *The Essay: Subject and Stances,* which Prentice Hall published almost twenty years ago in Maynard Mack's Literature Series. The climate for a collection of essays has changed considerably from what it was back then. In the ensuing years, there has been a remarkable revival of interest, at least in English departments, in the essay as a literary genre. A number of English departments have instituted courses in the essay, whereas in the mid-1970s, you would have had to search long and hard in college catalogues to find a listing of such a course. As the Bibliography at the back of this book reveals, a notable number of books and articles on the essay have been published just in the last ten years. Another sign of the revival is the annual publication, starting in 1986, of *The Best American Essays* under the general editorship of Robert Atwan.

*The Essay, Old and New* concentrates on the so-called familiar essay, a type of essay that we attempt to characterize, if not define, in our Introduction. That concentration has served to exclude from this collection such masters of critical and historical essays as John Dryden, Matthew Arnold, Thomas Babington Macaulay, Edmund Wilson, and George Steiner. It also excludes many of the kinds of journalistic writing that appear so often in anthologies designed for freshman English courses. But anyone who reads the full range of the prose pieces included in this book will remark about the amazing variety of the essays presented here. Since its beginnings with Michel de Montaigne, the essay—a term that derives from the French word meaning "a trial, a testing, an experiment"—has ventured into a plethora of new forms. In fact, those of you who were introduced to the essay very early in your schooling may question whether some of the twentieth-century prose pieces that we include can rightfully be called "familiar" or "personal" essays. Others of you, however, may regard the evolution of the essay into a variety of new forms as a mark of its vitality.

We designed this collection, first, for courses in the essay as a distinct literary form. For that reason, we have provided an Introduction that gives a brief history of the essay and an explanation of the nature of this literary form. Each essay is prefaced with a biographical sketch of the author and is followed by questions on the content or form of the essay. The collection is organized into thirteen chapters, each one dealing with a theme that essayists have written about for centuries. Each chapter is prefaced with a discussion of its theme, and within the chapter, the essays are arranged with the earliest examples first, thus illustrating the development of the form. Many of the essayists are part of the canon of English and American literature; but many of the essayists, especially those from the twentieth century, are new practitioners of the art. In the last chapter of the book, there are essays "On the Art of the Essay," all of them written by authors who are represented by another essay in one of the earlier chapters. The book concludes with a fairly extensive Bibliography, provided for those who want to delve more deeply into the history and theory of the essay.

This collection can also be used in writing courses, especially in those courses where the instructor wants to exercise students in writing the freer, more personal forms of prose. Unless students eventually become professional writers, they may have little or no occasion later on in life to write the kind of casual, free-form prose featured in this book, but indulging in this kind of writing can loosen up the flow of words, can engender confidence in fledgling writers, and can lead them to discoveries about themselves and the world of ideas.

Finally, this collection of essays can introduce readers—instructors and students alike—to some very pleasant, entertaining, stimulating, imaginative prose. Literacy empowers the reader and the writer, but it can also introduce the literate person to a whole new world of fantasy, ideas, and emotions. It is a commonplace that children are entranced by fiction, the world of make-believe that they find in fairy tales, stories, poems, and plays; as children grow older, they can discover another world of enchantment in the kind of reading presented in this book. So, we invite you to enjoy, enjoy.

In putting this book together, we owe many debts to many people. First of all, we owe a debt to those elementary, secondary, and college teachers who introduced us to the wonderful world of the essay and to the many authors who wrote the essays that we read and enjoyed. We owe a debt also to those reviewers who evaluated our manuscript at various stages and made helpful suggestions: William Allen, Ohio State University; Chris Anderson, Oregon State University; Mary Bly, University of California, Davis; Robert DiYanni, Pace University; Douglas Hesse, Illinois State University; Betsy Hilbert, Miami-Dade Community College; Charles Schuster, University of Wisconsin, Milwaukee; Michael Shugrue, College of Staten Island; and John Warnock, University of Arizona. We especially want to thank Robert Atwan, who judiciously guided us in choosing the final roster of essays. We owe many debts to the editorial staff of Blair Press: Nancy Perry, Leslie Cavaliere, and LeeAnn Einert; to Roberta Winston, who copy-edited the manuscript; and to Sally Steele, who saw it through production. Finally, we want to thank those who waited patiently for us to get done.

Sheryl L. Finkle
Northern Illinois University

Edward P. J. Corbett
Ohio State University

# Contents


Preface vii

Chronological Table of Contents xvii

Introduction xxi

**CHAPTER 1 On Personal Identity 1**

Abraham Cowley **Of Myself** 2

Jack London **What Life Means to Me** 6

Zora Neale Hurston **How It Feels to Be Colored Me** 14

Eudora Welty **The Little Store** 18

Shelby Steele **On Being Black and Middle Class** 26

**CHAPTER 2 On Family Relationships 39**

William Makepeace Thackeray **On Two Children in Black** 40

W. E. B. Du Bois **Of the Passing of the First-Born** 43

Sherwood Anderson **Discovery of a Father** 48

Joan Didion **On Going Home** 54

N. Scott Momaday **The Way to Rainy Mountain** 57

Alice Walker **Brothers and Sisters** 62

**CHAPTER 3 ON CHARACTER TYPES 67**

SAMUEL JOHNSON **THE HISTORY OF AN ADVENTURER IN LOTTERIES** 68
JOHN HENRY NEWMAN **A DEFINITION OF A GENTLEMAN** 72
H. L. MENCKEN **THE POLITICIAN** 75
DOROTHY PARKER **GOOD SOULS** 79
ELIAS CANETTI **THE TATTLETALE** 85

**CHAPTER 4 ON THE ANIMAL KINGDOM 87**

GILBERT WHITE **ON THE ENGLISH HOUSE-MARTIN** 88
AGNES REPPLIER **A KITTEN** 92
EDWARD HOAGLAND **THE COURAGE OF TURTLES** 99
BARRY LOPEZ **WOLF NOTES** 106
EMILY HAHN **CLEVER HANS** 109

**CHAPTER 5 ON TOWN AND COUNTRY 115**

CHARLES DICKENS **NIGHT WALKS** 116
HENRY DAVID THOREAU **THE PONDS** 124
ANNIE DILLARD **A FIELD OF SILENCE** 127
ALFRED KAZIN **THE BLOCK** 131
GRETEL EHRLICH **THE SMOOTH SKULL OF WINTER** 135
PAUL THEROUX **SUBTERRANEAN GOTHIC** 138

**CHAPTER 6 On Education 145**

Francis Bacon **Of Studies** 146
Benjamin Franklin **On Education** 148
Frederick Douglass **Learning to Read and Write** 152
James Thurber **University Days** 157
Adrienne Rich **Taking Women Students Seriously** 163
Richard Rodriguez **The Achievement of Desire** 171

**CHAPTER 7 On Mortality 179**

Michel de Montaigne **Of Practice** 180
William Hazlitt **On the Feeling of Immortality in Youth** 190
Virginia Woolf **The Death of the Moth** 197
E. B. White **Once More to the Lake** 200
Lewis Thomas **The Long Habit** 206
Richard Selzer **The Knife** 211

**CHAPTER 8 On the National Pastime 217**

Stephen Jay Gould **The Creation Myths of Cooperstown** 218
Wilfred Sheed **Confessions of a Sports Nut** 229
Doris Kearns Goodwin **Fathers, Daughters, and the Magic of Baseball** 238
Gerald Early **Baseball: The Ineffable National Pastime** 241
George F. Will **The Hard Blue Glow** 248
John Updike **Hub Fans Bid Kid Adieu** 254

**CHAPTER 9 ON LANGUAGE 259**

OLIVER GOLDSMITH **OF ELOQUENCE** 260
GEORGE ORWELL **POLITICS AND THE ENGLISH LANGUAGE** 267
HELEN KELLER **THE DAY LANGUAGE CAME INTO MY LIFE** 279
LANGSTON HUGHES **THAT WORD *BLACK*** 282
MAXINE HONG KINGSTON **THE SILENCE OF A CHINESE-AMERICAN SCHOOLGIRL** 284
RUSSELL BAKER **LITTLE RED RIDING HOOD REVISITED** 289

**CHAPTER 10 ON SOCIAL AND POLITICAL ISSUES 293**

JONATHAN SWIFT **A MODEST PROPOSAL** 294
MARY WOLLSTONECRAFT **A PLEA TO WOMEN TO CHANGE THEIR IMAGE** 302
G. K. CHESTERTON **TOMMY AND THE TRADITIONS** 305
WENDELL BERRY **THE TYRANNY OF CHARITY** 308
HANNAH ARENDT **POWER AND VIOLENCE** 315

**CHAPTER 11 ON FREEDOM OF OPINION 325**

JOHN STUART MILL **OF THE LIBERTY OF THOUGHT AND DISCUSSION** 326
MARK TWAIN **CORN-PONE OPINIONS** 333
DOROTHY THOMPSON **CONCERNING TOLERANCE** 338
WILLIAM F. BUCKLEY, JR., **WHY DON'T WE COMPLAIN?** 341

**CHAPTER 12 On the Sexes 347**

Daniel Defoe **Undesirable Husbands 348**
Joseph Addison **The Dissection of a Beau's Head 350**
Katherine Anne Porter **The Necessary Enemy 354**
Judy Brady **I Want a Wife 359**
Brigid Brophy **Women 361**
Scott Russell Sanders **The Men We Carry in Our Minds 368**

**CHAPTER 13 On the Art of the Essay 375**

Michel de Montaigne **Of Giving the Lie 376**
Virginia Woolf **The Modern Essay 380**
E. B. White **The Essayist and the Essay 389**
George Orwell **Why I Write 391**
Joan Didion **Why I Write 398**
Edward Hoagland **What I Think, What I Am 404**

Bibliography **409**
Index of Authors and Titles **419**

# Chronological Table of Contents

Authors are placed in the century with which they are traditionally associated. Within the century, authors are listed in the order of their birthdate. In the case of authors represented by two essays, the second essay appears in Chapter 13, "On the Art of the Essay."

## The Sixteenth and Seventeenth Centuries


Michel de Montaigne **Of Practice** 180

Michel de Montaigne **Of Giving the Lie** 376

Francis Bacon **Of Studies** 146

Abraham Cowley **Of Myself** 2


## The Eighteenth Century


Daniel Defoe **Undesirable Husbands** 348

Jonathan Swift **A Modest Proposal** 294

Joseph Addison **The Dissection of a Beau's Head** 350

Benjamin Franklin **On Education** 148

SAMUEL JOHNSON **THE HISTORY OF AN ADVENTURER IN LOTTERIES** 68
GILBERT WHITE **ON THE ENGLISH HOUSE-MARTIN** 88
OLIVER GOLDSMITH **OF ELOQUENCE** 260
MARY WOLLSTONECRAFT **A PLEA TO WOMEN TO CHANGE THEIR IMAGE** 302

## THE NINETEENTH CENTURY

WILLIAM HAZLITT **ON THE FEELING OF IMMORTALITY IN YOUTH** 190
JOHN HENRY NEWMAN **A DEFINITION OF A GENTLEMAN** 72
JOHN STUART MILL **OF THE LIBERTY OF THOUGHT AND DISCUSSION** 326
WILLIAM MAKEPEACE THACKERAY **ON TWO CHILDREN IN BLACK** 40
CHARLES DICKENS **NIGHT WALKS** 116
HENRY DAVID THOREAU **THE PONDS** 124
FREDERICK DOUGLASS **LEARNING TO READ AND WRITE** 152
MARK TWAIN **CORN-PONE OPINIONS** 333
AGNES REPPLIER **THE KITTEN** 92
W. E. B. DU BOIS **OF THE PASSING OF THE FIRST-BORN** 43

## THE TWENTIETH CENTURY

G. K. CHESTERTON **TOMMY AND THE TRADITIONS** 305
SHERWOOD ANDERSON **DISCOVERY OF A FATHER** 48
JACK LONDON **WHAT LIFE MEANS TO ME** 6

H. L. Mencken **The Politician** 75
Helen Keller **The Day Language Came into My Life** 279
Virginia Woolf **The Death of a Moth** 197
Virginia Woolf **The Modern Essay** 380
Katherine Anne Porter **The Necessary Enemy** 354
Dorothy Parker **Good Souls** 79
James Thurber **University Days** 157
Dorothy Thompson **Concerning Tolerance** 338
E. B. White **Once More to the Lake** 200
E. B. White **The Essayist and the Essay** 389
Zora Neale Hurston **How It Feels to Be Colored Me** 14
Langston Hughes **That Word *Black*** 282
George Orwell **Politics and the English Language** 267
George Orwell **Why I Write** 391
Emily Hahn **Clever Hans** 109
Elias Canetti **The Tattletale** 85
Hannah Arendt **Power and Violence** 315
Eudora Welty **The Little Store** 18
Lewis Thomas **The Long Habit** 206
Alfred Kazin **The Block** 131
Russell Baker **Little Red Riding Hood Revisited** 289
William F. Buckley, Jr. **Why Don't We Complain?** 341
Richard Selzer **The Knife** 211
Adrienne Rich **Taking Women Students Seriously** 163
Brigid Brophy **Women** 361
Wilfred Sheed **Confessions of a Sports Nut** 229
Edward Hoagland **The Courage of Turtles** 99
Edward Hoagland **What I Think, What I Am** 404
John Updike **Hub Fans Bid Kid Adieu** 254
Joan Didion **On Going Home** 54
Joan Didion **Why I Write** 398
N. Scott Momaday **The Way to Rainy Mountain** 57
Wendell Berry **The Tyranny of Charity** 308
Judy Brady **I Want a Wife** 359

MAXINE HONG KINGSTON **THE SILENCE OF A CHINESE-AMERICAN SCHOOLGIRL** 284
STEPHEN JAY GOULD **THE CREATION MYTHS OF COOPERSTOWN** 218
PAUL THEROUX **SUBTERRANEAN GOTHIC** 138
GEORGE F. WILL **THE HARD BLUE GLOW** 248
DORIS KEARNS GOODWIN **FATHERS, DAUGHTERS, AND THE MAGIC OF BASEBALL** 238
ALICE WALKER **BROTHERS AND SISTERS** 62
RICHARD RODRIGUEZ **THE ACHIEVEMENT OF DESIRE** 171
BARRY LOPEZ **WOLF NOTES** 106
ANNIE DILLARD **A FIELD OF SILENCE** 127
SCOTT RUSSELL SANDERS **THE MEN WE CARRY IN OUR MINDS** 368
SHELBY STEELE **ON BEING BLACK AND MIDDLE CLASS** 26
GRETEL EHRLICH **THE SMOOTH SKULL OF WINTER** 135
GERALD EARLY **BASEBALL: THE INEFFABLE NATIONAL PASTIME** 241

# INTRODUCTION

We are the beneficiaries—or, in some people's view, the victims—of the tremendous knowledge explosion that has occurred in the twentieth century. A good deal of that mushrooming knowledge is being recorded and transmitted by electronic media, such as records, films, audio- and videotapes, compact discs, radio, television, and computers. Even in this electronic age, however, much knowledge still reaches us through the medium of print. At no time in the history of the world have so much paper and ink been consumed to inform, instruct, influence, and entertain us. Literate people everywhere can—in fact, must—select from the avalanche of printed material what they will read; they cannot live a single day without reading something, if only a headline, a street sign, a billboard, a bumper sticker, a graffito, or the label on a can.

Fashions in the print medium, as in anything else, change from generation to generation. Epic poems, sermons, and short stories no longer attract the legions of readers they once did. Another genre that does not so readily find a publisher today as it once did is the one variously labeled *informal essay, personal essay, familiar essay, literary nonfiction,* or simply *essay*—terms that will be used interchangeably in this text. The term *essay* has become so elastic that it no longer clearly designates a distinctive kind of literary discourse. A combination of the common elements in the definitions given in six contemporary dictionaries would read something like the following: "An essay is a short literary composition in prose presenting an analytic or interpretative treatment of a single topic or theme from a limited or personal point of view." That composite definition, however, raises more questions than it answers. How short must a literary composition be to qualify as an essay? How does the "analytic or interpretative" treatment in an essay differ from that in a scientific treatise? an academic dissertation? a newspaper editorial? a magazine article? a piece of literary criticism? And isn't every literary composition written, to some degree, from a limited or personal point of view?

To pursue precise answers to questions like these is to run the risk of confusing, rather than clarifying, one's notion of what the essay is. Because the definition of the term *essay* has become as elusive as the definition of the term *short story,* it may be best to rely on the reader's intuitive sense of what an essay is or to trust that the reader will gain a sense of what an essay is by reading the examples of the genre in this text. The fact is that most readers can recognize an example of a genre, even though they may not be able to give a discriminating definition of it. Later in this Introduction, however, we shall attempt to differentiate the essay from other kinds of nonfiction prose that readers regularly encounter in the print medium.

In the past fifty years or so, the familiar essay has shared the fate of the short story. The number of periodicals that print short stories and familiar essays has declined noticeably, and even in periodicals that still print short stories and familiar essays, the number of pages devoted to these two genres has shrunk perceptibly. Apparently, editors are catering to the growing appetite for "factual articles." But although the balance of interest has shifted, some newspapers and magazines still print personal essays. Harry Golden's *The Carolina Israelite,* launched in 1942, was devoted exclusively to the informal essay, and such sections as "The Talk of the Town" in *The New Yorker,* "The Easy Chair" in *Harper's,* "Accent on Living" in the *Atlantic,* "Time Essay" in *Time,* and "My Turn" in *Newsweek* have frequently published informal essays. Some feature articles and syndicated columns also bear the earmarks of the familiar essay. The so-called New Journalism, which embraces such writers as Tom Wolfe, Norman Mailer, Truman Capote, Gay Talese, and Garry Wills, is viewed by some critics as a hybrid of reportorial and novelistic techniques, and the growing popularity of such writing—wherein we are subtly made aware of the controlling presence of the reporter—presaged the most recent revival of interest in the personal essay, which occurred in the 1980s.

Although some literary historians detect a precedent for the essay in such philosophical treatises of Cicero as *De Senectute (On Old Age)* (44 B.C.) and *De Amicitia (On Friendship)* (44 B.C.) and in the prose character sketches (fourth century B.C.) of Theophrastus, most of them attribute the invention of this literary form to Michel de Montaigne. Some notion of Montaigne's uncertainty about this new literary form can be gained from the word he chose to label his prose discourses. The French word *essai* originally meant "a trial, a testing, an experiment." By adopting the plural form *essais* as the title of his first collection in 1580, Montaigne intended to suggest to his readers the tentative, inchoate nature of his personal reflections on a variety of subjects. That sense of a probative rehearsal of one's views persisted for a long time and is implicit in the titles of such works as John Locke's philosophical treatise *Essay concerning Human Understanding* (1690) and Alexander Pope's didactic poem *An Essay on Criticism* (1711).

The notion of unsystematic probing of a subject that is implicit in Montaigne's use of the word *essai* is a common note in the discussion of the essay by essayists themselves. Carl Klaus in his "Essayists on the Essay" examined some forty published essayists and found an amazing commonality in their notions of the essay (see the Bibliography at the back of this book). A reiterative note in their discussions is the suggestion, as Klaus put it, of the "essay's naturalness, openness, or looseness as opposed to the methodicality, regularity, and strictly ordered quality of conventional prose discourse" (156). This notion of the essay rejecting a conventionalized form is reflected in many of the characterizing phrases that essayists used in speaking of the essay: Montaigne's "disjointed parts," Samuel Johnson's "loose sally of the mind," Joseph Addison's "the looseness and freedom of the Essay," G. K. Chesterton's "leisure and liberty," Alfred Kazin's "open form."

Francis Bacon is often cited as being the British promoter of the essay. After Bacon used the English word *Essays* for the title of his collection of "Counsels, Civil and Moral" in 1597, that word was firmly established as the label for a literary genre that flourished for the next three centuries and engaged some of the most talented writers in British and American literature. Although Bacon's essays seem to have a more regularized form than Montaigne's, we find Bacon using such phrases as "dispersed meditations" and "fragments of my conceits" in speaking of his own prose compositions.

In the late seventeenth and early eighteenth centuries, the essay received a renewed impetus from a number of cultural and social developments. The Theophrastian "prose character" became a popular species of the essay in the seventeenth century and later exerted a powerful influence on the development of typical and individualistic characters in the novels and periodical literature of the eighteenth century. The proliferation of movable-type printing presses, the advent of the cheap penny post, made possible by the building of a network of roads between cities and rural villages, the growing hunger of the emerging mercantile class for news and instruction joined to make the regular publication and dissemination of printed matter feasible and profitable. The very format of the periodical—usually folio half-sheets—lent itself to the printing of brief news items about banking transactions, ship arrivals, and diplomatic negotiations and of short, breezy essays on topics of contemporary interest. The news and the lively conversation that had formerly been confined to urban coffeehouses could now be easily broadcast to outlying towns and villages. In a number of professional papers that she has delivered or published in recent years, Shirley Brice Heath has been emphasizing the influence that letter writing and polite conversation had on the development of the essay in the eighteenth century.

This moment in the history of journalism was fortunate for the writers who were attracted to the new medium. There were, of course, hordes of hack writers who fed the insatiable presses with their scribblings, but there were also verbal artists who could turn copy that by its very nature was ephemeral into enduring literature. Had writers of the quality of Daniel Defoe, Joseph Addison, Richard Steele, Samuel Johnson, and Oliver Goldsmith thought it beneath their dignity to compose an essay against a relentless deadline, the development of modern journalism and of the essay might have been delayed for another century or more.

The creation in 1802 of the *Edinburgh Review* initiated a new era in the history of journalism and the essay. Periodicals like the *Edinburgh Review,* the *Quarterly Review, Fraser's Magazine,* and the *London Magazine* were founded to propagate a particular political, philosophical, religious, or literary point of view. But because they were monthlies or quarterlies and because an issue might contain 200–250 pages, these journals provided writers with the time and the space to compose and polish a long essay. Not only did the essay become longer and more polished, but it also became more sober in its tone, more impassioned in its rhythms, and more ornate in its style. In fact, the history of the essay from this point on becomes a history not of the development of new species of the essay but of changing styles. In his essay entitled "Style," Walter Pater called the kind of essay produced by early-nineteenth-century writers like William Hazlitt, Charles Lamb, and Thomas DeQuincey "imaginative prose" and pronounced it to be the "special art of the modern world." These Romantic prose writers took their inspiration from the sonorous, florid style of such seventeenth-century essayists as Jeremy Taylor and Sir Thomas Browne. Their baroque prose enjoyed a brief, intensive vogue but inspired few imitators among twentieth-century essayists. Mid-Victorian essayists such as Thomas Babington Macaulay, John Henry Newman, and Matthew Arnold cultivated a lucid, urbane style that struck a balance between the simple elegance of the best eighteenth-century writers and the mannered grandiloquence of the Romantic essayists. Later Victorian writers like Robert Louis Stevenson, Thomas Henry Huxley, and Walter Bagehot adopted even more noticeably the plain style of the eighteenth century, the kind of style that has clearly become dominant in twentieth-century journalism and essay writing.

Essays distinctly American did not begin to appear in abundance until later in the nineteenth century. As in other cultural activities, the "new England" essayists tended to look to established British writers for their models. The best of the eighteenth- and nineteenth-century American writers—writers such as Benjamin Franklin, Washington Irving, Henry David Thoreau, Oliver Wendell Holmes, and Ralph Waldo Emerson—may not have been slavish imitators of the British essayists, but when we read them, we are invariably reminded of some British counterpart. As a number of contemporary writers and critics have pointed out, it was Mark Twain's *Huckleberry Finn* (1884) that established a distinctly American prose style and spawned a host of imitators. Essayists too began to cultivate the new American tone and style, and as a result, essays began to appear, even anonymously, about which readers could confidently pronounce, "Those were written by an American."

What has been notably missing so far in this quick history of the familiar essay is the names of women. And indeed not many women essayists were admitted to the English and the American literary canon, mainly because not many women tried their hand at the essay. From a list of major and minor essayists that you found in a bibliography of the English and American essay (see the Bibliography at the back of this book), you might recognize the names of a dozen women. If you were a student of English and American literature, you might recognize, for instance, the names of such women as Anne Bradstreet, Lady Mary Wortley Montagu, May Wollstonecraft, Margaret Fuller, Frances Trollope, and Alice Meynell.

The reason for women's absence from the ranks of the major essayists for the greater part of the recorded history of English and American culture is that women were discouraged, even prevented, from going public in any of the arts. Every schoolchild now knows that during Shakespeare's time, young boys played the parts of women on the stage. During the late seventeenth century, women did act in Restoration plays, but it was not until late in the eighteenth century that acting on the stage was considered a respectable occupation for women. For an even longer time, women were discouraged from going public by publishing their writings. The first of the literary arts that women ventured into was the novel, but often women novelists adopted masculine pseudonyms, as did Mary Ann Evans, who adopted the pen name George Eliot when she published her novels in the nineteenth century. Women not only were blocked from getting a university education but were prevented from becoming teachers, even in the grammar schools. Sure, they could become governesses in private families, but the teachers in the public and private schools were men, many of them clergymen.

Women became essayists even later. Not until the last quarter of the nineteenth century do we find women essayists in notable numbers. (For instance, the last three women named above—Margaret Fuller, Frances Trollope, and Alice Meynell—were essayists in the late Victorian period.) Agnes Repplier was the most prominent of the women essayists who wrote and published in the early twentieth century, but in the second half of the twentieth century, many scintillating women essayists came to the fore. Now the best of the women essayists rank with the best of the men essayists.

The twentieth century has witnessed a marked shift in the kinds of nonfiction prose that predominate in our periodicals. The objective news story is, of course, the most prominent feature of daily newspapers and of weekly newsmagazines like *Time* and *Newsweek.* In the news media, as well as in weekly, monthly, and quarterly magazines, what is now taking up an increasing amount of space is the species of prose discourse called the *article.* The article is often a piece of in-depth reporting about an event, a personality, an institution, or a social phenomenon, based on firsthand observation, interviews, previously published material, or, in the journalist's jargon, legwork. Another kind of article is the so-called *think piece,* in which the author argues a thesis about a contemporary issue. A third kind is the *feature article,* usually a lighthearted human interest story involving much less investigation and research than the piece of in-depth reporting. Still another kind of article, usually found in prestigious monthlies or quarterlies like *Atlantic, Harper's, Partisan Review,* and *Daedalus,* is the *critical article,* either on a particular work by an artist (a writer, a painter, a musician, or the like) or on an artist's work in general.

Although articles of this kind are frequently referred to as essays, what distinguishes them from the kind of essay featured in this book is their impersonal tone. The authors of such articles strive to keep themselves out of their work. Even in the think piece, where the author is arguing his or her own view, the pronoun *I* seldom or never appears. Bylined syndicated columns come closest, perhaps, to matching the manner and tone of the familiar essay, because we detect in them the voice of the author. In the twentieth century, however, syndicated columnists have become specialists. They write exclusively on politics or economics or gardening or movies—to name just a few of the specialties. Familiar essayists, on the other hand, have always felt free to write about any subject that struck their fancy. They write not from a particular expertise but from an amateur's interest in any aspect of the human scene.

Although the article has become the dominant form of prose discourse in contemporary periodicals, the familiar essay, as the large number of twentieth-century selections in this text makes clear, has not entirely disappeared. By comparing these twentieth-century essays with the selections from earlier centuries, readers can discover for themselves how much the contemporary examples are different and how much they are the same. Readers who want to gain even more of a historical perspective on the evolution of the essay can do so by reading the biographical information in the headnotes and by reading some of the books and articles listed in "The History and/or the Art of the Essay" section of the Bibliography. Because most writers are represented in this book by only one essay, readers cannot acquire herein a sense of the range and development of any one essayist during his or her lifetime. To gain such a sense, readers would have to read a collection of an author's essays, many of which compilations are named in the headnotes.

In addition to giving students a historical sense of the variety and evolution of the essay as a distinct literary genre, we wanted also to provide them with models of a kind of prose discourse that unites the objective and the subjective. Objective writing has been the main kind of writing taught not only in journalism classes but also in English classes—in themes, reports, critiques, research papers, and dissertations. Indeed, such writing provides students with a valuable and useful discipline. It trains aspiring writers to observe carefully, to organize coherently, to report accurately, and to reason responsibly, and it is the kind of writing that they are called on to do most often in their college classes and later in their jobs. Yet many students feel bridled by the discipline of this kind of "expository" writing. They yearn to be free to express themselves, to be creative, to set their own forms, or even to be individualistically "formless." In recent years students have been encouraged by teachers and textbooks to engage in this kind of "freewriting." In many composition courses the emphasis has shifted from the *product* of writing to the *process* of writing, and writing has come to be viewed not simply as an act of communication but also as a means of self-discovery and self-expression.

The familiar essay, perhaps more than any other prose form, allows for the combination of the objective and the subjective kinds of writing, of the imaginative and the utilitarian types. In a sense, the familiar essay is the prose equivalent of the lyric poem—short, unified, and compact, conducive not only to transmitting the writer's view of "reality" but also to expressing the writer's emotions and personality. It allows for that combination of freedom and discipline necessary for writers to perform at the top of their bent. It allows them to write about a subject "off the top of their head" and to choose their own tack and tone in dealing with the subject, yet it also demands that they attend to all the elements in the rhetorical triad: the writer, the audience, and the message (the *I*, the *you*, and the *it*). By demanding that writers be concerned about all three of these elements, the familiar essay permits them to give vent to their individuality and imagination, yet constrains them to be responsible to their subject and sensitive to their readers. By practicing the composition of the familiar essay, aspiring writers may be able to avoid the pitfalls, on the one hand, of the formless, turn-on-the-spigot kind of writing and, on the other hand, of the voiceless, vapidly formularized, academic kind of writing. They may, in short, learn to compose a piece of prose that will please both themselves and their readers.

But note that word *compose*. There is an art to the familiar essay, even though it may be a concealed art. Despite its apparent ease and casualness, the familiar essay is still tightly controlled and deliberately, if idiosyncratically, structured by the writer. Familiar essayists enjoy a number of freedoms, but they still must make a number of crucial choices, and the making of choices marks the point where the "art" comes into play. An author is free to write about something as trivial as a bed pillow or as profound as immortality. Having chosen a subject, however, he or she is free to choose whether to treat that subject seriously or whimsically or satirically. That choice in turn forces or determines other choices—of stance, of voice, of diction, of organization.

What every writer eventually discovers is that with each successive choice, the range of freedom narrows and the constraints on subsequent choices increase. Paradoxically, however, the discipline of making choices ultimately gives a writer *real* freedom, because that discipline bestows on the writer the power to do what he or she wants to do. The best of the familiar essays have an air about them of pleasant, free-flowing conversation. The flow is indeed there; what the writers have concealed from us is all the channels they had to cut to ensure that easy flow.

# 1

# On Personal Identity

*There is a sense in which it is true to say that we spend a good portion of our life trying to discover who we are. But the period when the search for our personal identity is most intense and agonizing is the teenage years. At first, we come to know ourselves by keeping our minds and our physical senses open to the big buzzing world "out there." And so the child is constantly fascinated—and sometimes frightened—by the world of faces, objects, scenes, and sensations that impinge on his or her consciousness. But when we enter the adolescent years, we turn our attention inward to discover who we are and where we fit in that big buzzing world to which we have begun to acclimate ourselves. We become introspective, even solipsistic. By the time we approach young manhood or young womanhood, we begin to turn our attention outward again and to make the adjustments that may be necessary in order for us to integrate ourselves with the community in which we must live and survive. It is at this stage that we begin to verbalize about our discovery of self in relation to the outer world. All the writers represented in this section were well advanced in years when they wrote these essays about how they discovered themselves, their place in the world, and their relationship with other people. Surely, some, maybe all, of these essays will arouse in you memories of how* you *discovered who you are.*

# Of Myself

## ABRAHAM COWLEY

In the history of English literature, Abraham Cowley (1618–1667) is best remembered—even if not read—as one of the "metaphysical poets," whom Samuel Johnson characterized in his "Life of Cowley." Cowley attended Trinity College, Cambridge—the same college that Francis Bacon attended—but in 1643, during the Cromwellian civil war, he was expelled because of his Royalist sympathies—that is, as an advocate of the reigning monarch. He went first to Oxford and then, in 1646, to Paris, where he served as secretary for the exiled Queen Henrietta Marie and as emissary on several diplomatic missions. On his return to England in 1655, he was arrested and briefly imprisoned as a Royalist spy. After his release on bail, he returned to Oxford to study medicine. In 1656, he published *Miscellanies,* a collection of poetry that included his *Pindarique Odes* and the four books of *Davideis,* an epic in pentameter couplets on the biblical history of David. When Alexander Pope asked in 1737 in his *Epistle to Augustus,* "Who now reads Cowley?" he was alluding to Cowley's poetry. The same fate did not visit Cowley's collection of essays. Not published until 1668, the year after his death, his *Several Discourses by Way of Essays, in Verse and Prose* reached a twelfth edition by 1721. Cowley's essays bear more resemblance to Montaigne's essays than Bacon's do—a casual, personal, digressive manner, with many illustrative and supportive quotations from classical authors. What is particularly distinctive about "Of Myself"—as with many of his essays—is that Cowley mixes poetry—most of it his own—with his prose. As you read this essay about Cowley's search for his identity, see if you experience any disruption of your mood as the essay shifts from prose to poetry and back to prose.

It is a hard and nice[1] subject for a man to write of himself; it grates 1
his own heart to say anything of disparagement and the reader's ears to hear anything of praise from him. There is no danger from me of offending him in this kind; neither my mind, nor my body, nor my fortune allow me any materials for that vanity. It is sufficient for my own contentment that they have preserved me from being scandalous, or remarkable on the defective side. But besides that, I shall here speak of myself only in relation to the subject of these precedent discourses, and shall be likelier thereby to fall into the contempt than rise up to the estimation of most people. As far as my memory can return back into my past life, before I knew or was capable of guessing what the world, or glories, or business of it were, the natural affections of my soul gave me a secret bent of aversion from them, as some plants are said to turn away from others, by an antipathy

[1]*nice:* delicate. [Eds.]

imperceptible to themselves and inscrutable to man's understanding. Even when I was a very young boy at school,[2] instead of running about on holidays and playing with my fellows, I was wont to steal from them and walk into the fields, either alone with a book, or with some one companion, if I could find any of the same temper. I was then, too, so much an enemy to all constraint, that my masters could never prevail on me, by any persuasions or encouragements, to learn without book the common rules of grammar, in which they dispensed with me alone, because they found I made a shift to do the usual exercise out of my own reading and observation. That I was then of the same mind as I am now (which I confess I wonder at myself) may appear by the latter end of an ode[3] which I made when I was but thirteen years old, and which was then printed with many other verses. The beginning of it is boyish, but of this part which I here set down, if a very little were corrected, I should hardly now be much ashamed.

IX

This only grant me, that my means may lie
Too low for envy, for contempt too high.
   Some honor I would have,
Not from great deeds, but good alone.
The unknown are better than ill known.
   Rumor can ope the grave;
Acquaintance I would have, but when 't depends
Not on the number, but the choice of friends.

X

Books should, not business, entertain the light,
And sleep, as undisturbed as death, the night.
   My house a cottage, more
Than palace, and should fitting be
For all my use, no luxury.
   My garden painted o'er
With Nature's hand, not Art's; and pleasures yield,
Horace might envy in his Sabine field.

XI

Thus would I double my life's fading space,
For he that runs it well, twice runs his race.
   And in this true delight,
These unbought sports, this happy state,
I would not fear, nor wish my fate,
   But boldly say each night,
To-morrow let my sun his beams display,
Or in clouds hide them—I have lived to-day.

---

[2]*young boy at school:* Cowley entered Westminster School when he was about ten years old. [Eds.]

[3]The stanzas quoted form the conclusion of a poem entitled "A Vote," which appeared in "Sylva" of 1636. [Eds.]

2 You may see by it I was even then acquainted with the poets (for the conclusion is taken out of Horace),[4] and perhaps it was the immature and immoderate love of them which stamped first, or rather engraved, these characters in me. They were like letters cut into the bark of a young tree, which with the tree still grow proportionably. But how this love came to be produced in me so early is a hard question. I believe I can tell the particular little chance that filled my head first with such chimes of verse as have never since left ringing there. For I remember when I began to read, and to take some pleasure in it, there was wont to lie in my mother's parlor (I know not by what accident, for she herself never in her life read any book but of devotion), but there was wont to lie Spenser's works; this I happened to fall upon, and was infinitely delighted with the stories of the knights, and giants, and monsters, and brave houses, which I found everywhere there (though my understanding had little to do with all this); and by degrees with the tinkling of the rhyme and dance of the numbers, so that I think I had read him all over before I was twelve years old, and was thus made a poet as irremediably as a child is made a eunuch. With these affections of mind, and my heart wholly set upon letters, I went to the university, but was soon torn from thence by that violent public storm[5] which would suffer nothing to stand where it did, but rooted up every plant, even from the princely cedars to me, the hyssop. Yet I had as good fortune as could have befallen me in such a tempest; for I was cast by it into the family of one of the best persons, and into the court of one of the best princesses of the world. Now though I was here engaged in ways most contrary to the original design of my life, that is, into much company, and no small business, and into a daily sight of greatness, both militant and triumphant, for that was the state then of the English and French courts; yet all this was so far from altering my opinion, that it only added the confirmation of reason to that which was before but natural inclination. I saw plainly all the paint of that kind of life, the nearer I came to it; and that beauty which I did not fall in love with when, for aught I knew, it was real, was not like to bewitch or entice me when I saw that it was adulterate. I met with several great persons, whom I liked very well, but could not perceive that any part of their greatness was to be liked or desired, no more than I would be glad or content to be in a storm, though I saw many ships which rid safely and bravely in it. A storm would not agree with my stomach, if

---

[4]Odes," III, xxix, 41. [Eds.]

[5]*violent public storm:* Because of his sympathies with Charles I during the king's troubles with the House of Commons, Cowley had to leave Cambridge in 1643. The next year, he went to Paris as secretary to Lord Jermyn, the adviser of Queen Henrietta Maria, who is the "best princess" spoken of in the next sentence. [Eds.]

it did with my courage. Though I was in a crowd of as good company as could be found anywhere, though I was in business of great and honorable trust, though I ate at the best table, and enjoyed the best conveniences for present subsistence that ought to be desired by a man of my condition in banishment and public distresses, yet I could not abstain from renewing my old schoolboy's wish in a copy of verses to the same effect:—

> Well then; I now do plainly see,
> This busy world and I shall ne'er agree, etc.[6]

And I never then proposed to myself any other advantage from 3
His Majesty's happy restoration, but the getting into some moderately convenient retreat in the country, which I thought in that case I might easily have compassed, as well as some others, with no greater probabilities or pretences, have arrived to extraordinary fortunes. But I had before written a shrewd prophecy against myself, and I think Apollo inspired me in the truth, though not in the elegance of it:[7]—

> Thou, neither great at court nor in the war,
> Nor at th' exchange shalt be, nor at the wrangling bar;
> Content thyself with the small barren praise,
> Which neglected verse does raise.
> She spoke; and all my years to come
>     Took their unlucky doom.
> Their several ways of life let others chuse,
> Their several pleasures let them use;
> But I was born for Love and for a Muse.
>
> What Fate what boots it to contend?
> Such I began, such am, and so must end.
>     The star that did my being frame
>     Was but a lambent flame,
>     And some small light it did dispense,
>     But neither heat nor influence.
> No matter, Cowley; let proud Fortune see
> That thou canst her despise no less than she does thee.
>
> Let all her gifts the portion be
> Of folly, lust, and flattery,
> Fraud, extortion, calumny,
> Murder, infidelity,
> Rebellion and hypocrisy.
> Do thou not grieve nor blush to be,
> As all th' inspired tuneful men,
> And all thy great forefathers were, from Homer down to Ben.

---

[6]These lines are from "The Wish," one of the poems that Cowley published in 1647 under the collective title of *The Mistress.* [Eds.]

[7]The subsequent lines are quoted from "The Destiny," one of Cowley's *Pindarique Odes,* published in 1656. [Eds.]

However, by the failing of the forces which I had expected, I did not quit the design which I had resolved on; I cast myself into it *À corps perdu,*[8] without making capitulations or taking counsel of fortune. But God laughs at a man who says to his soul, "Take thy ease": I met presently not only with many little encumbrances and impediments, but with so much sickness (a new misfortune to me) as would have spoiled the happiness of an emperor as well as mine. Yet I do neither repent nor alter my course. *Non ego perfidum dixi sacramentum.*[9] Nothing shall separate me from a mistress which I have loved so long, and have now at last married, though she neither has brought me a rich portion, nor lived yet so quietly with me as I hoped from her.[10] 4

**IN RETROSPECT**

**1.** Few, if any, of the other essays in this collection present what Cowley's essay does: a mixture of prose and poetry, both written by the author. In the headnote to this essay, you were asked to consider whether you experienced any disruption of your mood as the essay shifted from prose to poetry and back to prose. From which of the two media did you learn more about Cowley? Explain.

**2.** By centering his essay on his interest in and facility for writing and then tracing the development of this interest and skill, Cowley gives us a sense of how he has come to define himself. In a brief written sketch entitled "Of Myself," experiment with Cowley's method of self-definition in order to introduce yourself to your classmates. What strikes you as definitive in your life? How has this "center," or definitive feature, evolved over time? Discuss with your classmates how easy or difficult it is for you to find a single satisfactory feature on which to focus your identity. Compare the various ways in which people in the class choose to define themselves. How might the diversity you have observed in the ways you define yourselves figure into the ways in which you might interact with texts and with one another throughout this course?

# *What Life Means to Me*

## JACK LONDON

Jack London (1876–1916), whose formal name was John Griffith London, was born in San Francisco. He finished his formal schooling at the age of fourteen, when he graduated from grade school.

---

[8] *À corps perdu:* the phrase can be translated here as "headlong." [Eds.]

[9] *Non ego . . . sacramentum:* I have not sworn a faithless oath (Horace, *Odes,* II, 17). [Eds.]

[10] The verses with which Cowley concluded his essay are omitted here. [Eds.]

Hanging out at the waterfront in Oakland, California, he scraped up enough money to buy a small boat, and in the company of some unemployed teenagers like himself, he raided oyster beds in the Bay and sold the stolen goods. Abandoning this unsavory occupation in 1893, he became a drifter for several years, going on an expedition to Japan in search of seals, tramping on foot across Canada and the United States, and taking time out briefly to put in a semester at the University of California. Returning to the Oakland waterfront, he became a militant socialist and revolutionist. He then joined the gold rush to the Klondike, and although he failed in that mining enterprise, he acquired a knowledge of the hard life in that frigid environment that figured in many of the short stories and novels that he later wrote and published. He wrote an astonishing number of short stories, novels, and nonfiction pieces and became famous and relatively rich. His two best-known novels are *The Call of the Wild* (1903) and *White Fang* (1906). The essay reprinted here gives an account of Jack London's attempt to find himself—or to find his niche in life. Born into the working class, he envied the well-born and the wealthy. He says in the second sentence of the essay, "Early I discovered enthusiasm, ambition, and ideals; and to satisfy these became the problem of my child-life." After reading the essay, go back over it to see if you can determine which of the three attributes named in that sentence influenced his successes in life and which influenced his disillusionments.

I was born in the working-class. Early I discovered enthusiasm, 1
ambition, and ideals; and to satisfy these became the problem of my child-life. My environment was crude and rough and raw. I had no outlook, but an uplook rather. My place in society was at the bottom. Here life offered nothing but sordidness and wretchedness, both of the flesh and the spirit; for here flesh and spirit were alike starved and tormented.

Above me towered the colossal edifice of society, and to my mind 2
the only way out was up. Into this edifice I early resolved to climb. Up above, men wore black clothes and boiled shirts, and women dressed in beautiful gowns. Also, there were good things to eat, and there was plenty to eat. This much for the flesh. Then there were the things of the spirit. Up above me, I knew, were unselfishness of the spirit, clean and noble thinking, keen intellectual living. I knew all this because I read "Seaside Library" novels, in which, with the exception of the villains and adventuresses, all men and women thought beautiful thoughts, spoke a beautiful tongue, and performed glorious deeds. In short, as I accepted the rising of the sun, I accepted that up above me was all that was fine and noble and gracious, all that gave decency and dignity to life, all that made life worth living and that remunerated one for his travail and misery.

But it is not particularly easy for one to climb up out of the 3
working-class—especially if he is handicapped by the possession of ideals and illusions. I lived on a ranch in California, and I was hard

put to find the ladder whereby to climb. I early inquired the rate of interest on invested money, and worried my child's brain into an understanding of the virtues and excellencies of that remarkable invention of man, compound interest. Further, I ascertained the current rates of wages for workers of all ages, and the cost of living. From all this data I concluded that if I began immediately and worked and saved until I was fifty years of age, I could then stop working and enter into participation in a fair portion of the delights and goodnesses that would then be open to me higher up in society. Of course, I resolutely determined not to marry, while I quite forgot to consider at all that great rock of disaster in the working-class world—sickness.

But the life that was in me demanded more than a meager existence of scraping and scrimping. Also, at ten years of age, I became a newsboy on the streets of a city, and found myself with a changed uplook. All about me were still the same sordidness and wretchedness, and up above me was still the same paradise waiting to be gained; but the ladder whereby to climb was a different one. It was now the ladder of business. Why save my earnings and invest in government bonds, when, by buying two newspapers for five cents, with a turn of the wrist I could sell them for ten cents and double my capital? The business ladder was the ladder for me, and I had a vision of myself becoming a baldheaded and successful merchant prince. 4

Alas for visions! When I was sixteen I had already earned the title of "prince." But this title was given me by a gang of cut-throats and thieves, by whom I was called "The Prince of the Oyster Pirates." And at that time I had climbed the first rung of the business ladder. I was a capitalist. I owned a boat and a complete oyster-pirating outfit. I had begun to exploit my fellow-creatures. I had a crew of one man. As captain and owner I took two-thirds of the spoils, and gave the crew one-third, though the crew worked just as hard as I did and risked just as much his life and liberty. 5

This one rung was the height I climbed up the business ladder. One night I went on a raid amongst the Chinese fishermen. Ropes and nets were worth dollars and cents. It was robbery, I grant, but it was precisely the spirit of capitalism. The capitalist takes away the possessions of his fellow-creatures by means of a rebate, or of a betrayal of trust, or by the purchase of senators and supreme-court judges. I was merely crude. That was the only difference. I used a gun. 6

But my crew that night was one of those inefficients against whom the capitalist is wont to fulminate, because, forsooth, such inefficients increase expenses and reduce dividends. My crew did both. What of his carelessness: he set fire to the big mainsail and totally destroyed it. There weren't any dividends that night, and the Chinese fishermen were richer by the nets and ropes we did not get. I 7 was bankrupt, unable just then to pay sixty-five dollars for a new mainsail. I left my boat at anchor and went off on a bay-pirate boat on a raid up the Sacramento River. While away on this trip, another gang of bay pirates raided my boat. They stole everything, even the anchors; and later on, when I recovered the drifting hulk, I sold it for twenty dollars. I had slipped back the one rung I had climbed, and never again did I attempt the business ladder.

From then on I was mercilessly exploited by other capitalists. I 8
had the muscle, and they made money out of it while I made but a very indifferent living out of it. I was a sailor before the mast, a longshoreman, a roustabout; I worked in canneries, and factories, and laundries; I mowed lawns, and cleaned carpets, and washed windows. And I never got the full product of my toil. I looked at the daughter of the cannery owner, in her carriage, and knew that it was my muscle, in part, that helped drag along that carriage on its rubber tires. I looked at the son of the factory owner, going to college, and knew that it was my muscle that helped, in part, to pay for the wine and good fellowship he enjoyed.

But I did not resent this. It was all in the game. They were the 9
strong. Very well, I was strong. I would carve my way to a place amongst them and make money out of the muscles of other men. I was not afraid of work. I loved hard work. I would pitch in and work harder than ever and eventually become a pillar of society.

And just then, as luck would have it, I found an employer that 10
was of the same mind. I was willing to work, and he was more than willing that I should work. I thought I was learning a trade. In reality, I had displaced two men. I thought he was making an electrician out of me; as a matter of fact, he was making fifty dollars per month out of me. The two men I had displaced had received forty dollars each per month; I was doing the work of both for thirty dollars per month.

This employer worked me nearly to death. A man may love 11
oysters, but too many oysters will disincline him toward that particular diet. And so with me. Too much work sickened me. I did not wish ever to see work again. I fled from work. I became a tramp, begging my way from door to door, wandering over the United States and sweating bloody sweats in slums and prisons.

I had been born in the working-class, and I was now, at the age of 12
eighteen, beneath the point at which I had started. I was down in the cellar of society, down in the subterranean depths of misery about which it is neither nice nor proper to speak. I was in the pit, the abyss, the human cesspool, the shambles and charnel-house of our civilization. This is the part of the edifice of society that society chooses to ignore. Lack of space compels me here to ignore it, and I shall say only that the things I there saw gave me a terrible scare.

I was scared into thinking. I saw the naked simplicities of the complicated civilization in which I lived. Life was a matter of food and shelter. In order to get food and shelter men sold things. The merchant sold shoes, the politician sold his manhood, and the representative of the people, with exceptions, of course, sold his trust; while nearly all sold their honor. Women, too, whether on the street or in the holy bond of wedlock, were prone to sell their flesh. All things were commodities, all people bought and sold. The one commodity that labor had to sell was muscle. The honor of labor had no price in the market-place. Labor had muscle, and muscle alone, to sell. 13

But there was a difference, a vital difference. Shoes and trust and honor had a way of renewing themselves. They were imperishable stocks. Muscle, on the other hand, did not renew. As the shoe merchant sold shoes, he continued to replenish his stock. But there was no way of replenishing the laborer's stock of muscle. The more he sold of his muscle, the less of it remained to him. It was his one commodity, and each day his stock of it diminished. In the end, if he did not die before, he sold out and put up his shutters. He was a muscle bankrupt, and nothing remained to him but to go down into the cellar of society and perish miserably. 14

I learned, further, that brain was likewise a commodity. It, too, was different from muscle. A brain seller was only at his prime when he was fifty or sixty years old, and his wares were fetching higher prices than ever. But a laborer was worked out or broken down at forty-five or fifty. I had been in the cellar of society, and I did not like the place as a habitation. The pipes and drains were unsanitary, and the air was bad to breathe. If I could not live on the parlor floor of society, I could, at any rate, have a try at the attic. It was true, the diet there was slim, but the air at least was pure. So I resolved to sell no more muscle, and to become a vender of brains. 15

Then began a frantic pursuit of knowledge. I returned to California and opened the books. While thus equipping myself to become a brain merchant, it was inevitable that I should delve into sociology. There I found, in a certain class of books, scientifically formulated, the simple sociological concepts I had already worked out for myself. Other and greater minds, before I was born, had worked out all that I had thought and a vast deal more. I discovered that I was a socialist. 16

The socialists were revolutionists, inasmuch as they struggled to overthrow the society of the present, and out of the material to build the society of the future. I, too, was a socialist and a revolutionist. I joined the groups of working-class and intellectual revolutionists, and for the first time came into intellectual living. Here I found keen-flashing intellects and brilliant wits; for here I met strong and alert-brained, withal horny-handed, members of the working-class; 17

unfrocked preachers too wide in their Christianity for any congregation of Mammon-worshippers; professors broken on the wheel of university subservience to the ruling class and flung out because they were quick with knowledge which they strove to apply to the affairs of mankind.

Here I found, also, warm faith in the human, glowing idealism, 18
sweetnesses of unselfishness, renunciation, and martyrdom—all the splendid, stinging things of the spirit. Here life was clean, noble, and alive. Here life rehabilitated itself, became wonderful and glorious; and I was glad to be alive. I was in touch with great souls who exalted flesh and spirit over dollars and cents, and to whom the thin wail of the starved slum child meant more than all the pomp and circumstance of commercial expansion and world empire. All about me were nobleness of purpose and heroism of effort, and my days and nights were sunshine and starshine, all fire and dew, with before my eyes, ever burning and blazing, the Holy Grail, Christ's own Grail, the warm human, long-suffering and maltreated, but to be rescued and saved at the last.

And I, poor foolish I, deemed all this to be a mere foretaste of the 19
delights of living I should find higher above me in society. I had lost many illusions since the day I read "Seaside Library" novels on the California ranch. I was destined to lose many of the illusions I still retained.

As a brain merchant I was a success. Society opened its portals to 20
me. I entered right in on the parlor floor, and my disillusionment proceeded rapidly. I sat down to dinner with the masters of society, and with the wives and daughters of the masters of society. The women were gowned beautifully, I admit; but to my naïve surprise I discovered that they were of the same clay as all the rest of the women I had known down below in the cellar. "The colonel's lady and Judy O'Grady were sisters under their skins"—and gowns.

It was not this, however, so much as their materialism, that 21
shocked me. It is true, these beautifully gowned, beautiful women prattled sweet little ideals and dear little moralities; but in spite of their prattle the dominant key of the life they lived was materialistic. And they were so sentimentally selfish! They assisted in all kinds of sweet little charities, and informed one of the fact, while all the time the food they ate and the beautiful clothes they wore were bought out of dividends stained with the blood of child labor, and sweated labor, and of prostitution itself. When I mentioned such facts, expecting in my innocence that these sisters of Judy O'Grady would at once strip off their blood-dyed silks and jewels, they became excited and angry, and read me preachments about the lack of thrift, the drink, and the innate depravity that caused all the misery in society's cellar.

When I mentioned that I couldn't quite see that it was the lack of thrift, the intemperance, and the depravity of a half-starved child of six that made it work twelve hours every night in a Southern cotton mill, these sisters of Judy O'Grady attacked my private life and called me an "agitator"—as though that, forsooth, settled the argument.

Nor did I fare better with the masters themselves. I had expected 22
to find men who were clean, noble, and alive, whose ideals were clean, noble, and alive. I went about amongst the men who sat in the high places—the preachers, the politicians, the business men, the professors, and the editors. I ate meat with them, drank wine with them, automobiled with them, and studied them. It is true, I found many that were clean and noble; but with rare exceptions, they were not *alive*. I do verily believe I could count the exceptions on the fingers of my two hands. Where they were not alive with rottenness, quick with unclean life, they were merely the unburied dead—clean and noble, like well-preserved mummies, but not alive. In this connection I may especially mention the professors I met, the men who live up to that decadent university ideal, "the passionless pursuit of passionless intelligence."

I met men who invoked the name of the Prince of Peace in their 23
diatribes against war, and who put rifles in the hands of Pinkertons with which to shoot down strikers in their own factories. I met men incoherent with indignation at the brutality of prize-fighting, and who, at the same time, were parties to the adulteration of food that killed each year more babies than even red-handed Herod had killed.

I talked in hotels and clubs and homes and Pullmans and 24
steamer-chairs with captains of industry, and marvelled at how little travelled they were in the realm of intellect. On the other hand, I discovered that their intellect, in the business sense, was abnormally developed. Also, I discovered that their morality, where business was concerned, was nil.

This delicate, aristocratic-featured gentleman, was a dummy di- 25
rector and a tool of corporations that secretly robbed widows and orphans. This gentleman, who collected fine editions and was an especial patron of literature, paid blackmail to a heavy-jowled, black-browed boss of a municipal machine. This editor, who published patent medicine advertisements and did not dare print the truth in his paper about said patent medicines for fear of losing the advertising, called me a scoundrelly demagogue because I told him that his political economy was antiquated and that his biology was contemporaneous with Pliny.

This senator was the tool and the slave, the little puppet of a 26
gross, uneducated machine boss; so was this governor and this supreme court judge; and all three rode on railroad passes. This man,

talking soberly and earnestly about the beauties of idealism and the goodness of God, had just betrayed his comrades in a business deal. This man, a pillar of the church and heavy contributor to foreign missions, worked his shop girls ten hours a day on a starvation wage and thereby directly encouraged prostitution. This man, who endowed chairs in universities, perjured himself in courts of law over a matter of dollars and cents. And this railroad magnate broke his word as a gentleman and a Christian when he granted a secret rebate to one of two captains of industry locked together in a struggle to the death.

It was the same everywhere, crime and betrayal, betrayal and 27
crime—men who were alive, but who were neither clean nor noble, men who were clean and noble but who were not alive. Then there was a great, hopeless mass, neither noble nor alive, but merely clean. It did not sin positively nor deliberately; but it did sin passively and ignorantly by acquiescing in the current immorality and profiting by it. Had it been noble and alive it would not have been ignorant, and it would have refused to share in the profits of betrayal and crime.

I discovered that I did not like to live on the parlor floor of society. 28
Intellectually I was bored. Morally and spiritually I was sickened. I remembered my intellectuals and idealists, my unfrocked preachers, broken professors, and clean-minded, class-conscious workingmen. I remembered my days and nights of sunshine and starshine, where life was all a wild sweet wonder, a spiritual paradise of unselfish adventure and ethical romance. And I saw before me, ever blazing and burning, the Holy Grail.

So I went back to the working-class, in which I had been born and 29
where I belonged. I care no longer to climb. The imposing edifice of society above my head holds no delights for me. It is the foundation of the edifice that interests me. There I am content to labor, crowbar in hand, shoulder to shoulder with intellectuals, idealists, and class-conscious workingmen, getting a solid pry now and again and setting the whole edifice rocking. Some day, when we get a few more hands and crowbars to work, we'll topple it over, along with all its rotten life and unburied dead, its monstrous selfishness and sodden materialism. Then we'll cleanse the cellar and build a new habitation for mankind, in which there will be no parlor floor, in which all the rooms will be bright and airy, and where the air that is breathed will be clean, noble, and alive.

Such is my outlook. I look forward to a time when man shall 30
progress upon something worthier and higher than his stomach, when there will be a finer incentive to impel men to action than the incentive of today, which is the incentive of the stomach. I retain my belief in the nobility and excellence of the human. I believe that spiritual sweetness and unselfishness will conquer the gross gluttony

of today. And last of all, my faith is in the working-class. As some Frenchman has said, "The stairway of time is ever echoing with the wooden shoe going up, the polished boot descending."

**IN RETROSPECT**

**1.** This essay tells us mainly about London's disillusionment with the members of the society in which he lived. Born into a working-class family, he aspired to become a member of the upper class. When, as a result of getting some education, he got a taste of upper-class life, he was disgusted by the behavior and the morality of the men and women he met in that environment. Ultimately, he became disillusioned by the materialism he found among the members of the privileged class. Does he end up totally disillusioned? If not, where does he end up putting his faith?

**2.** At the beginning of paragraph 12, London tells us that he had now reached the age of eighteen. Most of you who read this essay are at least eighteen. Compare your response to the life you have experienced up until now with London's response. Are you now upbeat about life, or do you now believe that life "sucks"? Give your reasons for your answer.

# *How It Feels to Be Colored Me*

## ZORA NEALE HURSTON

We cannot be sure whether Zora Neale Hurston was born in 1900, 1901, or 1903 (Hurston herself cited all three dates), but we are sure that she was born in Eatonville, Florida—reputed to be the first incorporated, all-black town in America—and that she died in Fort Pierce, Florida, on January 28, 1960. She died penniless, a neglected and forgotten writer once associated with the Harlem Renaissance, her four novels and two books of Afro-American folklore long out of print. Her biographer Robert E. Hemenway has said of her, "Zora Neale Hurston is one of the most significant unread authors in America, the author of two minor classics and four other major books." She attended Howard University in 1923–1924 and then went on to Barnard College, where she obtained a B.A. in 1928. The renowned anthropologist Franz Boaz, who was her teacher at Barnard, sent her back to Eatonville to collect the folklore that she could gather in that black community. She later collected folklore in Jamaica, Haiti, and Bermuda and in 1935 published one of her classic works, *Mules and Men,* in which she recorded what she had found during her years of patient research. In 1973 Alice Walker, a great admirer of Hurston, traveled to Eatonville to see what she could find out about the writer from the town's longtime residents. Walker reported her findings in an essay titled "Looking for Zora," published in the March 1975 issue of *Ms.* The autobiographical essay reprinted here first appeared in Hurston's *I Love Myself When I Am Laughing* (1928). A bright, vibrant personality emerges from this essay. After reading the essay, make a list of the character traits that make Hurston a distinct personality for you. How much of that personality is established by what she does and how much by what she says?

I am colored but I offer nothing in the way of extenuating circumstances except the fact that I am the only Negro in the United States whose grandfather on the mother's side was *not* an Indian chief. 1

I remember the very day that I became colored. Up to my thirteenth year I lived in the little Negro town of Eatonville, Florida. It is exclusively a colored town. The only white people I knew passed through the town going to or coming from Orlando. The native whites rode dusty horses, the Northern tourists chugged down the sandy village road in automobiles. The town knew the Southerners and never stopped cane chewing when they passed. But the Northerners were something else again. They were peered at cautiously from behind curtains by the timid. The more venturesome would come out on the porch to watch them go past and got just as much pleasure out of the tourists as the tourists got out of the village. 2

The front porch might seem a daring place for the rest of the town, but it was a gallery seat for me. My favorite place was atop the gate-post. Proscenium box for a born first-nighter. Not only did I enjoy the show, but I didn't mind the actors knowing that I liked it. I usually spoke to them in passing. I'd wave at them and when they returned my salute, I would say something like this: "Howdy-do-well-I-thank-you-where-you-goin'?" Usually automobile or the horse paused at this, and after a queer exchange of compliments, I would probably "go a piece of the way" with them, as we say in farthest Florida. If one of my family happened to come to the front in time to see me, of course negotiations would be rudely broken off. But even so, it is clear that I was the first "welcome-to-our-state" Floridian, and I hope the Miami Chamber of Commerce will please take notice. 3

During this period, white people differed from colored to me only in that they rode through town and never lived there. They liked to hear me "speak pieces" and sing and wanted to see me dance the parse-me-la, and gave me generously of their small silver for doing these things, which seemed strange to me for I wanted to do them so much that I needed bribing to stop. Only they didn't know it. The colored people gave no dimes. They deplored any joyful tendencies in me, but I was their Zora nevertheless. I belonged to them, to the nearby hotels, to the county—everybody's Zora. 4

But the changes came in the family when I was thirteen, and I was sent to school in Jacksonville. I left Eatonville, the town of the oleanders, as Zora. When I disembarked from the river-boat at Jack- 5 sonville, she was no more. It seemed that I had suffered a sea change. I was not Zora of Orange County anymore, I was now a little colored girl. I found it out in certain ways. In my heart as well as in the mirror, I became a fast brown—warranted not to rub nor run.

6 But I am not tragically colored. There is not great sorrow dammed up in my soul, nor lurking behind my eyes. I do not mind at all. I do not belong to the sobbing school of Negrohood who hold that nature somehow has given them a lowdown dirty deal and whose feelings are all hurt about it. Even in the helter-skelter skirmish that is my life, I have seen that the world is to the strong regardless of a little pigmentation more or less. No, I do not weep at the world—I am too busy sharpening my oyster knife.

7 Someone is always at my elbow reminding me that I am the granddaughter of slaves. It fails to register depression with me. Slavery is sixty years in the past. The operation was successful and the patient is doing well, thank you. The terrible struggle that made me an American out of a potential slave said "On the line!" The Reconstruction said "Get set!"; and the generation before said "Go!" I am off to a flying start and I must not halt in the stretch to look behind and weep. Slavery is the price I paid for civilization, and the choice was not with me. It is a bully adventure and worth all that I have paid through my ancestors for it. No one on earth ever had a greater chance for glory. The world to be won and nothing to be lost. It is thrilling to think—to know that for any act of mine, I shall get twice as much praise or twice as much blame. It is quite exciting to hold the center of the national stage, with the spectators not knowing whether to laugh or to weep.

8 The position of my white neighbor is much more difficult. No brown specter pulls up a chair beside me when I sit down to eat. No dark ghost thrusts its leg against mine in bed. The game of keeping what one has is never so exciting as the game of getting.

9 I do not always feel colored. Even now I often achieve the unconscious Zora of Eatonville before the Hegira. I feel most colored when I am thrown against a sharp white background.

10 For instance at Barnard. "Beside the waters of the Hudson" I feel my race. Among the thousand white persons, I am a dark rock surged upon, and overswept, but through it all, I remain myself. When covered by the waters, I am; and the ebb but reveals me again.

11 Sometimes it is the other way around. A white person set down in our midst, but the contrast is just as sharp for me. For instance, when I sit in the drafty basement that is The New World Cabaret with a white person, my color comes. We enter chatting about any little

nothing that we have in common and are seated by the jazz waiters. In the abrupt way that jazz orchestras have, this one plunges into a number. It loses no time in circumlocutions, but gets right down to business. It constricts the thorax and splits the heart with its tempo and narcotic harmonies. This orchestra grows rambunctious, rears on its hind legs and attacks the tonal veil with primitive fury, rending it, clawing it until it breaks through to the jungle beyond. I follow those heathen—follow them exultingly. I dance wildly inside myself; I yell within, I whoop; I shake my assegai above my head, I hurl it true to the mark *yeeeeooww!* I am in the jungle and living in the jungle way. My face is painted red and yellow and my body is painted blue. My pulse is throbbing like a war drum. I want to slaughter something—give pain, give death to what, I do not know. But the piece ends. The men of the orchestra wipe their lips and rest their fingers. I creep back slowly to the veneer we call civilization with the last tone and find the white friend sitting motionless in his seat, smoking calmly.

"Good music they have here," he remarks, drumming the table 12
with his fingertips.

Music. The great blobs of purple and red emotion have not 13
touched him. He has only heard what I felt. He is far away and I see him but dimly across the ocean and the continent that have fallen between us. He is so pale with his whiteness then and I am *so* colored.

At certain times I have no race, I am *me.* When I set my hat at a 14
certain angle and saunter down Seventh Avenue, Harlem City, feeling as snooty as the lions in front of the Forty-Second Street Library, for instance. So far as my feelings are concerned, Peggy Hopkins Joyce on the Boule Mich with her gorgeous raiment, stately carriage, knees knocking together in a most aristocratic manner, has nothing on me. The cosmic Zora emerges. I belong to no race nor time. I am the eternal feminine with its string of beads.

I have no separate feeling about being an American citizen and 15
colored. I am merely a fragment of the Great Soul that surges within the boundaries. My country, right or wrong.

Sometimes, I feel discriminated against, but it does not make me 16
angry. It merely astonishes me. How *can* any deny themselves the pleasure of my company? It's beyond me.

But in the main, I feel like a brown bag of miscellany propped 17
against a wall. Against a wall in company with other bags, white, red and yellow. Pour out the contents, and there is discovered a jumble of small things priceless and worthless. A first-water diamond, an empty spool, bits of broken glass, lengths of string, a key to a door long since crumbled away, a rusty knife-blade, old shoes saved for a

road that never was and never will be, a nail bent under the weight of things too heavy for any nail, a dried flower or two still a little fragrant. In your hand is the brown bag. On the ground before you is the jumble it held—so much like the jumble in the bags, could they be emptied, that all might be dumped in a single heap and the bags refilled without altering the content of any greatly. A bit of colored glass more or less would not matter. Perhaps that is how the Great Stuffer of Bags filled them in the first place—who knows?

### IN RETROSPECT

**1.** For most readers, this essay may be the most difficult one in this chapter to read and understand. The difficulty may stem from the structure of the essay and from the way in which the parts are related. The essay seems to fall into four parts, each of them separated by extra space between the paragraphs: part 1, paragraphs 1–5; part 2, paragraphs 6–10; part 3, paragraphs 11–13; and part 4, paragraphs 14–17. See if by yourself or in consultation with others who have read the essay you can determine what Hurston is doing in each of these parts and how these parts are related to one another.

**2.** One of the appealing features of this essay is the author's use of fresh, arresting metaphors. Here, for instance, are two of the metaphors: (a) "Proscenium box for a born first-nighter. Not only did I enjoy the show, but I didn't mind the actors knowing that I liked it" (paragraph 3) and (b) "No, I do not weep at the world—I am too busy sharpening my oyster knife" (paragraph 6). Maybe the most interesting figure of speech is the extended metaphor of the brown bag with its jumble of miscellany inside (in the final paragraph, paragraph 17). What does this metaphor—and the others in the essay—contribute to your understanding of the essay?

# *The Little Store*

## EUDORA WELTY

Eudora Welty (1909– ) was born in Jackson, Mississippi, and still lives there. As a beginning writer of fiction, she was strongly influenced by another Southern writer, Katherine Anne Porter, and like Porter, she is a keen observer of human character and an elegant stylist. Her first three collections of short stories were *The Curtain of Green* (1941), *The Wide Net* (1943), and *The Golden Apples,* (1949). Her first novel was *Delta Welty* (1946). A later short novel, *The Ponder Heart* (1954), was turned into a Broadway play by Jerome Chodorov and Joseph Fields in 1957. Her 1972 novel, *The Optimist's Daughter,* won the Pulitzer Prize. "The Little Store" is reprinted from a collection of her essays entitled *The Eye of the Story* (1978), a title that is a pun on the familiar phrase "the eye of the storm" (*eye* here equals the pronoun *I*). The *I* in "The Little Store" is Welty as a child growing up in Jackson. This piece of literary nonfiction exhibits Welty's talent for the kind of meticulous, revealing observation of scene and character that is exemplified in all her fiction. Like every child, Welty is struggling here to discover her identity and her place in the small corner of the earth in which she was born and raised.

Two blocks away from the Mississippi State Capitol, and on the same street with it, where our house was when I was a child growing up in Jackson, it was possible to have a little pasture behind your backyard where you could keep a Jersey cow, which we did. My mother herself milked her. A thrifty homemaker, wife, mother of three, she also did all her own cooking. And as far as I can recall, she never set foot inside a grocery store. It wasn't necessary. 1

For her regular needs, she stood at the telephone in our front hall and consulted with Mr. Lemly, of Lemly's Market and Grocery downtown, who took her order and sent it out on his next delivery. And since Jackson at the heart of it was still within very near reach of the open country, the blackberry lady clanged on her bucket with a quart measure at your front door in June without fail, the watermelon man rolled up to your house exactly on time for the Fourth of July, and down through the summer, the quiet of the early-morning streets was pierced by the calls of farmers driving in with their plenty. One brought his with a song, so plaintive we would sing it with him: 2

Milk, milk,
Buttermilk,
Snap beans—butterbeans—
Tender okra—fresh greens . . .
And buttermilk.

My mother considered herself pretty well prepared in her kitchen and pantry for any emergency that, in her words, might choose to present itself. But if she should, all of a sudden, need another lemon or find she was out of bread, all she had to do was call out, "Quick! Who'd like to run to the Little Store for me?" 3

I would. 4

She'd count out the change into my hand, and I was away. I'll bet the nickel that would be left over that all over the country, for those of my day, the neighborhood grocery played a similar part in our growing up. 5

Our store had its name—it was that of the grocer who owned it, whom I'll call Mr. Sessions—but "the Little Store" is what we called it 6 at home. It was a block down our street toward the capitol and a half a block further, around the corner, toward the cemetery. I knew even the sidewalk to it as well as I knew my own skin. I'd skipped my jumping-rope up and down it, hopped its length through mazes of hopscotch, played jacks in its islands of shade, serpentined along it on my Princess bicycle, skated it backward and forward. In the twilight I had dragged my steamboat by its string (this was home-made out of every new shoebox, with candle in the bottom lighted and shining through colored tissue paper pasted over windows scissored out in the shapes of the sun, moon, and stars) across every crack of the walk without letting it bump or catch fire. I'd "played out" on that street after supper with my brothers and friends as long as "first-dark" lasted; I'd caught its lightning bugs. On the first Armistice Day (and this will set the time I'm speaking of) we made our own parade down that walk on a single velocipede—my brother pedaling, our little brother riding the handlebars, and myself standing on the back, all with arms wide, flying flags in each hand. (My father snapped that picture as we raced by. It came out blurred.)

As I set forth for the Little Store, a tune would float toward me 7
from the house where there lived three sisters, girls in their teens, who ratted their hair over their ears, wore headbands like gladiators, and were considered to be very popular. They practiced for this in the daytime; they'd wind up the Victrola, leave the same record on they'd played before, and you'd see them bobbing past their dining-room windows while they danced with each other. Being three, they could go all day, cutting in:

> Everybody ought to know-oh
> How to do the Tickle-Toe
> (how to do the Tickle-Toe)—

they sang it and danced to it, and as I went by to the same song, I believed it.

A little further on, across the street, was the house where the 8
principal of our grade school lived—lived on, even while we were having vacation. What if she would come out? She would halt me in my tracks—she had a very carrying and well-known voice in Jackson, where she'd taught almost everybody—saying "Eudora Alice Welty, spell OBLIGE." OBLIGE was the word that she of course knew had kept me from making 100 on my spelling exam. She'd make me miss it again now, by boring her eyes through me from across the street. This was my vacation fantasy, one good way to scare myself on the way to the store.

Down near the corner waited the house of a little boy named 9
Lindsey. The sidewalk here was old brick, which the roots of a giant

chinaberry tree had humped up and tilted this way and that. On skates, you took it fast, in a series of skittering hops, trying not to touch ground anywhere. If the chinaberries had fallen and rolled in the cracks, it was like skating through a whole shooting match of marbles. I crossed my fingers that Lindsey wouldn't be looking.

During the big flu epidemic he and I, as it happened, were being nursed through our sieges at the same time. I'd hear my father and mother murmuring to each other, at the end of a long day, "And I wonder how poor little *Lindsey* got along today?" Just as, down the street, he no doubt would have to hear his family saying, "And I wonder how is poor *Eudora* by now?" I got the idea that a choice was going to be made soon between poor little Lindsey and poor Eudora, and I came up with a funny poem. I wasn't prepared for it when my father told me it wasn't funny and my mother cried that if I couldn't be ashamed for myself, she'd have to be ashamed for me: 10

> There was a little boy and his name was Lindsey.
> He went to heaven with the influinzy.

He didn't, he survived it, poem and all, the same as I did. But his chinaberries could have brought me down in my skates in a flying act of contrition before his eyes, looking pretty funny myself, right in front of his house.

Setting out in this world, a child feels so indelible. He only comes to find out later that it's all the others along his way who are making themselves indelible to him. 11

Our Little Store rose right up from the sidewalk; standing in a street of family houses, it alone hadn't any yard in front, any tree or flowerbed. It was a plain frame building covered over with brick. Above the door, a little railed porch ran across on an upstairs level and four windows with shades were looking out. But I didn't catch on to those. 12

Running in out of the sun, you met what seemed total obscurity inside. There were almost tangible smells—licorice recently sucked in a child's cheek, dill-pickle brine that had leaked through a paper sack in a fresh trail across the wooden floor, ammonia-loaded ice that had been hoisted from wet croker sacks and slammed into the icebox with its sweet butter at the door, and perhaps the smell of still-untrapped mice. 13

Then through the motes of cracker dust, cornmeal dust, the Gold Dust of the Gold Dust Twins that the floor had been swept out with, the realities emerged. Shelves climbed to high reach all the way around, set out with not too much of any one thing but a lot of things—lard, molasses, vinegar, starch, matches, kerosene, Octagon soap (about a year's worth of octagon-shaped coupons cut out and 14 saved brought a signet ring addressed to you in the mail. Furthermore, when the postman arrived at your door, he blew a whistle). It was up to you to remember what you came for, while your eye traveled from cans of sardines to ice cream salt to harmonicas to flypaper (over your head, batting around on a thread beneath the blades of the ceiling fan, stuck with its testimonial catch).

Its confusion may have been in the eye of its beholder. Enchant- 15
ment is cast upon you by all those things you weren't supposed to have need for, it lures you close to wooden tops you'd outgrown, boy's marbles and agates in little net pouches, small rubber balls that wouldn't bounce straight, frazzly kite-string, clay bubble-pipes that would snap off in your teeth, the stiffest scissors. You could contemplate those long narrow boxes of sparklers gathering dust while you waited for it to be the Fourth of July or Christmas, and noisemakers in the shape of tin frogs for somebody's birthday party you hadn't been invited to yet, and see that they were all marvelous.

You might not have even looked for Mr. Sessions when he came 16
around his store cheese (as big as a doll's house) and in front of the counter looking for you. When you'd finally asked him for, and received from him in its paper bag, whatever single thing it was that you had been sent for, the nickel that was left over was yours to spend.

Down at a child's eye level, inside those glass jars with mouths in 17
their sides through which the grocer could run his scoop or a child's hand might be invited to reach for a choice, were wineballs, all-day suckers, gumdrops, peppermints. Making a row under the glass of a counter were the Tootsie Rolls, Hershey Bars, Goo-Goo Clusters, Baby Ruths. And whatever was the name of those pastilles that came stacked in a cardboard cylinder with a cardboard lid? They were thin and dry, about the size of tiddly-winks, and in the shape of twisted rosettes. A kind of chocolate dust came out with them when you shook them out in your hand. Were they chocolate? I'd say rather they were brown. They didn't taste of anything at all, unless it was wood. Their attraction was the number you got for a nickel.

Making up your mind, you circled the store around and around, 18
around the pickle barrel, around the tower of Cracker Jack boxes; Mr. Sessions had built it for us himself on top of a packing case, like a house of cards.

If it seemed too hot for Cracker Jacks, I might get a cold drink. Mr. 19
Sessions might have already stationed himself by the cold-drinks barrel, like a mind reader. Deep in ice water that looked black as ink, murky shapes that would come up as Coca-Colas, Orange Crushes, and various flavors of pop were all swimming around together. When you gave the word, Mr. Sessions plunged his bare arm in to the elbow and fished out your choice, first try. I favored a locally bottled

concoction called Lake's Celery. (What else could it be called? It was made by a Mr. Lake out of celery. It was a popular drink here for years but was not known universally, as I found out when I arrived in New York and ordered one in the Astor bar.) You drank on the premises, with feet set wide apart to miss the drip, and gave him back his bottle.

But he didn't hurry you off. A standing scales was by the door, 20
with a stack of iron weights and a brass slide on the balance arm, that would weigh you up to three hundred pounds. Mr. Sessions, whose hands were gentle and smelled of carbolic, would lift you up and set your feet on the platform, hold your loaf of bread for you, and taking his time while you stood still for him, he would make certain of what you weighed today. He could even remember what you weighed last time, so you could subtract and announce how much you'd gained. That was goodbye.

Is there always a hard way to go home? From the Little Store, you 21
could go partway through the sewer. If your brothers had called you a scarecat, then across the next street beyond the Little Store, it was possible to enter this sewer by passing through a private hedge, climbing down into the bed of a creek, and going into its mouth on your knees. The sewer—it might have been no more than a "storm sewer"—came out and emptied here, where Town Creek, a sandy, most often shallow little stream that ambled through Jackson on its way to the Pearl River, ran along the edge of the cemetery. You could go in darkness through this tunnel to where you next saw light (if you ever did) and climb out through the culvert at your own street corner.

I was a scarecat, all right, but I was a reader with my own refuge 22
in storybooks. Making my way under the sidewalk, under the street and the street-car track, under the Little Store, down there in the wet dark by myself, I could be Persephone entering into my six-month sojourn underground—though I didn't suppose Persephone had to crawl, hanging onto a loaf of bread, and come out through the teeth of an iron grating. Mother Ceres would indeed be wondering where she could find me, and mad when she knew. "Now am I going to have to start marching to the Little Store for *myself?*"

I couldn't picture it. Indeed I'm unable today to picture the Little 23
Store with a grown person in it, except for Mr. Sessions and the lady who helped him, who belonged there. We children thought it was ours. The happiness of errands was in part that of running for the moment away from home, a free spirit. I believed the Little Store to be a center of the outside world, and hence of happiness—as I believed what I found in the Cracker Jack box to be a genuine prize, which was as simply as I believed in the Golden Fleece.

But a day came when I ran to the store to discover, sitting on the 24
front step, a grown person, after all—more than a grown person. It

was the Monkey Man, together with his monkey. His grinding-organ was lowered to the step beside him. In my whole life so far, I must have laid eyes on the Monkey Man no more than five or six times. An itinerant of rare and wayward appearances, he was not punctual like the Gipsies, who every year with the first cool days of fall showed up in the aisles of Woolworth's. You never knew when the Monkey Man might decide to favor Jackson, or which way he'd go. Sometimes you heard him as close as the next street, and then he didn't come up yours.

But now I saw the Monkey Man at the Little Store, where I'd 25
never seen him before. I'd never seen him sitting down. Low on that familiar doorstep, he was not the same any longer, and neither was his monkey. They looked just like an old man and an old friend of his that wore a fez, meeting quietly together, tired, and resting with their eyes fixed on some place far away, and not the same place. Yet their romance for me didn't have it in its power to waver. I wavered. I simply didn't know how to step around them, to proceed on into the Little Store for my mother's emergency as if nothing had happened. If I could have gone in there after it, whatever it was, I would have given it to them—putting it into the monkey's cool little fingers. I would have given them the Little Store itself.

In my memory they are still attached to the store—so are all the 26
others. Everyone I saw on my way seemed to me then part of my errand, and in a way they were. As I myself, the free spirit, was part of it too.

All the years we lived in that house where we children were born, 27
the same people lived in the other houses on our street too. People changed through the arithmetic of birth, marriage, and death, but not by going away. So families just accrued stories, which through the fullness of time, in those times, their own lives made. And I grew up in those.

But I didn't know there'd ever been a story at the Little Store, one 28
that was going on while I was there. Of course, all the time the Sessions family had been living right overhead there, in the upstairs rooms behind the little railed porch and the shaded windows; but I think we children never thought of that. Did I fail to see them as a family because they weren't living in an ordinary house? Because I so seldom saw them close together, or having anything to say to each other? She sat in the back of the store, her pencil over a ledger, while he stood and waited on children to make up their minds. They worked in twin black eyeshades, held on their gray heads by elastic bands. It may be harder to recognize kindness—or unkindness either—in a face whose eyes are in shadow. His face underneath his shade was as round as the little wooden wheels in the Tinker Toy

box. So was her face. I didn't know, perhaps didn't even wonder: were they husband and wife or brother and sister? Were they father and mother? There were a few other persons, of various ages, wandering singly in by the back door and out. But none of their relationships could I imagine, when I'd never seen them sitting down together around their own table.

The possibility that they had any other life at all, anything beyond 29
what we could see within the four walls of the Little Store, occurred to me only when tragedy struck their family. There was some act of violence. The shock to the neighborhood traveled to the children, of course; but I couldn't find out from my parents what had happened. They held it back from me, as they'd already held back many things, "until the time comes for you to know."

You could find out some of these things by looking in the un- 30
abridged dictionary and the encyclopedia—kept to hand in our dining room—but you couldn't find out there what had happened to the family who for all the years of your life had lived upstairs over the Little Store, who had never been anything but patient and kind to you, who never once had sent you away. All I ever knew was its aftermath: they were the only people ever known to me who simply vanished. At the point where their life overlapped into ours, the story broke off.

We weren't being sent to the neighborhood grocery for facts of 31
life, or death. But of course those are what we were on the track of, anyway. With the loaf of bread and the Cracker Jack prize, I was bringing home the intimations of pride and disgrace, and rumors and early news of people coming to hurt one another, while others practiced for joy—storing up a portion for myself of the human mystery.

## IN RETROSPECT

**1.** The headnote for "The Little Store" suggests that Welty's essay can be seen from the perspective either of the "eye" or of the "I." In order to make sense of the essay, how would you use the contrast that you observed between what Welty sees and what she says she fails to see? How does the "eye" or the "I" that you focus on the world around you compare with Welty's?

**2.** Throughout the essay, Welty keeps shifting the perspectives from which she describes or narrates things—a shift, for instance, from the point of view of a child to the point of view of an adult; a shift from past time to present time; a shift in tempo from quickly narrating events to leisurely narrating events. Examine some of these shifts in the essay. What does Welty accomplish with them, and how does she manage to maintain coherence despite these frequent and abrupt shifts?

# *On Being Black and Middle Class*

**SHELBY STEELE**

Shelby Steele (1946– ) is a professor of English at San Jose State University in California. In 1990 he published *The Content of Our Character: A New Vision of Race in America,* which in 1991 won the National Book Critics Circle Award for General Nonfiction. In the essay reprinted here, Steele, because he is an extraordinarily articulate writer, is able to make us understand and feel what it is like to be a member of a minority race in the United States during the second half of the twentieth century. In this essay, which first appeared in a 1988 issue of *Commentary,* Steele is telling us about not only his struggle to determine his identity in this society but also his problem in dealing with the double bind brought on by his race and by his class—by being both a black man and a member of the middle class in America during the turbulent 1960s. Where do Steele's primary loyalties reside? Can he reconcile his racial roots with his middle-class status? It is a poignant story that he tells us.

Not long ago a friend of mine, black like myself, said to me that 1
the term "black middle class" was actually a contradiction in terms. Race, he insisted, blurred class distinctions among blacks. If you were black, you were just black and that was that. When I argued, he let his eyes roll at my naiveté. Then he went on. For us, as black professionals, it was an exercise in self-flattery, a pathetic pretension, to give meaning to such a distinction. Worse, the very idea of class threatened the unity that was vital to the black community as a whole. After all, since when had white America taken note of anything but color when it came to blacks? He then reminded me of an old Malcolm X line that had been popular in the sixties. Question: What is a black man with a Ph.D.? Answer: A nigger.

For many years I had been on my friend's side of this argument. 2
Much of my conscious thinking on the old conundrum of race and class was shaped during my high school and college years in the race-charged sixties, when the fact of my race took on an almost religious significance. Progressively, from the midsixties on, more and more aspects of my life found their explanation, their justification, and their motivation in race. My youthful concerns about career, romance, money, values, and even styles of dress became subject to consultation with various oracular sources of racial wisdom. And these ranged from a figure as ennobling as Martin Luther King, Jr., to the underworld elegance of dress I found in jazz clubs on the South Side of Chicago. Everywhere there were signals, and in those days I considered myself so blessed with clarity and direction that I pitied my white classmates who found more embarrassment than guidance

in the fact of *their* race. In 1968, inflated by my new power, I took a mischievous delight in calling them culturally disadvantaged.

But now, hearing my friend's comment was like hearing a priest 3
from a church I'd grown disenchanted with. I understood him, but my faith was weak. What had sustained me in the sixties sounded monotonous and off the mark in the eighties. For me, race had lost much of its juju, its singular capacity to conjure meaning. And today, when I honestly look at my life and the lives of many other middle-class blacks I know, I can see that race never fully explained our situation in American society. Black though I may be, it is impossible for me to sit in my single-family house with two cars in the driveway and a swing set in the back yard and *not* see the role class has played in my life. And how can my friend, similarly raised and similarly situated, not see it?

Yet despite my certainty I felt a sharp tug of guilt as I tried to 4
explain myself over my friend's skepticism. He is a man of many comedic facial expressions and, as I spoke, his brow lifted in extreme moral alarm as if I were uttering the unspeakable. His clear implication was that I was being elitist and possibly (dare he suggest?) anti-black—crimes for which there might well be no redemption. He pretended to fear for me. I chuckled along with him, but inwardly I did wonder at myself. Though I never doubted the validity of what I was saying, I felt guilty saying it. Why?

After he left (to retrieve his daughter from a dance lesson) I 5
realized that the trap I felt myself in had a tiresome familiarity and, in a sort of slow-motion epiphany, I began to see its outline. It was like the suddenly sharp vision one has at the end of a burdensome marriage when all the long-repressed incompatibilities come undeniably to light.

What became clear to me is that people like myself, my friend, 6
and middle-class blacks generally are caught in a very specific double bind that keeps two equally powerful elements of our identity at odds with each other. The middle-class values by which we were raised—the work ethic, the importance of education, the value of property ownership, of respectability, of "getting ahead," of stable family life, of initiative, of self-reliance, etc.—are, in themselves, raceless and even assimilationist. They urge us toward participation in the American mainstream, toward integration, toward a strong identification with the society—and toward the entire constellation of qualities that are implied in the word "individualism." These values are almost rules for how to prosper in a democratic, free-enterprise society that admires and rewards individual effort. They tell us to work hard for ourselves and our families and to seek our opportunities whenever

they appear, inside or outside the confines of whatever ethnic group we may belong to.

But the particular pattern of racial identification that emerged in 7
the sixties and that still prevails today urges middle-class blacks (and all blacks) in the opposite direction. This pattern asks us to see ourselves as an embattled minority, and it urges an adversarial stance toward the mainstream, an emphasis on ethnic consciousness over individualism. It is organized around an implied separatism.

The opposing thrust of these two parts of our identity results in 8
the double bind of middle-class blacks. There is no forward movement on either plane that does not constitute backward movement on the other. This was the familiar trap I felt myself in while talking with my friend. As I spoke about class, his eyes reminded me that I was betraying race. Clearly, the two indispensable parts of my identity were a threat to each other.

Of course when you think about it, class and race are both similar 9
in some ways and also naturally opposed. They are two forms of collective identity with boundaries that intersect. But whether they clash or peacefully coexist has much to do with how they are defined. Being both black and middle class becomes a double bind when class and race are defined in sharply antagonistic terms, so that one must be repressed to appease the other.

But what is the "substance" of these two identities, and how does 10
each establish itself in an individual's overall identity? It seems to me that when we identify with any collective we are basically identifying with images that tell us what it means to be a member of that collective. Identity is not the same thing as the fact of membership in a collective; it is, rather, a form of self-definition, facilitated by images of what we wish our membership in the collective to mean. In this sense, the images we identify with may reflect the aspirations of the collective more than they reflect reality, and their content can vary with shifts in those aspirations.

But the process of identification is usually dialectical. It is just as 11
necessary to say what we are *not* as it is to say what we are—so that finally identification comes about by embracing a polarity of positive and negative images. To identify as middle class, for example, I must have both positive and negative images of what being middle class entails; then I will know what I should and should not be doing in order to be middle class. The same goes for racial identity.

In the racially turbulent sixties the polarity of images that came to 12
define racial identification was very antagonistic to the polarity that defined middle-class identification. One might say that the positive images of one lined up with the negative images of the other, so that

to identify with both required either a contortionist's flexibility or a dangerous splitting of the self. The double bind of the black middle class was in place.

The black middle class has always defined its class identity by 13
means of positive images gleaned from middle- and upper-class white society, and by means of negative images of lower-class blacks. This habit goes back to the institution of slavery itself, when "house" slaves both mimicked the whites they served and held themselves above the "field" slaves. But in the sixties the old bourgeois impulse to dissociate from the lower classes (the "we-they" distinction) backfired when racial identity suddenly called for the celebration of this same black lower class. One of the qualities of a double bind is that one feels it more than sees it, and I distinctly remember the tension and strange sense of dishonesty I felt in those days as I moved back and forth like a bigamist between the demands of class and race.

Though my father was born poor, he achieved middle-class 14
standing through much hard work and sacrifice (one of his favorite words) and by identifying fully with solid middle-class values—mainly hard work, family life, property ownership, and education for his children (all four of whom have advanced degrees). In his mind these were not so much values as laws of nature. People who embodied them made up the positive images in his class polarity. The negative images came largely from the blacks he had left behind because they were "going nowhere."

No one in my family remembers how it happened, but as time 15
went on, the negative images congealed into an imaginary character named Sam, who, from the extensive service we put him to, quickly grew to mythic proportions. In our family lore he was sometimes a trickster, sometimes a boob, but always possessed of a catalogue of sly faults that gave up graphic images of everything we should not be. On sacrifice: "Sam never thinks about tomorrow. He wants it now or he doesn't care about it." On work: "Sam doesn't favor it too much." On children: "Sam likes to have them but not to raise them." On money: "Sam drinks it up and pisses it out." On fidelity: "Sam has to have two or three women." On clothes: "Sam features loud clothes. He likes to see and be seen." And so on. Sam's persona amounted to a negative instruction manual in class identity.

I don't think that any of us believed Sam's faults were accurate 16
representations of lower-class black life. He was an instrument of self-definition, not of sociological accuracy. It never occurred to us that he looked very much like the white racist stereotype of blacks, or that he might have been a manifestation of our own racial self-hatred.

He simply gave us a counterpoint against which to express our aspirations. If self-hatred was a factor, it was not, for us, a matter of hating lower-class blacks but of hating what we did not want to be.

Still, hate or love aside, it is fundamentally true that my middle- 17
class identity involved a dissociation from images of lower-class black life and a corresponding identification with values and patterns of responsibility that are common to the middle class everywhere. These values sent me a clear message: be both an individual and a responsible citizen; understand that the quality of your life will approximately reflect the quality of effort you put into it; know that individual responsibility is the basis of freedom and that the limitations imposed by fate (whether fair or unfair) are no excuse for passivity.

Whether I live up to these values or not, I know that my accep- 18
tance of them is the result of lifelong conditioning. I know also that I share this conditioning with middle-class people of all races and that I can no more easily be free of it than I can be free of my race. Whether all this got started because the black middle class modeled itself on the white middle class is no longer relevant. For the middle-class black, conditioned by these values from birth, the sense of meaning they provide is as immutable as the color of his skin.

I started the sixties in high school feeling that my class-condition- 19
ing was the surest way to overcome racial barriers. My racial identity was pretty much taken for granted. After all, it was obvious to the world that I was black. Yet I ended the sixties in graduate school a little embarrassed by my class background and with an almost desperate need to be "black." The tables had turned. I knew very clearly (though I struggled to repress it) that my aspirations and my sense of how to operate in the world came from my class background, yet "being black" required certain attitudes and stances that made me feel secretly a little duplicitous. The inner compatibility of class and race I had known in 1960 was gone.

For blacks, the decade between 1960 and 1969 saw racial identi- 20
fication undergo the same sort of transformation that national identity undergoes in times of war. It became more self-conscious, more narrowly focused, more prescribed, less tolerant of opposition. It spawned an implicit party line, which tended to disallow competing forms of identity. Race-as-identity was lifted from the relative slumber it knew in the fifties and pressed into service in a social and political war against oppression. It was redefined along sharp adversarial lines and directed toward the goal of mobilizing the great mass of black Americans in this warlike effort. It was imbued with a strong moral authority, useful for denouncing those who opposed it and for

celebrating those who honored it as a positive achievement rather than as a mere birthright.

The form of racial identification that quickly evolved to meet the 21
challenge presented blacks as a racial monolith, a singular people with a common experience of oppression. Differences within the race, no matter how ineradicable, had to be minimized. Class distinctions were one of the first such differences to be sacrificed, since they not only threatened racial unity but also seemed to stand in contradiction to the principle of equality which was the announced goal of the movement for racial progress. The discomfort I felt in 1969, the vague but relentless sense of duplicity, was the result of a historical necessity that put my race and class at odds, that was asking me to cast aside the distinction of my class and identify with a monolithic view of my race.

If the form of this racial identity was the monolith, its substance 22
was victimization. The civil rights movement and the more radical splinter groups of the late sixties were all dedicated to ending racial victimization, and the form of black identity that emerged to facilitate this goal made blackness and victimization virtually synonymous. Since it was our victimization more than any other variable that identified and unified us, moreover, it followed logically that the purest black was the poor black. It was images of him that clustered around the positive pole of the race polarity; all other blacks were, in effect, required to identify with him in order to confirm their own blackness.

Certainly there were more dimensions to the black experience 23
than victimization, but no other had the same capacity to fire the indignation needed for war. So, again out of historical necessity, victimization became the overriding focus of racial identity. But this only deepened the double bind for middle-class blacks like me. When it came to class we were accustomed to defining ourselves against lower-class blacks and identifying with at least the values of middle-class whites; when it came to race we were now being asked to identify with images of lower-class blacks and to see whites, middle class or otherwise, as victimizers. Negative lining up with positive, we were called upon to reject what we had previously embraced and to embrace what we had previously rejected. To put it still more personally, the Sam figure I had been raised to define myself against had now become the "real" black I was expected to identify with.

The fact that the poor black's new status was only passively 24
earned by the condition of his victimization, not by assertive, positive action, made little difference. Status was status apart from the means by which it was achieved, and along with it came a certain power—

the power to define the terms of access to that status, to say who was black and who was not. If a lower-class black said you were not really "black"—a sellout, an Uncle Tom—the judgment was all the more devastating because it carried the authority of his status. And this judgment soon enough came to be accepted by many whites as well.

In graduate school I was once told by a white professor, "Well, 25
but . . . you're not really black. I mean, you're not disadvantaged." In his mind my lack of victim status disqualified me from the race itself. More recently I was complimented by a black student for speaking reasonably correct English, "proper" English as he put it. "But I don't know if I really want to talk like that," he went on. "Why not?" I asked. "Because then I wouldn't be black no more," he replied without a pause.

To overcome his marginal status, the middle-class black had to 26
identify with a degree of victimization that was beyond his actual experience. In college (and well beyond) we used to play a game called "nap matching." It was a game of one-upmanship, in which we sat around outdoing each other with stories of racial victimization, symbolically measured by the naps of our hair. Most of us were middle class and so had few personal stories to relate, but if we could not match naps with our own biographies, we would move on to those legendary tales of victimization that came to us from the public domain.

The single story that sat atop the pinnacle of racial victimization 27
for us was that of Emmett Till, the Northern black teenager who, on a visit to the South in 1955, was killed and grotesquely mutilated for supposedly looking at or whistling at (we were never sure which, though we argued the point endlessly) a white woman. Oh, how we probed his story, finding in his youth and Northern upbringing the quintessential embodiment of black innocence, brought down by a white evil so portentous and apocalyptic, so gnarled and hideous, that it left us with a feeling not far from awe. By telling his story and others like it, we came to *feel* the immutability of our victimization, its utter indigenousness, as a thing on this earth like dirt or sand or water.

Of course, these sessions were a ritual of group identification, a 28
means by which we, as middle-class blacks, could be at one with our race. But why were we, who had only a moderate experience of victimization (and that offset by opportunities our parents never had), so intent on assimilating or appropriating an identity that in so many ways contradicted our own? Because, I think, the sense of innocence that is always entailed in feeling victimized filled us with a corresponding feeling of entitlement, or even license, that helped us endure our vulnerability on a largely white college campus.

In my junior year in college I rode to a debate tournament with three white students and our faculty coach, an elderly English professor. The experience of being the lone black in a group of whites was so familiar to me that I thought nothing of it as our trip began. But then halfway through the trip the professor casually turned to me and, in an isn't-the-world-funny sort of tone, said that he had just refused to rent an apartment in a house he owned to a "very nice" black couple because their color would "offend" the white couple who lived downstairs. His eyebrows lifted helplessly over his hawkish nose, suggesting that he too, like me, was a victim of America's racial farce. His look assumed a kind of comradeship: he and I were above this grimy business of race, though for expediency we had occasionally to concede the world its madness. 29

My vulnerability in this situation came not so much from the professor's blindness to his own racism as from his assumption that I would participate in it, that I would conspire with him against my own race so that he might remain comfortably blind. Why did he think I would be amenable to this? I can only guess that he assumed my middle-class identity was so complete and all-encompassing that I would see his action as nothing more than a trifling concession to the folkways of our land, that I would in fact applaud his decision not to disturb propriety. Blind to both his own racism and to me—one blindness serving the other—he could not recognize that he was asking me to betray my race in the name of my class. 30

His blindness made me feel vulnerable because it threatened to expose my own repressed ambivalence. His comment pressured me to choose between my class identification, which had contributed to my being a college student and a member of the debating team, and my desperate desire to be "black." I could have one but not both; I was double-bound. 31

Because double binds are repressed there is always an element of terror in them: the terror of bringing to the conscious mind the buried duplicity, self-deception, and pretense involved in serving two masters. This terror is the stuff of vulnerability, and since vulnerability is one of the least tolerable of all human feelings, we usually transform it into an emotion that seems to restore the control of which it has robbed us; most often, that emotion is anger. And so, before the professor had even finished his little story, I had become a furnace of rage. The year was 1967, and I had been primed by endless hours of nap-matching to feel, at least consciously, completely at one with the victim-focused black identity. This identity gave me the license, and the impunity, to unleash upon this professor one of those volcanic eruptions of racial indignation familiar to us from the novels of Richard Wright. Like Cross Damon in *Outsider,* who kills in perfectly 32 righteous anger, I tried to annihilate the man. I punished him not according to the measure of his crime but according to the measure of my vulnerability, a measure set by the cumulative tension of years of repressed terror. Soon I saw that terror in *his* face, as he stared hollow-eyed at the road ahead. My white friends in the back seat, knowing no conflict between their own class and race, were astonished that someone they had taken to be so much like themselves could harbor a rage that for all the world looked murderous.

Though my rage was triggered by the professor's comment, it 33
was deepened and sustained by a complex of need, conflict, and repression in myself of which I had been wholly unaware. Out of my racial vulnerability I had developed the strong need of an identity with which to defend myself. The only such identity available was that of me as victim, him as victimizer. Once in the grip of this paradigm, I began to do far more damage to myself than he had done.

Seeing myself as a victim meant that I clung all the harder to my 34
racial identity, which, in turn, meant that I suppressed my class identity. This cut me off from all the resources my class values might have offered me. In those values, for instance, I might have found the means to a more dispassionate response, the response less of a victim attacked by a victimizer than of an individual offended by a foolish old man. As an individual I might have reported this professor to the college dean. Or I might have calmly tried to reveal his blindness to him, and possibly won a convert. (The flagrancy of his remark suggested a hidden guilt and even self-recognition on which I might have capitalized. Doesn't confession usually signal a willingness to face oneself?) Or I might have simply chuckled and then let my silence serve as an answer to his provocation. Would not my composure, in any form it might take, deflect into his own heart the arrow he'd shot at me?

Instead, my anger, itself the hair-trigger expression of a long- 35
repressed double bind, not only cut me off from the best of my own resources, it also distorted the nature of my true racial problem. The righteousness of this anger and the easy catharsis it brought buoyed the delusion of my victimization and left me as blind as the professor himself.

As a middle-class black I have often felt myself *contriving* to be 36
"black." And I have noticed this same contrivance in others—a certain stretching away from the natural flow of one's life to align oneself with a victim-focused black identity. Our particular needs are out of sync with the form of identity available to meet those needs. Middle-class blacks need to identify racially; it is better to think of ourselves as black and victimized than not black at all; so we contrive (more

unconsciously than consciously) to fit ourselves into an identity that denies our class and fails to address the true source of our vulnerability.

For me this once meant spending inordinate amounts of time at 37
black faculty meetings, though these meetings had little to do with my real racial anxieties or my professional life. I was new to the university, one of two blacks in an English department of over seventy, and I felt a little isolated and vulnerable, though I did not admit it to myself. But at these meetings we discussed the problems of black faculty and students within a framework of victimization. The real vulnerability we felt was covered over by all the adversarial drama the victim/victimized polarity inspired, and hence went unseen and unassuaged. And this, I think, explains our rather chronic ineffectiveness as a group. Since victimization was not our primary problem—the university had long ago opened its doors to us—we had to contrive to make it so, and there is not much energy in contrivance. What I got at these meetings was ultimately an object lesson in how fruitless struggle can be when it is not grounded in actual need.

At our black faculty meetings, the old equation of blackness with 38
victimization was ever present—to be black was to be a victim; therefore, not to be a victim was not to be black. As we contrived to meet the terms of this formula there was an inevitable distortion of both ourselves and the larger university. Through the prism of victimization the university seemed more impenetrable than it actually was, and we more limited in our powers. We fell prey to the victim's myopia, making the university an institution from which we could seek redress but which we could never fully join. And this mind-set often led us to look more for compensations for our supposed victimization than for opportunities we could pursue as individuals.

The discomfort and vulnerability felt by middle-class blacks in the 39
sixties, it could be argued, was a worthwhile price to pay considering the progress achieved during that time of racial confrontation. But what may have been tolerable then is intolerable now. Though changes in American society have made it an anachronism, the monolithic form of racial identification that came out of the sixties is still very much with us. It may be more loosely held, and its power to punish heretics has probably diminished, but it continues to catch middle-class blacks in a double bind, thus impeding not only their own advancement but even, I would contend, that of blacks as a group.

The victim-focused black identity encourages the individual to 40
feel that his advancement depends almost entirely on that of the group. Thus he loses sight not only of his own possibilities but of the

inextricable connection between individual effort and individual advancement. This is a profound encumbrance today, when there is more opportunity for blacks than ever before, for it reimposes limitations that can have the same oppressive effect as those the society has only recently begun to remove.

It was the emphasis on mass action in the sixties that made the 41
victim-focused black identity a necessity. But in the eighties and beyond, when racial advancement will come only through a multitude of individual advancements, this form of identity inadvertently adds itself to the forces that hold us back. Hard work, education, individual initiative, stable family life, property ownership—these have always been the means by which ethnic groups have moved ahead in America. Regardless of past or present victimization, these "laws" of advancement apply absolutely to black Americans also. There is no getting around this. What we need is a form of racial identity that energizes the individual by putting him in touch with both his possibilities and his responsibilities.

It has always annoyed me to hear from the mouths of certain 42
arbiters of blackness that middle-class blacks should "reach back" and pull up those blacks less fortunate than they—as though middle-class status were an unearned and essentially passive condition in which one needed a large measure of noblesse oblige to occupy one's time. My own image is of reaching back from a moving train to lift on board those who have no tickets. A noble enough sentiment—but might it not be wiser to show them the entire structure of principles, effort, and sacrifice that puts one in a position to buy a ticket any time one likes? This, I think, is something members of the black middle class can realistically offer to other blacks. Their example is not only a testament to possibility but also a lesson in method. But they cannot lead by example until they are released from a black identity that regards that example as suspect, that sees them as "marginally" black, indeed that holds *them* back by catching them in a double bind.

To move beyond the victim-focused black identity we must learn 43
to make a difficult but crucial distinction: between actual victimization, which we must resist with every resource, and identification with the victim's status. Until we do this we will continue to wrestle more with ourselves than with the new opportunities which so many paid so dearly to win.

**IN RETROSPECT**

**1.** Steele is especially skillful in giving us a sense of the agonizing double bind that some middle-class black people experience in American society. What kinds of double binds are you aware of in your own life? In what ways are these double binds similar to or different from those that Steele discusses?

What ideas in Steele's essay do you find particularly useful in understanding and dealing with your own multiple identities and with your understanding and treatment of others? How does one incorporate such ideas into daily living so that they are not forgotten shortly after their reading?

**2.** Like the other essayists in this section, Steele familiarizes us with his personal experiences. This essay differs from the rest, however, in its tone, its voice, and its diction. Point out how these features in Steele's essay differ from the same features in the other personal essays and what effect these differences have on your understanding and appreciation of the essay.

# 2

# On Family Relationships

*The previous chapter dealt with the period in which we human beings preoccupy ourselves with discovering who we are and how we fit into the physical and social world about us. Part of that discovery process consists of discovering other people. Naturally, the people we discover first and most thoroughly are our parents, our siblings, and perhaps other relatives. In short, we discover our families. A person's reactions to such discoveries can vary tremendously, depending largely on the kinds of relationships that develop within the family group. It is a rare child who does not revolt against his or her parents to some degree at some stage of life; it is also a rare child who does not readjust his or her attitude toward the parents at some later stage in life. All the writers in this chapter are talking, in one way or another, about familial relationships. The relationships may be puzzling or traumatic or comforting, but what all the relationships described here have in common is that they have been indelibly etched into the psyche of the person who shares those memories with us. What memories of your own family relationships are stirred by these essays?*

# *On Two Children in Black*

## WILLIAM MAKEPEACE THACKERAY

Many contemporary students would be able to identify William Makepeace Thackeray (1811–1863). They would know, for instance, that Thackeray was the Victorian novelist who wrote *Vanity Fair* (1847), a novel featuring two boarding-school friends, Amelia Sedley and Becky Sharp, characters who served Margaret Mitchell as the models for Melanie Hamilton and Scarlett O'Hara, respectively, in her famous novel *Gone with the Wind* (1936). They might also be able to supply such biographical information as that Thackeray was born in India but spent most of his life in England. They might not, however, be able to name such other novels of Thackeray as *Pendennis* (1848), *Henry Esmond* (1852) and its sequel *The Virginians* (1857), and *The Newcomes* (1853). They would undoubtedly not be able to cite *The Roundabout Papers* (1863), a collection of essays written for *Cornhill Magazine,* of which Thackeray was the editor from 1860 to 1862, or to tell us that "On Two Children in Black" was taken from that collection. One wonders whether this essay is a piece of reporting about an experience that Thackeray himself had while traveling on the Continent or whether Thackeray is passing on to his readers a report that he had heard from others about two young boys and their strange female and male guides. Thackeray was basically a satiric novelist. Was he being satiric in this essay? If so, what was he satirizing?

Now every word is true of this little anecdote, and I submit that 1
there lies in it a most curious and exciting little mystery. I am like a man who gives you the last bottle of his '25 claret. It is the pride of his cellar; he knows it, and he has a right to praise it. He takes up the bottle, fashioned so slenderly—takes it up tenderly, cants it with care, places it before his friends, declares how good it is, with honest pride, and wishes he had a hundred dozen bottles more of the same wine in his cellar. *Si quid novisti, &c.* I shall be very glad to hear from you. I protest and vow I am giving you the best I have.

Well, who those little boys in black were, I shall never probably 2
know, to my dying day. They were very pretty little men, with pale faces, and large melancholy eyes; and they had beautiful little hands, and little boots, and the finest little shirts, and black paletots lined with the richest silk; and they had picture-books in several languages, English, and French, and German, I remember. Two more aristocratic-looking little men I never set eyes on. They were travelling with a very handsome pale lady in mourning, and a maid-servant dressed in black, too; and on the lady's face there was the deepest grief. The little boys clambered and played about the carriage, and she sat watching. It was a railway-carriage from Frankfort to Heidelberg.

I saw at once that she was the mother of those children, and going to part from them. Perhaps I have tried parting with my own, and not found the business very pleasant. Perhaps I recollect driving down (with a certain trunk and carpet-bag on the box) with my own mother to the end of the avenue, where we waited—only a few minutes—until the whirring wheels of that "Defiance" coach were heard rolling towards us as certain as death. Twang goes the horn; up goes the trunk; down come the steps. Bah! I see the autumn evening: I hear the wheels now: I smart the cruel smart again: and, boy or man, have never been able to bear the sight of people parting from their children. 3

I thought these little men might be going to school for the first time in their lives; and Mamma might be taking them to the Doctor, and would leave them with many fond charges, and little wistful secrets of love, bidding the elder to protect his younger brother, and the younger to be gentle, and to remember to pray to God always for his mother, who would pray for her boy too. Our party made friends with these young ones during the little journey; but the poor lady was too sad to talk, except to the boys now and again, and sat in her corner, pale, and silently looking at them. 4

The next day, we saw the lady and her maid driving in the direction of the railway-station, *without the boys.* The parting had taken place, then. That night they would sleep among strangers. The little beds at home were vacant, and poor mother might go and look at them. Well, tears flow, and friends part, and mothers pray every night all over the world. I dare say we went to see Heidelberg Castle, and admired the vast shattered walls, and quaint gables; and the Neckar running its bright course through that charming scene of peace and beauty; and ate our dinner, and drank our wine with relish. The poor mother would eat but little *Abendessen* that night; and, as for the children—that first night at school—hard bed, hard words, strange boys bullying, and laughing, and jarring you with their hateful merriment—as for the first night at a strange school, we most of us remember what *that* is. And the first is not the *worst,* my boys, there's the rub. But each man has his share of troubles, and, I suppose, you must have yours. 5

From Heidelberg we went to Baden-Baden: and, I dare say, saw Madame de Schlangenbad and Madame de la Cruchecassée, and Count Punter, and Honest Captain Blackball. And whom should we see in the evening but our two little boys, walking on each side of a fierce, yellow-faced, bearded man! We wanted to renew our acquaintance with them, and they were coming forward quite pleased to greet us. But the father pulled back one of the little men by his 6 paletot, gave a grim scowl, and walked away. I can see the children now looking rather frightened away from us and up into the father's face, or the cruel uncle's—which was he? I think he was the father. So this was the end of them. Not school, as I at first had imagined. The mother was gone, who had given them the heaps of pretty books, and the pretty studs in the shirts, and the pretty silken clothes, and the tender—tender cares; and they were handed to this scowling practitioner of Trente-et-Quarante. Ah! this is worse than school. Poor little men! Poor mother sitting by the vacant little beds! We saw the children once or twice after, always in Scowler's company; but we did not dare to give each other any marks of recognition.

From Baden we went to Basle, and thence to Lucerne, and so over 7
the Saint Gothard into Italy. From Milan we went to Venice; and now comes the singular part of my story. In Venice there is a little court of which I forget the name: but in it is an apothecary's shop, whither I went to buy some remedy for the bites of certain animals which abound in Venice. Crawling animals, skipping animals, and humming flying animals: all three will have at you at once; and one night nearly drove me into a strait-waistcoat. Well, as I was coming out of the apothecary's with the bottle of spirits of hartshorn in my hand (it really does do the bites a great deal of good), whom should I light upon but one of my little Heidelberg-Baden boys!

I have said how handsomely they were dressed as long as they 8
were with their mother. When I saw the boy at Venice, who perfectly recognised me, his only garb was a wretched yellow cotton gown. His little feet, on which I had admired the little shiny boots, were *without shoe or stocking*. He looked at me, ran to an old hag of a woman, who seized his hand; and with her he disappeared down one of the thronged lanes of the city.

From Venice we went to Trieste (the Vienna railway at that time 9
was only opened as far as Laybach, and the magnificent Semmering Pass was not quite completed). At a station between Laybach and Graetz, one of my companions alighted for refreshment, and came back to the carriage saying:—

"There's that horrible man from Baden with the two little boys." 10

Of course, we had talked about the appearance of the little boy at 11
Venice, and his strangely altered garb. My companion said they were pale, wretched-looking, and *dressed quite shabbily.*

I got out at several stations, and looked at all the carriages. I could 12
not see my little men. From that day to this I have never set eyes on them. That is all my story. Who were they? What could they be? How can you explain that mystery of the mother giving them up; of the remarkable splendour and elegance of their appearance while under her care; of their barefooted squalor in Venice, a month afterwards; of

their shabby habiliments at Laybach? Had the father gambled away his money, and sold their clothes? How came they to have passed out of the hands of a refined lady (as she evidently was, with whom I first saw them) into the charge of quite a common woman like her with whom I saw one of the boys at Venice? Here is but one chapter of the story. Can any man write the next, or that preceding the strange one on which I happened to light? Who knows? The mystery may have some quite simple solution. I saw two children, attired like little princes, taken from their mother and consigned to other care; and a fortnight afterwards, one of them barefooted and like a beggar. Who will read this riddle of The Two Children in Black?

#### IN RETROSPECT

**1.** What we see displayed in this essay is a relationship between two young boys and three adults, two of whom may be the parents of the boys. But like the "I" of this narrative, we observe the relationship from, as it were, a distance. We encounter the boys four times; we observe what happens each time; and we make inferences about the relationship. Many of our observations of people outside our family circle are conducted in this manner. This narrative intrigues us because it leaves us with more questions than answers about the boys and the adults. In the last paragraph, the author articulates some of the questions we are left with. The ultimate question we are left with is, What point was Thackeray trying to make with this enigmatic narrative?

**2.** In the first paragraph the author claims that what he is about to relate is the absolute truth. Why does he spend a whole paragraph vowing that he is telling the truth? Is it because he anticipates that his readers will find the anecdote incredible? Could it be that he is fictionalizing the event? Could this be a short story rather than an essay? (To answer this last question, you may have to reread the Introduction in order to recall the characteristics of the kind of essays that are featured in this book.) Here's another question: As the headnote suggests, could Thackeray be satirizing some situation in the Victorian society of his day?

## *Of the Passing of the First-Born*

### W. E. B. DU BOIS

William Edward Burghardt Du Bois (1868–1963) was born in Massachusetts, a descendant of a French Huguenot and an African slave. He became a scholar of Latin and Greek in his early schooling. After receiving his Ph.D. from Harvard in 1895, Du Bois began teaching history and economics at Atlanta University and launched his unremitting campaign to win social justice for the members of his race. From 1910 to 1934 he edited *The Crisis,* a magazine devoted to the amelioration of the political and social lot of blacks everywhere. Among his many published works are *John Brown* (1909), *The Negro* (1915), *Black Reconstruction* (1935), *Color and Democracy: Colonies and Peace* (1945), the novel *Dark Princess* (1928), and the autobiography *Dusk at Dawn* (1940). In 1958, Du Bois was awarded the Lenin International Peace Prize. James Weldon Johnson, another noted champion of the rights of Afro-Americans during the early years of the twentieth century, said in his autobiography, *Along the Way* (1933), that Du Bois's *The Souls of Black Folk* (1903), from which the following is taken, is "a work which, I think, has had a greater effect upon and within the Negro race in America than any other single book published in this country since *Uncle Tom's Cabin.*" The poignant lament in this essay over the death of Du Bois's young son echoes the plangent note that white Americans had long heard but had not heeded in the blues, the spirituals, and the cottonfield chants. The prose style exhibited in this essay is as distinguished as any style that you will find in twentieth-century American literature. See if you can characterize the stylistic features of this essay.

*O sister, sister, thy first-begotten,*
*The hands that cling and the feet that follow,*
*The voice of the child's blood crying yet,*
Who hath remembered me? who hath forgotten?
*Thou hast forgotten, O summer swallow,*
*But the world shall end when I forget.*

—Swinburne

"Unto you a child is born," sang the bit of yellow paper that fluttered into my room one brown October morning. Then the fear of fatherhood mingled wildly with the joy of creation; I wondered how it looked and how it felt,—what were its eyes, and how its hair curled and crumpled itself. And I thought in awe of her,—she who had slept with Death to tear a man-child from underneath her heart, while I was unconsciously wandering. I fled to my wife and child, repeating the while to myself half wonderingly, "Wife and child? Wife and child?"—fled fast and faster than boat and steam-car, and yet must ever impatiently await them; away from the hard-voiced city, away from the flickering sea into my own Berkshire Hills that sit all sadly guarding the gates of Massachusetts. 1

Up the stairs I ran to the wan mother and whimpering babe, to the sanctuary on whose altar a life at my bidding had offered itself to win a life, and won. What is this tiny formless thing, this newborn wail from an unknown world,—all head and voice? I handle it curiously, and watch perplexed its winking, breathing, and sneezing. I did not love it then; it seemed a ludicrous thing to love; but her I loved, my girl-mother, she whom now I saw unfolding like the glory 2 of the morning—the transfigured woman. Through her I came to love the wee thing, as it grew strong; as its little soul unfolded itself in twitter and cry and half-formed word, and as its eyes caught the gleam and flash of life. How beautiful he was, with his olive-tinted flesh and dark gold ringlets, his eyes of mingled blue and brown, his perfect little limbs, and the soft voluptuous roll which the blood of Africa had moulded into his features! I held him in my arms, after we had sped far away to our Southern home,—held him, and glanced at the hot red soil of Georgia and the breathless city of a hundred hills, and felt a vague unrest. Why was his hair tinted with gold? An evil omen was golden hair in my life. Why had not the brown of his eyes crushed out and killed the blue?—for brown were his father's eyes, and his father's father's. And thus in the Land of the Color-line I saw, as it fell across my baby, the shadow of the Veil.

Within the Veil was he born, said I; and there within shall he 3
live,—a Negro and a Negro's son. Holding in that little head—ah, bitterly!—the unbowed pride of a hunted race, clinging with that tiny dimpled hand—ah, wearily!—to a hope not hopeless but unhopeful, and seeing with those bright wondering eyes that peer into my soul a land whose freedom is to us a mockery and whose liberty a lie. I saw the shadow of the Veil as it passed over my baby, I saw the cold city towering above the blood-red land. I held my face beside his little cheek, showed him the star-children and the twinkling lights as they began to flash, and stilled with an evensong the unvoiced terror of my life.

So sturdy and masterful he grew, so filled with bubbling life, so 4
tremulous with the unspoken wisdom of a life but eighteen months distant from the All-life,—we were not far from worshipping this revelation of the divine, my wife and I. Her own life builded and moulded itself upon the child; he tinged her every dream and idealized her every effort. No hands but hers must touch and garnish those little limbs; no dress or frill must touch them that had not wearied her fingers; no voice but hers could coax him off to Dreamland, and she and he together spoke some soft and unknown tongue and in it held communion. I too mused above this little white bed; saw the strength of my own arm stretched onward through the ages through the newer strength of his; saw the dream of my black fathers stagger a step onward in the wild phantasm of the world; heard in his baby voice the voice of the Prophet that was to rise within the Veil.

And so we dreamed and loved and planned by fall and winter, 5
and the full flush of the long Southern spring, till the hot winds rolled from the fetid Gulf, till the roses shivered and the still stern sun quivered its awful light over the hills of Atlanta. And then one night the little feet pattered wearily to the wee white bed, and the tiny

hands trembled; and a warm flushed face tossed on the pillow, and we knew baby was sick. Ten days he lay there,—a swift week and three endless days, wasting, wasting away. Cheerily the mother nursed him the first days, and laughed into the little eyes that smiled again. Tenderly then she hovered round him, till the smile fled away and Fear crouched beside the little bed.

Then the day ended not, and night was a dreamless terror, and joy and sleep slipped away. I hear now that Voice at midnight calling me from dull and dreamless trance,—crying, "The Shadow of Death! The Shadow of Death!" Out into the starlight I crept, to rouse the gray physician,—the Shadow of Death, the Shadow of Death. The hours trembled on; the night listened; the ghastly dawn glided like a tired thing across the lamplight. Then we two alone looked upon the child as he turned toward us with great eyes, and stretched his stringlike hands,—the Shadow of Death! And we spoke no word, and turned away. 6

He died at eventide, when the sun lay like a brooding sorrow above the western hills, veiling its face; when the winds spoke not, and the trees, the great green trees he loved, stood motionless. I saw his breath beat quicker and quicker, pause, and then his little soul leapt like a star that travels in the night and left a world of darkness in its train. The day changed not; the same tall trees peeped in at the windows, the same green grass glinted in the setting sun. Only in the chamber of death writhed the world's most piteous thing—a childless mother. 7

I shirk not. I long for work. I pant for a life full of striving. I am no coward, to shrink before the rugged rush of the storm, nor even quail before the awful shadow of the Veil. But hearken, O Death! Is not this my life hard enough,—is not that dull land that stretches its sneering web about me cold enough,—is not all the world beyond these four little walls pitiless enough, but that thou must needs enter here,—thou, O Death? About my head the thundering storm beat like a heartless voice, and the crazy forest pulsed with the curses of the weak; but what cared I, within my home beside my wife and baby boy? Wast thou so jealous of one little coign of happiness that thou must needs enter there,—thou, O Death? 8

A perfect life was his, all joy and love, with tears to make it brighter,—sweet as a summer's day beside the Housatonic. The world loved him; the women kissed his curls, the men looked gravely into his wonderful eyes, and the children hovered and fluttered about him. I can see him now, changing like the sky from sparkling laughter to darkening frowns, and then to wondering thoughtfulness as he watched the world. He knew no color-line, poor dear,—and the Veil, though it shadowed him, had not yet darkened half his sun. He loved 9 the white matron, he loved his black nurse; and in his little world walked souls alone, uncolored and unclothed. I—yea, all men—are larger and purer by the infinite breadth of that one little life. She who in simple clearness of vision sees beyond the stars said when he had flown, "He will be happy There; he ever loved beautiful things." And I, far more ignorant, and blind by the web of mine own weaving, sit alone winding words and muttering, "If still he be, and he be There, and there be a There, let him be happy, O Fate!"

Blithe was the morning of his burial, with bird and song and 10
sweet-smelling flowers. The trees whispered to the grass, but the children sat with hushed faces. And yet it seemed a ghostly unreal day,—the wraith of Life. We seemed to rumble down an unknown street behind a little white bundle of posies, with the shadow of a song in our ears. The busy city dinned about us; they did not say much, those pale-faced hurrying men and women; they did not say much,—they only glanced and said, "Niggers!"

We could not lay him in the ground there in Georgia, for the earth 11
there is strangely red, so we bore him away to the northward, with his flowers and his little folded hands. In vain, in vain!—for where, O God! beneath thy broad blue sky shall my dark baby rest in peace,—where Reverence dwells, and Goodness, and a Freedom that is free?

All that day and all that night there sat an awful gladness in my 12
heart,—nay, blame me not if I see the world thus darkly through the Veil,—and my soul whispers ever to me, saying, "Not dead, not dead, but escaped; not bond, but free." No bitter meanness now shall sicken his baby heart till it die a living death, no taunt shall madden his happy boyhood. Fool that I was to think or wish that this little soul should grow choked and deformed within the Veil! I might have known that yonder deep unworldly look that ever and anon floated past his eyes was peering far beyond this narrow Now. In the poise of his little curl-crowned head did there not sit all that wild pride of being which his father had hardly crushed in his own heart? For what, forsooth, shall a Negro want with pride amid the studied humiliations of fifty million fellows? Well sped, my boy, before the world had dubbed your ambition insolence, had held your ideals unattainable, and taught you to cringe and bow. Better far this nameless void that stops my life than the sea of sorrow for you.

Idle words; he might have borne his burden more bravely than 13
we,—aye, and found it lighter too, some day; for surely, surely this is not the end. Surely there shall yet dawn some mighty morning to lift the Veil and set the prisoned free. Not for me—I shall die in my bonds,—but for fresh young souls who have not known the night and waken to the morning; a morning when men ask of the workman, not "Is he white?" but "Can he work?" When men ask artists, not "Are

they black?" but "Do they know?" Some morning this may be, long, long years to come. But now there wails, on that dark shore within the Veil, the same deep voice, *Thou shalt forego!* And all have I foregone at that command, and with small complaint,—all save that fair young form that lies so coldly wed with death in the nest I had builded.

If one must have gone, why not I? Why may I not rest me from 14
this restlessness and sleep from this wide waking? Was not the world's alembic, Time, in his young hands, and is not my time waning? Are there so many workers in the vineyard that the fair promise of this little body could lightly be tossed away? The wretched of my race that line the alleys of the nation sit fatherless and unmothered; but Love sat beside his cradle, and in his ear Wisdom waited to speak. Perhaps now he knows the All-love, and needs not to be wise. Sleep, then, child,—sleep till I sleep and waken to a baby voice and the ceaseless patter of little feet—above the Veil.

### IN RETROSPECT

**1.** Most fathers would simply be sad about the death of a son, but by the end of this essay, Du Bois presents a different perspective about his son's death. What psychological transformation does Du Bois undergo in this essay? What is the "Veil"? And what role does the Veil play in Du Bois's response to his son's death?

**2.** There are a number of literary features in this piece of nonfiction: the poetic epigraph at the head of the essay; the capitalization of certain words *(Veil, Shadow, Dreamland);* the symbolism of golden curls and blue eyes. What significance do these features have in the essay? How do these features affect your interpretation of this account of the death of a firstborn son?

# *Discovery of a Father*

## SHERWOOD ANDERSON

Sherwood Anderson (1876–1941), born in Camden, Ohio, was a noted short story writer, novelist, poet, and newspaperman. As a young man living in Clyde, Ohio, he had an irregular education, and in 1896, he took off for Chicago, where he worked as a laborer. During the Spanish-American War, he served briefly in the army. After he was discharged from the army, he returned to Chicago and worked as a copywriter for an advertising agency. He then returned to Ohio and set up a paint factory in Elyria; when that business failed, he returned to his former job in advertising in Chicago. About this time Anderson became interested in the literary movement of the so-called Midwestern Naturalists, a group that included such writers as Carl Sandburg and Theodore Dreiser. In 1919, Anderson's most famous book, *Winesburg, Ohio,* was published. This volume—a collection of related stories about life in a small town—became popular with young people all over the country. Although Anderson later published many other books, only one of them, *Dark Laughter* (1925), became a best-seller. His vogue as a fiction writer went steadily downhill, but the style of his fiction had a marked influence on such writers as Ernest Hemingway, Thomas Wolfe, and John Steinbeck. After the success of his *Dark Laughter,* Anderson settled on a farm in Virginia and bought two weekly newspapers. The essay reprinted here, which came from his posthumously published *Memoirs* (1942), is a classic retelling of the age-old story of the lack of communication or the miscommunication that traditionally exists between fathers and their teenage sons. In reading the essay, think about what enabled Anderson and his father to rediscover or recover each other later in life.

One of the strangest relationships in the world is that between father and son. I know it now from having sons of my own. 1

A boy wants something very special from his father. You hear it said that fathers want their sons to be what they feel they cannot themselves be, but I tell you it also works the other way. I know that as a small boy I wanted my father to be a certain thing he was not. I wanted him to be a proud, silent, dignified father. When I was with other boys and he passed along the street, I wanted to feel a glow of pride: "There he is. That is my father." 2

But he wasn't such a one. He couldn't be. It seemed to me then that he was always showing off. Let's say someone in our town had got up a show. They were always doing it. The druggist would be in it, the shoe-store clerk, the horse doctor, and a lot of women and girls. My father would manage to get the chief comedy part. It was, let's say, a Civil War play and he was a comic Irish soldier. He had to do the most absurd things. They thought he was funny, but I didn't. 3

I thought he was terrible. I didn't see how Mother could stand it. She even laughed with the others. Maybe I would have laughed if it hadn't been my father. 4

Or there was a parade, the Fourth of July or Decoration Day. He'd be in that, too, right at the front of it, as Grand Marshal or something, on a white horse hired from a livery stable. 5

He couldn't ride for shucks. He fell off the horse and everyone hooted with laughter, but he didn't care. He even seemed to like it. I remember once when he had done something ridiculous, and right out on Main Street, too. I was with some other boys and they were laughing and shouting at him and he was shouting back and having 6 as good a time as they were. I ran down an alley back of some stores and there in the Presbyterian Church sheds I had a good long cry.

Or I would be in bed at night and Father would come home a little 7
lit up and bring some men with him. He was a man who was never alone. Before he went broke, running a harness shop, there were always a lot of men loafing in the shop. He went broke, of course, because he gave too much credit. He couldn't refuse it and I thought he was a fool. I had got to hating him.

There'd be men I didn't think would want to be fooling around 8
with him. There might even be the superintendent of our schools and a quiet man who ran the hardware store. Once, I remember, there was a white-haired man who was a cashier of the bank. It was a wonder to me they'd want to be seen with such a windbag. That's what I thought he was. I know now what it was that attracted them. It was because life in our town, as in all small towns, was at times pretty dull and he livened it up. He made them laugh. He could tell stories. He'd even get them to singing.

If they didn't come to our house they'd go off, say at night, to 9
where there was a grassy place by a creek. They'd cook food there and drink beer and sit about listening to his stories.

He was always telling stories about himself. He'd say this or that 10
wonderful thing happened to him. It might be something that made him look like a fool. He didn't care.

If an Irishman came to our house, right away father would say he 11
was Irish. He'd tell what county in Ireland he was born in. He'd tell things that happened there when he was a boy. He'd make it seem so real that, if I hadn't known he was born in southern Ohio, I'd have believed him myself.

If it was a Scotchman, the same thing happened. He'd get a burr 12
into his speech. Or he was a German or a Swede. He'd be anything the other man was. I think they all knew he was lying, but they seemed to like him just the same. As a boy that was what I couldn't understand.

And there was Mother. How could she stand it? I wanted to ask 13
but never did. She was not the kind you asked such questions.

I'd be upstairs in my bed, in my room above the porch, and 14
Father would be telling some of his tales. A lot of Father's stories were about the Civil War. To hear him tell it he'd been in about every battle. He'd known Grant, Sherman, Sheridan and I don't know how many others. He'd been particularly intimate with General Grant so that when Grant went East, to take charge of all the armies, he took Father along.

"I was an orderly at headquarters and Sam Grant said to me, 15
'Irve,' he said, 'I'm going to take you along with me.' "

It seems he and Grant used to slip off sometimes and have a quiet 16
drink together. That's what my father said. He'd tell about the day Lee surrendered and how, when the great moment came, they couldn't find Grant.

"You know," my father said, "about General Grant's book, his 17
memoirs. You've read of how he said he had a headache and how, when he got word that Lee was ready to call it quits, he was suddenly and miraculously cured.

"Huh," said Father. "He was in the woods with me. 18

"I was there with my back against a tree. I was pretty well corned. 19
I had got hold of a bottle of pretty good stuff.

"They were looking for Grant. He had got off his horse and come 20
into the woods. He found me. He was covered with mud.

"I had the bottle in my hand. What'd I care? The war was over. I 21
knew we had them licked."

My father said that he was the one who told Grant about Lee. An 22
orderly riding by had told him, because the orderly knew how thick he was with Grant. Grant was embarrassed.

"But, Irve, look at me. I'm all covered with mud," he said to 23
Father.

And then, my father said, he and Grant decided to have a drink 24
together. They took a couple of shots and then, because he didn't want Grant to show up potted before the immaculate Lee, he smashed the bottle against the tree.

"Sam Grant's dead now and I wouldn't want it to get out on 25
him," my father said.

That's just one of the kind of things he'd tell. Of course, the men 26
knew he was lying, but they seemed to like it just the same.

When we got broke, down and out, do you think he ever brought 27
anything home? Not he. If there wasn't anything to eat in the house, he'd go off visiting around at farm houses. They all wanted him. Sometimes he'd stay away for weeks, Mother working to keep us fed, and then home he'd come bringing, let's say, a ham. He'd got it from some farmer friend. He'd slap in on the table in the kitchen. "You bet I'm going to see that my kids have something to eat," he'd say, and Mother would just stand smiling at him. She'd never say a word about all the weeks and months he'd been away, not leaving us a cent for food. Once I heard her speaking to a woman in our street. Maybe the woman had dared to sympathize with her. "Oh," she said, "it's all right. He isn't ever dull like most of the men in this street. Life is never dull when my man is about."

But often I was filled with bitterness, and sometimes I wished he 28
wasn't my father. I'd even invent another man as my father. To protect my mother I'd make up stories of a secret marriage that for

some strange reason never got known. As though some man, say the president of a railroad company or maybe a Congressman, had married my mother, thinking his wife was dead and then it turned out she wasn't.

So they had to hush it up but I got born just the same. I wasn't 29
really the son of my father. Somewhere in the world there was a very dignified, quite wonderful man who was really my father. I even made myself half believe these fancies.

And then there came a certain night. Mother was away from 30
home. Maybe there was church that night. Father came in. He'd been off somewhere for two or three weeks. He found me alone in the house, reading by the kitchen table.

It had been raining and he was very wet. He sat and looked at me 31
for a long time, not saying a word. I was startled, for there was on his face the saddest look I had ever seen. He sat for a time, his clothes dripping. Then he got up.

"Come on with me," he said. 32

I got up and went with him out of the house. I was filled with 33
wonder but I wasn't afraid. We went along a dirt road that led down into a valley, about a mile out of town, where there was a pond. We walked in silence. The man who was always talking had stopped his talking.

I didn't know what was up and had the queer feeling that I was 34
with a stranger. I don't know whether my father intended it so. I don't think he did.

The pond was quite large. It was still raining hard and there were 35
flashes of lightning followed by thunder. We were on a grassy bank at the pond's edge when my father spoke, and in the darkness and rain his voice sounded strange.

"Take off your clothes," he said. Still filled with wonder, I began 36
to undress. There was a flash of lightning and I saw that he was already naked.

Naked, we went into the pond. Taking my hand, he pulled me in. 37
It may be that I was too frightened, too full of a feeling of strangeness, to speak. Before that night my father had never seemed to pay any attention to me.

"And what is he up to now?" I kept asking myself. I did not swim 38
very well, but he put my hand on his shoulder and struck out into the darkness.

He was a man with big shoulders, a powerful swimmer. In the 39
darkness I could feel the movements of his muscles. We swam to the far edge of the pond and then back to where we had left our clothes. The rain continued and the wind blew. Sometimes my father swam on his back, and when he did he took my hand in his large powerful

one and moved it over so that it rested always on his shoulder. Sometimes there would be a flash of lightning, and I could see his face quite clearly.

It was as it was earlier, in the kitchen, a face filled with sadness. There would be the momentary glimpse of his face, and then again the darkness, the wind and the rain. In me there was a feeling I had never known before. 40

It was a feeling of closeness. It was something strange. It was as though there were only we two in the world. It was as though I had been jerked suddenly out of myself, out of my world of the schoolboy out of a world in which I was ashamed of my father. 41

He had become blood of my blood; he the strong swimmer and I the boy clinging to him in the darkness. We swam in silence, and in silence we dressed in our wet clothes and went home. 42

There was a lamp lighted in the kitchen, and when we came in, the water dripping from us, there was my mother. She smiled at us. I remember that she called us "boys." "What have you boys been up to?" she asked, but my father did not answer. As he had begun the evening's experience with me in silence, so he ended it. He turned and looked at me. Then he went, I thought, with a new and strange dignity, out of the room. 43

I climbed the stairs to my room, undressed in darkness and got into bed. I couldn't sleep and did not want to sleep. For the first time I knew that I was the son of my father. He was a storyteller as I was to be. It may be that I even laughed a little softly there in the darkness. If I did, I laughed knowing that I would never again be wanting another father. 44

### IN RETROSPECT

**1.** In the early part of Anderson's essay, the boy mentions several characteristics of his father that displease him. Why do you believe the same features that endear his father to other members of the town are so repulsive to the boy? Do you support the boy's perception of his father's behavior? Why or why not?

**2.** At the end of the essay, we witness a sudden transformation in the boy's attitude toward his father. What happened to effect this change in the boy's attitude? Was the swim a remarkable gesture on his father's part, or did the boy just view the gesture in a remarkable way?

# *On Going Home*

## JOAN DIDION

Joan Didion (1934– ) was born in Sacramento, California, and was educated at the University of California at Berkeley. In 1964, she married John Gregory Dunne, the husband mentioned in her essay. She was an associate editor of *Vogue* from 1956 to 1963, contributed articles to *Holiday, Harper's Bazaar,* and *Life,* and wrote a regular column for the *Saturday Evening Post.* Among her published books are the novels *Run River* (1963), *Play It as It Lays* (1970), *A Book of Common Prayer* (1977), and *Democracy* (1984) and the collections of essays *Slouching towards Bethlehem* (1968), *The White Album* (1979), and *After Henry* (1992). A recent work of hers is the book of journalistic reporting called *Salvador* (1983). Thomas Wolfe entitled one of his novels *You Can't Go Home Again,* which is an echo of an old folk saying. In the following essay, Didion talks about that same fact of life: that once the young leave the nest and begin to make their own lives, it becomes increasingly difficult to return and adjust to the old family patterns. Many of the essays we read about family relationships talk about the anguish that people experience when they leave home and family. Although Didion may seem to be exploring a contrasting theme in her essay—that returning home is not a very pleasant experience—there really is no incompatibility between longing for home and family and, on returning home, finding it difficult to readjust to living there. It is just a fact of life that "you can't go home again," even though you miss home very much.

I am home for my daughter's first birthday. By "home" I do not mean the house in Los Angeles where my husband and I and the baby live, but the place where my family is, in the Central Valley of California. It is a vital although troublesome distinction. My husband likes my family but is uneasy in their house, because once there I fall into their ways, which are difficult, oblique, deliberately inarticulate, not my husband's ways. We live in dusty houses ("D-U-S-T," he once wrote with his finger on surfaces all over the house, but no one noticed it) filled with mementos quite without value to him (what could the Canton dessert plates mean to him? how could he have known about the assay scales, why should he care if he did know?), and we appear to talk exclusively about people we know who have been committed to mental hospitals, about people we know who have been booked on drunk-driving charges, and about property, particularly about property, land, price per acre and C-2 zoning and assessments and freeway access. My brother does not understand my husband's inability to perceive the advantage in the rather common real-estate transaction known as "sale-leaseback," and my husband in turn does not understand why so many of the people he hears about in my father's house have recently been committed to mental hospi- 1 tals or booked on drunk-driving charges. Nor does he understand that when we talk about sale-leasebacks and right-of-way condemnations we are talking in code about the things we like best, the yellow fields and the cottonwoods and the rivers rising and falling and the mountain roads closing when the heavy snow comes in. We miss each other's points, have another drink and regard the fire. My brother refers to my husband, in his presence, as "Joan's husband." Marriage is the classic betrayal.

Or perhaps it is not any more. Sometimes I think that those of us 2
who are now in our thirties were born into the last generation to carry the burden of "home," to find in family life the source of all tension and drama. I had by all objective accounts a "normal" and a "happy" family situation, and yet I was almost thirty years old before I could talk to my family on the telephone without crying after I had hung up. We did not fight. Nothing was wrong. And yet some nameless anxiety colored the emotional charges between me and the place that I came from. The question of whether or not you could go home again was a very real part of the sentimental and largely literary baggage with which we left home in the fifties; I suspect that it is irrelevant to the children born of the fragmentation after World War II. A few weeks ago in a San Francisco bar I saw a pretty young girl on crystal take off her clothes and dance for the cash price in an "amateur-topless" contest. There was no particular sense of moment about this, none of the effect of romantic degradation, of "dark journey," for which my generation strived so assiduously. What sense could that girl possibly make of, say, *Long Day's Journey into Night?* Who is beside the point?

That I am trapped in this particular irrelevancy is never more 3
apparent to me than when I am home. Paralyzed by the neurotic lassitude engendered by meeting one's past at every turn, around every corner, inside every cupboard, I go aimlessly from room to room. I decide to meet it head-on and clean out a drawer, and I spread the contents on the bed. A bathing suit I wore the summer I was seventeen. A letter of rejection from *The Nation,* an aerial photograph of the site for a shopping center my father did not build in 1954. Three teacups hand-painted with cabbage roses and signed "E.M.," my grandmother's initials. There is no final solution for letters of rejection from *The Nation* and teacups hand-painted in 1900. Nor is there any answer to snapshots of one's grandfather as a young man on skis, surveying around Donner Pass in the year 1910. I smooth out the snapshot and look into his face, and do and do not see my own. I close the drawer, and have another cup of coffee with my mother. We get along very well, veterans of a guerrilla war we never understood.

Days pass. I see no one. I come to dread my husband's evening call, not only because he is full of news of what by now seems to me our remote life in Los Angeles, people he has seen, letters which require attention, but because he asks what I have been doing, suggests uneasily that I get out, drive to San Francisco or Berkeley. Instead I drive across the river to a family graveyard. It has been vandalized since my last visit and the monuments are broken, overturned in the dry grass. Because I once saw a rattlesnake in the grass I stay in the car and listen to a country-and-Western station. Later I drive with my father to a ranch he has in the foothills. The man who runs his cattle on it asks us to the roundup, a week from Sunday, and although I know that I will be in Los Angeles I say, in the oblique way my family talks, that I will come. Once home I mention the broken monuments in the graveyard. My mother shrugs. 4

I go to visit my great-aunts. A few of them think now that I am my cousin, or their daughter who died young. We recall an anecdote about a relative last seen in 1948, and they ask if I still like living in New York City. I have lived in Los Angeles for three years, but I say that I do. The baby is offered a horehound drop, and I am slipped a dollar bill "to buy a treat." Questions trail off, answers are abandoned, the baby plays with the dust motes in a shaft of afternoon sun. 5

It is time for the baby's birthday party: a white cake, strawberry-marshmallow ice cream, a bottle of champagne saved from another party. In the evening, after she has gone to sleep, I kneel beside the crib and touch her face, where it is pressed against the slats, with mine. She is an open and trusting child, unprepared for and unaccustomed to the ambushes of family life, and perhaps it is just as well that I can offer her little of that life. I would like to give her more. I would like to promise her that she will grow up with a sense of her cousins and of rivers and of her great-grandmother's teacups, would like to pledge her a picnic on a river with fried chicken and her hair uncombed, would like to give her *home* for her birthday, but we live differently now and I can promise her nothing like that. I give her a xylophone and a sundress from Madeira, and promise to tell her a funny story. 6

**IN RETROSPECT**

**1.** Considering the experiences Didion reports in this essay and your own experiences with your family, how would you respond to the adage "you can't go home again?"

**2.** In the first sentence of the essay, Didion mentions that she has come home for her daughter's first birthday. She does not mention her daughter again until the final paragraph of the essay, where she talks about kneeling beside her daughter's crib on the evening after the birthday party. What is the significance of this final paragraph in relation to the rest of the essay?

# *The Way to Rainy Mountain*

## N. SCOTT MOMADAY

In 1969, N. Scott Momaday (1934–     ) won the Pulitzer Prize for his novel *House Made of Dawn.* In that same year, Momaday published *The Way to Rainy Mountain,* a collection of legends about the Kiowa Indians, his native tribe. Born in Lawton, Oklahoma, the site of Rainy Mountain, Momaday was raised on several Indian reservations. After graduating from the University of New Mexico, he went on to study at Stanford University, where he eventually earned an M.A. and a Ph.D. He has taught in the English Department at the University of California at Santa Barbara (1963–1969), at the University of California at Berkeley (1969–1973), at Stanford University (1973–1982), and at the University of Arizona (1982 to the present). In his poetry and in his autobiography, *The Names: A Memoir* (1976), he celebrates his Indian heritage, especially its oral traditions. In the following essay, which originally appeared in *The Reporter* in 1967 but which is reprinted here from *The Way to Rainy Mountain,* Momaday talks mainly about his grandmother, who had recently died, and relates incidents from her life to the general culture of the Kiowas. Ultimately, this essay becomes a loving but unsentimental tribute to his grandmother, who lived out her useful life in the beautiful Big Sky country of the western plains. As you read this essay, note the mixture of folklore, myth, history, anecdote, and personal narrative, all melded into a unified, coherent account of the legacy from Momaday's cultural background. This kind of blending of forms or genres may look easy as Momaday does it, but were you to attempt such amalgamation in writing about some personal experience in your own life, you might find it extremely difficult to bring off. Still, there is no harm in trying.

A single knoll rises out of the plain in Oklahoma, north and west of the Wichita range. For my people, the Kiowas, it is an old landmark, and they gave it the name Rainy Mountain. The hardest weather in the world is there. Winter brings blizzards, hot tornadic winds arise in the spring, and in summer the prairie is an anvil's edge. The grass turns brittle and brown, and it cracks beneath your feet. There are green belts along the rivers and creeks, linear groves of hickory and pecan, willow and witch hazel. At a distance in July or August the steaming foliage seems almost to writhe in fire. Great green and yellow grasshoppers are everywhere in the tall grass, popping up like corn to sting the flesh, and tortoises crawl about on the red earth, going nowhere in the plenty of time. Loneliness is an aspect of the land. All things in the plain are isolate; there is no confusion of objects in the eye, but *one* hill or *one* tree or *one* man. To look upon that landscape in the early morning, with the sun at your back, is to lose the sense of proportion. Your imagination comes to life, and this, you think, is where Creation was begun. 1

I returned to Rainy Mountain in July. My grandmother had died 2
in the spring, and I wanted to be at her grave. She had lived to be very old and at last infirm. Her only living daughter was with her when she died, and I was told that in death her face was that of a child.

I like to think of her as a child. When she was born, the Kiowas 3
were living the last great moment of their history. For more than a hundred years they had controlled the open range from the Smoky Hill River to the Red, from the headwaters of the Canadian to the fork of the Arkansas and Cimarron. In alliance with the Comanches, they had ruled the whole of the Southern Plains. War was their sacred business, and they were the finest horsemen the world has ever known. But warfare for the Kiowas was pre-eminently a matter of disposition rather than of survival, and they never understood the grim, unrelenting advance of the U.S. Cavalry. When at last, divided and ill provisioned, they were driven onto the Staked Plains in the cold of autumn, they fell into panic. In Palo Duro Canyon they abandoned their crucial stores to pillage and had nothing then but their lives. In order to save themselves, they surrendered to the soldiers at Fort Sill and were imprisoned in the old stone corral that now stands as a military museum. My grandmother was spared the humiliation of those high gray walls by eight or ten years, but she must have known from birth the affliction of defeat, the dark brooding of old warriors.

Her name was Aho, and she belonged to the last culture to evolve 4
in North America. Her forebears came down from the high country in western Montana nearly three centuries ago. They were a mountain people, a mysterious tribe of hunters whose language has never been classified in any major group. In the late seventeenth century they began a long migration to the south and east. It was a journey toward the dawn, and it led to a golden age. Along the way the Kiowas were befriended by the Crows, who gave them the culture and religion of the Plains. They acquired horses, and their ancient nomadic spirit was suddenly free of the ground. The acquired Tai-me, the sacred sun-dance doll, from that moment the object and symbol of their worship, and so shared in the divinity of the sun. Not least, they acquired the sense of destiny, therefore courage and pride. When they entered upon the Southern Plains they had been transformed. No longer were they slaves to the simple necessity of survival; they were a lordly and dangerous society of fighters and thieves, hunters and priests of the sun. According to their origin myth, they entered the world through a hollow log. From one point of view, their migration was the fruit of an old prophecy, for indeed they emerged from a sunless world.

Though my grandmother lived out her long life in the shadow of 5
Rainy Mountain, the immense landscape of the continental interior lay like memory in her blood. She could tell of the Crows, whom she had never seen, and of the Black Hills, where she had never been. I wanted to see in reality what she had seen more perfectly in the mind's eye, and drove fifteen hundred miles to begin my pilgrimage.

A dark mist lay over the Black Hills, and the land was like iron. At 6
the top of a ridge I caught sight of Devil's Tower upthrust against the gray sky as if in the birth of time the core of the earth had broken through its crust and the motion of the world was begun. There are things in nature that engender an awful quiet in the heart of man; Devil's Tower is one of them. Two centuries ago, because of their need to explain it, the Kiowas made a legend at the base of the rock. My grandmother said:

"Eight children were there at play, seven sisters and their brother. 7
Suddenly the boy was struck dumb; he trembled and began to run upon his hands and feet. His fingers became claws, and his body was covered with fur. There was a bear where the boy had been. The sisters were terrified; they ran, and the bear after them. They came to the stump of a great tree, and the tree spoke to them. It bade them climb upon it, and as they did so, it began to rise into the air. The bear came to kill them, but they were just beyond its reach. It reared against the tree and scored the bark all around with its claws. The seven sisters were borne into the sky, and they became the stars of the Big Dipper." From that moment, and so long as the legend lives, the Kiowas have kinsmen in the night sky. Whatever they were in the mountains, they could be no more. However tenuous their well-being, however much they had suffered and would suffer again, they had found a way out of the wilderness.

My grandmother had a reverence for the sun, a holy regard that 8
now is all but gone out of mankind. There was a wariness in her, and an ancient awe. She was a Christian in her later years, but she had come a long way about, and she never forgot her birthright. As a child she had been to the sun dances; she had taken part in that annual rite, and by it she had learned the restoration of her people in the presence of Tai-me. She was about seven when the last Kiowa sun dance was held in 1887 on the Washita River above Rainy Mountain Creek. The buffalo were gone. In order to consummate the ancient sacrifice—to impale the head of a buffalo bull upon the Tai-me tree—a delegation of old men journeyed into Texas, there to beg and barter for an animal from the Goodnight herd. She was ten when the Kiowas came together for the last time as a living sun-dance culture. They could find no buffalo; they had to hang an old hide from the sacred tree. Before the dance could begin, a company of soldiers rode

out from Fort Sill under orders to disperse the tribe. Forbidden without cause the essential act of their faith, having seen the wild herds slaughtered and left to rot upon the ground, the Kiowas backed away forever from the tree. That was July 20, 1890, at the great bend of the Washita. My grandmother was there. Without bitterness, and for as long as she lived, she bore a vision of deicide.

Now that I can have her only in memory, I see my grandmother in 9
the several postures that were peculiar to her: standing at the wood stove on a winter morning and turning meat in a great iron skillet; sitting at the south window, bent above her beadwork, and afterwards, when her vision failed, looking down for a long time into the fold of her hands; going out upon a cane, very slowly as she did when the weight of age came upon her, praying. I remember her most often at prayer. She made long, rambling prayers out of suffering and hope, having seen many things. I was never sure that I had the right to hear, so exclusive were they of all mere custom and company. The last time I saw her she prayed standing by the side of her bed at night, naked to the waist, the light of a kerosene lamp moving upon her dark skin. Her long black hair, always drawn and braided in the day, lay upon her shoulders and against her breasts like a shawl. I do not speak Kiowa, and I never understood her prayers, but there was something inherently sad in the sound, some merest hesitation upon the syllables of sorrow. She began in a high and descending pitch, exhausting her breath to silence; then again and again—and always the same intensity of effort, of something that is, and is not, like urgency in the human voice. Transported so in the dancing light among the shadows of her room, she seemed beyond the reach of time. But that was illusion; I think I knew then that I should not see her again.

Houses are like sentinels in the plain, old keepers of the weather 10
watch. There, in a very little while, wood takes on the appearance of great age. All colors wear soon away in the wind and rain, and then the wood is burned gray and the grain appears and the nails turn red with rust. The window panes are black and opaque; you imagine there is nothing within, and indeed there are many ghosts, bones given up to the land. They stand here and there against the sky, and you approach them for a longer time than you expect. They belong in the distance; it is their domain.

Once there was a lot of sound in my grandmother's house, a lot of 11
coming and going, feasting and talk. The summers there were full of excitement and reunion. The Kiowas are a summer people; they abide the cold and keep to themselves, but when the season turns and the land becomes warm and vital they cannot hold still; an old

love of going returns upon them. The aged visitors who came to my grandmother's house when I was a child were made of lean and leather, and they bore themselves upright. They wore great black hats and bright ample shirts that shook in the wind. They rubbed fat upon their hair and wound their braids with strips of colored cloth. Some of them painted their faces and carried the scars of old and cherished enmities. They were an old council of warlords, come to remind and be reminded of who they were. Their wives and daughters served them well. The women might indulge themselves; gossip was at once the mark and compensation of their servitude. They made loud and elaborate talk among themselves, full of jest and gesture, fright and false alarm. They went abroad in fringed and flowered shawls, bright beadwork and German silver. They were at home in the kitchen, and they prepared meals that were banquets.

There were frequent prayer meetings, and nocturnal feasts. 12
When I was a child I played with my cousins outside, where the lamplight fell upon the ground and the singing of the old people rose up around us and carried away into the darkness. There were a lot of good things to eat, a lot of laughter and surprise. And afterwards, when the quiet returned, I lay down with my grandmother and could hear the frogs away by the river and feel the motion of the air.

Now there is a funereal silence in the rooms, the endless wake of 13
some final word. The walls have closed in upon my grandmother's house. When I returned to it in mourning, I saw for the first time in my life how small it was. It was late at night, and there was a white moon, nearly full. I sat for a long time on the stone steps by the kitchen door. From there I could see out across the land; I could see the long row of trees by the creek, the low light upon the rolling plains, and the stars of the Big Dipper. Once I looked at the moon and caught sight of a strange thing. A cricket had perched upon the handrail, only a few inches away. My line of vision was such that the creature filled the moon like a fossil. It had gone there, I thought, to live and die, for there, of all places, was its small definition made whole and eternal. A warm wind rose up and purled like the longing within me.

The next morning, I awoke at dawn and went out on the dirt road 14
to Rainy Mountain. It was already hot, and the grasshoppers began to fill the air. Still, it was early in the morning, and birds sang out of the shadows. The long yellow grass on the mountain shone in the bright light, and a scissortail hied above the land. There, where it ought to be, at the end of a long and legendary way, was my grandmother's grave. She had at last succeeded to that holy ground. Here and there on the dark stones were ancestral names. Looking back once, I saw the mountain and came away.

**IN RETROSPECT**

1. Student writers are often told that professional writers combine various modes of discourse to accommodate multiple related purposes for writing—such as describing a particular context, explaining someone's motives, solving a problem, or analyzing a situation. What different aims do you see at work in Momaday's essay? How does Momaday develop coherence among the various aims of his writing?

2. In memorializing his grandmother, Momaday seems to treat her more as a symbol than as an individual. How do time, history, and imagination figure into Momaday's interpretation and description of his grandmother's life?

# *Brothers and Sisters*

## ALICE WALKER

Alice Walker (1944–     ) was one of eight children—five boys and three girls—born to parents who were sharecroppers in rural Georgia. She got her talent for fiction writing from her parents, both of whom were natural storytellers. Her two collections of short stories are *In Love and Trouble* (1973) and *You Can't Keep a Good Woman Down* (1981). Best known among her three novels is *The Color Purple* (1982), which won the American Book Award and the Pulitzer Prize. But Walker is also an accomplished essayist. The two collections to date of her essays are *In Search of Our Mothers' Gardens: Womanist Prose* (1983) and *Living by the Word* (1988). "Brothers and Sisters" was taken from *In Search of Our Mothers' Gardens.* In this essay, Walker tells us about how the girls and boys in her family were raised differently, with different codes of conduct and morality for each sex. Walker's mother believed that a father should teach his sons, and a mother should teach her daughters, the "facts of life"; in Walker's family, the father encouraged his sons to have promiscuous sex with women, whereas the mother closely monitored her daughters' behavior. Walker says at one point in the essay, "It was not until I became a student of women's liberation ideology that I could understand and forgive my father." What about her father do you think she had to understand and forgive?

We lived on a farm in the South in the fifties, and my brothers, 1
the four of them I knew (the fifth had left home when I was three years old), were allowed to watch animals being mated. This was not unusual; nor was it considered unusual that my older sister and I were frowned upon if we even asked, innocently, what was going on. One of my brothers explained the mating one day, using words my father had given him: "The bull is getting a little something on his

stick," he said. And he laughed. "What stick?" I wanted to know. "Where did he get it? How did he pick it up? Where did he put it?" All my brothers laughed.

I believe my mother's theory about raising a large family of five 2
boys and three girls was that the father should teach the boys and the mother teach the girls the facts, as one says, of life. So my father went around talking about bulls getting something on their sticks and she went around saying girls did not need to know about such things. They were "womanish" (a very bad way to be in those days) if they asked.

The thing was, watching the matings filled my brothers with an 3
aimless sort of lust, as dangerous as it was unintentional. They knew enough to know that cows, months after mating, produced calves, but they were not bright enough to make the same connection between women and their offspring.

Sometimes, when I think of my childhood, it seems to me a 4
particularly hard one. But in reality, everything awful that happened to me didn't seem to happen to *me* at all, but to my older sister. Through some incredible power to negate my presence around people I did not like, which produced invisibility (as well as an ability to appear mentally vacant when I was nothing of the kind), I was spared the humiliation she was subjected to, though at the same time, I felt every bit of it. It was as if she suffered for my benefit, and I vowed early in my life that none of the things that made existence so miserable for her would happen to me.

The fact that she was not allowed at official matings did not mean 5
she never saw any. While my brothers followed my father to the mating pens on the other side of the road near the barn, she stationed herself near the pigpen, or followed our many dogs until they were in a mating mood, or, failing to witness something there, she watched the chickens. On a farm it is impossible *not* to be conscious of sex, to wonder about it, to dream . . . but to whom was she to speak of her feelings? Not to my father, who thought all young women perverse. Not to my mother, who pretended all her children grew out of stumps she magically found in the forest. Not to me, who never found anything wrong with this lie.

When my sister menstruated she wore a thick packet of clean rags 6
between her legs. It stuck out in front like a penis. The boys laughed at her as she served them at the table. Not knowing any better, and because our parents did not dream of actually *discussing* what was going on, she would giggle nervously at herself. I hated her for giggling, and it was at those times I would think of her as dim-witted. She never complained, but she began to have strange fainting fits

whenever she had her period. Her head felt as if it were splitting, she said, and everything she ate came up again. And her cramps were so severe she could not stand. She was forced to spend several days of each month in bed.

My father expected all of his sons to have sex with women. "Like 7
bulls," he said, "a man *needs* to get a little something on his stick." And so, on Saturday nights, into town they went, chasing the girls. My sister was rarely allowed into town alone, and if the dress she wore fit too snugly at the waist, or if her cleavage dipped too far below her collarbone, she was made to stay home.

"But why can't I go too," she would cry, her face screwed up with 8
the effort not to wail.

"They're boys, your brothers, *that's* why they can go." 9

Naturally, when she got the chance, she responded eagerly to 10
boys. But when this was discovered she was whipped and locked up in her room.

I would go in to visit her. 11

"Straight Pine," she would say, "you don't know what it *feels* like 12
to want to be loved by a man."

"And if this is what you get for feeling like it I never will," I said, 13
with—I hoped—the right combination of sympathy and disgust.

"Men smell so good," she would whisper ecstatically. "And when 14
they look into your eyes, you just melt."

Since they were so hard to catch, naturally she thought almost 15
any of them terrific.

"Oh, that Alfred!" she would moon over some mediocre, square- 16
headed boy, "he's so *sweet!*" And she would take his ugly picture out of her bosom and kiss it.

My father was always warning her not to come home if she ever 17
found herself pregnant. My mother constantly reminded her that abortion was a sin. Later, although she never became pregnant, her period would not come for months at a time. The painful symptoms, however, never varied or ceased. She fell for the first man who loved her enough to beat her for looking at someone else, and when I was still in high school, she married him.

My fifth brother, the one I never knew, was said to be different 18
from the rest. He had not liked matings. He would not watch them. He thought the cows should be given a choice. My father had disliked him because he was soft. My mother took up for him. "Jason is just tender-hearted," she would say in a way that made me know he was her favorite; "he takes after me." It was true that my mother cried about almost anything.

Who was this oldest brother? I wondered. 19

"Well," said my mother, "he was someone who always loved 20

you. Of course he was a great big boy when you were born and out working on his own. He worked on a road gang building roads. Every morning before he left he would come in the room where you were and pick you up and give you the biggest kisses. He used to look at you and just smile. It's a pity you don't remember him."

I agreed. 21

At my father's funeral I finally "met" my oldest brother. He is tall 22
and black with thick gray hair above a young-looking face. I watched my sister cry over my father until she blacked out from grief. I saw my brothers sobbing, reminding each other of what a great father he had been. My oldest brother and I did not shed a tear between us. When I left my father's grave he came up and introduced himself. "You don't ever have to walk alone," he said, and put his arms around me.

One out of five ain't *too* bad, I thought, snuggling up. 23

But I didn't discover until recently his true uniqueness: He is the 24
only one of my brothers who assumes responsibility for all his children. The other four all fathered children during those Saturday-night chases of twenty years ago. Children—my nieces and nephews whom I will probably never know—they neither acknowledge as their own, provide for, or even see.

It was not until I became a student of women's liberation ideology 25
that I could understand and forgive my father. I needed an ideology that would define his behavior in context. The black movement had given me an ideology that helped explain his colorism (he *did* fall in love with my mother partly because she was so light; he never denied it). Feminism helped explain his sexism. I was relieved to know his sexist behavior was not something uniquely his own, but rather, an imitation of the behavior of the society around us.

All partisan movements add to the fullness of our understanding 26
of society as a whole. They never detract; or, in any case, one must not allow them to do so. Experience adds to experience. "The more things the better," as O'Connor and Welty both have said, speaking, one of marriage, the other of Catholicism.

I desperately needed my father and brothers to give me male 27
models I could respect, because white men (for example; being particularly handy in this sort of comparison)—whether in films or in person—offered man as dominator, as killer, and always as hypocrite.

My father failed because he copied the hypocrisy. And my 28
brothers—except for one—never understood they must represent half the world to me, as I must represent the other half to them.*

---

*Since this essay was written, my brothers have offered their name, acknowledgment, and some support to all their children. [Walker's note]

## IN RETROSPECT

**1.** The kind of double standard that Walker talks about in this essay has prevailed between men and women for centuries in various cultures. How does Walker's experience compare with your own? Why do you think the double standard has persisted? What do you predict about standards of behavior for men and women in the coming decade? On what do you base your predictions?

**2.** Walker says that she "needed an ideology that would define [her father's] behavior in a context" (paragraph 25). In what ideology—or ideologies—did she eventually find the basis for being able to understand and forgive her father? Is Walker's response to and use of these ideologies typical or atypical? Why so? Toward what other ends might Walker have used the ideologies that she found? Do her reasons for understanding and forgiving her father convince you? Why or why not?

# 3

# On Character Types

*The first three chapters of this book are concerned with the discoveries we make about people—first the discoveries about ourselves, next the discoveries about our families, and then the discoveries about people outside of ourselves and our families. At first, we tend to notice individuals. Then, as we meet more and more people, we begin to see people as groups or classes or communities—males and females, old people and young people, Italians and Germans, Catholics and Protestants and Jews, rich people and poor people. And then we progress to that sophisticated stage of abstraction where we begin to classify people according to types—busybodies and lazybodies, cheaters and pleasers and teasers, saints and sinners. All the essayists in this chapter are engaged in a genre that was initiated by the Greek philosopher Theophrastus, picked up by many English writers in the seventeenth century, and continued by every generation of writers since then. What these writers do is assemble a number of common characteristics of a type and combine them in a generalized portrait of a "character." We all do this kind of generalizing to some degree: "There goes a ne'er-do-well if I ever saw one" or "You'd better keep your hand on your wallet when you're speaking to that guy." Are there really character types, or are they just a figment of our imagination?*

# *The History of an Adventurer in Lotteries*

**SAMUEL JOHNSON**

Samuel Johnson (1709–1784), born in the cathedral town of Lichfield, in Staffordshire, England, was the son of a bookseller. Despite many physical disabilities, including partial blindness, young Sam Johnson developed in his father's bookshop a voracious appetite for books. Adam Smith remarked that when Johnson came up to Pembroke College, Oxford, at age eighteen, he "knew more books than any man alive." The erudition and wisdom that Johnson gained from his random reading stood him in good stead when he turned to writing as a livelihood. The man who was later to be awarded honorary degrees by both Trinity College in Dublin and Oxford University had to leave Pembroke after only eighteen months of residence because his money ran out. After coming to London in 1737, in the company of his former pupil, the famous actor David Garrick, Johnson went to work for Edward Cave, editor of *The Gentleman's Magazine.* The story of Johnson's struggles and disappointments in those early years and of his later triumphs has been unforgettably related in James Boswell's great biography, *The Life of Samuel Johnson* (1791). The essay reprinted here, with a title supplied by the editors of this collection, was one of the papers that Johnson produced for *The Rambler* every Tuesday and Friday from March 20, 1750, to March 17, 1752, while he was engaged in compiling his monumental *Dictionary.* This essay, in the tradition of "character" writing, depicts, in the words of a persona that Dr. Johnson has created, a man who has become addicted to gambling. The ponderous Latinate style of this essay was appropriate for the majestic Dr. Johnson, but it was never successfully managed by later imitators. If nobody today writes like Dr. Johnson, it may be because nobody else could or should.

To *The Rambler.*

Sir,

As I have passed much of life in disquiet and suspense, and lost many opportunities of advantage by a passion which I have reason to believe prevalent in different degrees over a great part of mankind, I cannot but think myself well qualified to warn those, who are yet uncaptivated of the danger which they incur by placing themselves within its influence. 1

I served an apprenticeship to a linen-draper, with uncommon reputation for diligence and fidelity; and at the age of three-and-twenty opened a shop for myself with a large stock, and such credit among all the merchants, who were acquainted with my master, that I could command whatever was imported curious or valuable. For five years I proceeded with success proportionate to close application 2 and untainted integrity; was a daring bidder at every sale, always paid my notes before they were due; and advanced so fast in commercial reputation that I was proverbially marked out as the model of young traders, and every one expected that a few years would make me an alderman.

In this course of even propensity, I was one day persuaded to buy 3
a ticket in the lottery. The sum was inconsiderable, part was to be repaid though fortune might fail to favour me, and therefore my established maxims of frugality did not restrain me from so trifling an experiment. The ticket lay almost forgotten till the time at which every man's fate was to be determined; nor did the affairs even then seem of any importance, till I discovered by the public papers that the number next to mine had conferred the great prize.

My heart leaped at the thoughts of such an approach of sudden 4
riches, which I considered myself, however contrarily to the laws of computation, as having missed by a single chance; and I could not forbear to revolve the consequences which such a bounteous allotment would have produced, if it had happened to me. This dream of felicity, by degrees, took possession of my imagination. The great delight of my solitary hours was to purchase an estate, and form plantations with money which once might have been mine, and I never met my friends but I spoiled their merriment by perpetual complaints of my ill luck.

At length another lottery was opened, and I had now so heated 5
my imagination with the prospect of a prize, that I should have pressed among the first purchasers, had not my ardour been withheld by deliberation upon the probability of success from one ticket rather than another. I hesitated long between even and off; considered the square and cubic numbers through the lottery; examined all those to which good luck had been hitherto annexed; and at last fixed upon one, which, by some secret relation to the events of my life, I thought predestined to make me happy. Delay in great affairs is often mischievous; the ticket was sold, and its possessor could not be found.

I returned to my conjectures, and after many arts of prognostica- 6
tion, fixed upon another chance, but with less confidence. Never did captive, heir, or lover, feel so much vexation from the slow pace of time, as I suffered between the purchase of my ticket and the distribution of the prizes. I solaced my uneasiness as well as I could, by frequent contemplation of approaching happiness; when the sun arose I knew it would set, and congratulated myself at night that I was so much nearer to my wishes. At last the day came, my ticket appeared, and rewarded all my care and sagacity with a despicable prize of fifty pounds.

My friends, who honestly rejoiced upon my success, were very 7
coldly received; I hid myself a fortnight in the country, that my chagrin might fume away without observation, and then returning to my shop, began to listen after another lottery.

With the news of a lottery I was soon gratified, and having now 8
found the vanity of conjecture and inefficacy of computation, I resolved to take the prize by violence, and therefore bought forty tickets, not omitting, however, to divide them between the even and odd numbers, that I might not miss the lucky class. Many conclusions did I form, and many experiments did I try to determine from which of those tickets I might most reasonably expect riches. At last, being unable to satisfy myself by any modes of reasoning, I wrote the numbers upon dice, and allotted five hours every day to the amusement of throwing them in a garret; and examining the event by an exact register, found, on the evening before the lottery was drawn, that one of my numbers had been turned up five times more than any of the rest in three hundred and thirty thousand throws.

This experiment was fallacious; the first day presented the hope- 9
ful ticket, a detestable blank. The rest came out with different fortune, and in conclusion I lost thirty pounds by this great adventure.

I had now wholly changed the cast of my behaviour and the 10
conduct of my life. The shop was for the most part abandoned to my servants, and if I entered it, my thoughts were so engrossed by my tickets that I scarcely heard or answered a question, but considered every customer as an intruder upon my meditations, whom I was in haste to dispatch. I mistook the price of my goods, committed blunders in my bills, forgot to file my receipts, and neglected to regulate my books. My acquaintances by degrees began to fall away; but I perceived the decline of my business with little emotion, because whatever deficience there might be in my gains I expected the next lottery to supply.

Miscarriage naturally produced diffidence; I began now to seek 11
assistance against ill luck, by an alliance with those that had been more successful. I inquired diligently at what office any prize had been sold, that I might purchase of a propitious vender; solicited those who had been fortunate in former lotteries, to partake with me in my new tickets, and whenever I met with one that had in any event of his life been eminently prosperous, I invited him to take a larger share. I had, by this rule of conduct, so diffused my interest, that I had a fourth part of fifteen tickets, an eighth of forty, and a sixteenth of ninety.

I waited for the decision of my fate with my former palpitations, 12
and looked upon the business of my trade with the usual neglect. The wheel at last was turned, and its revolutions brought me a long succession of sorrows and disappointments. I indeed often partook of

a small prize, and the loss of one day was generally balanced by the gain of the next; but my desires yet remained unsatisfied, and when one of my chances had failed, all my expectation was suspended on those which remained yet undetermined. At last a prize of five thousand pounds was proclaimed; I caught fire at the cry, and inquiring the number, found it to be one of my own tickets, which I had divided among those on whose luck I depended, and of which I had retained only a sixteenth part.

You will easily judge with what detestation of himself a man thus 13
intent upon gain reflected that he had sold a prize which was once in his possession. It was to no purpose that I represented to my mind the impossibility of recalling the past, or the folly of condemning an act which only its event, an event which no human intelligence could foresee, proved to be wrong. The prize which, though put in my hands, had been suffered to slip from me, filled me with anguish; and knowing that complaint would only expose me to ridicule, I gave myself up silently to grief, and lost by degrees my appetite and my rest.

My indisposition soon became visible: I was visited by my 14
friends, and among them by Eumathes, a clergyman, whose piety and learning gave him such an ascendant over me that I could not refuse to open my heart. There are, said he, few minds sufficiently firm to be trusted in the hands of chance. Whoever finds himself inclined to anticipate futurity, and exalt possibility to certainty, should avoid every kind of casual adventure, since his grief must be always proportionate to his hope. You have long wasted that time which, by a proper application, would have certainly, though moderately, increased your fortune, in a laborious and anxious pursuit of a species of gain which no labour or anxiety, no art or expedient, can secure or promote. You are now fretting away your life in repentance of an act against which repentance can give no caution but to avoid the occasion of committing it. Rouse from this lazy dream of fortuitous riches, which if obtained, you could scarcely have enjoyed, because they could confer no consciousness of desert; return to rational and manly industry, and consider the mere gift of luck as below the care of a wise man.

### IN RETROSPECT

**1.** Johnson is depicting a type of person that is still very much with us: a person inextricably addicted to gambling. The persona that Johnson created for this essay is the exemplar of that type of character. In what ways is this adventurer in lotteries like and unlike the typical player of the lottery today? What irony do you find in this man's professional interest (his main occupation) and his personal vice? How would you reconcile the polarities in this character?

**2.** Many readers today may be put off by Johnson's style—his polysyllabic diction, his long sentences, his copious use of semicolons. Take any paragraph of the letter and rewrite it in a way that makes it more appealing to you and to other contemporary readers but at the same time preserves the integrity of the text (that is, does not change what Johnson meant to say). What, if anything, do you now notice about the text that you did not notice prior to rewriting it? How difficult or easy is it to both preserve the text and alter its style? What features of your revision make the text easier to read? Why?

# *A Definition of a Gentleman*

## JOHN HENRY NEWMAN

John Henry Newman (1801–1890) was engaged almost all his long life in controversy and in the publication of controversial writings. Soon after he became a fellow at Oriel College, Oxford, he was caught up in the theological controversy between High Church Anglicans and Low Church Anglicans, and his major contribution to that so-called Oxford Movement was a series of "Tracts for the Times." The controversies between the Anglicans and the Roman Catholics prompted him to write a number of treatises in defense of the Anglican position, including *Lectures on the Prophetical Office of the Church*. Shortly after his conversion to Roman Catholicism in 1845, Newman became involved in the spirited arguments between the exponents of a liberal education and the exponents of a utilitarian education. In response to that controversy and to an invitation from Irish bishops to establish a Catholic university in Ireland, Newman wrote the classic statement on the nature and scope of a liberal education, which was originally delivered as a series of lectures in 1852 and was eventually published under the title *The Idea of a University* (1873). Most of Newman's writings were thus in the rhetorical tradition. But "A Definition of a Gentleman," which was a set piece in *The Idea of a University*, was in the tradition of "character writing," one of the subspecies of the familiar essay. This essay presents Newman's characterization of the type of person produced by a liberal education. Admirable as this person is, he does not represent Newman's ultimate ideal, because he lacks a grounding in religion. As Newman says in the final paragraph of the essay, "Such are some of the lineaments of the ethical character, which the cultivated intellect will form, apart from religious principle." This classic essay exhibits Newman's lucid, urbane, elegant prose style.

Hence it is that it is almost a definition of a gentleman to say he is 1 one who never inflicts pain. This description is both refined and, as far as it goes, accurate. He is mainly occupied in merely removing the obstacles which hinder the free and unembarrassed action of those about him; and he concurs with their movements rather than takes the initiative himself. His benefits may be considered as parallel to what are called comforts or conveniences in arrangements of a personal nature: like an easy chair or a good fire, which do their part in dispelling cold and fatigue, though nature provides both means of rest and animal heat without them. The true gentleman in like manner carefully avoids whatever may cause a jar or a jolt in the minds of those with whom he is cast;—all clashing of opinion, or collision of feeling, all restraint, or suspicion, or gloom, or resentment; his great concern being to make every one at their ease and at home. He has his eyes on all his company; he is tender towards the bashful, gentle towards the distant, and merciful towards the absurd; he can recollect to whom he is speaking; he guards against unseasonable allusions, or topics which may irritate; he is seldom prominent in conversation, and never wearisome. He makes light of favours while he does them, and seems to be receiving when he is conferring. He never speaks of himself except when compelled, never defends himself by a mere retort, he has no ears for slander or gossip, is scrupulous in imputing motives to those who interfere with him, and interprets every thing for the best. He is never mean or little in his disputes, never takes unfair advantage, never mistakes personalities or sharp sayings for arguments, or insinuates evil which he dare not say out. From a longsighted prudence, he observes the maxim of the ancient sage, that we should ever conduct ourselves towards our enemy as if he were one day to be our friend. He has too much good sense to be affronted at insults, he is too well employed to remember injuries, and too indolent to bear malice. He is patient, forbearing, and resigned, on philosophical principles; he submits to pain, because it is inevitable, to bereavement, because it is irreparable, and to death, because it is his destiny. If he engages in controversy of any kind, his disciplined intellect preserves him from the blundering discourtesy of better, perhaps, but less educated minds; who, like blunt weapons, tear and hack instead of cutting clean, who mistake the point in argument, waste their strength on trifles, misconceive their adversary, and leave the question more involved than they find it. He may be right or wrong in his opinion, but he is too clear-headed to be unjust; he is as simple as he is forcible, and as brief as he is decisive. Nowhere shall we find greater candour, consideration, indulgence: he throws himself into the minds of his opponents, he accounts for their mistakes. He knows the weakness of human reason as well as its strength, its province and its limits. If he be an unbeliever, he will be too profound and large-minded to ridicule religion or to act against it; he is too wise to be a dogmatist or fanatic in his infidelity. He respects piety and devotion; he even supports institutions as venerable, beautiful, or useful, to which he does not assent; he honours the ministers of religion, and it contents him to decline its mysteries without assailing or denouncing them. He is a friend of religious toleration, and that, not only because his philosophy has taught him to look on all forms of faith with an impartial eye, but also from the gentleness and effeminacy of feeling, which is the attendant on civilization.

Not that he may not hold a religion too, in his own way, even 2
when he is not a Christian. In that case his religion is one of imagination and sentiment; it is the embodiment of those ideas of the sublime, majestic, and beautiful, without which there can be no large philosophy. Sometimes he acknowledges the being of God, sometimes he invests an unknown principle or quality with the attributes of perfection. And this deduction of his reason, or creation of his fancy, he makes the occasion of such excellent thoughts, and the starting-point of so varied and systematic a teaching, that he even seems like a disciple of Christianity itself. From the very accuracy and steadiness of his logical powers, he is able to see what sentiments are consistent in those who hold any religious doctrine at all, and he appears to others to feel and to hold a whole circle of theological truths, which exist in his mind no otherwise than as a number of deductions.

Such are some of the lineaments of the ethical character, which 3
the cultivated intellect will form, apart from religious principle. They are seen within the pale of the Church and without it, in holy men, and in profligate; they form the *beau-ideal* of the world; they partly assist and partly distort the development of the Catholic. They may subserve the education of a St. Francis de Sales or a Cardinal Pole; they may be the limits of the contemplation of a Shaftesbury or a Gibbon. Basil and Julian were fellow-students at the schools of Athens; and one became the Saint and Director of the Church, the other her scoffing and relentless foe.

**IN RETROSPECT**

**1.** For many years, students who read this essay were told that the gentleman described by Newman in this essay was an ideal character whom everyone might strive to imitate. What traits of the gentleman that Newman describes are worthy of imitation from a contemporary perspective?

**2.** In this essay, Newman portrays an ideal product of a liberal education. What is your understanding of the goals of a liberal education from reading this essay and from your own experience? In recent years, sensitivity to differences spawned by ethnicity, gender, and class have been privileged over any notion of an ideal. What implications do these considerations have for Newman's essay?

# *The Politician*

## H. L. MENCKEN

Henry Louis Mencken (1880–1956) had such a driving ambition to be a professional writer that he camped in the editorial office of the *Baltimore Morning Herald* every evening for a month, pestering Max Ways, the city editor, to give him an assignment. After Mencken was hired as a reporter, his intense ambition and precocious talents won for him a rapid succession of promotions: Sunday editor at age twenty-one, city editor at twenty-three, managing editor at twenty-four, and editor in chief at twenty-five. When the *Morning Herald* folded in 1906, Mencken went over to the *Baltimore Sun,* the newspaper with which his name has become indelibly associated. Thereafter, his rise to fame and influence as a social and literary critic was meteoric. The "Wicked Wasp of Baltimore," as Mencken was dubbed, stung most of America's sacred cows, yet he recognized and promoted merit wherever he found it. With the literary criticism that he published in *The Smart Set* and the *American Mercury,* he brought to the attention of the American reading public such writers as Theodore Dreiser, Sinclair Lewis, James Branch Cabell, and Sherwood Anderson. Although a pesky critic of pedantry and pedagogy, Mencken produced a solid and enduring work of scholarship in his *The American Language,* first published in 1919 and subsequently revised and supplemented many times. The following essay, from *A Mencken Chrestomathy* (1949), in the tradition of the "character" essay, exhibits most of the traits of this iconoclastic, cantankerous social critic. Although Mencken wrote many extravagantly foolish sentences during his career, it can be said to his credit that he never wrote a dull one.

After damning politicians up hill and down dale for many years, as rogues and vagabonds, frauds and scoundrels, I sometimes suspect that, like everyone else, I often expect too much of them. Though faith and confidence are surely more or less foreign to my nature, I not infrequently find myself looking to them to be able, diligent, candid, and even honest. Plainly enough, that is too large an order, as anyone must realize who reflects upon the manner in which they reach public office. They seldom if ever get there by merit alone, at least in democratic states. Sometimes, to be sure, it happens, but only by a kind of miracle. They are chosen normally for quite different 1 reasons, the chief of which is simply their power to impress and enchant the intellectually underprivileged. It is a talent like any other, and when it is exercised by a radio crooner, a movie actor or a bishop, it even takes on a certain austere and sorry respectability. But it is obviously not identical with a capacity for the intricate problems of statecraft.

Those problems demand for their solution—when they are sol- 2
uble at all, which is not often—a high degree of technical proficiency, and with it there should go an adamantine kind of integrity, for the temptations of a public official are almost as cruel as those of a glamor girl or a dipsomaniac. But we train a man for facing them, not by locking him up in a monastery and stuffing him with wisdom and virtue, but by turning him loose on the stump. If he is a smart and enterprising fellow, which he usually is, he quickly discovers there that hooey pleases the boobs a great deal more than sense. Indeed, he finds that sense really disquiets and alarms them—that it makes them, at best, intolerably uncomfortable, just as a tight collar makes them uncomfortable, or a speck of dust in the eye, or the thought of Hell. The truth, to the overwhelming majority of mankind, is indistinguishable from a headache. After trying a few shots of it on his customers, the larval statesman concludes sadly that it must hurt them, and after that he taps a more humane keg, and in a little while the whole audience is singing "Glory, glory, hallelujah," and when the returns come in the candidate is on his way to the White House.

I hope no one will mistake this brief account of the political 3
process under democracy for exaggeration. It is almost literally true. I do not mean to argue, remember, that all politicians are villains in the sense that a burglar, a child-stealer, or a Darwinian are villains. Far from it. Many of them, in their private characters, are very charming persons, and I have known plenty that I'd trust with my diamonds, my daughter or my liberty, if I had any such things. I happen to be acquainted to some extent with nearly all the gentlemen, both Democrats and Republicans, who are currently itching for the Presidency, including the present incumbent, and I testify freely that they are all pleasant fellows, with qualities above rather than below the common. The worst of them is a great deal better company than most generals in the army, or writers of murder mysteries, or astrophysicists, and the best is a really superior and wholly delightful man—full of sound knowledge, competent and prudent, frank and enterprising, and quite as honest as any American can be without being clapped into a madhouse. Don't ask me what his name is, for I am not in politics. I can only tell you that he has been in public life a long while, and has not been caught yet.

But will this prodigy, or any of his rivals, ever unload any appre- 4
ciable amount of sagacity on the stump? Will any of them venture to

tell the plain truth, the whole truth and nothing but the truth about the situation of the country, foreign or domestic? Will any of them refrain from promises that he knows he can't fulfill—that no human being *could* fulfill? Will any of them utter a word, however obvious, that will alarm and alienate any of the huge packs of morons who now cluster at the public trough, wallowing in the pap that grows thinner and thinner, hoping against hope? Answer: maybe for a few weeks at the start. Maybe before the campaign really begins. Maybe behind the door. But not after the issue is fairly joined, and the struggle is on in earnest. From that moment they will all resort to demagogy, and by the middle of June of election year the only choice among them will be a choice between amateurs of that science and professionals.

They will all promise every man, woman and child in the country 5
whatever he, she or it wants. They'll all be roving the land looking for chances to make the rich poor, to remedy the irremediable, to succor the unsuccorable, to unscramble the unscrambleable, to dephlogisticate the undephlogisticable. They will all be curing warts by saying words over them, and paying off the national debt with money that no one will have to earn. When one of them demonstrates that twice two is five, another will prove that it is six, six and a half, ten, twenty, *n*. In brief, they will divest themselves of their character as sensible, candid and truthful men, and become simply candidates for office, bent only on collaring votes. They will all know by then, even supposing that some of them don't know it now, that votes are collared under democracy, not by talking sense but by talking nonsense, and they will apply themselves to the job with a hearty yo-heave-ho. Most of them, before the uproar is over, will actually convince themselves. The winner will be whoever promises the most with the least probability of delivering anything.

Some years ago I accompanied a candidate for the Presidency on 6
his campaign-tour. He was, like all such rascals, an amusing fellow, and I came to like him very much. His speeches, at the start, were full of fire. He was going to save the country from all the stupendous frauds and false pretenses of his rival. Every time that rival offered to rescue another million of poor fish from the neglects and oversights of God he howled his derision from the back platform of his train. I noticed at once that these blasts of common sense got very little applause, and after a while the candidate began to notice it too. Worse, he began to get word from his spies on the train of his rival that the rival was wowing them, panicking them, laying them in the aisles. They threw flowers, hot dogs and five-cent cigars at him. In places where the times were especially hard they tried to unhook the locomotive from his train, so that he'd have to stay with them awhile longer, and promise them some more. There were no Gallup polls in

those innocent days, but the local politicians had ways of their own for finding out how the cat was jumping, and they began to join my candidate's train in the middle of the night, and wake him up to tell him that all was lost, including honor. This had some effect upon him—in truth, an effect almost as powerful as that of sitting in the electric chair. He lost his intelligent manner, and became something you could hardly distinguish from an idealist. Instead of mocking he began to promise, and in a little while he was promising everything that his rival was promising, and a good deal more.

One night out in the Bible country, after the hullabaloo of the day 7
was over, I went into his private car along with another newspaper reporter, and we sat down to gabble with him. This other reporter, a faithful member of the candidate's own party, began to upbraid him, at first very gently, for letting off so much hokum. What did he mean by making promises that no human being on this earth, and not many of the angels in Heaven, could ever hope to carry out? In particular, what was his idea in trying to work off all those preposterous bile-beans and snake-oils on the poor farmers, a class of men who had been fooled and rooked by every fresh wave of politicians since Apostolic times? Did he really believe that the Utopia he had begun so fervently to preach would ever come to pass? Did he honestly think that farmers, as a body, would ever see all their rosy dreams come true, or that the share-croppers in their lower ranks would ever be more than a hop, skip and jump from starvation? The candidate thought awhile, took a long swallow of the coffin-varnish he carried with him, and then replied that the answer in every case was no. He was well aware, he said, that the plight of the farmers was intrinsically hopeless, and would probably continue so, despite doles from the treasury, for centuries to come. He had no notion that anything could be done about it by merely human means, and certainly not by political means: it would take a new Moses, and a whole series of miracles. "But you forget, Mr. Blank," he concluded sadly, "that our agreement in the premisses must remain purely personal. You are not a candidate for President of the United States. *I am.*" As we left him, his interlocutor, a gentleman grown gray in Washington and long ago lost to every decency, pointed the moral of the episode. "In politics," he said, "man must learn to rise above principle." Then he drove it in with another: "When the water reaches the upper deck," he said, "follow the rats."

## IN RETROSPECT

**1.** *Ethos* (the ethical appeal), *pathos* (the emotional appeal), and *logos* (the rational appeal) are three means of persuasion recognized by the classical rhetoricians. How might Mencken apply these terms to an analysis of presidential politics? What role did these means of appeal play in Mencken's writing of this essay?

**2.** In paragraphs 6 and 7, Mencken describes a particular politician that he knew. To what extent does this portrait of a particular politician coincide with the general type of politician Mencken describes earlier in the essay or with politicians that you are familiar with today?

# *Good Souls*

## DOROTHY PARKER

Dorothy Parker (1893–1967) was a poet, a short-story writer, and a drama critic. She began her writing career by becoming the drama critic of *Vanity Fair.* When she was dismissed from that job because her reviews were too brutal, she became a drama critic and book reviewer for *The New Yorker,* where she was shielded by the editor Harold Ross from the many complaints that came in about the harshness of her reviews. Parker soon became widely known for her sardonic, trenchant wit. For instance, she once said of Katharine Hepburn in one of her movie roles, "She ran the whole gamut of emotion from A to B." Parker published several collections of her poems and short stories. Eventually, all her verse was collected in *Not So Deep as a Well* (1936); all her short stories, in *Here Lies* (1939). All her major works were published in the volume from which this essay was taken, the *Viking Portable Dorothy Parker,* first published in 1944 and reissued in 1973 in a revised edition. You may be surprised by the character type that is satirized in this essay. How could anyone find fault with the kind of person who is commonly referred to as "a good soul"? Well, Parker could—and she does. Parker finds this kind of "Goody Two Shoes" insufferable. By the time you finish reading Parker's characterization, you too may find good souls insufferable. On the other hand, you may object, as earlier readers did to her drama and book reviews, to the unfairness of Parker's treatment of a familiar type of person.

*Their Characteristics. Habits. and Innumerable Methods of Removing the Joy from Life.*

All about us, living in our very families, it may be, there exists a 1
race of curious creatures. Outwardly, they possess no marked peculiarities: in fact, at a hasty glance, they may be readily mistaken for regular human beings. They are built after the popular design; they have the usual number of features, arranged in the conventional manner; they offer no variations on the general run of things in their habits of dressing, eating, and carrying on their business.

Yet, between them and the rest of the civilized world, there 2
stretches an impassable barrier. Though they live in the very thick of the human race, they are forever isolated from it. They are fated to go through life, congenital pariahs. They live out their little lives, mingling with the world, yet never a part of it.

They are, in short, Good Souls. 3

And the piteous thing about them is that they are wholly uncon- 4
scious of their condition. A Good Soul thinks he is just like anyone else. Nothing could convince him otherwise. It is heartrending to see him, going cheerfully about, even whistling or humming as he goes, all unconscious of his terrible plight. The utmost he can receive from the world is an attitude of good-humored patience, a perfunctory word of approbation, a praising with faint damns, so to speak—yet he firmly believes that everything is all right with him.

There is no accounting for Good Souls. 5

They spring up anywhere. They will suddenly appear in families 6
which, for generations, have had no slightest stigma attached to them. Possibly they are throw-backs. There is scarcely a family without at least one Good Soul somewhere in it at the present moment—maybe in the form of an elderly aunt, an unmarried sister, an unsuccessful brother, an indigent cousin. No household is complete without one.

The Good Soul begins early; he will show signs of his condition 7
in extreme youth. Go now to the nearest window, and look out on the little children playing so happily below. Any group of youngsters that you may happen to see will do perfectly. Do you observe the child whom all the other little dears make "it" in their merry games? Do you follow the child from whom the other little ones snatch the cherished candy, to consume it before his streaming eyes? Can you get a good look at the child whose precious toys are borrowed for indefinite periods by the other playful youngsters, and are returned to him in fragments? Do you see the child upon whom all the other kiddies play their complete repertory of childhood's winsome pranks—throwing bags of water on him, running away and hiding from him, shouting his name in quaint rhymes, chalking coarse legends on his unsuspecting back?

Mark that child well. He is going to be a Good Soul when he 8
grows up.

Thus does the doomed child go through early youth and adoles- 9
cence. So does he progress towards the fulfillment of his destiny. And then, some day, when he is under discussion, someone will say of him, "Well, he means well, anyway." That settles it. For him, that is the end. Those words have branded him with the indelible mark of his pariahdom. He has come into his majority; he is a full-fledged Good Soul.

The activities of the adult of the species are familiar to us all. 10
When you are ill, who is it that hastens to your bedside bearing molds of blanc-mange, which, from infancy, you have hated with unspeakable loathing? As usual, you are way ahead of me, gentle reader—it is indeed the Good Soul. It is the Good Souls who efficiently smooth out your pillow when you have just worked it into the comfortable shape, who creak about the room on noisy tiptoe, who tenderly lay on your fevered brow damp cloths which drip ceaselessly down your neck. It is they who ask, every other minute, if there isn't something that they can do for you. It is they who, at great personal sacrifice, spend long hours sitting beside your bed, reading aloud the continued stories in the *Woman's Home Companion,* or chatting cozily on the increase in the city's death rate.

In health, as in illness, they are always right there, ready to 11
befriend you. No sooner do you sit down, than they exclaim that they can see you aren't comfortable in that chair, and insist on your changing places with them. It is the Good Souls who just *know* that you don't like your tea that way, and who bear it masterfully away from you to alter it with cream and sugar until it is a complete stranger to you. At the table, it is they who always feel that their grapefruit is better than yours and who have to be restrained almost forcibly from exchanging with you. In a restaurant the waiter invariably makes a mistake and brings them something which they did not order—and which they refuse to have changed, choking it down with a wistful smile. It is they who cause traffic blocks, by standing in subway entrances arguing altruistically as to who is to pay the fare.

At the theater, should they be members of a box-party, it is the 12
Good Souls who insist on occupying the rear chairs; if the seats are in the orchestra, they worry audibly, all through the performance, about their being able to see better than you, until finally in desperation you grant their plea and change seats with them. If, by so doing, they can bring a little discomfort on themselves—sit in a draught, say, or behind a pillar—then their happiness is complete. To feel the genial glow of martyrdom—that is all that they ask of life.

Good Souls are punctilious in their observation of correct little 13
ceremonies. If, for example, they borrow a [one-penny] postage stamp, they immediately offer two pennies in return for it—they insist upon this business transaction. They never fail to remember birthdays—their little gift always brings with it a sharp stab of remembrance that you have blissfully ignored their own natal day. At the last moment, on Christmas Eve, comes a present from some Good Soul whose existence, in the rush of holiday shopping, you have completely overlooked. When they go away, be it only for an overnight stay, they never neglect to send postcards bearing views of the

principal buildings of the place to all their acquaintances; to their intimates, they always bring back some local souvenir—a tiny dish, featuring the gold-lettered name of the town; a thimble in an appropriate case, both bearing the name of their native city; a tie-rack with the name of its place of residence burned decoratively on its wood; or some such useful novelty.

14 The lives of Good Souls are crowded with Occasions, each with its own ritual which must be solemnly followed. On Mothers' Day, Good Souls conscientiously wear carnations; on St. Patrick's Day, they faithfully don boutonnieres of shamrocks; on Columbus Day, they carefully pin on miniature Italian flags. Every feast must be celebrated by the sending out of cards—Valentine's Day, Arbor Day, Groundhog Day, and all the other important festivals, each is duly observed. They have a perfect genius for discovering appropriate cards of greeting for the event. It must take hours of research.

15 If it's too long a time between holidays, then the Good Soul will send little cards or little mementoes, just by way of surprises. He is strong on surprises, anyway. It delights him to drop in unexpectedly on his friends. Who has not known the joy of those evenings when some Good Soul just runs in, as a surprise? It is particularly effective when a chosen company of other guests happens to be present—enough for two tables of bridge, say. This means that the Good Soul must sit wistfully by, patiently watching the progress of the rubber, or else must cut in at intervals, volubly voicing his desolation at causing so much inconvenience, and apologizing constantly during the evening.

16 His conversation, admirable though it is, never receives its just due of attention and appreciation. He is one of those who believe and frequently quote the exemplary precept that there is good in everybody; hanging in his bedchamber is the whimsically phrased, yet vital, statement, done in burned leather—"There is so much good in the worst of us and so much bad in the best of us that it hardly behooves any of us to talk about the rest of us." This, too, he archly quotes on appropriate occasions. Two or three may be gathered together, intimately discussing some mutual acquaintance. It is just getting really absorbing, when comes the Good Soul, to utter his dutiful, "We mustn't judge harshly—after all, we must always remember that many times our own actions may be misconstrued." Somehow, after several of these little reminders, there seems to be a general waning of interest; the little gathering breaks up, inventing quaint excuses to get away and discuss the thing more fully, adding a few really good details, some place where the Good Soul will not follow. While the Good Soul, pitifully ignorant of their evil purpose, glows with the warmth of conscious virtue, and settles himself to

read the Contributors' Club, in the *Atlantic Monthly,* with a sense of duty well done.

Yet it must not be thought that their virtue lifts Good Souls above 17
the enjoyment of popular pastimes. Indeed, it does not: they are enthusiasts on the subject of good, wholesome fun. They lavishly patronize the drama, in its cleaner forms. They flock to the plays of Miss Rachel Crothers, Miss Eleanor Porter, and Mr. Edward Childs Carpenter. They are passionate admirers of the art of Mr. William Hodge. In literature, they worship at the chaste shrines of Harold Bell Wright, Gene Stratton-Porter, Eleanor Hallowell Abbott, Alice Hegan Rice, and the other triple-named apostles of optimism. They have never felt the same towards Arnold Bennett since he sprung "The Pretty Lady" on them; they no longer give "The Human Machine" and "How to Live on Twenty-four Hours a Day" as birthday offerings to their friends. In poetry, though Tennyson, Whittier, and Longfellow stand for the highest, of course, they have marked leaning toward the later works of Mrs. Ella Wheeler Wilcox. They are continually meeting people who know her, encounters of which they proudly relate. Among humorists, they prefer Mr. Ellis Parker Butler.

Good Souls, themselves, are no mean humorists. They have a 18
time-honored formula of fun-making, which must be faithfully followed. Certain words or phrases must be whimsically distorted every time they are used. "Over the river," they dutifully say, whenever they take their leave. "Don't you cast any asparagus on me," they warn, archly; and they never fail to speak of "three times in concussion." According to their ritual, these screaming phrases must be repeated several times, for the most telling effect, and are invariably followed by hearty laughter from the speaker, to whom they seem eternally new.

Perhaps the most congenial role of the Good Soul is that of 19
advice-giver. He loves to take people aside and have serious little personal talks, all for their own good. He thinks it only right to point out faults or bad habits which are, perhaps unconsciously, growing on them. He goes home and laboriously writes long, intricate letters, invariably beginning, "Although you may feel that this is no affair of mine, I think that you really ought to know," and so on, indefinitely. In his desire to help, he reminds one irresistibly of Marcelline, who used to try so pathetically and so fruitlessly to be of some assistance in arranging the circus arena, and who brought such misfortunes on his own innocent person thereby.

The Good Souls will, doubtless, gain their reward in Heaven; on 20
this earth certainly, theirs is what is technically known as a rough deal. The most hideous outrages are perpetrated on them. "Oh, he

won't mind," people say. "He's a Good Soul." And then they proceed to heap the rankest impositions upon him. When Good Souls give a party, people who have accepted weeks in advance call up at the last second and refuse, without the shadow of an excuse save that of a subsequent engagement. Other people are invited to all sorts of entertaining affairs; the Good Soul, unasked, waves them a cheery good-bye and hopes wistfully that they will have a good time. His is the uncomfortable seat in the motor; he is the one to ride backwards in the train; he is the one who is always chosen to solicit subscriptions and make up deficits. People borrow his money, steal his servants, lose his golf balls, use him as a sort of errand boy, leave him flat whenever something more attractive offers—and carry it all off with their cheerful slogan. "Oh, he won't mind—he's a Good Soul."

And that's just it—Good Souls never do mind. After each fresh 21
atrocity they are more cheerful, forgiving and virtuous, if possible, than they were before. There is simply no keeping them down—back they come, with their little gifts, and their little words of advice, and their little endeavors to be of service, always anxious for more.

Yes, there can be no doubt about it—their reward will come to 22
them in the next world.

Would that they were even now enjoying it! 23

### IN RETROSPECT

**1.** Given Parker's reputation as a harsh critic of others, do you read her portrayal of good souls as a serious description of the character type, as satire, or as some combination of the two? Why?

**2.** In her portrayal of good souls, Parker rarely, if ever, makes a positive comment about the character. This character sketch may just represent Parker's impression of good souls, rather than an objective representation of a recognizable type. Compare Parker's sketch with the other character sketches in this chapter. To what extent are those other sketches representations of a character type, and to what extent do they reveal the perspective of the authors as well? What role does the author's attitude toward the character play in the representation of the character?

# *The Tattletale*

## ELIAS CANETTI

Elias Canetti (1905– ) was born in Russe, Bulgaria, the son of Jewish parents. He attended schools in England, Austria, Switzerland, and Germany and obtained a doctorate in philosophy at the University of Vienna. His literary reputation in Europe and the United States was primarily established by two of his books, both written in German: *Die Blendung* (translated in England as *Auto-da-fe* [1946] and in the United States as *The Tower of Babel* [1947]) and *Masse und Macht* (translated as *Crowds and Power* [1962]). Although Canetti has won many literary prizes during his career, in 1981 he was awarded both the Kafka Prize and the Nobel Prize. The essay reproduced here is taken from *Der Ohrenzeuge: 50 Charaktere* (1974) (translated into English by Neugroschel and published under the title *Earwitness: Fifty Characters* [1979]). This work is a collection of Canetti's exercises in a genre of literature that was introduced by the Greek writer Theophrastus. We have all encountered a tattletale—in fact, we may have met several in our lifetime. What is particularly notable about Canetti's characterization is its brevity. But brevity was the hallmark of this kind of writing from the beginning. The trick is to include just enough traits of the character being portrayed that the reader can say, "Oh, yes, I know the kind of person you're talking about." See if Canetti's characterization conforms to your concept of a tattletale.

The tattletale won't keep anything to himself if it could hurt someone's feelings. He hurries and gets a steal on other tattletales. Sometimes it is a bitter race, and even though not all of them start at the same point, he can sense how close the others are already and he outstrips them in gigantic leaps. He speaks very fast and it is a secret. No one must find out that he knows. He expects gratitude, and it consists in discretion. "I'm only telling you. It concerns only you." The tattletale knows when a position is threatened. Since he moves so quickly—he is very hurried—the threat grows en route. He arrives, and everything is safe and sure. "You're being dismissed." The victim blanches. "When?" he asks. And, "How can that be? No one's said anything to me." "It's being kept a secret. They're going to tell you at the very last moment. I had to warn you. But don't give me away." Then he gives a detailed speech on how awful it would be if he were given away, and before the victim even has time to fully gauge the danger he's in, he already feels sorry for the tattletale, that best friend of his. 1

The tattletale will overlook no insult uttered in anger, and he makes sure that it reaches the insultee. He is less anxious to carry back praise, but to show his good will, he occasionally forces himself 2 to do so. In such cases, he never hurries, he tarries where he is. Praise lies on his tongue like unsavory poison. Before spitting it out, he feels as if he were choking. Finally he speaks it, but very chastely, as though timid at the other man's nakedness.

Otherwise he knows neither shame nor disgust. "You've got to 3
defend yourself. You've got to do something! You can't just take it sitting down!" He likes to counsel the victim, if for no other reason than because it takes longer. His advice is such that it magnifies the victim's fear. After all, the only thing the tattletale cares about is other people's confidence, he cannot live without confidence.

#### IN RETROSPECT

**1.** As we noted in an earlier question, character sketches are as much a product of an author's impressions as of comprehensive, objective observation. Canetti's essay is very short and may thus seem incomplete to you. Some of the characteristics Canetti assigns to the tattletale may coincide with your concept of a tattletale, while others may not. Freewrite your own character sketch of the tattletale and then compare it with those of your classmates and Canetti.

**2.** Compare your responses to the generalities of the character sketches in this chapter with your responses to the more personal essays in chapters 1 and 2. Do you notice any distinctive *stylistic* differences between the essays in chapters 1 and 2 and the essays in this chapter? If so, how do you account for the differences you perceive?

# 4

# On the Animal Kingdom

*In chapters 2 and 3, we remarked that when people turn their gaze outward, they see other human beings, and they begin to react to and to classify the living creatures that they encounter. But there is something else to see "out there": the animal, mineral, and vegetable phenomena commonly called nature. Although nature is always out there for us to see, hear, smell, touch, or taste, it does not vie so actively for our attention as human beings do. We have to make a more conscious effort to observe nature; we have to train ourselves to perceive what is out there. When we do train ourselves to observe keenly, nature begins to reveal its awesome beauties and mysteries. All the essayists in this chapter are reporting on their observations of the animal world, and most of these essayists use nature to reveal things about humanity in general or about themselves in particular. Some of the authors are just amateur observers and reporters, such as Agnes Repplier, who reports about the antics of her feline pets. Gilbert White is one of the first of the keen observers of the animal world who merited the title of naturalist. All the other authors in this chapter are residents of the twentieth century who trained themselves, by habit or by formal schooling, to be observers and reporters of the animal kingdom.*

# *On the English House-Martin*

**GILBERT WHITE**

Gilbert White (1720–1793) was born in the village of Selborne, in Hampshire, England, and educated at Oriel College, Oxford. Although he had many opportunities to take on larger and wealthier parishes, White preferred to spend his life as the curate of a church in his beloved birthplace. An amateur naturalist, he closely observed the animal and vegetable life of his native village and in 1751 began to keep a *Garden Kalendar* and later a *Naturalist's Journal*. He resorted to these records of his observations in 1767 when he began to write a series of letters to two distinguished naturalists, Thomas Pennant and the Honorable Daines Barrington. Although cast in the form of letters to a single person, these prose descriptions of the flora and fauna of Selborne can be considered essays: First, they give vent to the author's distinct personal voice, and second, White soon realized that these personal letters would eventually be published for the delight and instruction of a much larger audience. These letter-essays contain a number of remarkable features: particularity and accuracy of observation, the serene disposition of the observer and his obvious affection for all he observed, the lucidity and charm of his expository style, free for the most part of the scientist's technical language. White set an exemplary precedent for the many essayists who subsequently wrote about the natural scene. The following essay on the English house-martin was originally addressed to Thomas Pennant.

Letter XVI

Selborne, Nov. 20, 1773.

Dear Sir,

1 In obedience to your injunctions I sit down to give you some account of the house-martin, or martlet; and, if my monography of this little domestic and familiar bird should happen to meet with your approbation, I may probably soon extend my inquiries to the rest of the *British hirundines*—the swallow, the swift, and the bank-martin.

2 A few house-martins begin to appear about the sixteenth of *April;* usually some few days later than the swallow. For some time after they appear the hirundines in general pay no attention to the business of nidification, but play and sport about, either to recruit from the fatigue of their journey, if they do migrate at all, or else that their blood may recover it's true tone and texture after it has been so long benumbed by the severities of winter. About the middle of *May,* if the weather be fine, the martin begins to think in earnest of providing a mansion for it's family. The crust or shell of this nest seems to be formed of such dirt or loam as comes most readily to hand, and is tempered and wrought together with little bits of broken straws to render it tough and tenacious. As this bird often builds against a perpendicular wall without any projecting ledge under, it requires it's

utmost efforts to get the first foundation firmly fixed, so that it may safely carry the superstructure. On this occasion the bird not only clings with it's claws, but partly supports itself by strongly inclining it's tail against the wall, making that a fulcrum; and thus steadied it works and plasters the materials into the face of the brick or stone. But then, that this work may not, while it is soft and green, pull itself down by it's own weight, the provident architect has prudence and forbearance enough not to advance her work too fast; but by building only in the morning, and by dedicating the rest of the day to food and amusement, gives it sufficient time to dry and harden. About half an inch seems to be sufficient layer for a day. Thus careful workmen when they build mud-walls (informed at first perhaps by this little bird) raise but a moderate layer at a time, and then desist; lest the work should become top-heavy, and so be ruined by it's own weight. By this method in about ten or twelve days is formed an hemispheric nest with a small aperture towards the top, strong, compact, and warm; and perfectly fitted for all the purposes for which it was intended. But then nothing is more common than for the house-sparrow, as soon as the shell is finished, to seize on it as it's own, to eject the owner, and to line it after it's own manner.

After so much labour is bestowed in erecting a mansion, as 3
Nature seldom works in vain, martins will breed on for several years together in the same nest, where it happens to be well sheltered and secure from the injuries of weather. The shell or crust of the nest is a sort of rustic-work full of knobs and protuberances on the outside; nor is the inside of those that I have examined smoothed with any exactness at all; but is rendered soft and warm, and fit for incubation, by a lining of small straws, grasses, and feathers; and sometimes by a bed of moss interwoven with wool. In this nest they tread, or engender, frequently during the time of building; and the hen lays from three to five white eggs.

At first when the young are hatched, and are in a naked and 4
helpless condition, the parent birds, with tender assiduity, carry out what comes away from their young. Were it not for this affectionate cleanliness the nestlings would soon be burnt up and destroyed in so deep and hollow a nest, by their own caustic excrement. In the quadruped creation the same neat precaution is made use of; particularly among dogs and cats, where the dams lick away what proceeds from their young. But in birds there seems to be a particular provision, that the dung of nestlings is enveloped in a tough kind of jelly, and therefore is the easier conveyed off without soiling or daubing. Yet, as nature is cleanly in all her ways, the young perform this office for themselves in a little time by thrusting their tails out at the aperture of their nest. As the young of small birds presently arrive at

their ἡλικία, or full growth, they soon become impatient of confinement, and sit all day with their heads out at the orifice, where the dams, by clinging to the nest, supply them with food from morning to night. For a time the young are fed on the wing by their parents; but the feat is done by so quick and almost imperceptible a slight, that a person must have attended very exactly to their motions before he would be able to perceive it. As soon as the young are able to shift for themselves, the dams immediately turn their thoughts to the business of a second brood: while the first flight, shaken off and rejected by their nurses, congregate in great flocks, and are the birds that are seen clustering and hovering on sunny mornings and evenings round towers and steeples, and on the roofs of churches and houses. These congregatings usually begin to take place about the first week in *August;* and therefore we may conclude that by that time the first flight is pretty well over. The young of this species do not quit their abodes all together; but the more forward birds get abroad some days before the rest. These approaching the eaves of buildings, and playing about before them, make people think that several old ones attend one nest. They are often capricious in fixing on a nesting-place, beginning many edifices, and leaving them unfinished; but when once a nest is completed in a sheltered place, it serves for several seasons. Those which breed in a ready finished house get the start in hatching of those that build new by ten days or a fortnight. These industrious artificers are at their labours in the long days before four in the morning: when they fix their materials they plaster them on with their chins, moving their heads with a quick vibratory motion. They dip and wash as they fly sometimes in the very hot weather, but not so frequently as swallows. It has been observed that martins usually build to a north-east or north-west aspect, that the heat of the sun may not crack or destroy their nests: but instances are also remembered where they bred for many years in vast abundance in an hot stifled inn-yard, against a wall facing to the south.

Birds in general are wise in their choice of situation: but in this 5
neighbourhood every summer is seen a strong proof to the contrary at an house without eaves in an exposed district, where some martins build year by year in the corners of the windows. But, as the corners of these windows (which face to the south-east and south-west) are too shallow, the nests are washed down every hard rain; and yet these birds drudge on to no purpose from summer to summer, without changing their aspect or house. It is a piteous sight to see them labouring when half their nest is washed away and bringing dirt . . . *"generis lapsi sarcire ruinas."* Thus is instinct a most wonderfully unequal faculty; in some instances so much above reason, in other respects so far below it! Martins love to frequent towns, espe-

cially if there are great lakes and rivers at hand; nay they even affect the close air of *London*. And I have not only seen them nesting in the *Borough,* but even in the *Strand* and *Fleet-street;* but then it was obvious from the dinginess of their aspect that their feathers partook of the filth of that sooty atmosphere. Martins are by far the least agile of the four species; their wings and tails are short, and therefore they are not capable of such surprising turns and quick and glancing evolutions as the swallow. Accordingly they make use of a placid easy motion in a middle region of the air, seldom mounting to any great height, and never sweeping long together over the surface of the ground or water. They do not wander far for food, but affect sheltered districts, over some lake, or under some hanging wood, or in some hollow vale, especially in windy weather. They breed the latest of all the swallow kind: in 1772 they had nestlings on to *October* the twenty-first, and are never without unfledged young as late as *Michaelmas.*

As the summer declines, the congregating flocks increase in num- 6
bers daily by the constant accession of the second broods; till at last they swarm in myriads upon myriads round the villages on the *Thames,* darkening the face of the sky as they frequent the aits of that river, where they roost. They retire, the bulk of them I mean, in vast flocks together about the beginning of *October:* but have appeared of late years in a considerable flight in this neighbourhood, for one day or two, as late as *November* the third and sixth, after they were supposed to have been gone for more than a fortnight. They therefore withdraw with us the latest of any species. Unless these birds are very short-lived indeed, or unless they do not return to the district where they are bred, they must undergo vast devastations some how, and some where; for the birds that return yearly bear no manner of proportion to the birds that retire.

House-martins are distinguished from their congeners by having 7
their legs covered with soft downy feathers down to their toes. They are no songsters; but twitter in a pretty inward soft manner in their nests. During the time of breeding they are often greatly molested with fleas.

I am, &c.

**IN RETROSPECT**

**1.** There are a number of interesting things about the vocabulary that White uses in this letter-essay. For one thing, he uses only a few technical terms in describing the habits and habitats of the house-martin: *quadruped, congeners,* and the Latin word *hirundines,* which biologists use to designate the genus of birds that includes the house-martin, the swallow, the swift, and the bank-martin. Once White uses a Greek word (printed in Greek letters), but he translates the word as "full growth." And once he uses a Latin phrase but does not translate it. Although occasionally he uses such "big words" as *monography, nidification,* and *assiduity,* for the most part he uses words that most literate persons would be familiar with. What does the vocabulary of this essay suggest to you about its writer (White) and about his knowledge of and attention to his intended reader (Pennant)?

**2.** Point to places in the essay that indicate how carefully and how repeatedly White had to observe the house-martins in order to be able to report what he did about this species of bird. How did the repeated and different types of observation contribute to the development of this essay?

# *A Kitten*

## AGNES REPPLIER

Anyone who traces the evolution of the essay from its beginnings in the sixteenth century is bound to remark on how few women distinguished themselves as essay writers before the last quarter of the nineteenth century. In her bibliography for *The Essay in American Literature* (1914), Adaline May Conway lists the names of about a hundred women in the thirty-two-page section on Minor Essayists, but of those, only about five would be even vaguely familiar to contemporary readers. In the five-page section on Major Modern Essayists, Conway lists only two women, one of whom is Agnes Repplier (1855–1950). Not only was Repplier the outstanding woman essayist of her time, but when the definitive history of the essay is written, she will undoubtedly stand as one of the supreme essayists of all time. Born in Philadelphia and educated at the Convent of the Sacred Heart in Torresdale, Pennsylvania, Repplier published her first collection of essays, *Books and Men,* in 1888. After that, she published dozens of collections of essays, in addition to her many biographical works and her historical study of types of humor, *In Pursuit of Laughter* (1936). With the grace, wit, and erudition of her essays, Repplier set a high standard for the many first-rate women essayists who succeeded her. In the following essay, taken from one of her many collections of essays, *The Dozy Hours and Other Papers* (1894), Repplier manifests her fascination with and love for cats, especially for the male kitten of her household mother cat Agrippina. Repplier describes in great detail Claudius Nero's mischievous but always-endearing antics. Indeed, she was so enamored of cats that she later wrote a whole book about them, *The Fireside Sphinx* (1902).

If 1

> The child is father of the man,

why is not the kitten father of the cat? If in the little boy there lurks the infant likeness of all that manhood will complete, why does not the kitten betray some of the attributes common to the adult puss? A puppy is but a dog, plus high spirits, and minus common sense. We never hear our friends say they love puppies, but cannot bear dogs. A kitten is a thing apart; and many people who lack the discriminating enthusiasm for cats, who regard these beautiful beasts with aversion and mistrust, are won over easily, and cajoled out of their prejudices by the deceitful wiles of kittenhood.

> The little actor cons another part,

and is the most irresistible comedian in the world. Its wide-open eyes gleam with wonder and mirth. It darts madly at nothing at all, and then, as though suddenly checked in the pursuit, prances sideways on its hind legs with ridiculous agility and zeal. It makes a vast pretense of climbing the rounds of a chair, and swings by the curtain like an acrobat. It scrambles up a table leg, and is seized with comic horror at finding itself full two feet from the floor. If you hasten to its rescue, it clutches you nervously, its little heart thumping against its furry sides, while its soft paws expand and contract with agitation and relief;

> And all their harmless claws disclose,
> Like prickles of an early rose.

Yet the instant it is back on the carpet it feigns to be suspicious of your interference, peers at you out of "the tail o' its ee," and scampers for protection under the sofa, from which asylum it presently emerges with cautious trailing steps, as though encompassed by fearful dangers and alarms. Its baby innocence is yet unseared. The evil knowledge of uncanny things which is the dark inheritance of cathood has not yet shadowed its round infant eyes. Where did witches find the mysterious beasts that sat motionless by their fires, and watched unblinkingly the waxen manikins dwindling in the flame? They never reared those companions of their solitude, for no witch could have endured to see a kitten gamboling on her hearthstone. A witch's kitten! That one preposterous thought proves how wide, how unfathomed, is the gap between feline infancy and age.

So it happens that the kitten is loved and cherished and caressed 2
as long as it preserves the beguiling mirthfulness of youth. Richelieu, we know, was wont to keep a family of kittens in his cabinet, that their grace and gayety might divert him from the cares of state, and from black moods of melancholy. Yet, with short-sighted selfishness, he banished these little friends when but a few months old, and gave

their places to younger pets. The first faint dawn of reason, the first indication of soberness and worldly wisdom, the first charming and coquettish pretenses to maturity, were followed by immediate dismissal. Richelieu desired to be amused. He had no conception of the finer joy which springs from mutual companionship and esteem. Even humbler and more sincere admirers, like Joanna Baillie, in whom we wish to believe Puss found a friend and champion, appear to take it for granted that the kitten should be the spoiled darling of the household, and the cat a social outcast, degraded into usefulness, and expected to work for her living. What else can be understood from such lines as these?

> Ah! many a lightly sportive child,
> Who hath, like thee, our wits beguiled,
> To dull and sober manhood grown,
> With strange recoil our hearts disown.
> Even so, poor Kit! must thou endure,
> When thou becomest a cat demure,
> Full many a cuff and angry word,
> Chid roughly from the tempting board.
> And yet, for that thou hast, I ween,
> So oft our favored playmate been,
> Soft be the change which thou shalt prove,
> *When time hath spoiled thee of our love;*
> Still be thou deemed, by housewife fat,
> A comely, careful, mousing cat,
> Whose dish is, for the public good,
> Replenished oft with savory food.

Here is a plain exposition of the utilitarian theory which Shakespeare is supposed to have countenanced because Shylock speaks of the "harmless, necessary cat." Shylock, forsooth! As if he, of all men in Christendom or Jewry, knew anything about cats! Small wonder that he was outwitted by Portia and Jessica, when an adroit little animal could so easily beguile him. But Joanna Baillie should never have been guilty of those smug commonplaces concerning the

> comely, careful, mousing cat,

remembering her own valiant Tabby who won Scott's respectful admiration by worrying and killing a dog. It ill became the possessor of an Amazonian cat, distinguished by Sir Walter's regard, to speak with such patronizing kindness of the race.

We can make no more stupid blunder than to look upon our pets 3
from the standpoint of utility. Puss, as a rule, is another Nimrod, eager for the chase, and unwearyingly patient in pursuit of her prey. But she hunts for her own pleasure, not for our convenience; and

when a life of luxury has relaxed her zeal, she often declines to hunt at all. I knew intimately two Maryland cats, well born and of great personal attractions. The sleek, black Tom was named Onyx, and his snow-white companion Lilian. Both were idle, urbane, fastidious, and self-indulgent as Lucullus. Now, into the house honored, but not served, by these charming creatures came a rat, which secured permanent lodgings in the kitchen, and speedily evicted the maid servants. A reign of terror followed, and after a few days of hopeless anarchy it occurred to the cook that the cats might be brought from their comfortable cushions upstairs and shut in at night with their hereditary foe. This was done, and the next morning, on opening the kitchen door, a tableau rivaling the peaceful scenes of Eden was presented to the view. On one side of the hearth lay Onyx, on the other, Lilian; and ten feet away, upright upon the kitchen table, sat the rat, contemplating them both with tranquil humor and content. It was apparent to him, as well as to the rest of the household, that he was an object of absolute, contemptuous indifference to those two lordly cats.

There is none of this superb unconcern in the joyous eagerness of 4
infancy. A kitten will dart in pursuit of everything that is small enough to be chased with safety. Not a fly on the window-pane, not a moth in the air, not a tiny crawling insect on the carpet, escapes its unwelcome attentions. It begins to "take notice" as soon as its eyes are open, and its vivacity, outstripping its dawning intelligence, leads it into infantile perils and wrong doing. I own that when Agrippina brought her first-born son—aged two days—and established him in my bedroom closet, the plan struck me at the start as inconvenient. I had prepared another nursery for the little Claudius Nero, and I endeavored for a while to convince his mother that my arrangements were best. But Agrippina was inflexible. The closet suited her in every respect; and, with charming and irresistible flattery, she gave me to understand, in the mute language I knew so well, that she wished her baby boy to be under my immediate protection. "I bring him to you because I trust you," she said as plainly as looks can speak. "Downstairs they handle him all the time, and it is not good for kittens to be handled. Here he is safe from harm, and here he shall remain." After a few weak remonstrances, the futility of which I too clearly understood, her persistence carried the day. I removed my clothing from the closet, spread a shawl upon the floor, had the door taken from its hinges, and resigned myself, for the first time in my life, to the daily and hourly companionship of an infant.

I was amply rewarded. People who require the household cat to 5
rear her offspring in some remote attic, or dark corner of the cellar, have no idea of all the diversion and pleasure that they lose. It is

delightful to watch the little blind, sprawling, feeble, helpless things develop swiftly into the grace and agility of kittenhood. It is delightful to see the mingled pride and anxiety of the mother, whose parental love increases with every hour of care, and who exhibits her young family as if they were infant Gracchi, the hope of all their race. During Nero's extreme youth, there were times, I admit, when Agrippina wearied both of his companionship and of her own maternal duties. Once or twice she abandoned him at night for the greater luxury of my bed, where she slept tranquilly by my side, unmindful of the little wailing cries with which Nero lamented her desertion. Once or twice the heat of early summer tempted her to spend the evening on the porch roof which lay beneath my windows, and I have passed some anxious hours awaiting her return, and wondering what would happen if she never came back, and I were left to bring up the baby by hand.

But as the days sped on, and Nero grew rapidly in beauty and intelligence, Agrippina's affection for him knew no bounds. She could hardly bear to leave him even for a little while, and always came hurrying back to him with a loud frightened mew, as if fearing he might have been stolen in her absence. At night she purred over him for hours, or made little gurgling noises expressive of ineffable content. She resented the careless curiosity of strangers, and was a trifle supercilious when the cook stole softly in to give vent to her fervent admiration. But from first to last she shared with me her pride and pleasure; and the joy in her beautiful eyes, as she raised them to mine, was frankly confiding and sympathetic. When the infant Claudius rolled for the first time over the ledge of the closet, and lay sprawling on the bedroom floor, it would have been hard to say which of us was the more elated at his prowess. A narrow pink ribbon of honor was at once tied around the small adventurer's neck, and he was pronounced the most daring and agile of kittens. From that day his brief career was a series of brilliant triumphs. He was a kitten of parts. Like one of Miss Austen's heroes, he had air and countenance. Less beautiful than his mother, whom he closely resembled, he easily eclipsed her in vivacity and the specious arts of fascination. Never were mother and son more unlike in character and disposition, and the inevitable contrast between kittenhood and cathood was enhanced in this case by a strong natural dissimilarity which no length of years could have utterly effaced. 6

Agrippina had always been a cat of manifest reserves. She was only six weeks old when she came to me, and had already acquired that gravity of demeanor, that air of gentle disdain, that dignified and somewhat supercilious composure, which won the respectful admiration of those whom she permitted to enjoy her acquaintance. Even in 7 moments of self-forgetfulness and mirth her recreations resembled those of the little Spanish Infanta, who, not being permitted to play with her inferiors, and having no equals, diverted herself as best she could with sedate and solitary sport. Always chary of her favors, Agrippina cared little for the admiration of her chosen circle; and, with a single exception, she made no friends beyond it.

Claudius Nero, on the contrary, thirsted for applause. Affable, 8
debonair, and democratic to the core, the caresses and commendations of a chance visitor or of a housemaid were as valuable to him as were my own. I never looked at him "showing off," as children say—jumping from chair to chair, balancing himself on the bedpost, or scrambling rapturously up the forbidden curtains,—without thinking of the young Emperor who contended in the amphitheater for the worthless plaudits of the crowd. He was impulsive and affectionate,—so, I believe was the Emperor for a time,—and as masterful as if born to the purple. His mother struggled hard to maintain her rightful authority, but it was in vain. He woke her from her sweetest naps; he darted at her tail, and leaped down on her from sofas and tables with the grace of a diminutive panther. Every time she attempted to punish him for these misdemeanors he cried piteously for help, and was promptly and unwisely rescued by some kind-hearted member of the family. After a while Agrippina took to sitting on her tail, in order to keep it out of his reach, and I have seen her many times carefully tucking it out of sight. She had never been a cat of active habits or of showy accomplishments, and the daring agility of the little Nero amazed and bewildered her. "A Spaniard," observes that pleasant gossip, James Howell, "walks as if he marched, and seldom looks upon the ground, as if he contemned it. I was told of a Spaniard who, having got a fall by a stumble, and broke his nose, rose up, and in a disdainful manner said, 'This comes of walking on the earth.' "

Now Nero seldom walked on the earth. At least, he never, if he 9
could help it, walked on the floor; but traversed a room in a series of flying leaps from chair to table, from table to lounge, from lounge to desk, with an occasional dash at the mantelpiece, just to show what he could do. It was curious to watch Agrippina during the performance of these acrobatic feats. Pride, pleasure, the anxiety of a mother, and the faint resentment of conscious inferiority struggled for mastership in her little breast. Sometimes, when Nero's radiant self-satisfaction grew almost insufferable, I have seen her eyelids narrow sullenly, and have wondered whether the Roman Empress ever looked in that way at her brilliant and beautiful son, when maternal love was withering slowly under the shadow of coming evil. Sometimes, when Nero had been prancing and paddling about with absurd and irresistible glee, attracting and compelling the attention of

everybody in the room, Agrippina would jump on my lap, and look in my face with an expression I thought I understood. She had never before valued my affection in all her little petted, pampered life. She had been sufficient for herself, and had merely tolerated me as a devoted and useful companion. But now that another had usurped so many of her privileges, I fancied there were moments when it pleased her to know that one subject, at least, was not to be beguiled from allegiance; that to one friend, at least, she always was and always would be the dearest cat in the world.

I am glad to remember that love triumphed over jealousy, and 10
that Agrippina's devotion to Nero increased with every day of his short life. The altruism of a cat seldom reaches beyond her kittens; but she is capable of heroic unselfishness, where they are concerned. I knew of a London beast, a homeless, forlorn vagrant, who constituted herself an out-door pensioner at the house of a friendly man of letters. This cat had a kitten, whose youthful vivacity won the hearts of a neighboring family. They adopted it willingly, but refused to harbor the mother, who still came for her daily dole to her only benefactor. Whenever a bit of fish or some other especial dainty was given her, this poor mendicant scaled the wall, and watched her chance to share it with her kitten, her little wealthy, greedy son, who gobbled it up as remorselessly as if he were not living on the fat of the land.

Agrippina would have been swift to follow such an example of 11
devotion. At dinner time she always yielded the precedence to Nero, and it became one of our daily tasks to compel the little lad to respect his mother's privileges. He scorned his saucer of milk, and from tenderest infancy aspired to adult food, making predatory incursions upon Agrippina's plate, and obliging us finally to feed them in separate apartments. I have seen him, when a very young kitten, rear himself upon his baby legs, and with his soft and wicked little paw strike his mother in the face until she dropped the piece of meat she had been eating, when he tranquilly devoured it. It was to prevent the recurrence of such scandalous scenes that two dining-rooms became a necessity in the family. Yet he was so loving and so lovable, poor little Claudius Nero! Why do I dwell on his faults, remembering, as I do, his winning sweetness and affability? Day after day, in the narrow city garden, the two cats played together, happy in each other's society, and never a yard apart. Night after night they retired at the same time, and slept upon the same cushion, curled up inextricably into one soft, furry ball. Many times I have knelt by their chair to bid them both good-night; and always, when I did so, Agrippina would lift her charming head, purr drowsily for a few seconds, and then nestle closer still to her first-born, with sighs of supreme satisfac-

tion. The zenith of her life had been reached. Her cup of contentment was full.

It is a rude world, even for little cats, and evil chances lie in wait 12 for the petted creatures we strive to shield from harm. Remembering the pangs of separation, the possibilities of unkindness or neglect, the troubles that hide in ambush on every unturned page. I am sometimes glad that the same cruel and selfish blow struck both mother and son, and that they lie together, safe from hurt or hazard, sleeping tranquilly and always, under the shadow of the friendly pines.

**IN RETROSPECT**

**1.** Repplier entitled her essay "A Kitten," suggesting that she is going to give us a general study of kittens. And at the beginning of the essay, she devotes three paragraphs to a generic discussion of kittens. Why, then, does she go on to devote eight paragraphs to a discussion of the relationship of a particular mother cat to her male kitten?

**2.** How do you respond to Repplier's attribution of human characteristics to cats and kittens and to her allusions to historical and literary figures? What do such attributions and allusions add to her depictions of her pets?

# *The Courage of Turtles*

## EDWARD HOAGLAND

After graduating from Harvard, Edward Hoagland (1932– ) spent the better part of a decade writing short stories and novels. But in recent years he has turned to writing essays, an avocation that he appraises in his essay on the essay in chapter 13, "What I Think, What I Am." To date, Hoagland has published five collections of his essays: *The Courage of Turtles* (1971), *Walking the Dead Diamond River* (1973), *Red Wolves and Black Bears* (1976), *The Tugman's Passage* (1982), and *Heart's Desire* (1988). Somebody once said, "Just reading the titles of Hoagland's books makes you want to read them." He spends his summers with his family in a small town in northern Vermont and spends the rest of the year in the heart of bustling Manhattan. In his fiction, Hoagland is a meticulous observer and reporter of the urban scene, but when he describes nature, as he does in many of his essays, he seems to put on a different pair of glasses. In the essay reprinted here, Hoagland turns his attention to the unlikely subject of turtles, and he delights and instructs us with detailed accounts of the habits and behaviors of these amphibious animals. Hoagland is the sort of "natural naturalist" that Aldo Leopold, himself a naturalist, called for in one of his essays.

Turtles are a kind of bird with the governor turned low. With the 1
same attitude of removal, they cock a glance at what is going on, as if they need only to fly away. Until recently they were also a case of virtue rewarded, at least in the town where I grew up, because, being humble creatures, there were plenty of them. Even when we still had a few bobcats in the woods the local snapping turtles, growing up to forty pounds, were the largest carnivores. You would see them through the amber water, as big as greeny wash basins at the bottom of the pond, until they faded into the inscrutable mud as if they hadn't existed at all.

When I was ten I went to Dr. Green's Pond, a two-acre pond 2
across the road. When I was twelve I walked a mile or so to Taggart's Pond, which was lusher, had big water snakes and a waterfall; and shortly after that I was bicycling way up to the adventuresome vastness of Mud Pond, a lake-sized body of water in the reservoir system of a Connecticut city, possessed of cat-backed little islands and empty shacks and a forest of pines and hardwoods along the shore. Otters, foxes, and mink left their prints on the bank; there were pike and perch. As I got older, the estates and forgotten back lots in town were parceled out and sold for nice prices, yet, though the woods had shrunk, it seemed that fewer people walked in the woods. The new residents didn't know how to find them. Eventually, exploring, they did find them, and it required some ingenuity and doubling around on my part to go for eight miles without meeting someone. I was grown by now, I lived in New York, and that's what I wanted on the occasional weekends when I came out.

Since Mud Pond contained drinking water I had felt confident 3
nothing untoward would happen there. For a long while the developers stayed away, until the drought of the mid-1960s. This event, squeezing the edges in, convinced the local water company that the pond wasn't a necessity as a catch basin, however; so they bulldozed a hole in the earthen dam, bulldozed the banks to fill in the bottom, and landscaped the flow of water that remained to wind like an English brook and provide a domestic view for the houses which were planned. Most of the painted turtles of Mud Pond, who had been inaccessible as they sunned on their rocks, wound up in boxes in boys' closets within a matter of days. Their footsteps in the dry leaves gave them away as they wandered forlornly. The snappers and the little musk turtles, neither of whom leave the water except once a year to lay their eggs, dug into the drying mud for another siege of hot weather, which they were accustomed to doing whenever the pond got low. But this time it was low for good; the mud baked over them and slowly entombed them. As for the ducks, I couldn't stroll in the woods and not feel guilty, because they were crouched beside

every stagnant pothole, or were slinking between the bushes with their heads tucked into their shoulders so that I wouldn't see them. If they decided I had, they beat their way up through the screen of trees, striking their wings dangerously, and wheeled about with that headlong, magnificent velocity to locate another poor puddle.

I used to catch possums and black snakes as well as turtles, and I kept dogs and goats. Some summers I worked in a menagerie with the big personalities of the animal kingdom, like elephants and rhinoceroses. I was twenty before these enthusiasms began to wane, and it was then that I picked turtles as the particular animal I wanted to keep in touch with. I was allergic to fur, for one thing, and turtles need minimal care and not much in the way of quarters. They're personable beasts. They see the same colors we do and they seem to see just as well, as one discovers in trying to sneak up on them. In the laboratory they unravel the twists of a maze with the hot-blooded rapidity of a mammal. Though they can't run as fast as a rat, they improve on their errors just as quickly, pausing at each crossroads to look left and right. And they rock rhythmically in place, as we often do, although they are hatched from eggs, not the womb. (A common explanation psychologists give for our pleasure in rocking quietly is that it recapitulates our mother's heartbeat *in utero*). 4

Snakes, by contrast, are dryly silent and priapic. They are smooth movers, legalistic, unblinking, and they afford the humor which the humorless do. But they make challenging captives; sometimes they don't eat for months on a point of order—if the light isn't right, for instance. Alligators are sticklers too. They're like war-horses, or German shepherds, and with their bar-shaped, vertical pupils adding emphasis, they have the *idée fixe* of eating, eating, even when they choose to refuse all food and stubbornly die. They delight in tossing a salamander up toward the sky and grabbing him in their long mouths as he comes down. They're so eager that they get the jitters, and they're too much of a proposition for a casual aquarium like mine. Frogs are depressingly defenseless: that moist, extensive back, with the bones almost sticking through. Hold a frog and you're holding its skeleton. Frogs' tasty legs are the staff of life to many animals—herons, raccoons, ribbon snakes—though they themselves are hard to feed. It's not an enviable role to be the staff of life, and after frogs you descend down the evolutionary ladder a big step to fish. 5

Turtles cough, burp, whistle, grunt and hiss, and produce social judgments. They put their heads together amicably enough, but then one drives the other back with the suddenness of two dogs who have been conversing in tones too low for an onlooker to hear. They pee in fear when they're first caught, but exercise both pluck and optimism 6 in trying to escape, walking for hundreds of yards within the confines of their pen, carrying the weight of that cumbersome box on legs which are cruelly positioned for walking. They don't feel that the contest is unfair; they keep plugging, rolling like sailorly souls—a bobbing, infirm gait, a brave, sea-legged momentum—stopping occasionally to study the lay of the land. For me, anyway, they manage to contain the rest of the animal world. They can stretch out their necks like a giraffe, or loom underwater like an apocryphal hippo. They browse on lettuce thrown on the water like a cow moose which is partly submerged. They have a penguin's alertness, combined with a build like a Brontosaurus when they rise up on tiptoe. Then they hunch and ponderously lunge like a grizzly going forward.

Baby turtles in a turtle bowl are a puzzle in geometrics. They're as 7
decorative as pansy petals, but they are also self-directed building blocks, propping themselves on one another in different arrangements, before upending the tower. The timid individuals turn fearless, or vice versa. If one gets a bit arrogant he will push the others off the rock and afterwards climb down into the water and cling to the back of one of those he has bullied, tickling him with his hind feet until he bucks like a bronco. On the other hand, when this same milder-mannered fellow isn't exerting himself, he will stare right into the face of the sun for hours. What could be more lionlike? And he's at home in or out of the water and does lots of metaphysical tilting. He sinks and rises, with an infinity of levels to choose from; or, elongating himself, he climbs out on the land again to perambulate, sits boxed in his box, and finally slides back in the water, submerging into dreams.

I have five of these babies in a kidney-shaped bowl. The hatch- 8
ling, who is a painted turtle, is not as large as the top joint of my thumb. He eats chicken gladly. Other goods he will attempt to eat but not with sufficient perseverance to succeed because he's so little. The yellow-bellied terrapin is probably a yearling, and he eats salad voraciously, but no meat, fish, or fowl. The Cumberland terrapin won't touch salad or chicken but eats fish and all of the meats except for bacon. The little snapper, with a black crenelated shell, feasts on any kind of meat, but rejects greens and fish. The fifth of the turtles is African. I acquired him only recently and don't know him well. A mottled brown, he unnerves the green turtles, dragging their food off to his lairs. He doesn't seem to want to be green—he bites the algae off his shell, hanging meanwhile at daring, steep, head-first angles.

The snapper was a Ferdinand until I provided him with deeper 9
water. Now he snaps at my pencil with his downturned and fearsome mouth, his swollen face like a napalm victim's. The Cumberland has

an elliptical red mark on the side of his green-and-yellow head. He is benign by nature and ought to be as elegant as his scientific name *(Pseudemys scripta elegans)*, except he has contracted a disease of the air bladder which has permanently inflated it; he floats high in the water at an undignified slant and can't go under. There may have been internal bleeding, too, because his carapace is stained along its ridge. Unfortunately, like flowers, baby turtles often die. Their mouths fill up with a white fungus and their lungs with pneumonia. Their organs clog up from the rust in the water, or diet troubles, and, like a dying man's, their eyes and heads become too prominent. Toward the end, the edge of the shell becomes flabby as felt and folds around them like a shroud.

While they live they're like puppies. Although they're vivacious, 10
they would be a bore to be with all the time, so I also have an adult wood turtle about six inches long. Her shell is the equal of any seashell for sculpturing, even a Cellini shell; it's like an old, dusty, richly engraved medallion dug out of a hillside. Her legs are salmon-orange bordered with black and protected by canted, heroic scales. Her plastron—the bottom shell—is splotched like a margay cat's coat, with black ocelli on a yellow background. It is convex to make room for the female organs inside, whereas a male's would be concave to help him fit tightly on top of her. Altogether, she exhibits every camouflage color on her limbs and shells. She has a turtleneck neck, a tail like an elephant's, wise old pachydermous hind legs, and the face of a turkey—except that when I carry her she gazes at the passing ground with a hawk's eyes and mouth. Her feet fit to the fingers of my hand, one to each one, and she rides looking down. She can walk on the floor in perfect silence, but usually she lets her shell knock portentously, like a footstep, so that she resembles some grand, concise, slow-moving id. But if an earthworm is presented, she jerks swiftly ahead, poises above it, and strikes like a mongoose, consuming it with wild vigor. Yet she will climb on my lap to eat bread or boiled eggs.

If put into a creek, she swims like a cutter, nosing forward to 11
intercept a strange turtle and smell him. She drifts with the current to go downstream, maneuvering behind a rock when she wants to take stock, or sinking to the nether levels, while bubbles float up. Getting out, choosing her path, she will proceed a distance and dig into a pile of humus, thrusting herself to the coolest layer at the bottom. The hole closes over her until it's as small as a mouse's hole. She's not as aquatic as a musk turtle, not quite as terrestrial as the box turtles in the same woods, but because of her versatility she's marvelous, she's everywhere. And though she breathes the way we breathe, with scarcely perceptible movements of her chest, sometimes instead she

pumps her throat ruminatively, like a pipe smoker sucking and puffing. She waits and blinks, pumping her throat, turning her head, then sets off like a loping tiger in slow motion, hurdling the jungly lumber, the pea vine and twigs. She estimates angles so well that when she rides over the rocks, sliding down a drop-off with her rugged front legs extended, she has the grace of a rodeo mare.

But she's well off to be with me rather than at Mud Pond. The 12
other turtles have fled—those that aren't baked into the bottom. Creeping up the brooks to sad, constricted marshes, burdened as they are with that box on their backs, they're walking into a setup where all their enemies move thirty times faster than they. It's like the nightmare most of us have whimpered through, where we are weighted down disastrously while trying to flee; fleeing our home ground, we try to run.

I've seen turtles in still worse straits. On Broadway, in New York 13
there is a penny arcade which used to sell baby terrapins that were scrawled with bon mots in enamel paint, such as KISS ME BABY. The manager turned out to be a wholesaler as well, and once I asked him whether he had any larger turtles to sell. He took me upstairs to a loft room devoted to the turtle business. There were desks for the paper work and a series of racks that held shallow tin bins atop one another, each with several hundred babies crawling around in it. He was a smudgy-complexioned, serious fellow and he did have a few adult terrapins, but I was going to school and wasn't actually planning to buy; I'd only wanted to see them. They were aquatic turtles, but here they went without water, presumably for weeks, lurching about in those dry bins like handicapped citizens, living on gumption. An easel where the artist worked stood in the middle of the floor. She had a palette and a clip attachment for fastening the babies in place. She wore a smock and a beret, and was homely, short, and eccentric-looking, with funny black hair, like some of the ladies who show their paintings in Washington Square in May. She had a cold, she was smoking, and her hand wasn't very steady, although she worked quickly enough. The smile that she produced for me would have looked giddy if she had been happier, or drunk. Of course the turtles' doom was sealed when she painted them, because their bodies inside would continue to grow but their shells would not. Gradually, invisibly, they would be crushed. Around us their bellies—two thousand belly shells—rubbed on the bins with a mournful momentous hiss.

Somehow there were so many of them I didn't rescue one. Years 14
later, however, I was walking on First Avenue when I noticed a basket of living turtles in front of a fish store. They were as dry as a heap of old bones in the sun; nevertheless, they were creeping over one another gimpily, doing their best to escape. I looked and was

touched to discover that they appeared to be wood turtles, my favorites, so I bought one. In my apartment I looked closer and realized that in fact this was a diamond-back terrapin, which was bad news. Diamondbacks are tidewater turtles from brackish estuaries, and I had no sea water to keep him in. He spent his days thumping interminably against the baseboards, pushing for an opening through the wall. He drank thirstily but would not eat and had none of the hearty, accepting qualities of wood turtles. He was morose, paler in color, sleeker, and more Oriental in the carved ridges and rings that formed his shell. Though I felt sorry for him, finally I found his unrelenting presence exasperating. I carried him, struggling in a paper bag, across town to the Morton Street Pier on the Hudson. It was August but gray and windy. He was very surprised when I tossed him in; for the first time in our association, I think, he was afraid. He looked afraid as be bobbed about on top of the water, looking up at me from ten feet below. Though we were both accustomed to his resistance and rigidity, seeing him still pitiful, I recognized that I must have done the wrong thing. At least the river was salty, but it was also bottomless; the waves were too rough for him, and the tide was coming in, bumping him against the pilings underneath the pier. Too late, I realized that he wouldn't be able to swim to a peaceful inlet in New Jersey, even if he could figure out which way to swim. But since, short of diving in after him, there was nothing I could do, I walked away.

**IN RETROSPECT**

**1.** In this essay, there are many occurrences of the pronoun *I*. Perhaps here more than in any other essay in this chapter, we are made conscious of the person who is describing what is observed. Does the writer's prominence in this essay detract from the pictures that we get of the many species of turtles that are described for us? For instance, the second paragraph is predominantly autobiographical. In your opinion, what purpose does this paragraph serve in an essay that purports to be about turtles? What, if anything, would be lost were this paragraph deleted?

**2.** Hoagland is not a professional zoologist. How do you think he acquired the store of information he provides in this essay? How does his means of acquiring such information affect his presentation of it and subsequently our interest in and understanding of the essay?

# *Wolf Notes*

**BARRY LOPEZ**

Barry Lopez (1945– ), born in upstate New York, received his undergraduate degree (*cum laude,* 1966) and his M.A.T. (Master of Arts in Teaching, 1968) from the University of Notre Dame. Having developed a liking for the West Coast when he lived with his family in California during his preteen years, he elected to do graduate work at the University of Oregon. As a graduate student of folklore, he became interested in some American Indian stories about the coyote as a trickster. Those studies led to the publication of Lopez's first book, *Giving Birth to Thunder, Sleeping with His Daughter: Coyote Builds North America* (1978). Finding the life of a writer more suitable to his temperament than the life of a scholar, Lopez terminated his graduate studies at the university, settled with his wife along the McKenzie River in Oregon, and devoted himself full-time to writing. His first major book, *Of Wolves and Men* (1978), resulted from a commission from the *Smithsonian.* This book of natural history, which Lopez wrote after conducting an extensive and intensive study of wolves in the Arctic, is reputed to be the most thoroughgoing treatise on wolves that has ever been published. Lopez has won an astonishing number of literary awards for this book and for his later books and articles. He is already classified as being in the same league as such other naturalist writers as Peter Matthiessen, Loren Eiseley, Joseph Wood Krutch, Edward Hoagland, and Edward Abbey. The essay here, from *Of Wolves and Men,* reveals how intensely Lopez observed the wolves in their arctic setting and how vividly he conveys to his readers what he observed and recorded.

Imagine a wolf moving through the northern woods. The movement, over a trail he has traversed many times before, is distinctive, unlike that of a cougar or a bear, yet he appears, if you are watching, sometimes catlike or bearlike. It is purposeful, deliberate movement. Occasionally the rhythm is broken by the wolf's pause to inspect a scent mark, or a move off the trail to paw among stones where a year before he had cached meat. 1

The movement down the trail would seem relentless if it did not appear so effortless. The wolf's body, from neck to hips, appears to float over the long, almost spindly legs and the flicker of wrists, a bicycling drift through the trees, reminiscent of the movement of water or of shadows. 2

The wolf is three years old. A male. He is of the subspecies *occidentalis,* and the trees he is moving among are spruce and subalpine fir on the eastern slope of the Rockies in northern Canada. He is light gray; that is, there are more blond and white hairs mixed with gray in the saddle of fur that covers his shoulders and extends down 3 his spine than there are black and brown. But there are silver and even red hairs mixed in, too.

It is early September, an easy time of year, and he has not seen 4
the other wolves in his pack for three or four days. He has heard no howls, but he knows the others are about, in ones and twos like himself. It is not a time of year for much howling. It is an easy time. The weather is pleasant. Moose are fat. Suddenly the wolf stops in mid-stride. A moment, then his feet slowly come alongside each other. He is staring into the grass. His ears are rammed forward, stiff. His back arches and he rears up and pounces like a cat. A deer mouse is pinned between his forepaws. Eaten. The wolf drifts on. He approaches a trail crossing, an undistinguished crossroads. His movement is now slower and he sniffs the air as though aware of a possibility for scents. He sniffs a scent post, a scrawny blueberry bush in use for years, and goes on.

The wolf weighs ninety-four pounds and stands thirty inches at 5
the shoulder. His feet are enormous, leaving prints in the mud along a creek (where he pauses to hunt crayfish but not with much interest) more than five inches long by just over four wide. He has two fractured ribs, broken by a moose a year before. They are healed now, but a sharp eye would notice the irregularity. The skin on his right hip is scarred, from a fight with another wolf in a neighboring pack when he was a yearling. He has not had anything but a few mice and a piece of arctic char in three days, but he is not hungry. He is traveling. The char was a day old, left on rocks along the river by bears.

The wolf is tied by subtle threads to the woods he moves 6
through. His fur carries seeds that will fall off, effectively dispersed, along the trail some miles from where they first caught in his fur. And miles distant is a raven perched on the ribs of a caribou the wolf helped kill ten days ago, pecking like a chicken at the decaying scraps of meat. A smart snowshoe hare that eluded the wolf and left him exhausted when he was a pup has been dead a year now, food for an owl. The den in which he was born one April evening was home to porcupines last winter.

It is now late in the afternoon. The wolf has stopped traveling, 7
has lain down to sleep on cool earth beneath a rock outcropping. Mosquitoes rest on his ears. His ears flicker. He begins to waken. He rolls on his back and lies motionless with his front legs pointed toward the sky but folded like wilted flowers, his back legs splayed, and his nose and tail curved toward each other on one side of his body. After a few moments he flops on his side, rises, stretches, and moves a few feet to inspect—minutely, delicately—a crevice in the

rock outcropping and finds or doesn't find what draws him there. And then he ascends the rock face, bounding and balancing momentarily before bounding again, appearing slightly unsure of the process—but committed. A few minutes later he bolts suddenly into the woods, achieving full speed, almost forty miles per hour, for forty or fifty yards before he begins to skid, to lunge at a lodgepole pine cone. He trots away with it, his head erect, tail erect, his hips slightly to one side and out of line with his shoulders, as though hindquarters were impatient with forequarters, the cone inert in his mouth. He carries it for a hundred feet before dropping it by the trail. He sniffs it. He goes on.

The underfur next to his skin has begun to thicken with the 8
coming of fall. In the months to follow it will becomes so dense between his shoulders it will be almost impossible to work a finger down to his skin. In seven months he will weigh less: eighty-nine pounds. He will have tried unsuccessfully to mate with another wolf in the pack. He will have helped kill four moose and thirteen caribou. He will have fallen through ice into a creek at twenty-two below zero but not frozen. He will have fought with other wolves.

He moves along now at the edge of a clearing. The wind coming 9
downvalley surrounds him with a river of odors, as if he were a migrating salmon. He can smell ptarmigan and deer droppings. He can smell willow and spruce and the fading sweetness of fireweed. Above, he sees a hawk circling, and farther south, lower on the horizon, a flock of sharp-tailed sparrows going east. He senses through his pads with each step the dryness of the moss beneath his feet, and the ridges of old tracks, some his own. He hears the sound his feet make. He hears the occasional movement of deer mice and voles. Summer food.

Toward dusk he is standing by a creek, lapping the cool water, 10
when a wolf howls—a long wail that quickly reaches pitch and then tapers, with several harmonics, long moments to a tremolo. He recognizes his sister. He waits a few moments, then, throwing his head back and closing his eyes, he howls. The howl is shorter and it changes pitch twice in the beginning, very quickly. There is no answer.

The female is a mile away and she trots off obliquely through the 11
trees. The other wolf stands listening, laps water again, then he too departs, moving quickly, quietly through the trees, away from the trail he had been on. In a few minutes the two wolves meet. They approach each other briskly, almost formally, tails erect and moving somewhat as deer move. When they come together they make high squeaking noises and encircle each other, rubbing and pushing, poking their noses into each other's neck fur, backing away to stretch,

chasing each other for a few steps, then standing quietly together, one putting a head over the other's back. And then they are gone, down a vague trail, the female first. After a few hundred yards they begin, simultaneously, to wag their tails.

In the days to follow, they will meet another wolf from the pack, a second female, younger by a year, and the three of them will kill a caribou. They will travel together ten or twenty miles a day, through the country where they live, eating and sleeping, birthing, playing with sticks, chasing ravens, growing old, barking at bears, scent-marking trails, killing moose, and staring at the way water in a creek breaks around their legs and flows on. 12

**IN RETROSPECT**

**1.** Lopez's essay "Wolf Notes" can be read in relation to Agnes Repplier's essay "A Kitten." In what ways are the essays similar and different in their treatment of the subject?

**2.** One of the stylistic features of this essay is the short sentences—perhaps more short sentences than can be found in any other essay in this anthology. What is the effect of these short sentences? Are short sentences particularly appropriate to the subject of this essay? Explain.

# *Clever Hans*

## EMILY HAHN

Emily Hahn (1905– ) was born in St. Louis, Missouri, and educated at the University of Wisconsin, Columbia University, and Oxford University. She was the first woman to be granted a B.S. in mining engineering at the University of Wisconsin, despite the protests of the all-male student body in the College of Engineering. Hahn's first job after graduation in 1926 was with an oil company in St. Louis; she also had a one-year stint as an instructor of geology at Hunter College in New York City. After working with the Red Cross in the Belgian Congo (now Zaire) for one year, Hahn became a correspondent for several newspapers in Europe and Africa. Moreover, she served as an instructor in English at three universities in China in the years just before the Japanese attack on Pearl Harbor precipitated the United States into World War II, and she spent nine years in China as a foreign correspondent for *The New Yorker.* Hahn published an extraordinary number of books on a variety of topics. "Clever Hans" was originally published in *The New Yorker* and later appeared in her book *Look Who's Talking! New Discoveries in Animal Communication* (1978). This essay is a contribution to the debunking of the popular notion that animals are capable of displaying human rationality. It concentrates on a clever horse in Germany who performed remarkable feats for an audience in response to verbal commands from his master, Wilhelm von Osten. The many professional people who witnessed Clever Hans's performances observed his actions accurately but made wrong inferences from what they observed. Finally, two psychologists from the University of Berlin conducted a rigorous scientific investigation of Hans's performances and discovered how he did what he did. Despite the exposé of von Osten, would you grant that Hans was nevertheless a very clever animal?

Language is only one form of communication. We ourselves have perfected several codes of facial expressions and gestures; anyone who doubts it has only to watch speakers on the television screen when the sound is off. Other species have developed various methods of communicating with one another. Some of these methods depend on sight, some on sound, some on scent, and some on touch. For a long time, we could not imagine such different modes; if an animal did not produce at least a fair approximation of our method of signalling—namely, speech—we gave up trying to get in touch with it. We could see and hear communication going on in the songs of birds, in the silent communication of horses, in the play of dogs and cats, but we stood outside. Over the years, many people have entertained a wistful regret that all this life was hidden from us—a circumstance that helps to explain the eagerness with which the world has always received rumors that some animal has been vouchsafed the gift of speech. 1

A generation before Descartes published his strictures on reason in animals, the Western world was fascinated by a white horse named Morocco, owned by one Mr. Banks, of London. Morocco, though not able to talk, evidently understood speech, for he did practically everything Banks told him to; among the men who marvelled at his talents were Shakespeare, Ben Jonson, and Sir Walter Raleigh. He could dance in time to music. If somebody rolled the dice and Banks asked Morocco what the total was, the horse tapped the ground with a hoof the right number of times. He could answer yes-or-no questions the same way, tapping once for yes and twice for no. He answered correctly when he was asked how old a bystander might be: the person would whisper his age to Banks, and, sure enough, Morocco would tap out the right answer. Very seldom did he make a mistake. Finally, a contemporary writer who specialized in magic and juggling tricks and knew how the thing was done wrote about it. He observed that Morocco, while he was performing, never took his eyes off his master, Banks, and that Banks stood very still until the horse had 2 pawed the ground the right number of times, and then, unobtrusively, he shrugged one shoulder. Whenever this happened, Morocco stopped tapping his hoof.

Milbourne Christopher, a modern writer whose subject is magic 3
and the like, has traced the career of Morocco and recounted two incidents that he admits may or may not be true. It was said that Banks took his wonderful animal to France and started giving performances there, but was soon arrested and charged with practicing witchcraft. This happened in Orléans. He was condemned to death by the court, but Morocco saved him by going up to a high official and kneeling down to him. Later, in Rome, according to an equally doubtful story that Christopher tells, Banks and Morocco were both burned at the stake.

Banks's horse may have been the first of his kind, but there has 4
been a long line of similarly conditioned performing animals, not necessarily equines. Near the end of the eighteenth century, New Yorkers were able to watch a star billed as the Learned Dog, and an equally accomplished pig was rapturously received here a few years later. Under the auspices of one Mr. William Frederick Pinchbeck, the pig could play card games, selecting any one of a number of cards that lay on the floor. In time, Pinchbeck himself exposed the secret method he used to aid the animal in making its selections: whenever the pig's snout hovered over the right card, the man sniffed, making a noise that was just loud enough for the animal to hear but was lost on the audience. Horses, however, seem to have been the most popular, for there were many of them. Christopher lists the Learned Little Horse, who entertained the public in Glasgow in 1764; the Military Horse of Knowledge, who could be seen in 1780 in England; Spottie, who appeared in Baltimore in 1807; and an Arabian animal, Mahomet, whose trainer, a Mr. E. L. Probasco, had taught him to add and subtract as fast as any human being, and who was first exhibited in 1889.

It was now time for the appearance of the most famous learned 5
horse of all, Clever (or, in his native German, Kluge) Hans. The difference between Hans and his renowned predecessors was that nobody seems to have thought of him as one of the show animals; he was in a class by himself. Or perhaps it was the people astonished by Hans's feats who were in a special class, insulated from the mob: they were intellectuals, who might never have heard of Spottie or Mahomet, and it is quite possible that they hadn't. At any rate, it seems certain that Hans's owner, a former mathematics teacher named Wilhelm von Osten, trained his animal in good faith. And the professors who examined Hans and wrote long papers about him did not link him up with the marvellous horses of Mr. Banks and Mr. Pro-

basco, though much of what Hans did was just like the feats of those other animals.

Every day, the wonderful horse was exhibited in a paved court- 6
yard that adjoined his stall, in a northern district of Berlin, next to Mr. von Osten's house. About noon, there would gather in the courtyard a select company of people who had been invited by Mr. von Osten—mathematicians, musicians, psychology professors, and others who had a valid reason for being there. No charge was ever made for the show; it was not, as I have said, that kind of thing at all. The pair of them would enter from the stall—Wilhelm von Osten, a white-haired man who was somewhere between sixty-five and seventy, holding Hans's bridle, and Hans himself, a good-looking trotting horse in fine condition, wearing merely a girth strap, a snaffle, and light headgear. He seemed very docile, though it was rumored that he sometimes showed flashes of bad temper. Von Osten handled him gently, with soft, encouraging words; he never used a whip. Now and then, after a correct reply, he would slip Hans a piece of bread or a carrot. If von Osten's questions were of the yes-or-no type, they were answered by a nod or a headshake on the part of Hans, who also indicated "up" and "down" with his head. Other questions, which were answered with hoof-tapping, had to be posed within the limits of the vocabulary with which he was familiar, but its scope was fairly wide and increased day by day. By means of the code that von Osten had taught him, the horse would transpose into numbers a variety of concepts—letters of the alphabet, tones of the musical scale, the names of playing cards—and use them appropriately. He mastered the cardinal numbers from one to one hundred and the ordinals to ten. He solved arithmetic problems. He could read German, though Mr. von Osten taught him only lower-case letters: when placards with several written words were put in front of him and he was told to do so, he indicated one word or another by pointing to it with his nose. He knew the value of all German coins. He carried the entire yearly calendar in his head and could give you the right date for any day you might mention. He recognized people from their photographs. In music, he had absolute tone consciousness, and could recognize a note sung to him as C, D, etc. (within the once-accented scale of C-major). There seemed no limit to his powers.

Not surprisingly, Hans captured the public fancy in Germany. He 7
was the subject of popular songs, and people could buy picture postcards of him and bring home little toy Hanses for the children. Nevertheless, there were some who doubted. Though no one had ever seen any signals pass between Mr. von Osten and his horse, there simply had to be signals, the skeptics said. Somebody suggested that the old mathematics master might be emitting the new

X-rays that everybody was talking about. Or was it that mysterious thing called "hypnotic suggestion"? At length, it was agreed that a thorough scientific inquiry should be made into the matter. Mr. von Osten, after a time, promised to cooperate with the examiners, and a number of men, some familiar with Hans and some who were not so intimate with the horse and his master, participated in the experiments. Two of the latter were Professor Stumpf, a psychologist, who was director of the Psychological Institute of the University of Berlin, and Oskar Pfungst, one of Stumpf's co-workers at the Psychological Institute, who later wrote a book about Hans. The rules were drawn up: every now and then, one of the gentlemen was to ask Hans something to which he himself did not have the answer. Also, the interrogators were to be switched from time to time. The stage was set, and the men arranged themselves with a questioner standing to Hans's right, equipped with bread, carrots, and lumps of sugar. With all due solemnity, a card with the figure 8 on it was produced and shown to the horse in such a way that the questioner couldn't see it. Hans tapped out fourteen. Next time, the questioner was allowed to look at the card. It was 8 again—and Hans tapped out eight. The next card said 4, and the questioner didn't see it. Hans tapped eight again. Whenever the questioner didn't see the card, Hans was wrong almost every time. Whenever he did, the horse was almost always right. There was no blinking at these facts: Hans could not count. Reading tests got the same results: Whenever the questioner didn't see the words, Hands didn't know them, but he made no mistakes when the man did see the words. So Hans couldn't read, either. He failed the test on calculation of dates; he failed in music, which was tested by someone playing a harmonica that spanned the once-accented octave.

Poor von Osten became increasingly dismayed as he saw his 8
wonderful horse fail time after time. Perhaps, he suggested, the secret lay in sound waves emitted by the questioner. No, it was later decided, that could not be the explanation, because at times it wasn't necessary to speak aloud to Hans—he would start tapping before the question was uttered. Just to make sure, however, they tried him with earmuffs. The earmuffs made no difference. No, it couldn't be sound waves. However mysteriously he did it, the gentlemen agreed, Hans did get hold of visual signals. To try the idea out, they put blinkers on him. Something different happened immediately. Hans didn't care for the blinkers, and made what were described as strenuous efforts to regain a view of his questioner, raging and tearing at the lines when they tried to tie him and make him stand still. Furthermore, his record of answers now became woefully bad. When they took the blinkers off, Hans calmed down. They asked him questions

in the old way, and now, at last, they noticed something that had never been observed before—that when a problem was posed to the horse he had a peculiar way of watching his questioner very closely, instead of looking at the object under consideration: the card or whatever it was.

Now that the examiners knew where to look, they soon had their 9
solution: Hans was watching his questioner's involuntary movements. Having set a problem, the questioner unconsciously leaned forward to count the hoof taps, and when the proper number had been reached, he relaxed; that is, he straightened himself with a slight upward jerk of the head. It was the smallest possible movement, but it was enough for Hans.

The discovery had wide repercussions in the scientific world. 10
Even today, researchers in the field of animal awareness are apt to say to one another over the results of some experiment, "You're sure that wasn't just a Clever Hans syndrome?" The affair may well have discouraged many people who wanted to find out more about animal communication.

#### IN RETROSPECT

**1.** The relationship of Hahn to her subject matter is notably different from the relationship of the other essayists in this chapter to their subjects. How would you characterize the difference? Point to instances in the essay where this difference is especially apparent.

**2.** The headnote to this essay remarks that the "many professional people who witnessed Clever Hans's performances observed his actions accurately but made wrong inferences from what they observed." Point out some of the instances of accurate observation but wrong inference. How were the wrong inferences corrected?

# 5

# On Town and Country

*Poets and fiction writers are noted for their keen observation of their environment. Because of their intensive observation of the scene and their command of language, these artists are able to make other people see what they see. Practitioners of the visual arts can also make us see the world "out there." They create a painting or a sketch of a person, a creature, a place, or a thing; or they take a photograph of someone or something out there; or they record what is out there on film or videotape. These pictures tend to be more objective—more realistic, if you will—than the pictures that writers give us, because they reproduce something in visual symbols that is closer to the actuality than the representation writers create by the use of verbal symbols. Whereas a photographer can present you with a snapshot of a tree, a writer has to conjure up a picture of a tree in your consciousness by setting down the verbal symbol* tree. *You actually see the tree the photographer captured on film; the tree that the writer makes you see, however, is the image conjured up in your mind by the familiar word* tree. *Ten people who read that word or hear it uttered are likely to conceive of ten different pictures of a tree. Three of the writers in this chapter are creating verbal pictures of a rural scene; the others are creating verbal pictures of an urban scene. Since many of you who read these essays will never have actually seen the landscapes that are being described in verbal symbols, it would be interesting for a group of you to compare the impressions of the scene that you receive from these verbal descriptions. How much of your attitude toward the scene is influenced by the writer's attitude?*

# *Night Walks*

## CHARLES DICKENS

Every schoolchild eventually hears the name Charles Dickens, a name as ubiquitous and inescapable as William Shakespeare or Mark Twain. Although the schoolchild may never get around to reading the literary works ascribed to those names, he or she can identify the persons who bear them. Charles Dickens (1812–1870) was a novelist during the Victorian period in England, the author of such books as *Oliver Twist, David Copperfield,* and *A Christmas Carol.* Most educated people know at least that much about Dickens. Those who go on to deepen their knowledge of English literature will read other novels by Dickens, will hear about the dramatic readings he gave from his books in England and America, and may read some of the sketches and essays that he wrote for the weekly periodical he founded, *Household Words,* and later collected in *All the Year Round* and *The Uncommercial Traveller.* "Night Walks" is a product of those series. Dickens describes in vivid detail his walks through the streets of London late at night. His accounts of the homeless vagrants that he encounters on his nocturnal perambulations will seem highly relevant to contemporary readers who in recent years have been hearing about, and seeing documentary films and telecasts about, the growing numbers of homeless people in the streets of our major cities.

Some years ago, a temporary inability to sleep, referable to a 1
distressing impression, caused me to walk about the streets all night for a series of several nights. The disorder might have taken a long time to conquer, if it had been faintly experimented on in bed; but, it was soon defeated by the brisk treatment of getting up directly after lying down, and going out, and coming home tired at sunrise.

In the course of those nights I finished my education in a fair 2
amateur experience of Houselessness. My principal object being to get through the night, the pursuit of it brought me into sympathetic relations with people who have no other object every night in the year.

The month was March, and the weather damp, cloudy, and cold. 3
The sun not rising before half-past five, the night perspective looked sufficiently long at half-past twelve: which was about my time for confronting it.

The restlessness of a great city, and the way in which it tumbles 4
and tosses before it can get to sleep, formed one of the first entertainments offered to the contemplation of us houseless people. It lasted about two hours. We lost a great deal of companionship when the late public houses turned their lamps out, and when the potmen thrust the last brawling drunkards into the street; but stray vehicles and stray people were left us after that. If we were very lucky, a policeman's rattle sprang, and a fray turned up; but, in general, surprisingly little of this diversion was provided. Except in the Haymarket, which is the worst-kept part of London, and about Kent

Street in the Borough, and along a portion of the line of the Old Kent Road, the peace was seldom violently broken. But, it was always the case that London, as if in imitation of individual citizens belonging to it, had expiring fits and starts of restlessness. After all seemed quiet, if one cab rattled by, half a dozen would surely follow; and Houselessness even observed that intoxicated people appeared to be magnetically attracted towards each other; so that we knew, when we saw one drunken object staggering against the shutters of a shop, that another drunken object would stagger up before five minutes were out, to fraternize or fight with it. When we made a divergence from the regular species of drunkard, the thin-armed, puff-faced, leaden-lipped gin-drinker, and encountered a rarer specimen of a more decent appearance, fifty to one but that specimen was dressed in soiled mourning. As the street experience in the night, so the street experience in the day; the common folk who come unexpectedly into a little property, come unexpectedly into a deal of liquor.

At length these flickering sparks would die away, worn out—the 5
last veritable sparks of waking life trailed from some late pieman or hot-potato man—and London would sink to rest. And then the yearning of the houseless mind would be for any sign of company, any lighted place, any movement, anything suggestive of any one being up—nay, even so much as awake, for the houseless eye looked out for lights in windows.

Walking the streets under the pattering rain, Houselessness 6
would walk and walk and walk, seeing nothing but the interminable tangle of streets, save at a corner, here and there, two policemen in conversation, or the sergeant or inspector looking after his men. Now and then in the night—but rarely—Houselessness would become aware of a furtive head peering out of a doorway a few yards before him, and, coming up with the head, would find a man standing bolt upright to keep within the doorway's shadow, and evidently intent upon no particular service to society. Under a kind of fascination, and in a ghostly silence suitable to the time, Houselessness and this gentleman would eye one another from head to foot, and so, without exchange of speech, part, mutually suspicious. Drip, drip, drip, from ledge and coping, splash from pipes and water-spouts, and by and by the houseless shadow would fall upon the stones that pave the way to Waterloo Bridge; it being in the houseless mind to have a halfpennyworth of excuse for saying "Good night" to the tollkeeper, and catching a glimpse of his fire. A good fire, and a good greatcoat and a good woolen neck-shawl, were comfortable things to see in conjunction with the tollkeeper; also his brisk wakefulness was excellent company when he rattled the change of halfpence down upon that metal table of his, like a man who defied the night, with all its sorrowful thoughts, and didn't care for the coming of dawn. There

was need of encouragement on the threshold of the bridge, for the bridge was dreary. The chopped-up murdered man had not been lowered with a rope over the parapet when those nights were; he was alive, and slept then quietly enough most likely, and undisturbed by any dream of where he was to come. But the river had an awful look, the buildings on the banks were muffled in black shrouds, and the reflected lights seemed to originate deep in the water, as if the spectres of suicides were holding them to show where they went down. The wild moon and clouds were as restless as an evil conscience in a tumbled bed, and the very shadow of the immensity of London seemed to lie oppressively upon the river.

Between the bridge and the two great theatres there was but the 7
distance of a few hundred paces, so the theatres came next. Grim and black within, at night, those great dry Wells, and lonesome to imagine, with the rows of faces faded out, the lights extinguished, and the seats all empty. One would think that nothing in them knew itself at such a time but Yorick's skull. In one of my night walks, as the church steeples were shaking the March winds and rain with the strokes of four, I passed the outer boundary of one of these great deserts, and entered it. With a dim lantern in my hand, I groped my well-known way to the stage, and looked over the orchestra—which was like a great grave dug for a time of pestilence—into the void beyond. A dismal cavern of an immense aspect, with the chandelier gone dead like everything else, and nothing visible, through mist and fog and space, but tiers of winding-sheets. The ground at my feet, where, when last there, I had seen the peasantry of Naples dancing among the vines, reckless of the burning mountain which threatened to overwhelm them, was now in possession of a strong serpent of engine-hose, watchfully lying in wait for the serpent Fire, and ready to fly at it if it showed its forked tongue. A ghost of a watchman, carrying a faint corpse-candle, haunted the distant upper gallery and flitted away. Retiring within the proscenium, and holding my light above my head towards the rolled-up curtain—green no more, but black as ebony—my sight lost itself in a gloomy vault, showing faint indications in it of a shipwreck of canvas and cordage. Methought I felt much as a diver might at the bottom of the sea.

In those small hours when there was no movement in the streets, 8
it afforded matter for reflection to take Newgate in the way, and, touching its rough stone, to think of the prisoners in their sleep, and then to glance in at the lodge over the spiked wicket, and see the fire and light of the watching turnkeys on the white wall. Not an inappropriate time, either, to linger by that wicked little Debtors' Door—shutting tighter than any other door one ever saw—which has been Death's Door to so many. In the days of the uttering of forged one-pound notes by people tempted up from the country, how many

hundreds of wretched creatures of both sexes—many quite innocent—swung out of a pitiless and inconsistent world, with the tower of yonder Christian church of St. Sepulchre monstrously before their eyes! Is there any haunting of the Bank Parlour, by the remorseful souls of old directors, in the nights of these later days, I wonder, or is it as quiet as this degenerate Aceldama of an Old Bailey?

To walk on to the Bank, lamenting the good old times and bemoan- 9
ing the present evil period, would be an easy next step, so I would take it, and would make my houseless circuit of the Bank, and give a thought to the treasure within; likewise to the guard of soldiers passing the night there, and nodding over the fire. Next, I went to Billingsgate, in some hope of market-people, but it proving as yet too early, crossed London Bridge, and got down by the water-side on the Surrey shore, among the buildings of the great brewery. There was plenty going on at the brewery; and the reek, and the smell of grains, and the rattling of the plump dray horses at their mangers, were capital company. Quite refreshed by having mingled with this good society, I made a new start with a new heart, setting the old King's Bench Prison before me for my next object, and resolving, when I should come to the wall, to think of poor Horace Kinch, and the Dry Rot in men.

A very curious disease the Dry Rot in men, and difficult to detect 10
the beginning of. It had carried Horace Kinch inside the wall of the old King's Bench Prison, and it had carried him out with his feet foremost. He was a likely man to look at, in the prime of life, well to do, as clever as he needed to be, and popular among many friends. He was suitably married, and had healthy and pretty children. But, like some fair-looking houses or fair-looking ships, he took the Dry Rot. The first strong external revelation of the Dry Rot in men is a tendency to lurk and lounge; to be at street corners without intelligible reason; to be going anywhere when met; to be about many places rather than at any; to do nothing tangible, but to have an intention of performing a variety of intangible duties tomorrow, or the day after. When this manifestation of the disease is observed, the observer will usually connect it with a vague impression once formed or received, that the patient was living a little too hard. He will scarcely have had leisure to turn it over in his mind, and form the terrible suspicion "Dry Rot," when he will notice a change for the worse in the patient's appearance: a certain slovenliness and deterioration which is not poverty, nor dirt, nor intoxication, nor ill-health, but simply Dry Rot. To this succeeds a smell as of strong waters in the morning; to that, a looseness respecting money; to that, a stronger smell as of strong waters at all times; to that, a looseness respecting everything; to that, a trembling of the limbs, somnolency, misery, and crumbling to pieces. As it is in wood, so it is in men. Dry Rot advances at a compound usury quite incalculable. A plank is found infected with it,

and the whole structure is devoted. Thus it had been with the unhappy Horace Kinch, lately buried by a small subscription. Those who knew him had not nigh done saying, "So well off, so comfortably established, with such hope before him—and yet, it is feared, with a slight touch of Dry Rot!" when lo! the man was all Dry Rot and dust.

From the dead wall associated on those houseless nights with this 11
too common story, I chose next to wander by Bethlehem Hospital; partly because it lay on my road round to Westminster; partly because I had a night fancy in my head which could be best pursued within sights of its walls and dome. And the fancy was this: Are not the sane and insane equal at night as the sane lie a-dreaming? Are not all of us outside this hospital, who dream, more or less in the condition of those inside it, every night of our lives? Are we not nightly persuaded, as they daily are, that we associate preposterously with kings and queens, emperors and empresses, and notabilities of all sorts? Do we not nightly jumble events and personages, and times and places, as these do daily? Are we not sometimes troubled by our own sleeping inconsistencies, and do we not vexedly try to account for them or excuse them, just as these do sometimes in respect of their waking delusions? Said an afflicted man to me, when I was last in a hospital like this, "Sir, I can frequently fly." I was half ashamed to reflect that so could I—by night. Said a woman to me on the same occasion, "Queen Victoria frequently comes to dine with me, and Her Majesty and I dine off peaches and macaroni in our nightgowns, and His Royal Highness the Prince Consort does us the honour to make a third on horseback in a Field-Marshal's uniform." Could I refrain from reddening with consciousness when I remembered the amazing royal parties I myself had given (at night), the unaccountable viands I had put on table, and my extraordinary manner of conducting myself on those distinguished occasions? I wonder that the great master who knew everything, when he called Sleep the death of each day's life, did not call Dreams the insanity of each day's sanity.

By this time I had left the hospital behind me, and was again 12
setting towards the river; and in a short breathing-space I was on Westminster Bridge, regaling my houseless eyes with the external walls of the British Parliament—the perfection of a stupendous institution, I know, and the admiration of all surrounding nations and succeeding ages, I do not doubt, but perhaps a little the better, now and then, for being pricked up to its work. Turning off into Old Palace Yard, the Courts of Law kept me company for a quarter of an hour; hinting in low whispers what numbers of people they were keeping awake, and how intensely wretched and horrible they were rendering the small hours to unfortunate suitors. Westminster Abbey was fine gloomy society for another quarter of an hour; suggesting a wonderful procession of its dead among the dark arches and pillars,

each century more amazed by the century following it than by all the centuries going before. And, indeed, in those houseless night walks—which even included cemeteries where watchmen went round among the graves at stated times, and moved the tell-tale handle of an index which recorded that they had touched it at such an hour—it was a solemn consideration what enormous hosts of dead belong to one old great city, and how, if they were raised while the living slept, there would not be the space of a pin's point in all the streets and ways for the living to come out into. Not only that, but the vast armies of dead would overflow the hills and valleys beyond the city, and would stretch away all round it, God knows how far.

When a church clock strikes on houseless ears in the dead of the 13
night, it may be at first mistaken for company, and hailed as such. But, as the spreading circles of vibration, which you may perceive at such time with great clearness, go opening out, for ever and ever afterwards widening, perhaps (as the philosopher has suggested) in external space, the mistake is rectified, and the sense of loneliness is profounder. Once—it was after leaving the Abbey, and turning my face north—I came to the great steps of St. Martin's Church as the clock was striking three. Suddenly, a thing that in a moment more I should have trodden upon without seeing, rose up at my feet with a cry of loneliness and houselessness, struck out of it by the bell, the like of which I never heard. We then stood face to face looking at one another, frightened by one another. The creature was like a beetle-browed hare-lipped youth of twenty, and it had a loose bundle of rags on, which it held together with one of its hands. It shivered from head to foot, and its teeth chattered, and as it started at me—persecutor, devil, ghost, whatever it thought me—it made with its whining mouth as if it were snapping at me, like a worried dog. Intending to give this ugly object money, I put out my hand to stay it—for it recoiled as it whined and snapped—and laid my hand upon its shoulder. Instantly, it twisted out of its garment, like the young man in the New Testament, and left me standing alone with its rags in my hand.

Covent Garden Market, when it was market morning, was won- 14
derful company. The great wagons of cabbages, with growers' men and boys lying asleep under them, and with sharp dogs from market-garden neighbourhoods looking after the whole, were as good as a party. But one of the worst night sights I know in London is to be found in the children who prowl about this place; who sleep in the baskets, fight for the offal, dart at any object they think they can lay their thieving hands on, dive under the carts and barrows, dodge the constables, and are perpetually making a blunt pattering on the pavement of the Piazza with the rain of their naked feet. A painful and unnatural result comes of the comparison one is forced to institute between the growth of corruption as displayed in the so much

improved and cared-for fruits of the earth, and the growth of corruption as displayed in these all-uncared-for (except inasmuch as ever-hunted) savages.

There was early coffee to be got about Covent Garden Market, 15
and that was more company—warm company, too, which was better. Toast of a very substantial quality was likewise procurable: though the tousled-headed man who made it, in an inner chamber within the coffee-room, hadn't got his coat on yet, and was so heavy with sleep that in every interval of toast and coffee he went off anew behind the partition into complicated crossroads of choke and snore, and lost his way directly. Into one of these establishments (among the earliest) near Bow Street there came one morning, as I sat over my houseless cup, pondering where to go next, a man in a high and long snuff-coloured coat, and shoes, and, to the best of my belief, nothing else but a hat, who took out of his hat a large cold meat-pudding; a meat-pudding so large that it was a very tight fit, and brought the lining of the hat out with it. This mysterious man was known by his pudding, for, on his entering, the man of sleep brought him a pint of hot tea, a small loaf, and a large knife and fork and plate. Left to himself in his box, he stood the pudding on the bare table, and, instead of cutting it, stabbed it, overhand, with the knife, like a mortal enemy; then took the knife out, wiped it on his sleeve, tore the pudding asunder with his fingers, and ate it all up. The remembrance of this man with the pudding remains with me as the remembrance of the most spectral person my houselessness encountered. Twice only was I in that establishment, and twice I saw him stalk in (as I should say, just out of bed, and presently going back to bed), take out his pudding, stab his pudding, wipe the dagger, and eat his pudding all up. He was a man whose figure promised cadaverousness, but who had an excessively red face, though shaped like a horse's. On the second occasion of my seeing him, he said huskily to the man of sleep, "Am I red tonight?" "You are," he uncompromisingly answered. "My mother," said the spectre, "was a red-faced woman that liked drink, and I looked at her hard when she laid in her coffin, and I took the complexion." Somehow, the pudding seemed an unwholesome pudding after that, and I put myself in its way no more.

When there was no market, or when I wanted variety, a railway 16
terminus, with the morning mails coming in, was remunerative company. But, like most of the company to be had in this world, it lasted only a very short time. The station lamps would burst out ablaze, the porters would emerge from places of concealment, the cabs and trucks would rattle to their places (the Post Office carts were already in theirs), and finally, the bell would strike up, and the train would come banging in. But there were few passengers and little luggage, and everything scuttled away with the greatest expedition. The loco-

motive post offices, with their great nets—as if they had been dragging the country for bodies—would fly open as to their doors, and would disgorge a smell of lamp, an exhausted clerk, a guard in a red coat, and their bags of letters; the engine would blow and heave and perspire, like an engine wiping its forehead, and saying what a run it had had; and within ten minutes the lamps were out, and I was houseless and alone again.

But now there were driven cattle on the highroad near, wanting 17
(as cattle always do) to turn into the midst of stone walls, and squeeze themselves through six inches' width of iron railing, and getting their heads down (also as cattle always do) for tossing-purchase at quite imaginary dogs, and giving themselves and every devoted creature associated with them a most extraordinary amount of unnecessary trouble. Now, too, the conscious gas began to grow pale with the knowledge that daylight was coming, and straggling workpeople were already in the streets, and, as waking life had become extinguished with the last pieman's sparks, so it began to be rekindled with the fires of the first street-corner breakfast-sellers. And so by faster and faster degrees, until the last degrees were very fast, the day came, and I was tired and could sleep. And it is not, as I used to think, going home at such times, the least wonderful thing in London, that, in the real desert region of the night, the houseless wanderer is alone there. I knew well enough where to find Vice and Misfortune of all kinds, if I had chosen; but they were put out of sight, and my houselessness had many miles upon miles of streets in which it could, and did, have its own solitary way.

## IN RETROSPECT

**1.** Dickens gives us not so much a physical picture of the city of London in the middle nineteenth century as a sense of the atmosphere of a sleeping city. If you look closely at this essay, you will find very few set pieces of description of buildings, streets, rivers, bridges, vehicles, or people. You may never have seen, firsthand or in photographs or films, any of the sections of London (even of contemporary London) that the wandering Dickens talks about, but you may get an *impression* of his nighttime London. What is the impression that you get of Dickens's nighttime London, and how did Dickens create that impression for you?

**2.** The images that Dickens gives us of the sleeping city are not so much snapshots as motion pictures. His essay is like a travel film or a documentary—scenes in motion. How does Dickens organize his travelogue in this fairly long essay? Go through the essay again and mark off the parts (giving the paragraph span of each part), and then indicate what Dickens is portraying in each part. If you do not know London, you may be unable to tell whether the progression of locations is orderly or random, but see if you can determine Dickens's principle of organization.

# *The Ponds*

## HENRY DAVID THOREAU

Henry David Thoreau (1817–1862) was born in Concord, Massachusetts, and was educated—at great financial sacrifice by his family—at Concord Academy and Harvard University. After he graduated from Harvard, Thoreau and his brother John opened a school in Concord, but after three years they had to give up that enterprise because of John's failing health. In 1841, Thoreau went to live in the home of Ralph Waldo Emerson, who introduced him to transcendentalism, a philosophy that had a great influence on Thoreau's life and writings. Thoreau became a nineteenth-century exponent of many of the values and causes espoused by young people in the 1960s: nonviolent civil disobedience, the anti-slavery movement, protests against the growing industrialization of American society, the shameful pollution of the environment, the back-to-nature mystique. He built himself a cabin near Walden Pond, where he lived from July 4, 1845, to September 6, 1847, because he wanted to experience life stripped down to its essentials so that he might "subdue and cultivate a few cubic feet of flesh" and "suck out all the marrow of life." "The Ponds" is one of the set-pieces in Thoreau's book *Walden* (1854). This piece is notable not only for the minuteness and vividness of Thoreau's description of the environs of his cabin at Walden but also for the many personal notes he intermingles with his descriptions of the scene. Although anyone who has as much time on his or her hands as Thoreau did at Walden Pond has the leisure to observe closely the microcosm of nature, it takes someone as skillful with words as Thoreau to re-create the experience for others. Thoreau's exemplary prose style was much influenced by the crispness and sententiousness that he observed in the Greek authors that he could read voraciously and readily. Among his other accomplishments as a writer, Thoreau was a great phrase-maker.

The scenery of Walden is on a humble scale, and, though very 1
beautiful, does not approach to grandeur, nor can it much concern one who has not long frequented it or lived by its shore; yet this pond is so remarkable for its depth and purity as to merit a particular description. It is a clear and deep green well, half a mile long and a mile and three quarters in circumference, and contains about sixty-one and a half acres; a perennial spring in the midst of pine and oak woods, without any visible inlet or outlet except by the clouds and evaporation. The surrounding hills rise abruptly from the water to the height of forty to eighty feet, though on the south-east and east they attain to about one hundred and one hundred and fifty feet respectively, within a quarter and a third of a mile. They are exclusively woodland. All our Concord waters have two colors at least, one when viewed at a distance, and another, more proper, close at hand. The first depends more on the light, and follows the sky. In clear weather, in summer, they appear blue at a little distance, especially if agitated, and at a great distance all

appear alike. In stormy weather they are sometimes of a dark slate color. The sea, however, is said to be blue one day and green another without any perceptible change in the atmosphere. I have seen our river, when, the landscape being covered with snow, both water and ice were almost as green as grass. Some consider blue "to be the color of pure water, whether liquid or solid." But, looking directly down into our waters from a boat, they are seen to be of very different colors. Walden is blue at one time and green at another, even from the same point of view. Lying between the earth and the heavens, it partakes of the color of both. Viewed from a hill-top it reflects the color of the sky, but near at hand it is of a yellowish tint next to the shore where you can see the sand, then a light green, which gradually deepens to a uniform dark green in the body of the pond. In some lights, viewed even from a hill-top, it is of a vivid green next to the shore. Some have referred this to the reflection of the verdure; but it is equally green there against the railroad sand-bank, and in the spring, before the leaves are expanded, and it may be simply the result of the prevailing blue mixed with the yellow of the sand. Such is the color of its iris. This is that portion, also, where in the spring, the ice being warmed by the heat of the sun reflected from the bottom, and also transmitted through the earth, melts first and forms a narrow canal about the still frozen middle. Like the rest of our waters, when much agitated, in clear weather, so that the surface of the waves may reflect the sky at the right angle, or because there is more light mixed with it, it appears at a little distance of a darker blue than the sky itself; and at such a time, being on its surface, and looking with divided vision, so as to see the reflection, I have discerned a matchless and indescribable light blue, such as watered or changeable silks and sword blades suggest, more cerulean than the sky itself, alternating with the original dark green on the opposite sides of the waves, which last appeared but muddy in comparison. It is a vitreous greenish blue, as I remember it, like those patches of the winter sky seen through cloud vistas in the west before sundown. Yet a single glass of its water held up to the light is as colorless as an equal quantity of air. It is well known that a large plate of glass will have a green tint, owing, as the makers say, to its "body," but a small piece of the same will be colorless. How large a body of Walden water would be required to reflect a green tint I have never proved. The water of our river is black or a very dark brown to one looking directly down on it, and, like that of most ponds, imparts to the body of one bathing in it a yellowish tinge; but this water is of such crystalline purity that the body of the bather appears of an alabaster whiteness, still more unnatural, which, as the limbs are magnified and distorted withal, produces a monstrous effect, making fit studies for a Michael Angelo.

2 The water is so transparent that the bottom can easily be discerned at the depth of twenty-five or thirty feet. Paddling over it, you may see, many feet beneath the surface, the schools of perch and shiners, perhaps only an inch long, yet the former easily distinguished by their transverse bars, and you think that they must be ascetic fish that find a subsistence there. Once, in the winter, many years ago, when I had been cutting holes through the ice in order to catch pickerel, as I stepped ashore I tossed my axe back on to the ice, but, as if some evil genius had directed it, it slid four or five rods directly into one of the holes, where the water was twenty-five feet deep. Out of curiosity, I lay down on the ice and looked through the hole, until I saw the axe a little on one side, standing on its head, with its helve erect and gently swaying to and fro with the pulse of the pond; and there it might have stood erect and swaying till in the course of time the handle rotted off, if I had not disturbed it. Making another hole directly over it with an ice chisel which I had, and cutting down the longest birch which I could find in the neighborhood with my knife, I made a slip-noose, which I attached to its end, and, letting it down carefully, passed it over the knob of the handle, and drew it by a line along the birch, and so pulled the axe out again.

3 The shore is composed of a belt of smooth rounded white stones like paving stones, excepting one or two short sand beaches, and is so steep that in many places a single leap will carry you into water over your head; and were it not for its remarkable transparency, that would be the last to be seen of its bottom till it rose on the opposite side. Some think it is bottomless. It is nowhere muddy, and a casual observer would say that there were no weeds at all in it; and of noticeable plants, except in the little meadows recently overflowed, which do not properly belong to it, a closer scrutiny does not detect a flag nor a bulrush, nor even a lily, yellow or white, but only a few small heart-leaves and potamogetons, and perhaps a water-target or two; all which however a bather might not perceive; and these plants are clean and bright like the element they grow in. The stones extend a rod or two into the water, and then the bottom is pure sand, except in the deepest parts, where there is usually a little sediment, probably from the decay of the leaves which have been wafted on to it so many successive falls, and a bright green weed is brought up on anchors even in midwinter.

4 We have one other pond just like this, White Pond in Nine Acre Corner, about two and a half miles westerly; but, though I am acquainted with most of the ponds within a dozen miles of this centre, I do not know a third of this pure and well-like character. Successive nations perchance have drank at, admired, and fathomed it, and passed away, and still its water is green and pellucid as ever. Not an intermitting spring! Perhaps on that spring morning when

Adam and Eve were driven out of Eden Walden Pond was already in existence, and even then breaking up in a gentle spring rain accompanied with mist and a southerly wind, and covered with myriads of ducks and geese, which had not heard of the fall, when still such pure lakes sufficed them. Even then it had commenced to rise and fall, and had clarified its waters and colored them of the hue they now wear, and obtained a patent of heaven to be the only Walden Pond in the world and distiller of celestial dews. Who knows in how many unremembered nations' literatures this has been the Castalian Fountain? or what nymphs presided over it in the Golden Age? It is a gem of the first water which Concord wears in her coronet.

#### IN RETROSPECT

**1.** In this descriptive piece, Thoreau concentrates on one aspect of the scene: the ponds at Walden. Although we get vivid, detailed pictures of the ponds, it is not snapshots that we get; rather, it is a composite picture of several aspects of the ponds. Trace the organization of this verbal picture. What are the parts? And what is done in each of the parts?

**2.** These are two questions that might be asked about any of the essays in this chapter: Why is the author giving us this verbal picture of this particular scene? And why would anyone want to read a verbal picture of this scene? In relation to "The Ponds," what is your response to each of these questions?

## *A Field of Silence*

### ANNIE DILLARD

Annie Dillard (1945–        ) was born in Pittsburgh, Pennsylvania, to Frank and Pam Doak. In 1965, she married the poet and novelist Richard Henry Wilde Dillard, and in 1975, the couple divorced. After obtaining an A.B. (1967) and an M.A. (1968) at Hollins College, Dillard taught poetry and creative writing at Western Washington State University; in 1979–1981 she was a Distinguished Visiting Professor at Wesleyan University in Connecticut. For her first published book of prose, *Pilgrim at Tinker Creek,* Dillard received the Pulitzer Prize in 1975, when she was only twenty-nine years old. Her first published book was a book of poems, *Tickets for a Prayer Wheel* (1974). *Holy the Firm* appeared in 1977, and *Encounters with Chinese Writers* appeared in 1984. Her *An American Childhood* (1987) is a memoir of her growing up in Pittsburgh; her *The Living* (1992), her first novel, is about life in the Pacific Northwest in the second half of the nineteenth century. In her Pulitzer Prize–winning book, Dillard describes herself as "a poet and a walker with a background in theology and a penchant for quirky facts." Are those characteristics evident in the essay printed here, "A Field of Silence"? The author with whom Dillard is most often compared is Henry David Thoreau. If you read Thoreau's essay "The Ponds" earlier in this chapter, you might find it instructive to compare Thoreau's essay with Dillard's to determine in what ways the two writers are similar. Hint: They would not frequently be compared with each other by literary critics were the only similarity between them the fact that they both write about the rural scene.

There is a place called "the farm" where I lived once, in a time that 1
was very lonely. Fortunately I was unconscious of my loneliness then, and felt it only deeply, bewildered, in the half-bright way that a puppy feels pain.

I loved the place, and still do. It was an ordinary farm, a calf- 2
raising, haymaking farm, and very beautiful. Its flat, messy pastures ran along one side of the central portion of a quarter-mile road in the central part of an island, an island in Puget Sound, so that from the high end of the road you could look west toward the Pacific, to the Sound and its hundred islands, and from the other end—and from the farm—you could see east to the water between you and the mainland, and beyond it the mainland's mountains slicked smooth with snow.

I liked the clutter about the place, the way everything blossomed 3
or seeded or rusted; I liked the hundred half-finished projects, the smells, and the way the animals always broke loose. It is calming to herd animals. Often a regular rodeo breaks out—two people and a clever cow can kill a morning—but still, it is calming. You laugh for a while, exhausted, and silence is restored; the beasts are back in their pastures, the fences not fixed but disguised as if they were fixed, ensuring the animals' temporary resignation; and a great calm descends, a lack of urgency, a sense of having to invent something to do until the next time you must run and chase cattle.

The farm seemed eternal in the crude way the earth does— 4
extending, that is, a very long time. The farm was as old as earth, always there, as old as the island, the Platonic form of "farm," of human society itself and at large, a piece of land eaten and replenished a billion summers, a piece of land worked on, lived on, grown over, plowed under, and stitched again and again, with fingers or with leaves, in and out and into human life's thin weave. I lived there once.

I lived there once and I have seen, from behind the barn, the long 5
roadside pastures heaped with silence. Behind the rooster, suddenly, I saw the silence heaped on the fields like trays. That day the green hayfields supported silence evenly sown; the fields bent just so under the even pressure of silence, bearing it, even, palming it aloft: cleared fields, part of a land, a planet, they did not buckle beneath the heel of silence, nor split up scattered to bits, but instead lay secret, disguised

as time and matter as though that were nothing, ordinary—disguised as fields like those which bear the silence only because they are spread, and the silence spreads over them, great in size.

I do not want, I think, ever to see such a sight again. That there is loneliness here I had granted, in the abstract—but not, I thought, inside the light of God's presence, inside his sanction, and signed by his name. 6

I lived alone in the farmhouse and rented; the owners, Angus and Lynn, in their twenties, lived in another building just over the yard. I had been reading and restless for two or three days. It was morning. I had just read at breakfast an Updike story, "Packed Dirt, Churchgoing, A Dying Cat, A Traded Car," which moved me. I heard our own farmyard rooster and two or three roosters across the street screeching. I quit the house, hoping at heart to see Lynn or Angus, but immediately to watch our rooster as he crowed. 7

It was Saturday morning late in the summer, in early September, clear-aired and still. I climbed the barnyard fence between the poultry and the pastures; I watched the red rooster, and the rooster, reptilian, kept one alert and alien eye on me. He pulled his extravagant neck to its maximum length, hauled himself high on his legs, stretched his beak as if he were gagging, screamed, and blinked. It was a ruckus. The din came from everywhere, and only the most rigorous application of reason could persuade me that it proceeded in its entirety from this lone and maniac bird. 8

After a pause, the roosters across the street would start, answering the proclamation, or cranking out another round, arrhythmically, interrupting. In the same way there is no pattern nor sense to the massed stridulations of cicadas; their skipped beats, enjambments, and failed alterations jangle your spirits, as though each of those thousand insects, each with identical feelings, were stubbornly deaf to the others, and loudly alone. 9

I shifted along the fence to see if Lynn or Angus was coming or going. To the rooster I said nothing, but only stared. And he stared at me: we were both careful to keep the wooden fence slat from our line of sight, so that his profiled eye and my two eyes could meet. From time to time I looked beyond the pastures to learn if anyone might be seen on the road. 10

When I was turned away in this manner, the silence gathered and struck me. It bashed me broadside from nowhere, as if I'd been hit by a plank. It dropped from the heavens above me like yard goods; ten acres of fallen, invisible sky choked the fields. The pastures on either side of the road turned green in surrealistic fashion, monstrous, impeccable, as if they were holding their breath. The roosters stopped. All the things of the world—the fields and the fencing, the road, a parked orange truck—were stricken and self-conscious. A world pressed down 11 on their surfaces, a world battered just within their surfaces, and that real world, so near to emerging, had got stuck.

There was only silence. It was the silence of matter caught in the 12
act and embarrassed. There were no cells moving, and yet there were cells. I could see the shape of the land, how it lay holding silence. Its poise and its stillness were unendurable, like the ring of the silence you hear in your skull when you're little and notice you're living, the ring which resumes later in life when you're sick.

There were flies buzzing over the dirt by the henhouse, moving 13
in circles and buzzing, black dreams in chips off the one long dream, the dream of the regular world. But the silent fields were the real world, eternity's outpost in time, whose look I remembered but never like this, this God-blasted, paralyzed day. I felt myself tall and vertical, in a blue shirt, self-conscious, and wishing to die. I heard the flies again; I looked at the rooster who was frozen looking at me.

Then at last I heard whistling, human whistling far on the air, and 14
I was not able to bear it. I looked around, heartbroken; only at the big yellow Charolais farm far up the road was there motion—a woman, I think, dressed in pink, and pushing a wheelbarrow easily over the grass. It must have been she who was whistling and heaping on top of the silence those hollow notes of song. But the slow sound of the music—the beautiful sound of the music ringing the air like a stone bell—was isolate and detached. The notes spread into the general air and became the weightier part of silence, silence's last straw. The distant woman and her wheelbarrow were flat and detached, like mechanized and pink-painted properties for a stage. I stood in pieces, afraid I was unable to move. Something had unhinged the world. The houses and roadsides and pastures were buckling under the silence. Then a Labrador, black, loped up the distant driveway, fluid and cartoonlike, toward the pink woman. I had to try to turn away. Holiness is a force, and like the others can be resisted. It was given, but I didn't want to see it, God or no God. It was as if God had said, "I am here, but not as you have known me. This is the look of silence, and of loneliness unendurable: it too has always been mine, and now will be yours." I was not ready for a life of sorrow, sorrow deriving from knowledge I could just as well stop at the gate.

I turned away, willful, and the whole show vanished. The real- 15
ness of things disassembled. The whistling became ordinary, familiar; the air above the fields released its pressure and the fields lay hooded as before. I myself could act. Looking to the rooster I whistled to him myself, softly, and some hens appeared at the chicken house window, greeted the day, and fluttered down.

Several months later, walking past the farm on the way to a 16
volleyball game, I remarked to a friend, by way of information, "There are angels in those fields." Angels! That silence so grave and

so stricken, that choked and unbearable green! I have rarely been so surprised at something I've said. Angels! What are angels? I had never thought of angels, in any way at all.

From that time I began to think of angels. I considered that sights such as I had seen of the silence must have been shared by the people who said they saw angels. I began to review the thing I had seen that morning. My impression now of those fields is of thousands of spirits—spirits trapped, perhaps, by my refusal to call them more fully, or by the paralysis of my own spirit at that time—thousands of spirits, angels in fact, almost discernible to the eye, and whirling. If pressed I would say they were three or four feet from the ground. Only their motion was clear (clockwise, if you insist); that, and their beauty unspeakable. 17

There are angels in those fields, and I presume, in all fields, and everywhere else. I would go to the lions for this conviction, to witness this fact. What all this means about perception, or language, or angels, or my own sanity, I have no idea. 18

### IN RETROSPECT

**1.** Carefully observe the way in which Dillard positions the descriptive words that she uses in this essay. For instance, in paragraph 15, instead of saying "I willfully turned away," Dillard says, "I turned away, willful." Instead of using the construction, "This is the look of silence, and of unendurable loneliness," Dillard writes, "This is the look of silence, and of loneliness unendurable" (paragraph 14). Find other instances of constructions that seem to you to be unusual, and talk with your classmates about Dillard's possible motivations for the placement of words in those constructions. What you may be getting at in speculating about Dillard's motivations is the effect she hoped to achieve by using this unusual syntax.

**2.** In the last paragraph of the essay, Dillard comments, "What all this means about perception, or language, or angels, or my own sanity, I have no idea." What do you think Dillard's experience on the farm has to do with perception, language, angels, and sanity? What are we to make of the audience, purpose, and effect of this essay, given this final statement by Dillard?

# *The Block*

## ALFRED KAZIN

Alfred Kazin (1915– ) is mainly a literary critic, one who has taught at many universities in the United States. The four best-known collections of his literary criticism are *On Native Grounds: An Interpretation of Modern American Prose Literature* (1942), *The Inmost Leaf* (1955), *Starting Out in the Thirties* (1962), and *Contemporaries*

(1962). Kazin's *New York Jew* (1978) presents a survey of the New York City literary and intellectual scene. *A Walker in the City* (1951), from which the following essay was taken, is an autobiographical work about Kazin's boyhood and adolescence in the Brownsville section of Brooklyn, New York, in the early years of the twentieth century. Whereas several of the other essays in this chapter depict a country scene, this one depicts an urban scene. Especially notable about this description is that it concentrates on the scene: The boy (Kazin) is the only human being we are made aware of; this is *his* block, and he wants us to see it and to understand what it meant to him while he was growing up there.

The block: *my* block. It was on the Chester Street side of our house, between the grocery and the back wall of the old drugstore, that I was hammered into the shape of the streets. Everything beginning at Blake Avenue would always wear for me some delightful strangeness and mildness, simply because it was not of my block, *the* block, where the clang of your head sounded against the pavement when you fell in a fist fight, and the rows of storelights on each side were pitiless, watching you. Anything away from the block was good: even a school you never went to, two blocks away: there were vegetable gardens in the park across the street. Returning from "New York," I would take the longest routes home from the subway, get off a station ahead of our own, only for the unexpectedness of walking through Betsy Head Park and hearing the gravel crunch under my feet as I went beyond the vegetable gardens, smelling the sweaty sweet dampness from the pool in summer and the dust on the leaves as I passed under the ailanthus trees. On the block itself everything rose up only to test me. 1

We worked every inch of it, from the cellars and the backyards to the sickening space between the roofs. Any wall, any stoop, any curving metal edge on a billboard sign made a place against which to knock a ball; any bottom rung of a fire escape ladder a goal in basketball; any sewer cover a base; any crack in the pavement a "net" for the tense sharp tennis that we played by beating a soft ball back and forth with our hands between the squares. Betsy Head Park two blocks away would always feel slightly foreign, for it belonged to the Amboys and the Bristols and the Hopkinsons as much as it did to us. *Our* life every day was fought out on the pavement and in the gutter, up against the walls of the houses and the glass fronts of the drugstore and the grocery, in and out of the fresh steaming piles of horse manure, the wheels of passing carts and automobiles, along the iron spikes of the stairway to the cellar, the jagged edge of the open garbage cans, the crumbly steps of the old farmhouses still left on one side of the street. 2

As I go back to the block now, and for a moment fold my body up again in its narrow arena—there, just there, between the black of the asphalt and the old women in their kerchiefs and flowered house- 3 dresses sitting on the tawny kitchen chairs—the back wall of the drugstore still rises up to test me. Every day we smashed a small black viciously hard regulation handball against it with fanatical cuts and drives and slams, beating and slashing at it almost in hatred for the blind strength of the wall itself. I was never good enough at handball, was always practicing some trick shot that might earn me esteem, and when I was weary of trying, would often bat a ball down Chester Street just to get myself to Blake Avenue. I have this memory of playing one-o'-cat by myself in the sleepy twilight, at a moment when everyone else had left the block. The sparrows floated down from the telephone wires to peck at every fresh pile of horse manure, and there was a smell of brine from the delicatessen store, of egg crates and of the milk scum left in the great metal cans outside the grocery, of the thick white paste oozing out from behind the fresh Hecker's Flour ad on the metal signboard. I would throw the ball in the air, hit it with my bat, then with perfect satisfaction drop the bat to the ground and run to the next sewer cover. Over and over I did this, from sewer cover to sewer cover, until I had worked my way to Blake Avenue and could see the park.

With each clean triumphant ring of my bat against the gutter 4
leading me on, I did the whole length of our block up and down, and never knew how happy I was just watching the asphalt rise and fall, the curve of the steps up to an old farmhouse. The farmhouses themselves were streaked red on one side, brown on the other, but the steps themselves were always gray. There was a tremor of pleasure at one place; I held my breath in nausea at another. As I ran after my ball with the bat heavy in my hand, the odd successiveness of things in myself almost choked me, the world was so full as I ran—past the cobblestoned yards into the old farmhouses, where stray chickens still waddled along the stones; past the little candy store where we went only if the big one on our side of the block was out of Eskimo Pies; past the three neighboring tenements where the last of the old women sat on their kitchen chairs yawning before they went up to make supper. Then came Mrs. Rosenwasser's house, the place on the block I first identified with what was farthest from home, and strangest, because it was a "private" house; then the fences around the monument works, where black cranes rose up above the yard and you could see the smooth gray slabs that would be cut and carved into tombstones, some of them already engraved with the names and dates and family virtues of the dead.

Beyond Blake Avenue was the pool parlor outside which we 5
waited all through the tense September afternoons of the World's Series to hear the latest scores called off the ticker tape—and where as we waited, banging a ball against the bottom of the wall and drinking water out of empty coke bottles, I breathed the chalk off the cues and

listened to the clocks ringing in the fire station across the street. There was an old warehouse next to the pool parlor; the oil on the barrels and the iron staves had the same rusty smell. A block away was the park, thick with the dusty gravel I liked to hear my shoes crunch in as I ran round and round the track; then a great open pavilion, the inside mysteriously dark, chill even in summer; there I would wait in the sweaty coolness before pushing on to the wading ring where they put up a shower on the hottest days.

Beyond the park the "fields" began, all those still unused lots 6
where we could still play hard ball in perfect peace—first shooing away the goats and then tearing up goldenrod before laying our bases. The smell and touch of those "fields," with their wild compost under the billboards of weeds, goldenrod, bricks, goat droppings, rusty cans, empty beer bottles, fresh new lumber, and damp cement, lives in my mind as Brownsville's great open door, the wastes that took us through to the west. I used to go round them in summer with my cousins selling near-beer to the carpenters, but always in a daze, would stare so long at the fibrous stalks of the goldenrod as I felt their harshness in my hand that I would forget to make a sale, and usually go off sick on the beer I drank up myself. Beyond! Beyond! Only to see something new, to get away from each day's narrow battleground between the grocery and the back wall of the drugstore! Even the other end of our block, when you got to Mrs. Rosenwasser's house and the monument works, was dear to me for the contrast. On summer nights, when we played Indian trail, running away from each other on prearranged signals, the greatest moment came when I could plunge into the darkness down the block for myself and hide behind the slabs in the monument works. I remember the air whistling around me as I ran, the panicky thud of my bones in my sneakers, and then the slabs rising in the light from the street lamps as I sped past the little candy store and crept under the fence.

In the darkness you could never see where the crane began. We 7
liked to trap the enemy between the slabs and sometimes jumped them from great mounds of rock just in from the quarry. A boy once fell to his death that way, and they put a watchman there to keep us out. This made the slabs all the more impressive to me, and I always aimed first for that yard whenever we played follow-the-leader. Day after day the monument works became oppressively more mysterious and remote, though it was only just down the block; I stood in front of it every afternoon on my way back from school, filling it with my fears. It was not death I felt there—the slabs were usually faceless. It was the darkness itself, and the wind howling around me whenever I stood poised on the edge of a high slab waiting to jump. Then I would take in, along with the fear, some amazement of joy that I had found my way out that far.

**IN RETROSPECT**

1. Another essay in this chapter that describes an urban scene is Dickens's "Night Walks." You can learn a great deal about how to manage a description of place by comparing Kazin's description of his neighborhood in Brownsville during the early part of the twentieth century with Dickens's description of London during the middle nineteenth century. What differences and similarities do you observe in the way these two writers describe the scene? What do these similarities and differences suggest to you about writing a description of a place?

2. What do you make of the fact that many of the aspects of the Brownsville neighborhood that Kazin describes are associated with games he played as a boy—especially the game of baseball?

# *The Smooth Skull of Winter*

**GRETEL EHRLICH**

Born in 1946, Gretel Ehrlich may be the youngest writer represented in this anthology, but she is definitely not immature when it comes to writing essays—she ranks with the best of the younger contemporary essayists. Ehrlich was born in Santa Barbara, California, and attended Bennington College; the University of California at Los Angeles, where she studied film; and the New School for Social Research. She now lives on a ranch in Wyoming. She was introduced to that "Big Sky" country when she was filming a documentary on Wyoming sheepherders for PBS (Public Broadcasting Service). While Ehrlich was engaged in that enterprise, the man she was in love with died of cancer in New York. Although she was devastated by his death, Ehrlich soaked up "the solace of open spaces"—a phrase that forms the title of the book from which this essay was taken. Donald Hall says of "The Smooth Skull of Winter" that "with its densely imagined landscape, [it] reads like a poem worked into the prose of an essay." And indeed it might be called a prose poem. Ehrlich began her writing career by writing poetry. Poets—the good ones, anyway—are noted for the intensity with which they observe the world around them and for the vividness with which they report perceptions of that world. You will *feel* the frigidity of winter through the warmth of Ehrlich's imagery. Just reflect on how much is conveyed to you by the startling metaphor of the "smooth skull" in the title of this essay.

Winter looks like a fictional place, an elaborate simplicity, a 1
Nabokovian invention of rarefied detail. Winds howl all night and day, pushing litters of storm fronts from the Beartooth to the Big Horn Mountains. When it lets up, the mountains disappear. The hayfield that runs east from my house ends in a curl of clouds that have fallen like sails luffing from sky to ground. Snow returns

across the field to me, and the cows, dusted with white, look like snowcapped continents drifting.

The poet Seamus Heaney said that landscape is sacramental, to 2
be read as text. Earth is instinct: perfect, irrational, semiotic. If I read winter right, it is a scroll—the white growing wider and wider like the sweep of an arm—and from it we gain a peripheral vision, a capacity for what Nabokov calls "those asides of spirit, those footnotes in the volume of life by which we know life and find it to be good."

Not unlike emotional transitions—the loss of a friend or the be- 3
ginnings of new work—the passage of seasons is often so belabored and quixotic as to deserve separate names so the year might be divided eight ways instead of four.

This fall ducks flew across the sky in great "V"s as if that one 4
letter were defecting from the alphabet, and when the songbirds climbed to the memorized pathways that route them to winter quarters, they lifted off in a confusion, like paper scraps blown from my writing room.

A Wyoming winter laminates the earth with white, then hardens 5
the lacquer work with wind. Storms come announced by what old-timers call "mare's tails"—long wisps that lash out from a snow cloud's body. Jack Davis, a packer who used to trail his mules all the way from Wyoming to southern Arizona when the first snows came, said, "The first snowball that hits you is God's fault; the second one is yours."

Every three days or so white pastures glide overhead and drop 6
themselves like skeins of hair to earth. The Chinese call snow that has drifted "white jade mountains," but winter looks oceanic to me. Snow swells, drops back, and hits the hulls of our lives with a course-bending sound. Tides of white are overtaken by tides of blue, and the logs in the woodstove, like sister ships, tick toward oblivion.

On the winter solstice it is thirty-four degrees below zero and 7
there is very little in the way of daylight. The deep ache of this audacious Arctic air is also the ache in our lives made physical. Patches of frostbite show up on our noses, toes, and ears. Skin blisters as if cold were a kind of radiation to which we've been exposed. It strips what is ornamental in us. Part of the ache we feel is also a softness growing. Our connections with neighbors—whether strong or tenuous, as lovers or friends—become too urgent to disregard. We rub the frozen toes of a stranger whose pickup has veered off the road; we open water gaps with a tamping bar and an ax; we splice a friend's frozen water pipe; we take mittens and blankets to the men who herd sheep. Twenty or thirty below makes the breath we exchange visible: all of mine for all of yours. It is the tacit way we express the intimacy no one talks about.

One of our recent winters is sure to make the history books 8
because of not the depth of snow but, rather, the depth of cold. For a month the mercury never rose above zero and at night it was fifty below. Cows and sheep froze in place and an oil field worker who tried taking a shortcut home was found next spring two hundred yards from his back door. To say you were snowed in didn't express the problem. You were either "froze in," "froze up," or "froze out," depending on where your pickup or legs stopped working. The day I helped tend sheep camp we drove through a five-mile tunnel of snow. The herder had marked his location for us by deliberately cutting his finger and writing a big "X" on the ice with his blood.

When it's fifty below, the mercury bottoms out and jiggles there 9
as if laughing at those of us still above ground. Once I caught myself on tiptoes, peering down into the thermometer as if there were an extension inside inscribed with higher and higher declarations of physical misery: ninety below to the power of ten and so on.

Winter sets up curious oppositions in us. Where a wall of snow 10
can seem threatening, it also protects our staggering psyches. All this cold has an anesthetizing effect: the pulse lowers and blankets of snow induce sleep. Though the rancher's workload is lightened in winter because of the short days, the work that does need to be done requires an exhausting patience. And while earth's sudden frigidity can seem to dispossess us, the teamwork on cold nights during calving, for instance, creates a profound camaraderie—one that's laced with dark humor, an effervescent lunacy, and unexpected fits of anger and tears. To offset Wyoming's Arctic seascape, a nightly flush of Northern Lights dances above the Big Horns, irradiating winter's pallor and reminding us that even though at this time of year we veer toward our various nests and seclusions, nature expresses itself as a bright fuse, irrepressible and orgasmic.

Winter is smooth-skulled, and all our skids on black ice are 11
cerebral. When we begin to feel cabin-feverish, the brain pistons thump against bone and mind irrupts—literally invading itself—unable to get fresh air. With the songbirds gone only scavengers are left: magpies, crows, eagles. As they pick on road-killed deer we humans are apt to practice the small cruelties on each other.

We suffer from snow blindness, selecting what we see and feel 12
while our pain whites itself out. But where there is suffocation and self-imposed ignorance, there is also refreshment—snow on flushed cheeks and a pristine kind of thinking. All winter we skate the small ponds—places that in summer are water holes for cattle and sheep—and here a reflection of mind appears, sharp, vigilant, precise. Thoughts, bright as frostfall, skate through our brains. In winter, consciousness looks like an etching.

### IN RETROSPECT

**1.** All the essays in this chapter make use of figures of speech, but perhaps none are as dense with them as Ehrlich's essay is. Here are just a few of her figures of speech:

"This fall ducks flew across the sky in great 'V's as if that one letter were defecting from the alphabet" (paragraph 4).

"A Wyoming winter laminates the earth with white, then hardens the lacquer work with wind" (paragraph 5).

"Winter is smooth-skulled" (paragraph 11).

"Thoughts, bright as frostfall, skate through our brains" (paragraph 12). Look at these metaphors and similies in the context in which they occur, and point out how they illuminate what the author is describing.

**2.** Student writers are often asked to "show" rather than "tell" what they mean in their writing. Besides using the figures of speech mentioned in the preceding question, how does Ehrlich make you *feel* the cold of Wyoming winters? Which of the various means of showing you the cold make you *feel* the cold most?

# *Subterranean Gothic*

## PAUL THEROUX

Paul Theroux (1941–     ) was born in Medford, Massachusetts, one of seven children. After graduating from Medford High School, he attended the University of Maine for one year and then transferred to the University of Massachusetts, where he earned a B.A. in 1963. He joined the Peace Corps and was sent to Malawi in South Africa; there he was a lecturer in English at Soche Hill College from 1963 to 1965. He later taught English at Makerere University in Kampala, Uganda (1965–1968), at the University of Singapore (1968–1971), and at the University of Virginia (1972–1973). Theroux now lives in London, England, with his wife and two sons and makes his living primarily as a professional writer. He has published twelve novels and four collections of short stories. At least three of his novels have been chosen as Book-of-the-Month Club selections. Two of his novels were made into movies: *The Mosquito Coast* in 1986 and *Doctor Slaughter* that same year under the title *Half Moon Street.* But it has been his travel books that have won the most literary prizes for him: *The Great Railway Bazaar: By Train through Asia* (1975), *The Old Patagonian Express: By Train through the Americas* (1979), *Sailing through China* (1984), *The Kingdom by the Sea: A Journey around Great Britain* (1985). *Sunrise with Seamonsters: Travels and Discoveries 1964–1984* (1985), from which the following essay was taken, is a collection of several of his essays that appeared in magazines over a twenty-year period. In the essay "Subterranean Gothic," Theroux describes a scene or experience that is very familiar to those who live in large cities, such as Boston, Chicago, and New York: the subway. Just as Charles Dickens describes the aboveground nighttime scene in nineteenth-century London, Paul Theroux depicts the underground scene in twentieth-century New York City.

When people say the subway frightens them they are not being silly or irrational. The subway is frightening. It is no good saying how cheap or how fast it is, because it looks disgusting and it stinks. It is also very easy to get lost on the subway, and the person who is lost in New York City has a serious problem. 1

New Yorkers make it their business to avoid getting lost. It is the stranger who sees people hurrying into the stairwell: subway entrances are just dark holes in the sidewalk—the stations are belowground. There is nearly always a bus-stop near the subway entrance. People waiting at a bus-stop have a special pitying gaze for people entering the subway. It is sometimes not pity, but fear, bewilderment, curiosity, or fatalism; often they look like miners' wives watching their menfolk going down the pit. 2

The stranger's sense of disorientation down below is immediate. The station is all tile and iron and dampness; it has bars and turnstiles and steel grates. It has the look of an old prison or a monkey cage. Buying a token the stranger may ask directions, but the token booth—reinforced, burglarproof, bulletproof—renders the reply incoherent. And subway directions are a special language. 3

"A-train . . . Downtown . . . Express to the Shuttle . . . Change at Ninety-sixth for the two . . . Uptown . . . The Lex . . . CC . . . LL . . . The Local . . ." 4

Most New Yorkers refer to the subway by the now obsolete forms "IND," "IRT," "BMT." No one intentionally tries to confuse the stranger; it is just that, where the subway is concerned, precise directions are very hard to convey. 5

Verbal directions are incomprehensible, written ones are defaced. The signboards and subway maps are indiscernible beneath layers of graffiti. That Andy Warhol, the stylish philistine, has said, "I love graffiti" is almost reason enough to hate them. One is warier still of Norman Mailer, who naively encouraged this public scrawling in his book *The Faith of Graffiti*. 6

Graffiti are destructive; they are anti-art; they are an act of violence, and they can be deeply menacing. They have displaced the subway signs and maps, blacked-out the windows of the trains, and obliterated the instructions. *In case of emergency*—is cross-hatched with a felt-tip; *These seats are for the elderly and disabled*—a yard-long signature obscures it; *The subway tracks are very dangerous. If the train should stop, do not*—the rest is black and unreadable. The stranger cannot rely on printed instructions or warnings, and there are few cars out of the six thousand on the system in which the maps have not been torn out. Assuming the stranger has boarded the train, he can only feel 7 panic when, searching for a clue to his route, he sees in the map-frame the message, *Guzmán—Ladrón, Maricón y Asesino.*

Panic: and so he gets off the train, and then his troubles really begin. 8

He may be in the South Bronx or the upper reaches of Broadway 9 on the Number One line, or on any one of a dozen lines that traverse Brooklyn. He gets off the train, which is covered in graffiti, and steps onto a station platform which is covered in graffiti. It is possible (this is true of many stations) that none of the signs will be legible. Not only will the stranger not know where he is, but the stairways will be splotched and stinking—no *Uptown,* no *Downtown,* no *Exit.* It is also possible that not a single soul will be around, and the most dangerous stations—ask any police officer—are the emptiest. Of course, the passenger might just want to sit on a broken bench and, taking Mailer's word for it, contemplate the *macho* qualities of the graffiti; on the other hand, he is more likely to want to get the hell out of there.

This is the story that most people tell of subway fear—the predica- 10 ment of having boarded the wrong train and gotten off at a distant station; of being on an empty platform, waiting for a train which shows no sign of coming. Then the vandalized station signs, the crazy semiliterate messages, the monkey scratches on the walls, the dampness, the neglect, the visible evidence of destruction and violence—they all combine to produce a sense of disgust and horror.

In every detail it is like a nightmare, complete with rats and mice 11 and a tunnel and a low ceiling. It is manifest suffocation straight out of Poe. And some of these stations have long platforms—you have to squint to see what is at the far end. These distances intensify a person's fear, and so do all the pillars behind which any ghoul could be lurking. Is it any wonder that, having once strayed into this area of subterranean gothic, people decide that the subway is not for them?

But those who tell this story seldom have a crime to report. They 12 have experienced shock, fear, and have gone weak at the knees. It is completely understandable—what is worse than being trapped underground?—but it has been a private little horror. In most cases the person will have come to no harm. But he will remember his fear on that empty station for the rest of his life.

When New Yorkers recount an experience like this they are 13 invariably speaking of something that happened on another line, not their usual route. Their own line is fairly safe, they'll say; it's cleaner than the others, it's got a little charm, it's kind of dependable, they've been taking it for years. Your line has crazy people on it, but my line has "characters." This sense of loyalty to a regularly-used line is the most remarkable thing about the subway passenger in New York. It is, in fact, a jungle attitude.

"New York is a jungle," the tourist says, and he believes he has 14 made a withering criticism. But all very large cities are jungles, which is to say that they are dense and dark and full of surprises and strange growths; they are hard to read, hard to penetrate; strange people live in them; and they contain mazy areas of great danger. The jungle aspect of cities (and of New York City in particular) is the most interesting thing about them—the way people behave in this jungle, and adapt to it; the way they change it or are changed by it.

15 In any jungle, the pathway is a priority. People move around New York in various ways, but the complexities of the subway have allowed the New Yorker to think of his own route as something personal, even *original*. No one uses maps on the subway—you seldom see any. Most subway passengers were shown how to ride it by parents or friends. Then habit turns it into instinct, just like a trot down a jungle path. The passenger knows where he is going because he never diverges from his usual route. But that is also why, unless you are getting off at precisely his stop, he cannot tell you how to get where you're going.

16 The only other way of learning how to use the subway is by maps and charts—teaching yourself. This very hard work requires imagination and intelligence. It means navigating in four dimensions. No one can do it idly, and I doubt that many people take up subway riding in their middle years.

17 In general, people have a sense of pride in their personal route; they may be superstitious about it and even a bit secretive. Vaguely fearful of other routes, they may fantasize about them—these "dangerous" lines that run through unknown districts. This provokes them to assign a specific character to the other lines. The IRT is the oldest line; for some people it is dependable, with patches of elegance (those beaver mosaics at Astor Place commemorating John Jacob Astor's fur business), and for others it is dangerous and dirty. One person praises the IND, another person damns it. "I've got a soft spot for the BMT," a woman told me, but found it hard to explain why. "Take the 'A' train," I was told. "That's the best one, like the song." But some of the worst stations are on the (very long) "A" line. The "CC," 8th Avenue local, was described to me as "scuzz"—disreputable—but this train, running from Bedford Park Boulevard, The Bronx, via Manhattan and Brooklyn, to Rockaway Park, Queens, covers a distance of 32.39 miles. The fact is that for some of these miles it is pleasant and for others it is not. There is part of one line that is indisputably bad; that is, the stretch of the "2" line (IRT) from Nostrand to New Lots Avenue. It is dangerous and ugly and when you get to New Lots Avenue you cannot imagine why you went. The police call this line "The Beast."

18 But people in the know—the police, the Transit Authority, the people who travel throughout the system—say that one line is pretty much like another.

19 "Is this line bad?" I asked Robert Huber of the Transit Authority, and pointed to the map in his office.

"The whole system is bad," he said. "From 1904 until just a few years ago it went unnoticed. People took it for granted. In 1975, the first year of the fiscal crisis, Mayor Beame ordered cutbacks. They started a program of deferred maintenance—postponed servicing and just attended to the most serious deficiencies. After four or five years of deferred maintenance, the bottom fell out. In January–February, 1981, twenty-five per cent of the trains were out of service, and things got worse—soon a thirty minute trip was taking an hour and a half. No one was putting any money into it. But of course they never had. It was under-capitalized from the beginning. Now there is decay everywhere, but there is also a real determination to reverse that trend and get it going right." 20

No train is entirely good or bad, crime-ridden or crime-free. The trains carry crime with them, picking it up in one area and bringing it to another. They pass through a district and take on the characteristics of that place. The South Bronx is regarded as a High Risk area, but seven lines pass through it, taking vandals and thieves all over the system. There is a species of vandalism that was once peculiar to the South Bronx: boys would swing on the stanchions—those chrome poles in the center of the car—and raising themselves sideways until they were parallel with the floor they would kick hard against a window and burst it. Now this South Bronx window-breaking technique is universal throughout the system. Except for the people who have the misfortune to travel on "The Beast" no one can claim that his train is much better or worse than any other. This business about one line being dependable and another being charming and a third being dangerous is just jungle talk. 21

The whiff of criminality, the atmosphere of viciousness, is so strong in the stations and trains that it does little good to say that, relatively speaking, crime is not that serious on the subway. Of course, many crimes go unreported on the subway, but this is also true outside the transit system. In one precinct they might have seventy-seven murders in a year, which makes the thirteen on the subway in 1981 look mild by comparison. In the same year there were thirty-five rapes and rape attempts (an attempt is classified as rape), which again, while nothing to crow about, is not as bad as is widely believed ("I'll bet they have at least one rape a day," a girl told me, and for that reason she never took the subway). The majority of subway crime is theft—bag-snatching; this is followed by robbery—the robber using a gun or knife. There are about thirty-two robberies or snatches a day in the system, and one or two cases of aggravated assault a day. This takes care of all "Part I Offenses"—the serious ones. 22

It is the obvious vandalism on the subways that conveys the feeling of lawlessness. Indeed, the first perception of subway crime came with the appearance of widespread graffiti in 1970. It was then 23 that passengers took fright and ridership, which had been declining slowly since the 'fifties, dropped rapidly. Passengers felt threatened, and newspapers gave prominence to subway crime. Although the "CC" line is over thirty-two miles long a passenger will be alarmed to hear that a crime has been committed on it, because this is *his* line, and the proprietorial feeling of a rider for his line is as strong as a jungle dweller for his regular path. Subway passengers are also very close physically to one another, but this is a city in which people are accustomed to quite a lot of space. On the subway you can hear the breathing of the person next to you—that is, when the train is at the station. The rest of the time it is impossible to hear anything except the thundering train, which is equally frightening.

"Violence underground attracts more coverage in the papers, but 24
it is foolish to imagine the subway is some sort of death trap." This statement was not made by anyone in the New York Transit Authority, but by Nadine Joly, the twenty-eight-year-old head of the Special Paris Metro Security Squad. She was speaking about the Paris Metro, but her sentiments are quite similar to those of Edward Silberfarb of the Transit Authority Police.

"The interest in subway crime is much greater than in street 25
crime," Mr. Silberfarb said. "Crime actually went down six per cent in September, but the paper reversed the statistic and reported it having gone up. Maybe they're looking for headlines."

The most frequent complaint of subway passengers is not about 26
crime. It is, by a wide margin, about delayed trains and slow service. The second largest category of complaint is about the discourtesy of conductors or token-sellers; and the third concerns unclean stations. "Mainly the smell of urine—it's really horrible at some stations," said Mr. Huber of the Transit Authority.

The perception of crime is widespread, and yet statistically the 27
experience of it is quite small.

"But what do those statistics matter to someone who is in a car 28
and a gang of six guys starts teasing and then threatening the passengers?" the New York lawyer Arthur S. Penn remarked to me. "Or that other familiar instance—you get into a car and there's one guy way down at the end sitting all by himself, and the rest of the people are crowded up this end of the car. You know from experience that the man who's sitting alone is crazy, and then, when the train pulls out, he starts screaming . . ."

Discomfort, anxiety, fear—these are the responses of most pas- 29
sengers. No wonder people complain that the trains are too slow: when one is fearful, every trip takes too long. In fact, these are among the fastest subway trains in the world. Stan Fischler, in his enthusiastic history of the system, *Uptown, Downtown* (1976), gives fifty-five mph as the top speed of an average express, such as the Harlem-

Bronx "D." The train going by sounds as if it is full of coal, but when one is inside, it can feel like a trip on "The Wild Mouse."

People's fears can be at odds with reality. It is interesting that the 30
two most famous movies with New York subway settings, *The Incident* (about a gang terrorizing a group of passengers on an express), and *The Taking of Pelham 1-2-3* (about the hijacking of an IRT train), are both preposterous. But as fantasies they give expression to widely-held fears of subway violence. (The famous chase in *The French Connection* starts at Bay 50th on the B-line and finishes deep in Bensonhurst on the West End line.)

Some people do get mugged—about twelve thousand a year. I 31
asked a uniformed police officer what reaction he got upon entering a car. "A big sigh of relief," he said. "You can actually hear it. People smile at me. They're relieved! But the ones who are the most pleased to see me are the handicapped people and the old people. They're the ones who get mugged mostly."

That is the disgraceful part: the victims of subway crime are most 32
often the old, the mentally retarded, the crippled, the blind, the weak. The majority of victims are women. Minorities comprise the next largest category of victim: a black person in a white area, an hispanic in a black area, a white in an hispanic area, and all the other grotesque permutations of race. Of course, the old and handicapped are also minorities, regarded as easy targets and defenseless. But cities can turn people into members of a minority group quite easily. What makes the New Yorker so instinctively wary is perhaps the thought that anyone who boards the wrong train, or gets off at the wrong stop, or walks one block too many, is capable of being in the minority.

## IN RETROSPECT

**1.** Given what you know about the term *gothic* and about characters in "gothic" works of fiction or art, what do you think makes Theroux's title for his essay, "Subterranean Gothic," aptly descriptive of this underground scene?

**2.** Consider Theroux's "Subterranean Gothic" and Kazin's "The Block" as contributions to a conversation about New York City. What contradictory voices do you hear within each essay? between them? What different facts and opinions are expressed about the city? What relationship do you perceive between the environment (the time and the place in which the speakers find themselves) and the speakers' interpretations of the city? As an outsider, what further observations or responses could you add to a conversation with the authors of, and the characters in, these essays?

# 6

# ON EDUCATION

*In a sense, each of the preceding chapters has been concerned with self-education or informal schooling. The essays in those chapters dealt with the various ways in which human beings, simply through experience and observation, get to know the world in which they live. But there comes a time in every civilized nation when human beings have to submit themselves for a number of years to formal schooling. In the United States and Canada, for instance, virtually every citizen now has the opportunity to get at least a grade-school education. Those of you now reading this introduction have been empowered, through whatever formal schooling you have been exposed to up to this point, with the marvelous skill of reading. Consequently, you can read the essays in this chapter, all of which deal, in various ways and from different perspectives, with getting educated. Francis Bacon, who is reputed to be the first notable English essayist, in his essay "Of Studies" is really talking about what it means to be literate. Some of the essays in this chapter address the difficulties experienced by minorities in our society in getting the kind of education that leads to the privileged state of literacy. A few of the essays deal with a particular experience that someone had in school. All of you who read these essays could tell us about some experience you had in school that would be worth our time to listen to.*

# *Of Studies*

## FRANCIS BACON

Francis Bacon (1561–1626) is commonly regarded as the originator of the essay as an English-language literary genre. Born in London, educated at Trinity College in Cambridge, and trained for the legal profession at Gray's Inn, Bacon might well have never turned his hand to writing. Because of his services in the courts of Queen Elizabeth and King James I, his public career advanced rapidly: from Solicitor General to Attorney General to Keeper of the Seal to Lord Chancellor. Bacon became Baron Verulam in 1618 and Viscount St. Albans in 1621. This meteoric ascent in government service ended in disgrace, however, when Bacon was convicted by Parliament of having accepted bribes while sitting on the judicial bench. Even at the height of his busy government service, Bacon pursued his interest in the "new science," an interest that culminated in the publication of his major philosophical works, *The Advancement of Advancement of Learning* (1605), *Novum Organum* (1620), and *De Augmentis* (1623). The "new science" was the result of the shift during the seventeenth century from the Aristotelian emphasis on the deductive method of learning to the inductive approach to learning favored by the physical sciences. Bacon's reputation as an important figure in the history of Western thought rests on these works, but his literary reputation was established by his *Essays or Counsels, Civil and Moral.* Although Bacon was inspired by Montaigne's *Essais,* his own essays do not exhibit Montaigne's strong personal tone. Their crisp, succinct, epigrammatic style did, however, establish a tone as distinctive as Montaigne's and won for Bacon a host of imitators and a secure place in the history of the essay. "Of Studies" is perhaps the best known and certainly the most quotable of Bacon's essays.

Studies serve for delight, for ornament, and for ability. Their chief use for delight is in privateness and retiring; for ornament, is in discourse; and for ability, is in the judgment and disposition of business. For expert men can execute and perhaps judge of particulars, one by one, but the general counsels and the plots and marshalling of affairs come best from those that are learned. To spend too much time in studies is sloth; to use them too much for ornament is affectation; to make judgment wholly by their rules is the humour of a scholar. They perfect nature, and are perfected by experience, for natural abilities are like natural plants that need pruning by study; and studies themselves do give forth directions too much at large, except they be bounded in by experience. Crafty men condemn studies; simple men admire them; and wise men use them, for they teach not their own use, but that is a wisdom without them and above them, won by observation. Read not to contradict and confute, nor to believe and take for granted, nor to find talk and discourse, but to weigh and consider. Some books are to be tasted, others to be swal- 1 lowed, and some few to be chewed and digested; that is, some books are to be read only in parts; others to be read, but not curiously, and some few to be read wholly and with diligence and attention. Some books also may be read by deputy, and extracts made of them by others, but that would be only in the less important arguments and the meaner sort of books; else distilled books are like common distilled waters, flashy things. Reading maketh a full man, conference a ready man, and writing an exact man. And therefore, if a man write little, he had need have a great memory; if he confer little, he had need have a present wit; and if he read little, he had need have much cunning, to seem to know that he doth not. Histories make men wise, poets witty, the mathematics subtile, natural philosophy deep, moral grave, logic and rhetoric able to contend. *Abeunt studia in mores.* Nay there is no stond or impediment in the wit but may be wrought out by fit studies, like as diseases of the body may have appropriate exercises. Bowling is good for the stone and reins, shooting for the lungs and breast; gentle walking for the stomach; riding for the head; and the like. So if a man's wit be wandering, let him study the mathematics, for in demonstrations, if his wit be called away never so little, he must begin again. If his wit be not apt to distinguish or find differences, let him study the schoolmen, for they are *cymini sectores.* If he be not apt to beat over matters and to call up one thing to prove and illustrate another, let him study the lawyers' cases. So every defect of the mind may have a special receipt.

## IN RETROSPECT

**1.** Bacon says, "Some books are to be tasted, others to be swallowed, and some few to be chewed and digested; that is, some books are to be read only in parts; others to be read, but not curiously [that is, carefully], and some few to be read wholly and with diligence and attention." Bacon first tells us how to read various kinds of books under the metaphor of eating (tasting, swallowing, chewing and digesting), and then he tells us *literally* how to read various kinds of books. Pick out some of the essays you have already read in this book and indicate which of them should be tasted, which swallowed, and which chewed and digested. Give the reasons for your choices.

**2.** Here is another of Bacon's parallel triplets: "Reading maketh a full man, conference [discussion or conversation] a ready man, and writing an exact man." Consider, along with your classmates, what Bacon means when he speaks of a "full man," a "ready man," and an "exact man." What role do you see reading, conference, and writing playing in your life? Would you say from your own experiences that Bacon is correct in his observations about the benefits of reading, conference, and writing? How might you make these activities work for you in aspects of your life outside the classroom?

# *On Education*

## BENJAMIN FRANKLIN

Benjamin Franklin (1706–1790) was a veritable prototype for the Horatio Alger stories of the middle nineteenth century. He rose from obscurity as a printer's apprentice in his half-brother's shop in Boston to worldwide renown as a scientist, inventor, statesman, diplomat, publisher, and writer. From his press in Philadelphia, Franklin issued both *The Pennsylvania Gazette* (1729–1766), a newspaper to which he contributed essays and character sketches, and *Poor Richard's Almanack* (1758–1773), the work that made his fame as a writer. His experiments with a kite in an electrical storm and his invention of the Franklin stove and of a new kind of clock are legendary. In 1757, Franklin was sent on a diplomatic mission to England. Returning to America, he became embroiled in the revolt of the American colonists against Great Britain. He participated in the First Continental Congress and had a hand in drafting the Declaration of Independence. During the Revolutionary War Franklin was sent to France to negotiate a treaty, and after General Burgoyne surrendered in 1778, Franklin was appointed as the American minister to the Court of France. The following essay was taken from his "Dogood Papers," a series of essays Franklin contributed to his half-brother's newspaper, the *New England Courant*. When "On Education" appeared in May 1722, Franklin was only sixteen years old. In style and technique, Franklin is here imitating his boyhood literary idol, Joseph Addison. He is also adopting a device that Addison used in some of his periodical essays: reporting on a dream that he tells us he had. In his dream, Franklin visited the "Temple of Learning," a pretentious academy to which members of the peasant class were eager to send their children. The point Franklin is making with his narrative is relevant to us today: the folly of forcing young people to get a college education even if they have no desire or talent for such advanced schooling. (Incidentally, Franklin's own formal education ended when he was just ten years old.)

Discoursing the other day at dinner with my reverend boarder, 1
formerly mentioned, whom for distinction's sake we will call by the name of Clericus, concerning the education of children, I asked his advice about my young son William, whether or not I had best bestow upon him academic learning, or, as our phrase is, "bring him up at our college." He persuaded me to do it by all means, using many weighty arguments with me, and answering all the objections that I could form against it; telling me withal, that he did not doubt that the lad would take his learning very well and not idle away his time as too many there nowadays do. These words of Clericus gave me a curiosity to inquire a little more strictly into the present circumstances of that famous seminary of learning, but the information which he gave me was neither pleasant, nor such as I expected.

As soon as dinner was over, I took a solitary walk into my 2
orchard, still ruminating on Clericus' discourse with much consideration, until I came to my usual place of retirement under the great apple tree where, having seated myself, and carelessly laid my head on a verdant bank, I fell by degrees into a soft and undisturbed slumber. My waking thoughts remained with me in my sleep, and before I awoke again, I dreamed the following dream.

I fancied I was traveling over pleasant and delightful fields and 3
meadows and through many small country towns and villages; and as I passed along, all places resounded with the fame of the Temple of Learning. Every peasant who had wherewithal was preparing to send one of his children at least to this famous place; and in this case most of them consulted their own purses instead of their children's capacities: so that I observed a great many, yea, the most part of those who were traveling thither, were little better than dunces and blockheads. Alas! Alas!

At length I entered upon a spacious plain, in the midst of which 4
was erected a large and stately edifice. It was to this that a great company of youths from all parts of the country were going; so stepping in among the crowd, I passed on with them, and presently arrived at the gate.

The passage was kept by two sturdy porters named Riches and 5
Poverty, and the latter obstinately refused to give entrance to any who had not first gained the favor of the former; so that I observed many who came even to the very gate were obliged to travel back again as ignorant as they came for want of this necessary qualification. However, as a spectator I gained admittance and with the rest entered directly into the temple.

In the middle of the great hall stood a stately and magnificent 6
throne, which was ascended to by two high and difficult steps. On the top of it sat Learning in awful state; she was appareled wholly in black and surrounded almost on every side with innumerable volumes in all languages. She seemed very busily employed in writing something on half a sheet of paper, called the *New England Courant.* On her right hand sat English, with a pleasant, smiling countenance, and handsomely attired; and on her left were seated several antique figures with their faces veiled. I was considerably puzzled to guess who they were, until one informed me (who stood beside me) that those figures on her left hand were Latin, Greek, Hebrew, etc., and that they were very much reserved, and seldom or never unveiled their faces here, and then to few or none, though most of those who have in this place acquired so much learning as to distinguish them from English, pretended to an intimate acquaintance with them. I then inquired of him what could be the reason why they continued

veiled, in this place especially. He pointed to the foot of the throne, where I saw Idleness, attended with Ignorance; and these, he informed me, were they who first veiled them and still kept them so.

Now I observed that the whole tribe who entered into the temple 7
with me began to climb the throne. But the work proving troublesome and difficult to most of them, they withdrew their hands from the plow, and contented themselves to sit at the foot, with Madam Idleness and her maid Ignorance, until those who were assisted by Diligence and docible Temper had well-nigh got up the first step. But the time drawing nigh in which they could no way avoid ascending, they were fain to crave the assistance of those who had got up before them, and who, for the reward perhaps of a pint of milk, or a piece of plum cake, lent the lubbers a helping hand, and sat them in the eye of the world upon a level with themselves.

The other step being in the same manner ascended, and the usual 8
ceremonies at an end, every beetle-skull seemed well satisfied with his own portion of learning, though perhaps he was even just as ignorant as ever. And now the time of their departure being come, they marched out-of-doors to make room for another company who waited for entrance. And I, having seen all that was to be seen, quitted the hall likewise and went to make my observations on those who were just gone out before me.

Some, I perceived, took to merchandising, others to traveling, 9
some to one thing, some to another, and some to nothing. And many of them from henceforth, for want of patrimony, lived as poor as church mice, being unable to dig and ashamed to beg; and to live by their wits it was impossible. But the most part of the crowd went along a large beaten path, which led to a temple at the further end of the plain, called the Temple of Theology. The business of those who were employed in this temple being laborious and painful, I wondered exceedingly to see so many go toward it. But while I was pondering this matter in my mind, I spied Pecunia behind a curtain, beckoning to them with her hand, which sight immediately satisfied me for whose sake it was that a great part of them (I will not say all) traveled that road. In this temple I saw nothing worth mentioning, except the ambitious and fraudulent contrivances of Plagius, who, notwithstanding he had been severely reprehended for such practices before, was diligently transcribing some eloquent paragraphs out of Tillotson's works, etc., to embellish his own.

Now I bethought myself in my sleep that it was time to be at 10
home; and as I fancied I was traveling back thither, I reflected in my mind on the extreme folly of those parents who, blind to their children's dullness and insensible of the solidity of their skulls, because they think their purses can afford it, will needs send them to the

Temple of Learning where, for want of a suitable genius, they learn little more than how to carry themselves handsomely and enter a room genteelly, which might as well be acquired at a dancing school and from whence they return, after abundance of trouble and charge, as great blockheads as ever, only more proud and self-conceited.

While I was in the midst of these unpleasant reflections, Clericus, 11
who with a book in his hand was walking under the trees, accidentally awoke me. To him I related my dream with all its particulars, and he, without much study, presently interpreted it, assuring me that it was a lively representation of Harvard College, et cetera.

I remain, sir,<br>Your humble servant,<br>Silence Dogood

**IN RETROSPECT**

**1.** Franklin wants to convince his readers that it is foolish for parents to force their children to get a college education, even if the children have no desire or talent for such advanced schooling. Why, then, does he not do what many people would do—namely, present a number of arguments in support of his thesis? Why does he resort to the dream technique?

**2.** In the first paragraph of this letter-essay, Clericus recommends that Silence Dogood send his son William to college and presents his arguments in support of his recommendation. In the final paragraph of the essay, Clericus interprets Dogood's dream for him and then assures Dogood that the dream was "a lively representation of Harvard College." What does Clericus mean by these words? Is Clericus confessing that as a result of hearing the dream, he no longer recommends that Dogood send William to college? What did Franklin intend his readers to understand from this final sentence of the essay?

# *Learning to Read and Write*

## FREDERICK DOUGLASS

Frederick Douglass (1817–1895) was born in Tuckahoe, Maryland, the son of a black slave and a white father. As a black slave himself, Douglass had many masters while he was growing up, but in 1838, he escaped from a Baltimore shipyard and fled to freedom up North. Largely self-educated—as the following essay makes clear—Douglass first came into public prominence in 1841, when he was invited to speak at an anti-slavery meeting. A national leader in the abolition movement, he became one of the most eloquent orators and most persuasive writers in the nation during the latter half of the nineteenth century. With the money he collected from a successful lecture tour in Great Britain, Douglass was able to start up a newspaper, the *North Star,* which he edited for seventeen years. He held various government offices, including the post of consul general to the Republic of Haiti. His most lasting legacy was his memoirs, *The Life and Times of Frederick Douglass* (1881; revised in 1892), from which "Learning to Read and Write" was taken. This essay tells the poignant tale of how Douglass, as a slave boy, struggled surreptitiously to become literate—and thereby empowered to shape his own destiny.

I lived in Master Hugh's family about seven years. During this time, I succeeded in learning to read and write. In accomplishing this, I was compelled to resort to various stratagems. I had no regular teacher. My mistress, who had kindly commenced to instruct me, had, in compliance with the advice and direction of her husband, not only ceased to instruct, but had set her face against my being instructed by anyone else. It is due, however, to my mistress to say of her, that she did not adopt this course of treatment immediately. She at first lacked the depravity indispensable to shutting me up in mental darkness. It was at least necessary for her to have some training in the exercise of irresponsible power, to make her equal to the task of treating me as though I were a brute. 1

My mistress was, as I have said, a kind and tender-hearted woman; and in the simplicity of her soul she commenced, when I first went to live with her, to treat me as she supposed one human being ought to treat another. In entering upon the duties of a slaveholder, she did not seem to perceive that I sustained to her the relation of a mere chattel, and that for her to treat me as a human being was not only wrong, but dangerously so. Slavery proved as injurious to her as it did to me. When I went there, she was a pious, warm, and tender-hearted woman. There was no sorrow or suffering for which she had not a tear. She had bread for the hungry, clothes for the naked, and comfort for every mourner that came within her reach. Slavery soon proved its ability to divest her of these heavenly qualities. Under its 2 influence, the tender heart became stone, and the lamblike disposition gave way to one of tiger-like fierceness. The first step in her downward course was in her ceasing to instruct me. She now commenced to practice her husband's precepts. She finally became even more violent in her opposition than her husband himself. She was not satisfied with simply doing as well as he had commanded; she seemed anxious to do better. Nothing seemed to make her more angry than to see me with a newspaper. She seemed to think that here lay the danger. I have had her rush at me with a face made all up of fury, and snatch from me a newspaper, in a manner that fully revealed her apprehension. She was an apt woman; and a little experience soon demonstrated, to her satisfaction, that education and slavery were incompatible with each other.

From this time I was most narrowly watched. If I was in a 3
separate room any considerable length of time, I was sure to be suspected of having a book, and was at once called to give an account of myself. All this, however, was too late. The first step had been taken. Mistress, in teaching me the alphabet, had given me the *inch,* and no precaution could prevent me from taking the *ell.*

The plan which I adopted, and the one by which I was most 4
successful, was that of making friends of all the little white boys whom I met in the street. As many of these as I could, I converted into teachers. With their kindly aid, obtained at different times and in different places, I finally succeeded in learning to read. When I was sent on errands, I always took my book with me, and by going one part of my errand quickly, I found time to get a lesson before my return. I used also to carry bread with me, enough of which was always in the house, and to which I was always welcome; for I was much better off in this regard than many of the poor white children in our neighborhood. This bread I used to bestow upon the hungry little urchins, who, in return, would give me that more valuable bread of knowledge. I am strongly tempted to give the names of two or three of those little boys, as a testimonial of the gratitude and affection I bear them; but prudence forbids—not that it would injure me, but it might embarrass them; for it is almost an unpardonable offence to teach slaves to read in this Christian country. It is enough to say of the dear little fellows, that they lived on Philpot Street, very near Durgin and Bailey's ship-yard. I used to talk this matter of slavery over with them. I would sometimes say to them, I wished I could be as free as they would be when they got to be men. "You will be free as soon as you are twenty-one, *but I am a slave for life!* Have not I as good a right to be free as you have?" These words used to trouble them; they would express for me the liveliest sympathy, and console me with the hope that something would occur by which I might be free.

I was now about twelve-years-old, and the thought of being *a* 5
*slave for life* began to bear heavily upon my heart. Just about this time, I got hold of a book entitled "The Columbian Orator." Every opportunity I got, I used to read this book. Among much of other interesting matter, I found in it a dialogue between a master and his slave. The slave was represented as having run away from his master three times. The dialogue represented the conversation which took place between them, when the slave was retaken the third time. In this dialogue, the whole argument in behalf of slavery was brought forward by the master, all of which was disposed of by the slave. The slave was made to say some very smart as well as impressive things in reply to his master—things which had the desired though unexpected effect; for the conversation resulted in the voluntary emancipation of the slave on the part of the master.

In the same book, I met with one of Sheridan's mighty speeches 6
on and in behalf of Catholic emancipation. These were choice documents to me. I read them over and over again with unabated interest. They gave tongue to interesting thoughts of my own soul, which had frequently flashed through my mind, and died away for want of utterance. The moral which I gained from the dialogue was the power of truth over the conscience of even a slaveholder. What I got from Sheridan was a bold denunciation of slavery, and a powerful vindication of human rights. The reading of these documents enabled me to utter my thoughts, and to meet the arguments brought forward to sustain slavery; but while they relieved me of one difficulty, they brought on another even more painful than the one of which I was relieved. The more I read, the more I was led to abhor and detest my enslavers. I could regard them in no other light than a band of successful robbers, who had left their homes, and gone to Africa, and stolen us from our homes, and in a strange land reduced us to slavery. I loathed them as being the meanest as well as the most wicked of men. As I read and contemplated the subject, behold! that very discontentment which Master Hugh had predicted would follow my learning to read had already come, to torment and sting my soul to unutterable anguish. As I writhed under it, I would at times feel that learning to read had been a curse rather than a blessing. It had given me a view of my wretched condition, without the remedy. It opened my eyes to the horrible pit, but to no ladder upon which to get out. In moments of agony, I envied my fellow-slaves for their stupidity. I have often wished myself a beast. I preferred the condition of the meanest reptile to my own. Anything, no matter what, to get rid of thinking! It was this everlasting thinking of my condition that tormented me. There was no getting rid of

it. It was pressed upon me by every object within sight or hearing, animate or inanimate. The silver trump of freedom had roused my soul to eternal wakefulness. Freedom now appeared, to disappear no more forever. It was heard in every sound, and seen in every thing. It was ever present to torment me with a sense of my wretched condition. I saw nothing without seeing it, I heard nothing without hearing it, and felt nothing without feeling it. It looked from every star, it smiled in every calm, breathed in every wind, and moved in every storm.

I often found myself regretting my own existence, and wishing 7
myself dead; and but for the hope of being free, I have no doubt but that I should have killed myself, or done something for which I should have been killed. While in this state of mind, I was eager to hear anyone speak of slavery. I was a ready listener. Every little while, I could hear something about the abolitionists. It was some time before I found what the word meant. It was always used in such connections as to make it an interesting word to me. If a slave ran away and succeeded in getting clear, or if a slave killed his master, set fire to a barn, or did anything very wrong in the mind of a slaveholder, it was spoken of as the fruit of *abolition.* Hearing the word in this connection very often, I set about learning what it meant. The dictionary afforded me little or no help. I found it was "the act of abolishing"; but then I did not know what was to be abolished. Here I was perplexed. I did not dare to ask anyone about its meaning, for I was satisfied that it was something they wanted me to know very little about. After a patient waiting, I got one of our city papers, containing an account of the number of petitions from the North, praying for the abolition of slavery in the District of Columbia, and of the slave trade between the States. From this time I understood the words *abolition* and *abolitionist,* and always drew near when that word was spoken, expecting to hear something of importance to myself and fellow-slaves. The light broke in upon me by degrees. I went one day down on the wharf of Mr. Waters; and seeing two Irishmen unloading a scow of stone, I went, unasked, and helped them. When we had finished, one of them came to me and asked me if I were a slave. I told him I was. He asked, "Are ye a slave for life?" I told him that I was. The good Irishman seemed to be deeply affected by the statement. He said to the other that it was a pity so fine a little fellow as myself should be a slave for life. He said it was a shame to hold me. They both advised me to run away to the North; that I should find friends there, and that I should be free. I pretended not to be interested in what they said, and treated them as if I did not understand them; for I feared they might be treacherous. White men have been

known to encourage slaves to escape, and then, to get the reward, catch them and return them to their masters. I was afraid that these seemingly good men might use me so; but I nevertheless remembered their advice, and from that time I resolved to run away. I looked forward to a time at which it would be safe for me to escape. I was too young to think of doing so immediately; besides, I wished to learn how to write, as I might have occasion to write my own pass. I consoled myself with the hope that I should one day find a good chance. Meanwhile, I would learn to write.

The idea as to how I might learn to write was suggested to me by 8
being in Durgin and Bailey's shipyard, and frequently seeing the ship carpenters, after hewing, and getting a piece of timber ready for use, write on the timber the name of that part of the ship for which it was intended. When a piece of timber was intended for the larboard side, it would be marked thus—"L." When a piece was for the starboard side, it would be marked thus—"S." A piece for the larboard side forward would be marked thus—"L.F." When a piece was for starboard side forward, it would be marked thus—"S.F." For larboard aft, it would be marked thus—"L.A." For starboard aft, it would be marked thus—"S.A." I sooned learned the names of these letters, and for what they were intended when placed upon a piece of timber in the shipyard. I immediately commenced copying them, and in a short time was able to make the four letters named. After that, when I met with any boy who I knew could write, I would tell him I could write as well as he. The next word would be, "I don't believe you. Let me see you try it." I would then make the letters which I had been so fortunate as to learn, and ask him to beat that. In this way I got a good many lessons in writing, which it is quite possible I should never have gotten it any other way. During this time, my copy-book was the board fence, brick wall, and pavement; my pen and ink was a lump of chalk. With these, I learned mainly how to write. I then commenced and continued copying the Italics in *Webster's Spelling Book,* until I could make them all without looking on the book. By this time, my little Master Thomas had gone to school, and learned how to write, and had written over a number of copy-books. These had been brought home, and shown to some of our near neighbors, and then laid aside. My mistress used to go to class meeting at the Wilk Street meeting-house every Monday afternoon, and leave me to take care of the house. When left thus, I used to spend the time in writing in the spaces left in master Thomas's copy-book, copying what he had written. I continued to do this until I could write a hand very similar to that of Master Thomas. Thus, after a long, tedious effort for years, I finally succeeded in learning how to write.

**IN RETROSPECT**

**1.** There seems to be some ambiguity present in this essay. From reading Douglass's essay, what do you understand the relationship between freedom and literacy to be? Is literacy a *cause* or an *effect* of freedom? Or is Douglass suggesting that some other kind of relationship exists between freedom and literacy?

**2.** Douglass gives us a much different picture of how people learn to read and write than we get from other writers in this chapter. How is Douglass's discussion of learning different from the other perceptions offered in this chapter? What does his account add to your understanding of how people learn?

# *University Days*

## JAMES THURBER

Everyone has his or her favorite piece by James Thurber (1894–1961)—whether it be an autobiographical sketch like "The Night the Bed Fell on Father," a short story like "The Secret Life of Walter Mitty," a satire like *Is Sex Necessary?*, a children's book like *The 13 Clocks*, a stage comedy like *The Male Animal*, or one of his cartoons, with its engaging cast of bewildered men, forceful women, and placid dogs. That kind of popularity bespeaks Thurber's achievements as an American humorist. Born in Columbus, Ohio, and educated at Ohio State University, Thurber joined the staff of *The New Yorker* in 1927, two years after its founding by Harold Ross. Most of his stories, essays, fables, and cartoons originally appeared in the pages of *The New Yorker* over the next thirty years. "University Days," one of his most frequently reprinted essays, appeared in his book *My Life and Hard Times*, after its original publication in *The New Yorker*. Everyone has some amusing or depressing tales to tell about school days at the elementary, secondary, or college level. In this essay, Thurber recounts the problems he had in many of his classes at Ohio State University. Many of his problems stemmed from the fact that, as a young boy, he lost the sight in one of his eyes as the result of an accident. In this essay, Thurber highlights the humorous, not the pathetic, side of the incidents that he recounts. His sketches are a good illustration of the saying that has become a threadbare platitude: Humor is just the flip side of pathos.

I passed all the other courses that I took at my University, but I 1
could never pass botany. This was because all botany students had to spend several hours a week in a laboratory looking through a microscope at plant cells, and I could never see through a microscope. I never once saw a cell through a microscope. This used to enrage my instructor. He would wander around the laboratory pleased with the progress all the students were making in drawing the involved and, so I am told, interesting structure of flower cells, until he came to me. I would just be standing there. "I can't see anything," I would say. He would begin patiently enough, explaining how anybody can see through a microscope, but he would always end up in a fury; claiming that I could *too* see through a microscope but just pretended that I couldn't. "It takes away from the beauty of flowers anyway," I used to tell him. "We are not concerned with beauty in this course," he would say. "We are concerned solely with what I may call the *mechanics* of flars." "Well," I'd say. "I can't see anything." "Try it just once again," he'd say, and I would put my eye to the microscope and see nothing at all, except now and again a nebulous milky substance—a phenomenon of maladjustment. You were supposed to see a vivid, restless clockwork of sharply defined plant cells. "I see what looks like a lot of milk," I would tell him. This, he claimed, was the result of my not having adjusted the microscope properly, so he would readjust it for me, or rather, for himself. And I would look again and see milk.

I finally took a deferred pass, as they called it, and waited a year 2
and tried again. (You had to pass one of the biological sciences or you couldn't graduate.) The professor had come back from vacation brown as a berry, bright-eyed, and eager to explain cell-structure again to his classes. "Well," he said to me, cheerily, when we met in the first laboratory hour of the semester, "we're going to see cells this time, aren't we?" "Yes, sir," I said. Students to the right of me and left of me and in front of me were seeing cells; what's more, they were quietly drawing pictures of them in their notebooks. Of course, I didn't see anything.

"We'll try it," the professor said to me, grimly, "with every 3
adjustment of the microscope known to man. As God is my witness, I'll arrange this glass so that you can see cells through it or I'll give up teaching. In twenty-two years of botony, I—" He cut off abruptly for he was beginning to quiver all over, like Lionel Barrymore, and he genuinely wished to hold onto his temper; his scenes with me had taken a great deal out of him.

So we tried it with every adjustment of the microscope known to 4
man. With only one of them did I see anything but blackness or the familiar lacteal opacity, and that time I saw, to my pleasure and amazement, a variegated constellation of flecks, specks, and dots.

These I hastily drew. The instructor, noting my activity, came from an adjoining desk, a smile on his lips and his eyebrows high in hope. He looked at my cell drawing. "What's that?" he demanded, with a hint of squeal in his voice. "That's what I saw," I said. "You didn't, you didn't, you *did*n't!" he screamed, losing control of his temper instantly, and he bent over and squinted into the microscope. His head snapped up. "That's your eye!" he shouted. "You've fixed the lens so that it reflects! You've drawn your eye!"

Another course that I didn't like, but somehow managed to pass, 5
was economics. I went to that class straight from the botany class, which didn't help me any in understanding either subject. I used to get them mixed up. But not as mixed up as another student in my economics class who came there direct from a physics laboratory. He was a tackle on the football team, named Bolenciecwcz. At that time Ohio State University had one of the best football teams in the country, and Bolenciecwcz was one of its outstanding stars. In order to be eligible to play it was necessary for him to keep up in his studies, a very difficult matter, for while he was not dumber than an ox he was not any smarter. Most of his professors were lenient and helped him along. None gave him more hints, in answering questions, or asked him simpler ones than the economics professor, a thin, timid man named Bassum. One day when we were on the subject of transportation and distribution, it came Bolenciecwcz's turn to answer a question. "Name one means of transportation," the professor said to him. No light came into the big tackle's eyes. "Just any means of transportation," said the professor. Bolenciecwcz sat staring at him. "That is," pursued the professor, "any medium, agency, or method of going from one place to another." Bolenciecwcz had the look of a man who is being led into a trap. "You may choose among steam, horse-drawn, or electrically propelled vehicles," said the instructor. "I might suggest the one which we commonly take in making long journeys across land." There was a profound silence in which everybody stirred uneasily, including Bolenciecwcz and Mr. Bassum. Mr. Bassum abruptly broke this silence in an amazing manner. "Choo-choo-choo," he said, in a low voice, and turned instantly scarlet. He glanced appealingly around the room. All of us, of course, shared Mr. Bassum's desire that Bolenciecwcz should stay abreast of the class in economics, for the Illinois game, one of the hardest and most important of the season, was only a week off. "Toot, toot, tootooooooot!" some student with a deep voice moaned, and we all looked encouragingly at Bolenciecwcz. Somebody else gave a fine imitation of a locomotive letting off steam. Mr. Bassum himself rounded off the little show. "Ding, dong, ding, dong," he said, hopefully. Bolenciecwcz was staring at the floor now, trying to think,

his great brow furrowed, his huge hands rubbing together, his face red.

"How did you come to college this year, Mr. Bolenciecwcz?" 6
asked the professor. "*Chuf*fa chuffa, *chuf*fa chuffa."

"M'father sent me," said the football player. 7

"What on?" asked Bassum. 8

"I git an 'lowance," said the tackle, in a low, husky voice, obvi- 9
ously embarrassed.

"No, no," said Bassum. "Name a means of transportation. What 10
did you *ride* here on?"

"Train," said Bolenciecwcz. 11

"Quite right," said the professor. "Now, Mr. Nugent, will you tell 12
us—"

If I went through anguish in botany and economics—for different 13
reasons—gymnasium work was even worse. I don't even like to think about it. They wouldn't let you play games or join in the exercises with your glasses on and I couldn't see with mine off. I bumped into professors, horizontal bars, agricultural students, and swinging iron rings. Not being able to see, I could take it but I couldn't dish it out. Also, in order to pass gymnasium (and you had to pass it to graduate) you had to learn to swim if you didn't know how. I didn't like the swimming pool, I didn't like swimming, and I didn't like the swimming instructor, and after all these years I still don't. I never swam but I passed my gym work anyway, by having another student give my gymnasium number (978) and swim across the pool in my place. He was a quiet, amiable blonde youth, number 473, and he would have seen through a microscope for me if we could have got away with it, but we couldn't get away with it. Another thing I didn't like about gymnasium work was that they made you strip the day you registered. It is impossible for me to be happy when I am stripped and being asked a lot of questions. Still, I did better than a lanky agricultural student who was cross-examined just before I was. They asked each student what college he was in—that is, whether Arts, Engineering, Commerce, or Agriculture. "What college are you in?" the instructor snapped at the youth in front of me. "Ohio State University," he said promptly.

It wasn't that agricultural student but it was another a whole lot 14
like him who decided to take up journalism, possibly on the ground that when farming went to hell he could fall back on newspaper work. He didn't realize, of course, that that would be very much like falling back full-length on a kit of carpenter's tools. Haskins didn't seem cut out for journalism, being too embarrassed to talk to anybody and unable to use a typewriter, but the editor of the college paper assigned him to the cow barns, the sheep house, the horse pavilion,

and the animal husbandry department generally. This was a genuinely big "beat," for it took up five times as much ground and got ten times as great a legislative appropriation as the College of Liberal Arts. The agricultural student knew animals, but nevertheless his stories were dull and colorlessly written. He took all afternoon on each one of them, on account of having to hunt for each letter on the typewriter. Once in a while he had to ask somebody to help him hunt. "C" and "L," in particular, were hard letters for him to find. His editor finally got pretty much annoyed at the farmer-journalist because his pieces were so uninteresting. "See here, Haskins," he snapped at him one day, "why is it we never have anything hot from you on the horse pavilion? Here we have two hundred head of horses on this campus—more than any other university in the Western Conference except Purdue—and yet you never get any real low-down on them. Now shoot over to the horse barns and dig up something lively." Haskins shambled out and came back in about an hour; he said he had something. "Well, start it off snappily," said the editor. "Something people will read." Haskins set to work and in a couple of hours brought a sheet of typewritten paper to the desk; it was a two-hundred word story about some disease that had broken out among the horses. Its opening sentence was simple but arresting. It read: "Who has noticed the sores on the tops of the horses in the animal husbandry building?"

15 Ohio State was a land grant university and therefore two years of military drill was compulsory. We drilled with old Springfield rifles and studied the tactics of the Civil War even though the World War was going on at the time. At 11 o'clock each morning thousands of freshmen and sophomores used to deploy over the campus, moodily creeping up on the old chemistry building. It was good training for the kind of warfare that was waged at Shiloh but it had no connection with what was going on in Europe. Some people used to think there was German money behind it, but they didn't dare say so or they would have been thrown in jail as German spies. It was a period of muddy thought and marked, I believe, the decline of higher education in the Middle West.

16 As a soldier I was never any good at all. Most of the cadets were glumly indifferent soldiers, but I was no good at all. Once General Littlefield, who was commandant of the cadet corps, popped up in front of me during regimental drill and snapped, "You are the main trouble with this university!" I think he meant that my type was the main trouble with the university but he may have meant me individually. I was mediocre at drill, certainly—that is, until my senior year. By that time I had drilled longer than anybody else in the Western Conference, having failed at military at the end of each preceding

year so that I had to do it all over again. I was the only senior still in uniform. The uniform which, when new, had made me look like an interurban railway conductor, now that it had become faded and too tight made me look like Bert Williams in his bellboy act. This had a definitely bad effect on my morale. Even so, I had become by sheer practice little short of wonderful at squad manoeuvres.

One day General Littlefield picked our company out of the whole regiment and tried to get it mixed up by putting it through one movement after another as fast as we could execute them: squads right, squads left, squads on right into line, squads right about, squads left front into line, etc. In about three minutes one hundred and nine men were marching in one direction and I was marching away from them at an angle of forty degrees, all alone. "Company, halt!" shouted General Littlefield, "That man is the only man who has it right!" I was made a corporal for my achievement. 17

The next day General Littlefield summoned me to his office. He was swatting flies when I went in. I was silent and he was silent too, for a long time. I don't think he remembered me or why he had sent for me, but he didn't want to admit it. He swatted some more flies, keeping his eyes on them narrowly before he let go with the swatter. "Button up your coat!" he snapped. Looking back on it now I can see that he meant me although he was looking at a fly, but I just stood there. Another fly came to rest on a paper in front of the general and began rubbing its hind legs together. The general lifted the swatter cautiously. I moved restlessly and the fly flew away. "You startled him!" barked General Littlefield, looking at me severely. I said I was sorry. "That won't help the situation!" snapped the General, with cold military logic. I didn't see what I could do except offer to chase some more flies toward his desk, but I didn't say anything. He stared out the window at the faraway figures of co-eds crossing the campus toward the library. Finally, he told me I could go. So I went. He either didn't know which cadet I was or else he forgot what he wanted to see me about. It may have been that he wished to apologize for having called me the main trouble with the university; or maybe he had decided to compliment me on my brilliant drilling of the day before and then at the last minute decided not to. I don't know. I don't think about it much any more. 18

**IN RETROSPECT**

**1.** Many of the incidents Thurber relates expose his ineptitude as a student, but indirectly these incidents also tell us something about others around him. From reading this essay, what have you learned about university-level education, and how does that learning correspond to your own experiences in college?

**2.** One of the notable features of this essay is Thurber's expert use of dialogue to tell a story or make a point. Choose an incident in your life and make a point about that incident by telling the story predominantly, if not exclusively, with dialogue—as you would, for instance, if you were writing the script of a play. Share your dialogue with several members of your class. Reflect on which dialogues seem most effective and why. What does dialogue allow you to accomplish that narration may not?

# *Taking Women Students Seriously*

## ADRIENNE RICH

If a group of people knowledgeable about the contemporary literary scene were asked to identify Adrienne Rich (1929–       ), virtually all of them would say, "She's a poet." And that response would ring the bell, because to date Rich has published at least nine collections of her poetry, one of which, *Diving into the Wreck,* won the National Book Award in 1974. A few of them might add, "She is a prominent and an insistent spokeswoman for the feminist movement." On the lecture circuit, if she is not reading from her poetry Rich is speaking on some issue espoused by feminists in this country. Yet not many people—if any—would speak of her as an essayist. Rich, however, has published a highly regarded collection of her essays, *On Lies, Secrets, and Silence: Selected Prose, 1966.* The essay reprinted here was first delivered as a lecture at a conference sponsored by the New Jersey College and University Coalition on Women's Education. As a woman student herself at Radcliffe College, Rich was taken very seriously. The esteemed British poet W. H. Auden recommended her first book of poems, *A Change of World,* for the Yale Series of Younger Poets Award, and a year after graduating from Radcliffe, Rich won a Guggenheim fellowship. Currently a professor of English at Stanford University, Rich undoubtedly takes her women students very seriously.

I see my function here today as one of trying to create a context, 1
delineate a background, against which we might talk about women as students and students as women. I would like to speak for a while about this background, and then I hope that we can have, not so much a question period, as a raising of concerns, a sharing of questions for which we as yet may have no answers, an opening of conversations which will go on and on.

When I went to teach at Douglass, a women's college, it was with a particular background which I would like briefly to describe to you. I had graduated from an all-girls' school in the 1940s, where the head and the majority of the faculty were independent, unmarried women. One or two held doctorates, but had been forced by the Depression (and by the fact that they were women) to take secondary school teaching jobs. These women cared a great deal about the life of the mind, and they gave a great deal of time and energy—beyond any limit of teaching hours—to those of us who showed special intellectual interest or ability. We were taken to libraries, art museums, lectures at neighboring colleges, set to work on extra research projects, given extra French or Latin reading. Although we sometimes felt "pushed" by them, we held those women in a kind of respect which even then we dimly perceived was not generally accorded to women in the world at large. They were vital individuals, defined not by their relationships but by their personalities; and although under the pressure of the culture we were all certain we wanted to get married, their lives did not appear empty or dreary to us. In a kind of cognitive dissonance, we knew they were "old maids" and therefore supposed to be bitter and lonely; yet we saw them vigorously involved with life. But despite their existence as alternate models of women, the *content* of the education they gave us in no way prepared us to survive as women in a world organized by and for men. 2

From that school, I went on to Radcliffe, congratulating myself that now I would have great men as my teachers. From 1947 to 1951, when I graduated, I never saw a single woman on a lecture platform, or in front of a class, except when a woman graduate student gave a paper on a special topic. The "great men" talked of other "great men," of the nature of Man, the history of Mankind, the future of Man; and never again was I to experience, from a teacher, the kind of prodding, the insistence that my best could be even better, that I had known in high school. Women students were simply not taken very seriously. Harvard's message to women was an elite mystification: we were, of course, part of Mankind; we were special achieving women, or we would not have been there; but of course our real goal was to marry—if possible, a Harvard graduate. 3

In the late sixties, I began teaching at the City College of New York—a crowded, public, urban, multiracial institution as far removed from Harvard as possible. I went there to teach writing in the SEEK Program, which predated Open Admissions and which was then a kind of model for programs designed to open up higher education to poor, black, and Third World students. Although during the next few years we were to see the original concept of SEEK diluted, then violently attacked and betrayed, it was for a short time 4 an extraordinary and intense teaching and learning environment. The characteristics of this environment were a deep commitment on the part of teachers to the minds of their students; a constant, active effort to create or discover the conditions for learning, and to educate ourselves to meet the needs of the new college population; a philosophical attitude based on open discussion of racism, oppression, and the politics of literature and language; and a belief that learning in the classroom could not be isolated from the student's experience as a member of an urban minority group in white America. Here are some of the kinds of questions we, as teachers of writing, found ourselves asking:

1. What has been the student's experience of education in the inadequate, often abusively racist public school system, which rewards passivity and treats a questioning attitude or independent mind as a behavior problem? What has been her or his experience in a society that consistently undermines the selfhood of the poor and the nonwhite? How can such a student gain that sense of self which is necessary for active participation in education? What does all this mean for us as teachers?
2. How do we go about teaching a canon of literature which has consistently excluded or depreciated nonwhite experience?
3. How can we connect the process of learning to write well with the student's own reality, and not simply teach her/him to write acceptable lies in standard English?

When I went to teach at Douglass College in 1976, and in teaching 5
women's writing workshops elsewhere, I came to perceive stunning parallels to the questions I had first encountered in teaching the so-called disadvantaged students at City. But in this instance, and against the specific background of the women's movement, the questions framed themselves like this:

1. What has been the student's experience of education in schools which reward female passivity, indoctrinate girls and boys in stereotypic sex roles, and do not take the female mind seriously? How does a woman gain a sense of her *self* in a system—in this case, patriarchal capitalism—which devalues work done by women, denies the importance and uniqueness of female experience, and is physically violent toward women? What does this mean for a woman teacher?
2. How do we, as women, teach women students a canon of literature which has consistently excluded or depreciated female expe-

rience, and which often expresses hostility to women and validates violence against us?

3. How can we teach women to move beyond the desire for male approval and getting "good grades" and seek and write their own truths that the culture has distorted or made taboo? (For women, of course, language itself is exclusive: I want to say more about this further on.)

In teaching women, we have two choices: to lend our weight to the forces that indoctrinate women to passivity, self-depreciation, and a sense of powerlessness, in which case the issue of "taking women students seriously" is a moot one; or to consider what we have to work against, as well as with, in ourselves, in our students, in the content of the curriculum, in the structure of the institution, in the society at large. And this means, first of all, taking ourselves seriously: Recognizing that central responsibility of a woman to herself, without which we remain always the Other, the defined, the object, the victim; believing that there is a unique quality of validation, affirmation, challenge, support, that one woman can offer another. Believing in the value and significance of women's experience, traditions, perceptions. Thinking of ourselves seriously, not as one of the boys, not as neuters, or androgynes, but *as women.* 6

Suppose we were to ask ourselves, simply: What does a woman need to know? Does she not, as a self-conscious, self-defining human being, need a knowledge of her own history, her much-politicized biology, an awareness of the creative work of women of the past, the skills and crafts and techniques and powers exercised by women in different times and cultures, a knowledge of women's rebellions and organized movements against our oppression and how they have been routed or diminished? Without such knowledge women live and have lived without context, vulnerable to the projections of male fantasy, male prescriptions for us, estranged from our own experience because our education has not reflected or echoed it. I would suggest that no biology, but ignorance of our selves, has been the key to our powerlessness. 7

But the university curriculum, the high-school curriculum, do not provide this kind of knowledge for women, the knowledge of Womankind, whose experience has been so profoundly different from that of Mankind. Only in the precariously budgeted, much-condescended-to area of women's studies is such knowledge available to women students. Only there can they learn about the lives and work of women other than the few select women who are included in the "mainstream" texts, usually misrepresented even when they do appear. Some students, at some institutions, manage to take a majority 8 of courses in women's studies, but the message from on high is that this is self-indulgence, soft-core education: the "real" learning is the study of Mankind.

If there is any misleading concept, it is that of "coeducation": that 9
because women and men are sitting in the same classrooms, hearing the same lectures, reading the same books, performing the same laboratory experiments, they are receiving an equal education. They are not, first because the content of education itself validates men even as it invalidates women. Its very message is that men have been the shapers and thinkers of the world, and that this is only natural. The bias of higher education, including the so-called sciences, is white and male, racist and sexist; and this bias is expressed in both subtle and blatant ways. I have mentioned already the exclusiveness of grammar itself: "The student should test himself on the above questions"; "The poet is representative. He stands among partial men for the complete man." Despite a few halfhearted departures from custom, what the linguist Wendy Martyna has named "He-Man" grammar prevails throughout the culture. The efforts of feminists to reveal the profound ontological implications of sexist grammar are routinely ridiculed by academicians and journalists, including the professedly liberal *Times* columnist Tom Wicker and the professed humanist Jacques Barzun. Sexist grammar burns into the brains of little girls and young women a message that the male is the norm, the standard, the central figure beside which we are the deviants, the marginal, the dependent variables. It lays the foundation for andro-centric thinking, and leaves men safe in their solipsistic tunnel-vision.

Women and men do not receive an equal education because 10
outside the classroom women are perceived not as sovereign beings but as prey. The growing incidence of rape on and off the campus may or may not be fed by the proliferations of pornographic magazines and X-rated films available to young males in fraternities and student unions; but it is certainly occurring in a context of widespread images of sexual violence against women, on billboards and in so-called high art. More subtle, more daily than rape is the verbal abuse experienced by the woman student on many campuses—Rutgers for example—where, traversing a street lined with fraternity houses, she must run a gauntlet of male commentary and verbal assault. The undermining of self, of a woman's sense of her right to occupy space and walk freely in the world, is deeply relevant to education. The capacity to think independently, to take intellectual risks, to assert ourselves mentally, is inseparable from our physical way of being in the world, our feelings of personal integrity. If it is dangerous for me to walk home late of an evening from the library, *because I am a woman and can be raped,* how self-possessed, how exuberant can I feel as I sit

working in that library? How much of my working energy is drained by the subliminal knowledge that, as a woman, I test my physical right to exist each time I go out alone? Of this knowledge, Susan Griffin has written:

> . . . more than rape itself, the fear of rape permeates our lives. And what does one do from day to day, with *this* experience, which says, without words and directly to the heart, *your existence, your experience, may end at any moment.* Your experience may end, and the best defense against this is not to be, to deny being in the body, as a self, to . . . avert your gaze, make yourself, as a presence in the world, less felt.

Finally, rape of the mind. Women students are more and more often now reporting sexual overtures by male professors—one part of our overall growing consciousness of sexual harassment in the workplace. At Yale a legal suit has been brought against the university by a group of women demanding an explicit policy against sexual advances toward female students by male professors. Most young women experience a profound mixture of humiliation and intellectual self-doubt over seductive gestures by men who have the power to award grades, open doors to grants and graduate school, or extend special knowledge and training. Even if turned aside, such gestures constitute mental rape, destructive to a woman's ego. They are acts of domination, as despicable as the molestation of the daughter by the father. 11

But long before entering college the woman student has experienced her alien identity in a world which misnames her, turns her to its own uses, denying her the resources she needs to become self-affirming, self-defined. The nuclear family teaches her that relationships are more important than selfhood or work; that "whether the phone rings for you, and how often," having the right clothes, doing the dishes, take precedence over study or solitude; that too much intelligence or intensity may make her unmarriageable; that marriage and children—service to others—are, finally, the points on which her life will be judged a success or a failure. In high school, the polarization between feminine attractiveness and independent intelligence comes to an absolute. Meanwhile, the culture resounds with messages. During Solar Energy Week in New York I saw young women wearing "ecology" T-shirts with the legend: CLEAN, CHEAP, AND AVAILABLE; a reminder of the 1960s antiwar button which read: CHICKS SAY YES TO MEN WHO SAY NO. Department store windows feature female mannequins in chains, pinned to the wall with legs spread, smiling in positions of torture. Feminists are depicted in the media as "shrill," "strident," "puritanical," or "humorless," and the lesbian choice—the choice of the woman-identified woman—as 12 pathological or sinister. The young woman sitting in the philosophy classroom, the political science lecture, is already gripped by tensions between her nascent sense of self-worth, and the battering force of messages like these.

Look at a classroom: look at the many kinds of women's faces, 13
postures, expressions. Listen to the women's voices. Listen to the silences, the unasked questions, the blanks. Listen to the small, soft voices, often courageously trying to speak up, voices of women taught early that tones of confidence, challenge, anger, or assertiveness are strident and unfeminine. Listen to the voices of the women and the voices of the men; observe the space men allow themselves, physically and verbally, the male assumption that people will listen, even when the majority of the group is female. Look at the faces of the silent, and of those who speak. Listen to a woman groping for language in which to express what is on her mind, sensing that the terms of academic discourse are not her language, trying to cut down her thought to the dimensions of a discourse not intended for her *(for it is not fitting that a woman speak in public);* or reading her paper aloud at breakneck speed, throwing her words away, deprecating her own work by a reflex prejudgment: *I do not deserve to take up time and space.*

As women teachers, we can either deny the importance of this 14
context in which women students think, write, read, study, project their own futures; or try to work with it. We can either teach passively, accepting these conditions, or actively, helping our students identify and resist them.

One important thing we can do is *discuss* the context. And this 15
need not happen only in a women's studies course; it can happen anywhere. We can refuse to accept passive, obedient learning and insist upon critical thinking. We can become harder on our women students, giving them the kinds of "cultural prodding" that men receive, but on different terms and in a different style. Most young women need to have their intellectual lives, their work, legitimized against the claims of family, relationships, the old message that a woman is always available for service to others. We need to keep our standards very high, not to accept a woman's preconceived sense of her limitations; we need to be hard to please, while supportive of risk-taking, because self-respect often comes only when exacting standards have been met. At a time when adult literacy is generally low, we need to demand more, not less, of women, both for the sake of their futures as thinking beings, and because historically women have always had to be better than men to do half as well. A romantic sloppiness, an inspired lack of rigor, a self-indulgent incoherence, are symptoms of female self-depreciation. We should help our women students to look very critically at such symptoms, and to understand where they are rooted.

Nor does this mean we should be training women students to "think like men." Men in general think badly: in disjuncture from their personal lives, claiming objectivity where the most irrational passions seethe, losing, as Virginia Woolf observed, their senses in the pursuit of professionalism. It is not easy to think like a woman in a man's world, in the world of the professions; yet the capacity to do that is a strength which we can try to help our students develop. To think like a woman in a man's world means thinking critically, refusing to accept the givens, making connections between facts and ideas which men have left unconnected. It means remembering that every mind resides in a body; remaining accountable to the female bodies in which we live; constantly retesting given hypotheses against lived experience. It means a constant critique of language, for as Wittgenstein (no feminist) observed, "The limits of my language are the limits of my world." And it means that most difficult thing of all: listening and watching in art and literature, in the social sciences, in all the descriptions we are given of the world, for the silences, the absences, the nameless, the unspoken, the encoded—for there we will find the true knowledge of women. And in breaking those silences, naming our selves, uncovering the hidden, making ourselves present, we begin to define a reality which resonates to *us,* which affirms *our* being, which allows the woman teacher and the woman student alike to take ourselves, and each other, seriously: meaning, to begin taking charge of our lives. 16

**IN RETROSPECT**

**1.** Rich says in paragraph 12 of her essay that "the woman student has experienced her alien identity in a world which misnames her, turns her to its own uses, denying her the resources she needs to become self-affirming, self-defined." It might be argued that our society is only now beginning to discuss the ways in which many people are marginalized. Drawing upon your own experiences, try to re-create for others what it feels like to be alienated, misnamed, misused, and denied the resources to become self-affirming and self-defined.

**2.** Rich argues that it is important to understand the context in which we think, write, read, study, and project the future. Write a case study of yourself as a learner in this class. Identify in some way the conditions of the class and the ways in which you benefit from or resist those conditions in the process of developing as a reader, writer, and learner. What do the multiple stories that members of your class share suggest about being a productive member of your own particular learning community?

# *The Achievement of Desire*

## RICHARD RODRIGUEZ

Richard Rodriguez (1944–        ), the son of Mexican-American immigrant parents, was born in San Francisco and attended Catholic elementary and secondary schools in Sacramento, California. After graduating from Stanford University, he did graduate work at Columbia University and at the Warburg Institute in London. He became a professor at the University of California at Berkeley after earning his Ph.D. there. In 1981, Rodriguez published *The Hunger of Memory: The Education of Richard Rodriguez.* In the essay reprinted here, which originally appeared in the November 1978 issue of *College English* and later was incorporated into *The Hunger of Memory,* Rodriguez argues that there is a cause-and-effect relationship between the education that he received as a young man and the subsequent course of his life. The "proofs" that he offers in support of his argument consist primarily of incidents (examples) from his life as a schoolboy, incidents that point up his growing awareness of the sharp contrasts between his home life and his school life, between his role as a "good student" and his role as a "dutiful son." Rodriguez keeps relating his own experiences to what Richard Hoggart had said in his book *The Uses of Literacy* (1957) about the life of a typical "scholarship boy."

What I am about to describe to you has taken me twenty years to admit: *The primary reason for my success in the classroom was that I couldn't forget that schooling was changing me and separating me from the life I had enjoyed before becoming a student.* (That simple realization!) For years I never spoke to anyone about this boyhood fear, my guilt and remorse. I never mentioned these feelings to my parents or my brothers. Nor to my teachers or classmates. From a very early age, I understood enough, just enough, about my experiences to keep what I knew vague, repressed, private, beneath layers of embarrassment. Not until the last months that I was a graduate student, nearly thirty years old, was it possible for me to think about the reasons for my success. Only then. At the end of my schooling, I needed to determine how far I had moved from my past. The adult finally confronted—and now must publicly say—what the child shuddered from knowing and could never admit to the faces which smiled at his every success. 1

At the end, in the British Museum (too distracted to finish my dissertation), for weeks I read, speed-read, books by sociologists and educationists only to find infrequent and brief mention of scholarship students, "successful working-class students." Then one day I came across Richard Hoggart's *The Uses of Literacy* and saw, in his descrip- 2 tion of the scholarship boy,[1] myself. For the first time I realized that there were others much like me, and I was able to frame the meaning of my academic failure and success.

What Hoggart understands is that the scholarship boy moves between environments, his home and the classroom, which are at cultural extremes, opposed. With his family, the boy has the pleasure of an exuberant intimacy—the family's consolation in feeling public alienation. Lavish emotions texture home life. *Then* at school the instruction is to use reason primarily. Immediate needs govern the pace of his parents' lives; from his mother and father he learns to trust spontaneity and non-rational ways of knowing. *Then* at school there is mental calm; teachers emphasize the value of a reflectiveness which opens a space between thinking and immediate action. 3

It will require years of schooling for the boy to sketch the cultural differences as abstractly as this. But he senses those differences early. Perhaps as early as the night he brings home some assignment from school and finds the house too noisy for study. 4

> He has to be more and more alone, if he is going to "get on." He will have, probably unconsciously, to oppose the ethos of the hearth, the intense gregariousness of the working-class family group. Since everything centres upon the living room, there is unlikely to be a room of his own; the bedrooms are cold and inhospitable, and to warm them or the front room, if there is one, would not only be expensive, but would require an imaginative leap—out of the tradition—which most families are not capable of making. There is a corner of the living-room table. On the other side Mother is ironing, the wireless is on, someone is singing a snatch of song or Father says intermittently whatever comes into his head. The boy has to cut himself off mentally so as to do his homework as well as he can.[2]

The next day, the lesson is as apparent at school. There are even rows of desks. The boy must raise his hand (and rehearse his thoughts) before speaking in a loud voice to an audience of students he barely knows. And there is time enough and silence to think about ideas ("big ideas") never mentioned at home.

Not for the working-class child alone is adjustment to the classroom difficult. Schooling requires of any student alteration of childhood habits. But the working-class child is usually least prepared for the change. Unlike most middle-class children, moreover, he goes 5

---

[1]For reasons of tone and verbal economy only, I employ the expression, scholarship *boy,* throughout this essay. I do not intend to imply by its usage that the experiences I describe belong to or are the concern solely of male students. [Rodriguez's note]

[2]Richard Hoggart, *The Uses of Literacy* (London: Chatto and Windus, 1957), p. 241. [Rodriguez's note]

home and sees in his parents a way of life that is not only different, but starkly opposed to that of the classroom. They talk and act in precisely the ways his teachers discourage. Without his extraordinary determination and the great assistance of others—at home and at school—there is little chance for success. Typically, most working-class children are barely changed by the classroom. The exception succeeds. Only a few become scholarship students. Of these, Richard Hoggart estimates, most manage a fairly graceful transition. They somehow learn to live in the two very different worlds of their day. There are some others, however, those Hoggart terms scholarship boys, for whom success comes with awkwardness and guilt.

Scholarship boy: good student, troubled son. The child is "mod- 6
erately endowed," intellectually mediocre, Hoggart suggests—though it may be more pertinent to note the special qualities of temperament in the boy. Here is a child haunted by the knowledge that one chooses to become a student. (It is not an inevitable or natural step in growing up.) And that, with the decision, he will separate himself from a life that he loves and even from his own memory of himself.

For a time, he wavers, balances allegiance. "The boy is himself 7
(until he reaches, say, the upper forms) very much of *both* the worlds of home and school. He is enormously obedient to the dictates of the world of school, but emotionally still strongly wants to continue as part of the family circle" (p. 241). Gradually, because he needs to spend more time studying, his balance is lost. He must enclose himself in the "silence" permitted and required by intense concentration. Thus, he takes the first step toward academic success. But a guilt sparks, flickers, then flares up within him. He cannot help feeling that he is rejecting the attractions of family life. (There is no logic here, only the great logic of the heart.)

From the very first days, through the years following, it will be 8
with his parents—the figures of lost authority, the persons toward whom he still feels intense emotion—that the change will most powerfully be measured. A separation will unravel between him and them. Not the separation, "the generation gap," caused by a difference of age, but one that results from cultural factors. The former is capable of being shortened with time, when the child, grown older, comes to repeat the refrain of the newly adult: "I realize now what my parents knew. . . ." Age figures in the separation of the scholarship boy from his parents, but in an odder way. Advancing in his studies, the boy notices that his father and mother have not changed as much as he. Rather, as he sees them, they often remind him of the person he was once, and the life he earlier shared with them. In a way he realizes what Romantics also know when they praise the working-class for the capacity for human closeness, qualities of passion and

spontaneity, that the rest of us share in like measure only in the earliest part of our youth. For Romantics, this doesn't make working-class life childish. Rather, it becomes challenging just because it is an *adult* way of life.

The scholarship boy reaches a different conclusion. He cannot 9
afford to admire his parents. (How could he and still pursue such a contrary life?) He permits himself embarrassment at their lack of education. And to evade nostalgia for the life he has lost, he concentrates on the benefits education will give him. He becomes an especially ambitious student. "[The scholarship boy] tends to make a father-figure of his form master" (p. 243), Hoggart writes with the calm prose of the social scientist. His remark only makes me remember with what urgency I *idolized* my teachers.

I began imitating their accents, using their diction, trusting their 10
every direction. Any books they told me to read, I read—and then waited for them to tell me which books I enjoyed. I was awed by how much they knew. I copied their most casual opinions; I memorized all that they taught. I stayed after school and showed up on Saturdays in order "to help"—to get their attention. It was always their encouragement that mattered to me. *They* understood exactly what my achievements entailed. My memory clutched and caressed each word of praise they bestowed so that, still today, their compliments come quickly to mind.

I cannot forget either, though it is tempting to want to forget, 11
some of the scenes at home which followed my resolution to seek academic success. During the crucial first months, the shy, docile, obedient student came home a shrill and precocious son—as though he needed to prove (to himself? to his parents?) that he had made the right choice. After a while, I developed quiet tact. I grew more calm. I became a conventionally dutiful son; politely affectionate; cheerful enough; even—for reasons beyond choosing—my father's favorite. And in many ways, much about my home life was easy, calm, comfortable, happy in the rhythm of the family's routine: the noises of radios and alarm clocks, the errands, the rituals of dinner and going to bed in flannel pyjamas.

But withheld from my parents was most of what deeply mattered 12
to me: the extraordinary experience of my education. My father or mother would wonder: "What did you learn today?" Or say: "Tell us about your new courses." I would barely respond. "Just the usual things. . . ." (Silence. Silence!) In place of the sounds of intimacy which once flowed easily between us there was the silence. (The toll of my guilt and my loss.) After dinner, I would rush away to a bedroom with papers and books. As often as possible I resisted parental pleas to "save lights" by coming to the kitchen to work. I

kept so much, so often to myself. Sad. Guilty for the excitement of coming upon new ideas, new possibilities. Eager. Fascinated. I hoarded the pleasures of learning. Alone for hours. Enthralled. Afraid. Quiet (the house noisy), I rarely looked away from my books—or back on my memories. Times when relatives visited and the front rooms were warmed by Spanish sounds, I slipped out of the house.

It mattered that education was changing me. It never ceased to 13
matter. I would not have become a scholarship boy had it not mattered so much.

Walking to school with classmates sometimes, I would hear them 14
tell me that their parents read to them at night. Strange-sounding books like *Winnie the Pooh.* Immediately, I asked them: "What is it like?" But the question only confused my companions. So I learned to keep it to myself and silently imagined the scene of parent and child reading together.

One day—I must have been nine or ten years old at the time—my 15
mother asked for a "nice" book to read. ("Something not too hard that you think I might like.") Carefully, I chose one. I think it was Willa Cather's *My Antonia.* But when, several weeks later, I happened to see it next to her bed, unread except for the first few pages, I was furious with impatience. And then suddenly I wanted to cry; I grabbed up the book and took it back to my room.

"Why didn't you tell us about the award?" my mother scolded— 16
though her face was softened with pride. At the grammar school ceremony, some days later, I felt such contrary feelings. (There is no simple roadmap through the heart of the scholarship boy.) Nervously, I heard my father speak to my teacher and felt my familiar shame of his accent. Then guilty for the shame. My instructor was so soft-spoken and her words were edged clear. I admired her until it seemed to me that she spoke too carefully. Sensing that she was condescending to them, I was suddenly resentful. Protective. I tried to move my parents away. "You must both be so proud of him," she said. They quickly answered in the affirmative. They were proud. "We are proud of all our children." Then, this afterthought: "They sure didn't get their brains from us." I smiled. The three of them laughed.

But tightening the irony into a knot was the knowledge that my 17
parents were always behind me. In many ways, they made academic success possible. They evened the path. They sent their children to parochial schools because "the nuns teach better." They paid a tuition they couldn't afford. They spoke English at home. ("*¡Hablanos en* English!") Their voices united to urge me past my initial resistance to

the classroom. They always wanted for my brothers and me the chances they never had.

It saddened my mother to learn about Mexican-American parents 18
who wanted their children to start working after finishing high school. In schooling she recognized the key to job advancement. And she remembered her past. As a girl, new to America, she had been awarded a diploma by high school teachers too busy or careless to notice that she hardly spoke English. On her own she determined to learn to type. That skill got her clean office jobs and encouraged an optimism about the possibility of advancement. (Each morning when her sisters put on uniforms for work, she chose a bright-colored dress.) She became an excellent speller—of words she mispronounced. ("And I've never been to college," she would say smiling when her children asked about a word they didn't want to look up in a dictionary.)

When her youngest child started going to high school, my mother 19
found full-time employment. She worked for the (California) state government, in civil service positions, positions carefully numbered and acquired by examinations. The old ambition of her youth was still bright then. She consulted bulletin boards for news of new jobs, possible advancement. Then one day saw mention of something called an "anti-poverty agency." A typing job. A glamorous job—part of the governor's staff. ("A knowledge of Spanish desired.") She applied without hesitation and grew nervous only when the job was suddenly hers.

"Everyone comes to work all dressed up," she reported at night. 20
And didn't need to say more than that her co-workers wouldn't let her answer the phone. She was only a typist. Though a fast typist. And an excellent speller. There was a letter one day to be sent to a Washington cabinet officer. On the dictating tape my mother heard mention of "urban guerillas." She typed (the wrong word, correctly): "gorillas." Everyone was shocked. The mistake horrified the anti-poverty bureaucrats who, several days later, returned her to her previous position. She would go no further. She willed her ambition to her children.

After one of her daughters got a job ironing for some rich people 21
we knew, my mother was nervous with fear. ("I don't want you wearing a uniform.") Another summer, when I came home from college, she refused to let me work as a gardener. "You can do much better than that," she insisted. "You've got too much education now." I complied with her wish, though I really didn't think of schooling as job-training. It's true that I planned by that time to become a teacher, but it wasn't an occupation I aimed for as much as something more elusive and indefinite: I wanted to know as much as my teachers; to

possess their confidence and authority; even to assume a professor's persona.

For my father, education had a value different from that it had for 22
my mother. He chuckled when I claimed to be tired by reading and writing. It wasn't real work I did, he would say. "You'll never know what real work is." His comment would recall in my mind his youth. Orphaned when he was eight, he began working after two years in school. He came to America in his twenties, dreaming of returning to school and becoming an engineer. ("Work for my hands and my head.") But there was no money and too little energy at the end of a day for more than occasional night-school courses in English and arithmetic. Days were spent in factories. He no longer expected ever to become an engineer. And he grew pessimistic about the ultimate meaning of work or the possibility of ever escaping its claims. ("But look at all you've accomplished," his best friend once said to him. My father said nothing, and only smiled weakly.)

But I would see him looking at me with opened-mouth curiosity 23
sometimes when I glanced up from my books. Other times, I would come upon him in my bedroom, standing at my desk or bookshelves, fingering the covers of books, opening them to read a few lines. He seemed aware at such moments of some remarkable possibility implied by academic activity. (Its leisure? Its splendid uselessness?) At the moment our eyes met, we each looked quickly away and never spoke.

Such memories as these slammed together in the instant of hear- 24
ing that familiar refrain (all scholarship boys hear) from strangers and friends: "Your parents must be so proud." Yes, my parents were happy at my success. They also were proud. The night of the awards ceremony my mother's eyes were brighter than the trophy I won. Pushing back the hair from my forehead, she whispered that I had "shown" the *gringos.* Years later, my father would wonder why I never displayed my awards and diplomas. He said that he liked to go to doctors' offices and notice the schools they had attended. My awards got left in closets. The golden figure atop a trophy was broken, wingless, after hitting the ground. Medals were put into a jar. My father found my high school diploma when it was about to be thrown out with the trash. He kept it afterwards with his own things.

"We are proud of all of our children." 25

**IN RETROSPECT**

**1.** "The Achievement of Desire" reads largely like a short story about Rodriguez's life as a student. If this piece of writing is basically a narrative, what is it doing in a collection of familiar essays? In other words, how does this piece qualify as an essay, as defined in the Introduction to this collection?

**2.** Several voices speak out on education in this essay. Whose voices are they, how are they presented, and how does Rodriguez use the differences between them to help us understand what he is getting at in this essay?

# 7

# On Mortality

*The one certain, inexorable event in the life of every organism on this planet is death. Even birth is not a predictable event for any organism. Understandably, much has been written and said about human death, but some people are more concerned about death than others. Elderly people and people afflicted with a fatal disease are preoccupied by the subject. Young people, on the other hand, rarely, if ever, think about death. In the vigor of their vitality, they regard death as a distant, even an improbable, event. For that reason, discussions about death should be less forbidding to young people than it is to those for whom the Grim Reaper seems to be lurking just around the corner. Since young people can read about death or listen to sermons about death with great equanimity, it should be salutary for them to be confronted from time to time with reminders about the eventual termination of their sojourn in this vale of tears. But they probably would not take up an essay on death to read unless they were required to do so. If you are required to read essays in this chapter, you will probably discover that reading about death can be a rewarding experience. Some of the greatest essayists of all time are represented herein, among them, Michel de Montaigne, the reputed originator of the essay as a literary form, and William Hazlitt, one of the most renowned English essayists of the nineteenth century; Hazlitt's selection talks about youths' assurance of their immortality. If you can overcome your innate distaste for the macabre, you will be fascinated with the rest of the essays in this chapter.*

# *Of Practice*

## MICHEL DE MONTAIGNE

Michel de Montaigne (1533–1592) is the acknowledged originator of the literary form known as the essay, in particular the kind of personal essay featured in this collection. Born in Périgord, France, Montaigne was subjected to an intensive classical education: The tutor hired by Montaigne's father was instructed to speak only Latin to the boy until he was six years old. As a young man, Montaigne served as counselor in the *Parlement* in Bordeaux, where he formed a close friendship with a young judge, Etienne de la Boétie, who encouraged Montaigne to study philosophy. Boétie's premature death profoundly affected Montaigne's subsequent life and writings. In 1571, Montaigne retired to his estate in Dordogne, where he devoted himself to a systematic program of reading and writing. Books 1 and 2 of his *Essais* appeared in 1580; in 1588, a revised edition of those two books, along with book 3, was published; and in 1595, a posthumous edition of the *Essais* incorporated all the additions and changes that Montaigne had previously made. In the essay reprinted here, Montaigne ruminates about death. He observes that life holds many painful experiences against which we can fortify ourselves by practicing the experience or some experience analogous to it. But he wonders whether any of us can prepare ourselves for the ultimate experience of all human beings: death. He suggests that the experience of sleep can perhaps prepare us for death, since sleep has many of the semblances of death. He then recounts for us, at some length, the experience he had one day when he was violently knocked off the horse he was riding and became comatose. He describes not only the physical sensations he felt on waking from his unconscious state but also some of the mental sensations he experienced. In the latter part of the essay, Montaigne goes on to justify this kind of introspective writing about himself. In essence, he is here explaining the value of the kind of personal writing he practices.

Reasoning and education, though we are willing to put our trust in them, can hardly be powerful enough to lead us to action, unless besides we exercise and form our soul by experience to the way we want it to go; otherwise, when it comes to the time for action, it will undoubtedly find itself at a loss. That is why, among the philosophers, those who have wanted to attain some greater excellence have not been content to await the rigors of Fortune in shelter and repose, for fear she might surprise them inexperienced and new to the combat; rather they have gone forth to meet her and have flung themselves deliberately into the test of difficulties. Some of them have abandoned riches to exercise themselves in a voluntary poverty; others have sought labor and a painful austerity of life to toughen themselves against toil and trouble; others have deprived themselves 1 of the most precious parts of the body, such as sight and the organs of generation, for fear that their services, too pleasant and easy, might relax and soften the firmness of their soul.

But for dying, which is the greatest task we have to perform, 2
practice cannot help us. A man can, by habit and experience, fortify himself against pain, shame, indigence, and such other accidents; but as for death, we can try it only once: we are all apprentices when we come to it.

In ancient times there were men who husbanded their time so 3
excellently that they tried to taste and savor it even at the point of death, and strained their minds to see what this passage was; but they have not come back to tell us news of it:

> No man awakes
> Whom once the icy end of living overtakes.
> Lucretius

Canius Julius, a Roman nobleman of singular virtue and firm- 4
ness, after being condemned to death by that scoundrel Caligula, gave this among many prodigious proofs of his resoluteness. As he was on the point of being executed, a philosopher friend of his asked him: "Well, Canius, how stands your soul at this moment? What is it doing? What are your thoughts?" "I was thinking," he replied, "about holding myself ready and with all my powers intent to see whether in that instant of death, so short and brief, I shall be able to perceive any dislodgment of the soul, and whether it will have any feeling of its departure; so that, if I learn anything about it, I may return later, if I can, to give the information to my friends." This man philosophizes not only unto death, but even in death itself. What assurance it was, and what proud courage, to want his death to serve as a lesson to him, and to have leisure to think about other things in such a great business!

> Such sway he had over his dying soul.
> Lucan

It seems to me, however, that there is a certain way of familiariz- 5
ing ourselves with death and trying it out to some extent. We can have an experience of it that is, if not entire and perfect, at least not useless, and that makes us more fortified and assured. If we cannot reach it, we can approach it, we can reconnoiter it; and if we do not penetrate as far as its fort, at least we shall see and become acquainted with the approaches to it.

It is not without reason that we are taught to study even our sleep 6
for the resemblance it has with death. How easily we pass from

waking to sleeping! With how little sense of loss we lose consciousness of the light and of ourselves! Perhaps the faculty of sleep, which deprives us of all action and all feeling, might seem useless and contrary to nature, were it not that thereby Nature teaches us that she has made us for dying and living alike, and from the start of life presents to us the eternal state that she reserves for us after we die, to accustom us to it and take away our fear of it.

7 But those who by some violent accident have fallen into a faint and lost all sensation, those, in my opinion, have been very close to seeing death's true and natural face. For as for the instant and point of passing away, it is not to be feared that it carries with it any travail or pain, since we can have no feeling without leisure. Our sufferings need time, which in death is so short and precipitate that it must necessarily be imperceptible. It is the approaches that we have to fear, and these may fall within our experience.

8 Many things seem to us greater in imagination than in reality. I have spent a good part of my life in perfect and entire health; I mean not merely entire, but even blithe and ebullient. This state, full of verdure and cheer, made me find the thought of illnesses so horrible that when I came to experience them I found their pains mild and easy compared with my fears.

9 Here is what I experience every day: if I am warmly sheltered in a nice room during a stormy and tempestuous night, I am appalled and distressed for those who are then in the open country; if I am myself outside, I do not even wish to be anywhere else.

10 The mere idea of being always shut up in a room seemed to me unbearable. Suddenly I had to get used to being there a week, or a month, full of agitation, alteration, and weakness. And I have found that in time of health I used to pity the sick much more than I now think I deserve to be pitied when I am sick myself; and that the power of my apprehension made its object appear almost half again as fearful as it was in its truth and essence. I hope that the same thing will happen to me with death, and that it is not worth the trouble I take, the many preparations that I make, and all the many aids that I invoke and assemble to sustain the shock of it. But at all events, we can never be well enough prepared.

11 During our third civil war, or the second (I do not quite remember which), I went riding one day about a league from my house, which is situated at the very hub of all the turmoil of the civil wars of France. Thinking myself perfectly safe, and so near my home that I needed no better equipage, I took a very easy but not very strong horse. On my return, when a sudden occasion came up for me to use this horse for a service to which it was not accustomed, one of my men, big and strong, riding a powerful work horse who had a desperately hard

mouth and was moreover fresh and vigorous—this man, in order to show his daring and get ahead of his companions, spurred his horse at full speed up the path behind me, came down like a colossus on the little man and little horse, and hit us like a thunderbolt with all his strength and weight, sending us both head over heels. So that there lay the horse bowled over and stunned, and I ten or twelve paces beyond, dead, stretched on my back, my face all bruised and skinned, my sword, which I had had in my hand, more than ten paces away, my belt in pieces, having no more motion or feeling than a log. It is the only swoon that I have experienced to this day.

Those who were with me, after having tried all the means they 12
could to bring me round, thinking me dead, took me in their arms and were carrying me with great difficulty to my house, which was about half a French league from there. On the way, and after I had been taken for dead for more than two full hours, I began to move and breathe; for so great an abundance of blood had fallen into my stomach that nature had to revive its forces to discharge it. They set me up on my feet, where I threw up a whole bucketful of clots of pure blood, and several times on the way I had to do the same thing. In so doing I began to recover a little life, but it was bit by bit and over so long a stretch of time that my first feelings were much closer to death than to life:

> Because the shaken soul, uncertain yet
> Of its return, is still not firmly set.
>
> Tasso

This recollection, which is strongly implanted on my soul, showing me the face and idea of death so true to nature, reconciles me to it somewhat.

When I began to see anything, it was with a vision so blurred, 13
weak, and dead, that I still could distinguish nothing but the light,

> As one 'twixt wakefulness and doze,
> Whose eyes now open, now again they close.
>
> Tasso

As for the functions of the soul, they were reviving with the same progress as those of the body. I saw myself all bloody, for my doublet was stained all over with the blood I had thrown up. The first thought that came to me was that I had gotten a harquebus shot in the head; indeed several were being fired around us at the time of the accident. It seemed to me that my life was hanging only by the tip of my lips; I closed my eyes in order, it seemed to me, to help push it out, and took pleasure in growing languid and letting myself go. It was an idea that was only floating on the surface of my soul, as delicate and feeble as all the rest, but in truth not only free from distress but mingled with that sweet feeling that people have who let themselves slide into sleep.

I believe that this is the same state in which people find them- 14
selves whom we see fainting with weakness in the agony of death; and I maintain that we pity them without cause, supposing that they are agitated by grievous pains or have their soul oppressed by painful thoughts. This has always been my view, against the opinion of many, and even of Etienne de La Boétie, concerning those whom we see thus prostrate and comatose as their end approaches, or overwhelmed by the length of the disease, or by a stroke of apoplexy, or by epilepsy—

> This do we often see:
> A man, struck, as by lightning, by some malady,
> Falls down all foaming at the mouth, shivers and rants;
> He moans under the torture, writhes his muscles, pants,
> And in fitful tossing exhausts his weary limbs
>
> Lucretius

—or wounded in the head: When we hear them groan and from time to time utter poignant sighs, or see them make certain movements of the body, we seem to see signs that they still have some consciousness left; but I have always thought, I say, that their soul and body were buried in sleep.

> He lives, and is unconscious of his life.
>
> Ovid

And I could not believe that with so great a paralysis of the limbs, and so great a failing of the senses, the soul could maintain any force within by which to be conscious of itself; and so I believed that they had no reflections to torment them, nothing able to make them judge and feel the misery of their condition, and that consequently they were not much to be pitied.

I can imagine no state so horrible and unbearable for me as to 15
have my soul alive and afflicted, without means to express itself. I should say the same of those who are sent to execution with their tongue cut out, were it not that in this sort of death the most silent seems to be the most becoming, if it goes with a firm, grave countenance; and the same of those miserable prisoners who fall into the hands of the villainous murdering soldiers of these days, who torture them with every kind of cruel treatment to force them to pay some excessive and impossible ransom, keeping them meanwhile in a

condition and in a place where they have no means whatever of expressing or signifying their thoughts and their misery.

The poets have portrayed some gods as favorable to the deliv- 16
erance of those who thus drag out a lingering death:

> I bear to Pluto, by decree,
> This lock of hair, and from your body set you free.
> Virgil

Nonetheless, the short and incoherent words and replies that are extorted from them by dint of shouting about their ears and storming at them, or the movements that seem to have some connection with what is asked them, are not evidence that they are alive, at least fully alive. So it happens to us in the early stages of sleep, before it has seized us completely, to sense as in a dream what is happening around us, and to follow voices with a blurred and uncertain hearing which seems to touch on only the edges of the soul; and following the last words spoken to us, we make answers that are more random than sensible.

Now I have no doubt, now that I have tried this out by experi- 17
ence, that I judged this matter rightly all along. For from the first, while wholly unconscious, I was laboring to rip open my doublet with my nails (for I was not in armor); and yet I know that I felt nothing in my imagination that hurt me; for there are many movements of ours that do not come from our will:

> And half-dead fingers writhe and seize the sword again.
> Virgil

Thus those who are falling throw out their arms in front of them, by a natural impulse which makes our limbs lend each other their services and have stirrings apart from our reason:

> They say that chariots bearing scythes will cut so fast
> That severed limbs are writhing on the ground below
> Before the victim's soul and strength can ever know
> Or even feel the pain, so swift has been the hurt.
> Lucretius

My stomach was oppressed with the clotted blood; my hands flew to it of their own accord, as they often do where we itch, against the intention of our will.

There are many animals, and even men, whose muscles we can 18
see contract and move after they are dead. Every man knows by experience that there are parts that often move, stand up, and lie

down, without his leave. Now these passions which touch only the rind of us cannot be called ours. To make them ours, the whole man must be involved; and the pains which the foot or the hand feel while we are asleep are not ours.

As I approached my house, where the alarm of my fall had 19
already come, and the members of my family had met me with the outcries customary in such cases, not only did I make some sort of answer to what was asked me, but also (they say) I thought of ordering them to give a horse to my wife, whom I saw stumbling and having trouble on the road, which is steep and rugged. It would seem that this consideration must have proceeded from a wide-awake soul; yet the fact is that I was not there at all. These were idle thoughts, in the clouds, set in motion by the sensations of the eyes and ears; they did not come from within me. I did not know, for all that, where I was coming from or where I was going, nor could I weigh and consider what I was asked. These are slight effects which the senses produce of themselves, as if by habit; what the soul contributed was in a dream, touched very lightly, and merely licked and sprinkled, as it were, by the soft impression of the senses.

Meanwhile my condition was, in truth, very pleasant and peace- 20
ful; I felt no affliction either for others or for myself; it was a languor and an extreme weakness, without any pain. I saw my house without recognizing it. When they had put me to bed, I felt infinite sweetness in this repose, for I had been villainously yanked about by those poor fellows, who had taken the pains to carry me in their arms over a long and very bad road, and had tired themselves out two or three times in relays. They offered me many remedies, of which I accepted none, holding it for certain that I was mortally wounded in the head. It would, in truth, have been a very happy death; for the weakness of my understanding kept me from having any judgment of it, and that of my body from having any feeling of it. I was letting myself slip away so gently, so gradually and easily, that I hardly ever did anything with less of a feeling of effort.

When I came back to life and regained my powers, 21

> When my senses at last regained their strength.
> Ovid

which was two or three hours later, I felt myself all of a sudden caught up again in the pain, my limbs being all battered and bruised by my fall, and I felt so bad two or three nights after that I thought I was going to die all over again, but by a more painful death; and I still feel the effect of the shock of that collision.

I do not want to forget this, that the last thing I was able to recover was the memory of this accident; I had people repeat to me several times where I was going, where I was coming from, at what time it had happened to me, before I could take it in. As for the manner of my fall, they concealed it from me and made up other versions for the sake of the man who had been the cause of it. But a long time after, and the next day, when my memory came to open up and picture to me the state I had been in at the instant I had perceived that horse bearing down on me (for I had seen him at my heels and thought I was a dead man, but that thought had been so sudden that I had no time to be afraid), it seemed to me that a flash of lightning was striking my soul with a violent shock, and that I was coming back from the other world. 22

This account of so trivial an event would be rather pointless, were it not for the instruction that I have derived from it for myself; for in truth, in order to get used to the idea of death, I find there is nothing like coming close to it. Now as Pliny says, each man is a good education to himself, provided he has the capacity to spy on himself from close up. What I write here is not my teaching, but my study; it is not a lesson for others, but for me. 23

And yet it should not be held against me if I publish what I write. What is useful to me may also by accident be useful to another. Moreover, I am not spoiling anything, I am using only what is mine. And if I play the fool, it is at my expense and without harm to anyone. For it is a folly that will die with me, and will have no consequences. We have heard of only two or three ancients who opened up this road, and even of them we cannot say whether their manner in the least resembled mine, since we know only their names. No one since has followed their lead. It is a thorny undertaking, and more so than it seems, to follow a movement so wandering as that of our mind, to penetrate the opaque depths of its innermost folds, to pick out and immobilize the innumerable flutterings that agitate it. And it is a new and extraordinary amusement, which withdraws us from the ordinary occupations of the world, yes, even from those most recommended. 24

It is many years now that I have had only myself as object of my thoughts, and I have been examining and studying only myself; and if I study anything else, it is in order promptly to apply it to myself, or rather within myself. And it does not seem to me that I am making a mistake if—as is done in the other sciences, which are incomparably less useful—I impart what I have learned in this one, though I am hardly satisfied with the progress I have made in it. There is no description equal in difficulty, or certainly in usefulness, to the de- 25 scription of oneself. Even so one must spruce up, even so one must present oneself in an orderly arrangement, if one would go out in public. Now, I am constantly adorning myself, for I am constantly describing myself.

Custom has made speaking of oneself a vice, and obstinately 26
forbids it out of hatred for the boasting that seems always to accompany it. Instead of blowing a child's nose, as we should, this amounts to pulling it off.

> Flight from a fault will lead us into crime.
> Horace

I find more harm than good in this remedy. But even if it were true that it is presumptuous, no matter what the circumstances, to talk to the public about oneself, I still must not, according to my general plan, refrain from an action that openly displays this morbid quality, since it is in me; nor may I conceal this fault, which I not only practice but profess. However, to say what I think about it, custom is wrong to condemn wine because many get drunk on it. We can misuse only things which are good. And I believe that the rule against speaking of oneself applies only to the vulgar form of this failing. Such rules are bridles for calves, with which neither the saints, whom we hear speaking so boldly about themselves, nor the philosophers, nor the theologians curb themselves. Nor do I, though I am none of these. If they do not write about themselves expressly, at least when the occasion leads them to it they do not hesitate to put themselves prominently on display. What does Socrates treat of more fully than himself? To what does he lead his disciples' conversation more often than to talk about themselves, not about the lesson of their book, but about the essence and movement of their soul? We speak our thoughts religiously to God, and to our confessor, as our neighbors[1] do to the whole people. But, someone will answer, we speak only our self-accusations. Then we speak everything: for our very virtue is faulty and fit for repentance.

My trade and my art is living. He who forbids me to speak about 27
it according to my sense, experience, and practice, let him order the architect to speak of buildings not according to himself but according to his neighbor; according to another man's knowledge, not according to his own. If it is vainglory for a man himself to publish his own merits, why doesn't Cicero proclaim the eloquence of Hortensius, Hortensius that of Cicero?

[1] The Protestants. [Montaigne's note]

Perhaps they mean that I should testify about myself by works and deeds, not by bare words. What I chiefly portray is my cogitations, a shapeless subject that does not lend itself to expression in actions. It is all I can do to couch my thoughts in this airy medium of words. Some of the wisest and most devout men have lived avoiding all noticeable actions. My actions would tell more about fortune than about me. They bear witness to their own part, not to mine, unless it be by conjecture and without certainty: they are samples, which display only details. I expose myself entire: my portrait is a cadaver on which the veins, the muscles, and the tendons appear at a glance, each part in its place. One part of what I am was produced by a cough, another by a pallor or a palpitation of the heart—in any case dubiously. It is not my deeds that I write down; it is myself, it is my essence. 28

I hold that a man should be cautious in making an estimate of himself, and equally conscientious in testifying about himself—whether he rates himself high or low makes no difference. If I seemed to myself good and wise or nearly so, I would shout it out at the top of my voice. To say less of yourself than is true is stupidity, not modesty. To pay yourself less than you are worth is cowardice and pusillanimity, according to Aristotle. No virtue is helped by falsehood, and truth is never subject to error. To say more of yourself than is true is not always presumption; it too is often stupidity. To be immoderately pleased with what you are, to fall therefore into an undiscerning self-love, is in my opinion the substance of this vice. The supreme remedy to cure it is to do just the opposite of what those people prescribe who, by prohibiting talking about oneself, even more strongly prohibit thinking about oneself. The pride lies in the thought; the tongue can have only a very slight share in it. 29

It seems to them that to be occupied with oneself means to be pleased with oneself, that to frequent and associate with oneself means to cherish oneself too much. That may be. But this excess arises only in those who touch themselves no more than superficially; who observe themselves only after taking care of their business; who call it daydreaming and idleness to be concerned with oneself, and making castles in Spain to furnish and build oneself; who think themselves something alien and foreign to themselves. 30

If anyone gets intoxicated with his knowledge when he looks beneath him, let him turn his eyes upward toward past ages, and he will lower his horns, finding there so many thousands of minds that trample him underfoot. If he gets into some flattering presumption about his valor, let him remember the lives of the two Scipios, so many armies, so many nations, all of whom leave him so far behind them. No particular quality will make a man proud who balances it 31 against the many weaknesses and imperfections that are also in him, and, in the end, against the nullity of man's estate.

Because Socrates alone had seriously digested the precept of his 32
god—to know himself—and because by that study he had come to despise himself, he alone was deemed worthy of the name *wise*. Whoever knows himself thus, let him boldly make himself known by his own mouth.

**IN RETROSPECT**

**1.** One of the points that Montaigne makes in "Of Practice" is that our fearful anticipation of certain events in our life often proves to be worse than the reality. To convince us of this thesis, Montaigne tells us about an event in his life that brought him as close as he has ever been to the most feared event in most people's lives: death. Review the particulars of Montaigne's account of the event and see if you can discover why this experience relieved him of his natural fear of death.

**2.** If you have taken a writing class, you were undoubtedly told that your essays and paragraphs should be marked by unity. How deliberately unified is Montaigne's essay? How might one tie the medley of subjects in this essay into a unified whole? How necessary is it to do so? What conclusions might you draw about the concept of unity as a result of your reading of and reflecting on this essay?

# *On the Feeling of Immortality in Youth*

## WILLIAM HAZLITT

William Hazlitt (1778–1830) was born in Maidstone, England, the son of a Unitarian minister. Though he aspired to be a painter, his association with such contemporaries as Samuel Taylor Coleridge, William Wordsworth, and Charles Lamb converted him to the pursuit of a literary career. Hazlitt's many essays, published during the last twenty years of his life, can be classified into three groups: (a) essays on art and drama, (b) essays of literary criticism, and (c) familiar essays on miscellaneous subjects. Hazlitt is one of the most prolific and garrulous of the English essayists of the first half of the nineteenth century: The standard edition of his complete works runs to twenty-one volumes. And not only did Hazlitt write many works, but he wrote at great length—it is impossible to find a short essay among his published works. One sign of his garrulity is his long, dense paragraphs. For instance, the long essay reprinted here comprises only *five* paragraphs. Yet despite the copiousness of his prose, Hazlitt is rarely difficult or boring to read. In the following essay Hazlitt examines the psychology of why young people seldom contemplate their inevitable death, and he agrees that young people's not brooding over their mortality is healthy.

No young man believes he shall ever die. It was a saying of my brother's, and a fine one. There is a feeling of Eternity in youth which makes us amends for everything. To be young is to be as one of the Immortals. One half of time indeed is spent—the other half remains in store for us with all its countless treasures, for there is no line drawn, and we see no limit to our hopes and wishes. We make the coming age our own— 1

> The vast, the unbounded prospect lies before us.

Death, old age, are words without a meaning, a dream, a fiction, with which we have nothing to do. Others may have undergone, or may still undergo them—we "bear a charmed life," which laughs to scorn all such idle fancies. As, in setting out on a delightful journey, we strain our eager sight forward,

> Bidding the lovely scenes at distance hail,

and see no end to prospect after prospect, new objects presenting themselves as we advance, so in the outset of life we see no end to our desires nor to the opportunities of gratifying them. We have as yet found no obstacle, no disposition to flag, and it seems that we can go on so for ever. We look round in a new world, full of life and motion, and ceaseless progress, and feel in ourselves all the vigour and spirit to keep pace with it, and do not foresee from any present signs how we shall be left behind in the race, decline into old age, and drop into the grave. It is the simplicity and, as it were, abstractedness of our feelings in youth that (so to speak) identifies us with Nature and (our experience being weak and our passions strong) makes us fancy ourselves immortal like it. Our short-lived connexion with being, we fondly flatter ourselves, is an indissoluble and lasting union. As infants smile and sleep, we are rocked in the cradle of our desires, and hushed into fancied security by the roar of the universe around us—we quaff the cup of life with eager thirst without draining it, and joy and hope seem ever mantling to the brim—objects press around us, filling the mind with their magnitude and with the throng of desires that wait upon them, so that there is no room for the thoughts of death. We are too much dazzled by the gorgeousness and novelty of the bright waking dream about us to discern the dim shadow lingering for us in the distance. Nor would the hold that life has taken of us permit us to detach our thoughts that way, even if we could. We are too much absorbed in present objects and pursuits. While the spirit of youth remains unimpaired, ere "the wine of life is drunk," we are like people intoxicated or in a fever, who are hurried away by the violence of their own sensations: it is only as present objects begin to pall upon the sense, as we have been disappointed in our favourite pursuits, cut off from our closest ties, that we by degrees become weaned from the world, that passion loosens its hold upon futurity, and that we begin to contemplate as in a glass darkly the possibility of parting with it for good. Till then, the example of others has no effect upon us. Casualties we avoid; the slow approaches of age we play at *hide and seek* with. Like the foolish fat scullion in Sterne, who hears that Master Bobby is dead, our only reflection is, "So am not I!" The idea of death, instead of staggering our confidence, only seems to strengthen and enhance our sense of the possession and enjoyment of life. Others may fall around us like leaves, or be mowed down by the scythe of Time like grass; these are but metaphors to the unreflecting, buoyant ears and overweening presumption of youth. It is not till we see the flowers of Love, Hope, and Joy withering around us, that we give up the flattering delusions that before led us on, and that the emptiness and dreariness of the prospect before us reconciles us hypothetically to the silence of the grave.

Life is indeed a strange gift, and its privileges are most myste- 2
rious. No wonder when it is first granted to us, that our gratitude, our admiration, and our delight should prevent us from reflecting on our own nothingness, or from thinking it will ever be recalled. Our first and strongest impressions are borrowed from the mighty scene that is opened to us, and we unconsciously transfer its durability as well as its splendour to ourselves. So newly found, we cannot think of parting with it yet, or at least put off that consideration *sine die*. Like a rustic at a fair, we are full of amazement and rapture, and have no thought of going home, or that it will soon be night. We know our existence only by ourselves, and confound our knowledge with the objects of it. We and Nature are therefore one. Otherwise the illusion, the "feast of reason and the flow of soul," to which we are invited, is a mockery and a cruel insult. We do not go from a play till the last act is ended, and the lights are about to be extinguished. But the fairy face of Nature still shines on: shall we be called away before the curtain falls, or ere we have scarce had a glimpse of what is going on? Like children, our step-mother Nature holds us up to see the raree-show of the universe, and then, as if we were a burden to her to support, lets us fall down again. Yet what brave sublunary things does not this pageant present, like a ball or fête of the universe!

To see the golden sun, the azure sky, the outstretched ocean; to walk upon the green earth, and be lord of a thousand creatures; to look down yawning precipices or over distant sunny vales; to see the world spread out under one's feet on a map; to bring the stars near; to view the smallest insects through a microscope; to read history, and consider the revolutions of empire and the successions of generations; to hear the glory of Tyre, of Sidon, of Babylon, and of Susa, and so say all these were before me and are now nothing; to say I exist in such a point of time, and in such a point of space; to be a spectator and a part of its ever-moving scene; to witness the change of season, of spring and autumn, of winter and summer; to feel hot and cold, pleasure and pain, beauty and deformity; right and wrong; to be sensible to the accidents of Nature; to consider the mighty world of eye and ear; to listen to the stock-dove's notes amid the forest deep; to journey over moor and mountain; to hear the midnight sainted choir; to visit lighted halls, or the cathedral's gloom, or sit in crowded theatres and see life itself mocked; to study the works of art and refine the sense of beauty to agony; to worship fame, and to dream of immortality; to look upon the Vatican, and to read Shakespear; to gather up the wisdom of the ancients, and to pry into the future; to listen to the trump of war, the shout of victory; to question history as to the movements of the human heart; to seek for truth; to plead the cause of humanity; to overlook the world as if time and Nature poured their treasures at our feet—to be and to do all this, and then in a moment to be nothing—to have it all snatched from us as by a juggler's trick, or a phantasmagoria! There is something in this transition from all to nothing that shocks us and damps the enthusiasm of youth new flushed with hope and pleasure, and we cast the comfortless thought as far from us as we can. In the first enjoyment of the estate of life we discard the fear of debts and duns, and never think of the final payment of our great debt to Nature. Art we know is long; life, we flatter ourselves, should be so too. We see no end of the difficulties and delays we have to encounter: perfection is slow of attainment, and we must have time to accomplish it in. The fame of the great names we look up to is immortal: and shall not we who contemplate it imbibe a portion of ethereal fire, the *divinae particula aurae,* which nothing can extinguish? A wrinkle in Rembrandt or in Nature takes whole days to resolve itself into its component parts, its softenings and its sharpnesses; we refine upon our perfections, and unfold the intricacies of Nature. What a prospect for the future! What a task have we not begun! And shall we be arrested in the middle of it? We do not count our time thus employed lost, or our pains thrown away; we do not flag or grow tired, but gain new vigour at our endless task. Shall Time, then, grudge us to finish what we have 3 begun, and have formed a compact with Nature to do? Why not fill up the blank that is left us in this manner? I have looked for hours at a Rembrandt without being conscious of the flight of time, but with ever new wonder and delight, have thought that not only my own but another existence I could pass in the same manner. This rarefied, refined existence seemed to have no end, nor stint, nor principle of decay in it. The print would remain long after I who looked on it had become the prey of worms. The thing seems in itself out of all reason: health, strength, appetite are opposed to the idea of death, and we are not ready to credit it till we have found our illusions vanished, and our hopes grown cold. Objects in youth, from novelty, etc., are stamped upon the brain with such force and integrity that one thinks nothing can remove or obliterate them. They are riveted there, and appear to us as an element of our nature. It must be a mere violence that destroys them, not a natural decay. In the very strength of this persuasion we seem to enjoy an age by anticipation. We melt down years into a single moment of intense sympathy, and by anticipating the fruits defy the ravages of time. If, then, a single moment of our lives is worth years, shall we set any limits to its total value and extent? Again, does it not happen that so secure do we think ourselves of an indefinite period of existence, that at times, when left to ourselves, and impatient of novelty, we feel annoyed at what seems to us the slow and creeping progress of time, and argue that if it always moves at this tedious snail's pace it will never come to an end? How ready are we to sacrifice any space of time which separates us from a favourite object, little thinking that before long we shall find it move too fast.

For my part, I started in life with the French Revolution, and I 4
have lived, alas! to see the end of it. But I did not foresee this result. My sun arose with the first dawn of liberty, and I did not think how soon both must set. The new impulse to ardour given to men's minds imparted a congenial warmth and glow to mine; we were strong to run a race together, and I little dreamed that long before mine was set, the sun of liberty would turn to blood, or set once more in the night of despotism. Since then, I confess, I have no longer felt myself young, for with that my hopes fell.

I have since turned my thoughts to gathering up some of the 5
fragments of my early recollections, and putting them into a form to which I might occasionally revert. The future was barred to my progress, and I turned for consolation and encouragement to the past. It is thus that, while we find our personal and substantial identity vanishing from us, we strive to gain a reflected and vicarious one in our thoughts: we do not like to perish wholly, and wish to bequeath our names, at least, to posterity. As long as we can make

our cherished thoughts and nearest interests live in the minds of others, we do not appear to have retired altogether from the stage. We still occupy the breasts of others, and exert an influence and power over them, and it is only our bodies that are reduced to dust and powder. Our favourite speculations still find encouragement, and we make as great a figure in the eye of the world, or perhaps a greater than in our lifetime. The demands of our self-love are thus satisfied, and these are the most imperious and unremitting. Besides, if by our intellectual superiority we survive ourselves in this world, by our virtues and faith we may attain an interest in another, and a higher state of being, and may thus be recipients at the same time of men and of angels.

> E'en from the tomb the voice of Nature cries,
> E'en in our ashes live their wonted fires.

As we grow old, our sense of the value of time becomes vivid. Nothing else, indeed, seems of any consequence. We can never cease wondering that that which has ever been should cease to be. We find many things remain the same: why then should there be change in us. This adds a convulsive grasp of whatever is, a sense of fallacious hollowness in all we see. Instead of the full, pulpy feeling of youth tasting existence and every object in it, all is flat and vapid, – a whited sepulchre, fair without but full of ravening and all uncleanness within. The world is a witch that puts us off with false shows and appearances. The simplicity of youth, the confiding expectation, the boundless raptures, are gone: we only think of getting out of it as well as we can, and without any great mischance or annoyance. The flush of illusion, even the complacent retrospect of past joys and hopes, is over; if we can slip out of life without indignity, can escape with little bodily infirmity, and frame our minds to the calm and respectable composure of *still-life* before we return to absolute nothingness, it is as much as we can expect. We do not die wholly at our deaths: we have mouldered away gradually long before. Faculty after faculty, interest after interest, attachment after attachment disappear: we are torn from ourselves while living, year after year sees us no longer the same, and death only consigns the last fragment of what we were to the grave. That we should wear out by slow stages, and dwindle at last into nothing, is not wonderful, when even in our prime our strongest impressions leave little trace but for the moment, and we are the creatures of petty circumstance. How little effect is made on us in our best days by the books we have read, the scenes we have witnessed, the sensations we have gone through! Think only of the feelings we experience in reading a fine romance (one of Sir Walter's, for instance); what beauty, what sublimity, what interest, what heart-rending emotions! You would suppose the feelings you then experienced would last for ever, or subdue the mind to their own harmony and tone: while we are reading it seems as if nothing could ever put us out of our way, or trouble us: – the first splash of mud that we get on entering the street, the first twopence we are cheated out of, the feeling vanishes clean out of our minds, and we become the prey of petty and annoying circumstance. The mind soars to the lofty: it is at home in the grovelling, the disagreeable, and the little. And yet we wonder that age should be feeble and querulous, – that the freshness of youth should fade away. Both worlds would hardly satisfy the extravagance of our desires and of our presumption.

### IN RETROSPECT

**1.** The headnote to this essay remarks on the long, dense paragraphs Hazlitt writes. Select an unusually long, dense paragraph from this essay. Analyze the paragraph carefully. Is it unified – that is, are all the sentences in the paragraph dealing with one topic? Analyze how Hazlitt expands the paragraph. Can you break up the long paragraph into two or three shorter paragraphs? If so, how? After all this analysis, what is your final judgment about Hazlitt's style of writing?

**2.** In looking at Montaigne's essay "Of Practice," we remarked on its rambling structure, the kind of structure that became a hallmark of his *essais*. In Hazlitt's essay, we may be witnessing another tradition, the practice of copiousness, a practice in which Renaissance schoolboys were rigorously exercised. To promote the ability to pour out an abundance of words on a subject, the schoolmasters had their pupils keep commonplace books in which they copied down passages they read from books and essays written by a variety of authors. The commonplace book then became a reservoir of ideas to resort to when the writer was assigned to write on a certain subject. On first reading Hazlitt's essay, you may feel that Hazlitt is repeating the same theme over and over again. Go back to the essay and see if you can find instances where Hazlitt is not just being repetitive but is indeed fruitfully filling out his theme about youths' feelings of immortality. How do the seemingly repetitive sentences actually develop the essay?

# *The Death of the Moth*

## VIRGINIA WOOLF

Virginia Woolf (1882–1941) is certainly better known to contemporary readers than her husband, Leonard Woolf, who founded the Hogarth Press in London, and her father, Sir Leslie Stephens, who among other things edited the multivolume *Dictionary of National Biography,* a monumental reference work. A member of the "Bloomsbury Group"—composed of a number of talented writers, artists, and philosophers who began meeting about 1906 in the Stephenses' home in London—and an early experimenter in stream-of-consciousness fiction, Woolf is known for such innovative novels as *Mrs. Dalloway* (1922), *To the Lighthouse* (1927), *Orlando* (1928), and *The Waves* (1931). She was also a pioneer in the feminist movement of the twentieth century. A great many of her essays were ventures in literary criticism, such as the essays in her *Common Reader: First Series* (1925) and *Common Reader: Second Series* (1932). In 1941, in a fit of depression over the war and her wavering health, Woolf committed suicide by drowning herself. *The Death of the Moth and Other Essays,* from which the following essay was taken, was published posthumously by her husband in 1942. In this essay, Woolf's sensitive and poetic disposition is manifested in the meticulous and affectionate way in which she observed the fluttering moth and in her vivid, sensuous report of its fading struggle against death.

Moths that fly by day are not properly to be called moths; they do not excite that pleasant sense of dark autumn nights and ivy-blossom which the commonest yellow-underwing asleep in the shadow of the curtain never fails to rouse in us. They are hybrid creatures, neither gay like butterflies nor sombre like their own species. Nevertheless the present specimen, with his narrow hay-colored wings, fringed with a tassel of the same color, seemed to be content with life. It was a pleasant morning, mid-September, mild, benignant, yet with a keener breath than that of the summer months. The plough was already scoring the field opposite the window, and where the share had been, the earth was pressed flat and gleamed with moisture. Such vigor came rolling in from the fields and the down beyond that it was difficult to keep the eyes strictly turned upon the book. The rooks too were keeping one of their annual festivities; soaring round the tree tops until it looked as if a vast net with thousands of black knots in it had been cast up into the air; which, after a few moments sank slowly down upon the trees until every twig seemed to have a knot at the end of it. Then, suddenly, the net would be thrown into the air again in a wider circle this time, with the utmost clamor and vociferation, as though to be thrown into the air and settle slowly down upon the tree tops were a tremendously exciting experience. 1

2 The same energy which inspired the rooks, the ploughmen, the horses, and even, it seemed, the lean bare-backed downs, sent the moth fluttering from side to side of his square of the window-pane. One could not help watching him. One was, indeed, conscious of a queer feeling of pity for him. The possibilities of pleasure seemed that morning so enormous and various that to have only a moth's part in life, and a day moth's at that, appeared a hard fate, and his zest in enjoying his meagre opportunities to the full, pathetic. He flew vigorously to one corner of his compartment, and, after waiting there a second, flew across to the other. What remained for him but to fly to a third corner and then to a fourth? That was all he could do, in spite of the size of the downs, the width of the sky, the far-off smoke of houses, and the romantic voice, now and then, of a steamer out at sea. What he could do he did. Watching him, it seemed as if a fibre, very thin but pure, of the enormous energy of the world had been thrust into his frail and diminutive body. As often as he crossed the pane, I could fancy that a thread of vital light became visible. He was little or nothing but life.

3 Yet, because he was so small, and so simple a form of the energy that was rolling in at the open window and driving its way through so many narrow and intricate corridors in my own brain and in those of other human beings, there was something marvelous as well as pathetic about him. It was as if someone had taken a tiny bead of pure life and decking it as lightly as possible with down and feathers, had set it dancing and zigzagging to show us the true nature of life. Thus displayed one could not get over the strangeness of it. One is apt to forget all about life, seeing it humped and bossed and garnished and cumbered so that it has to move with the greatest circumspection and dignity. Again, the thought of all that life might have been had he been born in any other shape caused one to view his simple activities with a kind of pity.

4 After a time, tired by his dancing apparently, he settled on the window ledge in the sun, and, the queer spectacle being at an end, I forgot about him. Then, looking up, my eye was caught by him. He was trying to resume his dancing, but seemed either so stiff or so awkward that he could only flutter to the bottom of the window-pane; and when he tried to fly across it he failed. Being intent on other matters I watched these futile attempts for a time without thinking, unconsciously waiting for him to resume his flight, as one waits for a machine, that has stopped momentarily, to start again without considering the reason of its failure. After perhaps a seventh attempt he slipped from the wooden ledge and fell, fluttering his wings, onto his back on the window sill. The helplessness of his attitude roused me. It flashed upon me he was in difficulties; he could

no longer raise himself; his legs struggled vainly. But, as I stretched out a pencil, meaning to help him to right himself, it came over me that the failure and awkwardness were the approach of death. I laid the pencil down again.

The legs agitated themselves once more. I looked as if for the 5
enemy against which he struggled. I looked out of doors. What had happened there? Presumably it was midday, and work in the fields had stopped. Stillness and quiet had replaced the previous animation. The birds had taken themselves off to feed in the brooks. The horses stood still. Yet the power was there all the same, massed outside indifferent, impersonal, not attending to anything in particular. Somehow it was opposed to the little hay-colored moth. It was useless to try to do anything. One could only watch the extraordinary efforts made by those tiny legs against an oncoming doom which could, had it chosen, have submerged an entire city, not merely a city, but masses of human beings; nothing, I knew, had any chance against death. Nevertheless after a pause of exhaustion the legs fluttered again. It was superb this last protest, and so frantic that he succeeded at last in righting himself. One's sympathies, of course, were all on the side of life. Also, when there was nobody to care or to know, this gigantic effort on the part of an insignificant little moth, against a power of such magnitude, to retain what no one else valued or desired to keep, moved one strangely. Again, somehow, one saw life, a pure bead. I lifted the pencil again, useless though I knew it to be. But even as I did so, the unmistakable tokens of death showed themselves. The body relaxed, and instantly grew stiff. The struggle was over. The insignificant little creature now knew death. As I looked at the dead moth, this minute wayside triumph of so great a force over so mean an antagonist filled me with wonder. Just as life had been strange for a few minutes before, so death was now as strange. The moth having righted himself now lay most decently and uncomplainingly composed. O yes, he seemed to say, death is stronger than I am.

**IN RETROSPECT**

**1.** Given that this essay is entitled "The Death of a Moth," why do you think Woolf devotes more paragraphs to discussing the life of the moth than to discussing its death? That is, how do you reconcile the title of the essay with what the author does in the essay?

**2.** What observation about the moth draws Woolf's attention to the moth, and what role does that observation play in her commentary on the moth's death and on death in general?

# *Once More to the Lake*

## E. B. WHITE

Elwyn Brooks White (1899–1985) was one of a group of gifted writers who joined the staff of *The New Yorker* soon after it was founded by its first editor, Harold Ross, in 1925. In 1929, White published a volume of poetry, *The Lady Is Cold,* and, in collaboration with James Thurber, the humorous satire *Is Sex Necessary?* White later published three classic children's books, *Stuart Little* (1945), *Charlotte's Web* (1952), and *The Trumpet of the Swan* (1970). In 1959, he revived and revised *The Elements of Style,* a small textbook written by William Strunk, Jr., an English professor who had taught White at Cornell University in 1919. This textbook became a runaway best-seller, one that has proved to be an invaluable guide for countless students and professional writers. In 1938, White moved with his wife and young son to an old farmhouse on the Maine coast, where he remained for five years. During that period, he made a monthly contribution to *Harper's Magazine,* under the heading "One Man's Meat." Although a long time span exists between the first great naturalist writer, Gilbert White, and the twentieth-century E. B. White, the two writers share a remarkable affinity in method and style—the same kind of careful, sympathetic observation of the natural scene and the same kind of clear, vibrant prose style. The essay that follows, which first appeared in the August 1941 issue of *Harper's Magazine,* is, however, more than just a vivid description of a rustic scene. The Whites went annually, in August, "once more to the lake." Going to the lake with his son, White is amazed at how similar the scene and the activities are to those he had experienced when he went there with his own father. There is continuity in the experience, a kind of immortality. But in the final scene, as White watches his son put on a soggy bathing suit to go swimming in the lake after a summer rainstorm, the writer feels "the chill of death." Mortality infuses the continuity.

One summer, along about 1904, my father rented a camp on a lake in Maine and took us all there for the month of August. We all got ringworm from some kittens and had to rub Pond's Extract on our arms and legs night and morning, and my father rolled over in a canoe with all his clothes on; but outside of that the vacation was a success and from then on none of us ever thought there was any place in the world like that lake in Maine. We returned summer after summer—always on August 1st for one month. I have since become a salt-water man, but sometimes in summer there are days when the restlessness of the tides and the fearful cold of the sea water and the incessant wind which blows across the afternoon and into the evening make me wish for the placidity of a lake in the woods. A few weeks ago this feeling got so strong I bought myself a couple of bass 1 hooks and a spinner and returned to the lake where we used to go, for a week's fishing and to revisit old haunts.

I took along my son, who had never had any fresh water up his 2
nose and who had seen lily pads only from train windows. On the journey over to the lake I began to wonder what it would be like. I wondered how time would have marred this unique, this holy spot—the coves and streams, the hills that the sun set behind, the camps and the paths behind the camps. I was sure the tarred road would have found it out and I wondered in what other ways it would be desolated. It is strange how much you can remember about places like that once you allow your mind to return into the grooves which lead back. You remember one thing, and that suddenly reminds you of another thing. I guess I remembered clearest of all the early mornings, when the lake was cool and motionless, remembered how the bedroom smelled of the lumber it was made of and of the wet woods whose scent entered through the screen. The partitions in the camp were thin and did not extend clear to the top of the rooms, and as I was always the first up I would dress softly so as not to wake the others, and sneak out into the sweet outdoors and start out in the canoe, keeping close along the shore in the long shadows of the pines. I remembered being very careful never to rub my paddle against the gunwale for fear of disturbing the stillness of the cathedral.

The lake had never been what you would call a wild lake. There 3
were cottages sprinkled around the shores, and it was in farming country although the shores of the lake were quite heavily wooded. Some of the cottages were owned by nearby farmers, and you would live at the shore and eat your meals at the farmhouse. That's what our family did. But although it wasn't wild, it was a fairly large and undisturbed lake and there were places in it which, to a child at least, seemed infinitely remote and primeval.

I was right about the tar; it led to within half a mile of the shore. 4
But when I got back there, with my boy, and we settled into a camp near a farmhouse and into the kind of summertime I had known, I could tell that it was going to be pretty much the same as it had been before—I knew it, lying in bed the first morning, smelling the bedroom, and hearing the boy sneak quietly out and go off along the shore in a boat. I began to sustain the illusion that he was I, and therefore, by simple transposition, that I was my father. This sensation persisted, kept cropping up all the time we were there. It was not an entirely new feeling, but in this setting it grew much stronger. I seemed to be living a dual existence. I would be in the middle of some simple act, I would be picking up a bait box or laying down a table fork, or I would be saying something, and suddenly it would be not I

but my father who was saying the words or making the gesture. It gave me a creepy sensation.

We went fishing the first morning. I felt the same damp moss 5
covering the worms in the bait can, and saw the dragonfly alight on the tip of my rod as it hovered a few inches from the surface of the water. It was the arrival of this fly that convinced me beyond any doubt that everything was as it always had been, that the years were a mirage and there had been no years. The small waves were the same, chucking the rowboat under the chin as we fished at anchor, and the boat was the same boat, the same color green and the ribs broken in the same places, and under the floor-boards the same fresh-water leavings and débris—the dead helgramite, the wisps of moss, the rusty discarded fishhook, the dried blood from yesterday's catch. We stared silently at the tips of our rods, at the dragonflies that came and went. I lowered the tip of mine into the water, tentatively, pensively dislodging the fly, which darted two feet away, poised, darted two feet back, and came to rest again a little farther up the rod. There had been no years between the ducking of this dragonfly and the other one—the one that was part of memory. I looked at the boy, who was silently watching his fly, and it was my hands that held his rod, my eyes watching. I felt dizzy and didn't know which rod I was at the end of.

We caught two bass, hauling them in briskly as though they were 6
mackerel, pulling them over the side of the boat in a businesslike manner without any landing net, and stunning them with a blow on the back of the head. When we got back for a swim before lunch, the lake was exactly where we had left it, the same number of inches from the dock, and there was only the merest suggestion of a breeze. This seemed an utterly enchanted sea, this lake you could leave to its own devices for a few hours and come back to, and find that it had not stirred, this constant and trustworthy body of water. In the shallows, the dark, water-soaked sticks and twigs, smooth and old, were undulating in clusters on the bottom against the clean ribbed sand, and the track of the mussel was plain. A school of minnows swam by, each minnow with its small individual shadow, doubling the attendance, so clear and sharp in the sunlight. Some of the other campers were in swimming, along the shore, one of them with a cake of soap, and the water felt thin and clear and unsubstantial. Over the years there had been this person with the cake of soap, this cultist, and there he was. There had been no years.

Up to the farmhouse to dinner through the teeming, dusty field, 7
the road under our sneakers was only a two-track road. The middle track was missing, the one with the marks of the hooves and the splotches of dried, flaky manure. There had always been three tracks

to choose from in choosing which track to walk in; now the choice was narrowed down to two. For a moment I missed terribly the middle alternative. But the way led past the tennis court and something about the way it lay there in the sun reassured me; the tape had loosened along the backline, the alleys were green with plantains and other weeds, and the net (installed in June and removed in September) sagged in the dry noon, and the whole place steamed with midday heat and hunger and emptiness. There was a choice of pie for dessert, and one was blueberry and one was apple, and the waitresses were the same country girls, there having been no passage of time, only the illusion of it as in a dropped curtain—the waitresses were still fifteen; their hair had been washed, that was the only difference—they had been to the movies and seen the pretty girls with the clean hair.

Summertime, oh summertime, pattern of life indelible, the fade- 8
proof lake, the woods unshatterable, the pasture with the sweetfern and the juniper forever and ever, summer without end; this was the background, and the life along the shore was the design, the cottages with their innocent and tranquil design, their tiny docks with the flagpole and the American flag floating against the white clouds in the blue sky, the little paths over the roots of the trees leading from camp to camp and the paths leading back to the outhouses and the can of lime for sprinkling, and at the souvenir counters at the store the miniature birch-bark canoes and the post cards that showed things looking a little better than they looked. This was the American family at play, escaping the city heat, wondering whether the newcomers in the camp at the head of the cove were "common" or "nice," wondering whether it was true that the people who drove up for Sunday dinner at the farmhouse were turned away because there wasn't enough chicken.

It seemed to me, as I kept remembering all this, that those times 9
and those summers had been infinitely precious and worth saving. There had been jollity and peace and goodness. The arriving (at the beginning of August) had been so big a business in itself, at the railway station the farm wagon drawn up, the first smell of the pine-laden air, the first glimpse of the smiling farmer, and the great importance of the trunks and your father's enormous authority in such matters, and the feel of the wagon under you for the long ten-mile haul, and at the top of the last long hill catching the first view of the lake after eleven months of not seeing this cherished body of water. The shouts and cries of the other campers when they saw you, and the trunks to be unpacked, to give up their rich burden. (Arriving was less exciting nowadays, when you sneaked up in your car and parked it under a tree near the camp and took out the bags and in

five minutes it was all over, no fuss, no loud wonderful fuss about trunks.)

Peace and goodness and jollity. The only thing that was wrong now, really, was the sound of the place, an unfamiliar nervous sound of the outboard motors. This was the note that jarred, the one thing that would sometimes break the illusion and set the years moving. In those other summertimes all motors were inboard; and when they were at a little distance, the noise they made was a sedative, an ingredient of summer sleep. They were one-cylinder and two-cylinder engines, and some were make-and-break and some were jump-spark, but they all made a sleepy sound across the lake. The one-lungers throbbed and fluttered, and the twin-cylinder ones purred and purred, and that was a quiet sound too. But now the campers all had outboards. In the daytime, in the hot mornings, these motors made a petulant, irritable sound; at night, in the still evening when the afterglow hit the water, they whined about one's ears like mosquitoes. My boy loved our rented outboard, and his great desire was to achieve singlehanded mastery over it, and authority, and he soon learned the trick of choking it a little (but not too much), and the adjustment of the needle valve. Watching him I would remember the things you could do with the old one-cylinder engine with the heavy flywheel, how you could have it eating out of your hand if you got really close to it spiritually. Motor boats in those days didn't have clutches, and you would make a landing by shutting off the motor at the proper time and coasting in with a dead rudder. But there was a way of reversing them, if you learned the trick, by cutting the switch and putting it on again exactly on the final dying revolution of the flywheel, so that it would kick back against compression and begin reversing. Approaching a dock in a strong following breeze, it was difficult to slow up sufficiently by the ordinary coasting method, and if a boy felt he had complete mastery over his motor, he was tempted to keep it running beyond its time and then reverse it a few feet from the dock. It took a cool nerve, because if you threw the switch a twentieth of a second too soon you would catch the flywheel when it still had speed enough to go up past center, and the boat would leap ahead, charging bull-fashion at the dock. 10

We had a good week at the camp. The bass were biting well and the sun shone endlessly, day after day. We would be tired at night and lie down in the accumulated heat of the little bedrooms after the long hot day and the breeze would stir almost imperceptibly outside and the smell of the swamp drift through the rusty screens. Sleep would come easily and in the morning the red squirrel would be on the roof, tapping out his gay routine. I kept remembering everything, 11 lying in bed in the morning—the small steamboat that had a long rounded stern like the lip of a Ubangi, and how quietly she ran on the moonlight sails, when the older boys played their mandolins and the girls sang and we ate doughnuts dipped in sugar, and how sweet the music was on the water in the shining night, and what it had felt like to think about girls then. After breakfast we would go up to the store and the things were in the same place—the minnows in a bottle, the plugs and spinners disarranged and pawed over by the youngsters from the boys' camp, the fig newtons and the Beeman's gum. Outside, the road was tarred and cars stood in front of the store. Inside, all was just as it had always been, except there was more Coca-Cola and not so much Moxie and root beer and birch beer and sarsaparilla. We would walk out with a bottle of pop apiece and sometimes the pop would backfire up our noses and hurt. We explored the streams, quietly, where the turtles slid off the sunny logs and dug their way into the soft bottom; and we lay on the town wharf and fed worms to the tame bass. Everywhere we went I had trouble making out which was I, the one walking at my side, the one walking in my pants.

One afternoon while we were there at that lake a thunderstorm 12
came up. It was like the revival of an old melodrama that I had seen long ago with childish awe. The second-act climax of the drama of the electrical disturbance over a lake in America had not changed in any important respect. This was the big scene, still the big scene. The whole thing was so familiar, the first feeling of oppression and heat and a general air around camp of not wanting to go very far away. In midafternoon (it was all the same) a curious darkening of the sky, and a lull in everything that had made life tick; and then the way the boats suddenly swung the other way at their moorings with the coming of a breeze out of the new quarter, and the premonitory rumble. Then the kettle drum, then the snare, then the bass drum and cymbals, then crackling light against the dark, and the gods grinning and licking their chops in the hills. Afterward the calm, the rain steadily rustling in the calm lake, the return of light and hope and spirits, and the campers running out in joy and relief to go swimming in the rain, their bright cries perpetuating the deathless joke about how they were getting simply drenched, and the children screaming with delight at the new sensation of bathing in the rain, and the joke about getting drenched linking the generations in a strong indestructible chain. And the comedian who waded in carrying an umbrella.

When the others went swimming my son said he was going in 13
too. He pulled his dripping trunks from the line where they had hung all through the shower, and wrung them out. Languidly, and with no

thought of going in, I watched him, his hard little body, skinny and bare, saw him wince slightly as he pulled up around his vitals the small, soggy, icy garment. As he buckled the swollen belt suddenly my groin felt the chill of death.

### IN RETROSPECT

**1.** In this essay, White recounts a series of experiences that he had with his son the summer that he returned to the scene of his own boyhood vacations. After every experience that White recounts for us, he makes the same observation—though in different words, of course. What is the theme of White's repeated observation?

**2.** William Shawn, editor of *The New Yorker* at the time of White's death, has said that White's style was "singular, colloquial, clear, unforced, thoroughly American and utterly beautiful." Examine this essay carefully. Cite passages that you find particularly stylistically appealing. Which, if any, of the adjectives Shawn uses help to explain why you are drawn to the passage? What effect does the passage have on you as a reader? Having read some of White's language, what do you think each of the adjectives Shawn uses means? How would you recognize language that is "American" or "unforced" if you saw it again? What makes White's use of language "singular" or beautiful"?

# *The Long Habit*

## LEWIS THOMAS

Lewis Thomas (1913–     ) was born in Flushing, New York, the son of a surgeon. He obtained his B.S. at Princeton University and his M.D. at Harvard University and has held professional positions at hospitals in Boston and New York and teaching positions at various American universities. In 1971, Thomas launched another career for himself when he began writing a column titled "Notes of a Biology Watcher" for the prestigious *New England Journal of Medicine.* Some of the pieces from that column were published in 1974 in Thomas's first collection of essays, *Lives of a Cell: Notes of a Biology Watcher.* His second collection of essays, *The Medusa and the Snail: More Notes of a Biology Watcher,* was published in 1979. In the essay reprinted here, from *Lives of a Cell,* Thomas reflects philosophically on humankind's "long habit" of dying. Thomas bears a remarkable similarity to the seventeenth-century physician and essay writer Sir Thomas Browne, whom Thomas cites in his essay. First, both are medical doctors, and both achieved literary fame by writing about mortality. Second, the literary work that gained Sir Thomas Browne admittance to the canon of English literature was *Urn Burial* (1658)—

a treatise on the various modes that the British have adopted throughout history for disposing of their dead—and the meditative tone of this treatise is arguably similar to the tone of many of Thomas's essays. And third, although Browne writes in a quaint Elizabethan style and Thomas in a distinctly modern style, the level of eloquence in both writers' styles is of the same high order.

We continue to share with our remotest ancestors the most tan- 1
gled and evasive attitudes about death, despite the great distance we have come in understanding some of the profound aspects of biology. We have as much distaste for talking about personal death as for thinking about it; it is an indelicacy, like talking in mixed company about venereal disease or abortion in the old days. Death on a grand scale does not bother us in the same special way: we can sit around a dinner table and discuss war, involving 60 million volatilized human deaths, as though we were talking about bad weather; we can watch abrupt bloody death every day, in color, on films and television, without blinking back a tear. It is when the numbers of dead are very small, and very close, that we begin to think in scurrying circles. At the very center of the problem is the naked cold deadness of one's own self, the only reality in nature of which we can have absolute certainty, and it is unmentionable, unthinkable. We may be even less willing to face the issue at first hand than our predecessors because of a secret new hope that maybe it will go away. We like to think, hiding the thought, that with all the marvelous ways in which we seem now to lead nature around by the nose, perhaps we can avoid the central problem if we just become, next year, say, a bit smarter.

"The long habit of living," said Thomas Browne, "indisposeth us 2
to dying." These days, the habit has become an addiction: we are hooked on living; the tenacity of its grip on us, and ours on it, grows in intensity. We cannot think of giving it up, even when living loses its zest—even when we have lost the zest for zest.

We have come a long way in our technologic capacity to put death 3
off, and it is imaginable that we might learn to stall it for even longer periods, perhaps matching the life-spans of the Abkhasian Russians, who are said to go on, springily, for a century and a half. If we can rid ourselves of some of our chronic, degenerative diseases, and cancer, strokes, and coronaries, we might go on and on. It sounds attractive and reasonable, but it is no certainty. If we became free of disease, we would make a much better run of it for the last decade or so, but might still terminate on about the same schedule as now. We may be like the genetically different lines of mice, or like Hayflick's different tissue-culture lines, programmed to die after a predetermined number of days, clocked by their genomes. If this is the way it is, some of

us will continue to wear out and come unhinged in the sixth decade, and some much later, depending on genetic timetables.

If we ever do achieve freedom from most of today's diseases, or 4
even complete freedom from disease, we will perhaps terminate by drying out and blowing away on a light breeze, but we will still die.

Most of my friends do not like this way of looking at it. They 5
prefer to take it for granted that we only die because we get sick, with one lethal ailment or another, and if we did not have our diseases we might go on indefinitely. Even biologists choose to think this about themselves, despite the evidences of the absolute inevitability of death that surround their professional lives. Everything dies, all around, trees, plankton, lichens, mice, whales, flies, mitochondria. In the simplest creatures it is sometimes difficult to see it as death, since the strands of replicating DNA they leave behind are more conspicuously the living parts of themselves than with us (not that it is fundamentally any different, but it seems so). Flies do not develop a ward round of diseases that carry them off, one by one. They simply age, and die, like flies.

We hanker to go on, even in the face of plain evidence that long, 6
long lives are not necessarily pleasurable in the kind of society we have arranged thus far. We will be lucky if we can postpone the search for new technologies for a while, until we have discovered some satisfactory things to do with the extra time. Something will surely have to be found to take the place of sitting on the porch re-examining one's watch.

Perhaps we would not be so anxious to prolong life if we did not 7
detest so much the sickness of withdrawal. It is astonishing how little information we have about this universal process, with all the other dazzling advances in biology. It is almost as though we wanted not to know about it. Even if we could imagine the act of death in isolation, without any preliminary stage of being struck down by disease, we would be fearful of it.

There are signs that medicine may be taking a new interest in the 8
process, partly from curiosity, partly from an embarrassed realization that we have not been handling this aspect of disease with as much skill as physicians once displayed, back in the days before they became convinced that disease was their solitary and sometimes defeatable enemy. It used to be the hardest and most important of all the services of a good doctor to be on hand at the time of death and to provide comfort, usually in the home. Now it is done in hospitals, in secrecy (one of the reasons for the increased fear of death these days may be that so many people are totally unfamiliar with it; they never actually see it happen in real life). Some of our technology permits us to deny its existence, and we maintain flickers of life for long stretches

in one community of cells or another, as though we were keeping a flag flying. Death is not a sudden-all-at-once affair; cells go down in sequence, one by one. You can, if you like, recover and grow them out in cultures. It takes hours, even days, before the irreversible word finally gets around to all the provinces.

We may be about to rediscover that dying is not such a bad thing 9
to do after all. Sir William Osler took this view: he disapproved of people who spoke of the agony of death, maintaining that there was no such thing.

In a nineteenth-century memoir on an expedition in Africa, there 10
is a story by David Livingstone about his own experience of near-death. He was caught by a lion, crushed across the chest in the animal's great jaws, and saved in the instant by a lucky shot from a friend. Later, he remembered the episode in clear detail. He was so amazed by the extraordinary sense of peace, calm, and total painlessness associated with being killed that he constructed a theory that all creatures are provided with a protective physiologic mechanism, switched on at the verge of death, carrying them through in a haze of tranquility.

I have seen agony in death only once, in a patient with rabies; he 11
remained acutely aware of every stage in the process of his own disintegration over a twenty-four-hour period, right up to his final moment. It was as though, in the special neuropathology of rabies, the switch had been prevented from turning.

We will be having new opportunities to learn more about the 12
physiology of death at first hand, from the increasing numbers of cardiac patients who have been through the whole process and then back again. Judging from what has been found out thus far, from the first generation of people resuscitated from cardiac standstill (already termed the Lazarus syndrome), Osler seems to have been right. Those who remember parts or all of their episodes do not recall any fear, or anguish. Several people who remained conscious throughout, while appearing to have been quite dead, could only describe a remarkable sensation of detachment. One man underwent coronary occlusion with cessation of the heart and dropped for all practical purposes dead in front of a hospital; within a few minutes his heart had been restarted by electrodes and he breathed his way back into life. According to his account, the strangest thing was that there were so many people around him, moving so urgently, handling his body with such excitement, while all his awareness was of quietude.

In a recent study of the reaction to dying in patients with obstruc- 13
tive disease of the lungs, it was concluded that the process was considerably more shattering for the professional observers than the observed. Most of the patients appeared to be preparing themselves

with equanimity for death, as though intuitively familiar with the business. One elderly woman reported that the only painful and distressing part of the process was in being interrupted; on several occasions she was provided with conventional therapeutic measures to maintain oxygenation or restore fluids and electrolytes, and each time she found the experience of coming back harrowing; she deeply resented the interference with her dying.

I find myself surprised by the thought that dying is an all-right 14
thing to do, but perhaps it should not surprise. It is, after all, the most ancient and fundamental of biologic functions, with its mechanisms worked out with the same attention to detail, the same provision for the advantage of the organism, the same abundance of genetic information for guidance through the stages, that we have long since become accustomed to finding in all the crucial acts of living.

Very well. But even so, if the transformation is a coordinated, 15
integrated physiologic process in its initial, local stages, there is still that permanent vanishing of consciousness to be accounted for. Are we to be stuck forever with this problem? Where on earth does it go? Is it simply stopped dead in its tracks, lost in humus, wasted? Considering the tendency of nature to find uses for complex and intricate mechanisms, this seems to me unnatural. I prefer to think of it as somehow separated off at the filaments of its attachment, and then drawn like an easy breath back into the membrane of its origin, a fresh memory for a biospherical nervous system, but I have no data on the matter.

This is for another science, another day. It may turn out, as some 16
scientists suggest, that we are forever precluded from investigating consciousness by a sort of indeterminacy principle that stipulates that the very act of looking will make it twitch and blur out of sight. If this is true, we will never learn. I envy some of my friends who are convinced about telepathy; oddly enough, it is my European scientist acquaintances who believe it most freely and take it most lightly. All their aunts have received Communications, and there they sit, with proof of the motility of consciousness at their fingertips, and the making of a new science. It is discouraging to have had the wrong aunts, and never the ghost of a message.

## IN RETROSPECT

**1.** How do Thomas's comments on death compare with Woolf's in her essay "The Death of a Moth"? Having read these two essays, how do you feel about the prospect of death? Have your feelings about death changed as a result of reading these essays? If so, how? If not, why not?

**2.** One source of the appeal of this essay for many people is its tone. That tone is achieved largely by Thomas's playful, even irreverent use of language—such as his final phrase, "ghost of a message." What phrases or sentences particularly appeal to you? Cite some of these arresting phrases or sentences. Do you see any opportunities for playing with language that Thomas overlooked? If so, why might he have passed up these opportunities?

# *The Knife*

## RICHARD SELZER

Richard Selzer (1928–      ) was born in Troy, New York, the son of a family doctor. He obtained a B.S. at Union College in 1948, earned an M.D. at Albany Medical College in 1953, and did post doctoral work at Yale University from 1957 to 1960. For many years thereafter, he maintained a private practice in general surgery. His first published book, *Rituals of Surgery* (1974), was a collection of short stories; today he is best known as a writer of essays, usually on some aspect of medical practice. Selzer was once a frequent contributor to such popular magazines as *Mademoiselle, Harper's, Redbook,* and *American Review,* and in 1975, he received the National Magazine Award from Columbia University's School of Journalism for a series of essays published in *Esquire.* His second and third books, *Mortal Lessons* (1977) and *Confessions of a Knife* (1979), firmly established his fame as an essayist. Selzer is often compared with Lewis Thomas; both essayists write prose that the ordinary, literate layperson can read and enjoy. But because of his rather flamboyant style and his tendency to write about "the visceral side of medicine," some critics rank Selzer a peg below Thomas as an essayist. Compile a list of the features of Selzer's writing that you think might draw readers' attention more to the style of his essays than to their substance. You might then assemble some arguments to support your contention that Selzer's style is either *inferior* to or merely *different* from Thomas's style.

One holds the knife as one holds the bow of a cello or a tulip—by 1
the stem. Not palmed nor gripped nor grasped, but lightly, with the tips of the fingers. The knife is not for pressing. It is for drawing across the field of skin. Like a slender fish, it waits, at the ready, then, go! It darts, followed by a fine wake of red. The flesh parts, falling away to yellow globules of fat. Even now, after so many times, I still marvel at its power—cold, gleaming, silent. More, I am still struck with a kind of dread that it is I in whose hand the blade travels, that

my hand is its vehicle, that yet again this terrible steel-bellied thing and I have conspired for a most unnatural purpose, the laying open of the body of a human being.

A stillness settles in my heart and is carried to my hand. It is the 2
quietude of resolve layered over fear. And it is this resolve that lowers us, my knife and me, deeper and deeper into the person beneath. It is an entry into the body that is nothing like a caress; still, it is among the gentlest of acts. Then stroke and stroke again, and we are joined by other instruments, hemostats and forceps, until the wound blooms with strange flowers whose looped handles fall to the sides in steely array.

There is sound, the tight click of clamps fixing teeth into severed 3
blood vessels, the snuffle and gargle of the suction machine clearing the field of blood for the next stroke, the litany of monosyllables with which one prays his way down and in: *clamp, sponge, suture, tie, cut.* And there is color. The green of the cloth, the white of the sponges, the red and yellow of the body. Beneath the fat lies the fascia, the tough fibrous sheet encasing the muscles. It must be sliced and the red beef of the muscles separated. Now there are retractors to hold apart the wound. Hands move together, part, weave. We are fully engaged, like children absorbed in a game or the craftsmen of some place like Damascus.

Deeper still. The peritoneum, pink and gleaming and mem- 4
branous, bulges into the wound. It is grasped with forceps, and opened. For the first time we can see into the cavity of the abdomen. Such a primitive place. One expects to find drawings of buffalo on the walls. The sense of trespassing is keener now, heightened by the world's light illuminating the organs, their secret colors revealed—maroon and salmon and yellow. The vista is sweetly vulnerable at this moment, a kind of welcoming. An arc of the liver shines high and on the right, like a dark sun. It laps over the pink sweep of the stomach, from whose lower border the gauzy omentum is draped, and through which veil one sees, sinuous, slow as just-fed snakes, the indolent coils of the intestine.

You turn aside to wash your gloves. It is a ritual cleansing. One 5
enters this temple doubly washed. Here is man as microcosm, representing in all his parts the earth, perhaps the universe.

I must confess that the priestliness of my profession has even 6
been impressed on me. In the beginning there are vows, taken with all solemnity. Then there is the endless harsh novitiate of training, much fatigue, much sacrifice. At last one emerges as celebrant, standing close to the truth lying curtained in the Ark of the body. Not surplice and cassock but mask and gown are your regalia. You hold

no chalice, but a knife. There is no wine, no wafer. There are only the facts of blood and flesh.

And if the surgeon is like a poet, then the scars you have made on 7
countless bodies are like verses into the fashioning of which you have poured your soul. I think that if years later I were to see the trace from an old incision of mine, I should know it at once, as one recognizes his pet expressions.

But mostly you are a traveler in a dangerous country, advancing 8
into the moist and jungly cleft your hands have made. Eyes and ears are shuttered from the land you left behind; mind empties itself of all other thought. You are the root of groping fingers. It is a fine hour for the fingers, their sense of touch so enhanced. The blind must know this feeling. Oh, there is risk everywhere. One goes lightly. The spleen. No! No! Do not touch the spleen that lurks below the left leaf of the diaphragm, a manta ray in a coral cave, its bloody tongue protruding. One poke and it might rupture, exploding with sudden hemorrhage. The filmy omentum must not be torn, the intestine scraped or denuded. The hand finds the liver, palms it, fingers running along its sharp lower edge, admiring. Here are the twin mounds of the kidneys, the apron of the omentum hanging in front of the intestinal coils. One lifts it aside and the fingers dip among the loops, searching, mapping territory, establishing boundaries. Deeper still, and the womb is touched, then held like a small muscular bottle—the womb and its earlike appendages, the ovaries. How they do nestle in the cup of a man's hand, their power all dormant. They are frailty itself.

There is a hush in the room. Speech stops. The hands of the 9
others, assistants and nurses, are still. Only the voice of the patient's respiration remains. It is the rhythm of a quiet sea, the sound of waiting. Then you speak, slowly, the terse entries of a Himalayan climber reporting back.

"The stomach is okay. Greater curvature clean. No sign of ulcer. 10
Pylorus, duodenum fine. Now comes the gallbladder. No stones. Right kidney, left, all right. Liver . . . uh-oh."

Your speech lowers to a whisper, falters, stops for a long, long 11
moment, then picks up again at the end of a sigh that comes through your mask like a last exhalation.

"Three big hard ones in the left lobe, one on the right. Metastatic 12
deposits. Bad, bad. Where's the primary? Got to be coming from somewhere."

The arm shifts direction and the fingers drop lower and lower 13
into the pelvis—the body impaled now upon the arm of the surgeon to the hilt of the elbow.

"Here it is." 14

The voice goes flat, all business now. 15

"Tumor in the sigmoid colon, wrapped all around it, pretty tight. 16
We'll take out a sleeve of the bowel. No colostomy. Not that, anyway. But, God, there's a lot of it down there. Here, you take a feel."

You step back from the table, and lean into a sterile basin of 17
water, resting on stiff arms, while the others locate the cancer. . . .

What is it, then, this thing, the knife, whose shape is virtually the 18
same as it was three thousand years ago, but now with its head grown detachable? Before steel, it was bronze. Before bronze, stone—then back into unremembered time. Did man invent it or did the knife precede him here, hidden under ages of vegetation and hoofprints, lying in wait to be discovered, picked up, used?

The scalpel is in two parts, the handle and the blade. Joined, it is 19
six inches from tip to tip. At one end of the handle is a narrow notched prong upon which the blade is slid, then snapped into place. Without the blade, the handle has a blind, decapitated look. It is helpless as a trussed maniac. But slide on the blade, click it home, and the knife springs instantly to life. It is headed now, edgy, leaping to mount the fingers for the gallop to its feast.

Now is the moment from which you have turned aside, from 20
which you have averted your gaze, yet toward which you have been hastened. Now the scalpel sings along the flesh again, its brute run unimpeded by germs or other frictions. It is a slick slide home, a barracuda spurt, a rip of embedded talon. One listens, and almost hears the whine—nasal, high, delivered through that gleaming metallic snout. The flesh splits with its own kind of moan. It is like the penetration of rape.

The breasts of women are cut off, arms and legs sliced to the bone 21
to make ready for the saw, eyes freed from sockets, intestines lopped. The hand of the surgeon rebels. Tension boils through his pores, like sweat. The flesh of the patient retaliates with hemorrhage, and the blood chases the knife wherever it is withdrawn.

Within the belly a tumor squats, toadish, fungoid. A gray mother and 22
her brood. The only thing it does not do is croak. It too is hacked from its bed as the carnivore knife lips the blood, turning in it in a kind of ecstasy of plenty, a gluttony after a long fast. It is just for this that the knife was created, tempered, heated, its violence beaten into paper-thin force.

At last a little thread is passed into the wound and tied. The 23
monstrous booming fury is stilled by a tiny thread. The tempest is silenced. The operation is over. On the table, the knife lies spent, on its side, the bloody meal smear-dried upon its flanks. The knife rests.

And waits. 24

## IN RETROSPECT

**1.** Someone has said, "Richard Selzer is the writer who brings us closest to the physical side of medicine." It might also be said that of all the writers in this chapter, Selzer is the one who brings us closest to the physical side of death. In what ways does Selzer bring us close to the physical side of death in "The Knife"?

**2.** Death is a very difficult experience to describe, because, as Montaigne says in "Of Practice," those who have seen "what this passage [into death] was . . . have not come back to tell us news of it" (paragraph 3). Examine the different ways in which all the authors in this chapter approach the subject of death in order to give their readers some sense of what death is like.

# 8

# On the National Pastime

*Since the beginning of civilization, people have enjoyed participating in and watching athletic contests. The Olympic Games, for instance, had their foundation in the athletic contests held in Homer's time (c. eighth century* B.C.*). For a number of reasons, more people, in any culture, become avid spectators of sports than regular participants in such games. In the twentieth century, the number of spectators of major athletic events has increased at an astounding rate. Today, not only do we have stadiums where 50,000–100,000 people sit and watch a football game or a soccer match or a baseball game, but we also have television sets that enable thousands, even millions, of additional fans to witness the same contest. Presented in this chapter are essays about only one sport, the sport that has traditionally been dubbed America's "national pastime," baseball. For some reason, more memorable essays have been written about baseball than about any other athletic contest—with the possible exception of boxing. Although other sports draw larger crowds and attract more boisterous fans than baseball does, it is hard to find another sport that attracts so many devoted lovers of the game as baseball does. Every essayist represented in this chapter is a diehard lover of the game. The chapter begins with relatively general essays about the sport and gradually moves to more particular examinations of it, ending with John Updike's classic depiction of Ted Williams's last baseball game in Boston's Fenway Park in September 1960. Enjoy, enjoy!*

# *The Creation Myths of Cooperstown*

**STEPHEN JAY GOULD**

Stephen Jay Gould (1941– ), born in New York City, did his undergraduate work at Antioch College and his graduate work at Columbia University. Gould is usually classified as a paleontologist, someone associated with the branch of geology that deals with prehistoric forms of life (dinosaurs, for instance) through a study of plant and animal fossils. As such, Gould's main preoccupation is with evolutionary theory. At Harvard University, he teaches geology, biology, and the history of science. Since most of his writings are on natural history, it is appropriate that most of his essays have appeared in *Natural History,* the monthly magazine of the American Museum of Natural History. What is notable about the essays Gould wrote for that magazine is that they can be read and understood by the literate public. Consequently, he commands a large and wide-ranging readership. These essays have been collected in four books: *Ever Since Darwin* (1977), *The Panda's Thumb* (1980), *Hen's Teeth and Horses' Toes* (1983), and *The Flamingo's Smile* (1985). "The Creation Myths of Cooperstown," Gould's essay about the evolution of the American sport of baseball, appeared in *Natural History* in 1989 and was reprinted in *The Best American Essays 1990,* edited by Justin Kaplan. This essay exemplifies the prevailing virtues of Gould's writings: his exemplary lucidity, his passion for determining the truth about a phenomenon, his persistent interest in the evolutionary history of whatever he is studying. What ultimately emerges from this scientific study is Gould's love for the game of baseball.

You may either look upon the bright side and say that hope springs eternal or, taking the cynic's part, you may mark P. T. Barnum as an astute psychologist for his proclamation that suckers are born every minute. The end result is the same: you can, Honest Abe notwithstanding, fool most of the people all of the time. How else to explain the long and continuing compendium of hoaxes—from the medieval shroud of Turin to Edwardian Piltdown Man to an ultramodern array of flying saucers and astral powers—eagerly embraced for their consonance with our hopes or their resonance with our fears? 1

Some hoaxes make a sufficient mark upon history that their products acquire the very status initially claimed by fakery—legitimacy (although as an object of human or folkloric, rather than natural, history. I once held the bones of Piltdown Man and felt that I was handling an important item of Western culture). 2

The Cardiff Giant, the best American entry for the title of paleontological hoax turned into cultural history, now lies on display in a shed behind a barn at the Farmer's Museum in Cooperstown, New York. This gypsum man, more than ten feet tall, was "discovered" by 3 workmen digging a well on a farm near Cardiff, New York, in October 1869. Eagerly embraced by a gullible public, and ardently displayed by its creators at fifty cents a pop, the Cardiff Giant caused a brouhaha around Syracuse, and then nationally, for the few months of its active life between exhumation and exposure.

The Cardiff Giant was the brainchild of George Hull, a cigar 4
manufacturer (and general rogue) from Binghamton, New York. He quarried a large block of gypsum from Fort Dodge, Iowa, and shipped it to Chicago, where two marble cutters fashioned the rough likeness of a naked man. Hull made some crude and minimal attempts to give his statue an aged appearance. He chipped off the carved hair and beard because experts told him that such items would not petrify. He drove darning needles into a wooden block and hammered the statue, hoping to simulate skin pores. Finally, he dumped a gallon of sulfuric acid all over his creation to simulate extended erosion. Hull then shipped his giant in a large box back to Cardiff.

Hull, as an accomplished rogue, sensed that his story could not 5
hold for long and, in that venerable and alliterative motto, got out while the getting was good. He sold a three-quarter interest in the Cardiff Giant to a consortium of highly respectable businessmen, including two former mayors of Syracuse. These men raised the statue from its original pit on November 5 and carted it off to Syracuse for display.

The hoax held on for a few more weeks, and Cardiff Giant fever 6
swept the land. Debate raged in newspapers and broadsheets between those who viewed the giant as a petrified fossil and those who regarded it as a statue wrought by an unknown and wondrous prehistoric race. But Hull had left too many tracks—at the gypsum quarries in Fort Dodge, at the carver's studio in Chicago, along the roadways to Cardiff (several people remembered seeing an awfully large box passing on a cart just days before the supposed discovery). By December, Hull was ready to recant, but held his tongue a while longer. Three months later, the two Chicago sculptors came forward, and the Cardiff Giant's brief rendezvous with fame and fortune ended.

The common analogy of the Cardiff Giant with Piltdown Man 7
works only to a point (both were frauds passed off as human fossils) and fails in one crucial respect. Piltdown was cleverly wrought and fooled professionals for forty years, while the Cardiff Giant was preposterous from the start. How could a man turn to solid gypsum while preserving all his soft anatomy, from cheeks to toes to penis? Geologists and paleontologists never accepted Hull's statue. O. C. Marsh, later to achieve great fame as a discoverer of dinosaurs,

echoed a professional consensus in his unambiguous pronouncement: "It is of very recent origin and a decided humbug."

Why, then, was the Cardiff Giant so popular, inspiring a wave of 8
interest and discussion as high as any tide in the affairs of men during its short time in the sun? If the fraud had been well executed, we might attribute this great concern to the dexterity of the hoaxers (just as we grant grudging attention to a few of the most accomplished art fakers for their skills as copyists). But since the Cardiff Giant was so crudely done, we can only attribute its fame to the deep issue, the raw nerve, touched by the subject of its fakery—human origins. Link an absurd concoction to a noble and mysterious subject and you may prevail, at least for a while. My opening reference to P. T. Barnum was not meant sarcastically; he was one of the great practical psychologists of the nineteenth century—and his motto applies with special force to the Cardiff Giant: "No humbug is great without truth at bottom." (Barnum made a copy of the Cardiff Giant and exhibited it in New York City. His mastery of hype and publicity assured that his model far outdrew the "real" fake when the original went on display at a rival establishment in the same city.)

For some reason (to be explored but not resolved in this essay), we 9
are powerfully drawn to the subject of beginnings. We yearn to know about origins, and we readily construct myths when we do not have data (or we suppress data in favor of legend when a truth strikes us as too commonplace). The hankering after an origin myth has always been especially strong for the closest subject of all—the human race. But we extend the same psychic need to our accomplishments and institutions—and we have origin myths and stories for the beginning of hunting, of language, of art, of kindness, of war, of boxing, bowties, and brassieres. Most of us know that the Great Seal of the United States pictures an eagle holding a ribbon reading *e pluribus unum.* Fewer would recognize the motto on the other side (check it out on the back of a dollar bill): *annuit coeptis*—"he smiles on our beginning."

Cooperstown may house the Cardiff Giant, but the fame of this 10
small village in central New York does not rest upon its celebrated namesake, author James Fenimore, or its lovely Lake Otsego or the Farmer's Museum. Cooperstown is "on the map" by virtue of a different origin myth—one more parochial but no less powerful for many Americans than the tales of human beginnings that gave life to the Cardiff Giant. Cooperstown is the sacred founding place in the official myth about the origin of baseball.

Origin myths, since they are so powerful, can engender enor- 11
mous practical problems. Abner Doubleday, as we shall soon see, most emphatically did not invent baseball at Cooperstown in 1839 as the official tale proclaims; in fact, no one invented baseball at any

moment or in any spot. Nonetheless, this creation myth made Cooperstown the official home of baseball, and the Hall of Fame, with its associated museum and library, set its roots in this small village, inconveniently located near nothing in the way of airports or accommodations. We all revel in bucolic imagery on the field of dreams, but what a hassle when tens of thousands line the roads, restaurants, and port-a-potties during the annual Hall of Fame weekend, when new members are enshrined and two major league teams arrive to play an exhibition game at Abner Doubleday Field, a sweet little ten-thousand-seater in the middle of town. Put your compass point at Cooperstown, make your radius at Albany—and you'd better reserve a year in advance if you want any accommodation within the enormous resulting circle.

After a lifetime of curiosity, I finally got the opportunity to wit- 12
ness this annual version of forty students in a telephone booth or twenty circus clowns in a Volkswagen. Since Yaz (former Boston star Carl Yastrzemski to the uninitiated) was slated to receive baseball's Nobel in 1989, and his old team was playing in the Hall of Fame game, and since I'm a transplanted Bostonian (although still a New Yorker and not-so-secret Yankee fan at heart), Tom Heitz, chief of the wonderful baseball library at the Hall of Fame, kindly invited me to joint the sardines in this most lovely of all cans.

The silliest and most tendentious of baseball writing tries to wrest 13
profundity from the spectacle of grown men hitting a ball with a stick by suggesting linkages between the sport and deep issues of morality, parenthood, history, lost innocence, gentleness, and so on, seemingly ad infinitum. (The effort reeks of silliness because baseball is profound all by itself and needs no excuses; people who don't know this are not fans and are therefore unreachable anyway.) When people ask me how baseball imitates life, I can only respond with what the more genteel newspapers used to call a "barnyard epithet," but now, with growing bravery, usually render as "bullbleep." Nonetheless, baseball is a major item of our culture, and it does have a long and interesting history. Any item or institution with these two properties must generate a set of myths and stories (perhaps even some truths) about its beginnings. And the subject of beginnings is the bread and butter of this column on evolution in the broadest sense. I shall make no woolly analogies between baseball and life; this is an essay on the origins of baseball, with some musings on why beginnings of all sorts hold such fascination for us. (I thank Tom Heitz not only for the invitation to Cooperstown at its yearly acme but also for drawing the contrast between creation and evolution stories of baseball, and for supplying much useful information from his unparalleled storehouse.)

Stories about beginnings come in only two basic modes. An 14
entity either has an explicit point of origin, a specific time and place of creation, or else it evolves and has no definable moment of entry into the world. Baseball provides an interesting example of this contrast because we know the answer and can judge received wisdom by the two chief criteria, often opposed, of external fact and internal hope. Baseball evolved from a plethora of previous stick-and-ball games. It has no true Cooperstown and no Doubleday. Yet we seem to prefer the alternative model of origin by a moment of creation—for then we can have heroes and sacred places. By contrasting the myth of Cooperstown with the fact of evolution, we can learn something about our cultural practices and their frequent disrespect for truth.

The official story about the beginning of baseball is a creation 15
myth, and a review of the reasons and circumstances of its fabrication may give us insight into the cultural appeal of stories in this mode. A. G. Spalding, baseball's first great pitcher during his early career, later founded the sporting goods company that still bears his name and became one of the great commercial moguls of America's gilded age. As publisher of the annual *Spalding's Official Base Ball Guide,* he held maximal power in shaping both public and institutional opinion on all facets of baseball and its history. As the sport grew in popularity, and the pattern of two stable major leagues coalesced early in our century, Spalding and others felt the need for clarification (or merely for codification) of opinion on the hitherto unrecorded origins of an activity that truly merited its common designation as America's "national pastime."

In 1907, Spalding set up a blue ribbon committee to investigate 16
and resolve the origins of baseball. The committee, chaired by A. G. Mills and including several prominent businessmen and two senators who had also served as presidents of the National League, took much testimony but found no smoking gun for a beginning. Then, in July 1907, Spalding himself transmitted to the committee a letter from an Abner Graves, then a mining engineer in Denver, who reported that Abner Doubleday had, in 1839, interrupted a marbles game behind the tailor's shop in Cooperstown, New York, to draw a diagram of a baseball field, explain the rules of the game, and designate the activity by its modern name of "base ball" (then spelled as two words).

Such "evidence" scarcely inspired universal confidence, but the 17
commission came up with nothing better—and the Doubleday myth, as we shall soon see, was eminently functional. Therefore, in 1908, the Mills Commission reported its two chief findings: first, "that base ball had its origins in the United States"; and second, "that the first scheme for playing it, according to the best evidence available to date, was devised by Abner Doubleday, at Cooperstown, New York, in

1839." This "best evidence" consisted only of "a circumstantial statement by a reputable gentleman"—namely Graves's testimony as reported by Spalding himself.

When cited evidence is so laughably insufficient, one must seek 18
motivations other than concern for truth value. The key to underlying reasons stands in the first conclusion of Mills's committee: hoopla and patriotism (cardboard version) decreed that a national pastime must have an indigenous origin. The idea that baseball had evolved from a wide variety of English stick-and-ball games—although true—did not suit the mythology of a phenomenon that had become so quintessentially American. In fact, Spalding had long been arguing, in an amiable fashion, with Henry Chadwick, another pioneer and entrepreneur of baseball's early years. Chadwick, born in England, had insisted for years that baseball had developed from the British stick-and-ball game called rounders; Spalding had vociferously advocated a purely American origin, citing the Colonial game of "one old cat" as a distant precursor, but holding that baseball itself represented something so new and advanced that a pinpoint of origin—a creation myth—must be sought.

Chadwick considered the matter of no particular importance, argu- 19
ing (with eminent justice) that an English origin did not "detract one iota from the merit of its now being unquestionably a thoroughly American field sport, and a game too, which is fully adapted to the American character." (I must say that I have grown quite fond of Mr. Chadwick, who certainly understood evolutionary change and its chief principle that historic origin need not match contemporary function.) Chadwick also viewed the committee's whitewash as a victory for his side. He labeled the Mills report as "a masterful piece of special pleading which lets my dear old friend Albert [Spalding] escape a bad defeat. The whole matter was a joke between Albert and myself."

We may accept the psychic need for an indigenous creation myth, 20
but why Abner Doubleday, a man with no recorded tie to the game and who, in the words of Donald Honig, probably "didn't know a baseball from a kumquat"? I had wondered about this for years, but only ran into the answer serendipitously during a visit to Fort Sumter in the harbor of Charleston, South Carolina. There, an exhibit on the first skirmish of the Civil War points out that Abner Doubleday, as captain of the Union artillery, had personally sighted and given orders for firing the first responsive volley following the initial Confederate attack on the fort. Doubleday later commanded divisions at Antietam and Fredericksburg, became at least a minor hero at Gettysburg, and retired as a brevet major general. In fact, A. G. Mills, head of the commission, had served as part of an honor guard when Doubleday's body lay in state in New York City, following his death in 1893.

If you have to have an American hero, could anyone be better 21
than the man who fired the first shot (in defense) of the Civil War? Needless to say, this point was not lost on the members of Mills's committee. Spalding, never one to mince words, wrote to the committee when submitting Graves's dubious testimony: "It certainly appeals to the American pride to have had the great national game of base ball created and named by a Major General in the United States Army." Mills then concluded in his report: "Perhaps in the years to come, in view of the hundreds of thousands of people who are devoted to base ball, and the millions who will be, Abner Doubleday's fame will rest evenly, if not quite as much, upon the fact that he was its inventor . . . as upon his brilliant and distinguished career as an officer in the Federal Army."

And so, spurred by a patently false creation myth, the Hall of 22
Fame stands in the most incongruous and inappropriate locale of a charming little town in central New York. Incongruous and inappropriate, but somehow wonderful. Who needs another museum in the cultural maelstroms (and summer doldrums) of New York, Boston, or Washington? Why not a major museum in a beautiful and bucolic setting? And what could be more fitting than the spatial conjunction of two great American origin myths—the Cardiff Giant and the Doubleday Fable? Thus, I too am quite content to treat the myth gently, while honesty requires fessing up. The exhibit on Doubleday in the Hall of Fame Museum sets just the right tone in its caption: "In the hearts of those who love baseball, he is remembered as the lad in the pasture where the game was invented. Only cynics would need to know more." Only in the hearts; not in the minds.

Baseball evolved. Since the evidence is so clear (as epitomized 23
below), we must ask why these facts have been so little appreciated for so long, and why a creation myth like the Doubleday story ever gained a foothold. Two major reasons have conspired: first, the positive block of our attraction to creation stories; second, the negative impediment of unfamiliar sources outside the usual purview of historians. English stick-and-ball games of the nineteenth century can be roughly classified into two categories along social lines. The upper and educated classes played cricket, and the history of this sport is copiously documented because the literati write about their own interests, and because the activities of men in power are well recorded (and constitute virtually all of history, in the schoolboy version). But the ordinary pastimes of rural and urban working people can be well nigh invisible in conventional sources of explicit commentary. Working people played a different kind of stick-and-ball game, existing in various forms and designated by many names, including "rounders" in western England, "feeder" in London, and "base ball"

in southern England. For a large number of reasons, forming the essential difference between cricket and baseball, cricket matches can last up to several days (a batsman, for example, need not run after he hits the ball and need not expose himself to the possibility of being put out every time he makes contact). The leisure time of working people does not come in such generous gobs, and the lower-class stick-and-ball games could not run more than a few hours.

Several years ago, at the Victoria and Albert Museum in London, 24
I learned an important lesson from an excellent exhibit on the late-nineteenth-century history of the British music hall. This is my favorite period (Darwin's century, after all), and I consider myself tolerably well informed on cultural trends of the time. I can sing any line from any of the Gilbert and Sullivan operas (a largely middle-class entertainment), and I know the general drift of high cultural interests in literature and music. But here was a whole world of entertainment for millions, a world with its heroes, its stars, its top forty songs, its gaudy theaters—and I knew nothing, absolutely nothing, about it. I felt chagrined, but my ignorance had an explanation beyond personal insensitivity (and the exhibit had been mounted explicitly to counteract the selective invisibility of certain important trends in history). The music hall was the chief entertainment of Victorian working classes, and the history of working people is often invisible in conventional written sources. It must be rescued and reconstituted from different sorts of data; in this case, from posters, playbills, theater accounts, persistence of some songs in the oral tradition (most were never published as sheet music), recollections of old-timers who knew the person who knew the person . . .

The early history of baseball—the stick-and-ball game of working 25
people—presents the same problem of conventional invisibility—and the same promise of rescue by exploration of unusual sources. Work continues and intensifies as the history of sport becomes more and more academically respectable, but the broad outlines (and much fascinating detail) are not well established. As the upper classes played a codified and well-documented cricket, working people played a largely unrecorded and much more diversified set of stick-and-ball games ancestral to baseball. Many sources, including primers and boys' manuals, depict games recognizable as precursors to baseball well into the early eighteenth century. Occasional references even spill over into high culture. In *Northanger Abbey,* written at the close of the eighteenth century, Jane Austen remarks: "It was not very wonderful that Catherine . . . should prefer cricket, base ball, riding on horseback, and running about the country, at the age of fourteen, to books." As this quotation illustrates, the name of the game is no more Doubleday's than the form of play.

These ancestral styles of baseball came to America with early 26
settlers and were clearly well established by Colonial times. But they were driven ever further underground by Puritan proscriptions of sport for adults. They survived largely as children's games and suffered the double invisibility of location among the poor and the young. But two major reasons brought these games into wider repute and led to a codification of standard forms quite close to modern baseball between the 1820s and the 1850s. First, a set of social reasons, from the decline of Puritanism to increased concern about health and hygiene in crowded cities, made sport an acceptable activity for adults. Second, middle-class and professional people began to take up these early forms of baseball, and with this upward social drift came teams, leagues, written rules, uniforms, stadiums, guidebooks: in short, all the paraphernalia of conventional history.

I am not arguing that these early games could be called baseball 27
with a few trivial differences (evolution means substantial change, after all), but only that they stand in a complex lineage, better called a nexus, from which modern baseball emerged, eventually in a codified and canonical form. In those days before instant communication, every region had its own version, just as every set of outdoor steps in New York City generated a different form of stoopball in my youth, without threatening the basic identity of the game. These games, most commonly called town ball, differed from modern baseball in substantial ways. In the Massachusetts Game, a codification of the late 1850s drawn up by ballplayers in New England towns, four bases and three strikes identify the genus, but many specifics are strange by modern standards. The bases were made of wooden stakes projecting four feet from the ground. The batter (called the striker) stood between first and fourth base. Sides changed after a single out. One hundred runs (call tallies), not higher score after a specified number of innings, spelled victory. The field contained no foul lines, and balls hit in any direction were in play. Most importantly, runners were not tagged out but were retired by "plugging," that is, being hit with a thrown ball while running between bases. Consequently, since baseball has never been a game for masochists, balls were soft—little more than rags stuffed into leather covers—and could not be hit far. (Tom Heitz has put together a team of Cooperstown worthies to re-create town ball for interested parties and prospective opponents. Since few others groups are well schooled in this lost art, Tom's team hasn't been defeated in ages, if ever. "We are the New York Yankees of town ball," he told me. His team is called, quite appropriately in general but especially for this essay, The Cardiff Giants.)

Evolution is continual change, but not insensibly gradual transi- 28
tion; in any continuum, some points are always more interesting than others. The conventional nomination for most salient point in this

particular continuum goes to Alexander Joy Cartwright, leader of a New York team that started to play in lower Manhattan, eventually rented some changing rooms and a field in Hoboken (just a quick ferry ride across the Hudson), and finally drew up a set of rules in 1845, later known as the New York Game. Cartwright's version of town ball is much closer to modern baseball, and many clubs followed his rules—for standardization became ever more vital as the popularity of early baseball grew and opportunity for play between regions increased. In particular, Cartwright introduced two key innovations that shaped the disparate forms of town ball into a semblance of modern baseball. First, he eliminated plugging and introduced tagging in the modern sense; the ball could now be made harder, and hitting for distance became an option. Second, he introduced foul lines, again in the modern sense, as his batter stood at a home plate and had to hit the ball within lines defined from home through first and third bases. The game could now become a spectator sport because areas close to the field but out of action could, for the first time, be set aside for onlookers.

The New York Game may be the highlight of a continuum, but it 29
provides no origin myth for baseball. Cartwright's rules were followed in various forms of town ball. His New York Game still included many curiosities by modern standards (twenty-one runs, called aces, won the game, and balls caught on one bounce were outs). Moreover, our modern version is an amalgam of the New York Game plus other town ball traditions, not Cartwright's baby grown up by itself. Several features of the Massachusetts Game entered the modern version in preference to Cartwright's rules. Balls had to be caught on the fly in Boston, and pitchers threw overhand, not underhand as in the New York Game (and in professional baseball until the 1880s).

Scientists often lament that so few people understand Darwin 30
and the principles of biological evolution. But the problem goes deeper. Too few people are comfortable with evolutionary modes of explanation in any form, I do not know why we tend to think so fuzzily in this area, but one reason must reside in our social and psychic attraction to creation myths in preference to evolutionary stories—for creation myths, as noted before, identify heroes and sacred places, while evolutionary stories provide no palpable, particular thing as a symbol for reverence, worship, or patriotism. Still, we must remember—and an intellectual's most persistent and nagging responsibility lies in making this simple point over and over again, however noxious and bothersome we render ourselves thereby—that truth and desire, fact and comfort, have no necessary, or even preferred, correlation (so rejoice when they do coincide).

To state the most obvious example in our current political tur- 31
moil. Human growth is a continuum, and no creation myth can

define an instant for the origin of an individual life. Attempts by anti-abortionists to designate the moment of fertilization as the beginning of personhood make no sense in scientific terms (and also violate a long history of social definitions that traditionally focused on the quickening, or detected movement, of the fetus in the womb). I will admit—indeed, I emphasized as a key argument of this essay—that not all points on a continuum are equal. Fertilization is a more interesting moment than most, but it no more provides a clean definition of origin than the most interesting moment of baseball's continuum—Cartwright's codification of the New York Game—defines the beginning of our national pastime. Baseball evolved and people grow; both are continua without definable points of origin. Probe too far back and you reach absurdity, for you will see Nolan Ryan on the hill when the first ape hit a bird with a stone; or you will define both masturbation and menstruation as murder—and who will then cast the first stone? Look for something in the middle, and you find nothing but continuity—always a meaningful "before," and always a more modern "after." (Please note that I am not stating an opinion on the vexatious question of abortion—an ethical issue that can only be decided in ethical terms. I only point out that one side has rooted its case in an argument from science that is not only entirely irrelevant to the proper realm of resolution but also happens to be flat-out false in trying to devise a creation myth within a continuum.)

And besides, why do we prefer creation myths to evolutionary stories? I find all the usual reasons hollow. Yes, heroes and shrines are all very well, but is there not grandeur in the sweep of continuity? Shall we revel in a story for all humanity that may include the sacred ball courts of the Aztecs, and perhaps, for all we know, a group of *Homo erectus* hitting rocks or skulls with a stick or a femur? Or shall we halt beside the mythical Abner Doubleday, standing behind the tailor's shop in Cooperstown, and say "behold the man"—thereby violating truth and, perhaps even worse, extinguishing both thought and wonder? 32

**IN RETROSPECT**

**1.** This essay is primarily about the origins of the game of baseball. Why, then, does Gould spend paragraphs 3–8 talking about the hoax of the Cardiff Giant?

**2.** Gould says that in his essay he is going to explore the contrast between creation myths and evolution stories about the origins of baseball. Having read this essay, compile a list of the similarities and differences that you detected in the facts, interpretations, and purposes of creation myths and evolution stories of baseball. What effect, if any, does the knowledge of *both* have on your interpretation of or response to baseball? How might that effect be altered if an event other than baseball were being discussed? Consider other origins—for instance, origins of humanity, the church, the Bible, a particular law, or a Shakespeare play. What impact does the existence of a creation myth, an evolution story, or both have on your interpretations of these things? Is there any harm in choosing to believe one type of origin over another—especially when facts about origins are not certain? Explain.

# *Confessions of a Sports Nut*

**WILFRID SHEED**

Wilfrid Sheed (1930– ) is a member of a noted British family of writers and publishers. His mother, Maisie Ward, is the esteemed biographer of G. K. Chesterton, John Henry Newman, and Robert Browning and the cofounder, with her husband, Frank Sheed, of the publishing house Sheed & Ward. Though born in London, Sheed came to the United States in 1940 and, during his teenage years, became fascinated with American sports, especially baseball. His aspirations to participate in sports were cut short, however, when he fell victim to polio. After a lengthy convalescence, he returned to England and obtained a B.A. and an M.A. at Lincoln College, Oxford. Returning to the United States in 1947, Sheed served as a movie or drama critic for such magazines as *Jubilee, Commonweal,* and *Esquire.* He gained steadily in stature and reputation as a novelist with the publication of *The Hack* (1963), *Office Politics* (1966), *Max Jamison* (1970), *People Will Always Be Kind* (1973), and *The Boys of Winter* (1987). In 1972, he became a member of the editorial board of the Book-of-the-Month Club. With his uncommon mastery of diction and syntax, Sheed has become one of the most trenchant prose stylists on the contemporary scene. In the following essay, he tells us how he became addicted to sports, especially baseball.

They took away my cricket bat at the age of nine and told me I 1
wouldn't be needing it any more. Out of kindness they didn't tell me I wouldn't need my soccer ball, either. Otherwise, I don't think I would have come to America at all. I would have lied about my age and joined the horse marines.

Exile is an ugly business at any age. Harold Pinter, the play- 2
wright, carted his bat with him all over England to remind him of the past (he must have been eight when he started out). I was forced to hand mine over at the frontier, and with it the long summer evenings, the boys with the dangling suspenders, the whole Fanny-by-

gaslight world of cricket; my life for the next few years would be a hunt for fresh symbols, a bat and ball I could believe in.

Baseball dismayed me at first blush almost as much as the big cars 3
and the big faces in the street. In the dictionary of the senses *cricket* stood for twilight, silence, flutter. (See also *Swans*). *Baseball* equalled noonday, harsh, noise, clatter. (See *Geese*). That was how it looked at first—boys milling around dusty lots jabbering and hitching at their pants. But as I kept craning from train windows and car windows in my first days in America, I noticed something promising: that nothing ever seemed to be happening at that particular moment—the same basic principle as cricket. The pitcher peering in to get the sign, the ritual chant of the infield, the whispered consultations and then, if you were very lucky, a foul tip, before you were whisked out of range. Baseball was not as busy as it seemed but lived, like the mother game, on pregnant pauses. This, plus the fact that it happened to be in season and you played it with a bat and ball, made it look like my best bet.

Unfortunately, the place where we first lived was an almost 4
deserted village, so there was no one to play with. There was one boy about a mile down the road. He straightened out my batting stance and filled me in on the First World War, too, but he was five years older than I, with his own life to live, so I couldn't bother him too often.

Instead, I became perhaps the outstanding solitary baseball 5
player of my generation, whaling fungoes down the long, narrow garden and plodding after them, chattering to myself and whaling them back again. Anything pulled or sliced got lost, so my first encounter with American botany was staring sightless through it, hunting the tawny baseball. When that palled, I would chalk a strike zone on the garage door and lob a tennis ball at it. Already I had the style, though God knows where it came from: the mock aggression and inscrutable loneliness. Gary Cooper high on a hill, twitching his cap, shaking off the sign: nodding, rearing, firing. Clunk, against the old garage door. The manner came with my first glove.

Another thing that stoked my love affair was the statistics. I like a 6
game that has plenty of statistics, the more inconsequential the better, and I began soaking up baseball records like a sea sponge before I even knew what they meant. I liked the way you could read *around* baseball, without ever getting to the game at all. I devoured a long piece in the old *Satevepost* about Hank Greenberg, baseball's most eligible bachelor, and another about young Ted Williams, who only shaved twice a week. Official baseball sneaked up on me through its trivia. My learned friend up the road took me, at last, to an actual game at Shibe Park, and I was hooked for fair. It was the St. Louis

Browns vs. the Philadelphia Athletics, hardly an offering to stir the blood, but more than enough to stir mine. The Brownies built up a big lead, but the A's, led by Wally Moses and Bob Johnson, staged one of their rare comebacks and pulled it out of the fire. The sand-lot games I had seen so far had not been beautiful to look at, only intellectually interesting (I used phrases like that occasionally, a real little snot in some ways); but here we had something as elegant as the Radio City Rockettes—explosively elegant and almost as fussily stylish as cricket.

Baseball became my constant, obsessive companion after that. Up 7
and down the garden, faster and faster, first as Dick Siebert, the A's first baseman, then as Arky Vaughan, whose name and dour appearance I fancied, then right-handed as Jimmy Foxx. And at night I played out whole games in my head, in which I was always the quiet, unobtrusive professional (I detested showboating) who hit the penultimate single or made a key play in the *eighth* inning. It was as if I'd brought my cricket bat with me, after all.

The point about this was that it was all what D. H. Lawrence 8
would have called "baseball in the head." When I came to play with other boys in the next few years, I continued my solipsistic ways, trotting out quietly to my position, chewing all the gum that my mouth would hold and gazing around with mild, shrewd eyes; or, for a time, grinning like Stan Hack, the Cub third baseman—a steady player on a steady club, the way I wanted to spend eternity.

A sociologist might (and I would probably agree with him, having 9
just made him up) explain my choice of this particular type of athlete quite simply. Baseball was my social passport, and a slight averageness is good on a passport. It means that the officials look at you less closely. Who is that guy over there? Maybe he'd like to play. Say—he's quietly efficient, isn't he? I remember standing around picnic sites and county fairs, wistfully, with my glove half concealed under my arm as if I didn't mean anything by it. I was slightly ashamed of my accent and bitterly ashamed of my first name; but baseball did not judge you by those things. The Statue of Liberty, bat in hand, said, "Try this, kid."

Sometimes, magically, it happened. I was rather light for a ball- 10
player in spite of weighing myself a lot. I knew the names of all the light ballplayers (the Waner brothers were a special comfort), but still, 80 pounds was 80 pounds, and even with the most graceful swing in town I could rarely nudge the ball past second base. However, I waited out numerous walks, if there happened to be an umpire, fielded as well as the pebbles allowed and always looked a little better than the clumsy lout they had buried in right field. Afterwards they went their way, into houses I knew nothing about, to a life that contained other things besides baseball; and I went mine.

In the fall of '41 I left for boarding school. Although the baseball season was still raging, I found that it was all over as far as my new school was concerned. I felt as if I had lost a friend. My companion of the long, silent summer was replaced by a harsh, grunting affair, where people shouted like drill sergeants and made a big thing of getting in shape, being in shape, staying in shape. Suck in your gut, get those knees up. 11

I saw right away that football was the enemy. If 80 pounds was of dubious value in summer, it was downright ludicrous in fall. Beyond that, I distrusted the atmosphere of the game, all that crouching and barking. It was a side of America that might have appealed to a little German boy, but hardly to me. The essential solitude of baseball gave way to the false heartiness, the just-feel-that-stomach toughness. We only played touch football that year but, even so, managed to make a military thing of it. 12

God knows how, I came to love football anyway. The finished product, the game itself, transcended all the midweek drivel. I had seen the previous winter one game, in which Whizzer (now Sir Whizzer or Lord Byron) White scored two touchdowns against the woebegone Eagles of Philadelphia, and I guess I liked it all right. I drew some crayon pictures of it, anyway, showing little Davey O'Brien being smothered by Lions. 13

But there was an actuality to the game as played that was quite different from the game as watched or the game as planned. I became second-string quarterback in our rather peculiar school and got to run back a kickoff in a quasi-real game. Huddled in the lee of a gland case, a 250-pound eighth-grader, I made our only considerable gain of the day. I relished the swooping, shifting patterns that had to be diagnosed instantly, the hilarity of each yard gained, the pleasure of doing something you've practiced and getting it right. 14

It was quite different from my dreamy, poetic, half-mad relationship with baseball. This was crisp and outgoing, hep-two-three-four, and based on the realities of the game, not on some dream of it. Yet it filled the same social purpose. It became a shortcut, or substitute, for mastering the local culture. I still didn't know how to talk to these people but while I was playing I didn't have to. The soundless pat on the back, the "nice going, Sheed"—you could be any manner of clod, or even an English boy, and it didn't matter. I remember blocking a punt with my stomach and writhing in agony, and feeling it was worth it for the brief respect I commanded. 15

This was canceled on another occasion, which is still almost too painful to describe, and which I write here only that it may be of help to others: that is, to any 80-pound English refugees who happen to be reading this. The setting was a pickup game played in semi-darkness. 16

The agreed-on goal line was a fuzzy patch of trees off in the middle distance, I'm still not sure where. My team was losing 12–0, and it was understood that the next play would be the last one: hence meaningless, a lame-duck exercise. Their man threw a long pass. I intercepted it and stepped backward, some place in the area of the goal line.

Triumphant hands were clapped on me, and I was told that I had 17
just handed two points to the enemy. Would (and I have woulded this would often since) that Zeus had smitten my tongue at that moment. The game would have been forgotten–12–0, 14–0, who cared–and I would have been spared three lousy years. As it was, I said in fruitiest Cockney, "How was I supposed to know where the goal line was?"

Wrong thing to say. I heard no more about it that day. The saying 18
went underground for a while, and when it emerged the context had been garbled slightly. I was now alleged to have run the wrong way, like Riegel in the Rose Bowl, and to have capped it, in what was now a horrible whine: "'Ow was Aye suppowsed to know which why the gowl was!" Well, O.K., I was used to that by now, in an Irish school. But this legend so grabbed the popular imagination that I was still hearing it three years later from boys who had just entered the school.

The moral of this tragedy is that sport as a Julien Sorel passport 19
has its treacherous side. It can bestow curses as carelessly as blessings, and the curses stick. However, those first two years would have been grim without sports, which played an unnaturally large part in my life, and still do in my mind, because they were, at times, all I had.

As to my life as a fan, that, too, was a social passport, and 20
therefore doctored slightly. "Hey, how come you know so much about baseball?" could be a friendly question or it could be weighted with menace. Like a professional dumb blonde, I found there were circles where it paid to keep my knowledge to myself, even though it burned in the mouth and even though some fat fool was deluding the crowd with wrong statistics.

It was, though, an acceptable subject, and there weren't too many 21
of those. I did not understand cars, had not been camping last summer, had a non-cooking mother: subject after subject broke in my hands. Only sports could be trusted. Fate had presented me with three frowsy teams to talk about: the Phillies, A's, and Eagles, all usually cemented into their respective last places. (I was foolishly pleased when a friend said, "Don't the A's usually finish around sixth?" The A's never finished anywhere near sixth.). Pennsylvania University was some small consolation–I saw it beat Army, Harvard,

Cornell on various weekends—but hardly enough. My own social position was too sensitive to burden with three risible teams, so I decided to diversify. I took on board the Brooklyn Dodgers and the Washington Redskins. Sammy Baugh was a man I could identify with. Lean and steel-eyed, my winter self.

On balance, I would say that playing games didn't do much for my character. It gives one a highly specialized confidence and a highly qualified cooperativeness, but in return it makes one incurably childish. Intellectually, it teaches you that you can't argue with a fact, a mixed blessing. However, being a Brooklyn fan was useful. It taught me to suffer. The Dodgers immediately and definitely broke my heart. I had barely become a fan when Mickey Owen dropped the third strike and gave a World Series game away. Then the next season, 1942, Peter Reiser banged his head on the wall and the Bums blew a ten-game lead over the Cardinals. The Dodgers came to Philadelphia on July 4 strutting like gods and pasted the local scarecrows 14–0 and 5–4. Reiser hit the neatest, mellowest little home run you ever saw. Medwick, Camilli—players twice as big, twice as regal as any since. 22

On the Sunday after Labor Day the Cardinals came in. They had beaten the Dodgers the day previous, on Whitey Kurowski's home run, to reach first place for the first time. The Dodgers were playing two with Cincinnati. There was strangling doom in the air. I knew, everyone knew, what was going to happen. All afternoon I watched the scoreboard. The Phillies were managing to split with the Cards, an unlikely reprieve, but the Dodgers went down slowly, inexorably to total defeat. 23

I was insane with grief. It was worse than the fall of France, and the feelings were not dissimilar: the same sense of irreversible momentum and crushed dreams. It seemed strange even then that a misfortune suffered by a random collection of strangers could hurt so much. Yet for days I was sick with sorrow and actually tried to forget about baseball: a trick I wasn't to master for another twenty years. I recovered in time to root lustily for the Cardinals in the World Series. A defeat for the Yankees was already sweeter than a victory for anyone else. Hence, there was an element of vindictive nihilism in my baseball thinking, which was to run riot when Walter O'Malley took his team from Brooklyn to L.A. some sixteen years later, and which has dominated since that time. 24

In the fall of '43 we moved to New York. The Philadelphia hermitage was over. No more mowing lawns and hoeing vegetable beds in our victory garden to pay my way to Shibe Park, no more early-morning trolley rides to Frankford and long subways rides from there in order to get the whole of batting practice and two games for 25 my buck and a quarter. I had not realized what a grueling regimen this was until I took a friend with a medium interest in baseball along for company. Even though we saw Ted Williams strike out three times on the knuckle ball and then hit a home run in the tenth, my friend never once mentioned baseball again.

But now I was in New York, the capital of baseball, and my appetite raged wantonly, like some Thomas Wolfe character in Europe, prowling the streets and roaring. In those days every barbershop had a radio, every butcher shop—the whole block was a symphony of baseball. 26

To be young in Paris, to be coming up for thirteen in New York! Unfortunately, the game itself was not in such hot shape right then. The stars were wafting, or drafting, away and being replaced by squinting, shambling defectives like the ones I had left behind in Philadelphia. The Dodgers tried out a sixteen-year-old shortstop. The lordly Yankees were reduced to the likes of Joe Buzas and Ossie Grimes. The St. Louis Browns actually had a one-armed centerfielder. The hottest player in town was an aging retread called Phil Weintraub. You had to love baseball to survive those years. 27

But I liked going to the parks anyway. They offered the cultural continuity of churches. You could slip into one in a strange city and pick up the ceremony right away. College football stadiums made me nervous with their brutal cliquishness, and professional football stadiums always gave me rotten seats—the same one, it seemed like, high up and to the left, in back of the goal line. But ball parks were home and still are, a place where I understand what my neighbors are up to, even after a year abroad. 28

The football scene was a slight improvement over Godforsaken Philadelphia. The wartime Giants must have been one of the dullest teams in history, with their off-tackle smashes and their defensive genius. But they were usually able to make a game of it. I saw Don Hutson *throw* a touchdown pass off an end-around reverse, and my hero, Sammy Baugh, quick-kick 66 yards to the Giants' four. You didn't seem to see things like that in Philadelphia. 29

My own playing career mooned along all this while, striking me, at least, as promising. I had become a spottily effective left end, running solemn little down-and-outs and tackling with bravura (I found I wasn't afraid of head-on tackles, which put one in the elite automatically). I discovered that basketball yielded to humorless determination better than most games and I once succeeded in sinking seventeen foul shots in a row. But the game had no great emotional interest; it was more like a bar game of skill that whiles away the evenings. I liked the hot gymnasiums and the feel of the floor underfoot, and it was fun fretting about the score, but the game left no 30 resonance afterwards. Fast breaks and the swishing of the strings—a thin collection of memories.

Baseball continued to intoxicate, worse than ever; tossing the ball 31
among snowdrifts at the beginning of spring, the sweet feeling in the hands when you connected and sent it scudding over the winter grass, the satisfaction of turning your back on a fly and turning round again in more or less the right place to catch it. I had grown off my 80-pound base and was now a gawky fanatic of 105 or so; willing to field for hours, taking my glove everywhere, pounding an endless pocket into it, scavenging for a game.

This sport, which I had needed so badly on arrival, was now 32
making me pay for its favors. I was enslaved to it, like Emil Jennings to Marlene Dietrich. My life had become seriously lopsided. I refused to go swimming because it interfered with my career—tightened the skin on the chest and all that. I looked at the countryside with blank eyes. My father admonished me to throw away my baseball magazines after one reading, but I hid them like an addict. I don't recall reading anything else at all. Nothing, not even the war, interested me any more.

In my new neighborhood my passport was honored handsomely. 33
I was the best shortstop, in an admittedly skimpy field, and I was always sure of a game. I didn't bother to make friends in any other context, seeing myself as an aloof professional who never mixed business with pleasure. I took an ascetic view of people who goofed off and had a mortal horror of games degenerating into horseplay. "Come on, let's play ball," I would say austerely, like some Dominican friar behind on his autos-da-fé. My father, who spent half the war in each country, took me to see a cricket match in Van Cortlandt Park, and it struck me as a vague, ramshackle game. We got into a discussion over the concept "not cricket." It seemed to me ridiculous not to take every advantage you could in a game. The slyness and bluff of baseball were as beautiful to me as the winging ball.

How long this would have lasted, I have no way of knowing. I 34
might have snapped out of it in a year or two, under pressure of girls and such, or followed it glumly until some awakening in a Class A minor league. I contracted polio at the age of fourteen, and my career was over just like that. I ran a fever and for the first couple of nights I could see nothing in it but sports images: football highlights, baseball highlights, boxing (I was the only boy in school who had rooted for Louis over Conn, so I had the films of the fight in my repertoire), all rushing through my head like the Gadarene swine on their way to the sea. I was allowed to switch sports, but not the main subject. My obsession had to play itself out.

When calmness returned, I found my interest in sports had fix- 35
ated, frozen, at that particular point. I was to remain a fourteen-year-old fan for the next twenty years. I continued thinking that the life of a professional ballplayer was attractive long after a sensible man would have abandoned the notion. I returned to England for a while and became a cricket nut all over again.

Yet it wasn't really the same. I knew now that my bat had been 36
taken for good and I had better find something else to do. Sports still raged, but in one lobe only. The other was liberated, free to grow up if it could. And my interest in sport was more house-trained and philosophical: no more wrist-slashing over defeat, no more hero worship, an occasional thin smile while losing at pool—all in all, about as much maturity as you can expect from a hardened sports addict.

But when I see some Negro or Puerto Rican kid making basket 37
catches or running like an arrow, breaking the language barrier and waving his passport, I feel like saying O.K., but don't take it too seriously, don't let this be all. Sports are socially useful, up to a strictly limited point. I stopped being a foreigner the moment I blocked that kick, and a moment is sometimes all it takes. But blocking kicks or whacking baseballs only gets you so far. (Don't bring those muddy boots in the living room.) The mockery starts up again the minute you leave the park.

I thought sports had made me an American but in some ways 38
they actually retarded the process. I played them like an English colonial officer, exhausting himself with some amusing native game and missing too many other things. Having said that, let me double back on it: if you had to limit yourself to one aspect of American life, the showdowns between pitcher and hitter, quarterback and defense, hustler and fish, would tell you more about politics, manners, style in this country than any one other thing. Sports constitute a code, a language of the emotions, and a tourist who skips the stadiums will not recoup his losses at Lincoln Center and Grant's Tomb.

**IN RETROSPECT**

**1.** With the title of this selection, Sheed puts his essay in the tradition of confession literature, a genre that goes back as far as the *Confessions* of Saint Augustine in the Middle Ages. Confession literature has always appealed to a large audience of readers. In the United States, during the first half of the twentieth century, a number of confession magazines were published to satisfy the appetite for this kind of literature. Taking the place of these magazines in the second half of the twentieth century have been certain talk shows, such as those hosted by Phil Donohue, Oprah Winfrey, and Geraldo Rivera. While Sheed's confessions are not of the lurid sort that frequently populate the confessions magazines and the talk shows, they are revelations about a certain aspect of his life. Why do people read "confessions"? Why do people read narratives—such as those in this chapter—that deal with someone's participation in sports?

**2.** As this chapter's headnotes point out, Gould is a scientific writer, and Sheed is a literary writer. Compare and contrast the two essays by these writers. How do their professional dispositions affect their depictions of baseball?

## *Fathers, Daughters, and the Magic of Baseball*

**DORIS KEARNS GOODWIN**

Doris Kearns Goodwin (1943–        ) was born in Rockville Centre, New York. She took an undergraduate degree, magna cum laude, at Colby College in 1964 and a Ph.D. in political science at Harvard University in 1968. In the early 1960s, Goodwin was an intern in the State Department in Washington, D.C., served for a while as a special assistant to Willard Wirtz, and then became a special assistant to President Lyndon B. Johnson, who later chose her as his official biographer. Goodwin published her unflattering biography of him, *Lyndon Johnson and the American Dream,* in 1976. In 1987 she published her highly praised biography *The Fitzgeralds and the Kennedys: An American Saga.* Goodwin has served as the host of a television show and as a political analyst for the news desk at another TV station. Since 1969, she has been a professor of government at Harvard University. "Fathers, Daughters, and the Magic of Baseball" was first published in the *Boston Globe* in 1986. Just as Joyce Carol Oates was introduced to boxing by her father and later wrote a book of essays about boxing, Goodwin was introduced to baseball by her father—and here reminisces about those magical days of summer when, as a young girl, she lived and relived baseball games with her father.

The game of baseball has always been linked in my mind with the mystic texture of childhood, with the sounds and smells of summer nights and with the memories of my father. 1

My love for baseball was born the first day my father took me to Ebbets Field in Brooklyn. Riding in the trolley car, he seemed as excited as I was. He never stopped talking; now describing for me the street in Brooklyn where he had grown up, now recalling the first 2 game he had been taken to by his own father, now recapturing for me his favorite memories from the Dodgers of his youth—the Dodgers of Casey Stengel, Zach Wheat, and Jimmy Johnston.

3 In the evenings, when my dad came home from work, we would sit together on our porch and relive the events of that afternoon's game, which I had so carefully preserved in the large, red scorebook I'd been given for my seventh birthday. I can still remember how proud I was to have mastered all those strange and wonderful symbols that permitted me to recapture, in miniature form, the every movement of Jackie Robinson and Pee Wee Reese, Duke Snider and Gil Hodges. But the real power of that scorebook lay in the responsibility it entailed. For all though my childhood, my father kept from me the knowledge that the daily papers printed daily box scores, allowing me to believe that without my personal renderings of all those games he missed while he was at work, he would be unable to follow our team in the only proper way a team should be followed—day by day, inning by inning. In other words, without me, his love for baseball would be forever incomplete.

4 To be sure, there were risks involved in making a commitment as boundless as mine. For me, as for all too many Brooklyn fans, the presiding memory of "the boys of summer" was the memory of the final playoff game in 1951 against the Giants. Going into the ninth the Dodgers held a 4–1 lead. Then came two singles and a double, placing the winning run at the plate with Bobby Thomson at bat. As manager Dressen replaced pitcher Carl Erskine with Ralph Branca, my older sister, with maddening foresight, predicted the forever famous Thomas homer. This prediction left me so angry, imagining that with her words she had somehow brought it about, that I would not speak to her for days.

5 So the seasons of my childhood passed until that miserable summer when the Dodgers were taken away to Los Angeles by the unforgivable O'Malley, leaving all our rash hopes and dreams of glory behind. And then came a summer of still deeper sadness when my father died. Suddenly my feelings for baseball seemed an aspect of my departing youth, along with my childhood freckles and my favorite childhood haunts, to be left behind when I went away to college and never came back.

6 Then one September day, having settled into teaching at Harvard, I agreed, half reluctantly, to go to Fenway Park. There it was again: the cozy ballfield scaled to human dimensions so that every word of encouragement and every scornful yell could be heard on the field; the fervent crowd that could, with equal passion, curse a player for today's failures after cheering his heroics the day before; the team that always seemed to break your heart in the last week of the season.

It took only a matter of minutes before I found myself directing all my old intensities toward my new team—the Boston Red Sox.

I am often teased by my women friends about my obsession, but 7
just as often, in the most unexpected places—in academic conferences, in literary discussions, at the most elegant dinner parties—I find other women just as crazily committed to baseball as I am, and the discovery creates an instant bond between us. All at once, we are deep in conversation, mingling together the past and the present, as if the history of the Red Sox had been our history too.

There we stand, one moment recollecting the unparalleled perfor- 8
mance of Carl Yazstremski in '67, the next sharing ideas on how the present lineup should be changed; one moment recapturing the splendid career of "the Splendid Splinter," the next complaining about the manager's decision to pull the pitcher the night before. And then, invariably, comes the most vivid memory of all, the frozen image of Carlton Fisk as he rounded first in the sixth game of the '75 World Series, an image as intense in its evocation of triumph as the image of Dodger pitcher Ralph Branca weeping in the dugout is in its portrayal of heartache.

There is another, more personal memory associated with Carlton 9
Fisk, for he was, after all the years I had followed baseball, the first player I actually met in person. Apparently he had read the biography I had written on Lyndon Johnson and wanted to meet me. Yet when the meeting took place, I found myself reduced to the shyness of childhood. There I was, a professor at Harvard, accustomed to speaking with presidents of the United States, and yet, standing beside this young man in a baseball uniform, I was speechless.

Finally, Fisk said that it might have been an awesome experience 10
to work with a man of such immense power as President Johnson—and with that, I was at last able to stammer out, with a laugh, "Not as awesome as the thought that I am really standing here talking with you."

Perhaps I have circled back to my childhood, but if this is so, I am 11
certain that my journey through time is connected in some fundamental way to the fact that I am now a parent myself, anxious to share with my three sons the same ritual I once shared with my father.

For in this linkage between the generations rests the magic of 12
baseball, a game that has defied the ravages of modern life, a game that is still played today by the same basic rules and at the same pace as it was played 100 years ago. There is something deeply satisfying in the knowledge of this continuity.

And there is something else as well that I have experienced sitting 13
in Fenway Park with my small boys on a warm summer's day. If I close my eyes against the sun, all at once I am back at Ebbets Field, a

young girl once more in the presence of my father, watching the players of my youth on the grassy field below. There is magic in this moment, for when I open my eyes and see my sons in the place where my father once sat, I feel an invisible bond between our three generations, an anchor of loyalty linking my sons to the grandfather whose face they never saw, but whose person they have already come to know through this most timeless of all sports, the game of baseball.

**IN RETROSPECT**

**1.** Sheed and Goodwin both talk about the part baseball played in their lives, and both of them gave up baseball for a time because of something that happened in their lives—Sheed's polio and Goodwin's father's death. Why is it that baseball, perhaps more than any other major sport, is so intimately tied up with other aspects of people's lives?

**2.** In paragraph 9, Goodwin speaks about her first meeting with the celebrated baseball player Carlton Fisk. What irony do you see in the fact that this highly articulate woman, who taught at Harvard University and was on speaking terms with President Johnson and other high-ranking officials in Washington society, was rendered speechless in the presence of a baseball player? Does the adulation for baseball and for baseball heroes transcend gender boundaries and power structures?

# *Baseball: The Ineffable National Pastime*

## GERALD EARLY

Gerald Early (1952–        ), born in Philadelphia, Pennsylvania, earned a B.A. (cum laude) at the University of Pennsylvania in 1974 and a master's degree (1980) and a Ph.D. (1982) at Cornell University. He is now at Washington University, where he teaches English and African and Afro-American studies. He was a script advisor for the Warner Brothers Communications television series "The Mississippi" (1983). Two of his books are *Tuxedo Junction: Essays on American Culture* (1990) and *The Culture of Bruising: Essays on Literature, Prizefighting, and Modern American Culture* (1991). Early has been represented twice in *Best American Essays:* in the 1986 volume edited by Elizabeth Hardwick and in the 1989 volume edited by Geoffrey Wolff. "Baseball: The Ineffable National Pastime" is excerpted from an essay that was included in *Openings: Original Essays by Contemporary Soviet and American Writers* (1990), edited by Robert Atwan and

Valeri Vinokurov. As Early tells us in the first paragraph of his essay, "There is little here about the sport [of baseball] itself. The examination is centered on baseball's political, social, and cultural meaning." He talks about what baseball has meant to him in his personal and professional life and about its place in the life of American citizens. Those of you who love baseball will find yourselves frequently saying "Me too" while reading this essay. Those of you who have not developed a love of baseball may come to understand, from reading this essay, why some people develop a consuming interest in a sport, even though they may be only a spectator of that sport.

*The most marvelous gift of sports is its faculty for making heroes of underdogs, of lifting the downtrodden up to solid ground.*
—A.S. Young, *Negro Firsts in Sports* (1963)

*For they had much rather see us engaged in those degrading sports, than to see us behaving like intellectual, moral, and accountable beings.*
—Frederick Douglass, *Narrative of the Life of Frederick Douglass, An American Slave* (1845)

The following tableaus are about baseball, one of the sports I know best, and one that (along with boxing) perhaps defines and reflects the complexities of American culture better than any other. There is little here about the sport itself. The examination is centered on baseball's political, social, and cultural meaning. I leave it to wiser and more scholarly heads than mine to talk about sports as philosophy, as play, as performance, as economic enterprise, or in relation to American history. 1

It is one of the persistent ironies in our culture that athletic endeavor, such a speechless act, should generate such need for narrative, for language, for story—from the coach's pep talk to the sportswriter's column; from the television sports announcers who describe actions readily seen to sports talk shows and "open lines" that discuss events which, for the most part, are settled on the field of play. What is remarkable about the rise of professional sports in America (beyond the increasingly exacting specialization among athletes themselves) is that the popularity of athletics would not have been possible without the progressive technology of endlessly reproducing discourse about it: newspapers, radio, television, VCRs. The far-reaching varieties of discourse about sports signify not only our commitment to athletics but also our commitment to language as metaexperience; once the athletic event has ended, the discourse about it displaces the event. The event becomes the shadow. 2

Everyone knows, for instance, that as a young man Ronald Reagan worked as a baseball announcer. He was a very good one, 3 describing games he himself did not see, simply embellishing stark summations he received off a ticker tape. There he sat at the microphone, speaking threads and threads of narrative, shaping drama like a blind Homer. It is fitting that this collective fantasizing should revolve around baseball, which promotes a gamut of fantasies from old-timers' games and daydreamers' camps to card and board games, from professional sports' most publicized All-Star Games to computer matchups. What Reagan did as a broadcaster is what most rabid baseball fans do; namely, work backward from the facts and statistics and reconstruct the entire narrative structure of ball games, for ball games are insistently and relentlessly narrative. One must not simply *know* baseball; one must *tell* it. Baseball is one of two sports that seek to be an omnipresent—and sometimes ominous—metalanguage. (Boxing is the other.) It is in this maze of fantasy that the hero of Robert Coover's *The Universal Baseball Association, Inc., J. Henry Waugh, Prop.* (1968) finds himself. Our enjoyment of baseball, and of sports generally, is inextricably bound to story, to rhetoric, to conversation, to dialogue, to pure fussing about how the event actually was and how it should be told. The Greeks were right: in a fundamental and timeless way, sports are about our being human, about our being what we are. Only a barbarian would hate sports.

"Sports give people things to talk about other than the inadequacy 4
and unhappiness of their lives," someone once told me. Sports do even more: they give people, specifically men, a language *in* which to talk as well as a language *about* which to prate. Often, sitting in the company of older men during my boyhood, I wondered what would there be to talk about if professional sports did not exist. Discussion and argument were bountiful and eternal about all sorts of questions athletic: how big were Sonny Liston's fists; which was the better local high school basketball team, West Philadelphia or Overbrook; which records did Wilt Chamberlain set at Overbrook High; were the Washington Redskins a racist team; why did the Philadelphia Eagles trade Sonny Jurgenson; who was the better Eagle running back, Timmy Brown or Tom Woodeshick; why could local light heavyweight Harold Johnson never beat Archie Moore; why could local middleweight Bennie Briscoe never win a title; who was the better center, Bill Russell or Wilt Chamberlain; why was Joey Giardello a pretty good fighter "for a white boy"; who was the better baseball player, Hank Aaron, Willie Mays, or Roberto Clemente; why were the current crop of black ball players (circa the early and middle 1960s) not as good as the old Negro league players; why were current black ball players better than current white ball players; why were old-time Negro league players better than old-time white players; who was the best fighter, Jack Johnson, Sugar Ray Robinson, or Joe Louis?

Around and around the talk went, swirls and eddies, torrents 5
and streams, which, as a youngster, I found both fascinating and enriching, foolish and funny, learned and exhibitionist by turns. "Dammit, nigger, can't you get it through your thick head? Wasn't no way on earth Louis was gonna beat Lil Arthur! Ain't nobody was ever born who was a better defensive fighter than Jack Johnson. Johnson could be hitting you all upside your head and peeling a grape at the same time." "I knows I'm right, man! Josh Gibson got better numbers than Babe Ruth and you can look it up. I got the book at home, man. The book don't lie." "I don't care what nobody say. I *know* that Satchel Paige, in his prime, was a better pitcher than Bob Gibson 'cause I seen 'em both pitch. I know what I'm talking about." "It take about five white guys to bring down Jim Brown excepting maybe Sam Huff. You got to give the devil his due there. That Huff is a bad white boy." "How come ain't no colored middle linebackers is what I wants to know. Some colored boys out there be badder than Huff if they give us the chance."

But I was shaken once when, sitting around with the cronies in 6
the local barbershop, one of the guys, Raymond, I think, jumped up and shouted, "Why y'all always sitting around talkin' about these goddam sports? Why don't you talk about something natural that a man is supposed to talk about—like a woman, or a bottle of Scotch, or how the world ain't treatin' you right? All this here talking about these jocks and these games ain't natural; it ain't a natural way for one man to talk to another." The fact that the vast majority of athletes experience defeat more commonly than they do victory is why the mystical insistence on unnaturalness is sport's great fascination and great virtue. Alas, the athlete replicates a holistic yet puzzling human experience by giving us the male (and some females) whose vocation and condition are identical. There are two explicit and distinct memories I have of baseball and language.

As a child I remember never discussing baseball with my grand- 7
father, a native of the Bahamas, a short, stern, very black man who, I was told by other family members, was, in his youth, a follower of Marcus Garvey, although I never heard him utter a political word in his life and he has seemed a particularly accommodating man around whites. I recall one incident I was told several times: during the Depression, in order to feed his quite large family, my grandfather, in desperation, tried to steal some sausages from the local white grocer by stuffing them in his pocket. Such ineptitude made his discovery nearly inevitable. It was painfully embarrassing for him to have to plead his case to the white grocer because my grandfather has always prided himself on being an honest man and on being able to feed his family. The grocer knew my grandfather well and times were hard for

everyone, so he did not have him arrested. He simply sent him home. Family members tell the story with a great deal of good-natured humor, although he has never found it funny. I do not recall ever having a real conversation with my grandfather during my entire life, certainly not during my entire childhood. I was too afraid of him.

Yet despite the silence of our relationship he took me to profes- 8
sional baseball games every summer as he was an ardent fan of the sport; in fact, he introduced me to the sport. I remember many a sunny Sunday afternoon (we always seemed to go on a Sunday after church), sitting in Connie Mack Stadium's bleacher section, watching the Philadelphia Phillies play; Johnny Callison making grand catches in right field; Art Mahaffey and his curious windup; Don Demeter fouling balls off his left foot; Dick Stuart, old "Dr. Strangeglove," hitting a homer; the voices of Byrum Saam and Bill Campbell, the Phillies sports announcers, on radios around the park; Frank Thomas having a racial run-in with Richie (later Dick) Allen; the colorful southpaw Bo Belinsky, who once dated Mamie Van Doren and who, along with pitcher Dean Chance, was, if not one of the playboys of the Western world, certainly one of the most publicized playboys of professional baseball; the less colorful southpaw Dennis Bennet, who never made it; the deadly way Wes Covington cocked his bat before swinging; the two great years Jack Baldshun had as a relief pitcher before being traded away to mediocrity and obscurity.

I hated the Phillies as a boy; virtually every black person I knew 9
felt the same, recalling how the team had treated Jackie Robinson when he first broke into the National League. My grandfather, however, silent and strict-looking, handing out the sandwiches and drinks for our lunch with his usual authority, liked the Phillies a great deal. Perhaps that is why we never spoke to each other about the games. Once, during a twilight double header against the Dodgers (in which Sandy Koufax pitched the first game, winning six to two), he bought me a Phillies yearbook. This was unusual for two reasons: first, we almost never went to night games and, second, he almost never bought anything at the ball park. I had ambivalent feelings about the book; I felt especially treated because my grandfather bought it for me, yet I remember always intensely disliking the *smell* of it. The book always smelled new, even after I had had it for several years. I never read that yearbook; I do not recall even opening it except while standing before my grandfather a few moments after he bought it. I thanked him profusely for buying it. My grandfather bought the book because he knew I liked books about baseball. In fact, I liked them almost more than I liked the game itself.

The books that most readily come to mind from my childhood are 10
Dr. Seuss's *The Cat in the Hat;* L. Frank Baum's *The Wizard of Oz;*

Edward Ormondroyd's *David and the Phoenix;* and seemingly miles of juvenile baseball biographies. I would occasionally, if only for the sake of variety, read the biography of an athlete from another sport—the lives of Red Grange, Oscar Robertson, Bobby Hull, A. J. Foyt (if one can consider him an athlete), Benny Leonard, and others. But the baseball biographies were my favorites, and having such books written for young boys was, I suppose, a very profitable market for publishers. Henry Aaron, Willie Mays, Babe Ruth, Lou Gehrig, Joe DiMaggio, Ty Cobb, Walter Johnson, Cy Young, Grover Cleveland Alexander, Felipe Alou, Mickey Mantle—all were presented in ghost-written, antiseptic volumes that were simply longer versions of articles in *The Sporting News* or *Boys' Life.* (Many of the books were autobiographies, but I made no distinction as a boy between self-narrative and reportorial narrative; since all were ghostwritten and all were, in some essential ways, fraudulent works, their core attraction was their *narrativity,* not their authenticity. Or let me say that the books' authenticity was located in something far larger and much more gripping than the normal consideration we give to the nature of biographical writing.) During my boyhood and adolescence, my love for these books was so intense that I once had a fistfight with my friend William Bradshaw over a Warren Spahn biography he had been given. I knew he was not interested in baseball and I wanted him to give the book to me. In fact, I demanded it. He refused to give it to me, so we fought. He, being both stronger and bigger, easily beat me. What is so surprising and dismaying about this in retrospect is that I was very shy and timid as a boy. It is still hard for me to comprehend how I could have been so aggressive about something that did not belong to me.

I learned a certain sort of factual information from these books, 11
the sort of information that a boy who loved baseball would want: year-by-year statistics, career statistics, teams played for, best games played, and the like. But it was not for this information alone that I read these books, information that, after all, was condensed on the back of the baseball cards I sometimes collected. It was the sheer redundancy of the paradigmatic lesson, the comfort of knowing that each player's life was like every other player's, that producing the odd oxymoron of dull, rooted inspiration. You had to work hard to succeed, the books taught incessantly. You had to be single-minded and dedicated. You had to live a pure, clean life. You had to marry your teenage sweetheart. If you worked hard, you would be rewarded sooner or later. The books became better, infinitely more interesting than watching the games themselves in which I could see many of these athletes play. The games began to seem, in my youthful mind, like the end product, although I still enjoyed them a lot. It was far

more vital to learn the story of how a man became an athlete. Once he achieved success, his story was finished. There was something like the Ben Franklin father-to-son story in all of this, and something that reminded me, years later, of F. Scott Fitzgerald's Jay Gatsby writing out his day's schedule, as a boy, on the cover of *Hopalong Cassidy*. I did something similar, writing out a schedule for success when I was about thirteen, on the cover of a juvenile biography of Roy Campanella.

It did not occur to me until I taught *The Great Gatsby* and Heming- 12
way's *The Sun Also Rises* in a freshman English class that the connection between sports and literature is central to understanding what sports are and why they exist. On one level, those books are about the very imposture of our national character and our national myth: blacks, Jews, and Catholics as athletes and sportsmen in *The Sun Also Rises;* the fake yachtsman, fake polo-player Gatsby, whose name change resonates with ethnic overtones; the rich, hard, Yale football star. Tom Buchanan, self-centered and racist; the woman's golf pro Jordan Baker, who cheats and feels no responsibility for her recklessness. These books are the absolute unraveling (unwriting and rewriting) of the American myth through sports. (It is surely no accident that these books were published in the 1920s, the golden age of American professional and amateur sports, both in terms of mass popularity and the production of mass sportswriting in newspapers.)

Obviously, reading those baseball biographies as a child gave me 13
a very usable mythology of male heroism, much more usable than, say, Greek legends or tall tales of the American frontier. The books also provided me with an orientation toward the culture I was to live in as a man, an orientation that was valuable, if not always honest or harmless. Indeed, the true value of the books as cultural orientation may center in the fact that they are dishonest—one must learn, in some ways, to negotiate their simplistic moralizing, which so distorts the real issues of real life. That I never read sports *fiction* as a child is also quite telling: for me, nothing could be made up that was more exciting than the re-creation of a real athletic career. And the re-creation of that young man-career became, over and over, simply the recitation of games, the story of games. We know that sports are an essential part of our cultural history and social fabric, but it is my contention that the sheer narratability of sports, or, at least, our fixation with their narratability, is, whether we are sports fans or not, the incessant reinvention of ourselves as males in relation to our national myth. The meaning of sports biography (and autobiography) is indelibly tied to its narrative dramatization of our national character as a rite of beautiful young manhood.

About two years ago I saw my grandfather while I was revisiting 14
Philadelphia. It has never been easy for us to talk, but I felt very

genial, possibly because my children were with me. I remember turning the conversation to baseball, after he had asked me about living in St. Louis. I talked about the Phillies and was in fact eager to show that I still kept up with the game and even with the local team. When I asked him about their chances that year he gave me a curious, almost childlike look, a wan smile, and said, "Oh, I don't know," as if he hardly thought about baseball anymore. I felt momentarily nonplussed. But his eyes seemed almost sad at my discomfort as our conversation fell away, almost as if he felt sorry for me, as if, in the calm center of wisdom, he knew, always knew from my childhood and before, what I would only come to know years later: What is there to say about games anyway?

### IN RETROSPECT

**1.** As the headnote points out, Early says in the first paragraph of his essay, "There is little here about the sport [of baseball] itself. The examination is centered on baseball's political, social, and cultural meaning." After reading the essay, can you answer these three questions: (a) What is the *political* meaning of baseball? (b) What is the *social* meaning of baseball? (c) What is the *cultural* meaning of baseball? Can you point to specific paragraphs where Early talks about the *political* meaning of baseball? the *social* meaning of baseball? the *cultural* meaning of baseball?

**2.** In paragraphs 7–9 and again in the final paragraph (14) of the essay, Early talks about his relationship to his grandfather. Although the grandfather was the one who introduced him to baseball and took him to baseball games in Philadelphia, Early's relationship with his grandfather was always strained. Why was this relationship strained?

# *The Hard Blue Glow*

## GEORGE F. WILL

George F. Will (1941–     ) was born and raised in Champaign-Urbana, the home of the University of Illinois, where his father taught. He received his B.A. from Trinity College at Oxford University, spent two more years (1962–1964) studying at Magdalen College at Oxford, and went on to obtain a Ph.D. from Princeton University in 1967. He taught political philosophy at Michigan State University in 1967–1968. Will is best known to readers as a political columnist who writes for more than five hundred newspapers in this country and for *Newsweek;* to television viewers he is best known as a political analyst on David Brinkley's "This Week." As a political commentator, Will is not very popular with liberals, because he usually takes a conservative stand on national and international issues. But he is widely respected for his intelligence, his knowledge of history, and his consummate skill as a debater. Will is also an incorrigible lover of baseball. Although as a native of Illinois he roots mainly for the Chicago Cubs, he has an astounding store of knowledge about all major-league teams, past and present. One reason Will's book *Men at Work: The Craft of Baseball* is such a delight to diehard baseball fans is that it is filled with the kind of statistical and historical lore that lovers of baseball dote on, the kinds of facts that constitute the stuff of trivia questions. The introduction to his book, which is reprinted here, presents one loving fan's assessment of the national pastime but, like all the subsequent chapters in the book, is filled as well with the kind of detailed information about players that helps to explain the mania in this country for collecting baseball cards.

A few years ago, in the Speaker's Dining Room in the U.S. 1
Capitol, a balding, hawk-nosed Oklahoma cattleman rose from the luncheon table and addressed his host, Tip O'Neill. The man who rose was Warren Spahn, the winningest left-hander in the history of baseball. Spahn was one of a group of former All-Stars who were in Washington to play in an old-timers' game. Spahn said: "Mr. Speaker, baseball is a game of failure. Even the best batters fail about 65 percent of the time. The two Hall of Fame pitchers here today [Spahn, 363 wins, 245 losses; Bob Gibson, 251 wins, 174 losses] lost more games than a team plays in a full season. I just hope you fellows in Congress have more success than baseball players have."

The fellows in Congress don't, and they know it. There are no 2
.400 hitters in Washington. And players in the game of government are spared the sort of remorselessly objective measurement of their performance that ball players see in box scores everyday. But Washington does have lots of baseball fans. In October, 1973, Potter Stewart, Associate Justice of the Supreme Court and avid Cincinnati Reds fan, was scheduled to hear oral arguments at the time of the Reds-Mets play-off game. He asked his clerks to pass him batter-by-batter bulletins. One read: "Kranepool flies to right. Agnew resigns." (Baseball also holds the attention of people at the other end of the system of justice. When Richard T. Cooper, a murderer, was on the threshold of California's death chamber, his final remarks included: "I'm very unhappy about the Giants.")

Because baseball is a game of failure, and hence a constantly 3
humbling experience, it is good that the national government is well stocked with students of the national pastime. There also is a civic interest served by having the population at large leavened by millions of fans. They are spectators of a game that rewards, and thus elicits, a remarkable level of intelligence from those who compete. To be an

intelligent fan is to participate in something. It is an activity, a form of appreciating that is good for the individual's soul, and hence for society.

Proof of the genius of ancient Greece is that it understood base- 4
ball's future importance. Greek philosophers considered sport a religious and civic—in a word, moral—undertaking. Sport, they said, is morally serious because mankind's noblest aim is the loving contemplation of worthy things, such as beauty and courage. By witnessing physical grace, the soul comes to understand and love beauty. Seeing people compete courageously and fairly helps emancipate the individual by educating his passions.

Being a serious baseball fan, meaning an informed and attentive 5
and observant fan, is more like carving than whittling. It is doing something that makes demands on the mind of the doer. Is there any other sport in which the fans say they "take in" a game? As in, "Let's take in a game tomorrow night." I think not. That is a baseball locution because there is a lot to ingest and there is time—although by no means too much time—to take it in.

Of all the silly and sentimental things said about baseball, none is 6
sillier than the description of the game as "unhurried" or "leisurely." Or (this from folks at the serious quarterlies) that baseball has "the pace of America's pastoral past." This is nonsense on stilts. Any late-twentieth-century academic who thinks that a nineteenth-century farmer's day was a leisurely, unhurried stroll from sunup to sundown needs a reality transplant. And the reality of baseball is that the action involves blazing speeds and fractions of seconds. Furthermore, baseball is as much a mental contest as a physical one. The pace of the action is relentless: There is barely enough time between pitches for all the thinking that is required, and that the best players do, in processing the changing information about the crucial variables.

In a sense, sports are not complicated. Even the infield fly rule 7
can be mastered, in time, without a master's degree from MIT. The object of a sport can be put simply. You put a ball in an end zone or through a hoop, or you put a puck in a net, and prevent the other fellows from doing so. Sports are not complicated in their objectives, but in execution they have layers of complexities and nuances. There is a lot of thought involved, however much many players deny or disguise that fact. When Dizzy Dean heard, before the 1934 World Series, that the Tigers' manager, Mickey Cochrane, was conducting a series of team meetings, Dean said, "If them guys are thinking, they're as good as licked right now." (The Cardinals beat the Tigers in seven games.) But even in his era Dean was one of baseball's cartoon characters, a caricature sent up from central casting, a Ring Lardner creation come to life. And certainly Dean bore no resemblance to

most of the men who rise to the top of today's baseball and stay there for a while.

It has been said that the problem with many modern athletes is 8
that they take themselves seriously and their sport lightly. That cannot be said of the men discussed in this book. This book treats the elements of the game by examining four men in terms of functions dictated by the order of the game. A manager assembles a team, trains it, devises a lineup for a particular game and controls his team's conduct during the game. A pitcher throws the ball, a batter hits it, a fielder handles it. During the time I was writing this book I attended games and conducted interviews in 11 major league cities, from Canada to Southern California. I liken the experience to being guided through an art gallery by a group of patient docents who were fine painters and critics. Such tutors teach the skill of seeing. To see, to really *see* what a painter has put on canvas requires learning to think the way the painter thought. My baseball guides have been players, managers, coaches, front office personnel, writers, broadcasters, and others of the small community of baseball.

Many players do not practice what they preach. They preach a 9
simplicity sharply at odds with their real attention to the fine points. A pitcher will say, "I just try to move the ball around and throw strikes." A hitter will describe himself as of the "see ball, hit ball" school. But when players are prompted to talk about what they do, the complexity emerges. Baseball is an exacting profession with a technical vocabulary and a distinctive mode of reasoning. It involves constant attention to the law of cumulation, which is: A lot of little things add up, through 162 games, 1,458 innings, to big differences. A 162-game season is, like life, an exercise in cumulation.

It was an architect who said that God is in the details. It could 10
have been a professional athlete, particularly a baseball player, most likely a catcher. Catchers, who have the game arrayed in front of them and are in on every pitch, not only work harder than other everyday players, they are required to think more. Ten of the 26 major league managers on Opening Day, 1989, had done some catching in their playing careers. It was, naturally, a catcher (Wes Westrum of the New York Giants) who said that baseball is like church: "Many attend but few understand."

Rick Dempsey, a catcher, is the sort of player whose natural skills 11
were never such that he looked like a candidate for longevity in the major leagues. Yet 1989 was his twenty-first season. He is the sort of player often called a journeyman, and he certainly has journeyed, from Minnesota to the Yankees to the Orioles to the Indians, and in the spring of 1988 he talked his way into a tryout with the Dodgers. In the autumn he was in the World Series. It was his third Series. He

played in all seven games of the Orioles' loss to the Pirates in 1979 and was the MVP of the 1983 Series in which the Orioles beat the Phillies in five games. Talking to Roger Angell of *The New Yorker* at the 1988 Series, Dempsey made clear the mental makeup that makes for survival in baseball:

> You have to play this game right. You have to think right. You're not trying to pull the ball all the time. You're not thinking, Hey, we're going to kill them tomorrow—because that may not happen. You're not looking to do something all on your own. You've got to take it one game at a time, one hitter at a time. You've got to go on doing the things you've talked about and agreed about beforehand. You can't get three outs at a time or five runs at a time. You've got to concentrate on each play, each hitter, each pitch. All this makes the game much slower and much clearer. It breaks down to its smallest part. If you take the game like that—one pitch, one hitter, one inning at a time, and then one *game* at a time—the next thing you know, you look up and you've won.

Winning is not everything. Baseball—its beauty, its craftsmanship, its exactingness—is an *activity* to be loved, as much as ballet or fishing or politics, and loving it is a form of participation. But this book is not about romance. Indeed, it is an antiromantic look at a game that brings out the romantic in the best of its fans.

A. Bartlett Giamatti was to the Commissioner's office what Sandy 12
Koufax was to the pitcher's mound: Giamatti's career had the highest ratio of excellence to longevity. If his heart had been as healthy as his soul—if his heart had been as strong as it was warm—Giamatti would one day have been ranked among commissioners the way Walter Johnson is ranked (by correct thinkers) among pitchers: as the best, period. Baseball's seventh commissioner, who was the first to have taught Renaissance literature at Yale, was fond of noting the etymological fact that the root of the word "paradise" is an ancient Persian word meaning "enclosed park or green." Ballparks exist, he said, because there is in humanity "a vestigial memory of an enclosed green space as a place of freedom or play." Perhaps. Certainly ballparks are pleasant places for the multitudes. But for the men who work there, ballparks are for hard, sometimes dangerous, invariably exacting business. Physically strong and fiercely competitive men make their living in those arenas. Most of these men have achieved, at least intermittently, the happy condition of the fusion of work and play. They get physical pleasure and emotional release and fulfillment from their vocation. However, Roy Campanella's celebrated aphorism—that there has to be a lot of little boy in a man who plays baseball—needs a corollary. There has to be a lot of hardness in a man who plays—who works at—this boys' game.

Success in life has been described as the maintained ecstasy of 13
burning with a hard, gemlike flame. The image recurs. In his famous essay on Ted Williams's final game, "Hub Fans Bid Kid Adieu," John Updike wrote of Williams radiating "the hard blue glow of high purpose." Updike said, "For me, Williams is the classic ballplayer of the game on a hot August weekday before a small crowd, when the only thing at stake is the tissue-thin difference between a thing done well and a thing done ill." Baseball, played on a field thinly populated with men rhythmically shifting from languor to tension, is, to Updike's eyes, an essentially lonely game. The cool mathematics of individual performances are the pigments coloring the long season of averaging out. Baseball heroism comes not from flashes of brilliance but rather, Updike says, from "the players who always *care,*" about themselves and their craft.

The connection between character and achievement is one of the 14
fundamental fascinations of sport. Some say that sport builds character. Others say that sport reveals character. But baseball at its best puts good character on display in a context of cheerfulness. Willie Stargell, the heart of the order during the Pirates' salad days in the 1970s, insisted that baseball is, or at any rate ought to be, fun. Walking wearily through the Montreal airport after a night game, he said, "I ain't complaining. I asked to be a ball player." Indeed, it is likely that a higher percentage of ball players than of plumbers or lawyers or dentists or almost any other group are doing what they passionately enjoy doing. On another occasion Stargell said, "The umpire says 'Play ball,' not 'Work ball.' " (Actually, the rule book requires the umpire to call out only the word "play.") But professional baseball is work.

Happiness has been called "the sweet exaltation of work." What 15
follows are the stories of four men who are happy in their work. From an appreciation of that work, many millions of people derive a happiness worth pursuing. This book is intended to help that pursuit. It also is a deep bow, not just to the particular players about whom I have written, but to all the baseball people who transmit the game, remarkably intact, through the whirl of American change. This book is a thank-you note. There is a book with the wonderful title *Baseball, I Gave You the Best Years of My Life.* What do we spectators give baseball besides the price of a seat and the respect implicit in paying attention? Baseball's best practitioners give in return the gift of virtues made vivid. This gift is a thing of beauty and joy forever, or at least until the next game, which is much the same thing as forever because the seasons stretch into forever. Yes, I know, I know. Even the continents drift. Nothing lasts. But baseball does renew itself constantly as youth

comes knocking at the door, and in renewal it becomes better. To see why this is so, come along and see some baseball men at work.

**IN RETROSPECT**

**1.** Early says in his essay that "the majority of athletes experience defeat more commonly than they do victory," and Will quotes Warren Spahn, "the winningest left-hander in the history of baseball," as saying that "baseball is a game of failure." What do these two writers mean when they say that sports are an enterprise of failure? If baseball is a game of failure, why are so many people attracted to it? What other occupations might similarly be characterized as games of failure?

**2.** "The Hard Blue Glow," the title of Will's introduction to his book *Men at Work: The Craft of Baseball,* is taken from John Updike's essay "Hub Fans Bid Kid Adieu," an excerpt from which is reprinted in this chapter. What image does the metaphor of a "hard blue glow" conjure up for you, and in what way is that image pertinent to baseball? (See paragraph 13 of Will's essay.)

# *Hub Fans Bid Kid Adieu*

## JOHN UPDIKE

Born in Shillington, Pennsylvania, John Updike (1932–      ) attended Harvard University and the Ruskin School of Drawing and Fine Art, in Oxford, England. From 1955 to 1957, he was on the staff of *The New Yorker,* to which he contributed poems, stories, and literary reviews. Updike's first major publication was a volume of poetry, *The Carpentered Hen* (1958), but novels like *The Poorhouse Fair* (1959), *Rabbit, Run* (1960), *The Centaur* (winner of the National Book Award in 1964), and *Couples* (1968) and short story collections like *The Same Door* (1959) and *Pigeon Feathers* (1962) established his position as one of America's premier writers of fiction. If there is any single essay for which Updike will be remembered by posterity, it is his classic "Hub Fans Bid Kid Adieu." This essay presents Updike's account of his visit to Boston's Fenway Park on Wednesday, September 28, 1960, when the seventh-place Red Sox were playing the last home game of the season against the Baltimore Orioles and when more than ten thousand fans would get their last look at the fabulous Ted Williams. In this brief selection from that twenty-page essay, Updike describes the climactic moment of that ball game and shows us how sports reporting can be turned into a piece of literature.

Williams was third in the batting order, so he came up in the 1
bottom of the first inning, and Steve Barber, a young pitcher born two months before Williams began playing in the major leagues, offered him four pitches, at all of which he disdained to swing, since none of them were within the strike zone. This demonstrated simultaneously that Williams' eyes were razor-sharp and that Barber's control wasn't. Shortly, the bases were full, with Williams on second. "Oh, I hope he gets held up at third! That would be wonderful," the girl beside me moaned, and, sure enough, the man at bat walked and Williams was delivered into our foreground. He struck the pose of Donatello's David, the third-base bag being Goliath's head. Fiddling with his cap, swapping small talk with the Oriole third baseman (who seemed delighted to have him drop in), swinging his arms with a sort of prancing nervousness, he looked fine—flexible, hard, and not unbecomingly substantial through the middle. The long neck, the small head, the knickers whose cuffs were worn down near his ankles—all these clichés of sports cartoon iconography were rendered in the flesh.

With each pitch, Williams danced down the baseline, waving his 2
arms and stirring dust, ponderous but menacing, like an attacking goose. It occurred to about a dozen humorists at once to shout. "Steal home! Go, go!" Williams' speed afoot was never legendary. Lou Clinton, a young Sox outfielder, hit a fairly deep fly to center field. Williams tagged up and ran home. As he slid across the plate, the ball, thrown with unusual heft by Jackie Brandt, the Oriole center fielder, hit him on the back.

"Boy, he was really loafing, wasn't he?" one of the collegiate 3
voices behind me said.

"It's cold," the other voice explained. "He doesn't play well when 4
it's cold. He likes heat. He's a hedonist."

The run that Williams scored was the second and last of the 5
inning. Gus Triandos, of the Orioles, quickly evened the score by plunking a home run over the handy left-field wall. Williams, who had had this wall at his back for twenty years,[1] played the ball flawlessly. He didn't budge. He just stood still, in the center of the little patch of grass that his patient footsteps had worn brown, and, limp with lack of interest, watched the ball pass overhead. It was not a very interesting game. Mike Higgins, the Red Sox manager, with nothing to lose, had restricted his major-league players to the left-field line—along with Williams, Frank Malzone, a first-rate third

[1]In his second season (1940) he was switched to left field, to protect his eyes from the right-field sun. [Updike's note]

baseman, played the game—and had peopled the rest of the terrain with unpredictable youngsters fresh, or not so fresh, off the farm. Other than Williams' recurrent appearances at the plate, the *maladresse* of the Sox infield was the sole focus of suspense; the second baseman turned every grounder into a juggling act, while the shortstop did a breathtaking impersonation of an open window. With this sort of assistance, the Orioles wheeled their way into a 4–2 lead. They had early replaced Barber with another young pitcher, Jack Fisher. Fortunately (as it turned out), Fisher is no cutie; he is willing to burn the ball through the strike zone, and inning after inning this tactic punctured Higgins' string of test balloons.

Whenever Williams appeared at the plate—pounding the dirt 6
from his cleats, gouging a pit in the batter's box with his left foot, wringing resin out of the bat handle with his vehement grip, switching the stick at the pitcher with an electric ferocity—it was like having a familiar Leonardo appear in a shuffle of *Saturday Evening Post* covers. This man, you realized—and here, perhaps, was the difference, greater than the difference in gifts—really desired to hit the ball. In the third inning, he hoisted a high fly to deep center. In the fifth, we thought he had it; he smacked the ball hard and high into the heart of his power zone, but the deep right field in Fenway and the heavy air and a casual east wind defeated him. The ball died. Al Pilarcik leaned his back against the big "380" pained on the right-field wall and caught it. On another day, in another park, it would have been gone. (After the game, Williams said, "I didn't think I could hit one any harder than that. The conditions weren't good.")

The afternoon grew so glowering that in the sixth inning the arc 7
lights were turned on—always a wan sight in the day time, like the burning headlights of a funeral procession. Aided by the gloom, Fisher was slicing through the Sox rookies, and Williams did not come to bat in the seventh. He was second up in the eighth. This was almost certainly his last time to come to the plate in Fenway Park, and instead of merely cheering, as we had at his three previous appearances, we stood, all of us, and applauded. I had never before heard pure applause in a ballpark. No calling, no whistling, just an ocean of handclaps, minute after minute, burst after burst, crowding and running together in continuous succession like the pushes of surf at the edge of the sand. It was a sombre and considered tumult. There was not a boo in it. It seemed to renew itself out of a shifting set of memories as the Kid, the Marine, the veteran of feuds and failures and injuries, the friend of children, and the enduring old pro evolved down the bright tunnel of twenty-two summers toward this moment. At last, the umpire signalled for Fisher to pitch; with the other players, he had been frozen in position. Only Williams had moved

during the ovation, switching his bat impatiently, ignoring everything except his cherished task. Fisher wound up, and the applause sank into a hush.

Understand that we were a crowd of rational people. We knew 8
that a home run cannot be produced at will; the right pitch must be perfectly met and luck must ride with the ball. Three innings before, we had seen a brave effort fail. The air was soggy, the season was exhausted. Nevertheless, there will always lurk, around the corner in a pocket of our knowledge of the odds, an indefensible hope, and this was one of the times, which you now and then find in sports, when a density of expectation hangs in the air and plucks an event out of the future.

Fisher, after his unsettling wait, was low with the first pitch. He 9
put the second one over, and Williams swung mightily and missed. The crowd grunted, seeing that classic swing, so long and smooth and quick, exposed. Fisher threw the third time, Williams swung again, and there it was. The ball climbed on a diagonal line into the vast volume of air over center field. From my angle, behind third base, the ball seemed less an object in flight than the tip of a towering, motionless construct, like the Eiffel Tower or the Tappan Zee Bridge. It was in the books while it was still in the sky. Brandt ran back to the deepest corner of the outfield grass, the ball descended beyond his reach and struck in the crotch where the bullpen met the wall, bounced chunkily, and vanished.

Like a feather caught in a vortex, Williams ran around the square 10
of bases at the center of our beseeching screaming. He ran as he always ran out home runs—hurriedly, unsmiling, head down, as if our praise were a storm of rain to get out of. He didn't tip his cap. Though we thumped, wept, and chanted "We want Ted" for minutes after he hid in the dugout, he did not come back. Our noise for some seconds passed beyond excitement into a kind of immense open anguish, a wailing, a cry to be saved. But immortality is nontransferable. The papers said that the other players, and even the umpires on the field, begged him to come out and acknowledge us in some way, but he refused. Gods do not answer letters.

### IN RETROSPECT

**1.** The excerpt reprinted here that Updike originally published in *The New Yorker* is a superb piece of reporting, a report that you might find on the front page of a sports page the day after a memorable ball game. But what is this specimen of sports reporting doing in a book on the familiar essay? How does this piece differ—if it does differ—from the straight, factual account of a ball game that you could find on the front page of your local newspaper any morning in summertime? Where is the personal note that we keep insisting is one of the hallmarks of the familiar essay? What does the dual identity of this piece of writing suggest to you about the definition of genres?

**2.** How do you interpret the last sentence of the excerpt printed here ("Gods do not answer letters")—a sentence in which Updike seems to be offering an explanation for Williams's refusal to acknowledge the crowd's ovations? What impression of Williams does this sentence, along with the whole final paragraph, leave us with?

# 9

# On Language

*The use of language is being exemplified in all of the chapters of this book. Essayists are one of the groups of people in our society who are vitally concerned about the fresh, precise, responsible use of language in the public arena. Nothing is more painful to them than clichés, platitudes, jargon, equivocations, and lies. They are well aware, of course, from their own experience in acquiring, extending, and perfecting their use of the language, how difficult it is to become a skillful verbal artist. This chapter leads off with an essay by Oliver Goldsmith on the oldest art dealing with the skillful use of language: the art of rhetoric, or, to use the eighteenth-century term, eloquence. George Orwell picks up the discussion with his exposure of the abuses of the English language in the public arena. Helen Keller and Maxine Hong Kingston each talk about the difficulties that certain groups of people have in acquiring the language of the mainstream culture, while Langston Hughes addresses the subtle prejudices embedded in that language. And Russell Baker considers some of the aberrations in the use of language—jargon and regionalisms, to be specific. If you can read these essays, you have acquired that most valuable of linguistic skills—literacy, the ability to read and write a particular language. Think of all the people in the world, even those living in your own society, for whom these pages are a blank. To get an idea of what a handicap illiteracy can be, just imagine seeing a street sign, billboard, or newspaper written in a language that is unfamiliar to you—for instance, Greek or Arabic or Chinese. You would feel utterly helpless.*

# *Of Eloquence*

## OLIVER GOLDSMITH

Oliver Goldsmith (1730–1774) was born in Ireland, the son of an Anglican clergyman. Rejected for ordination after receiving his undergraduate degree at Trinity College in Dublin, he studied medicine sporadically at Edinburgh and Leyden. In 1755–1756 Goldsmith traveled on foot through France, Switzerland, and Italy, often earning his bread-and-board by entertaining villagers with his stories and flute playing. When the destitute Goldsmith failed to obtain a medical position, he turned to journalism. The best examples of Goldsmith's essays are found in *The Bee,* a small periodical that he published during October and November 1759, and in his "Chinese Letters," which he published in John Newbery's *Public Ledger* and later collected under the title *Citizen of the World.* Goldsmith was an amazingly prolific writer, and judging by the enduring contributions he made to several literary genres—biography *(Life of Richard Nash),* criticism *(An Essay on the Theatre),* poetry *(The Deserted Village),* the novel *(The Vicar of Wakefield),* drama *(She Stoops to Conquer)*—we might pronounce him the most versatile of the eighteenth-century English writers. In the following essay, Goldsmith is talking about the art of rhetoric, the art governing the oratory of the public forum and the courtroom, the art that was first codified by the ancient Greeks. The art of oral discourse became the art of written discourse when people learned how to inscribe words on manuscript pages and especially after printing was invented. Goldsmith was himself a master of eloquence in the written form. Because of the ease, geniality, and lucidity of his prose style, his essays are reminiscent of the essays of Richard Steele, the collaborator with Joseph Addison on the popular *Tatler* and *Spectator* papers, and prefigure the essays of the popular nineteenth-century essayists Washington Irving and Charles Lamb.

Of all kinds of success, that of an orator is the most pleasing. 1
Upon other occasions, the applause we deserve is conferred in our absence, and we are insensible of the pleasure we have given; but in eloquence the victory and the triumph are inseparable. We read our own glory in the face of every spectator; the audience is moved; the antagonist is defeated; and the whole circle bursts into unsolicited applause.

The rewards which attend excellence in this way are so pleasing, 2
that numbers have written professed treatises to teach us the art; schools have been established with no other intent; rhetoric has taken place among the institutions; and pedants have ranged under proper heads, and distinguished with long learned names, *some* of the strokes of nature, or of passion, which orators have used. I say only *some,* for a folio volume could not contain all the figures which have

been used by the truly eloquent; and scarce a good speaker or writer but makes use of some that are peculiar or new.

3 Eloquence has preceded the rules of rhetoric, as languages have been formed before grammar. Nature renders men eloquent in great interests, or great passions. He that is sensibly touched, sees things with a very different eye from the rest of mankind. All nature to him becomes an object of comparison and metaphor, without attending to it; he throws life into all, and inspires his audience with a part of his own enthusiasm.

4 It has been remarked, that the lower parts of mankind generally express themselves most figuratively, and that tropes are found in the most ordinary forms of conversation. Thus, in every language, the heart burns; the courage is roused; the eyes sparkle; the spirits are cast down; passion inflames, pride swells, and pity sinks the soul. Nature everywhere speaks in those strong images, which, from their frequency, pass unnoticed.

5 Nature it is which inspires those rapturous enthusiasms, those irresistible turns; a strong passion, a pressing danger, calls up all the imagination, and gives the orator irresistible force. Thus, a captain of the first caliphs, seeing his soldiers fly, cried out, "Whither do you run? the enemy are not there! You have been told that the caliph is dead; but God is still living. He regards the brave, and will reward the courageous. Advance!"

6 *A man, therefore, may be called eloquent, who transfers the passion or sentiment with which he is moved himself, into the breast of another;* and this definition appears the more just, as it comprehends the graces of silence and of action. An intimate persuasion of the truth to be proved, is the sentiment and passion to be transferred; and he who effects this, is truly possessed of the talent of eloquence.

7 I have called eloquence a talent, and not an art, as so many rhetoricians have done, as art is acquired by exercise and study, and eloquence is the gift of nature. Rules will never make either a work or a discourse eloquent; they only serve to prevent faults, but not to introduce beauties; to prevent those passages which are truly eloquent and dictated by nature from being blended with others which might disgust, or at least abate our passion.

8 What we clearly conceive, says Boileau, we can clearly express. I may add, that what is felt with emotion is expressed also with the same movements; the words arise as readily to paint our emotions as to express our thoughts with perspicuity. The cool care an orator takes to express passions which he does not feel, only prevents his rising into that passion he would seem to feel. In a word, to feel your subject thoroughly, and to speak without fear, are the only rules of

eloquence, properly so called, which I can suffer. Examine a writer of genius on the most beautiful parts of his work, and he will always assure you, that such passages are generally those which have given him the least trouble, for they came as if by inspiration. To pretend that cold and didactic precepts will make a man eloquent is only to prove that he is incapable of eloquence.

But, as in being perspicuous, it is necessary to have a full idea of 9
the subject, so in being eloquent it is not sufficient, if I may so express it, to feel by halves. The orator should be strongly impressed, which is generally the effect of a fine and exquisite sensibility, and not that transient and superficial emotion which he excites in the greatest part of his audience. It is even impossible to affect the hearers in any great degree without being affected ourselves. In vain it will be objected, that many writers have had the art to inspire their readers with a passion for virtue, without being virtuous themselves, since it may be answered, that sentiments of virtue filled their minds at the time they were writing. They felt the inspiration strongly while they praised justice, generosity, or good-nature; but, unhappily for them, these passions might have been discontinued, when they laid down the pen. In vain will it be objected again, that we can move without being moved, as we can convince without being convinced. It is much easier to deceive our reason than ourselves: a trifling defect in reasoning may be overseen, and lead a man astray, for it requires reason and time to detect the falsehood; but our passions are not easily imposed upon,—our eyes, our ears, and every sense, are watchful to detect the imposture.

No discourse can be eloquent that does not elevate the mind. 10
Pathetic eloquence, it is true, has for its only object to affect; but I appeal to men of sensibility, whether their pathetic feelings are not accompanied with some degree of elevation. We may then call eloquence and sublimity the same thing, since it is impossible to be one without feeling the other. From hence it follows, that we may be eloquent in any language, since no language refuses to paint those sentiments with which we are thoroughly impressed. What is usually called sublimity of style, seems to be only an error. Eloquence is not in the words, but in the subject; and in great concerns, the more simply anything is expressed, it is generally the more sublime. True eloquence does not consist, as the rhetoricians assure us, in saying great things in a sublime style, but in a simple style; for there is, properly speaking, no such thing as a sublime style; the sublimity lies only in the things; and when they are not so, the language may be turgid, affected, metaphorical,—but not affecting.

What can be more simply expressed than the following extract 11
from a celebrated preacher, and yet what was ever more sublime?

Speaking of the small number of the elect, he breaks out thus among his audience:

> —"Let me suppose that this was the last hour of us all—that the heavens were opening over our heads—that time was passed, and eternity begun—that Jesus Christ in all His glory, that Man of Sorrows, in all His glory, appeared on the tribunal, and that we were assembled here to receive our final decree of life, or death eternal! Let me ask, impressed with terror like you, and not separating my lot from yours, but putting myself in the same situation in which we must all one day appear before God, our judge,—let me ask, if Jesus Christ should now appear to make that terrible separation of the just from the unjust, do you think the greatest number would be saved? Do you think the number of the elect would even be equal to that of the sinners? Do you think, if all our works were examined with justice, would He find ten just persons in this great assembly? Monsters of ingratitude! would He find one?"

Such passages as these are sublime in every language. The expression may be less speaking, or more indistinct, but the greatness of the idea still remains. In a word, we may be eloquent in every language and in every style, since elocution is only an assistant, but not a constitutor of eloquence.

Of what use, then, will it be said, are all the precepts given us 12
upon this head, both by the ancients and moderns? I answer, that they cannot make us eloquent, but they will certainly prevent us from becoming ridiculous. They can seldom procure a single beauty, but they may banish a thousand faults. The true method of an orator is not to attempt always to move, always to affect, to be continually sublime, but at proper intervals to give rest both to his own and the passions of his audience. In these periods of relaxation, or of preparation rather, rules may teach him to avoid anything low, trivial, or disgusting. Thus criticism, properly speaking, is intended not to assist those parts which are sublime, but those which are naturally mean and humble, which are composed with coolness and caution, and where the orator rather endeavours not to offend than attempts to please.

I have hitherto insisted more strenuously on that eloquence 13
which speaks to the passions, as it is a species of oratory almost unknown in England. At the bar it is quite discontinued, and I think with justice. In the senate it is used but sparingly, as the orator speaks to enlightened judges. But in the pulpit, in which the orator should chiefly address the vulgar, it seems strange that it should be entirely laid aside.

The vulgar of England are, without exception, the most barbarous 14
and the most unknowing of any in Europe. A great part of their ignorance may be chiefly ascribed to their teachers, who, with the

most pretty gentlemanlike serenity, deliver their cool discourses, and address the reason of men who have never reasoned in all their lives. They are told of cause and effect, of beings self-existent, and the universal scale of beings. They are informed of the excellence of the Bangorian Controversy, and the absurdity of an intermediate state. The spruce preacher reads his lucubration without lifting his nose from the text, and never ventures to earn the shame of an enthusiast.

By this means, though his audience feel not one word of all he 15
says, he earns, however, among his acquaintance, the character of a man of sense; among his acquaintance only, did I say? nay, even with his bishop.

The polite of every country have several motives to induce them 16
to a rectitude of action,—the love of virtue for its own sake, the shame of offending, and the desire of pleasing. The vulgar have one,—the enforcements of religion; and yet those who should push this motive home to their hearts, are basely found to desert their post. They speak to the squire, the philosopher, and the pedant; but the poor, those who really want instruction, are left uninstructed.

I have attended most of our pulpit orators, who, it must be 17
owned, write extremely well upon the text they assume. To give them their due also, they read their sermons with elegance and propriety; but this goes but a very short way in true eloquence. The speaker must be moved. In this, in this alone, our English divines are deficient. Were they to speak to a few calm, dispassionate hearers, they certainly use the properest methods of address; but their audience is chiefly composed of the poor, who must be influenced by motives of reward and punishment, and whose only virtues lie in self-interest or fear.

How, then, are such to be addressed? Not by studied periods, or 18
cold disquisitions; not by the labours of the head, but the honest spontaneous dictates of the heart. Neither writing a sermon with regular periods, and all the harmony of elegant expression—neither reading it with emphasis, propriety, and deliberation—neither pleasing with metaphor, simile, or rhetorical fustian—neither arguing coolly, and untying consequences united in *à priori,* nor bundling up inductions *à posteriori*—neither pedantic jargon, nor academical trifling, can persuade the poor. Writing a discourse coolly in the closet, then getting it by memory, and delivering it on Sundays, even that will not do. What then, is to be done? I know of no expedient to speak—to speak at once intelligibly and feelingly—except to understand the language: to be convinced of the truth of the object—to be perfectly acquainted with the subject in view—to prepossess yourself with a low opinion of your audience—and to do the rest extempore.

By this means, strong expressions, new thoughts, rising passions, and the true declamatory style, will naturally ensue.

Fine declamation does not consist in flowery periods, delicate 19
allusions, or musical cadences, but in a plain, open, loose style, where the periods are long and obvious; where the same thought is often exhibited in several points of view: all this, strong sense, a good memory, and a small share of experience, will furnish to every orator; and without these, a clergyman may be called a fine preacher, a judicious preacher, and a man of sound sense; he may make his hearers admire his understanding, but will seldom enlighten theirs.

When I think of the Methodist preachers among us, how seldom 20
they are endued with common sense, and yet how often and how justly they affect their hearers, I cannot avoid saying within myself, had these been bred gentlemen, and been endued with even the meanest share of understanding, what might they not effect! Did our bishops, who can add dignity to their expostulations, testify the same fervour, and *entreat* their hearers, as well as *argue,* what might not be the consequence! The vulgar, by which I mean the bulk of mankind, would then have a double motive to love religion; first, from seeing its professors honoured here, and next, from the consequences hereafter. At present the enthusiasms of the poor are opposed to law; did law conspire with their enthusiasms, we should not only be the happiest nation upon earth, but the wisest also.

Enthusiasm in religion, which prevails only among the vulgar, 21
should be the chief object of politics. A society of enthusiasts, governed by reason, among the great, is the most indissoluble, the most virtuous, and the most efficient of its own decrees that can be imagined. Every country, possessed of any degree of strength, has had its enthusiasms, which ever serve as laws among the people. The Greeks had their *Kalokagathia,* the Romans their *Amor Patriæ,* and we the truer and firmer bond of the *Protestant Religion.* The principle is the same in all: how much, then, is it the duty of those whom the law has appointed teachers of this religion, to enforce its obligations, and to raise those enthusiasms among people, by which alone political society can subsist?

From eloquence, therefore, the morals of our people are to expect 22
emendation; but how little can they be improved by men who get into the pulpit rather to show their parts than convince us of the truth of what they deliver; who are painfully correct in their style, musical in their tones; where every sentiment, every expression, seems the result of meditation and deep study.

Tillotson has been commended as the model of pulpit eloquence; 23
thus far he should be imitated, where he generally strives to convince

rather than to please; but to adopt his long, dry, and sometimes tedious discussions, which serve to amuse only divines, and are utterly neglected by the generality of mankind—to praise the intricacy of his periods, which are too long to be spoken—to continue his cool phlegmatic manner of enforcing every truth—is certainly erroneous. As I said before, the good preacher should adopt no model, write no sermons, study no periods; let him but understand his subject, the language he speaks, and be convinced of the truths he delivers. It is amazing to what heights eloquence of this kind may reach! This is that eloquence the ancients represented as lightning, bearing down every opposer; this the power which has turned whole assemblies into astonishment, admiration, and awe—that is described by the torrent, the flame, and every other instance of irresistible impetuosity.

But to attempt such noble heights, belongs only to the truly great, 24
or the truly good. To discard the lazy manner of reading sermons, or speaking sermons by rote; to set up singly against the opposition of men who are attached to their own errors, and to endeavour to be great, instead of being prudent, are qualities we seldom see united. A minister of the Church of England, who may be possessed of good sense, and some hopes of preferment, will seldom give up such substantial advantages for the empty pleasure of improving society. By his present method he is liked by his friends, admired by his dependants, not displeasing to his bishop; he lives as well, eats and sleeps as well, as if a real orator, and an eager asserter of his mission: he will hardly, therefore, venture all this, to be called, perhaps, an enthusiast; nor will he depart from customs established by the brotherhood, when, by such a conduct, he only singles himself out for their contempt.

## IN RETROSPECT

**1.** In paragraph 11 of this essay, Goldsmith quotes several sentences from a sermon by a "celebrated preacher." Using the standards that Goldsmith sets in this essay for what constitutes an eloquent, sublime discourse, indicate why Goldsmith admires this sermon. (In making your judgments, remember that some of the usages in the eighteenth century governing spelling, punctuation, and even grammar are different from the usages prevailing in our society in the twentieth century.)

**2.** Goldsmith has certain characteristic but sometimes unusual ways of joining parts of a sentence. For instance, in the first sentence of paragraph 2 and in the second sentence of paragraph 4, he uses *semicolons* to join the parts of his sentences. But in the third sentence of paragraph 18 and in the next-to-last sentence of paragraph 18, he uses *dashes* to join the parts of his sentences.

Do you think that in Goldsmith's system, these marks of punctuation are interchangeable, or do these "joiners" serve different functions? Give reasons for your answer.

# *Politics and the English Language*

**GEORGE ORWELL**

George Orwell was the pen name of Eric Blair (1903–1950). Born in Bengal, India, Orwell was brought to England as a young boy and educated at Eton. His experiences as a member of the Indian Imperial Police in Burma from 1922 to 1927 are recounted in his novel *Burmese Days* and in such oft-reprinted essays as "Shooting an Elephant" and "A Hanging." His experiences in a series of menial jobs are related in *Down and Out in Paris and London* (1933), and his experiences as a soldier on the Republican side (the Communist side) during the Spanish civil war are recorded in *Homage to Catalonia* (1938). Although Orwell professed to be a "democratic socialist," he expressed his growing disillusionment with the objectives and methods of international communism in two famous novels, *Animal Farm* (1945) and *Nineteen Eighty-Four* (1949). Because so much of Orwell's nonfiction prose is reportorial or polemical, it is difficult to find an example of a familiar essay in his collected works. But the essay "Politics and the English Language," which may be his most frequently reprinted essay, can qualify as the kind of essay featured in this anthology. In this essay, Orwell laments the shabby state of the English language in public life, analyzes the reasons for this decadence, and offers practical advice about how to reverse the decline. Orwell has often been compared with Jonathan Swift, whose essay appears in chapter 10 of this book. Although Orwell's essay does not exemplify the Swiftian mode of satire, it does exemplify the Swiftian style—clear, crisp, concrete prose.

Most people who bother with the matter at all would admit that 1
the English language is in a bad way, but it is generally assumed that we cannot by conscious action do anything about it. Our civilization is decadent and our language—so the argument runs—must inevitably share in the general collapse. It follows that any struggle against the abuse of language is a sentimental archaism, like preferring candles to electric light or hansom cabs to aeroplanes. Underneath this lies the half-conscious belief that language is a natural growth and not an instrument which we shape for our own purposes.

Now, it is clear that the decline of a language must ultimately 2
have political and economic causes: it is not due simply to the bad influence of this or that individual writer. But an effect can become a

cause, reinforcing the original cause and producing the same effect in an intensified form, and so on indefinitely. A man may take to drink because he feels himself to be a failure, and then fail all the more completely because he drinks. It is rather the same thing that is happening to the English language. It becomes ugly and inaccurate because our thoughts are foolish, but the slovenliness of our language makes it easier for us to have foolish thoughts. The point is that the process is reversible. Modern English, especially written English, is full of bad habits which spread by imitation and which can be avoided if one is willing to take the necessary trouble. If one gets rid of these habits one can think more clearly, and to think clearly is a necessary first step toward political regeneration: so that the fight against bad English is not frivolous and is not the exclusive concern of professional writers. I will come back to this presently, and I hope that by that time the meaning of what I have said here will have become clearer. Meanwhile, here are five specimens of the English language as it is now habitually written.

These five passages have not been picked out because they are 3
especially bad—I could have quoted far worse if I had chosen—but because they illustrate various of the mental vices from which we now suffer. They are a little below the average, but are fairly representative samples. I number them so that I can refer back to them when necessary:

> (1) I am not, indeed, sure whether it is not true to say that the Milton who once seemed not unlike a seventeenth-century Shelley had not become, out of an experience ever more bitter in each year, more alien *[sic]* to the founder of that Jesuit sect which nothing could induce him to tolerate.
>
> Professor Harold Laski
> (Essay in *Freedom of Expression)*

> (2) Above all, we cannot play ducks and drakes with a native battery of idioms which prescribes such egregious collocations of vocables as the basic *put up with* for *tolerate* or *put at a loss* for *bewilder.*
>
> Professor Lancelot Hogben *(Interglossa)*

> (3) On the one side we have the free personality: by definition it is not neurotic, for it has neither conflict nor dream. Its desires, such as they are, are transparent, for they are just what institutional approval keeps in the forefront of consciousness; another institutional pattern would alter their number and intensity; there is little in them that is natural, irreducible, or culturally dangerous. But *on the other side,* the social bond itself is nothing but the mutual reflection of these self-secure integrities. Recall the definition of love. Is not this the very picture of a small academic? Where is there a place in this hall of mirrors for either personality or fraternity?
>
> Essay on psychology in *Politics* (New York)

> (4) All the "best people" from the gentlemen's clubs, and all the frantic fascist captains, united in common hatred of Socialism and bestial horror of the rising tide of the mass revolutionary movement, have turned to acts of provocation, to foul incendiarism, to medieval legends of poisoned wells, to legalize their own destruction of proletarian organizations, and rouse the agitated petty-bourgeoisie to chauvinistic fervor on behalf of the fight against the revolutionary way out of the crisis.
>
> Communist pamphlet

> (5) If new spirit *is* to be infused into this old country, there is one thorny and contentious reform which must be tackled, and that is the humanization and galvanization of the B.B.C. Timidity here will bespeak canker and atrophy of the soul. The heart of Britain may be sound and of strong beat, for instance, but the British lion's roar at present is like that of Bottom in Shakespeare's *Midsummer Night's Dream*—as gentle as any sucking dove. A virile new Britain cannot continue indefinitely to be traduced in the eyes, or rather ears, of the world by the effete languors of Langham Place, brazenly masquerading as "standard English." When the Voice of Britain is heard at nine o'clock, better far and infinitely less ludicrous to hear aitches honestly dropped than the present priggish, inflated, inhibited, school-ma'amish arch braying of blameless bashful mewing maidens!
>
> Letter in *Tribune*

4 Each of these passages has faults of its own, but, quite apart from avoidable ugliness, two qualities are common to all of them. The first is staleness of imagery; the other is lack of precision. The writer either has a meaning and cannot express it, or he inadvertently says something else, or he is almost indifferent as to whether his words mean anything or not. This mixture of vagueness and sheer incompetence is the most marked characteristic of modern English prose, and especially of any kind of political writing. As soon as certain topics are raised, the concrete melts into the abstract and no one seems able to think of turns of speech that are not hackneyed: prose consists less and less of *words* chosen for the sake of their meaning, and more and more of *phrases* tacked together like the sections of a prefabricated henhouse. I list below, with notes and examples, various of the tricks by means of which the work of prose-construction is habitually dodged:

5 *Dying metaphors.* A newly invented metaphor assists thought by evoking a visual image, while on the other hand a metaphor which is technically "dead" (e.g., *iron resolution*) has in effect reverted to being an ordinary word and can generally be used without loss of vividness. But in between these two classes there is a huge dump of worn-out metaphors which have lost all evocative power and are merely

used because they save people the trouble of inventing phrases for themselves. Examples are: *Ring the changes on, take up the cudgels for, toe the line, ride roughshod over, stand shoulder to shoulder with, play into the hands of, no axe to grind, grist to the mill, fishing in troubled waters, on the order of the day, Achilles' heel, swan song, hotbed.* Many of these are used without knowledge of their meaning (what is a "rift," for instance?), and incompatible metaphors are frequently mixed, a sure sign that the writer is not interested in what he is saying. Some metaphors now current have been twisted out of their original meaning without those who use them ever being aware of the fact. For example, *toe the line* is sometimes written *tow the line.* Another example is *the hammer and the anvil,* now always used with the implication that the anvil gets the worst of it. In real life it is always the anvil that breaks the hammer, never the other way about: a writer who stopped to think what he was saying would be aware of this, and would avoid perverting the original phrase.

*Operators or verbal false limbs.* These save the trouble of picking out 6
appropriate verbs and nouns, and at the same time pad each sentence with extra syllables which give it an appearance of symmetry. Characteristic phrases are *render inoperative, militate against, make contact with, be subjected to, give grounds for, have the effect of, play a leading part (role) in, make itself felt, take effect, exhibit a tendency to, serve the purpose of,* etc., etc. The key-note is the elimination of simple verbs. Instead of being a single word, such as *break, stop, spoil, mend, kill,* a verb becomes a *phrase,* made up of a noun or adjective tacked on to some general-purpose verb such as *prove, serve, form, play, render.* In addition, the passive voice is wherever possible used in preference to the active, and noun constructions are used instead of gerunds (*by examination of* instead of *by examining*). The range of verbs is further cut down by means of the *-ize* and *de-* formations, and the banal statements are given an appearance of profundity by means of the *not un-* formation. Simple conjunctions and prepositions are replaced by such phrases as *with respect to, having regard to, the fact that, by dint of, in view of, in the interests of, on the hypothesis that;* and the ends of sentences are saved from anticlimax by such resounding commonplaces as *greatly to be desired, cannot be left out of account, a development to be expected in the near future, deserving of serious consideration, brought to a satisfactory conclusion,* and so on and so forth.

*Pretentious diction.* Words like *phenomenon, element, individual* (as 7
noun), *objective, categorical, effective, virtual, basic, primary, promote, constitute, exhibit, exploit, utilize, eliminate, liquidate,* are used to dress up simple statements and give an air of scientific impartiality to

biased judgments. Adjectives like *epoch-making, epic, historic, unforgettable, triumphant, age-old, inevitable, inexorable, veritable,* are used to dignify the sordid process of international politics, while writing that aims at glorifying war usually takes on an archaic color, its characteristic words being: *realm, throne, chariot, mailed fist, trident, sword, shield, buckler, banner, jackboot, clarion.* Foreign words and expressions such as *cul de sac, ancien régime, deus ex machina, mutatis mutandis, status quo, gleichschaltung, weltanschauung,* are used to give an air of culture and elegance. Except for the useful abbreviations *i.e., e.g.,* and *etc.,* there is no real need for any of the hundreds of foreign phrases now current in English. Bad writers, and especially scientific, political, and sociological writers, are nearly always haunted by the notion that Latin or Greek words are grander than Saxon ones, and unnecessary words like *expedite, ameliorate, predict, extraneous, deracinated, clandestine, subaqueous,* and hundreds of others constantly gain ground from their Anglo-Saxon opposite numbers.[1] The jargon peculiar to Marxist writing *(hyena, hangman, cannibal, petty bourgeois, these gentry, lackey, flunkey, mad dog, White Guard,* etc.) consists largely of words and phrases translated from Russian, German, or French; but the normal way of coining a new word is to use a Latin or Greek root with the appropriate affix and, where necessary, the *-ize* formation. It is often easier to make up words of this kind *(deregionalize, impermissible, extra-marital, nonfragmentary* and so forth) than to think up the English words that will cover one's meaning. The result, in general, is an increase in slovenliness and vagueness.

*Meaningless words.* In certain kinds of writing, particularly in art criticism and literary criticism, it is normal to come across long passages which are almost completely lacking in meaning.[2] Words like *romantic, plastic, values, human, dead, sentimental, natural, vitality,* as used in art criticism, are strictly meaningless, in the sense that they not only do not point to any discoverable object, but are hardly ever expected to do so by the reader. When one critic writes, "The outstanding feature of Mr. X's work is its living quality," while another writes, "The immediately striking thing about Mr. X's work is its 8

[1]An interesting illustration of this is the way in which the English flower names which were in use till very recently are being ousted by Greek ones, *snapdragon* becoming *antirrhinum, forget-me-not* becoming *myosotis,* etc. It is hard to see any practical reason for this change of fashion: it is probably due to an instinctive turning away from the more homely word and a vague feeling that the Greek word is scientific. [Orwell's note]

[2]Example: "Comfort's catholicity of perception and image, strangely Whitmanesque in range, almost the exact opposite in aesthetic compulsion, continues to evoke that trembling atmospheric accumulative hinting at a cruel, an inexorably serene timelessness. . . . Wrey Gardiner scores by aiming at simple bull's eyes with precision. Only they are not so simple, and through this contented sadness runs more than the surface bittersweet of resignation." *(Poetry Quarterly.)* [Orwell's note]

peculiar deadness," the reader accepts this as a simple difference of opinion. If words like *black* and *white* were involved, instead of the jargon words *dead* and *living,* he would see at once that language was being used in an improper way. Many political words are similarly abused. The word *Fascism* has now no meaning except in so far as it signifies "something not desirable." The words *democracy, socialism, freedom, patriotic, realistic, justice,* have each of them several different meanings which cannot be reconciled with one another. In the case of a word like *democracy,* not only is there no agreed definition, but the attempt to make one is resisted from all sides. It is almost universally felt that when we call a country democratic we are praising it: consequently the defenders of every kind of régime claim that it is a democracy, and fear that they might have to stop using the word if it were tied down to any one meaning. Words of this kind are often used in a consciously dishonest way. That is, the person who uses them has his own private definition, but allows his hearer to think he means something quite different. Statements like *Marshall Pétain was a true patriot, The Soviet press is the freest in the world, The Catholic Church is opposed to persecution,* are almost always made with intent to deceive. Other words used in variable meanings, in most cases more or less dishonestly, are: *class, totalitarian, science, progressive, reactionary, bourgeois, equality.*

Now that I have made this catalogue of swindles and perversions, 9
let me give another example of the kind of writing that they lead to. This time it must of its nature be an imaginary one. I am going to translate a passage of good English into modern English of the worst sort. Here is a well-known verse from *Ecclesiastes:*

> I returned and saw under the sun, that the race is not to the swift, nor the battle to the strong, neither yet bread to the wise, nor yet riches to men of understanding, nor yet favor to men of skill; but time and chance happeneth to them all.

Here it is in modern English: 10

> Objective consideration of contemporary phenomena compels the conclusion that success or failure in competitive activities exhibits no tendency to be commensurate with innate capacity, but that a considerable element of the unpredictable must invariably be taken into account.

This is a parody, but not a very gross one. Exhibit (3), above, for 11
instance, contains several patches of the same kind of English. It will be seen that I have not made a full translation. The beginning and ending of the sentence follow the original meaning fairly closely, but in the middle the concrete illustration—race, battle, bread—dissolve into the vague phrase "success or failure in competitive activities."

This had to be so, because no modern writer of the kind I am discussing—no one capable of using phrases like "objective consideration of contemporary phenomena"—would ever tabulate his thoughts in that precise and detailed way. The whole tendency of modern prose is away from concreteness. Now analyze these two sentences a little more closely. The first contains forty-nine words but only sixty syllables, and all its words are those of everyday life. The second contains thirty-eight words of ninety syllables: eighteen of its words are from Latin roots and one from Greek. The first sentence contains six vivid images, and only one phrase ("time and chance") that could be called vague. The second contains not a single fresh, arresting phrase, and in spite of its ninety syllables it gives only a shortened version of the meaning contained in the first. Yet without a doubt it is the second kind of sentence that is gaining ground in modern English. I do not want to exaggerate. This kind of writing is not yet universal, and outcrops of simplicity will occur here and there in the worst-written page. Still, if you or I were told to write a few lines on the uncertainty of human fortunes, we should probably come much nearer to my imaginary sentence than to the one from *Ecclesiastes.*

As I have tried to show, modern writing at its worst does not consist in picking out words for the sake of their meaning and inventing images in order to make the meaning clearer. It consists in gumming together long strips of words which have already been set in order by someone else, and making the results presentable by sheer humbug. The attraction of this way of writing is that it is easy. It is easier—even quicker, once you have the habit—to say *In my opinion it is not an unjustifiable assumption that* than to say *I think.* If you use ready-made phrases, you not only don't have to hunt about for words; you also don't have to bother with the rhythms of your sentences, since these phrases are generally so arranged as to be more or less euphonious. When you are composing in a hurry—when you are dictating to a stenographer, for instance, or making a public speech—it is natural to fall into a pretentious, Latinized style. Tags like *a consideration which we should do well to bear in mind* or *a conclusion to which all of us would readily assent* will save many a sentence from coming down with a bump. By using stale metaphors, similes, and idioms, you save much mental effort, at the cost of leaving your meaning vague, not only for your reader but for yourself. This is the significance of mixed metaphors. The sole aim of a metaphor is to call up a visual image. When these images clash—as in *The Fascist octopus has sung its swan song, the jackboot is thrown into the melting pot*—it can be taken as certain that the writer is not seeing a mental image of the objects he is naming; in other words he is not really thinking. Look 12 again at the examples I gave at the beginning of this essay. Professor Laski (1) uses five negatives in fifty-three words. One of these is superfluous, making nonsense of the whole passage, and in addition there is the slip—*alien* for akin—making further nonsense, and several avoidable pieces of clumsiness which increase the general vagueness. Professor Hogben (2) plays ducks and drakes with a battery which is able to write prescriptions, and, while disapproving of the everyday phrase *put up with,* is unwilling to look *egregious* up in the dictionary and see what it means; (3), if one takes an uncharitable attitude towards it, is simply meaningless: probably one could work out its intended meaning by reading the whole of the article in which it occurs. In (4), the writer knows more or less what he wants to say, but an accumulation of stale phrases chokes him like tea leaves blocking a sink. In (5), words and meaning have almost parted company. People who write in this manner usually have a general emotional meaning—they dislike one thing and want to express solidarity with another—but they are not interested in the detail of what they are saying. A scrupulous writer, in every sentence that he writes, will ask himself at least four questions, thus: What am I trying to say? What words will express it? What image or idiom will make it clearer? Is this image fresh enough to have an effect? And he will probably ask himself two more: Could I put it more shortly? Have I said anything that is avoidably ugly? But you are not obliged to go to all this trouble, You can shirk it by simply throwing your mind open and letting the ready-made phrases come crowding in. They will construct your sentences for you—even think your thoughts for you, to a certain extent—and at need they will perform the important service of partially concealing your meaning even from yourself. It is at this point that the special connection between politics and the debasement of language becomes clear.

In our time it is broadly true that political writing is bad writing. 13
Where it is not true, it will generally be found that the writer is some kind of rebel, expressing his private opinions and not a "party line." Orthodoxy, of whatever color, seems to demand a lifeless, imitative style. The political dialects to be found in pamphlets, leading articles, manifestoes, White Papers and the speeches of undersecretaries do, of course, vary from party to party, but they are all alike in that one almost never finds in them a fresh, vivid, home-made turn of speech. When one watches some tired hack on the platform mechanically repeating the familiar phrases—*bestial atrocities, iron heel, bloodstained tyranny, free peoples of the world, stand shoulder to shoulder*—one often has a curious feeling that one is not watching a live human being but some kind of dummy: a feeling which suddenly becomes stronger at moments when the light catches the speaker's spectacles and turns them into blank discs which seem to have no eyes behind them. And this is not altogether fanciful. A speaker who uses that kind of

phraseology has gone some distance towards turning himself into a machine. The appropriate noises are coming out of his larynx, but his brain is not involved as it would be if he were choosing his words for himself. If the speech he is making is one that he is accustomed to make over and over again, he may be almost unconscious of what he is saying, as one is when one utters the responses in church. And this reduced state of consciousness, if not indispensable, is at any rate favorable to political conformity.

In our time, political speech and writing are largely the defense of 14
the indefensible. Things like the continuance of British rule in India, the Russian purges and deportations, the droppings of the atom bombs on Japan, can indeed be defended, but only by arguments which are too brutal for most people to face, and which do not square with the professed aims of political parties. Thus political language has to consist largely of euphemism, question-begging, and sheer cloudy vagueness. Defenseless villages are bombarded from the air, the inhabitants driven out into the countryside, the cattle machine-gunned, the huts set on fire with incendiary bullets: this is called *pacification*. Millions of peasants are robbed of their farms and sent trudging along the roads with no more than they can carry: this is called *transfer of population* or *rectification of frontiers*. People are imprisoned for years without trial, or shot in the back of the neck or sent to die of scurvy in Arctic lumber camps: this is called *elimination of unreliable elements*. Such phraseology is needed if one wants to name things without calling up mental pictures of them. Consider for instance some comfortable English professor defending Russian totalitarianism. He cannot say outright, "I believe in killing off your opponents when you can get good results by doing so." Probably, therefore, he will say something like this:

> While freely conceding that the Soviet régime exhibits certain features which the humanitarian may be inclined to deplore, we must, I think, agree that a certain curtailment of the right to political opposition is an unavoidable concomitant of transitional periods, and that the rigors which the Russian people have been called upon to undergo have been amply justified in the sphere of concrete achievement.

The inflated style is itself a kind of euphemism. A mass of Latin 15
words falls upon the facts like soft snow, blurring the outlines and covering up all the details. The great enemy of clear language is insincerity. When there is a gap between one's real and one's declared aims, one turns as it were instinctively to long words and exhausted idioms, like a cuttlefish squirting out ink. In our age there is no such thing as "keeping out of politics." All issues are political issues, and politics itself is a mass of lies, evasions, folly, hatred and schizophrenia. When the general atmosphere is bad, language must suffer.

I should expect to find—this is a guess which I have not sufficient knowledge to verify—that the German, Russian, and Italian languages have all deteriorated in the last ten or fifteen years, as a result of dictatorship.

But if thought corrupts language, language can also corrupt 16
thought. A bad usage can spread by tradition and imitation, even among people who should and do know better. The debased language that I have been discussing is in some ways very convenient. Phrases like *a not unjustifiable assumption, leaves much to be desired, would serve no good purpose, a consideration which we should do well to bear in mind,* are a continuous temptation, a packet of aspirins always at one's elbow. Look back through this essay, and for certain you will find that I have again and again committed the very faults I am protesting against. By this morning's post I have received a pamphlet dealing with conditions in Germany. The author tells me that he "felt impelled" to write it. I open it at random, and here is almost the first sentence that I see: "[The Allies] have an opportunity not only of achieving a radical transformation of Germany's social and political structure in such a way as to avoid a nationalistic reaction in Germany itself, but at the same time of laying the foundations of a co-operative and unified Europe." You see, he "feels impelled" to write—feels, presumably, that he has something new to say—and yet his words, like cavalry horses answering the bugle, group themselves automatically into the familiar dreary pattern. This invasion of one's mind by ready-made phrases *(lay the foundations, achieve a radical transformation)* can only be prevented if one is constantly on guard against them, and every such phrase anaesthetizes a portion of one's brain.

I said earlier that the decadence of our language is probably 17
curable. Those who deny this would argue, if they produced an argument at all, that language merely reflects existing social conditions, and that we cannot influence its development by any direct tinkering with words and constructions. So far as the general tone or spirit of a language goes, this may be true, but it is not true in detail. Silly words and expressions have often disappeared, not through any evolutionary process but owing to the conscious action of a minority. Two recent examples were *explore every avenue* and *leave no stone unturned,* which were killed by the jeers of a few journalists. There is a long list of flyblown metaphors which could similarly be got rid of if enough people would interest themselves in the job; and it should also be possible to laugh the *not un-* formation out of existence,[3] to reduce the amount of Latin and Greek in the average sentence, to

[3]One can cure oneself of the *not un-* formation by memorizing this sentence: *A not unblack dog was chasing a not unsmall rabbit across a not ungreen field.* [Orwell's note]

drive out foreign phrases and strayed scientific words, and, in general, to make pretentiousness unfashionable. But all these are minor points. The defense of the English language implies more than this, and perhaps it is best to start by saying what it does *not* imply.

To begin with it has nothing to do with archaism, with the 18
salvaging of obsolete words and turns of speech, or with the setting up of a "standard English" which must never be departed from. On the contrary, it is especially concerned with the scrapping of every word or idiom which has outworn its usefulness. It has nothing to do with correct grammar and syntax, which are of no importance so long as one makes one's meaning clear, or with the avoidance of Americanisms, or with having what is called a "good prose style." On the other hand it is not concerned with fake simplicity and the attempt to make written English colloquial. Nor does it even imply in every case preferring the Saxon word to the Latin one, though it does imply using the fewest and shortest words that will cover one's meaning. What is above all needed is to let the meaning choose the word, and not the other way about. In prose, the worst thing one can do with words is to surrender to them. When you think of a concrete object, you think wordlessly, and then, if you want to describe the thing you have been visualizing you probably hunt about till you find the exact words that seem to fit it. When you think of something abstract you are more inclined to use words from the start, and unless you make a conscious effort to prevent it, the existing dialect will come rushing in and do the job for you, at the expense of blurring or even changing your meaning. Probably it is better to put off using words as long as possible and get one's meaning as clear as one can through pictures or sensations. Afterward one can choose—not simply *accept*—the phrases that will best cover the meaning, and then switch round and decide what impression one's words are likely to make on another person. This last effort of the mind cuts out all stale or mixed images, all prefabricated phrases, needless repetitions, and humbug and vagueness generally. But one can often be in doubt about the effect of a word or a phrase, and one needs rules that one can rely on when instinct fails. I think the following rules will cover most cases:

(i) Never use a metaphor, simile, or other figure of speech which you are used to seeing in print.
(ii) Never use a long word where a short one will do.
(iii) If it is possible to cut a word out, always cut it out.
(iv) Never use the passive where you can use the active.
(v) Never use a foreign phrase, a scientific word, or a jargon word if you can think of an everyday English equivalent.
(vi) Break any of these rules sooner than say anything outright barbarous.

These rules sound elementary, and so they are, but they demand a deep change of attitude in anyone who has grown used to writing in the style now fashionable. One could keep all of them and still write bad English, but one could not write the kind of stuff that I quoted in those five specimens at the beginning of this article.

I have not here been considering the literary use of language, but 19
merely language as an instrument for expressing and not for concealing or preventing thought. Stuart Chase and others have come near to claiming that all abstract words are meaningless, and have used this as a pretext for advocating a kind of political quietism. Since you don't know what Fascism is, how can you struggle against Fascism? One need not swallow such absurdities as this, but one ought to recognize that the present political chaos is connected with the decay of language, and that one can probably bring about some improvement by starting at the verbal end. If you simplify your English, you are freed from the worst follies of orthodoxy. You cannot speak any of the necessary dialects, and when you make a stupid remark its stupidity will be obvious, even to yourself. Political language—and with variations this is true of all political parties, from Conservatives to Anarchists—is designed to make lies sound truthful and murder respectable, and to give an appearance of solidity to pure wind. One cannot change this all in a moment, but one can at least change one's own habits, and from time to time one can even, if one jeers loudly enough, send some worn-out and useless phrase—some *jackboot, Achilles' heel, hotbed, melting pot, acid test, veritable inferno,* or other lump of verbal refuse—into the dustbin where it belongs.

#### IN RETROSPECT

**1.** In paragraph 2 of this essay, Orwell discusses the relationship between politics and language. How does he characterize this relationship? What implications does this discussion have for you as a writer? for you as a reader of the other essays in this book on the familiar essay?

**2.** At the end of paragraph 18, Orwell lists six suggestions for curing the "decadence" of the English language. Form groups of four to five class members, and in each group, experiment with at least three of the five passages that Orwell cites in paragraph 3. Try to revise each passage in terms of the six suggestions Orwell offers for writing clear prose. Compare your revisions with those offered by other groups in the class. Consider which revisions are most satisfactory, and give reasons for your judgments.

# *The Day Language Came into My Life*

## HELEN KELLER

Helen Keller (1880–1968) was born a normal child in Tuscumbia, Alabama, but at the age of nineteen months she contracted a disease that left her blind and deaf. Despite her handicap, which left her half-wild in her isolated state, she grew up to become—thanks to the extraordinary help she received, at age seven, from her teacher Anne Sullivan—a legend and an inspiration to other handicapped people throughout the world. Because of that empowering help, Keller began her formal schooling when she was fourteen. She made so much progress that after graduation from secondary school she was admitted to Radcliffe, the prestigious college for women, from which she graduated cum laude in 1904. Because of her keen concern for social issues, Keller joined the Socialist party, but in 1921, she decided that she could best serve humanity by devoting herself to helping the blind and the deaf. She subsequently received many awards and acclaims for her work in behalf of the American Foundation for the Blind. Among those awards was the Presidential Medal of Freedom that she received from Lyndon Johnson in 1964. Mark Twain, whose writings Keller greatly admired, once said of her that she was the most marvelous woman since Joan of Arc. In 1954, the movie *The Unconquered* was made of her life, and in 1959, William Gibson staged his play *The Miracle Worker,* which among other things dramatized that marvelous moment when Anne Sullivan made Keller aware of language. That moment is also narrated in the essay that follows, from Keller's *The Story of My Life* (1902).

The most important day I remember in all my life is the one on which my teacher, Anne Mansfield Sullivan, came to me. I am filled with wonder when I consider the immeasurable contrast between the two lives which it connects. It was the third of March 1887, three months before I was seven years old. 1

On the afternoon of that eventful day, I stood on the porch, dumb, expectant. I guessed vaguely from my mother's signs and from the hurrying to and fro in the house that something unusual was about to happen, so I went to the door and waited on the steps. The afternoon sun penetrated the mass of honeysuckle that covered the porch and fell on my upturned face. My fingers lingered almost unconsciously on the familiar leaves and blossoms which had just come forth to greet the sweet southern spring. I did not know what the future held of marvel or surprise for me. Anger and bitterness had preyed upon me continually for weeks and a deep languor had succeeded this passionate struggle. 2

Have you ever been at sea in a dense fog, when it seemed as if a tangible white darkness shut you in, and the great ship, tense and anxious, groped her way toward the shore with plummet and sound- 3 ing-line, and you waited with beating heart for something to happen? I was like that ship before my education began, only I was without compass or sounding-line and had no way of knowing how near the harbor was. "Light! give me light!" was the wordless cry of my soul, and the light of love shone on me in that very hour.

I felt approaching footsteps. I stretched out my hand as I sup- 4
posed to my mother. Someone took it, and I was caught up and held close in the arms of her who had come to reveal all things to me, and, more than all things else, to love me.

The morning after my teacher came she led me into her room and 5
gave me a doll. The little blind children at the Perkins Institution had sent it and Laura Bridgman had dressed it; but I did not know this until afterward. When I had played with it a little while, Miss Sullivan slowly spelled into my hand the word "d-o-l-l." I was at once interested in this finger play and tried to imitate it. When I finally succeeded in making the letters correctly I was flushed with childish pleasure and pride. Running downstairs to my mother I held up my hand and made the letters for doll. I did not know that I was spelling a word or even that words existed; I was simply making my fingers go in monkeylike imitation. In the days that followed I learned to spell in this uncomprehending way a great many words, among them *pin, hat, cup* and a few verbs like *sit, stand* and *walk.* But my teacher had been with me several weeks before I understood that everything has a name.

One day, while I was playing with my new doll, Miss Sullivan 6
put my big rag doll into my lap also, spelled "d-o-l-l" and tried to make me understand that "d-o-l-l" applied to both. Earlier in the day we had had a tussle over the words "m-u-g" and "w-a-t-e-r." Miss Sullivan had tried to impress it upon me that "m-u-g" is *mug* and that "w-a-t-e-r" is *water,* but I persisted in confounding the two. In despair she had dropped the subject for the time, only to renew it at the first opportunity. I became impatient at her repeated attempts and, seizing the new doll, I dashed it upon the floor. I was keenly delighted when I felt the fragments of the broken doll at my feet. Neither sorrow nor regret followed my passionate outburst. I had not loved the doll. In the still, dark world in which I lived there was no strong sentiment or tenderness. I felt my teacher sweep the fragments to one side of the hearth, and I had a sense of satisfaction that the cause of my discomfort was removed. She brought me my hat, and I knew I was going out into the warm sunshine. This thought, if a wordless sensation may be called a thought, made me hop and skip with pleasure.

We walked down the path to the well-house, attracted by the 7
fragrance of the honeysuckle with which it was covered. Some one

was drawing water and my teacher placed my hand under the spout. As the cool stream gushed over one hand she spelled into the other the word *water*, first slowly, then rapidly. I stood still, my whole attention fixed upon the motions of her fingers. Suddenly I felt a misty consciousness as of something forgotten—a thrill of returning thought; and somehow the mystery of language was revealed to me. I knew then that "w-a-t-e-r" meant the wonderful cool something that was flowing over my hand. The living word awakened my soul, gave it light, hope, joy, set it free! There were barriers still, it is true, but barriers that could in time be swept away.

I left the well-house eager to learn. Everything had a name, and 8
each name gave birth to a new thought. As we returned to the house every object which I touched seemed to quiver with life. That was because I saw everything with the strange, new sight that had come to me. On entering the door I remembered the doll I had broken. I felt my way to the hearth and picked up the pieces. I tried vainly to put them together. Then my eyes filled with tears; for I realized what I had done, and for the first time I felt repentance and sorrow.

I learned a great many new words that day. I do not remember 9
what they all were; but I do know that *mother, father, sister, teacher* were among them—words that were to make the world blossom for me, "like Aaron's rod, with flowers." It would have been difficult to find a happier child than I was as I lay in my crib at the close of that eventful day and lived over the joys it had brought me, and for the first time longed for a new day to come.

## IN RETROSPECT

**1.** In this essay, Keller demonstrates the power that language has to convey to herself and to others experiences that she never had through sight or sound. Consider the following sentence from paragraph 3: "Have you ever been at sea in a dense fog, when it seemed as if a tangible white darkness shut you in, and the great ship, tense and anxious, groped her way toward the shore with plummet and sounding-line, and you waited with beating heart for something to happen?" Even if Keller later in life had had the experience of being at sea in a dense fog, how would she know that fog was *white* and that the ship *groped* its way toward the shore? In answering this question, consider how the acquisition of language empowers a person to experience life in all its ramifications.

**2.** A person does not have to be completely deprived of the faculty of language to empathize with Keller. Recall an experience in which you lacked the command of language that would have enabled you to participate in a discussion. What were your frustrations on that occasion, and how did you overcome your handicap—if you did do so—in order to join in the discussion?

# *That Word* Black

## LANGSTON HUGHES

Langston Hughes (1902–1967) was born in Joplin, Missouri. As a literary figure, he is best known as a poet, an eloquent and influential poet of the Harlem Renaissance of the 1920s. Among his many collections of poetry are *Weary Blues* (1926), *Shakespeare in Harlem* (1942), *Montage of a Dream Deferred* (1951), and *Ask Your Mama* (1961). He also wrote a play, *Mulatto* (1935), which was later produced in a musical version, *The Barrier* (1950). He also published a novel, *Not without Laughter* (1930), and a short-story collection, *The Ways of White Folks* (1934). In the essay "That Word *Black*," the main speaker is Simple, a character Hughes created for a series of satirical sketches that he wrote for a black newspaper. In the sketch reproduced here, Simple explores a cultural phenomenon: the connotations that attach themselves to certain words in any language over time. Simple remarks on the bad connotations that have attached themselves to such words in American English as *blackmail, blacklist, blackball, black market, black sheep,* and *black mark.* In Simple's dictionary, such words would instead carry the word *white.* Are good and bad connotations a conscious or an unconscious creation of a people living in a certain culture?

"This evening," said Simple, "I feel like talking about the word *black.*" 1

"Nobody's stopping you, so go ahead. But what you really ought to have is a soap-box out on the corner of 126th and Lenox where the rest of the orators hang out." 2

"They expresses some good ideas on that corner," said Simple, "but for my ideas I do not need a crowd. Now, as I were saying, the word *black,* white folks have done used that word to mean something bad so often until now when the N.A.A.C.P asks for civil rights for the black man, they think they must be bad. Looking back into history, I reckon it all started with a *black* cat meaning bad luck. Don't let one cross your path! 3

"Next, somebody got up a *blacklist* on which you get if you don't vote right. Then when lodges come into being, the folks they didn't want in them got *black-balled.* If you kept a skeleton in your closet, you might get *black-mailed.* And everything bad was *black.* When it came down to the unlucky ball on the pool table, the eight-rock, they made it the *black* ball. So no wonder there ain't no equal rights for the *black* man." 4

"All you say is true about the odium attached to the word *black,*" I said. "You've even forgotten a few. For example, during the war if you bought something under the table, illegally, they said you were trading on the *black* market. In Chicago, if you're a gangster, the *Black* 5

*Hand Society* may take you for a ride. And certainly if you don't behave yourself, your family will say you're a *black* sheep. Then if your mama burns a *black* candle to change the family luck, they call it *black* magic."

"My mama never did believe in voodoo so she did not burn no 6
black candles," said Simple.

"If she had, that would have been a *black* mark against her." 7

"Stop talking about my mama. What I want to know is, where do 8
white folks get off calling everything bad *black?* If it is a dark night, they say it's *black* as hell. If you are mean and evil, they say you got a *black* heart. I would like to change all that around and say that the people who Jim Crow me have got a *white* heart. People who sell dope to children have got a *white* mark against them. And all the white gamblers who were behind the basketball fix are the *white* sheep of the sports world. God knows there was few, if any, Negroes selling stuff on the black market during the war, so why didn't they call it the *white* market? No, they got to take me and my color and turn it into everything *bad.* According to white folks, black is bad.

"Wait till my day comes! In my language, bad will be *white.* 9
Blackmail will be *white* mail. Black cats will be good luck, and *white* cats will be bad. If a *white* cat crosses your path, look out! I will take the black ball for the cue ball and let the *white* ball be the unlucky eight-rock. And on my blacklist—which will be a *white* list then—I will put everybody who ever Jim Crowed me from Rankin to Hitler, Talmadge to Malan, South Carolina to South Africa.

"I am black. When I look in the mirror, I see myself, daddy-o, but 10
I am not ashamed. God made me. He did not make us no badder than the rest of the folks. The earth is black and all kinds of good things comes out of the earth. Trees and flowers and fruit and sweet potatoes and corn and all that keeps mens alive comes right up out of the earth—good old black earth. Coal is black and it warms your house and cooks your food. The night is black, which has a moon, and a million stars, and is beautiful. Sleep is black which gives you rest, so you wake up feeling good. I am black. I feel very good this evening.

"What is wrong with black?" 11

**IN RETROSPECT**

**1.** Everything in Hughes's essay is presented in tandem: two people participate in a dialogue interchangeably; two colors (black and white) are explored; two connotations (positive and negative) are provided for each color; two races are discussed; two views of these races are implied; and a mirror image is presented in the last paragraph of the essay. What do we learn about the craft of this essayist from his use of this duality?

**2.** After reading this essay, how would you answer the question posed in the headnote: "Are good and bad connotations a conscious or an unconscious creation of a people living in a certain culture"? Present supporting arguments for your answer. What other words carry, as the word *black* does, strong connotations today? Are these connotations conscious or unconscious? How might they influence your thoughts and feelings?

# *The Silence of a Chinese-American Schoolgirl*

## MAXINE HONG KINGSTON

Maxine Hong Kingston (1940– ) was born in Stockton, California, to Chinese parents. Hong is her maiden name; she acquired the surname Kingston when she married the actor Earll Kingston in 1962, while she was working for an A.B. at the University of California at Berkeley. After obtaining a teaching certificate in 1965, Kingston began teaching high school in Hayward, California. She subsequently taught English at a number of high schools in Hawaii and in 1969 taught English as a second language at Honolulu Business College. From 1970 to 1977, Kingston was a teacher of English language arts at the Mid-Pacific Institute in Honolulu; in 1977 she became a visiting associate professor of English at the University of Hawaii at Manoa. Her two best-known published works are *The Woman Warrior: Memoirs of a Girlhood among Ghosts* (1976), from which the following essay was taken, and *China Men* (1980). Although these works are classified as nonfiction, they are, as many literary critics point out, a unique blend of fiction and nonfiction. Much of Kingston's writing reflects the influence of the many "story-talkers" she encountered in the Chinese-American community in which she grew up. It is ironic that the "silent" young girl described in the following essay, which bears a title assigned to it by the editors of this collection, became an accomplished teacher of English Language Arts and an esteemed writer.

When I went to kindergarten and had to speak English for the first time, I became silent. A dumbness—a shame—still cracks my voice in two, even when I want to say "hello" casually, or ask an easy question in front of the check-out counter, or ask directions of a bus driver. I stand frozen, or I hold up the line with the complete, grammatical sentence that comes squeaking out at impossible length. "What did you say?" says the cab driver, or "Speak up," so I have to 1 perform again, only weaker the second time. A telephone call makes my throat bleed and takes up that day's courage. It spoils my day with self-disgust when I hear my broken voice come skittering out into the open. It makes people wince to hear it. I'm getting better, though. Recently I asked the postman for special-issue stamps; I've waited since childhood for postmen to give me some of their own accord. I am making progress, a little every day.

2 My silence was thickest—total—during the three years that I covered my school paintings with black paint. I painted layers of black over houses and flowers and suns, and when I drew on the blackboard, I put a layer of chalk on top. I was making a stage curtain, and it was the moment before the curtain parted or rose. The teachers called my parents to school, and I saw they had been saving my pictures, curling and cracking, all alike and black. The teachers pointed to the pictures and looked serious, talked seriously too, but my parents did not understand English. ("The parents and teachers of criminals were executed," said my father.) My parents took the pictures home. I spread them out (so black and full of possibilities) and pretended the curtains were swinging open, flying up, one after another, sunlight underneath, mighty operas.

3 During the first silent year I spoke to no one at school, did not ask before going to the lavatory, and flunked kindergarten. My sister also said nothing for three years, silent in the playground and silent at lunch. There were other quiet Chinese girls not of our family, but most of them got over it sooner than we did. I enjoyed the silence. At first it did not occur to me I was supposed to talk or to pass kindergarten. I talked at home and to one or two of the Chinese kids in class. I made motions and even made some jokes. I drank out of a toy saucer when the water spilled out of the cup, and everybody laughed, pointing at me, so I did it some more. I didn't know that Americans don't drink out of saucers.

4 I liked the Negro students (Black Ghosts) best because they laughed the loudest and talked to me as if I were a daring talker too. One of the Negro girls had her mother coil braids over her ears Shanghai-style like mine; we were Shanghai twins except that she was covered with black like my paintings. Two Negro kids enrolled in Chinese school, and the teachers gave them Chinese names. Some Negro kids walked me to school and home, protecting me from the Japanese kids, who hit me and chased me and stuck gum in my ears. The Japanese kids were noisy and tough. They appeared one day in kindergarten, released from concentration camp, which was a tic-tac-toe mark, like barbed wire, on the map.

5 It was when I found out I had to talk that school became a misery, that the silence became a misery. I did not speak and felt bad each

time that I did not speak. I read aloud in first grade, though, and heard the barest whisper with little squeaks come out of my throat. "Louder," said the teacher, who scared the voice away again. The other Chinese girls did not talk either, so I knew the silence had to do with being a Chinese girl.

Reading out loud was easier than speaking because we did not have to make up what to say, but I stopped often, and the teacher would think I'd gone quiet again. I could not understand "I." The Chinese "I" has seven strokes, intricacies. How could the American "I," assuredly wearing a hat like the Chinese, have only three strokes, the middle so straight? Was it out of politeness that this writer left off the strokes the way a Chinese has to write her own name small and crooked? No, it was not politeness; "I" is a capital and "you" is lower-case. I stared at that middle line and waited so long for its black center to resolve into tight strokes and dots that I forgot to pronounce it. The other troublesome word was "here," no strong consonant to hang on to, and so flat, when "here" is two mountainous ideographs. The teacher, who had already told me every day how to read "I" and "here," put me in the low corner under the stairs again, where the noisy boys usually sat. 6

When my second grade class did a play, the whole class went to the auditorium except the Chinese girls. The teacher, lovely and Hawaiian, should have understood about us, but instead left us behind in the classroom. Our voices were too soft or nonexistent, and our parents never signed the permission slips anyway. They never signed anything unnecessary. We opened the door a crack and peeked out, but closed it again quickly. One of us (not me) won every spelling bee, though. 7

I remember telling the Hawaiian teacher, "We Chinese can't sing 'land where our fathers died.' " She argued with me about politics, while I meant because of curses. But how can I have that memory when I couldn't talk? My mother says that we, like the ghosts, have no memories. 8

After American school, we picked up our cigar boxes, in which we had arranged books, brushes, and an inkbox neatly, and went to Chinese school, from 5:00 to 7:30 P.M. There we chanted together, voices rising and falling, loud and soft, some boys shouting, everybody reading together, reciting together and not alone with one voice. When we had a memorization test, the teacher let each of us come to his desk and say the lesson to him privately, while the rest of the class practiced copying or tracing. Most of the teachers were men. The boys who were so well behaved in the American school played tricks on them and talked back to them. The girls were not mute. They screamed and yelled during recess, when there were no rules; 9

they had fistfights. Nobody was afraid of children hurting themselves or of children hurting school property. The glass doors to the red and green balconies with the gold joy symbols were left wide open so that we could run out and climb the fire escapes. We played capture-the-flag in the auditorium, where Sun Yat-sen and Chiang Kai-shek's pictures hung at the back of the stage, the Chinese flag on their left and the American flag on their right. We climbed the teak ceremonial chairs and made flying leaps off the stage. One flag headquarters was behind the glass door and the other on stage right. Our feet drummed on the hollow stage. During recess the teachers locked themselves up in their offices with the shelves of books, copybooks, inks from China. They drank tea and warmed their hands at a stove. There was no play supervision. At recess we had the school to ourselves, and also we could roam as far as we could go—downtown, Chinatown stores, home—as long as we returned before the bell rang.

At exactly 7:30 the teacher again picked up the brass bell that sat 10
on his desk and swung it over our heads, while we charged down the stairs, our cheering magnified in the stairwell. Nobody had to line up.

Not all of the children who were silent at American school found 11
voice at Chinese school. One new teacher said each of us had to get up and recite in front of the class, who was to listen. My sister and I had memorized the lesson perfectly. We said it to each other at home, one chanting, one listening. The teacher called on my sister to recite first. It was the first time a teacher had called on the second-born to go first. My sister was scared. She glanced at me and looked away; I looked down at my desk. I hoped that she could do it because if she could, then I would have to. She opened her mouth and a voice came out that wasn't a whisper, but it wasn't a proper voice either. I hoped that she would not cry, fear breaking up her voice like twigs underfoot. She sounded as if she were trying to sing through weeping and strangling. She did not pause or stop to end the embarrassment. She kept going until she said the last word, and then she sat down. When it was my turn, the same voice came out, a crippled animal running on broken legs. You could hear splinters in my voice, bones rubbing jagged against one another. I was loud, though. I was glad I didn't whisper.

How strange that the emigrant villagers are shouters, hollering 12
face to face. My father asks, "Why is it I can hear Chinese from blocks away? Is it that I understand the language? Or is it they talk loud?" They turn the radio up full blast to hear the operas, which do not seem to hurt their ears. And they yell over the singers that wail over the drums, everybody talking at once, big arm gestures, spit flying. You can see the disgust on American faces looking at women like that. It isn't just the loudness. It is the way Chinese sounds, ching-

chong ugly, to American ears, not beautiful like Japanese sayonara words with the consonants and vowels as regular as Italian. We make guttural peasant noise and have Ton Duc Thang names you can't remember. And the Chinese can't hear Americans at all; the language is too soft and western music unhearable. I've watched a Chinese audience laugh, visit, talk-story, and holler during a piano recital, as if the musician could not hear them. A Chinese-American, somebody's son, was playing Chopin, which has no punctuation, no cymbals, no gongs. Chinese piano music is five black keys. Normal Chinese women's voices are strong and bossy. We American-Chinese girls had to whisper to make ourselves American-feminine. Apparently we whispered even more softly than the Americans. Once a year the teachers referred my sister and me to speech therapy, but our voices would straighten out, unpredictably normal, for the therapists. Some of us gave up, shook our heads, and said nothing, not one word. Some of us could not even shake our heads. At times shaking my head no is more self-assertion than I can manage. Most of us eventually found some voice, however faltering. We invented an American-feminine speaking personality.

#### IN RETROSPECT

**1.** In this essay, Kingston occasionally quotes something that she or some other person said. Do you suppose she is quoting the exact words that she or someone else spoke, or is she, like a fiction writer, inventing dialogue that represents the substance of what was said? Is it legitimate in an essay to use the techniques of fiction writers?

**2.** Kingston describes a situation in which she was silenced and gives us a sense of the implications of that silencing. Discuss with your classmates various ways in which people can be silenced. Have you or has anyone you know ever been silenced in some way? If so, talk about the experience on paper, indicating how it felt and what you think it meant to have been silenced. Share this writing with your classmates, and discuss ways to continue the conversation about silencing that Kingston has begun.

# *Little Red Riding Hood Revisited*

## RUSSELL BAKER

Russell Baker (1925– ) was born in Morrisville, a rural town in Virginia. In his two autobiographical books, *Growing Up* (1982) and *The Good Times* (1989), he talks about his boyhood days in New Jersey and Baltimore and about his early days as a newspaperman. After graduating as an English major from Johns Hopkins University and serving a brief stint in the navy, Baker became a reporter for the *Baltimore Sun*. Eventually, he became the *Baltimore Sun's* London reporter, and then in 1954, he became a reporter on congressional politics in Washington, D.C., for the *New York Times*. But Baker soon became bored with the political arena and was given the chance in 1962 to write the "Observer" column in the *Times*. For the next twenty years, three times a week, he wrote essays for that column, most of them informal and some of them humorous. Baker has published several collections of his essays, including *All Things Considered* (1965) and *So This Is Depravity* (1980). He has won the Pulitzer Prize twice, the first time in 1979 for commentary on the national scene and the second time in 1982 for his autobiography *Growing Up*. From the many essays Baker has written on a variety of topics, we have chosen a piece that satirizes the jargon that has infected so much of the prose written in the business and academic world today. Baker has taken the familiar fairy tale of "Little Red Riding Hood" and translated its simple language into the stale, pretentious words and phrases characteristic of much of the writing that appears in professional journals—and even, alas, in some of our newspapers. Appraise what effect Baker's version of the fairy tale has on you.

In an effort to make the classics accessible to contemporary readers, I am translating them into the modern American language. Here is the translation of "Little Red Riding Hood": 1

Once upon a point in time, a small person named Little Red Riding Hood initiated plans for the preparation, delivery and transportation of foodstuffs to her grandmother, a senior citizen residing at a place of residence in a forest of indeterminate dimension. 2

In the process of implementing this program, her incursion into the forest was in mid-transportation process when it attained interface with an alleged perpetrator. This individual, a wolf, made inquiry as to the whereabouts of Little Red Riding Hood's goal as well as inferring that he was desirous of ascertaining the contents of Little Red Riding Hood's foodstuffs basket, and all that. 3

"It would be inappropriate to lie to me," the wolf said, displaying his huge jaw capability. Sensing that he was a mass of repressed hostility intertwined with acute alienation, she indicated. 4

5 "I see you indicating," the wolf said, "but what I don't see is whatever it is you're indicating at, you dig?"

6 Little Red Riding Hood indicated more fully, making one thing perfectly clear—to wit, that it was to her grandmother's residence and with a consignment of foodstuffs that her mission consisted of taking her to and with.

7 At this point in time the wolf moderated his rhetoric and proceeded to grandmother's residence. The elderly person was then subjected to the disadvantages of total consumption and transferred to residence in the perpetrator's stomach.

8 "That will raise the old woman's consciousness," the wolf said to himself. He was not a bad wolf, but only a victim of an oppressive society, a society that not only denied wolves' rights, but actually boasted of its capacity for keeping the wolf from the door. An interior malaise made itself manifest inside the wolf.

9 "Is that the national malaise I sense within my digestive tract?" wondered the wolf. "Or is it the old person seeking to retaliate for her consumption by telling wolf jokes to my duodenum?" It was time to make a judgment. The time was now, the hour had struck, the body lupine cried out for decision. The wolf was up to the challenge. He took two stomach powders right away and got into bed.

10 The wolf had adopted the abdominal-distress recovery posture when Little Red Riding Hood achieved his presence.

11 "Grandmother," she said, "your ocular implements are of an extraordinary order of magnitude."

12 "The purpose of this enlarged viewing capability," said the wolf, "is to enable your image to register a more precise impression upon my sight systems."

13 "In reference to your ears," said Little Red Riding Hood, "it is noted with the deepest respect that far from being underprivileged, their elongation and enlargement appear to qualify you for unparalleled distinction."

14 "I hear you loud and clear, kid," said the wolf, "but what about these new choppers?"

15 "If it is not inappropriate," said Little Red Riding Hood, "it might be observed that with your new miracle masticating products you may even be able to chew taffy again."

16 This observation was followed by the adoption of an aggressive posture on the part of the wolf and the assertion that it was also possible for him, due to the high efficiency ratio of his jaw, to consume little persons, plus, as he stated, his firm determination to do so at once without delay and with all due process and propriety, notwithstanding the fact that the ingestion of one entire grand-

mother had already provided twice his daily recommended cholesterol intake.

There ensued flight by Little Red Riding Hood accompanied by 17
pursuit in respect to the wolf and a subsequent intervention on the part of a third party, heretofore unnoted in the record.

Due to the firmness of the intervention, the wolf's stomach un- 18
derwent ax-assisted aperture with the result that Red Riding Hood's grandmother was enabled to be removed with only minor discomfort.

The wolf's indigestion was immediately alleviated with such ef- 19
fectiveness that he signed a contract with the intervening third party to perform with the grandmother in a television commercial demonstrating the swiftness of this dramatic relief for stomach discontent.

"I'm going to be on television," cried grandmother. 20

And they all joined her happily in crying, "What a phenomena!" 21

### IN RETROSPECT

**1.** Referring to the six rules about the use of language that Orwell gives us at the end of paragraph 18 in his essay "Politics and the English Language," find out how many of those rules Baker violates in his version of "Little Red Riding Hood." Quote the passages from Baker's version that you think break the rules.

**2.** Baker's translation preserves the substance of "Little Red Riding Hood," a fairy tale most readers are familiar with. What is the difference in the effect that the story has on you in Baker's version? What do you think was Baker's purpose in translating this classic tale into a style that is different from the one in which you first experienced the story?

# 10

# On Social and Political Issues

*Many of the essays in this book discuss contemporary situations or mores. The writers in this chapter are exposing a particular irregularity or injustice in society that needs to be corrected. They are exercising their command of rhetoric, or eloquence, that Oliver Goldsmith was talking about in chapter 9. They have noted a lamentable situation in their environment and want to arouse the citizenry to do something about it. In a democratic society, citizens can do something to correct a lamentable situation, and speakers and writers are free to inform and arouse the citizenry. In a tyrannical government, by contrast, speakers and writers are effectively silenced, and citizens are afraid to rise up in protest. In an oligarchy, such as existed in eighteenth-century England, speakers and writers may have to resort to subtle ways of arousing the citizenry. To arouse the citizenry and the government to do something to correct the crushing poverty of the Irish peasantry, Jonathan Swift had to resort to the device of irony—saying one thing but meaning something quite different. There is a double whammy in Swift's essay "A Modest Proposal."* The I, *the persona in that essay, is really serious in proposing that the Irish poor sell their infant children to the rich to be eaten. But Swift, the author, has quite the opposite intention: He wants to so shock the powers-that-be about the miserable condition of the Irish poor that they will do something to ameliorate the condition of the poor and prevent them from resorting to the proposal that they sell their infant children for food. The writers of the other essays in this chapter employ other rhetorical strategies to influence the attitudes and actions of their readers.*

# *A Modest Proposal*

## JONATHAN SWIFT

Like his compatriot Richard Steele (1672–1729), a popular essayist of the first quarter of the eighteenth century, Jonathan Swift (1667–1745) was born in Dublin, Ireland, and was virtually orphaned from the time of his infancy. Seven months after his father's death, Swift became a ward of his uncles for most of his boyhood. The seven desultory years he spent at Trinity College in Dublin were enough to qualify him for a master's degree, but he left the university in 1689, without taking his degree, to accept the position of secretary to Sir William Temple at Moor Park. Here for the next ten years, Swift read insatiably in Temple's well-stocked library and absorbed some valuable lessons in the intrigues of court affairs. The next fifteen years of Swift's life witness a succession of ups and downs for him in his quest for political office, of feverish political pamphlets, of brilliant satirical works (such as his *Tale of a Tub* and *Battle of the Books*), and of enigmatic relationships of Esther Johnson ("Stella"), Jane Waring ("Varina"), and Esther Vanhomrigh ("Vanessa"). The death of Queen Anne in 1714 shattered Swift's hopes of obtaining a prestigious position in the Tory government, and he settled in Dublin as the Dean of St. Patrick's Cathedral. Swift became a hero to the Irish because of the vigor and effectiveness with which he fought for many of their causes. "A Modest Proposal," one of the essays he wrote on behalf of the Irish, is "topical" in the sense that it was written in response to a contemporary situation, but the personal voice is not as pronounced here as in most of the essays in this volume, partly because the *I* in this piece is not Swift but a persona who is himself being satirized. Irony, a favorite device of the familiar essayist, was never managed more skillfully than it is in this frequently anthologized essay.

It is a melancholy object to those who walk through this great 1
town or travel in the country, when they see the streets, the roads, and cabin doors, crowded with beggars of the female sex, followed by three, four, or six children, all in rags and importuning every passenger for an alms. These mothers, instead of being able to work for their honest livelihood, are forced to employ all their time in strolling to beg sustenance for their helpless infants: who as they grow up either turn thieves for want of work, or leave their dear native country to fight for the pretender in Spain, or sell themselves to the Barbadoes.

I think it is agreed by all parties that this prodigious number of 2
children in the arms, or on the backs, or at the heels of their mothers, and frequently of their fathers, is in the present deplorable state of the kingdom a very great additional grievance; and, therefore, whoever could find out a fair, cheap, and easy method of making these children sound, useful members of the commonwealth, would deserve

so well of the public as to have his statue set up for a preserver of the nation.

But my intention is very far from being confined to provide only 3
for the children of professed beggars; it is of a much greater extent,
and shall take in the whole number of infants at a certain age who are
born of parents in effect as little able to support them as those who
demand our charity in the streets.

As to my own part, having turned my thoughts for many years 4
upon this important subject, and maturely weighed the several
schemes of our projectors, I have always found them grossly mistaken in their computation. It is true, a child just dropped from its
dam may be supported by her milk for a solar year, with little other
nourishment; at most not above the values of *2s.*, which the mother
may certainly get, or the value in scraps, by her lawful occupation of
begging; and it is exactly at one year old that I propose to provide for
them in such a manner as instead of being a charge upon their
parents or the parish, or wanting food and raiment for the rest of their
lives, they shall on the contrary contribute to the feeding, and partly
to the clothing, of many thousands.

There is likewise another great advantage in my scheme, that it 5
will prevent those voluntary abortions, and that horrid practice of
women murdering their bastard children, alas! too frequent among
us! sacrificing the poor innocent babes I doubt more to avoid the
expense than the shame, which would move tears and pity in the
most savage and inhuman breast.

The number of souls in this kingdom being usually reckoned one 6
million and a half, of these I calculate there may be about 200,000
couple whose wives are breeders; from which number I subtract
30,000 couple who are able to maintain their own children (although I
apprehend there cannot be so many, under the present distress of the
kingdom); but this being granted, there will remain 170,000 breeders.
I again subtract 50,000 for those women who miscarry, or whose
children die by accident or disease within the year. There only remain
120,000 children of poor parents annually born. The question therefore is, how this number shall be reared and provided for? which, as I
have already said, under the present situation of affairs, is utterly
impossible by all the methods hitherto proposed. For we can neither
employ them in handicraft or agriculture; we neither build houses (I
mean in the country) nor cultivate land; they can very seldom pick up
a livelihood by stealing, till they arrive at six years old, except where
they are of towardly parts; although I confess they learn the rudi-
ments much earlier; during which time they can, however, be properly looked upon only as probationers; as I have been informed by a
principal gentleman in the county of Cavan, who protested to me that

he never knew above one or two instances under the age of six, even in a part of the kingdom so renowned for the quickest proficiency in that art.

I am assured by our merchants, that a boy or a girl before twelve 7
years old is no saleable commodity; and even when they come to this age they will not yield above *3l.* or *3l. 2s. 6d.* at most on the exchange; which cannot turn to account either to the parents or kingdom, the charge of nutriment and rags having been at least four times that value.

I shall now therefore humbly propose my own thoughts, which I 8
hope will not be liable to the least objection.

I have been assured by a very knowing American of my acquain- 9
tance in London, that a young healthy child well nursed is at a year old a most delicious, nourishing, and wholesome food, whether stewed, roasted, baked, or broiled; and I make no doubt that it will equally serve in a fricassee or a ragout.

I do therefore humbly offer it to public consideration that of the 10
120,000 children already computed, 20,000 may be reserved for breed, whereof only one-fourth part to be males; which is more than we allow to sheep, black cattle, or swine; and my reason is, that these children are seldom the fruits of marriage, a circumstance not much regarded by our savages; therefore one male will be sufficient to serve four females. That the remaining 100,000 may, at a year old, be offered in sale to the persons of quality and fortune through the kingdom; always advising the mother to let them suck plentifully in the last month, so as to render them plump and fat for a good table. A child will make two dishes at an entertainment for friends; and when the family dines alone, the fore or hind quarter will make a reasonable dish, and seasoned with a little pepper or salt will be very good boiled on the fourth day, especially in winter.

I have reckoned upon a medium that a child just born will weigh 11
12 pounds, and in a solar year, if tolerably nursed, will increase to 28 pounds.

I grant this food will be somewhat dear, and therefore very 12
proper for landlords, who, as they have already devoured most of the parents, seem to have the best title to the children.

Infant's flesh will be in season throughout the year, but more 13
plentiful in March, and a little before and after: for we are told by a grave author, an eminent French physician, that fish being a prolific diet, there are more children born in Roman Catholic countries about nine months after Lent than at any other season; therefore, reckoning a year after Lent, the markets will be more glutted than usual, because the number of popish infants is at least three to one in this

kingdom: and therefore it will have one other collateral advantage, by lessening the number of papists among us.

I have already computed the charge of nursing a beggar's child (in 14
which list I reckon all cottages, laborers, and four-fifths of the farmers) to be about *2s.* per annum, rags included; and I believe no gentleman would repine to give *10s.* for the carcass of a good fat child, which, as I have said, will make four dishes of excellent nutritive meat, when he has only some particular friend or his own family to dine with him. Thus the squire will learn to be a good landlord, and grow popular among the tenants; the mother will have *8s.* net profit, and be fit for work till she produces another child.

Those who are more thrifty (as I must confess the times require) 15
may flay the carcass; the skin of which artificially dressed will make admirable gloves for ladies, and summer boots for fine gentlemen.

As to our city of Dublin, shambles may be appointed for this 16
purpose in the most convenient parts of it, and butchers we may be assured will not be wanting: although I rather recommend buying the child alive, and dressing them hot from the knife as we do roasting pigs.

A very worthy person, a true lover of his country, and whose 17
virtues I highly esteem, was lately pleased in discoursing on this matter to offer a refinement upon my scheme. He said that many gentlemen of this kingdom, having of late destroyed their deer, he conceived that the want of venison might be well supplied by the bodies of young lads and maidens, not exceeding fourteen years of age nor under twelve; so a great a number of both sexes in every country being now ready to starve for want of work and service; and these to be disposed of by their parents, if alive, or otherwise by their nearest relations. But with due deference to so excellent a friend and so deserving a patriot, I cannot be altogether in his sentiments; for as to the males, my American acquaintance assured me from frequent experience that their flesh was generally tough and lean, like that of our school-boys by continual exercise, and their taste disagreeable; and to fatten them would not answer the charge. Then as to the females, it would, I think, with humble submission be a loss to the public, because they soon would become breeders themselves: and besides, it is not improbable that some scrupulous person might be apt to censure such a practice (although indeed very unjustly), as a little bordering upon cruelty; which, I confess, has always been with me the strongest objection against any project, how well soever intended.

But in order to justify my friend, he confessed that this expedient 18
was put into his head by the famous Psalmanazar, a native of the

island Formosa, who came from thence to London about twenty years ago: and in conversation told my friend, that in his country when any young person happened to be put to death, the executioner sold the carcass to persons of quality as a prime dainty; and that in his time the body of a plump girl of fifteen, who was crucified for an attempt to poison the emperor, was sold to his imperial majesty's prime minister of state, and other great mandarins of the court, in joints from the gibbet, at 400 crowns. Neither indeed can I deny, that if the same use were made of several plump young girls in this town, who without one single groat to their fortunes cannot stir abroad without a chair, and appear at playhouse and assemblies in foreign fineries which they never will pay for, the kingdom would not be the worse.

Some persons of a desponding spirit are in great concern about 19
that vast number of poor people, who are aged, diseased, or maimed, and I have been desired to employ my thoughts what course may be taken to ease the nation of so grievous an encumbrance. But I am not in the least pain upon that matter, because it is very well known that they are every day dying and rotting by cold and famine, and filth and vermin, as fast as can be reasonably expected. And as to the young laborers, they are now in as hopeful a condition: they cannot get work, and consequently pine away for want of nourishment, to a degree that if at any time they are accidentally hired to common labor, they have not strength to perform it; and thus the country and themselves are happily delivered from the evils to come.

I have too long digressed, and therefore, shall return to my 20
subject. I think the advantages by the proposal which I have made are obvious and many, as well as of the highest importance.

For first, as I have already observed, it would greatly lessen the 21
number of papists, with whom we are yearly overrun, being the principal breeders of the nation as well as our most dangerous enemies; and who stay at home on purpose to deliver the kingdom to the Pretender, hoping to take their advantage by the absence of so many good Protestants, who have chosen rather to leave their country than stay at home and pay tithes against their conscience to an Episcopal curate.

Secondly, The poor tenants will have something valuable of their 22
own, which by law may be made liable to distress and help to pay their landlord's rent, their corn and cattle being already seized, and money a thing unknown.

Thirdly, Whereas the maintenance of 100,000 children from two 23
years old and upward, cannot be computed at less than *10s.* a-piece per annum, the nation's stock will be thereby increased £50,000 per annum, beside the profit of a new dish introduced to the tables of all

gentlemen of fortune in the kingdom who have any refinement in taste. And the money will circulate among ourselves, the goods being entirely of our own growth and manufacture.

Fourthly, The constant breeders, beside the gain of *8s.* sterling 24
per annum by the sale of their children, will be rid of the charge of maintaining them after the first year.

Fifthly, This food would likewise bring great custom to taverns, 25
where the vintners will certainly be so prudent as to procure the best receipts for dressing it to perfection, and consequently have their houses frequented by all the fine gentlemen, who justly value themselves upon their knowledge in good eating; and a skillful cook, who understands how to oblige his guests, will contrive to make it as expensive as they please.

Sixthly, This would be a great inducement to marriage, which all 26
wise nations have either encouraged by rewards or enforced by laws and penalties. It would increase the care and tenderness of mothers toward their children, when they were sure of a settlement for life to the poor babes, provided in some sort by the public, to their annual profit instead of expense. We should see an honest emulation among the married women, which of them would bring the fattest child to the market. Men would become as fond of their wives during the time of their pregnancy as they are now of their mares in foal, their cows in calf, their sows when they are ready to farrow; nor offer to beat or kick them (as is too frequent a practice) for fear of a miscarriage.

Many other advantages might be enumerated. For instance, the 27
addition of some thousand carcasses in our exportation of barreled beef, the propagation of swine's flesh, and improvement in the art of making good bacon, so much wanted among us by the great destruction of pigs, too frequent at our table; which are no way comparable in taste or magnificence to a well-grown, fat, yearling child, which roasted whole will make a considerable figure at a lord mayor's feast or any other public entertainment. But this and many others I omit, being studious of brevity.

Supposing that 1000 families in this city would be constant cus- 28
tomers for infants' flesh, besides others who might have it at merry-meetings, particularly at weddings and christenings, I compute that Dublin would take off annually about 20,000 carcasses; and the rest of the kingdom (where probably they will be sold somewhat cheaper) the remaining 80,000.

I can think of no one objection that will possibly be raised against 29
this proposal, unless it should be urged that the number of people will be thereby much lessened in the kingdom. This I freely own, and it was indeed one principal design in offering it to the world. I desire the reader will observe, that I calculate my remedy for this one

individual kingdom of Ireland and for no other that ever was, is, or I think ever can be upon earth. Therefore let no man talk to me of other expedients: of taxing our absentees at *5s.* a pound: of using neither clothes nor household furniture except what is of our own growth and manufacture: of utterly rejecting the materials and instruments that promote foreign luxury: of curing the expensiveness of pride, vanity, idleness, and gaming in our women: of introducing a vein of parsimony, prudence, and temperance: of learning to love our country, in the want of which we differ even from LAPLANDERS and the inhabitants of TOPINAMBOO: of quitting our animosities and factions, nor acting any longer like the Jews, who were murdering one another at the very moment their city was taken: of being a little cautious not to sell our country and conscience for nothing: of teaching landlords to have at least one degree of mercy toward their tenants: lastly, of putting a spirit of honesty, industry, and skill into our shopkeepers; who, if a resolution could now be taken to buy only our native goods, would immediately unite to cheat and exact upon us in the price, the measure, and the goodness, nor could ever yet be brought to make one fair proposal of just dealing, though often and earnestly invited to it.

30 Therefore I repeat, let no man talk to me of these and the like expedients, till he has at least some glimpse of hope that there will be ever some hearty and sincere attempt to put them in practice.

31 But as to myself, having been wearied out for many years with offering vain, idle, visionary thoughts, and at length utterly despairing of success, I fortunately fell upon this proposal; which, as it is wholly new, so it has something solid and real, of no expense and little trouble, full in our own power, and whereby we can incur no danger in disobliging ENGLAND. For this kind of commodity will not bear exportation, the flesh being of too tender a consistence to admit a long continuance in salt, although perhaps I could name a country which would be glad to eat up our whole nation without it.

32 After all, I am not so violently bent upon my own opinion as to reject any offer proposed by wise men, which shall be found equally innocent, cheap, easy, and effectual. But before something of that kind shall be advanced in contradiction to my scheme, and offering a better, I desire the author or authors will be pleased maturely to consider two points. First, as things now stand, how they will be able to find food and raiment for 100,000 useless mouths and backs. And secondly, there being a round million of creatures in human figure throughout this kingdom, whose subsistence put into a common stock would leave them in debt 2,000,000*l.* sterling, adding those who are beggars by profession to the bulk of farmers, cottagers, and laborers, with the wives and children who are beggars in effect; I

desire those politicians who dislike my overture, and may perhaps be so bold as to attempt an answer, that they will first ask the parents of these mortals, whether they would not at this day think it a great happiness to have been sold for food at a year old in the manner I prescribe, and thereby have avoided such a perpetual scene of misfortunes as they have since gone through by the oppression of landlords, the impossibility of paying rent without money or trade, the want of common sustenance, with neither house nor clothes to cover them from the inclemencies of the weather, and the most inevitable prospect of entailing the like or greater miseries upon their breed for ever.

I profess, in the sincerity of my heart, that I have not the least 33
personal interest in endeavoring to promote this necessary work, having no other motive than the public good of my country, by advancing our trade, providing for infants, relieving the poor, and giving some pleasure to the rich. I have no children by which I can propose to get a single penny; the youngest being nine years old, and my wife past child-bearing.

## IN RETROSPECT

**1.** Look at the arrangement of material in Swift's essay. At what point does the persona, the proposer, actually make his proposal? What precedes the proposal? At what point in the essay do you begin to realize the "down side" of the proposal? How would you account for the way Swift organized his essay? Is he, for instance, satirizing form as much as content in the essay? Explain.

**2.** We know what the persona, the *I* in this essay, is advocating. But do we ever learn what Swift, the author of "A Modest Proposal," advocates? If you will look closely at the essay, you will find a paragraph where the *I* speaks about the measures that Swift advocates in order to better the lot of the peasants in Ireland. Is this list of measures that Swift advocates obtrusive enough that attentive readers would not miss what Swift actually espouses in the essay? All of this subtlety is part of the irony of this highly political discourse. What role, if any, do you see irony playing in political discourses today? Who uses irony in our society, and how do they use it?

# *A Plea to Women to Change Their Image*

## MARY WOLLSTONECRAFT

Mary Wollstonecraft (1759–1797) was born in London, the second of seven children. Her early life was quite unsettled, mainly because her father, who thought he could make a living being a gentleman farmer, failed a number of times but also because the family had to move about between farms in England and Wales. Wollstonecraft's adult life was even more troublesome. She tried her hand at being first a schoolteacher and then a governess, but both occupations proved to be miserable experiences for her. She had an unfortunate love affair with an American named Gilbert Imlay, who fathered her first child, Fanny. When Imlay proved unfaithful to her, Wollstonecraft tried to commit suicide by jumping into the Thames River but was rescued. In the last ten years of her life, however, she hit her stride intellectually and published nine books, two of them novels. The first work that brought her to public attention was *A Vindication of the Rights of Men* (1790), an angry reply she wrote in response to Edmund Burke's *Reflections on the French Revolution.* But her most influential work—a work that the radical reformer William Godwin said made her the most famous woman in Europe for a time—was *A Vindication of the Rights of Women* (1792), from which the essay reprinted here was taken. In March 1797 Wollstonecraft married Godwin, and in August of the same year, she gave birth to her daughter Mary, who later became the wife of the poet Percy Bysshe Shelley and the author of the novel *Frankenstein.* But less than two weeks later, Wollstonecraft died from a fever brought on by the childbirth. Listen to the eloquent words of this tragic woman as she makes her plea to women to improve their image and status in this world. She may very well be the earliest of the feminist writers.

My own sex, I hope, will excuse me, if I treat them like rational 1
creatures, instead of flattering their *fascinating* graces, and viewing them as if they were in a state of perpetual childhood, unable to stand alone. I earnestly wish to point out in what true dignity and human happiness consists—I wish to persuade women to endeavour to acquire strength, both of mind and body, and to convince them that the soft phrases, susceptibility of heart, delicacy of sentiment, and refinement of taste, are almost synonymous with epithets of weakness, and that those beings who are only the objects of pity and that kind of love, which has been termed its sister, will soon become objects of contempt.

Dismissing, then, those pretty feminine phrases, which the men 2
condescendingly use to soften our slavish dependence, and despising that weak elegancy of mind, exquisite sensibility, and sweet docility of manners, supposed to be the sexual characteristics of the weaker

vessel, I wish to shew that elegance is inferior to virtue, that the first object of laudable ambition is to obtain a character as a human being, regardless of the distinction of sex; and that secondary views should be brought to this simple touchstone.

This is a rough sketch of my plan; and should I express my 3
conviction with the energetic emotions that I feel whenever I think of the subject, the dictates of experience and reflection will be felt by some of my readers. Animated by this important object, I shall disdain to cull my phrases or polish my style;—I aim at being useful, and sincerity will render me unaffected; for, wishing rather to persuade by the force of my arguments, than dazzle by the elegance of my language, I shall not waste my time in rounding periods, or in fabricating the turgid bombast of artificial feelings, which, coming from the head, never reach the heart. I shall be employed about things, not words! and, anxious to render my sex more respectable members of society, I shall try to avoid that flowery diction which has slided from essays into novels, and from novels into familiar letters and conversation.

These pretty superlatives, dropping glibly from the tongue, viti- 4
ate the taste, and create a kind of sickly delicacy that runs away from simple unadorned truth; and a deluge of false sentiments and overstretched feelings, stifling the natural emotions of the heart, render the domestic pleasures insipid, that ought to sweeten the exercise of those severe duties, which educate a rational and immortal being for a nobler field of action.

The education of women has, of late, been more attended to than 5
formerly; yet they are still reckoned a frivolous sex, and ridiculed or pitied by the writers who endeavour by satire or instruction to improve them. It is acknowledged that they spend many of the first years of their lives in acquiring a smattering of accomplishments; meanwhile strength of body and mind are sacrificed to libertine notions of beauty, to the desire of establishing themselves,—the only way women can rise in the world,—by marriage. And this desire making mere animals of them, when they marry they act as such children may be expected to act:—they dress, they paint, and nickname God's creatures. Surely these weak beings are only fit for a seraglio!—Can they be expected to govern a family with judgment, or take care of the poor babes whom they bring into the world?

If then it can be fairly deduced from the present conduct of the 6
sex, from the prevalent fondness for pleasure which takes place of ambition, and those nobler passions that open and enlarge the soul; that the instruction which women have hitherto received has only tended, with the constitution of civil society, to render them insignificant objects of desire—mere propagators of fools!—if it can be proved

that in aiming to accomplish them, without cultivating their understandings, they are taken out of their sphere of duties, and made ridiculous and useless when the short-lived bloom of beauty is over,[1] I presume that *rational* men will excuse me for endeavouring to persuade them to become more masculine and respectable.

Indeed the word masculine is only a bugbear: there is little reason 7
to fear that women will acquire too much courage or fortitude; for their apparent inferiority with respect to bodily strength, must render them, in some degree, dependent on men in the various relations of life; but why should it be increased by prejudices that give a sex to virtue, and confound simple truths and sensual reveries?

Women are, in fact, so much degraded by mistaken notions of 8
female excellence, that I do not mean to add a paradox when I assert, that this artificial weakness produces a propensity to tyrannize, and gives birth to cunning, the natural opponent of strength, which leads them to play off those contemptible infantile airs that undermine esteem even whilst they excite desire. Let men become more chaste and modest, and if women do not grow wiser in the same ratio, it will be clear that they have weaker understandings. It seems scarcely necessary to say, that I now speak of the sex in general. Many individuals have more sense than their male relatives; and, as nothing preponderates where there is a constant struggle for an equilibrium, without it has naturally more gravity, some women govern their husbands without degrading themselves, because intellect will always govern.

## IN RETROSPECT

**1.** Wollstonecraft is one of the pioneers of the feminist movement, advocating women's rights as early as the last half of the eighteenth century. The social climate then for such a movement was much different from what it is today. What strategy does Wollstonecraft use in this essay to rouse women to do something to improve their status and esteem in society? In what ways is her strategy different from the strategies used by feminist writers in the second half of the twentieth century?

**2.** A distinctive voice emerges from this essay. That distinctive voice comes through to us largely through the essay's style. Point out those features of Wollstonecraft's style which help to establish that voice.

---

[1]A lively writer, I cannot recollect his name, asks what business women turned of forty have to do in the world? [Wollstonecraft's note]

# *Tommy and the Traditions*

## G. K. CHESTERTON

Gilbert Keith Chesterton (1874–1936) was one of a group of talented British journalists and creative writers at the turn of the century, a group that included George Bernard Shaw, H. G. Wells, Max Beerbohm, and Hilaire Belloc. A veritable tun of a man, Falstaffian in his girth and his gusto, Chesterton preferred to fight his battles with the pen. In addition to his polemical prose, in which he defended his Catholicism and his conservative political and economic views, Chesterton wrote short stories, novels, poetry, biography, literary criticism, and, in his Father Brown stories, one of the classic series of detective fiction. In the following essay Chesterton argues that the poor are more often right in their views than the educated or the rich are. The impetus for arguing this thesis was Chesterton's experience of hearing a woman who lived in a run-down section of London say to her son, "Now, Tommy, run away and play." The most pronounced mannerism of Chesterton's style is the prevalence of paradoxes. A paradox can be defined as a statement that seems to be contradictory or absurd but is actually true. Here, for instance, is one of the many paradoxes in this essay: "The only way to make less of death is to make more of it." The basic "moral" of Chesterton's disquisition in this essay can be summed up in a paradox that reads something like this: "Whereas the rich and the educated treat their work as play and their play as work, the poor regard their work as work and their play as play." So when the mother told her son Tommy to run away and play, she was uttering "eternal commonsense."

A little while ago I was trying to convince the writers and readers of an excellent Socialist paper that the democracy was very decent after all. I did not succeed. The Socialist writers and readers were really delightful, and even playful people; but they could not swallow such a paradox as the statement that the poor are really right and the rich really wrong. In those quarters (in consequence) there has ever since been a disposition to connect my name with gin, a drink which I dislike, and with wife-beating, a pastime for which I lack the adequate energy. I have often wondered whether it would be worth while to try and explain again why I think that the poor are really quite right; and I was suddenly precipitated into the enterprise this morning. The impulse was only this—that as I walked past a dreary row of dwellings I heard a slatternly woman say to a very big child, "Now, Tommy, run away and play." She did not say it brutally, but with a hearty and healthy impatience, such as is natural to her sex. 1

I want to make one more attempt to revive the dead tradition of democracy by discussing what was involved in that remark. First, we must get it into our heads that a thing can be a superstition and still be 2 true. Ten thousand people may recite a thing as a lie, and it may still be a truth, in spite of their saying it. Thus Liberalism is true; but many Liberals are mere myths. Christianity can be believed; but some Christians are quite incredible. A hypocrite can hand on a truth. The Whigs of the early eighteenth century handed on the theory of liberty and self-government, though there was practically not one of them who was not a dirty courtier and a corrupt tyrant. The fashionable French priests of the later eighteenth century handed on the tradition of Catholicism, though there was hardly one of them who was not an atheist. But when democracy came, it was glad the Whigs had kept the tradition of Algernon Sydney. When the Catholic revival came, it was glad the French clergy had kept the tradition of St. Louis. Therefore, when I say that the poor have the right tradition I do not mean necessarily that they are going on in exactly the right way. I do not even mean that they think they are going on in the right way. As a matter of fact, they don't. The great difficulty is to persuade the poor that they are as right as they are.

I mean that just as there was an important truth in the Whig 3
Parliaments even when they were corrupt, just as there was an important truth in the Christian religion even when the Christians did not think so, so there is a truth which the poor possess in their misery and confusion, which we do not possess in our largest schemes of social reform. The point is not that they have gone specially right; but that they have stayed tolerably right while we have gone specially wrong.

I have often urged instances of this. For the sake of clearness I will 4
repeat one of them only. The very poor are always despised and rebuked because of their fuss and expenditure on funerals. Only today I saw that a public body refused aid to those who had gone any length in such expenditure. Now I do not mean that their crape is my abstract conception of robes of mourning, or that the conversation of Mrs. Brown with Mrs. Jones over the coffin has the dignity of "Lycidas." I do not even say that educated people could not do it better. I say that they are not trying to do it at all. Educated people have got some chilly fad to the effect that making a fuss about death is morbid or vulgar. The educated people are entirely wrong on the fundamental point of human psychology. The uneducated people are entirely right on the point.

The one way to make bereavement tolerable is to make it impor- 5
tant. To gather your friends, to have a gloomy festival, to talk, to cry, to praise the dead—all that does change the atmosphere, and carry human nature over the open grave. The nameless torture is to try and treat it as something private and casual, as our elegant stoics do. That is at once pride and pain and hypocrisy. The only way to make less of death is to make more of it. The poor have this blind tradition, and

will not be torn away from it. They do it in a bad social system; they do it in a bad way; but they have all humanity behind them, and in the noise and heat of their houses of mourning is the smoke of the baked meats of Hamlet and the dust and echo of the funeral games of Patroclus.

Now take a more cheerful instance: the poor have, in practice, a 6
certain view of work and play. And it is the right view; the root view of all mankind. I do not mean that their work and play are better; they are not. They do not play specially well; and they work as little as they can, and so should I in their shoes. What they have got right is the philosophy; the original principle of the thing. They differ from us and from the aristocracy (pardon the distinction) simply in this: that their work is work and their play is play. Work is doing what you do not like; play is doing what you like. The whole point of work is law; the whole point of play is liberty. There should be hours of labour, and they should be laborious; there should be hours of freedom, and they should be free.

That sounds simple enough: but the educated classes cannot 7
understand it. The educationalists cannot understand it. The public schools cannot understand it. The whole English upper class is built on the negation of it. A gentleman is taught to treat half his work as play (diplomacy, Parliament, finance), and then to treat more than half his play as work, by training for matches and bursting blood vessels in a race. He is taught to play at politics and work at cricket. At the English schools (as Mr. Maurice Baring sketched very cleverly in an article), a game has practically ceased to be a game; it has become a specially dull lesson, where boys are bored by having to look interested. But the athletic school is not alone to blame; the intellectual educationalists are quite as bad. They want to make children's play significant and instructive. They arrange children in Pre-Raphaelite patterns. They make them dance ethically or yell aesthetically. They want to follow children when they play, and make their games useful. They might as well follow them when they sleep, and make their dreams useful. Play is a rest, like sleep.

The woman who said "Run away and play" to Tommy on the 8
doorstep was the weary guardian of an eternal commonsense. Probably Tommy had a bad time sometimes; probably she made him work; but at least she did not make him play. She let him play. He fed on loneliness and liberty. That hour of play at least was not Froebel's contribution or Dr. Arnold's contribution to Tommy. That hour was Tommy's contribution to Tommy. I do not know whether I have succeeded, or ever shall succeed, in conveying what I mean about these people, and how they hold a battered shape of truth, while we hold perfected forms of error. But at least my work for this Friday evening is done. I shall run away and play.

**IN RETROSPECT**

**1.** In this essay Chesterton points out the conflicting values of the rich and the poor. We hear a great deal today about the sociopolitical values of various classes. Who are the groups of people in our society, other than the rich and the poor, who, in Chesterton's words, either "hold perfected forms of error" or "hold a battered shape of truth" (paragraph 8)?

**2.** Chesterton is noted for his heavy use of paradox, which may be defined as a statement that at first glance seems to be nonsensical but on second look strikes us as being a shining truth. Here are two of Chesterton's paradoxes: "A thing can be a superstition and still be true (paragraph 2)", and "The only way to make less of death is to make more of it (paragraph 5)." Search out additional examples of paradox in this essay, commenting on their rhetorical effectiveness.

# *The Tyranny of Charity*

**WENDELL BERRY**

Wendell Berry (1934– ) was born in Henry County, Kentucky. Although he has had a distinguished career as a professor of English at the University of Kentucky since 1964, he is best known to the outside world as an accomplished poet, novelist, and essayist. To date, he has published more than twenty-five books, several of them dealing with the despoliation of the environment, especially in his native Kentucky. The title of this essay, "The Tyranny of Charity," should raise an eyebrow in everyone who comes to the essay. We have all been taught that charity is a good thing. The Bible tells us, "So there remain faith, hope, and charity, but the greatest of these is charity" (I Corinthians, 13:13). How could anyone consider this virtue to be tyranny? Berry concentrates in this essay on a furniture maker in Eastern Kentucky who has been reduced to poverty by the coal companies that exploited the resources of the land and then put the miners out of work and on welfare. You will have to read the essay to find out why Berry believes that the government's giving the furniture maker food instead of tools can be considered an act of tyranny. It is a powerful essay.

The furniture maker is at work in the shade of some box elder trees that grow on the slope of the roadfill out at the end of his yard. Two chair posts, held by a system of pegs and wedges as in a vise, are on the puncheon bench in front of him. He is cutting the mortises into which he will later insert hewn slats to make the back of the chair. He uses a sharpened screwdriver as a chisel, driving it with a heavy hand ax. Nearby is another sort of homemade vise, this one made by 1 pinning the longer member of an inverted treefork into a mortise in another puncheon bench, so that the shape is roughly that of the figure 4. This he uses to hold pieces to be shaped with a drawing knife; he sits in a low chair at the end of the bench, holding his foot against the leg of the 4, by that leverage supplying the holding power of the vise.

From the tree in the woods to the finished chair, the materials are 2
handled by no hands but the furniture maker's own. In the process he uses only a few simple tools: a crosscut saw, an ax, a hand ax, a drawing knife, an auger, a pocketknife, a rasp, and the screw-driver sharpened into a mortising chisel. He also has a press that he uses to set the desired curves into chair backs and rockers. One needs to see him at work in order to understand how adequately his patient craftsmanship performs tasks that are usually done now by machines.

While he works, four of his children, who have come there to the 3
shady place with him, play with the tools he is not using or swing in the swings he has made for them in the box elders.

Held in such narrow focus, revealing only the man at work and 4
the few primitive tools, the scene might be thought to belong to some happily simple time in the past. But it is not in the past, and it is not happy. It belongs to the coal country of East Kentucky in the summer of 1965; it belongs to the tragedy of that country and its people, and to the shame, acknowledged or not, of what some still like to call "the American way of life."

The furniture maker, who moved down onto the state road in the 5
hope that he might sell some of his work to passers-by and travelers, lives in an old scale house once used by a coal company to weigh trucks. The house is built of rough-sawed lumber, covered with the rather flimsy material called brick siding; it has had no upkeep for years, and one can see that in cold weather it must be difficult to heat. The yard is partly a fill of coal rubble, dumped and leveled around the house, which stands bare in the hot sun. It is the most meager home site imaginable, starkly and heavily ugly, sterile and coal-stained and raw. The children who play and swing there in the shade are poorly clothed. Only the seven-year-old girl attends school, but the furniture maker and his wife will be dependent again this fall on the uneasy charity that gives away secondhand clothes. The furniture maker speaks of his distress over the presence of a "store" in the child's school. The store sells popsicles and candy and such to the children, and it is one of the furniture maker's cruel burdens, for it requires him either to send the child to school with nickels he can't afford or to have the family's poverty made painfully obvious to her—and all her classmates—every day.

Unable to live by his work, the furniture maker is dependent on 6
the government's welfare program, the benefits of which are somewhat questionable, since if he sells any of his work his welfare payments are diminished accordingly, and so he stands little or no chance of improving his situation by his own effort. Only the workman's loving pride in his work can explain why he has continued to make any effort at all.

Getting out of the car there at the edge of the road, standing up to 7
face that black yard and the bitter shambles of a house, you are inclined to forget the good you know of the place, and to be overcome by a foreboding of hopelessness that by being theirs is also mysteriously yours. It becomes a strong temptation to get back into the car and drive away, to take refuge in the thousand lies we have invented to justify the divine right to be mindlessly rich.

But once you have come upon the furniture maker at his work 8
this initial pressing of futility is, if not replaced, at least driven back by the excellence of the workmanship being accomplished with those crude tools in defiance of the poverty of place and circumstance. And this is supported by the sight of a large well-tended garden down in the creek bottom; the furniture maker is attempting to sell some of the produce in a makeshift stand beside the road, and his wife has been busy canning and preserving.

There comes the awareness, as it still must come here and there 9
throughout the Kentucky mountains, that as a measure of the depth of misery there still remains a height of pride—a sort of last stand of hopefulness shaped in a neat garden, a few flowers in bloom. It may be only because of this that the misery itself does not yet represent the dead end of vision. One can bear the knowledge of the furniture maker's situation because there remains in the man himself the promise as well as the hope of something better.

Though the furniture maker's house and household wear the 10
look of long poverty that is commonplace in the region, there are significant differences between his predicament and that of most. For while most of the poor have become so because of the lack of employment, the furniture maker still applies himself industriously to his work. And while most are handicapped by lack of skills, the furniture maker is a consummate craftsman. While the mentality of most has been conditioned by a long dependence on coal company and union, the furniture maker is self-employed and in full possession of the discipline and pride of the craftsman who is his own boss. And in a region, moreover, which has suffered a thorough social upheaval in the change from a dependence on the land to a dependence on industry, the furniture maker came to his work by inheritance. Asked

how he learned his craft, he replies: "It come to me from my ancestors."

The furniture maker's predicament is that though he has work, it 11
is work that is very near to being useless and meaningless. He is prevented, as I have said, from using it to augment his income from the welfare program. And he is bound to the program by his inability to make a living entirely from his work. He lacks, for one thing, a dependable market. Such furniture as he makes is either not sufficiently valued by enough people to assure a market, or the affluent passers-by who are his potential customers simply refuse to believe that anything of value could be produced in such a place. For another thing, he is so slowed by his old tools that he could hardly make more furniture than he does even if he had more customers. It takes him, for instance, about a month to make one of the large rocking chairs that bring from seventy to ninety dollars. He can sell only three or four of these a year, and most of his time is taken up by articles from which he earns much less.

For fear that this will seem to anyone to be a sentimental defense 12
of an anachronism, I hurry to say that this man's work, particularly in his chairs, is among the finest I have ever seen. The chairs are certainly the strongest and best-made of their kind that I know of. They are beautifully proportioned and balanced. Such ornamentation as is used is modest, and tasteful in a way that transcends fashionableness. They are made to last a lifetime and more, and their strength is achieved without expense of grace. It is hard to think of a room, rich or poor, that would not be dignified by the presence of one of them, and impossible to imagine a householder who would need to condescend to own one.

This, then, is an exceptional man. But if his troubles are not 13
typical of the region, they are nevertheless indigenous to it, and are peculiarly revealing of the region's troubles. His fate cannot be separated from the fate of his land. Like every poor man in East Kentucky, he is suffering from the deficiency of schools and opportunities in a land sold out by the greed of its elected officials, and systematically plundered by the coal companies. If the truth were not already available to anyone who cares to know it in Harry Caudill's *Night Comes to the Cumberlands,* it would be almost mathematically demonstrable that a land of such wealth could have been reduced to such poverty only by fraud. (The region itself is *not* poor; the big money did not come there to get lost.) That the land and its people could have been so far brought down is explainable only by the failure of governors to govern and legislators to legislate and judges to judge in the interest of those they are sworn to serve—only by the subser-

vience of our governmental ideals to the stupidity and greed of officials who have been willing to justify, by a spurious rhetoric of free enterprise, the right of the rich to get richer, by any means, at anybody's expense.

It is not possible to escape the irony of the fact that the furniture 14
maker—a man of skill and industry, whose craft is itself one of the valuable resources of his region and nation, and who is engaged constantly in making products of great beauty and usefulness—is destitute in America, now. This, it must be remembered, is the very man whose promise the American government was established to redeem. By all our public claims he ought to be one of the prime beneficiaries of our system. As it is, he is its victim. And if *he,* with his skill and his devoted effort, has wound up under the heels of the exploiters, what hope can there be for those who are less able?

The reaction of good sense to this man's predicament can only be 15
to ask: Instead of food stamps, why not tools? The food-stamp program, set up as it is to neutralize whatever income is earned by personal effort, is clearly stifling to ambition, making it certainly much easier, if not more remunerative as well, to do nothing. On the other hand, the few power tools that would be necessary to increase the man's productivity (perhaps enough to make him independent of government giveaways) would probably cost a good deal less than a year's supply of food stamps. The gift of tools, which would honor the capacity of the man to survive the troubles of his region and to support himself, would look toward a just end of the federal intervention in the region. The gift of food alone, whether or not limited to an established minimum, can lead only to an endless dependence on governmental charity—in which case charity becomes no more than a subtle form of oppression. If a man continues long in direct and absolute dependence on the government for the necessities of life, he ceases to be a citizen and becomes a slave.

The federal government has made no attempt to deal with the 16
furniture maker in terms of his particular abilities and needs. And the Division of Arts and Crafts of the state government, which would be thought the most logical source of help, seems completely puzzled by him; his output is too small, the quality and price too high. The state seems prepared to encourage only such arts and crafts as can be mass-produced at dime-store prices. One gathers that the emphasis is entirely on sales, and that no consideration at all is given to the quality of the work or the integrity of the workman. The Division's sole impulse in dealing with the furniture maker is to "change" him—which is to say, to diminish and cheapen him. His only hope, the Division feels, is to reduce the quality of his work in order to raise the volume and lower the price, or make something more marketable—

souvenir whistles, for instance. Nobody seems to have considered the possibility that it would be most natural, and even most expedient, to help him to make a living by doing what he already does supremely well. Nobody seems to know how he might get hold of some tools.

The truth is that the furniture maker is the dependent of his 17
region in a more meaningful and crucial way than he ever will be the dependent of any government. And the measures that will lead to his recovery are those that will lead to the recovery of the region.

But at this moment East Kentucky is caught in the relentless grind 18
of governmental cross-purposes. The federal government is there, carrying out various programs to assure that everybody will eat. Under the circumstances, that is commendable. But it is commendable only as a temporary expedient. To be worthy of admiration in any final sense, government help will have to accomplish the result of making itself unnecessary. It must be acknowledged both by the government and by the people that the charity programs can do no more than the minimum—can only prevent starvation. An agency or bureau or institution cannot exercise taste and judgment, cannot be motivated by love or compassion, cannot value a man for his industry or his art or his pride; they are abstractions themselves and must deal with people as abstractions.

To give a man bread when he needs a tool is as inept and unfeeling 19
as to give him a stone when he needs bread, and this painful clumsiness is inherent in the generalizations of the social planners and the organized charities. Their most "humane" endeavors almost necessarily involve an attitude toward humanity that debases it. The tendency to deal with individual citizens exclusively in terms of the abstractions of their class or conditions is to strike at the very foundation of American liberty, which was established to safeguard the possibility and the right of escape from such abstractions—the right to become exceptional. For the government to treat the furniture maker simply as one of the Appalachian poor is not only to insult and threaten him as an individual but to work at the destruction of the possibility that such craftsmen will ever live in the country again. To wage a "War on Poverty" in such a way as to encourage the exceptional to become ordinary would seem to imply an expectancy of defeat.

The furniture maker possesses the skill and the industry and the 20
pride that make envisionable for him the personal triumph on which most of our ideas of human worth and dignity depend: the triumph of making a living in the work of one's choice, by one's own effort, by the use of one's own gifts. And this triumph is completely beyond the reach of any government or bureau. It cannot be achieved except by a man's own doing. What government can do—and this has always

been one of the acknowledged functions of government—is to create and protect a condition in which personal effort is meaningful.

But having established and given extravagant publicity to the 21
necessarily superficial expedient of feeding the hungry, the government seems to be doing little to bring about the economic health of the region. It can be said, in fact, that the government is tacitly abetting the further gutting of the region by the coal companies. The history of the greed and irresponsibility of these companies in East Kentucky does not need repeating. It only needs to be added that as this is being written strip mining is going on there at an unprecedented rate—in a silence of federal power that seriously threatens all corrective efforts of the state. And it needs to be said that this sort of mining involves not only the further departure of the region's wealth, with little or no benefit to the region, but also the irreparable destruction of the region itself.

In the face of this crisis, which demands prompt and decisive 22
action, the federal government has embarked on a two-year "study." For two years, then, nothing is likely to be done. And the bulldozers will grind on in a destructiveness surpassing that of any war or natural calamity; the mine owners will grow richer; the people will grow poorer; the possibilities of the region will be steadily and rapidly diminished. To anyone who has watched a strip mine being worked or has seen the results—the huge dead gashes in the mountainsides, timbered slopes inundated by avalanches of sterile overburden, streams poisoned by acids and choked with rocks and mud, wells made unfit for use, the land and the homes of citizens destroyed—this two-year study is baffling and astonishing. It is not possible to imagine why it should take two years to "study" a situation that could be shown to be critical—to anyone with a live intelligence—in two days. Here again one smells the stench of the political fraud and bureaucratic paralysis that have begun to seem as natural to the region as coal.

Since the federal government is the largest customer (through 23
T.V.A.) of strip-mined coal, and consequently the chief depressor of coal prices and the chief discourager of the less destructive deep mining, one must wonder if there is any real intention to do more for the region than to ask the best and the worst to come together to eat out of the government's hand.

**IN RETROSPECT**

**1.** Berry recommends that, instead of giving the furniture maker and his family food stamps, the government give them a set of modern tools. Why would a set of tools be a better gift than food for this man and his family? In what sense does Berry consider the government's act of charity to be an act of tyranny?

**2.** Berry makes a pronounced use of oppositions in this essay, marked by such adversatives as *though . . . nevertheless, either . . . or, on the one hand . . . on the other hand, even if,* and *but* and by the use of contrasting situations. Discuss how the use of these polarities helps Berry to make his point and to give coherence to his essay.

# *Power and Violence*

## HANNAH ARENDT

Hannah Arendt (1906–1975), born in Germany, was educated at various German universities, including those at Koenigsberg, Marburg, and Freiburg; she obtained a doctorate in philosophy at Heidelberg University. In 1950, she became a naturalized citizen of the United States and taught at such institutions as Princeton University, the University of Chicago, Columbia University, and the University of California at Berkeley. She wrote and published an astonishing number of books, both in German and in English, among them *The Human Condition* (1958), *The Jew as Pariah: Jewish Identity and Politics in the Modern Age* (1978), and the three-volume *The Life of the Mind* (1978–1981). Perhaps her best-known and most controversial book was *Eichmann in Jerusalem: A Report on the Banality of Evil* (1963), a book that developed from a series of essays *The New Yorker* commissioned her to write about the trial of Adolf Eichmann, one of Hitler's henchmen during World War II and one of the major promoters of the Nazi concentration camps. "Power and Violence," the essay reprinted here, was taken from Arendt's 1970 book *On Violence.* In this long, closely reasoned essay, Arendt explores the history and meaning of two concepts, power and violence. Although she carries on the discussion at a fairly high philosophical level, she writes in a nontechnical language that is comprehensible to the ordinary literate layperson. One of the appeals of this distinguished academic is that she could communicate successfully with literate citizens about important and highly complex ideas. A common note about all writers of familiar essays is their ability to communicate with a wide range of readers on a variety of topics.

It is, I think, a rather sad reflection on the present state of political science that our terminology does not distinguish among such key words as "power," "strength," "force," "authority," and, finally, "violence"—all of which refer to distinct, different phenomena and would hardly exist unless they did. (In the words of d'Entrèves, "might, power, authority: these are all words to whose exact implications no 1 great weight is attached in current speech; even the greatest thinkers sometimes use them at random. Yet it is fair to presume that they refer to different properties, and their meaning should therefore be carefully assessed and examined. . . . The correct use of these words is a question not only of logical grammar, but of historical perspective.") To use them as synonyms not only indicates a certain deafness to linguistic meanings, which would be serious enough, but it has also resulted in a kind of blindness to the realities they correspond to. In such a situation it is always tempting to introduce new definitions, but—though I shall briefly yield to temptation—what is involved is not simply a matter of careless speech. Behind the apparent confusion is a firm conviction in whose light all distinctions would be, at best, of minor importance: the conviction that the most crucial political issue is, and always has been, the question of Who rules Whom? Power, strength, force, authority, violence—these are but words to indicate the means by which man rules over man; they are held to be synonyms because they have the same function. It is only after one ceases to reduce public affairs to the business of dominion that the original data in the realm of human affairs will appear, or, rather, reappear, in their authentic diversity.

These data, in our context, may be enumerated as follows: 2

*Power* corresponds to the human ability not just to act but to act in 3
concert. Power is never the property of an individual; it belongs to a group and remains in existence only so long as the group keeps together. When we say of somebody that he is "in power" we actually refer to his being empowered by a certain number of people to act in their name. The moment the group, from which the power originated to begin with (*potestas in populo,* without a people or group there is no power), disappears, "his power" also vanishes. In current usage, when we speak of a "powerful man" or a "powerful personality," we already use the word "power" metaphorically; what we refer to without metaphor is "strength."

*Strength* unequivocally designates something in the singular, an 4
individual entity; it is the property inherent in an object or person and belongs to its character, which may prove itself in relation to other things or persons, but is essentially independent of them. The strength of even the strongest individual can always be overpowered by the many, who often will combine for no other purpose than to ruin strength precisely because of its peculiar independence. The almost instinctive hostility of the many toward the one has always, from Plato to Nietzsche, been ascribed to resentment, to the envy of the weak for the strong, but this psychological interpretation misses the point. It is in the nature of a group and its power to turn against independence, the property of individual strength.

*Force,* which we often use in daily speech as a synonym for 5
violence, especially if violence serves as a means of coercion, should be reserved, in terminological language, for the "forces of nature" or the "force of circumstances" (*la force des choses*), that is, to indicate the energy released by physical or social movements.

*Authority,* relating to the most elusive of these phenomena and 6
therefore, as a term, most frequently abused, can be vested in persons—there is such a thing as personal authority, as, for instance, in the relation between parent and child, between teacher and pupil—or it can be vested in offices, as, for instance, in the Roman senate (*auctoritas in senatu*) or in the hierarchical offices of the Church (a priest can grant valid absolution even though he is drunk). Its hallmark is unquestioning recognition by those who are asked to obey; neither coercion nor persuasion is needed. (A father can lose his authority either by beating his child or by starting to argue with him, that is, either by behaving to him like a tyrant or by treating him as an equal.) To remain in authority requires respect for the person or the office. The greatest enemy of authority, therefore, is contempt, and the surest way to undermine it is laughter.

*Violence,* finally, as I have said, is distinguished by its instrumen- 7
tal character. Phenomenologically, it is close to strength, since the implements of violence, like all other tools, are designed and used for the purpose of multiplying natural strength until, in the last stage of their development, they can substitute for it.

It is perhaps not superfluous to add that these distinctions, 8
though by no means arbitrary, hardly ever correspond to watertight compartments in the real world, from which nevertheless they are drawn. Thus institutionalized power in organized communities often appears in the guise of authority, demanding instant, unquestioning recognition; no society could function without it. (A small, and still isolated, incident in New York shows what can happen if authentic authority in social relations has broken down to the point where it cannot work any longer even in its derivative, purely functional form. A minor mishap in the subway system—the doors on a train failed to operate—turned into a serious shutdown on the line lasting four hours and involving more than fifty thousand passengers, because when the transit authorities asked the passengers to leave the defective train, they simply refused.) Moreover, nothing, as we shall see, is more common than the combination of violence and power, nothing less frequent than to find them in their pure and therefore extreme form. From this, it does not follow that authority, power, and violence are all the same.

Still it must be admitted that it is particularly tempting to think of 9
power in terms of command and obedience, and hence to equate

power with violence, in a discussion of what actually is only one of power's special cases—namely, the power of government. Since in foreign relations as well as domestic affairs violence appears as a last resort to keep the power structure intact against individual challengers—the foreign enemy, the native criminal—it looks indeed as though violence were the prerequisite of power and power nothing but a façade, the velvet glove which either conceals the iron hand or will turn out to belong to a paper tiger. On closer inspection, though, this notion loses much of its plausibility. For our purpose, the gap between theory and reality is perhaps best illustrated by the phenomenon of revolution.

Since the beginning of the century theoreticians of revolution 10
have told us that the chances of revolution have significantly decreased in proportion to the increased destructive capacities of weapons at the unique disposition of governments. The history of the last seventy years, with its extraordinary record of successful and unsuccessful revolutions, tells a different story. Were people mad who even tried against such overwhelming odds? And, leaving out instances of full success, how can even a temporary success be explained? The fact is that the gap between state-owned means of violence and what people can muster by themselves—from beer bottles to Molotov cocktails and guns—has always been so enormous that technical improvements make hardly any difference. Textbook instructions on "how to make a revolution" in a step-by-step progression from dissent to conspiracy, from resistance to armed uprising, are all based on the mistaken notion that revolutions are "made." In a contest of violence against violence the superiority of the government has always been absolute; but this superiority lasts only as long as the power structure of the government is intact—that is, as long as commands are obeyed and the army or police forces are prepared to use their weapons. When this is no longer the case, the situation changes abruptly. Not only is the rebellion not put down, but the arms themselves change hands—sometimes, as in the Hungarian revolution, within a few hours. (We should know about such things after all these years of futile fighting in Vietnam, where for a long time, before getting massive Russian aid, the National Liberation Front fought us with weapons that were made in the United States.) Only after this has happened, when the disintegration of the government in power has permitted the rebels to arm themselves, can one speak of an "armed uprising," which often does not take place at all or occurs when it is no longer necessary. Where commands are no longer obeyed, the means of violence are of no use; and the question of this obedience is not decided by the command-obedience relation but by opinion, and, of course, by the number of those who share it. Every-

thing depends on the power behind the violence. The sudden dramatic breakdown of power that ushers in revolutions reveals in a flash how civil obedience—to laws, to rulers, to institutions—is but the outward manifestation of support and consent.

Where power has disintegrated, revolutions are possible but not 11
necessary. We know of many instances when utterly impotent regimes were permitted to continue in existence for long periods of time—either because there was no one to test their strength and reveal their weakness or because they were lucky enough not to be engaged in war and suffer defeat. Disintegration often becomes manifest only in direct confrontation; and even then, when power is already in the street, some group of men prepared for such an eventuality is needed to pick it up and assume responsibility. We have recently witnessed how it did not take more than the relatively harmless, essentially nonviolent French students' rebellion to reveal the vulnerability of the whole political system, which rapidly disintegrated before the astonished eyes of the young rebels. Unknowingly they had tested it; they intended only to challenge the ossified university system, and down came the system of governmental power, together with that of the huge party bureaucracies—*"une sorte de désintégration de toutes les hiérarchies."* It was a textbook case of a revolutionary situation that did not develop into a revolution because there was nobody, least of all the students, prepared to seize power and the responsibility that goes with it. Nobody except, of course, de Gaulle. Nothing was more characteristic of the seriousness of the situation than his appeal to the army, his journey to see Massu and the generals in Germany, a walk to Canossa, if there ever was one, in view of what had happened only a few years before. But what he sought and received was support, not obedience, and the means were not commands but concessions. If commands had been enough, he would never have had to leave Paris.

No government exclusively based on the means of violence has 12
ever existed. Even the totalitarian ruler, whose chief instrument of rule is torture, needs a power basis—the secret police and its net of informers. Only the development of robot soldiers, which, as previously mentioned, would eliminate the human factor completely and, conceivably, permit one man with a push button to destroy whomever he pleased, could change this fundamental ascendancy of power over violence. Even the most despotic domination we know of, the rule of master over slaves, who always outnumbered him, did not rest on superior means of coercion as such, but on a superior organization of power—that is, on the organized solidarity of the masters. Single men without others to support them never have enough power to use violence successfully. Hence, in domestic affairs, vio-

lence functions as the last resort of power against criminals or rebels—that is, against single individuals who, as it were, refuse to be overpowered by the consensus of the majority. And as for actual warfare, we have seen in Vietnam how an enormous superiority in the means of violence can become helpless if confronted with an ill-equipped but well-organized opponent who is much more powerful. This lesson, to be sure, was there to be learned from the history of guerrilla warfare, which is at least as old as the defeat in Spain of Napoleon's still-unvanquished army.

To switch for a moment to conceptual language: Power is indeed 13
of the essence of all government, but violence is not. Violence is by nature instrumental; like all means, it always stands in need of guidance and justification through the end it pursues. And what needs justification by something else cannot be the essence of anything. The end of war—end taken in its twofold meaning—is peace or victory; but to the question And what is the end of peace? there is no answer. Peace is an absolute, even though in recorded history periods of warfare have nearly always outlasted periods of peace. Power is in the same category; it is, as they say, "an end in itself." (This, of course, is not to deny that governments pursue policies and employ their power to achieve prescribed goals. But the power structure itself precedes and outlasts all aims, so that power, far from being the means to an end, is actually the very condition enabling a group of people to think and act in terms of the means-end category.) And since government is essentially organized and institutionalized power, the current question What is the end of government? does not make much sense either. The answer will be either question-begging—to enable men to live together—or dangerously utopian—to promote happiness or to realize a classless society or some other nonpolitical ideal, which if tried out in earnest cannot but end in some kind of tyranny.

Power needs no justification, being inherent in the very existence 14
of political communities; what it does need is legitimacy. The common treatment of these two words as synonyms is no less misleading and confusing than the current equation of obedience and support. Power springs up whenever people get together and act in concert, but it derives its legitimacy from the initial getting together rather than from any action that then may follow. Legitimacy, when challenged, bases itself on an appeal to the past, while justification relates to an end that lies in the future. Violence can be justifiable, but it never will be legitimate. Its justification loses in plausibility the farther its intended end recedes into the future. No one questions the use of violence in self-defense, because the danger is not only clear but also present, and the end justifying the means is immediate.

15 Power and violence, though they are distinct phenomena, usually appear together. Wherever they are combined, power, we have found, is the primary and predominant factor. The situation, however, is entirely different when we deal with them in their pure states—as, for instance, with foreign invasion and occupation. We saw that the current equation of violence with power rests on government's being understood as domination of man over man by means of violence. If a foreign conqueror is confronted by an impotent government and by a nation unused to the exercise of political power, it is easy for him to achieve such domination. In all other cases the difficulties are great indeed, and the occupying invader will try immediately to establish Quisling governments, that is, to find a native power base to support his dominion. The head-on clash between Russian tanks and the entirely nonviolent resistance of the Czechoslovak people is a textbook case of a confrontation between violence and power in their pure states. But while domination in such an instance is difficult to achieve, it is not impossible. Violence, we must remember, does not depend on numbers or opinions, but on implements, and the implements of violence, as I mentioned before, like all other tools, increase and multiply human strength. Those who oppose violence with mere power will soon find that they are confronted not by men but by men's artifacts, whose inhumanity and destructive effectiveness increase in proportion to the distance separating the opponents. Violence can always destroy power; out of the barrel of a gun grows the most effective command, resulting in the most instant and perfect obedience. What never can grow out of it is power.

16 In a head-on clash between violence and power, the outcome is hardly in doubt. If Ghandi's enormously powerful and successful strategy of nonviolent resistance had met with a different enemy—Stalin's Russia, Hitler's Germany, even prewar Japan, instead of England—the outcome would not have been decolonization, but massacre and submission. However, England in India and France in Algeria had good reasons for their restraint. Rule by sheer violence comes into play where power is being lost; it is precisely the shrinking power of the Russian government, internally and externally, that became manifest in its "solution" of the Czechoslovak problem—just as it was the shrinking power of European imperialism that became manifest in the alternative between decolonization and massacre. To substitute violence for power can bring victory, but the price is very high; for it is not only paid by the vanquished, it is also paid by the victor in terms of his own power. This is especially true when the victor happens to enjoy domestically the blessings of constitutional government. Henry Steele Commager is entirely right: "If we

subvert world order and destroy world peace we must inevitably subvert and destroy our own political institutions first." The much-feared boomerang effect of the "government of subject races" (Lord Cromer) on the home government during the imperialist era meant that rule by violence in faraway lands would end by affecting the government of England, that the last "subject race" would be the English themselves. The recent gas attack on the campus at Berkeley, where not just tear gas but also another gas, "outlawed by the Geneva Convention and used by the Army to flush out guerrillas in Vietnam," was laid down while gas-masked Guardsmen stopped anybody and everybody "from fleeing the gassed area," is an excellent example of this "backlash" phenomenon. It has often been said that impotence breeds violence, and psychologically this is quite true, at least of persons possessing natural strength, moral or physical. Politically speaking, the point is that loss of power becomes a temptation to substitute violence for power—in 1968 during the Democratic convention in Chicago we could watch this process on television—and that violence itself results in impotence. Where violence is no longer backed and restrained by power, the well-known reversal in reckoning with means and ends has taken place. The means, the means of destruction, now determine the end—with the consequence that the end will be the destruction of all power.

Nowhere is the self-defeating factor in the victory of violence over 17
power more evident than in the use of terror to maintain domination, about whose weird successes and eventual failures we know perhaps more than any generation before us. Terror is not the same as violence; it is, rather, the form of government that comes into being when violence, having destroyed all power, does not abdicate but, on the contrary, remains in full control. It has often been noticed that the effectiveness of terror depends almost entirely on the degree of social atomization. Every kind of organized opposition must disappear before the full force of terror can be let loose. This atomization—an outrageously pale, academic word for the horror it implies—is maintained and intensified through the ubiquity of the informer, who can be literally omnipresent because he no longer is merely a professional agent in the pay of the police but potentially every person one comes into contact with. How such a fully developed police state is established and how it works—or, rather, how nothing works where it holds sway—can now be learned in Aleksandr I. Solzhenitsyn's *The First Circle,* which will probably remain one of the masterpieces of twentieth-century literature and certainly contains the best documentation on Stalin's regime in existence. The decisive difference between totalitarian domination, based on terror, and tyrannies and dictatorships, established by violence, is that the former turns not only

against its enemies but against its friends and supporters as well, being afraid of all power, even the power of its friends. The climax of terror is reached when the police state begins to devour its own children, when yesterday's executioner becomes today's victim. And this is also the moment when power disappears entirely. There exist now a great many plausible explanations for the de-Stalinization of Russia—none, I believe, so compelling as the realization by the Stalinist functionaries themselves that a continuation of the regime would lead, not to an insurrection, against which terror is indeed the best safeguard, but to paralysis of the whole country.

To sum up: politically speaking, it is insufficient to say that power 18
and violence are not the same. Power and violence are opposites; where the one rules absolutely, the other is absent. Violence appears where power is in jeopardy, but left to its own course it ends in power's disappearance. This implies that it is not correct to think of the opposite of violence as nonviolence; to speak of nonviolent power is actually redundant. Violence can destroy power; it is utterly incapable of creating it. Hegel's and Marx's great trust in the dialectical "power of negation," by virtue of which opposites do not destroy but smoothly develop into each other because contradictions promote and do not paralyze development, rests on a much older philosophical prejudice: that evil is no more than a privative *modus* of the good, that good can come out of evil; that, in short, evil is but a temporary manifestation of a still-hidden good. Such time-honored opinions have become dangerous. They are shared by many who have never heard of Hegel or Marx, for the simple reason that they inspire hope and dispel fear—a treacherous hope used to dispel legitimate fear. By this, I do not mean to equate violence with evil; I only want to stress that violence cannot be derived from its opposite, which is power, and that in order to understand it for what it is, we shall have to examine its roots and nature.

## IN RETROSPECT

**1.** Early in this essay (paragraphs 3–7), Arendt defines such terms as *power, strength, force, authority,* and *violence.* Why does she bother to define *strength, force,* and *authority* in an essay that, according to the title, focuses on *power* and *violence?*

**2.** You may have had difficulty understanding Arendt's essay. You can often make an appreciable gain in your reading skill if you determine *why* you had difficulty reading a particular text. For instance, if you had difficulty reading Arendt's essay, was it due to (a) her style? (b) the level of her diction? (c) the nature of the subject matter? (d) the organization of the essay? (e) the use of several unexplained allusions? (f) other causes?

# 11

# On Freedom of Opinion

*In chapter 10 we witnessed writers who were intent on exposing social and political situations in their society and on rousing the citizenry to do something to correct those situations. Yet it takes more than just a democratic form of government for people to be able to stand up and, through an expenditure of words, attempt to move others to act. There must also be a climate in which freedom of expression prevails for everyone—even for those expressing unpopular or shocking or treasonous views. In short, there must be tolerance for expressions of opinion from a wide spectrum of perspectives—even fools must be allowed to speak out. In the essays that follow, John Stuart Mill leads off with his classic statement on liberty of thought and discussion. Mark Twain, Dorothy Thompson, and William F. Buckley, Jr., subsequently sound the same note from different perspectives. You should be thankful that you live in a society where essays like these can be printed to be read by anybody who can read.*

# *Of the Liberty of Thought and Discussion*

## JOHN STUART MILL

John Stuart Mill (1806–1873) was the son of the famous James Mill, who not only educated his son but later got him a job as a clerk in the British East India Company, an occupation that supported Mill while he did his intellectual work. "Of the Liberty of Thought and Discussion" is an excerpt from chapter 2 of Mill's influential book *On Liberty,* published in 1859. The views expressed in this essay are based on utilitarianism, a philosophy first formulated by Jeremy Bentham in 1780. Bentham preached that the basic principle governing morals and legislation was "the greatest happiness of the greatest number" of people. Thus, whenever we are called upon to judge the validity of any law, we should try to determine whether that law is likely to contribute to the welfare of not a certain class of people but the greatest number of people in that society. Mill introduced some modifications of that basic principle, but he subscribed to its main thrust. In this essay, he argues that no government or executive of a government has the right to prescribe what opinion the citizens may hear or hold. One can recognize that this view is the foundation of freedom of the press and opposition to censorship. After reading Mill's closely reasoned views, you might ask yourself—or your classmates—the classic question that ultimately comes up in every discussion of freedom of opinion: Would Mill defend a person's right to yell "Fire!" in a crowded theater?

The time, it is to be hoped, is gone by, when any defence would 1
be necessary of the "liberty of the press" as one of the securities against corrupt or tyrannical government. No argument, we may suppose, can now be needed, against permitting a legislature or an executive, not identified in interest with the people, to prescribe opinions to them, and determine what doctrines or what arguments they shall be allowed to hear. This aspect of the question, besides, has been so often and so triumphantly enforced by preceding writers, that it needs not be specially insisted on in this place. Though the law of England, on the subject of the press, is as servile to this day as it was in the time of the Tudors, there is little danger of its being actually put in force against political discussion, except during some temporary panic, when fear of insurrection drives ministers and judges from their propriety; and, speaking generally, it is not, in constitutional countries, to be apprehended, that the government, whether completely responsible to the people or not, will often attempt to control the expression of opinion, except when in doing so it makes itself the organ of the general intolerance of the public. Let us suppose, therefore, that the government is entirely at one with the

people, and never thinks of exerting any power of coercion unless in agreement with what it conceives to be their voice. But I deny the right of the people to exercise such coercion, either by themselves or by their government. The power itself is illegitimate. The best government has no more title to it than the worst. It is as noxious, or more noxious, when exerted in accordance with public opinion, than when in opposition to it. If all mankind minus one were of one opinion, and only one person were of the contrary opinion, mankind would be no more justified in silencing that one person, than he, if he had the power, would be justified in silencing mankind. Were an opinion a personal possession of no value except to the owner; if to be obstructed in the enjoyment of it were simply a private injury, it would make some difference whether the injury was inflicted only on a few persons or on many. But the peculiar evil of silencing the expression of an opinion is, that it is robbing the human race; posterity as well as the existing generation; those who dissent from the opinion, still more than those who hold it. If the opinion is right, they are deprived of the opportunity of exchanging error for truth: if wrong, they lose, what is almost as great a benefit, the clearer perception and livelier impression of truth, produced by its collision with error.

It is necessary to consider separately these two hypotheses, each 2
of which has a distinct branch of the argument corresponding to it. We can never be sure that the opinion we are endeavouring to stifle is a false opinion; and if we were sure, stifling it would be an evil still.

First: the opinion which it is attempted to suppress by authority 3
may possibly be true. Those who desire to suppress it, of course deny its truth; but they are not infallible. They have no authority to decide the question for all mankind, and exclude every other person from the means of judging. To refuse a hearing to an opinion, because they are sure that it is false, is to assume that *their* certainty is the same thing as *absolute* certainty. All silencing of discussion is an assumption of infallibility. Its condemnation may be allowed to rest on this common argument, not the worse for being common.

Unfortunately for the good sense of mankind, the fact of their 4
fallibility is far from carrying the weight in their practical judgment which is always allowed to it in theory; for while every one well knows himself to be fallible, few think it necessary to take any precautions against their own fallibility, or admit the supposition that any opinion, of which they feel very certain, may be one of the examples of the error to which they acknowledge themselves to be liable. Absolute princes, or others who are accustomed to unlimited deference, usually feel this complete confidence in their own opinions on nearly all subjects. People more happily situated, who sometimes hear their opinions disputed, and are not wholly unused to

being set right when they are wrong, place the same unbounded reliance only on such of their opinions as are shared by all who surround them, or to whom they habitually defer; for in proportion to a man's want of confidence in his own solitary judgment, does he usually repose, with implicit trust, on the infallibility of "the world" in general. And the world, to each individual, means the part of it with which he comes in contact; his party, his sect, his church, his class of society; the man may be called, by comparison, almost liberal and large-minded to whom it means anything so comprehensive as his own country or his own age. Nor is his faith in this collective authority at all shaken by his being aware that other ages, countries, sects, churches, classes, and parties have thought, and even now think, the exact reverse. He devolves upon his own world the responsibility of being in the right against the dissentient worlds of other people; and it never troubles him that mere accident has decided which of these numerous worlds is the object of his reliance, and that the same causes which make him a Churchman in London, would have made him a Buddhist or a Confucian in Pekin. Yet it is as evident in itself, as any amount of argument can make it, that ages are no more infallible than individuals; every age having held many opinions which subsequent ages have deemed not only false but absurd; and it is as certain that many opinions now general will be rejected by future ages, as it is that many, once general, are rejected by the present.

The objection likely to be made to this argument would probably 5
take some such form as the following. There is no greater assumption of infallibility in forbidding the propagation of error, than in any other thing which is done by public authority on its own judgment and responsibility. Judgment is given to men that they may use it. Because it may be used erroneously, are men to be told that they ought not to use it at all? To prohibit what they think pernicious, is not claiming exemption from error, but fulfilling the duty incumbent on them, although fallible, of acting on their conscientious conviction. If we were never to act on our opinions, because those opinions may be wrong, we should leave all our interests uncared for, and all our duties unperformed. An objection which applies to all conduct can be no valid objection to any conduct in particular. It is the duty of governments, and of individuals, to form the truest opinions they can; to form carefully, and never impose them upon others unless they are quite sure of being right. But when they are sure (such reasoners may say), it is not conscientiousness but cowardice to shrink from acting on their opinions, and allow doctrines which they honestly think dangerous to the welfare of mankind, either in this life or in another, to be scattered abroad without restraint, because other

people, in less enlightened times, have persecuted opinions now believed to be true. Let us take care, it may be said, not to make the same mistake: but governments and nations have made mistakes in other things, which are not denied to be fit subjects for the exercise of authority: they have laid on bad taxes, made unjust wars. Ought we therefore to lay on no taxes, and, under whatever provocation, make no wars? Men and governments, must act to the best of their ability. There is no such thing as absolute certainty, but there is assurance sufficient for the purposes of human life. We may, and must, assume our opinion to be true for the guidance of our own conduct: and it is assuming no more when we forbid bad men to pervert society by the propagation of opinions which we regard as false and pernicious.

I answer, that it is assuming very much more. There is the 6
greatest difference between presuming an opinion to be true, because, with every opportunity for contesting it, it has not been refuted, and assuming its truth for the purpose of not permitting its refutation. Complete liberty of contradicting and disproving our opinion is the very condition which justifies us in assuming its truth for purposes of action; and on no other terms can a being with human faculties have any rational assurance of being right.

When we consider either the history of opinion, or the ordinary 7
conduct of human life, to what is it to be ascribed that the one and the other are no worse than they are? Not certainly to the inherent force of the human understanding; for, on any matter not self-evident, there are ninety-nine persons totally incapable of judging of it for one who is capable; and the capacity of the hundredth person is only comparative; for the majority of the eminent men of every past generation held many opinions now known to be erroneous, and did or approved numerous things which no one will now justify. Why is it, then, that there is on the whole a preponderance among mankind of rational opinions and rational conduct? If there really is this preponderance—which there must be unless human affairs are, and have always been, in an almost desperate state—it is owing to a quality of the human mind, the source of everything respectable in man either as an intellectual or as a moral being, namely, that his errors are corrigible. He is capable of rectifying his mistakes by discussion and experience. Not by experience alone. There must be discussion, to show how experience is to be interpreted. Wrong opinions and practices gradually yield to fact and argument; but facts and arguments, to produce any effect on the mind, must be brought before it. Very few facts are able to tell their own story, without comments to bring out their meaning. The whole strength and value, then, of human judgment, depending on the one property, that it can be set right when it is wrong, reliance can be placed on it only when the means of

setting it right are kept constantly at hand. In the case of any person whose judgment is really deserving of confidence, how has it become so? Because he has kept his mind open to criticism on his opinions and conduct. Because it has been his practice to listen to all that could be said against him; to profit by as much of it as was just, and expound to himself, and upon occasion to others, the fallacy of what was fallacious. Because he has felt, that the only way in which a human being can make some approach to knowing the whole of a subject, is by hearing what can be said about it by persons of every variety of opinion, and studying all modes in which it can be looked at by every character of mind. No wise man ever acquired his wisdom in any mode but this; nor is it in the nature of human intellect to become wise in any other manner. The steady habit of correcting and completing his own opinion by collating it with those of others, so far from causing doubt and hesitation in carrying it into practice, is the only stable foundation for a just reliance on it: for, being cognisant of all that can, at least obviously, be said against him, and having taken up his position against all gainsayers—knowing that he has sought for objections and difficulties, instead of avoiding them, and has shut out no light which can be thrown upon the subject from any quarter—he has a right to think his judgment better than that of any person, or any multitude, who have not gone through a similar process.

It is not too much to require that what the wisest of mankind, 8
those who are best entitled to trust their own judgment, find necessary to warrant their relying on it, should be submitted to by that miscellaneous collection of a few wise and many foolish individuals, called the public. The most intolerant of churches, the Roman Catholic Church, even at the canonisation of a saint, admits, and listens patiently to, a "devil's advocate." The holiest of men, it appears, cannot be admitted to posthumous honours, until all that the devil could say against him is known and weighed. If even the Newtonian philosophy were not permitted to be questioned, mankind could not feel as complete assurance of its truth as they now do. The beliefs which we have most warrant for have no safeguard to rest on, but a standing invitation to the whole world to prove them unfounded. If the challenge is not accepted, or is accepted and the attempt fails, we are far enough from certainty still; but we have done the best that the existing state of human reason admits of; we have neglected nothing that could give the truth a chance of reaching us: if the lists are kept open, we may hope that if there be a better truth, it will be found when the human mind is capable of receiving it; and in the meantime we may rely on having attained such approach to truth as is possible in our own day. This is the amount of certainty attainable by a fallible being, and this the sole way of attaining it.

Strange it is, that men should admit the validity of the arguments 9
for free discussion, but object to their being "pushed to an extreme"; not seeing that unless the reasons are good for an extreme case, they are not good for any case. Strange that they should imagine that they are not assuming infallibility, when they acknowledge that there should be free discussion on all subjects which can possibly be *doubtful,* but think that some particular principle or doctrine should be forbidden to be questioned because it is so *certain,* that is, because *they are certain* that it is certain. To call any proposition certain, while there is any one who would deny its certainty if permitted, but who is not permitted, is to assume that we ourselves, and those who agree with us, are the judges of certainty, and judges without hearing the other side.

In the present age—which has been described as "destitute of 10
faith, but terrified at scepticism"—in which people feel sure, not so much that their opinions are true, as that they should not know what to do without them—the claims of an opinion to be protected from public attack are rested not so much on its truth, as on its importance to society. There are, it is alleged, certain beliefs so useful, not to say indispensable, to well-being that it is as much the duty of governments to uphold those benefits, as to protect any other of the interests of society. In a case of such necessity, and so directly in the line of their duty, something less than infallibility may, it is maintained, warrant, and even bind, governments to act on their own opinion, confirmed by the general opinion of mankind. It is also often argued, and still oftener thought, that none but bad men would desire to weaken these salutary beliefs; and there can be nothing wrong, it is thought, in restraining bad men, and prohibiting what only such men would wish to practise. This mode of thinking makes the justification of restraints on discussion not a question of the truth of doctrines, but of their usefulness; and flatters itself by that means to escape the responsibility of claiming to be an infallible judge of opinions. But those who thus satisfy themselves, do not perceive that the assumption of infallibility is merely shifted from one point to another. The usefulness of an opinion is itself matter of opinion: as disputable, as open to discussion, and requiring discussion as much as the opinion itself. There is the same need of an infallible judge of opinions to decide an opinion to be noxious, as to decide it to be false, unless the opinion condemned has full opportunity of defending itself. And it will not do to say that the heretic may be allowed to maintain the utility or harmlessness of his opinion, though forbidden to maintain its truth. The truth of an opinion is part of its utility. If we would know whether or not it is desirable that a proposition should be believed, is it possible to exclude the consideration of whether or not

it is true? In the opinion, not of bad men, but of the best men, no belief which is contrary to truth can be really useful; and can you prevent such men from urging that plea, when they are charged with culpability for denying some doctrine which they are told is useful, but which they believe to be false? Those who are on the side of received opinions never fail to take all possible advantage of this plea: you do not find *them* handling the question of utility as if it could be completely abstracted from that of truth: on the contrary, it is, above all, because their doctrine is "the truth," that the knowledge or the belief of it is held to be so indispensable. There can be no fair discussion of the question of usefulness when an argument so vital may be employed on one side, but not on the other. And in point of fact, when law or public feeling do not permit the truth of an opinion to be disputed, they are just as little tolerant of a denial of its usefulness. The utmost they allow is an extenuation of its absolute necessity, or of the positive guilt of rejecting it.

### IN RETROSPECT

**1.** Mill is dealing with one of the fundamental principles of a democratic society: every citizen's right to freedom of thought and expression. And the essay is also exposing the principles underlying all the discussions in this chapter about freedom of opinion. After one reads this essay, one can express any opinion about it that one thinks fit—"This is a brilliant essay," "John Stuart Mill is a foolish and dangerous man," "In my opinion, no citizen has the right to advocate the overthrow of the duly elected government of the country," and so on. One may be challenged to defend one's opinion, but according to Mill, one should not be forbidden to voice one's opinion. Where do *you* stand on the issue of liberty of thought and discussion? Are there any points on which your opinion about these issue differs from Mill's?

**2.** Aristotle wrote his treatise on rhetoric because he recognized that communities of people often have to make crucial decisions on the basis of something less than certainty—that is, on the basis of opinion or probability, rather than of demonstrated fact or certified truth. For instance, is this man guilty of the crime with which he is charged? Will the passage of this new tax law bring us out of our current recession, as this woman claims? Having read Mill's essay, what part do you believe rhetoric plays in the function of a democratic government?

# *Corn-pone Opinions*

## MARK TWAIN

Mark Twain, the pseudonym of Samuel Langhorne Clemens (1835–1910), established his fame with such works as *Tom Sawyer, Huckleberry Finn, Roughing It, Innocents Abroad,* and "The Celebrated Jumping Frog of Calaveras County," some or all of which most American schoolchildren have read by the time they graduate from high school. In fact, so great was Twain's popularity and influence that such literary figures as T. S. Eliot, Ernest Hemingway, H. L. Mencken, and Bernard De Voto have said in effect that all distinctly American humor stems from Twain. Born in Florida, Missouri, Twain moved with his family to Hannibal, Missouri, in 1839. There he became fascinated with the mighty Mississippi and absorbed the material for his later novels about mischievous boyhood adventures. As he tells us in *Life on the Mississippi,* he aspired to be a riverboat pilot, but when the Civil War closed down the riverboat operations, he went with his brother to Nevada, where he began his career as a humorist in the frontier tradition. In 1870, Twain married Olivia Langdon and settled in Hartford, Connecticut. Although he became increasingly frustrated and pessimistic in this Eastern milieu, it was during this period that he wrote all of his great novels. The bankruptcy of a publishing firm that he established in partnership with Charles L. Webster forced Twain onto the lecture circuit, throughout the United States and Europe, to help him discharge his debts. In the 1960s, Hal Holbrook re-created this aspect of Twain's life in *Mark Twain the Lecturer,* a monologue that Holbrook performed in hundreds of civic and university theaters across the country. The following essay exhibits Twain's opinion about how human beings acquire their viewpoints, fashions, positions, and convictions in life. As he says, "We are creatures of outside influences; as a rule we do not think, we only imitate."

Fifty years ago, when I was a boy of fifteen and helping to inhabit a Missourian village on the banks of the Mississippi, I had a friend whose society was very dear to me because I was forbidden by my mother to partake of it. He was a gay and impudent and satirical and delightful young black man—a slave—who daily preached sermons from the top of his master's woodpile, with me for sole audience. He imitated the pulpit style of the several clergymen of the village, and did it well, and with fine passion and energy. To me he was a wonder. I believed he was the greatest orator in the United States and would some day be heard from. But it did not happen; in the distribution of rewards he was overlooked. It is the way, in this world. 1

He interrupted his preaching, now and then, to saw a stick of wood; but the sawing was a pretense—he did it with his mouth; exactly imitating the sound the bucksaw makes in shrieking its way through the wood. But it served its purpose; it kept his master from 2 coming out to see how the work was getting along. I listened to the sermons from the open window of a lumber room at the back of the house. One of his texts was this:

> You tell me whar a man gits his corn pone, en I'll tell you what his 'pinions is.

I can never forget it. It was deeply impressed upon me. By my 3
mother. Not upon my memory, but elsewhere. She had slipped in upon me while I was absorbed and not watching. The black philosopher's idea was that a man is not independent, and cannot afford views which might interfere with his bread and butter. If he would prosper, he must train with the majority; in matters of large moment, like politics and religion, he must think and feel with the bulk of his neighbors, or suffer damage in his social standing and in his business prosperities. He must restrict himself to corn-pone opinions—at least on the surface. He must get his opinions from other people; he must reason out none for himself; he must have no first-hand views.

I think Jerry was right, in the main, but I think he did not go far 4
enough.

1. It was his idea that a man conforms to the majority view of his locality by calculation and intention.

This happens, but I think it is not the rule.

2. It was his idea that there is such a thing as a first-hand opinion; an original opinion; an opinion which is coldly reasoned out in a man's head, by a searching analysis of the facts involved, with the heart unconsulted, and the jury room closed against outside influences. It may be that such an opinion has been born somewhere, at some time or other, but I suppose it got away before they could catch it and stuff it and put it in the museum.

I am persuaded that a coldly-thought-out and independent ver- 5
dict upon a fashion in clothes, or manners, or literature, or politics, or religion, or any other matter that is projected into the field of our notice and interest, is a most rare thing—if it has indeed ever existed.

A new thing in costume appears—the flaring hoopskirt, for exam- 6
ple—and the passers-by are shocked, and the irreverent laugh. Six months later everybody is reconciled; the fashion has established itself; it is admired, now, and no one laughs. Public opinion resented it before, public opinion accepts it now, and is happy in it. Why? Was the resentment reasoned out? Was the acceptance reasoned out? No. The instinct that moves to conformity did the work. It is our nature to conform; it is a force which not many can successfully resist. What is its seat? The inborn requirement of self-approval. We all have to bow to that; there are no exceptions. Even the woman who refuses from

she could not wear the skirt and have her own approval; and that she *must* have, she cannot help herself. But as a rule our self-approval has its source in but one place and not elsewhere—the approval of other people. A person of vast consequences can introduce any kind of novelty in dress and the general world will presently adopt it—moved to do it, in the first place, by the natural instinct to passively yield to that vague something recognized as authority, and in the second place by the human instinct to train with the multitude and have its approval. An empress introduced the hoopskirt, and we know the result. A nobody introduced the bloomer, and we know the result. If Eve should come again, in her ripe renown, and reintroduce her quaint styles—well, we know what would happen. And we should be cruelly embarrassed, along at first.

The hoopskirt runs its course and disappears. Nobody reasons 7
about it. One woman abandons the fashion; her neighbor notices this and follows her lead; this influences the next woman; and so on and so on, and presently the skirt has vanished out of the world, no one knows how nor why, nor cares, for that matter. It will come again, by and by and in due course it will go again.

Twenty-five years ago, in England, six or eight wine glasses stood 8
grouped by each person's plate at a dinner party, and they were used, not left idle and empty; to-day there are but three or four in the group, and the average guest sparingly uses about two of them. We have not adopted this new fashion yet, but we shall do it presently. We shall not think it out; we shall merely conform, and let it go at that. We get our notions and habits and opinions from outside influences; we do not have to study them out.

Our table manners, and company manners, and street manners 9
change from time to time, but the changes are not reasoned out; we merely notice and conform. We are creatures of outside influences; as a rule we do not think, we only imitate. We cannot invent standards that will stick; what we mistake for standards are only fashions, and perishable. We may continue to admire them, but we drop the use of them. We notice this in literature. Shakespeare is a standard, and fifty years ago we used to write tragedies which we couldn't tell from—from somebody else's; but we don't do it any more, now. Our prose standard, three quarters of a century ago, was ornate and diffuse; some authority or other changed it in the direction of compactness and simplicity, and conformity followed, without argument. The historical novel starts up suddenly, and sweeps the land. Everybody writes one, and the nation is glad. We had historical novels before; but nobody read them, and the rest of us conformed—without reasoning it out. We are conforming in the other way, now, because it is another case of everybody.

The outside influences are always pouring in upon us, and we are 10
always obeying their orders and accepting their verdicts. The Smiths like the new play; the Joneses go to see it, and they copy the Smith verdict. Morals, religions, politics, get their following from surrounding influences and atmospheres, almost entirely; not from study, not from thinking. A man must and will have his own approval first of all, in each and every moment and circumstance of his life—even if he must repent of a self-approved act the moment after its commission, in order to get his self-approval *again:* but, speaking in general terms, a man's self-approval in the large concerns of life has its source in the approval of the peoples about him, and not in a searching personal examination of the matter. Mohammedans are Mohammedans because they are born and reared among that sect, not because they have thought it out and can furnish sound reasons for being Mohammedans; we know why Catholics are Catholics; why Presbyterians are Presbyterians; why Baptists are Baptists; why Mormons are Mormons; why thieves are thieves; why monarchists are monarchists; why Republicans are Republicans and Democrats, Democrats. We know it is a matter of association and sympathy, not reasoning and examination; that hardly a man in the world has an opinion upon morals, politics, or religion which he got otherwise than through his associations and sympathies. Broadly speaking, there are none but corn-pone opinions. And broadly speaking, corn-pone stands for self-approval. Self-approval is acquired mainly from the approval of other people. The result is conformity. Sometimes conformity has a sordid business interest—the bread-and-butter interest—but not in most cases, I think. I think that in the majority of cases it is unconscious and not calculated; that it is born of the human being's natural yearning to stand well with his fellows and have their inspiring approval and praise—a yearning which is commonly so strong and so insistent that it cannot be effectually resisted, and must have its way.

A political emergency brings out the corn-pone opinion in fine 11
force in its two chief varieties—the pocketbook variety, which has its origin in self-interest, and the bigger variety, the sentimental variety—the one which can't bear to be outside the pale; can't bear to be in disfavor; can't endure the averted face and the cold shoulder; wants to stand well with his friends, wants to be smiled upon, wants to be welcome, wants to hear the precious words, "*He's* on the right track!" Uttered, perhaps by an ass, but still an ass of high degree, an ass whose approval is gold and diamonds to a smaller ass, and confers glory and honor and happiness, and membership in the herd. For these gauds many a man will dump his life-long principles into the street, and his conscience along with them. We have seen it happen. In some millions of instances.

Men think they think upon great political questions, and they do; but they think with their party, not independently; they read its literature, but not that of the other side; they arrive at convictions, but they are drawn from a partial view of the matter in hand and are of no particular value. They swarm with their party, they feel with their party, they are happy in their party's approval; and where the party leads they will follow, whether for right and honor, or through blood and dirt and a mush of mutilated morals. 12

In our late canvass half of the nation passionately believed that in silver lay salvation, the other half as passionately believed that that way lay destruction. Do you believe that a tenth part of the people, on either side, had any rational excuse for having an opinion about the matter at all? I studied that mighty question to the bottom—came out empty. Half of our people passionately believes in high tariff, the other half believe otherwise. Does this mean study and examination, or only feeling? The latter, I think. I have deeply studied that question, too—and didn't arrive. We all do no end of feeling, and we mistake it for thinking. And out of it we get an aggregation which we consider a boon. Its name is Public Opinion. It is held in reverence. It settles everything. Some think it the Voice of God. 13

**IN RETROSPECT**

**1.** As the headnote points out, this essay presents Twain's opinion about how people acquire their viewpoints, fashions, positions, and convictions in life. Is Twain's opinion about these matters just another example of a corn-pone opinion? Before you try to give an answer to that question, make sure you understand what Twain means by the term "corn-pone opinion." For a clue as to the meaning of that term, look at what the young black man says in paragraph 2 and then at what Twain says in paragraph 3. Explain, in your own words, what "corn-pone opinion" means and then answer the question asked in the second sentence above.

**2.** What relationship does Twain's concept of "corn-pone opinions" have to Mill's belief in the liberty of thought and discussion? Do the two writers' views proceed from the same or from different assumptions about the legitimacy of opinions and their expression? Explain.

# *Concerning Tolerance*

**DOROTHY THOMPSON**

Dorothy Thompson (1894–1961), born in Lancaster, New York, was known principally as a journalist and columnist. From 1920 to 1928 she was a foreign correspondent, based primarily in Vienna and Berlin, for the Philadelphia *Public Ledger* and the New York *Evening Post*. Later the column she wrote for the New York *Herald Tribune* was syndicated in more than two hundred newspapers. Among the books Thompson published were *The New Russia* (1928), *I Saw Hitler* (1932), *Let the Record Speak* (1939), and the collection of essays—originally published in the *Ladies' Home Journal*—from which the following essay was taken, *The Courage to Be Happy* (1957). From 1928 until 1942 Thompson was married to the American novelist Sinclair Lewis. She was always an aggressive and outspoken writer. The following essay, "Concerning Tolerance," is a good example of her pungent style. It is indicative of Thompson's persistent common sense that in this essay, she approves of only a limited tolerance, even in a country as democratic as our own.

1 The open mind has been greatly praised, but somebody once said that an open mind was often a mind with nothing in it. It has also been said that "to understand all is to forgive all," but it is perhaps truer to say that to understand nothing is to forgive everything.

2 Every saw and every truism needs inspection. Words need periodic inspection. And one word that needs some reconsideration is the great word "tolerance." For it has been abused past recognition. From being a positive expression of respect for other people's rights, it has become a weasel word for the avoidance of responsibility.

3 The Latin root of the word "tolerance" refers to things that can be borne, endured, are supportable. The intrinsic meaning of "tolerance" is the capacity to sustain and endure, as of hardship. From this comes the inferential meaning of patience with the opinions and practices of those who differ. It is interesting that the word is used in connection with the coining of money and with machinery, to indicate the margin within which coins may deviate from the fixed standard, or the dimensions or parts of a machine from the norm.

4 But the word "tolerance" does not suggest that everything is supportable and that any amount of deviation is allowable. It suggests that one's principles and standards should be tempered with patience, and with readiness to subject them to modification, through practical or intellectual tests. But it does not suggest that one should have no principles or standards. In the contemporary world, I find that for many people this is, however, exactly what they mean by

tolerance: a vapid openness to the condoning of anything. Tolerance carried to this conclusion is anarchy. It is not an instrument of civilization, but an instrument of barbarism.

5 We are not tolerant of diphtheria bacilli, tuberculosis germs, or cancer cells. We do not assert their right also to live and work. We know that they cannot continue to exist if the organism which they have entered, or in which they have grown, is also to continue to exist. Therefore we eradicate them with the greatest intolerance. We know that there is no way for noncancerous tissue to come to an agreement with cancerous tissue. There is no possible *modus vivendi* between them. Therefore, a cancer is eradicated.

6 But in our social and political life we seem to think that democracy is only a casual host for the entertainment of all conceivable viewpoints and organizations, including those whose clear intention is to destroy the host. Instead of allowing that margin, even a very wide margin, for variation which is the essence of tolerance, we entertain those in whom there is no speck of tolerance whatsoever for democracy itself, or for tolerance itself, and who seek to substitute for ordered popular government under law a regime of dictatorship and violence.

7 The margin of tolerance in a democracy, or in any other organized and civilized state ruled by law, stops when standards essential to the continuance of an orderly and civilized community are seriously menaced. It is impossible, for instance, to continue any sort of orderly, civilized, and legal community at all if the police powers are captured, by whatever legal methods, by gangsters, and then used to destroy the law, the courts, private property, all civilian immunities, and to kill people arbitrarily, without indictment or trial.

8 It is of not the slightest consequence, for instance, that the American Communist Party is a legal organization, that it pays lip service to democracy—and, indeed, calls itself democracy's agent—and that it does not seek to make its way by throwing bombs or by other acts of violence, but uses instead the legal methods of persuasion and organization, assisted by more dubious instruments of slander and intimidation. Its object is what is important, and its object is to destroy the law, and to substitute for law the absolute dictatorship of a party itself dictatorially ruled, and acting as the self-appointed agents of what they choose to delineate as the proletariat, or "working masses." This is demonstrably the object of the Communist Party. This is the actual form of organization that exists in Soviet Russia, and it is a form of organization that has been consistently praised and never denounced by any Communist Party leader—or by any one of them who has continued thereafter to hold his position. The American Communist

Party is in alliance with the Communist Party of Russia. And, therefore, the American Communist Party is outside the bounds of possible tolerance by anyone who is not a Communist, for the achievement of its object is incompatible with the continuance of our existence as a civilized community ruled by law.

Exactly the same thing holds true for the German-American Bund 9
and its kindred and supporting organizations. The legality of their methods does not obscure the fact that their object is to destroy the essential integrity of this country both as an independent power and as an organized commonwealth. If anyone doubts that, after what has happened in Central Europe, he is verging on feeble-mindedness. Their program is to deprive millions of our citizens of their citizenship rights and make them "subjects" of the rest of us. The pattern of society which is their model is the dictatorship of a gang, knowing no limitations of ethics or law, and ruling with total arbitrariness. As I write these lines, this regime, if you can call it a regime, is engaged on an international plunder expedition.

It is impossible to tolerate the absolutely incompatible. Tolerating 10
then leads either to the destruction of order and civilization by capitulation, or to civil war. It cannot possibly lead anywhere else. You cannot make a "pact" with Communism or Nazism. They demand all or nothing; that is their nature. Therefore there is, in respect of them, no supportable plea for the rights of civil liberty. Al Capone could not appeal to civil liberties for the right openly to organize his gang, with the protection of the police. No state can tolerate that which is hostile to the very concept of the state as such.

In this country we can tolerate every political group, from the 11
right to the left, Socialists and Bourbons, provided they are not acting as agents of foreign powers and do not have as their object the substitution of the legally ordered society by the rule of violence. To extend tolerance to such is to abdicate intelligence and prepare for the extermination of tolerance itself.

### IN RETROSPECT

**1.** You do not have to read very far into Thompson's essay to realize that she does not totally agree with Mill's views on freedom of thought and expression. What are the differences in their views on this matter? Summarize the arguments they present in support of their differing views.

**2.** In question 1, we suggested that Thompson and Mill present different views on freedom of thought and discussion. Now we ask you to consider how the tone and the style of these two essays promote the aims of their authors.

# *Why Don't We Complain?*

**WILLIAM F. BUCKLEY, JR.**

William F. Buckley, Jr. (1925–     ), is one of ten children of a wealthy lawyer who had made his money in Texas oil. In what we can now regard as a forecast of his later controversial career, Buckley at age six wrote a letter to the king of England demanding that England pay its war debt to the United States. Buckley received his early education at St. Thomas More School in London and at Millbrook School in New York. After serving in the navy during World War II, he attended Yale University, where he concentrated on history, political science, and economics; wrote provocative articles for the *Yale Daily News;* and participated on the debating team that defeated the Oxford University team. Buckley first came into national prominence in 1951 with the publication of *God and Man at Yale,* a book in which he brashly pointed out what from his viewpoint as a Roman Catholic and a political conservative he considered to be the weaknesses in Yale's curriculum. He became an associate editor of the *American Mercury* in 1952, published *McCarthy and His Enemies* in 1954 and *Up from Liberalism* in 1959, and in 1955 founded the *National Review,* a journal of conservative opinion designed to counteract such liberal journals as the *New Republic* and the *Nation.* An ardent skier and motorcycle rider, Buckley also delights in playing the piano and a seventeenth-century clavichord that his father gave him as a graduation present. Although many liberals differ violently with Buckley's political and social views, they respect him for his forthrightness, his undeniable skill at debating, and his quaint but elegant style, characterized by its pungency and sometimes polysyllabic diction. Here is an example of an essay from his quill.

It was the very last coach and the only empty seat on the entire train, so there was no turning back. The problem was to breathe. Outside, the temperature was below freezing. Inside the railroad car the temperature must have been about 85 degrees. I took off my overcoat, and a few minutes later my jacket, and noticed that the car was flecked with the white shirts of the passengers. I soon found my hand moving to loosen my tie. From one end of the car to the other, as we rattled through Westchester County, we sweated; but we did not moan. 1

I watched the train conductor appear at the head of the car. "Tickets, all tickets, please!" In a more virile age, I thought, the passengers would seize the conductor and strap him down on a seat over the radiator to share the fate of his patrons. He shuffled down the aisle, picking up tickets, punching commutation cards. *No one addressed a word to him.* He approached my seat, and I drew a deep breath of resolution. "Conductor," I began with a considerable edge to my voice. . . . Instantly the doleful eyes of my seatmate turned 2 tiredly from his newspaper to fix me with a resentful stare: what question could be so important as to justify my sibilant intrusion into his stupor? I was shaken by those eyes. I am incapable of making a discreet fuss, so I mumbled a question about what time were we due in Stamford (I didn't even ask whether it would be before or after dehydration could be expected to set in), got my reply, and went back to my newspaper and to wiping my brow.

The conductor had nonchalantly walked down the gauntlet of 3
eighty sweating American freemen, and not one of them had asked him to explain why the passengers in that car had been consigned to suffer. There is nothing to be done when the temperature *outdoors* is 85 degrees, and indoors the air conditioner has broken down; obviously when that happens there is nothing to do, except perhaps curse the day that one was born. But when the temperature outdoors is below freezing, it takes a positive act of will on somebody's part to set the temperature *indoors* at 85. Somewhere a valve was turned too far, a furnace overstocked, a thermostat maladjusted: something that could easily be remedied by turning off the heat and allowing the great outdoors to come indoors. All this is so obvious. What is not obvious is what has happened to the American people.

It isn't just the commuters, whom we have come to visualize as a 4
supine breed who have got on to the trick of suspending their sensory faculties twice a day while they submit to the creeping dissolution of the railroad industry. It isn't just they who have given up trying to rectify irrational vexations. It is the American people everywhere.

A few weeks ago at a large movie theatre I turned to my wife and 5
said, "The picture is out of focus." "Be quiet," she answered. I obeyed. But a few minutes later I raised the point again, with mounting impatience. "It will be all right in a minute," she said apprehensively. (She would rather lose her eyesight than be around when I make one of my infrequent scenes.) I waited, it was *just* out of focus—not glaringly out, but out. My vision is 20-20, and I assume that is the vision, adjusted, of most people in the movie house. So, after hectoring my wife throughout the first reel, I finally prevailed upon her to admit that it *was* off, and very annoying. We then settled down, coming to rest on the presumption that: a) someone connected with the management of the theatre must soon notice the blur and make the correction; or b) that someone seated near the rear of the house would make the complaint in behalf of those of us up front; or c) that—any minute now—the entire house would explode into catcalls and foot stamping, calling dramatic attention to the irksome distortion.

What happened was nothing. The movie ended, as it had begun, 6
*just* out of focus, and as we trooped out, we stretched our faces in a

variety of contortions to accustom the eye to the shock of normal focus.

I think it is safe to say that everybody suffered on that occasion. 7
And I think it is safe to assume that everyone was expecting someone else to take the initiative in going back to speak to the manager. And it is probably true even that if we had supposed the movie would run right through the blurred image, someone surely would have summoned up the purposive indignation to get up out of his seat and file his complaint.

But notice that no one did. And the reason no one did is because 8
we are all increasingly anxious in America to be unobtrusive, we are reluctant to make our voices heard, hesitant about claiming our rights; we are afraid that our cause is unjust, or that if it is not unjust, that it is ambiguous; or if not even that, that it is too trivial to justify the horrors of a confrontation with Authority; we will sit in an oven or endure a racking headache before undertaking a head-on, I'm-here-to-tell-you complaint. That tendency to passive compliance, to a heedless endurance, is something to keep one's eyes on—in sharp focus.

I myself can occasionally summon the courage to complain, but I 9
cannot, as I have intimated, complain softly. My own instinct is so strong to let the thing ride, to forget about it—to expect that someone will take the matter up, when the grievance is collective, in my behalf—that it is only when the provocation is at a very special key, whose vibrations touch simultaneously a complexus of nerves, allergies, and passions, that I catch fire and find the reserves of courage and assertiveness to speak up. When that happens, I get quite carried away. My blood gets hot, my brow wet, I become unbearably and unconscionably sarcastic and bellicose; I am girded for a total showdown.

Why should that be? Why could not I (or anyone else) on that 10
railroad coach have said simply to the conductor, "Sir"—I take that back: that sounds sarcastic—"Conductor, would you be good enough to turn down the heat? I am extremely hot. In fact I tend to get hot every time the temperature reaches 85 degr—" Strike that last sentence. Just end it with the simple statement that you are extremely hot, and let the conductor infer the cause.

Every New Year's Eve I resolve to do something about the 11
Milquetoast in me and vow to speak up, calmly, for my rights, and for the betterment of our society, on every appropriate occasion. Entering last New Year's Eve I was fortified in my resolve because that morning at breakfast I had had to ask the waitress three times for a glass of milk. She finally brought it—after I had finished my eggs, which is when I don't want it any more. I did not have the manliness

to order her to take the milk back, but settled instead for a cowardly sulk, and ostentatiously refused to drink the milk—though I later paid for it—rather than state plainly to the hostess, as I should have, why I had not drunk it, and would not pay for it.

So by the time the New Year ushered out the Old, riding in on my 12
morning's indignation and stimulated by the gastric juices of resolution that flow so faithfully on New Year's Eve, I rendered my vow. Henceforward I would conquer my shyness, my despicable disposition to supineness. I would speak out like a man against the unnecessary annoyances of our time.

Forty-eight hours later, I was standing in line at the ski repair 13
store in Pico Peak, Vermont. All I needed, to get on with my skiing, was the loan, for one minute, of a small screwdriver, to tighten a loose binding. Behind the counter in the workshop were two men. One was industriously engaged in serving the complicated requirements of a young lady at the head of the line, and obviously he would be tied up for quite a while. The other—"Jiggs," his workmate called him—was a middle-aged man, who sat in a chair puffing a pipe, exchanging small talk with his working partner. My pulse began its telltale acceleration. The minutes ticked on. I stared at the idle shopkeeper, hoping to shame him into action, but he was impervious to my telepathic reproof and continued his small talk with his friend, brazenly insensitive to the nervous demands of six good men who were raring to ski.

Suddenly my New Year's Eve resolution struck me. It was now or 14
never. I broke from my place in line and marched to the counter. I was going to control myself. I dug my nails into my palms. My effort was only partially successful:

"If you are not too busy," I said icily, "would you mind handing 15
me a screwdriver?"

Work stopped and everyone turned his eyes on me, and I experi- 16
enced the mortification I always feel when I am the center of centripetal shafts of curiosity, resentment, perplexity.

But the worst was yet to come. "I am sorry, sir," said Jiggs 17
defensively, moving the pipe from his mouth. "I am not supposed to move. I have just had a heart attack." That was the signal for a great whirring noise that descended from heaven. We looked, stricken, out the window, and it appeared as though a cyclone had suddenly focused on the snowy courtyard between the shop and the ski lift. Suddenly a gigantic army helicopter materialized, and hovered down to a landing. Two men jumped out of the plane carrying a stretcher, tore into the ski shop, and lifted the shopkeeper onto the stretcher. Jiggs bade his companion good-by, was whisked out the door, into the plane, up to the heavens, down—we learned—to a near-by army

hospital. I looked up manfully—into a score of man-eating eyes. I put the experience down as a reversal.

As I write this, on an airplane, I have run out of paper and need to reach into my briefcase under my legs for more. I cannot do this until my empty lunch tray is removed from my lap. I arrested the stewardess as she passed empty-handed down the aisle on the way to the kitchen to fetch the lunch trays for the passengers up forward who haven't been served yet. "Would you please take my tray?" "Just a *moment, sir!*" she said, and marched on sternly. Shall I tell her that since she is headed for the kitchen *anyway,* it could not delay the feeding of the other passengers by more than two seconds necessary to stash away my empty tray? Or remind her that not fifteen minutes ago she spoke unctuously into the loudspeaker the words undoubtedly devised by the airline's highly paid public relations counselor: "If there is anything I or Miss French can do for you to make your trip more enjoyable, *please* let us—" I have run out of paper. 18

I think the observable reluctance of the majority of Americans to assert themselves in minor matters is related to our increased sense of helplessness in an age of technology and centralized political and economic power. For generations, Americans who were too hot, or too cold, got up and did something about it. Now we call the plumber, or the electrician, or the furnace man. The habit of looking after our own needs obviously had something to do with the assertiveness that characterized the American family familiar to readers of American literature. With the technification of life goes our direct responsibility for our material environment, and we are conditioned to adopt a position of helplessness not only as regards the broken air conditioner, but as regards the overheated train. It takes an expert to fix the former, but not the latter; yet these distinctions, as we withdraw into helplessness, tend to fade away. 19

Our notorious political apathy is a related phenomenon. Every year, whether the Republican or the Democratic Party is in office, more and more power drains away from the individual to feed vast reservoirs in far-off places; and we have less and less say about the shape of events which shape our future. From this alienation of personal power comes the sense of resignation with which we accept the political dispensations of a powerful government whose hold upon us continues to increase. 20

An editor of a national weekly news magazine told me a few years ago that as few as a dozen letters of protest against an editorial stance of his magazine was enough to convene a plenipotentiary meeting of the board of editors to review policy. "So few people complain, or make their voices heard," he explained to me, "that we assume a dozen letters represent the inarticulated views of thousands 21 of readers." In the past ten years, he said, the volume of mail has noticeably decreased, even though the circulation of his magazine has risen.

When our voices are finally mute, when we have finally sup- 22
pressed the natural instinct to complain, whether the vexation is trivial or grave, we shall have become automatons, incapable of feeling. When Premier Khrushchev first came to this country late in 1959 he was primed, we are informed, to experience the bitter resentment of the American people against his tyranny, against his persecutions, against the movement which is responsible for the great number of American deaths in Korea, for billions in taxes every year, and for life everlasting on the brink of disaster; but Khrushchev was pleasantly surprised, and reported back to the Russian people that he had been met with overwhelming cordiality (read: apathy), except, to be sure, for "a few fascists who followed me around with their wretched posters, and should be horsewhipped."

I may be crazy, but I say there would have been lots more posters 23
in a society where train temperatures in the dead of winter are not allowed to climb to 85 degrees without complaint.

**IN RETROSPECT**

**1.** Buckley's procedure in this essay is to present a number of instances where he and others had good reasons for complaining about a situation in which they found themselves but ended up not complaining at all. After presenting each incident, he asks, "Why don't we complain?" How does Buckley explain our failure to complain in these circumstances? Comment on the plausibility of his explanations.

**2.** How do you respond to the *ethos,* or personality of the author, that emerges through the prose of this essay? Do you like the person who is speaking? Are you amused by this man? Is this a person you would like to meet and talk with? Do you like his style of writing? How does his style compare with the style of one or more of the other writers in this chapter? How do your reactions to the personality of this writer affect your response to his arguments?

# 12

# On the Sexes

*Down through the ages, there must have been some kind of relationship between the sexes; otherwise, the world would not have been populated to the extent that it has been. But anyone familiar with world history knows that the relationship between the sexes has not always been amicable, equal, and productive. In fact, that relationship is still not universally amicable, equal, and productive. There are still places on this planet where women do not have access to the higher levels of education, where women do not enjoy the privilege of voting, where women are treated like chattel property. Indeed, even in our "enlightened" age, many women still do not command equal pay for equal work. In many countries now, however, the lot of women has been vastly improved: Women can vote, women can get a university education, women have access to the professions, and women have been able to induce some husbands to share the responsibility of rearing children. The feminist movement in the past twenty-five years or so has helped to improve the relationships between men and women, although it has destabilized the traditional gender relations. In this chapter, three eloquent women are speaking about the situation from the female perspective. The three men represented in this chapter—two from the eighteenth century and one from the twentieth century—are promoting, in their own ways, the improvement of relationships between men and women. Who says the twain shall never meet?*

# *Undesirable Husbands*

## DANIEL DEFOE

Daniel Defoe (1660–1731) was born in St. Giles parish, just outside the walls of London. As the son of a Dissenter (that is, a Protestant who did not subscribe to the doctrines and forms of the established church in England and Scotland), he could not attend Oxford or Cambridge. At the Dissenters' academy at Newington Green, however, for five years the young Defoe, under the tutelage of the Reverend Charles Morton, was exposed to an amazing range of humane and useful studies. In the early 1680s, Defoe quit school and set himself up as a hosiery merchant, the first of many business ventures in which he engaged and eventually failed. There followed a succession of mercenary engagements as a soldier, a pamphleteer, and a secret agent for both the Whig and the Tory parties. Defoe's extraordinary verbal facility made it inevitable that he try to make a living by writing. Although literary historians may never succeed in determining how many separate works he wrote during his lifetime, the more than five hundred works that have already been cataloged probably establish Defoe as the most prolific of all English writers. Most of this outpouring of words was ephemeral hackwork, but such books as *The Shortest Way with the Dissenters* and *Journal of the Plague Years* and the novels written in a five-year period after Defoe reached the age of fifty-nine (*Robinson Crusoe, Captain Singleton, Moll Flanders, Colonel Jacque,* and *Roxana*) secured for him an irrevocable position in the English literary pantheon. "Undesirable Husbands" appeared in the October 4, 1707, issue of *The Review,* a newspaper that Defoe founded in 1704, that continued publication until 1713, and that Defoe wrote most of the copy for. This essay, in the "character" tradition, portrays four types of reprehensible husbands. While these men are types rather than individuals, readers today probably know specimens of each type.

It is but seldom that I have taken up any part of this paper with 1
answering questions, and that is now and then to divert you. But I think the following question, as it was most seriously proposed, so it may be of very good service to abundance of good people to have it answered. As to the ladies who are concerned in it, if they are not pleased I am sorry for it. The question, in short, was not proposed in a letter, but in conversation, and is promised an answer in this paper for the good of others, viz.:

What is the worst sort of husband a sober woman can marry? 2

I confess this question has led me a long way about, into the 3
great, great variety of bad husbands of the age, with which many a poor lady is intolerably plagued throughout, as the wise man calls it, the years of her pilgrimage under the sun, the best of which kinds are bad enough. As

1. There is the drunken husband, whose picture it would take up 4
a whole volume to describe; his drunken passions, his drunken humours, his drunken smell, his drunken bed-fellowship, and above all, his drunken love. O! An amorous drunkard when he comes home fully gorged and staggers into bed to a modest, a nice, and a virtuous wife must needs have a great many charms in it such as my pen cannot bear the stench of relating.

2. There is the debauched husband who, having a sober, young, 5
pleasant and beautiful wife, slights and abandons her to take up with an ugly, a tawdry, nasty, and noisome strumpet, and convinces the world that lust is blinder than love. This sort of wretch has but one act of kindness to his wife which distinguishes him from other brutes of his kind, and that is that coming home laden with vice and rottenness, he gives his honest wife an ill disease that lifts her out of the world, putting her out of his reach, and out of her torment all together.

3. There is the fighting husband. I confess this is a strange crea- 6
ture that, when anything has put him in a passion abroad, comes and vents his thunder and lightning at home; that having not a heart to fight with a man, for generally speaking such fellows are always cowards, must come home and fight with his wife. These are excellent sort of people, and ought all to come to the same preferment one lately did in these parts who, beating his wife a little too much the poor woman took it so ill that she killed him for it. That is, she died, and he was hanged for the murder, as he deserved.

4. The extravagant husband. This is the *ill husband,* properly so- 7
called, or as the word is generally received. This is a blessed fellow too, and his way is that he spends his money in roaring, gaming, and drinking, when the poor woman sits quietly at home, waking and sighing for his company. If he is poor, as 'tis a wonder he should be rich, he feasts himself and his gang at the taverns and ale houses while the unhappy wife wants bread at home for his children. If he is an artist, he won't work; if he has a shop, he won't mind it; if business, it runs at random; the sot dreams away his time, ruins himself, and starves his family. The end of this wretch is generally to run away from her into the army or navy, and so dies like a rake, or perhaps takes up his lodgings nearer home in a gaol.

Well, good people, here are four sorts of ill husbands, and take 8
one of them where you will, the best of them is bad enough, and hard is that woman's case, especially if she be a woman of any merit, whose lot it is; but yet I think my first rate is behind still; there is yet a bad husband that is worse than all these, and a woman of sense had better take up with any of these than with him, and that's a *fool*

*husband*. The drunkard, the debauched, the fighting, and the extravagant; these may all have something attendant which in the intervals of their excesses may serve to alleviate and make a little amends to the poor woman, and held her to carry through the afflicting part; but a fool has something always about him that makes him intolerable; he is ever contemptible and uninterruptedly ridiculous—it is like a handsome woman with some deformity about her that makes all the rest be rejected. If he is kind, it is so apish, so below the rate of manhood, so surfeiting, and so disagreeable, that like an ill smell, it makes the face wrinkle at it; if he be froward, he is so unsufferably insolent that there is no bearing it; his passions are all flashes, struck out of him like fire from a flint. If it be anger, 'tis sullen and senseless; if love, 'tis coarse and brutish. He is in good, wavering; in mischief, obstinate; in society, empty; in management, unthinking; in manners, sordid; in error, incorrigible; and in everything ridiculous.

Wherefore upon the whole, my answer is in short, that the worst thing a sober woman can be married to is a FOOL. Of whom whoever has the lot, Lord have mercy, and a cross should be set on the door as of a house infected with the plague. 9

**IN RETROSPECT**

**1.** One of the most common relationships between the sexes is that of husband and wife. Here, operating in the tradition of "character" writing, specimens of which we saw in chapter 3 of this book, Defoe gives us portraits of some undesirable husbands. Why does Defoe consider the fifth type, the "fool husband," to be the worst? Which of these types do you consider to be the worst—and why?

**2.** If this essay were written from a twentieth-century perspective, how might it be different—different, for instance, in the types portrayed, in its tone, in its style, or in other ways? In writing a similar essay, what else might you include to complete your picture of undesirable husbands?

# *The Dissection of a Beau's Head*

## JOSEPH ADDISON

Joseph Addison (1672–1719) was born in Wiltshire, England, and educated at the Charterhouse and later at Queen's College and Magdalen College, Oxford. From 1699 to 1703 he traveled on the Continent to prepare himself for a diplomatic career. On his return to England, he found the Whigs out of power, but *The Campaign*, a poem he wrote to celebrate Marlborough's victory at Blenheim, won for him an appointment by the Tories as Commissioner of Appeal in Excise. This was the first of many high-level positions that Addison held in the government, such as Chief Secretary for Ireland, Secretary of State, and Lord Commissioner of Trade. Addison won a measure of contemporary renown for his English and Latin poetry and for his tragedy *Cato* (1713), but he won lasting fame for his collaboration with Richard Steele on two periodicals, the *Tatler* and the *Spectator.* The *Spectator* appeared six times a week from March 1, 1711, to December 6, 1712; after a two-year hiatus, it was revived by Addison and ran for six more months, from June 18, 1714, to December 20, 1714. Although Steele wrote most of the essays for the *Tatler,* Addison wrote the majority of the essays for the *Spectator.* None of the *Tatler* or *Spectator* essays bore a title (we have supplied one here); each issue carried a number, a date, and an epigraph (often in Latin). "The Dissection of a Beau's Head," from the January 15, 1712, issue of the *Spectator,* is an essay in the long tradition of "characters," detailed and mildly satiric descriptions of familiar character types. This tradition was established by Theophrastus, a Greek philosopher and a one-time pupil of Aristotle's, and was one of the influences on the development of the English essay. Using the device of an imaginary dissection of a beau's head, Addison gives us his version of the characteristics of an eighteenth-century fop or dandy, or what we might today call a ladies' man or womanizer.

*tribus Anticyris caput insanabile*
Juvenal

I was Yesterday engaged in an Assembly of Virtuosos, where one of them produced many curious Observations, which he had lately made in the Anatomy of an humane Body. Another of the Company communicated to us several wonderful Discoveries, which he had also made on the same Subject, by the Help of very fine Glasses. This gave Birth to a great Variety of uncommon Remarks, and furnished Discourse for the remaining Part of the Day. 1

The different Opinions which were started on this Occasion, presented to my Imagination so many new Ideas, that by mixing with those which were already there, they employed my Fancy all the last Night, and composed a very wild extravagant Dream. 2

I was invited, methought, to the Dissection of a *Beau's Head,* and of a *Coquet's Heart,* which were both of them laid on a Table before us. An imaginary Operator opened the first with a great deal of Nicety, which, upon a cursory and superficial View, appeared like the Head of another Man; but, upon applying our Glasses to it, we made a very odd Discovery, namely, that what we looked upon as Brains, were not such in Reality, but an Heap of strange Materials wound up in that Shape and Texture, and packed together with wonderful Art in the several Cavities of the Skull. For, as *Homer* tells us, that the Blood 3 of the Gods is not real Blood, but only Something like it; so we found that the Brain of a Beau is not real Brain, but only Something like it.

The *Pineal Gland,* which many of our Modern Philosophers sup- 4
pose to be the Seat of the Soul, smelt very strong of Essence and Orange-Flower Water, and was encompas'd with a Kind of horny Substance, cut into a thousand little Faces or Mirrours, which were imperceptible to the naked Eye; insomuch that the Soul, if there had been any here, must have been always taken up in contemplating her own Beauties.

We observed a large *Antrum* or Cavity in the *Sinciput,* that was 5
filled with Ribbons, Lace and Embroidery, wrought together in a most curious Piece of Network, the Parts of which were likewise imperceptible to the naked Eye. Another of these *Antrums* or Cavities was stuffed with invisible Billet-doux, Love-Letters, pricked Dances, and other Trumpery of the same Nature. In another we found a Kind of Powder, which set the whole Company a Sneezing, and by the Scent discovered it self to be right *Spanish.* The several other Cells were stored with Commodities of the same Kind, of which it would be tedious to give the Reader an exact Inventory.

There was a large Cavity on each Side of the Head, which I must 6
not omit. That on the right Side was filled with Fictions, Flatteries and Falsehoods, Vows, Promises and Protestations; that on the left with Oaths and Imprecations. There issued out a *Duct* from each of these Cells, which ran into the Root of the Tongue, where both joined together, and passed forward in one common *Duct* to the Tip of it. We discovered several little Roads or Canals running from the Ear into the Brain, and took particular Care to trace them out through their several Passages. One of them extended it self to a Bundle of Sonnets and little Musical Instruments. Others ended in several Bladders which were filled either with Wind or Froth. But the large Canal entered into a great Cavity of the Skull, from whence there went another Canal into the Tongue. This great Cavity was filled with a Kind of spongy Substance, which the *French* Anatomists call *Galimatias,* and the *English* Nonsense.

The Skins of the Forehead were extremly tough and thick, and, 7
what very much surpris'd us, had not in them any single Blood-Vessel that we were able to discover, either with or without our Glasses; from whence we concluded, that the Party when alive must have been entirely deprived of the Faculty of Blushing.

The *Os Cribriforme* was exceedingly stuffed, and in some Places 8
damaged with Snuff. We could not but take Notice in particular of that small Muscle, which is not often discovered in Dissections, and draws the Nose upwards, when it expresses the Contempt which the Owner of it has, upon seeing any Thing he does not like, or hearing

any Thing he does not understand. I need not tell my learned Reader, that is that Muscle which performs the Motion so often mentioned by the *Latin* Poets, when they talk of a Man's cocking his Nose, or playing the Rhinoceros.

We did not find any Thing very remarkable in the Eye, saving only, that the *Musculi Amatorii,* or as we may translate it into *English,* the *Ogling Muscles,* were very much worn and decayed with Use; whereas on the contrary, the *Elevator* or the Muscle which turns the Eye towards Heaven, did not appear to have been used at all. 9

I have only mentioned in this Dissection such new Discoveries as we were able to make, and have not taken any Notice of those Parts which are to be met with in common Heads. As for the Skull, the Face, and indeed the whole outward Shape and Figure of the Head, we could not discover any Difference from what we observe in the Heads of other Men. We were informed, that the Person to whom this Head belonged, has passed for a *Man* above five and thirty Years; during which Time he eat and drank like other People, dressed well, talked loud, laught frequently, and on particular Occasions had acquitted himself tolerably at a Ball or an Assembly, to which one of the Company added, that a certain Knot of Ladies took him for a Wit. He was cut off in the Flower of his Age, by the Blow of a Paring-Shovel, having been surprised by an eminent Citizen, as he was tendering some Civilities to his Wife. 10

When we had thoroughly examin'd this Head with all its Apartments, and its several Kinds of Furniture, we put up the Brain, such as it was, into its proper Place, and laid it aside under a broad Piece of Scarlet Cloth, in order to be *prepared,* and kept in a great Repository of Dissections, our Operator telling us that the Preparation would not be so difficult as that of another Brain, for that he had observed several of the little Pipes and Tubes which ran through the Brain were already filled with a Kind of mercurial Substance, which he looked upon to be true Quick Silver. 11

He applied himself in the next Place to the *Coquet's Heart,* which he likewise laid open with great Dexterity. There occurred to us many Particularities in this Dissection; but being unwilling to burden my Reader's Memory too much, I shall reserve this Subject for the Speculation of another Day. 12

**IN RETROSPECT**

**1.** Addison characterizes an eighteenth-century beau through an imaginary examination of the man's brain. What Addison does in this essay is turn all of the beau's traits into physical features. Along with a few of your classmates, select a concept, a character, or an object that you would like to define, describe, or satirize and experiment with Addison's technique of revealing characteristics of your subject through the metaphor of physical features.

**2.** What is Addison's point in exposing the characteristics of a beau? Just what does Addison satirize about this character type? And what contribution does he make to the conversation these essays create about the relationship between men and women?

# *The Necessary Enemy*

## KATHERINE ANNE PORTER

The reader may already have noticed how many writers who achieved their fame primarily as novelists, short story writers, dramatists, or poets are represented by essays in this volume. Apparently, imaginative writers have found the familiar essay a compatible form, and indeed a great deal of creativity is involved in writing the familiar essay. For a long time, it appeared that at least one American writer would be accorded major literary status as a writer exclusively of short fiction. The short stories and novellas that Katherine Anne Porter (1890–1980) published in such collections as *Flowering Judas* (1930), *Pale Horse, Pale Rider* (1939), and *The Leaning Tower* (1944) were such finely polished gems that most critics were disposed to grant her a place in the Temple of Fame solely on her achievement in short fiction forms. But Porter must have felt that she needed to prove her mettle by attempting the longer forms, for in 1962, she published *Ship of Fools,* a bulky novel she had been working on for twenty years. What many readers may not have realized is that throughout her literary career, she had also been trying her hand at that miniature form of literature known as the essay. She published her first collection of essays, articles, and book reviews in *The Days Before* (1952). A considerably expanded collection appeared in 1970 in *The Collected Essays and Occasional Writings of Katherine Anne Porter.* In the following essay from that 1970 volume, Porter explores the psychology of human character with the same subtlety and perceptiveness that she displayed in her stories. The grace and precision of style are there too.

She is a frank, charming, fresh-hearted young woman who mar- 1
ried for love. She and her husband are one of those gay, good-looking young pairs who ornament this modern scene rather more in profusion perhaps than ever before in our history. They are handsome, with a talent for finding their way in their world, they work at things that interest them, their tastes agree and their hopes. They intend in all good faith to spend their lives together, to have children and do well by them and each other—to be happy, in fact, which for them is

the whole point of their marriage. And all in stride, keeping their wits about them. Nothing romantic, mind you; their feet are on the ground.

Unless they were this sort of person, there would be not much point to what I wish to say; for they would seem to be an example of the high-spirited, right-minded young whom the critics are always invoking to come forth and do their duty and practice all those sterling old-fashioned virtues which in every generation seem to be falling into disrepair. As for virtues, these young people are more or less on their own, like most of their kind; they get very little moral or other aid from their society; but after three years of marriage this very contemporary young woman finds herself facing the oldest and ugliest dilemma of marriage. 2

She is dismayed, horrified, full of guilt and forebodings because she is finding out little by little that she is capable of hating her husband, whom she loves faithfully. She can hate him at times as fiercely and mysteriously, indeed in terribly much the same way, as often she hated her parents, her brothers and sisters, whom she loves, when she was a child. Even then it had seemed to her a kind of black treacherousness in her, her private wickedness that, just the same, gave her her only private life. That was one thing her parents never knew about her, never seemed to suspect. For it was never given a name. They did and said hateful things to her and to each other as if by right, as if in them it was a kind of virtue. But when they said to her, "Control your feelings," it was never when she was amiable and obedient, only in the black times of her hate. So it was her secret, a shameful one. When they punished her, sometimes for the strangest reasons, it was, they said, only because they loved her—it was for her good. She did not believe this, but she thought herself guilty of something worse than ever they had punished her for. None of this really frightened her: the real fright came when she discovered that at times her father and mother hated each other; this was like standing on the doorsill of a familiar room and seeing in a lightning flash that the floor was gone, you were on the edge of a bottomless pit. Sometimes she felt that both of them hated her, but that passed, it was simply not a thing to be thought of, much less believed. She thought she had outgrown all this, but here it was again, an element in her own nature she could not control, or feared she could not. She would have to hide from her husband, if she could, the same spot in her feelings she had hidden from her parents, and for the same no doubt disreputable, selfish reason: she wants to keep his love. 3

Above all, she wants him to be absolutely confident that she loves him, for that is the real truth, no matter how unreasonable it sounds, and no matter how her own feelings betray them both at times. She 4 depends recklessly on his love; yet while she is hating him, he might very well be hating her as much or even more, and it would serve her right. But she does not want to be served right, she wants to be loved and forgiven—that is, to be sure he would forgive her anything, if he had any notion of what she had done. But best of all she would like not to have anything in her love that should ask for forgiveness. She doesn't mean about their quarrels—they are not so bad. Her feelings are out of proportion, perhaps. She knows it is perfectly natural for people to disagree, have fits of temper, fight it out; they learn quite a lot about each other that way, and not all of it disappointing either. When it passes, her hatred seems quite unreal. It always did.

Love. We are early taught to say it. I love you. We are trained to 5
the thought of it as if there were nothing else, or nothing else worth having without it, or nothing worth having which it could not bring with it. Love is taught, always by precept, sometimes by example. Then hate, which no one meant to teach us, comes of itself. It is true that if we say I love you, it may be received with doubts, for there are times when it is hard to believe. Say I hate you, and the one spoken to believes it instantly, once for all.

Say I love you a thousand times to that person afterward and 6
mean it every time, and still it does not change the fact that once we said I hate you, and meant that too. It leaves a mark on that surface love had worn so smooth with its eternal caresses. Love must be learned, and learned again and again; there is no end to it. Hate needs no instruction, but waits only to be provoked . . . hate, the unspoken word, the unacknowledged presence in the house, that faint smell of brimstone among the roses, that invisible tongue-tripper, that unkempt finger in every pie, that sudden oh-so-curiously *chilling* look—could it be boredom?—on your dear one's features, making them quite ugly. Be careful: love, perfect love, is in danger.

If it is not perfect, it is not love, and if it is not love, it is bound to 7
be hate sooner or later. This is perhaps a not too exaggerated statement of the extreme position of Romantic Love, more especially in America, where we are all brought up on it, whether we know it or not. Romantic Love is changeless, faithful, passionate, and its sole end is to render the two lovers happy. It has no obstacles save those provided by the hazards of fate (that is to say, society), and such sufferings as the lovers may cause each other are only another word for delight: exciting jealousies, thrilling uncertainties, the ritual dance of courtship within the charmed closed circle of their secret alliance; all *real* troubles come from without, they face them unitedly in perfect confidence. Marriage is not the end but only the beginning of true happiness, cloudless, changeless to the end. That the candidates for

this blissful condition have never seen an example of it, nor ever knew anyone who had, makes no difference. That is the ideal and they will achieve it.

How did Romantic Love manage to get into marriage at last, 8
where it was most certainly never intended to be? At its highest it was tragic: the love of Héloïse and Abélard. At its most graceful, it was the homage of the trouvère for his lady. In its most popular form, the adulterous strayings of solidly married couples who meant to stray for their own good reasons, but at the same time do nothing to upset the property settlements or the line of legitimacy; at its most trivial, the pretty trifling of shepherd and shepherdess.

This was generally condemned by church and state and a word of 9
fear to honest wives whose mortal enemy it was. Love within the sober, sacred realities of marriage was a matter of personal luck, but in any case, private feelings were strictly a private affair having, at least in theory, no bearing whatever on the fixed practice of the rules of an institution never intended as a recreation ground for either sex. If the couple discharged their religious and social obligations, furnished forth a copious progeny, kept their troubles to themselves, maintained public civility and died under the same roof, even if not always on speaking terms, it was rightly regarded as a successful marriage. Apparently this testing ground was too severe for all but the stoutest spirits; it too was based on an ideal, as impossible in its way as the ideal Romantic Love. One good thing to be said for it is that society took responsibility for the conditions of marriage, and the sufferers within its bonds could always blame the system, not themselves. But Romantic Love crept into the marriage bed, very stealthily, by centuries, bringing its absurd notions about love as eternal springtime and marriage as a personal adventure meant to provide personal happiness. To a Western romantic such as I, though my views have been much modified by painful experience, it still seems to me a charming work of the human imagination, and it is a pity its central notion has been taken too literally and has hardened into a convention as cramping and enslaving as the older one. The refusal to acknowledge the evils in ourselves which therefore are implicit in any human situation is as extreme and unworkable a proposition as the doctrine of total depravity; but somewhere between them, or maybe beyond them, there does exist a possibility for reconciliation between our desires for impossible satisfactions and the simple unalterable fact that we also desire to be unhappy and that we create our own sufferings; and out of these sufferings we salvage our fragments of happiness.

Our young woman who has been taught that an important part of 10
her human nature is not real because it makes trouble and interferes

with her peace of mind and shakes her self-love, has been very badly taught; but she has arrived at a most important stage of her re-education. She is afraid her marriage is going to fail because she has not love enough to face its difficulties; and this because at times she feels a painful hostility toward her husband, and cannot admit its reality because such an admission would damage in her own eyes her view of what love should be, an absurd view, based on her vanity of power. Her hatred is real as her love is real, but her hatred has the advantage at present because it works on a blind instinctual level, it is lawless; and her love is subjected to a code of ideal conditions, impossible by their very nature of fulfillment, which prevents its free growth and deprives it of its right to recognize its human limitations and come to grips with them. Hatred is natural in a sense that love, as she conceives it, a young person brought up in the tradition of Romantic Love, is not natural at all. Yet it did not come by hazard, it is the very imperfect expression of the need of the human imagination to create beauty and harmony out of chaos, no matter how mistaken its notion of these things may be, nor how clumsy its methods. It has conjured love out of the air, and seeks to preserve it by incantations; when she spoke a vow to love and honor her husband until death, she did a very reckless thing, for it is not possible by any act of the will to fulfill such an engagement. But it was the necessary act of faith performed in defense of a mode of feeling, the statement of honorable intention to practice as well as she is able the noble, acquired faculty of love, that very mysterious overtone to sex which is the best thing in it. Her hatred is part of it, the necessary enemy and ally.

## IN RETROSPECT

**1.** Who or what is the necessary enemy in Porter's essay? Why is it an *enemy?* And in what sense is it *necessary* (an indispensable enemy? an inevitable enemy? an important enemy?)?

**2.** Throughout this essay Porter is examining the love-hate relationships that a woman experiences both in her family life and in her married life. How does your own experience confirm or negate Porter's notion about the love-hate relationship? In what ways is the love-hate relationship similar or different for men?

# *I Want a Wife*

## JUDY BRADY

Judy Brady (1937–      ) was born in San Francisco and received her higher education at the University of Iowa. She was married in 1960 and raised two daughters. After she was divorced, she had to take employment as a secretary so that she could support her family and go to school at night. Although she has said that she is not a writer (she earned a Bachelor of Fine Arts degree in painting at the University of Iowa), she has published a number of articles on political and social issues for a variety of magazines. The essay reprinted here was originally published in the December 1971 issue of *Ms.* and subsequently became one of the most frequently reprinted essays by a contemporary author. One of the reasons for the unusual popularity of this essay is the startling perspective from which the author writes: Here is a *woman* proclaiming that she wants a wife. Another reason this essay has proved to be so compelling for many readers is the clever strategy the author uses: She repeats the phrase (really it's a sentence) "I want a wife" at least thirty times in order to underscore the stereotyped expectations that have come to be associated with a wife in our society.

I belong to that classification of people known as wives. I am A 1
Wife. And, not altogether incidentally, I am a mother.

Not too long ago a male friend of mine appeared on the scene 2
fresh from a recent divorce. He had one child, who is, of course, with his ex-wife. He is looking for another wife. As I thought about him while I was ironing one evening, it suddenly occurred to me that I, too, would like to have a wife. Why do I want a wife?

I would like to go back to school so that I can become economi- 3
cally independent, support myself, and, if need be, support those dependent upon me. I want a wife who will work and send me to school. And while I am going to school I want a wife to take care of my children. I want a wife to keep track of the children's doctor and dentist appointments. And to keep track of mine, too. I want a wife to make sure my children eat properly and are kept clean. I want a wife who will wash the children's clothes and keep them mended. I want a wife who is a good nurturant attendant to my children, who arranges for their schooling, makes sure that they have an adequate social life with their peers, takes them to the park, the zoo, etc. I want a wife who takes care of the children when they are sick, a wife who arranges to be around when the children need special care, because, of course, I cannot miss classes at school. My wife must arrange to lose time at work and not lose the job. It may mean a small cut in my wife's income from time to time, but I guess I can tolerate that.

Needless to say, my wife will arrange and pay for the care of the children while my wife is working.

4 I want a wife who will take care of *my* physical needs. I want a wife who will keep my house clean. A wife who will pick up after my children, a wife who will pick up after me. I want a wife who will keep my clothes clean, ironed, mended, replaced when need be, and who will see to it that my personal things are kept in their proper place so that I can find what I need the minute I need it. I want a wife who cooks the meals, a wife who is a *good* cook. I want a wife who will plan the menus, do the necessary grocery shopping, prepare the meals, serve them pleasantly, and then do the cleaning up while I do my studying. I want a wife who will care for me when I am sick and sympathize with my pain and loss of time from school. I want a wife to go along when our family takes a vacation so that someone can continue to care for me and my children when I need a rest and change of scene.

5 I want a wife who will not bother me with rambling complaints about a wife's duties. But I want a wife who will listen to me when I feel the need to explain a rather difficult point I have come across in my course of studies. And I want a wife who will type my papers for me when I have written them.

6 I want a wife who will take care of the details of my social life. When my wife and I are invited out by my friends, I want a wife who will take care of the babysitting arrangements. When I meet people at school that I like and want to entertain, I want a wife who will have the house clean, will prepare a special meal, serve it to me and my friends, and not interrupt when I talk about things that interest me and my friends. I want a wife who will have arranged that the children are fed and ready for bed before my guests arrive so that the children do not bother us. I want a wife who takes care of the needs of my guests so that they feel comfortable, who makes sure that they have an ashtray, that they are passed the hors d'oeuvres, that they are offered a second helping of the food, that their wine glasses are replenished when necessary, that their coffee is served to them as they like it. And I want a wife who knows that sometimes I need a night out by myself.

7 I want a wife who is sensitive to my sexual needs, a wife who makes love passionately and eagerly when I feel like it, a wife who makes sure that I am satisfied. And, of course, I want a wife who will not demand sexual attention when I am not in the mood for it. I want a wife who assumes the complete responsibility for birth control, because I do not want more children. I want a wife who will remain sexually faithful to me so that I do not have to clutter up my intellectual life with jealousies. And I want a wife who understands that *my*

sexual needs may entail more than strict adherence to monogamy. I must, after all, be able to relate to people as fully as possible.

If, by chance, I find another person more suitable as a wife than 8
the wife I already have, I want the liberty to replace my present wife with another one. Naturally, I will expect a fresh, new life; my wife will take the children and be solely responsible for them so that I am left free.

When I am through with school and have a job, I want my wife to 9
quit working and remain at home so that my wife can more fully and completely take care of a wife's duties.

My God, who *wouldn't* want a wife? 10

### IN RETROSPECT

**1.** To make some judgment about the perspective of this essay, examine the needs and the priorities given to those needs that Brady lays out. What kind of perspective do we get in this essay? That is, does Brady play turnabout with a man's perspective? Does she present a feminist's perspective? Does she present a personal perspective? Or is there a blend of these perspectives? Explain and defend your judgment about the perspective of this essay.

**2.** What significance do you ascribe to Brady's tone in the essay and to her objectification of a marriage partner?

# *Women*

## BRIGID BROPHY

Brigid Brophy (1929– ) was born in London, England. Her father was the English novelist John Brophy. His precocious daughter studied classics on a Jubilee scholarship at St. Hugh College, Oxford, for four terms in 1947–1948, but she left Oxford without taking a degree. As a novelist, short-story writer, critic, biographer, and dramatist, Brophy has a list of publications as long as a person's arm. Her most notable biography is *Mozart the Dramatist: A New View of Mozart, His Operas, and His Age* (1964). Her novel *Hackenfeller's Ape* won the Cheltenham Literary Festival Prize for a first novel in 1954. *Her Black Ship to Hell* won the *London Magazine* Prize for prose in 1962. To date, Brophy's most puckish book, which she wrote in conjunction with Charles Osborne and her husband, Michael Levey, is *Fifty Works of English and American Literature We Could Do Without* (1967). As a feminist, a pacifist, an anti-vivisectionist, and a vegetarian—to name only a few of the issues she has taken a firm stand on—Brophy has written some very strong, uncompromising prose. As she said of herself in an interview with the *Guardian*, "I am really most interested in intensity. I cannot stand anything that is lukewarm." We get an example of her pugnacious prose in the following essay, in which she challenges the prevailing notion that women have finally won their social and political freedom. Someone has called her "the H. L. Mencken among women writers"—though she would probably object to being rated in relation to a man instead of on her own merits.

All right, nobody's disputing it. Women are free. At least, they *look* free. They even feel free. But in reality women in the western, industrialised world today are like the animals in a modern zoo. There are no bars. It appears that cages have been abolished. Yet in practice women are still kept in their place just as firmly as the animals are kept in their enclosures. The barriers which keep them in now are invisible. 1

It is about forty years since the pioneer feminists, several of whom were men, raised such a rumpus by rattling the cage bars—or created such a conspicuous nuisance by chaining themselves to them—that society was at least obliged to pay attention. The result was that the bars were uprooted, the cage thrown open: whereupon the majority of the women who had been held captive decided they would rather stay inside anyway. 2

To be more precise, they *thought* they decided; and society, which can with perfect truth point out "Look, no bars," *thought* it was giving them the choice. There are no laws and very little discrimination to prevent western, industrialised women from voting, being voted for or entering the professions. If there are still comparatively few women lawyers and engineers, let alone women presidents of the United States, what are women to conclude except that this is the result either of their own free choice or of something inherent in female nature? 3

Many of them do draw just this conclusion. They have come back to the old argument of the anti-feminists, many of whom were women, that women are unfit by nature for life outside the cage. And in letting this old wheel come full cycle women have fallen victim to one of the most insidious and ingenious confidence tricks ever penetrated. 4

In point of fact, neither female nature nor women's individual free choice has been put to the test. As American Negroes have discovered, to be officially free is by no means the same as being actually and psychologically free. A society as adept as ours has become at propaganda—whether political or commercial—should know that "persuasion," which means the art of launching myths and artificially inducing inhibitions, is every bit as effective as force of law. No doubt the reason society eventually agreed to abolish its anti- 5 women laws was that it had become confident of commanding a battery of hidden dissuaders which would do the job just as well. Cage bars are clumsy methods of control, which excite the more rebellious personalities inside to rattle them. Modern society, like the modern zoo, has contrived to get rid of the bars without altering the fact of imprisonment. All the zoo architect needs to do is run a zone of hot or cold air, whichever the animal concerned cannot tolerate, round the cage where the bars used to be. Human animals are not less sensitive to social climate.

The ingenious point about the new-model zoo is that it deceives 6
both sides of the invisible barrier. Not only can the animal not see how it is imprisoned; the visitor's conscience is relieved of the unkindness of keeping animals shut up. He can say "Look, no bars round the animals," just as society can say "Look, no laws restricting women" even while it keeps women rigidly in place by zones of fierce social pressure.

There is, however, one great difference. A woman, being a think- 7
ing animal, may actually be more distressed because the bars of her cage cannot be seen. What relieves society's conscience may afflict hers. Unable to perceive what is holding her back, she may accuse herself and her whole sex of craven timidity because women have not jumped at what has the appearance of an offer of freedom. Evidently quite a lot of women have succumbed to guilt of this sort, since in recent years quite an industry has arisen to assuage it. Comforting voices make the air as thick and reassuring as cotton wool while they explain that there is nothing shameful in not wanting a career, that to be intellectually unadventurous is no sin, that taking care of home and family may be personally "fulfilling" and socially valuable.

This is an argument without a flaw: except that it is addressed 8
exclusively to women. Address it to both sexes and instantly it becomes progressive and humane. As it stands, it is merely anti-woman prejudice revamped.

That many women would be happier not pursuing careers or 9
intellectual adventures is only part of the truth. The whole truth is that many *people* would be. If society had the clear sight to assure men as well as women that there is no shame in preferring to stay non-competitively and non-aggressively at home, many masculine neuroses and ulcers would be avoided, and many children would enjoy the benefit of being brought up by a father with a talent for the job instead of by a mother with no talent for it but a sense of guilt about the lack.

But society does nothing so sensible. Blindly it goes on insisting 10
on the tradition that men are the ones who go out to work and adventure—an arrangement which simply throws talent away. All

the home-making talent which happens to be born inside male bodies is wasted; and our businesses and governments are staffed quite largely by people whose aptitude for the work consists solely of their being what is, by tradition, the right sex for it.

The pressures society exerts to drive men out of the house are very nearly as irrational and unjust as those by which it keeps women in. The mistake of the early reformers was to assume that men were emancipated already and that therefore reform need ask only for the emancipation of women. What we ought to do now is go right back to scratch and demand the emancipation of both sexes. It is only because men are not free themselves that they have found it necessary to cheat women by the deception which makes them appear free when they are not. 11

The zones of hot and cold air which society uses to perpetuate its uneconomic and unreasonable state of affairs are the simplest and most effective conceivable. Society is playing on our sexual vanity. Just as the sexual regions are the most vulnerable part of the body, sexuality is the most vulnerable part of the Ego. Tell a man that he is not a real man, or a woman that she is not one hundred per cent woman, and you are threatening both with not being attractive to the opposite sex. No one can bear not to be attractive to the opposite sex. That is the climate which the human animal cannot tolerate. 12

So society has us all at its mercy. It has only to murmur to the man that staying at home is a feminine characteristic, and he will be out of the house like a bullet. It has only to suggest to the woman that logic and reason are the province of the masculine mind, whereas "intuition" and "feeling" are the female *forte,* and she will throw her physics textbooks out of the window, barricade herself into the house, and give herself up to having wishy-washy poetical feelings while she arranges the flowers. 13

She will, incidentally, take care that her feelings *are* wishy-washy. She has been persuaded that to have cogent feelings, of the kind which really do go into great poems (most of which are by men), would make her an unfeminine woman, a woman who imitates men. In point of fact, she would not be imitating men as such, most of whom have never written a line of great poetry, but poets, most of whom so far happen to be men. But the bad logic passes muster with her because part of the mythology she has swallowed ingeniously informs her that logic is not her *forte.* 14

Should a woman's talent or intelligence be so irrepressible that she insists on producing cogent works of art or watertight meshes of argument, she will be said to have "a mind like a man's." This is simply current idiom; translated, it means "a good mind." The use of the idiom contributes to an apparently watertight proof that all good 15 minds are masculine, since whenever they occur in women they are described as "like a man's."

What is more, this habit of thought actually contributes to perpet- 16
uating a state of affairs where most good minds really do belong to men. It is difficult for a woman to *want* to be intelligent when she has been told that to be so will make her like a man. She inclines to think an intelligence would be as unbecoming to her as a moustache; and many women have tried in furtive privacy to disembarrass themselves of intellect as though it were facial hair.

Discouraged from growing "a mind like a man's," women are 17
encouraged to have thoughts and feelings of a specifically feminine tone. For society is cunning enough not to place its whole reliance on threatening women with blasts of icy air. It also flatters them with a zone of hot air. The most deceptive and cynical of its blandishments is the notion that women have some specifically feminine contribution to make to culture. Unfortunately, as culture had already been shaped and largely built up by men before the invitation was issued, this leaves women little to do. Culture consists of reasoned thought and works of art composed to cogent feeling and imagination. There is only one way to be reasonable, and that is to reason correctly; and the only kind of art which is any good is good art. If women are to eschew reason and artistic imagination in favour of "intuition" and "feeling," it is pretty clear what is meant. "Intuition" is just a polite name for bad reasoning, and "feeling" for bad art.

In reality, the whole idea of a specifically feminine—or, for the 18
matter of that, masculine—contribution to culture is a contradiction of culture. A contribution to culture is not something which could not have been made by the other sex—it is something which could not have been made by any other *person*. Equally, the notion that anyone, of either sex, can create good art out of simple feeling, untempered by discipline, is a philistine one. The arts are a sphere where women seem to have done well; but really they have done *too* well—too well for the good of the arts. Instead of women sharing the esteem which ought to belong to artists, art is becoming smeared with femininity. We are approaching a philistine state of affairs where the arts are something which it is nice for women to take up in their spare time—men having slammed out of the house to get on with society's "serious" business, like making money, administering the country and running the professions.

In that "serious" sphere it is still rare to encounter a woman. A 19
man sentenced to prison would probably feel his punishment was redoubled by indignity if he were to be sentenced by a woman judge under a law drafted by a woman legislator—and if, on admission, he were to be examined by a woman prison doctor. If such a thing

happened every day, it would be no indignity but the natural course of events. It has never been given the chance to become the natural course of events and never will be so long as women remain persuaded it would be unnatural of them to want it.

20 So brilliantly has society contrived to terrorise women with this threat that certain behaviour is unnatural and unwomanly that it has left them no time to consider—or even sheerly observe—what womanly nature really is. For centuries errant superstitions were accepted as natural law. The physiological fact that only women can secrete milk for feeding babies was extended into the pure myth that it was women's business to cook for and wait on the entire family. The kitchen became woman's "natural" place because, for the first few months of her baby's life, the nursery really was. To this day a woman may suspect that she is unfeminine if she can discover in herself no aptitude or liking for cooking. Fright has thrown her into such a muddle that she confuses having no taste for cookery with having no breasts, and conversely assumes that nature has endowed the human female with a special handiness with frying pans.

21 Even psycho-analysis, which in general has been the greatest benefactor of civilisation since the wheel, has unwittingly reinforced the terrorisation campaign. The trouble was that it brought with it from its origin in medical therapy a criterion of normality instead of rationality. On sheer statistics every pioneer, genius and social reformer, including the first woman who demanded to be let out of the kitchen and into the polling booth, is abnormal, along with every lunatic and eccentric. What distinguishes the genius from the lunatic is that the genius's abnormality is justifiable by reason or aesthetics. If a woman who is irked by confinement to the kitchen merely looks round to see what other women are doing and finds they are accepting their kitchens, she may well conclude that she is abnormal and had better enlist her psycho-analyst's help towards "living with" her kitchen. What she ought to ask is whether it is rational for women to be kept to the kitchen, and whether nature really does insist on that in the way it insists women have breasts. And in a far-reaching sense to ask that question is much more normal and natural than learning to "live with" the handicap of women's inferior social status. The normal and natural thing for human beings is not to tolerate handicaps but to reform society and to circumvent or supplement nature. We don't learn to live minus a leg; we devise an artificial limb.

22 That, indeed, is the crux of the matter. Not only are the distinctions we draw between male nature and female nature largely arbitrary and often pure superstition: they are completely beside the point. They ignore the essence of *human* nature. The important question is not whether women are or are not less logical by nature than

men, but whether education, effort and the abolition of our illogical social pressures can improve on nature and make them (and, incidentally, men as well) *more* logical. What distinguishes human from any other animal nature is its ability to be unnatural. Logic and art are not natural or instinctive activities; but our nature includes a propensity to acquire them. It is not natural for the human body to orbit the earth; but the human mind has a natural adventurousness which enables it to invent machines whereby the body can do so. There is, in sober fact, no such creature as a natural man. Go as far back as they will, the archaeologists cannot come on a wild man in his natural habitat. At his most primitive, he has already constructed himself an artificial habitat, and decorated it not by a standardised instinctual method, as birds build nests, but by individualised—that is, abnormal—works of art or magic. And in doing so he is not limited by the fingers nature gave him; he has extended their versatility by making tools.

Civilisation consists not necessarily in defying nature but in mak- 23
ing it possible for us to do so if we judge it desirable. The higher we can lift our noses from the grindstone of nature, the wider the area we have of choice; and the more choices we have freely made, the more individualised we are. We are at our most civilised when nature does not dictate to us, as it does to animals and peasants, but when we can opt to fall in with it or better it. If modern civilisation has invented methods of education which make it possible for men to feed babies and for women to think logically, we are betraying civilisation itself if we do not set both sexes free to make a free choice.

**IN RETROSPECT**

**1.** Compare Brophy's essay with Brady's, commenting on the style, the tone, the content, and the method of treating the subject in both essays. How is each of these women looking at the world around her? What are the basic differences in the two views of the man-woman relationship presented in these essays?

**2.** The most prominent metaphor in Brophy's essay is that of the cage. She works variations of that metaphor, from a cage with bars to a cage without bars, to fit the changing nature of the man-woman relationship. Show how her varied use of this metaphor enables her to project her view of the evolving relationships between men and women and to present her arguments in support of her thesis.

# *The Men We Carry in Our Minds*

## SCOTT RUSSELL SANDERS

Scott Russell Sanders (1945– ) was born in Memphis, Tennessee. He earned a summa cum laude B.A. at Brown University and a Ph.D. at Cambridge University in England in 1971. He is now a professor of English at Indiana University. A versatile writer, Sanders has written science fiction, realistic fiction, children's stories, literary criticism, historical novels, folktales, and essays. Among his published books are *D. H. Lawrence: The World of the Major Novels* (1974), *Wilderness Plots: Tales about the Settlement of the American Land* (1983), *Fetching the Dead: Stories* (1984), *Stone Country* (1985), *Hear the Wind Blow: American Folksongs Retold* (1985), and *The Paradise of Bombs* (1987), the book from which the following essay was taken. He has won a number of awards and grants, among them a Woodrow Wilson fellowship, a Marshall scholarship, and a Bennett fellowship in creative writing. Sanders once said in an interview, "In all of my work, regardless of period or style, I am concerned with the ways in which human beings come to terms with the practical problems of living on a small planet, in nature and in communities. I am concerned with the life people make together, in marriages and families and towns, more than with the life of isolated individuals." The essay "The Men We Carry in Our Minds" reflects that concern. Sanders shows himself to be aware of the tensions between men and women, but in the essay, he accounts for why he understands men better than he understands women. After reading this essay, however, you will know that Sanders is not a sexist.

"This must be a hard time for women," I say to my friend Anneke. "They have so many paths to choose from, and so many voices calling them." 1

"I think it's a lot harder for men," she replies. 2

"How do you figure that?" 3

"The women I know feel excited, innocent, like crusaders in a just cause. The men I know are eaten up with guilt." 4

We are sitting at the kitchen table drinking sassafras tea, our hands wrapped around the mugs because this April morning is cool and drizzly. "Like a Dutch morning," Anneke told me earlier. She is Dutch herself, a writer and midwife and peacemaker, with the round face and sad eyes of a woman in a Vermeer painting who might be waiting for the rain to stop, for a door to open. She leans over to sniff a sprig of lilac, pale lavender, that rises from a vase of cobalt blue. 5

"Women feel such pressure to be everything, do everything," I say. "Career, kids, art, politics. Have their babies and get back to the office a week later. It's as if they're trying to overcome a million years' worth of evolution in one lifetime." 6

"But we help one another. We don't try to lumber on alone, like so many wounded grizzly bears, the way men do." Anneke sips her tea. I gave her the mug with the owls on it, for wisdom. "And we have this deep-down sense that we're in the *right*—we've been held back, passed over, used—while men feel they're in the wrong. Men are the ones who've been discredited, who have to search their souls." 7

I search my soul. I discover guilty feelings aplenty—towards the poor, the Vietnamese, Native Americans, the whales, an endless list of debts—a guilt in each case that is as bright and unambiguous as a neon sign. But toward women I feel something more confused, a snarl of shame, envy, wary tenderness, and amazement. This muddle troubles me. To hide my unease I say, "You're right, it's tough being a man these days." 8

"Don't laugh." Anneke frowns at me, mournful-eyed, through the sassafras steam. "I wouldn't be a man for anything. It's much easier being the victim. All the victim has to do is break free. The persecutor has to live with his past." 9

How deep is that past? I find myself wondering after Anneke has left. How much of an inheritance do I have to throw off? Is it just the beliefs I breathed in as a child? Do I have to scour memory back through father and grandfather? Through St. Paul? Beyond Stonehenge and into the twilit caves? I'm convinced the past we must contend with is deeper even than speech. When I think back on my childhood, on how I learned to see men and women, I have a sense of ancient, dizzying depths. The back roads of Tennessee and Ohio where I grew up were probably closer, in their sexual patterns, to the campsites of Stone Age hunters than to the genderless cities of the future into which we are rushing. 10

The first men, besides my father, I remember seeing were black convicts and white guards, in the cottonfield across the road from our farm on the outskirts of Memphis. I must have been three or four. The prisoners wore dingy gray-and-black zebra suits, heavy as canvas, sodden with sweat. Hatless, stooped, they chopped weeds in the fierce heat, row after row, breathing the acrid dust of boll-weevil poison. The overseers wore dazzling white shirts and broad shadowy hats. The oiled barrels of their shotguns flashed in the sunlight. Their faces in memory are utterly blank. Of course those men, white and black, have become for me an emblem of racial hatred. But they have also come to stand for the twin poles of my early vision of manhood—the brute toiling animal and the boss. 11

When I was a boy, the men I knew labored with their bodies. They were marginal farmers, just scraping by, or welders, steel- 12 workers, carpenters; they swept floors, dug ditches, mined coal, or drove trucks, their forearms ropy with muscle; they trained horses, stoked furnaces, built tires, stood on assembly lines wrestling parts onto cars and refrigerators. They got up before light, worked all day long whatever the weather, and when they came home at night they looked as though somebody had been whipping them. In the evenings and on weekends they worked on their own places, tilling gardens that were lumpy with clay, fixing broken-down cars, hammering on houses that were always too drafty, too leaky, too small.

The bodies of the men I knew were twisted and maimed in ways 13
visible and invisible. The nails of their hands were black and split, the hands tattooed with scars. Some had lost fingers. Heavy lifting had given many of them finicky backs and guts weak from hernias. Racing against conveyor belts had given them ulcers. Their ankles and knees ached from years of standing on concrete. Anyone who had worked for long around machines was hard of hearing. They squinted, and the skin of their faces was creased like the leather of old work gloves. There were times, studying them, when I dreaded growing up. Most of them coughed, from dust or cigarettes, and most of them drank cheap wine or whiskey, so their eyes looked bloodshot and bruised. The fathers of my friends always seemed older than the mothers. Men wore out sooner. Only women lived into old age.

As a boy I also knew another sort of men, who did not sweat and 14
break down like mules. They were soldiers, and so far as I could tell they scarcely worked at all. During my early school years we lived on a military base, an arsenal in Ohio, and every day I saw GIs in the guardshacks, on the stoops of barracks, at the wheels of olive drab Chevrolets. The chief fact of their lives was boredom. Long after I left the Arsenal I came to recognize the sour smell the soldiers gave off as that of souls in limbo. They were all waiting—for wars, for transfers, for leaves, for promotions, for the end of their hitch—like so many braves waiting for the hunt to begin. Unlike the warriors of older tribes, however, they would have no say about when the battle would start or how it would be waged. Their waiting was broken only when they practiced for war. They fired guns at targets, drove tanks across the churned-up fields of the military reservation, set off bombs in the wrecks of old fighter planes. I knew this was all play. But I also felt certain that when the hour for killing arrived, they would kill. When the real shooting started, many of them would die. This was what soldiers were *for,* just as a hammer was for driving nails.

Warriors and toilers: those seemed, in my boyhood vision, to be 15
the chief destinies for men. They weren't the only destinies, as I learned from having a few male teachers, from reading books, and from watching television. But the men on television—the politicians,

the astronauts, the generals, the savvy lawyers, the philosophical doctors, the bosses who gave orders to both soldiers and laborers—seemed as remote and unreal to me as the figures in tapestries. I could no more imagine growing up to become one of these cool, potent creatures than I could imagine becoming a prince.

16 A nearer and more hopeful example was that of my father, who had escaped from a red-dirt farm to a tire factory, and from the assembly line to the front office. Eventually he dressed in a white shirt and tie. He carried himself as if he had been born to work with his mind. But his body, remembering the earlier years of slogging work, began to give out on him in his fifties, and it quit on him entirely before he turned sixty-five. Even such a partial escape from man's fate as he had accomplished did not seem possible for most of the boys I knew. They joined the army, stood in line for jobs in the smoky plants, helped build highways. They were bound to work as their fathers had worked, killing themselves or preparing to kill others.

17 A scholarship enabled me not only to attend college, a rare enough feat in my circle, but even to study in a university meant for the children of the rich. Here I met for the first time young men who had assumed from birth that they would lead lives of comfort and power. And for the first time I met women who told me that men were guilty of having kept all the joys and privileges of the earth for themselves. I was baffled. What privileges? What joys? I thought about the maimed, dismal lives of most of the men back home. What had they stolen from their wives and daughters? The right to go five days a week, twelve months a year, for thirty or forty years to a steel mill or a coal mine? The right to drop bombs and die in war? The right to feel every leak in the roof, every gap in the fence, every cough in the engine, as a wound they must mend? The right to feel, when the lay-off comes or the plant shuts down, not only afraid but ashamed?

18 I was slow to understand the deep grievances of women. This was because, as a boy, I had envied them. Before college, the only people I had ever known who were interested in art or music or literature, the only ones who read books, the only ones who ever seemed to enjoy a sense of ease and grace were the mothers and daughters. Like the menfolk, they fretted about money, they scrimped and made-do. But, when the pay stopped coming in, they were not the ones who had failed. Nor did they have to go to war, and that seemed to me a blessed fact. By comparison with the narrow, ironclad days of fathers, there was an expansiveness, I thought, in the days of mothers. They went to see neighbors, to shop in town, to run errands at school, at the library, at church. No doubt, had I looked harder at their lives, I would have envied them less. It was not

my fate to become a woman, so it was easier for me to see the graces. Few of them held jobs outside the home, and those who did filled thankless roles as clerks and waitresses. I didn't see, then, what a prison a house could be, since houses seemed to me brighter, handsomer places than any factory. I did not realize—because such things were never spoken of—how often women suffered from men's bullying. I did learn about the wretchedness of abandoned wives, single mothers, widows; but I also learned about the wretchedness of lone men. Even then I could see how exhausting it was for a mother to cater all day to the needs of young children. But if I had been asked, as a boy, to choose between tending a baby and tending a machine, I think I would have chosen the baby. (Having now tended both, I know I would choose the baby.)

So I was baffled when the women at college accused me and my sex of having cornered the world's pleasures. I think something like my bafflement has been felt by other boys (and by girls as well) who grew up in dirt-poor farm country, in mining country, in black ghettos, in Hispanic barrios, in the shadows of factories, in Third World nations—any place where the fate of men is as grim and bleak as the fate of women. Toilers and warriors. I realize now how ancient these identities are, how deep the tug they exert on men, the undertone of a thousand generations. The miseries I saw, as a boy, in the lives of nearly all men I continue to see in the lives of many—the body-breaking toil, the tedium, the call to be tough, the humiliating powerlessness, the battle for a living and for territory. 19

When the women I met at college thought about the joys and privileges of men, they did not carry in their minds the sort of men I had known in my childhood. They thought of their fathers, who were bankers, physicians, architects, stockbrokers, the big wheels of the big cities. These fathers rode the train to work or drove cars that cost more than any of my childhood houses. They were attended from morning to night by female helpers, wives, and nurses and secretaries. They were never laid off, never short of cash at month's end, never lined up for welfare. These fathers made decisions that mattered. They ran the world. 20

The daughters of such men wanted to share in this power, this glory. So did I. They yearned for a say over their future, for jobs worthy of their abilities, for the right to live at peace, unmolested, whole. Yes, I thought, yes yes. The difference between me and these daughters was that they saw me, because of my sex, as destined from birth to become like their fathers, and therefore as an enemy to their desires. But I knew better. I wasn't an enemy, in fact or in feeling. I was an ally. If I had known, then, how to tell them so, would they have believed me? Would they now? 21

## IN RETROSPECT

**1.** The first nine paragraphs of Sanders's essay reproduce a conversation he had with Anneke, a Dutch friend of his. What is the import of their conversation? In what way does this conversation set up what follows in the essay?

**2.** Sanders gives us an assessment of the man-woman relationship from a masculine point of view. A good part of his present attitude toward men and women was shaped by his experience of growing up in rural areas of Tennessee and Ohio. His deepest memories of those days were of men—men who were either, as he puts it, "toilers or warriors." How did these early experiences shape Sanders's attitude toward men and women? Reflect on the image of men and woman that you carry with you from the early years of your life. What effect does this essay and your reflections on your own experiences have on your reactions to the essays in this chapter?

# 13

# On the Art of the Essay

*Artists of any kind impress us mainly through the products of their art; some, however, have also been able to educate us by talking about the* processes *of their art. Although successful practitioners of an art are not inevitably or invariably the best teachers, our natural disposition is to listen attentively when they discuss the principles and mechanics of their art. There is an art of the essay just as surely as there is an art of the poem, the play, or the short story. All of the essayists in this chapter have exhibited a product of their art in one or another of the previous chapters in this book; now these same essayists tell us how they or others operate as essayists and, indirectly, how aspiring essayists might become proficient practitioners of the art. As the ancient rhetoricians maintained, we learn any art or craft by exposure to some combination of precepts, imitation, and practice. The essays in this anthology provide us with an opportunity to learn by observation and imitation. By listening to the essayists in this chapter talk about their art and by analyzing other essays in the anthology, we can learn the precepts—the principles and mechanisms—of the art. By attempting to write essays ourselves, we can learn by practice. Go for the gold.*

# *Of Giving the Lie*

## MICHEL DE MONTAIGNE

As we pointed out in the headnote to chapter 7's essay "Of Practice," Michel de Montaigne (1533–1592) is the acknowledged originator of the literary form known as the essay. The collection of the literary discourses that he entitled *Essais* (a French word meaning "trials, attempts, gropings") appeared in three books written and revised between 1580 and 1595. The selection reprinted here exemplifies the rationale, the tone, and the manner, if not the style (remember, you are reading a translation from the French) of Montaigne's essays. No subject was too trivial or too profound for Montaigne to write about, but every subject was treated in the highly personal, charmingly casual manner that is the hallmark of this kind of prose discourse. As Montaigne said in one of the early essays in Book 1 of his opus, "Thus, gentle reader, I myself am the groundwork of my book." In the following essay, Montaigne justifies this kind of egotistical writing. What better way to get the rationale of this kind of writing than from the pen of the originator?

Yes, but someone will tell me that this plan of using oneself as a 1 subject to write about would be excusable in rare and famous men who by their reputation had aroused some desire to know them. That is certain; I admit it; and I know full well that to see a man of the common sort, an artisan will hardly raise his eyes from his work, whereas to see a great and prominent personage arrive in a city, men leave workshops and stores empty. It ill befits anyone to make himself known save him who has qualities to be imitated, and whose life and opinions may serve as a model. In the greatness of their deeds Caesar and Xenophon had something to found and establish their narrative upon, as on a just and solid base. Desirable therefore would be the journals of Alexander the Great, and the commentaries that Augustus, Cato, Sulla, Brutus, and others left about their deeds. People love and study the figures of such men, even in bronze and stone.

This remonstrance is very true, but it concerns me only very 2 little:

> Only to friends do I recite, and on request,
> Not to all men, or everywhere. Some will not rest,
> And keep reciting in the Forum or the baths.
>
> Horace

I am not building here a statue to erect at the town crossroads, or in a church or a public square:

> I do not aim to swell my page full-blown
> With windy trifles. . . .
> We two talk alone.
>
> Persius

This is for a nook in a library, and to amuse a neighbor, a relative, a friend, who may take pleasure in associating and conversing with me again in this image. Others have taken courage to speak of themselves because they found the subject worthy and rich; I, on the contrary, because I have found mine so barren and so meager that no suspicion of ostentation can fall upon my plan.

I willingly judge the actions of others; I give little chance to judge 3
mine because of their nullity. I do not find so much good in myself that I cannot tell it without blushing.

What a satisfaction it would be to me to hear someone tell me, in 4
this way, of the habits, the face, the expression, the favorite remarks, and the fortunes of my ancestors! How attentive I would be! Truly it would spring from a bad nature to be scornful of even the portraits of our friends and predecessors, the form of their clothes and their armor. I keep their handwriting, their seal, the breviary and a peculiar sword that they used, and I have not banished from my study some long sticks that my father ordinarily carried in his hand. *A father's coat and his ring are the more dear to his children the more they loved him* [Saint Augustine].

However, if my descendants have other tastes, I shall have ample 5
means for revenge: for they could not possibly have less concern about me than I shall have about them by that time.

All the contact I have with the public in this book is that I borrow 6
their tools of printing, as being swifter and easier. In recompense, perhaps I shall keep some pat of butter from melting in the market place.

> Lest tunny-fish and olives lack a robe.
>
> Martial

> To mackerel I'll often give a shirt.
>
> Catullus

And if no one reads me, have I wasted my time, entertaining 7
myself for so many idle hours with such useful and agreeable thoughts? In modeling this figure upon myself, I have had to fashion and compose myself so often to bring myself out, that the model itself has to some extent grown firm and taken shape. Painting myself for others, I have painted my inward self with colors clearer than my

original ones. I have no more made my book than my book has made me—a book consubstantial with its author, concerned with my own self, an integral part of my life; not concerned with some third-hand, extraneous purpose, like all other books. Have I wasted my time by taking stock of myself so continually, so carefully? For those who go over themselves only in their minds and occasionally in speech do not penetrate to essentials in their examination as does a man who makes that his study, his work, and his trade, who binds himself to keep an enduring account, with all his faith, with all his strength.

Indeed, the most delightful pleasures are digested inwardly, 8
avoid leaving any traces, and avoid the sight not only of the public but of any other person.

How many times has this task diverted me from annoying cogita- 9
tions! And all frivolous ones should be counted as annoying. Nature has made us a present of a broad capacity for entertaining ourselves apart, and often calls us to do so, to teach us that we owe ourselves in part to society, but in the best part to ourselves. In order to train my fancy even to dream with some order and purpose, and in order to keep it from losing its way and roving with the wind, there is nothing like embodying and registering all the little thoughts that come to it. I listen to my reveries because I have to record them. How many times, irritated by some action that civility and reason kept me from reproving openly, have I disgorged it here, not without ideas of instructing the public! And indeed, these poetic lashes—

> Bang in the eye, bang on the snout,
> Bang on the back of the apish lout!
>
> Marot

—imprint themselves even better on paper than on living flesh. What if I lend a slightly more attentive ear to books, since I have been lying in wait to pilfer something from them to adorn or support my own?

I have not studied one bit to make a book; but I have studied a bit 10
because I had made it, if it is studying a bit to skim over and pinch, by his head or his feet, now one author, now another; not at all to form my opinions, but certainly to assist, second, and serve those which I formed long ago.

But whom shall we believe when he talks about himself, in so 11
corrupt an age, seeing that there are few or none whom we can believe when they speak of others, where there is less incentive for lying? The first stage in the corruption of morals is the banishment of truth; for, as Pindar said, to be truthful is the beginning of a great virtue, and is the first article that Plato requires in the governor of his Republic. Our truth of nowadays is not what is, but what others can

be convinced of; just as we call "money" not only that which is legal, but also any counterfeit that will pass. Our nation has long been reproached for this vice; for Salvianus of Massilia, who lived in the time of the Emperor Valentinian, says that to the French lying and perjury are not a vice but a manner of speaking. If a man wanted to go this testimony one better, he could say that it is now a virtue to them. Men form and fashion themselves for it as for an honorable practice; for dissimulation is among the most notable qualities of this century.

Thus I have often considered what could be the source of that 12
custom, which we observe so religiously, of feeling more bitterly offended when reproached with this vice, which is so common among us, than with any other; and that it should be the worst insult that can be given us in words, to reproach us with lying. On that, I find that it is natural to defend ourselves most for the defects with which we are most besmirched. It seems that in resenting the accusation and growing excited about it, we unburden ourselves to some extent of the guilt; if we have it in fact, at least we condemn it in appearance.

Would it not also be that this reproach seems to involve coward- 13
ice and lack of courage? Is there any more obvious cowardice than to deny our own word? Worse yet, to deny what we know?

Lying is an ugly vice, which an ancient paints in most shameful 14
colors when he says that it is giving evidence of contempt for God, and at the same time of fear of men. It is not possible to represent more vividly the horror, the vileness, and the profligacy of it. For what can you imagine uglier than being a coward toward men and bold toward God? Since mutual understanding is brought about solely by way of words, he who breaks his word betrays human society. It is the only instrument by means of which our wills and thoughts communicate, it is the interpreter of our soul. If it fails us, we have no more hold on each other, no more knowledge of each other. If it deceives us, it breaks up all our relations and dissolves all the bonds of our society.

Certain nations of the new Indies (there is no use mentioning 15
their names, which are no more; for the desolation of their conquest—a monstrous and unheard-of case—has extended even to the entire abolition of the names and former knowledge of the places) offered to their gods human blood, but only such as was drawn from their tongue and ears, in expiation of the sin of falsehood, heard as well as uttered.

That worthy fellow from Greece used to say that children play 16
with knucklebones, men with words.

As for the varied etiquette of giving the lie, and our laws of honor 17
in that matter, and the changes they have undergone, I shall put off

till another time telling what I know about that, and shall meanwhile learn, if I can, at what time the custom began of weighing and measuring words so exactly, and attaching our honor to them. For it is easy to see that it did not exist in olden times among the Romans and the Greeks. And it has often seemed to me novel and strange to see them giving each other the lie and insulting each other, without having a quarrel over it. The laws of their duty took some other path than ours. Caesar is called now a robber, now a drunkard, to his face. We see how free are the invectives they use against each other, I mean the greatest warlords of both nations, where words are avenged merely by words, and do not lead to other consequences.

**IN RETROSPECT**

**1.** In "Of Giving the Lie," Montaigne devotes paragraphs 11–17 to discussing the vice of lying. Why do you think he discusses lying in an essay in which he announces that he plans to make himself the subject of all his essays?

**2.** At least five times in this essay, Montaigne does what your writing teacher may have discouraged or even forbidden you from doing: He writes a one-sentence paragraph (see paragraphs 3, 5, 8, 10, and 16). Speculate about what function these undeveloped paragraphs might be performing in the essay.

# *The Modern Essay*

## VIRGINIA WOOLF

Virginia Woolf (1882–1941) is the author of the essay "Death of a Moth," reprinted in chapter 7 of this book. In the essay appearing here, which is a review of *Modern English Essays,* a five-volume edition of essays edited by Ernest Rhys (see our Bibliography), Woolf talks about the essay as a distinct form of literature, characterizes that distinctive form, and discusses the merits or demerits of some of the essayists represented in Rhys's collection. The boundaries of Rhys's collection of *modern* essays range from 1837, the beginning of the Victorian age, to 1920. All the essayists discussed are British writers. Because only a few of those British essayists are represented in the present anthology, Woolf's appraisals of them may not be very interesting or meaningful to you—unless you are familiar with those authors from your previous reading. But what should be interesting and meaningful to you is Woolf's analysis of the distinctive marks and merits of the essay as a literary form. In this essay on the essay, Woolf manifests that she is one of the premier essayists—even on her own terms—in the history of the essay.

As Mr. Rhys truly says, it is unnecessary to go profoundly into 1
the history and origin of the essay—whether it derives from Socrates or Siranney the Persian—since, like all living things, its present is more important than its past. Moreover, the family is widely spread; and while some of its representatives have risen in the world and wear their coronets with the best, others pick up a precarious living in the gutter near Fleet Street. The form, too, admits variety. The essay can be short or long, serious or trifling, about God and Spinoza, or about turtles and Cheapside. But as we turn over the pages of these five little volumes, containing essays written between 1870 and 1920, certain principles appear to control the chaos, and we detect in the short period under review something like the progress of history.

Of all forms of literature, however, the essay is the one which 2
least calls for the use of long words. The principle which controls it is simply that it should give pleasure; the desire which impels us when we take it from the shelf is simply to receive pleasure. Everything in an essay must be subdued to that end. It should lay us under a spell with its first word, and we should only wake, refreshed, with its last. In the interval we may pass through the most various experiences of amusement, surprise, interest, indignation; we may soar to the heights of fantasy with Lamb or plunge to the depths of wisdom with Bacon, but we must never be roused. The essay must lap us about and draw its curtain across the world.

So great a feat is seldom accomplished, though the fault may well 3
be as much on the reader's side as on the writer's. Habit and lethargy have dulled his palate. A novel has a story, a poem rhyme; but what art can the essayist use in these short lengths of prose to sting us wide awake and fix us in a trance which is not sleep but rather an intensification of life—a basking, with every faculty alert, in the sun of pleasure? He must know—that is the first essential—how to write. His learning may be as profound as Mark Pattison's, but in an essay it must be so fused by the magic of writing that not a fact juts out, not a dogma tears the surface of the texture. Macaulay in one way, Froude in another, did this superbly over and over again. They have blown more knowledge into us in the course of one essay than the innumerable chapters of a hundred text-books. But when Mark Pattison has to tell us, in the space of thirty-five little pages, about Montaigne, we feel that he had not previously assimilated M. Grün. M. Grün was a gentleman who once wrote a bad book. M. Grün and his book should have been embalmed for our perpetual delight in amber. But the

process is fatiguing; it requires more time and perhaps more temper than Pattison had at his command. He served M. Grün up raw, and he remains a crude berry among the cook meats, upon which our teeth must grate for ever. Something of the sort applies to Matthew Arnold and a certain translator of Spinoza. Literal truth-telling and finding fault with a culprit for his good are out of place in an essay, where everything should be for our good and rather for eternity than for the March number of the *Fortnightly Review*. But if the voice of the scold should never be heard in this narrow plot, there is another voice which is as a plague of locusts—the voice of a man stumbling drowsily among loose words, clutching aimlessly at vague ideas, the voice, for example, of Mr. Hutton in the following passage:

> Add to this that his married life was very brief, only seven years and a half, being unexpectedly cut short, and that his passionate reverence for his wife's memory and genius—in his own words, "a religion"—was one which, as he must have been perfectly sensible; he could not make to appear otherwise than extravagant, not to say an hallucination, in the eyes of the rest of mankind, and yet that he was possessed by an irresistible yearning to attempt to embody it in all the tender and enthusiastic hyperbole of which it is so pathetic to find a man who gained his fame by his "dry-light" a master, and it is impossible not to feel that the human incidents in Mr. Mill's career are very sad.

A book could take that blow, but it sinks an essay. A biography in two volumes is indeed the proper depositary; for there, where the licence is so much wider, and hints and glimpses of outside things make part of the feast (we refer to the old type of Victorian volume), these yawns and stretches hardly matter, and have indeed some positive value of their own. But that value, which is contributed by the reader, perhaps illicitly, in his desire to get as much into the book from all possible sources as he can, must be ruled out here. 4

There is no room for the impurities of literature in an essay. Somehow or other, by dint of labour or bounty of nature, or both combined, the essay must be pure—pure like water or pure like wine, but pure from dullness, deadness, and deposits of extraneous matter. Of all writers in the first volume, Walter Pater best achieves this arduous task, because before setting out to write his essay ("Notes on Leonardo da Vinci") he has somehow contrived to get his material fused. He is a learned man, but it is not knowledge of Leonardo that remains with us, but a vision, such as we get in a good novel where everything contributes to bring the writer's conception as a whole before us. Only here, in the essay, where the bounds are so strict and facts have to be used in their nakedness, the true writer like Walter Pater makes these limitations yield their own quality. Truth will give 5 it authority; from its narrow limits he will get shape and intensity; and then there is no more fitting place for some of those ornaments which the old writers loved and we, by calling them ornaments, presumably despise. Nowadays nobody would have the courage to embark on the once famous description of Leonardo's lady who has

> learned the secrets of the grave; and has been a diver in deep seas and keeps their fallen day about her; and trafficked for strange webs with Eastern merchants; and, as Leda, was the mother of Helen of Troy, and, as Saint Anne, the mother of Mary. . . .

The passage is too thumb-marked to slip naturally into the context. But when we come unexpectedly upon "the smiling of women and the motion of great waters," or upon "full of the refinement of the dead, in sad, earth-coloured raiment, set with pale stones," we suddenly remember that we have ears and we have eyes, and that the English language fills a long array of stout volumes with innumerable words, many of which are of more than one syllable. The only living Englishman who ever looks into these volumes is, of course, a gentleman of Polish extraction. But doubtless our abstention saves us much gush, much rhetoric, much high-stepping and cloud-prancing, and for the sake of the prevailing sobriety and hard-headedness we should be willing to barter the splendour of Sir Thomas Browne and the vigour of Swift.

Yet, if the essay admits more properly than biography or fiction of 6
sudden boldness and metaphor, and can be polished till every atom of its surface shines, there are dangers in that too. We are soon in sight of ornament. Soon the current, which is the life-blood of literature, runs slow; and instead of sparkling and flashing or moving with a quieter impulse which has a deeper excitement, words coagulate together in frozen sprays which, like the grapes on a Christmas-tree, glitter for a single night, but are dusty and garish the day after. The temptation to decorate is great where the theme may be of the slightest. What is there to interest another in the fact that one has enjoyed a walking tour, or has amused oneself by rambling down Cheapside and looking at the turtles in Mr. Sweeting's shop window? Stevenson and Samuel Butler chose very different methods of exciting our interest in these domestic themes. Stevenson, of course, trimmed and polished and set out his matter in the traditional eighteenth-century form. It is admirably done, but we cannot help feeling anxious, as the essay proceeds, lest the material may give out under the craftsman's fingers. The ingot is so small, the manipulation so incessant. And perhaps that is why the peroration—

> To sit still and contemplate—to remember the faces of women without desire, to be pleased by the great deeds of men without envy, to

> be everything and everywhere in sympathy and yet content to remain where and what you are—

has the sort of insubstantiality which suggests that by the time he got to the end he had left himself nothing solid to work with. Butler adopted the very opposite method. Think your own thoughts, he seems to say, and speak them as plainly as you can. These turtles in the shop window which appear to leak out of their shells through heads and feet suggest a fatal faithfulness to a fixed idea. And so, striding unconcernedly from one idea to the next, we traverse a large stretch of ground; observe that a wound in the solicitor is a very serious thing; that Mary Queen of Scots wears surgical boots and is subject to fits near the Horse Shoe in Tottenham Court Road; take it for granted that no one really cares about Aeschylus; and so, with many amusing anecdotes and some profound reflections, reach the peroration, which is that, as he had been told not to see more in Cheapside than he could get into twelve pages of the *Universal Review,* he had better stop. And yet obviously Butler is at least as careful of our pleasure as Stevenson; and to write like oneself and call it not writing is a much harder exercise in style than to write like Addison and call it writing well.

But, however much they differ individually, the Victorian essay- 7
ists yet had something in common. They wrote at greater length than is now usual, and they wrote for a public which had not only time to sit down to its magazine seriously, but a high, if peculiarly Victorian, standard of culture by which to judge it. It was worth while to speak out upon serious matters in an essay; and there was nothing absurd in writing as well as one possibly could when, in a month or two, the same public which had welcomed the essay in a magazine would carefully read it once more in a book. But a change came from a small audience of cultivated people to a larger audience of people who were not quite so cultivated. The change was not altogether for the worse. In volume III we find Mr. Birrell and Mr. Beerbohm. It might even be said that there was a reversion to the classic type, and that the essay by losing its size and something of its sonority was approaching more nearly the essay of Addison and Lamb. At any rate, there is a great gulf between Mr. Birrell on Carlyle and the essay which one may suppose that Carlyle would have written upon Mr. Birrell. There is little similarity between *A Cloud of Pinafores,* by Max Beerbohm, and *A Cynic's Apology,* by Leslie Stephen. But the essay is alive; there is no reason to despair. As the conditions change so the essayist, most sensitive of all plants to public opinion, adapts himself, and if he is good makes the best of the change, and if he is bad the worst. Mr. Birrell is certainly good; and so we find that, though he has dropped a

considerable amount of weight, his attack is much more direct and his movement more supple. But what did Mr. Beerbohm give to the essay and what did he take from it? That is a much more complicated question, for here we have an essayist who has concentrated on the work and is without doubt the prince of his profession.

What Mr. Beerbohm gave was, of course, himself. This presence, 8
which has haunted the essay fitfully from the time of Montaigne, had been in exile since the death of Charles Lamb. Matthew Arnold was never to his readers Matt, nor Walter Pater affectionately abbreviated in a thousand homes to Wat. They gave us much, but that they did not give. Thus, some time in the 'nineties, it must have surprised readers accustomed to exhortation, information, and denunciation to find themselves familiarly addressed by a voice which seemed to belong to a man no larger than themselves. He was affected by private joys and sorrows, and had no gospel to preach and no learning to impart. He was himself, simply and directly, and himself he has remained. Once again we have an essayist capable of using the essayist's most proper but most dangerous and delicate tool. He has brought personality into literature, not unconsciously and impurely, but so consciously and purely that we do not know whether there is any relation between Max the essayist and Mr. Beerbohm the man. We only know that the spirit of personality permeates every word that he writes. The triumph is the triumph of style. For it is only by knowing how to write that you can make use in literature of your self; that self which, while it is essential to literature, is also its most dangerous antagonist. Never to be yourself and yet always—that is the problem. Some of the essayists in Mr. Rhys' collection, to be frank, have not altogether succeeded in solving it. We are nauseated by the sight of trivial personalities decomposing in the eternity of print. As talk, no doubt, it was charming, and certainly the writer is a good fellow to meet over a bottle of beer. But literature is stern; it is no use being charming, virtuous, or even learned and brilliant into the bargain, unless, she seems to reiterate, you fulfil her first condition—to know how to write.

This art is possessed to perfection by Mr. Beerbohm. But he has 9
not searched the dictionary for polysyllables. He has not moulded firm periods or seduced our ears with intricate cadences and strange melodies. Some of his companions—Henley and Stevenson, for example—are momentarily more impressive. But *A Cloud of Pinafores* had in it that indescribable inequality, stir, and finally expressiveness which belong to life and to life alone. You have not finished with it because you have read it, any more than friendship is ended because it is time to part. Life wells up and alters and adds. Even things in a book-case change if they are alive; we find ourselves wanting to meet

them again; we find them altered. So we look back upon essay after essay by Mr. Beerbohm, knowing that, come September or May, we shall sit down with them and talk. Yet it is true that the essayist is the most sensitive of all writers to public opinion. The drawing-room is the place where a great deal of reading is done nowadays, and the essays of Mr. Beerbohm lie, with an exquisite appreciation of all that the position exacts, upon the drawing-room table. There is no gin about; no stronger tobacco; no puns, drunkenness, or insanity. Ladies and gentlemen talk together, and some things, of course, are not said.

But if it would be foolish to attempt to confine Mr. Beerbohm to one room, it would be still more foolish, unhappily, to make him, the artist, the man who gives us only his best, the representative of our age. There are no essays by Mr. Beerbohm in the fourth or fifth volumes of the present collection. His age seems already a little distant, and the drawing-room table, as it recedes, begins to look rather like an altar where, once upon a time, people deposited offerings—fruit from their own orchards, gifts carved with their own hands. Now once more the conditions have changed. The public needs essays as much as ever, and perhaps even more. The demand for the light middle not exceeding fifteen hundred words, or in special cases seventeen hundred and fifty, much exceeds the supply. Where Lamb wrote one essay and Max perhaps writes two, Mr. Belloc at a rough computation produces three hundred and sixty-five. They are very short, it is true. Yet with what dexterity the practised essayist will utilise his space—beginning as close to the top of the sheet as possible, judging precisely how far to go, when to turn, and how, without sacrificing a hair's breadth of paper, to wheel about and alight accurately upon the last word his editor allows! As a feat of skill it is well worth watching. But the personality upon which Mr. Belloc, like Mr. Beerbohm, depends suffers in the process. It comes to us not with the natural richness of the speaking voice, but strained and thin and full of mannerisms and affectations, like the voice of a man shouting through a megaphone to a crowd on a windy day. "Little friends, my readers," he says in the essay called "An Unknown Country," and he goes on to tell us how— 10

> There was a shepherd the other day at Findon Fair who had come from the east by Lewes with sheep, and who had in his eyes that reminiscence of horizons which makes the eyes of shepherds and of mountaineers different from the eyes of other men. . . . I went with him to hear what he had to say, for shepherds talk quite differently from other men.

Happily this shepherd had little to say, even under the stimulus of the inevitable mug of beer, about the Unknown Country, for the only remark that he did make proves him either a minor poet, unfit 11 for the care of sheep, or Mr. Belloc himself masquerading with a fountain pen. That is the penalty which the habitual essayist must now be prepared to face. He must masquerade. He cannot afford the time either to be himself or to be other people. He must skim the surface of thought and dilute the strength of personality. He must give us a worn weekly halfpenny instead of a solid sovereign once a year.

But it is not Mr. Belloc only who has suffered from the prevailing conditions. The essays which bring the collection to the year 1920 may not be the best of their authors' work, but, if we except writers like Mr. Conrad and Mr. Hudson, who have strayed into essay writing accidentally, and concentrate upon those who write essays habitually, we shall find them a good deal affected by the change in their circumstances. To write weekly, to write daily, to write shortly, to write for busy people catching trains in the morning or for tired people coming home in the evening, is a heartbreaking task for men who know good writing from bad. They do it, but instinctively draw out of harm's way anything precious that might be damaged by contact with the public, or anything sharp that might irritate its skin. And so, if one reads Mr. Lucas, Mr. Lynd, or Mr. Squire in the bulk, one feels that a common greyness silvers everything. They are as far removed from the extravagant beauty of Walter Pater as they are from the intemperate candour of Leslie Stephen. Beauty and courage are dangerous spirits to battle in a column and a half; and thought, like a brown paper parcel in a waistcoat pocket, has a way of spoiling the symmetry of an article. It is a kind, tired, apathetic world for which they write, and the marvel is that they never cease to attempt, at least, to write well. 12

But there is no need to pity Mr. Clutton Brock for this change in the essayist's conditions. He has clearly made the best of his circumstances and not the worst. One hesitates even to say that he has had to make any conscious effort in the matter, so naturally has he effected the transition from the private essayist to the public, from the drawing-room to the Albert Hall. Paradoxically enough, the shrinkage in size has brought about a corresponding expansion of individuality. We have no longer the "I" of Max and of Lamb, but the "we" of public bodies and other sublime personages. It is "we" who go to hear the *Magic Flute;* "we" who ought to profit by it; "we," in some mysterious way, who, in our corporate capacity, once upon a time actually wrote it. For music and literature and art must submit to the same generalisation or they will not carry to the farthest recesses of the Albert Hall. That the voice of Mr. Clutton Brock, so sincere and so disinterested, carries such a distance and reaches so many without pandering to the weakness of the mass or its passions must be a matter of legitimate satisfaction to us all. But while "we" are gratified, 13

"I," that unruly partner in the human fellowship, is reduced to despair. "I" must always think things for himself, and feel things for himself. To share them in a diluted form with the majority of well-educated and well-intentioned men and women is for him sheer agony; and while the rest of us listen intently and profit profoundly, "I" slips off to the woods and the fields and rejoices in a single blade of grass or a solitary potato.

In the fifth volume of modern essays, it seems, we have got some 14
way from pleasure and the art of writing. But in justice to the essayists of 1920 we must be sure that we are not praising the famous because they have been praised already and the dead because we shall never meet them wearing spats in Piccadilly. We must know what we mean when we say that they can write and give us pleasure. We must compare them; we must bring out the quality. We must point to this and say it is good because it is exact, truthful, and imaginative:

> Nay, retire men cannot when they would; neither will they, when it were Reason; but are impatient of Privateness, even in age and sickness, which require the shadow: like old Townsmen: that will still be sitting at their street door, though thereby they offer Age to Scorn. . . .

and to this, and say it is bad because it is loose, plausible, and commonplace:

> With courteous and precise cynicism on his lips, he thought of quiet virginal chambers, of waters singing under the moon, of terraces where taintless music sobbed into the open night, of pure maternal mistresses with protecting arms and vigilant eyes, of fields slumbering in the sunlight, of leagues of ocean heaving under warm tremulous heavens, of hot ports, gorgeous and perfumed. . . .

It goes on, but already we are bemused with sound and neither feel nor hear. The comparison makes us suspect that the art of writing has for backbone some fierce attachment to an idea. It is on the back of an idea, something believed in with conviction or seen with precision and thus compelling words to its shape, that the diverse company which included Lamb and Bacon, and Mr. Beerbohm and Hudson, and Vernon Lee and Mr. Conrad, and Leslie Stephen and Butler and Walter Pater reaches the farther shore. Very various talents have helped or hindered the passage of the idea into words. Some scrape through painfully; others fly with every wind favouring. But Mr. Belloc and Mr. Lucas and Mr. Lynd and Mr. Squire are not fiercely attached to anything in itself. They share the contemporary dilemma—that lack of an obstinate conviction which lifts ephemeral sounds through the misty sphere of anybody's language to the land where there is a perpetual marriage, a perpetual union. Vague as all definitions are, a good essay must have this permanent quality about it; it must draw its curtain round us, but it must be a curtain that shuts us in, not out.

### IN RETROSPECT

**1.** Woolf says in paragraph 9, "Even things in a book-case change if they are alive; we find ourselves wanting to meet them again; we find them altered. So we look back upon essay after essay . . . knowing that come September or May, we shall sit down with them and talk." Select an essay that compels you to have a "talk" with it again. Reread the essay, noting places that you relish again and places where your reading seems to have changed. Find out how many people in your class chose the same essay to reread. Get into a group with those people and compare their reading reports with yours. How is your reading altered yet again by your conversation with other readers?

**2.** Woolf also says in paragraph 9 that "the essayist is the most sensitive of all writers to public opinion. . . . Ladies and gentlemen talk together, and some things, of course, are not said." See if you can find places in the essays in this book where (a) things are not said that might be said, (b) things are said more politely than the writer might have wished them to be said, or (c) things are said so subtly that while some readers get the message the author is trying to convey, other readers do not get that message at all.

# *The Essayist and the Essay*

## E. B. WHITE

E. B. White (1899–1985)—represented in chapter 7 of this anthology by "Once More to the Lake"—is one of the supreme American essayists of this century. When an artist like White speaks up, it behooves us to listen. In "The Essayist and the Essay," he talks about the great variety of essays, about the relatively low estate of the essayist in America, about the egoism of the essayist, and about the delights of this relaxed, unstructured form of writing. White kept on writing essays until he was eighty-five, when, much to the sorrow of his legions of readers, he died. Nevertheless, because of the legacy of his writings, White is immortal. Read what he has to say here about the art form that he loved.

The essayist is a self-liberated man, sustained by the childish belief that everything he thinks about, everything that happens to him, is of general interest. He is a fellow who thoroughly enjoys his work, just as people who take bird walks enjoy theirs. Each new excursion of the essayist, each new "attempt," differs from the last and takes him into new country. This delights him. Only a person who is congenitally self-centered has the effrontery and the stamina to write essays. 1

There are as many kinds of essays as there are human attitudes or poses, as many essay flavors as there are Howard Johnson ice creams. The essayist arises in the morning and, if he has work to do, selects his garb from an unusually extensive wardrobe: he can pull on any sort of shirt, be any sort of person, according to his mood or his subject matter—philosopher, scold, jester, raconteur, confidant, pundit, devil's advocate, enthusiast. I like the essay, have always liked it, and even as a child was at work, attempting to inflict my young thoughts and experiences on others by putting them on paper. I early broke into print in the pages of *St. Nicholas.* I tend still to fall back on the essay form (or lack of form) when an idea strikes me, but I am not fooled about the place of the essay in twentieth-century American letters—it stands a short distance down the line. The essayist, unlike the novelist, the poet, and the playwright, must be content in his self-imposed role of second-class citizen. A writer who has his sights trained on the Nobel Prize or other earthly triumphs had best write a novel, a poem, or a play, and leave the essayist to ramble about, content with living a free life and enjoying the satisfactions of a somewhat undisciplined existence. (Dr. Johnson called the essay "an irregular, undigested piece"; this happy practitioner has no wish to quarrel with the good doctor's characterization.) 2

There is one thing the essayist cannot do, though—he cannot indulge himself in deceit or in concealment, for he will be found out in no time. Desmond MacCarthy, in his introductory remarks to the 1928 E. P. Dutton & Company edition of Montaigne, observes that Montaigne "had the gift of natural candour. . . ." It is the basic ingredient. And even the essayist's escape from discipline is only a partial escape: the essay, although a relaxed form, imposes its own disciplines, raises its own problems, and these disciplines and problems soon become apparent and (we all hope) act as a deterrent to anyone wielding a pen merely because he entertains random thoughts or is in a happy or wandering mood. 3

I think some people find the essay the last resort of the egoist, a much too self-conscious and self-serving form for their taste; they feel that it is presumptuous of a writer to assume that his little excursions or his small observations will interest the reader. There is some justice 4 in their complaint. I have always been aware that I am by nature self-absorbed and egotistical; to write of myself to the extent I have done indicates a too great attention to my own life, not enough to the lives of others. I have worn many shirts, and not all of them have been a good fit. But when I am discouraged or downcast I need only fling open the door of my closet, and there, hidden behind everything else, hangs the mantle of Michel de Montaigne, smelling slightly of camphor.

### IN RETROSPECT

**1.** White agrees with Samuel Johnson's characterization of the essay as being "an irregular, undigested piece" (paragraph 2). Look at Johnson's essay in chapter 3 and White's essay in chapter 7 and see whether either essay strikes you as being "an irregular, undigested piece." There is a great variety of essays in this collection. Can you find among them some that are definitely *not* examples of "an irregular, undigested piece" but are examples of a regular, digested piece? In his essay "Of Studies," reprinted in chapter 6, Francis Bacon says that some books should be "chewed and digested." Bacon there is talking about readers. Would he advocate that writers too should chew and digest what they are composing?

**2.** White emphasizes a point about the essay that we remarked about in our Introduction, in some of our headnotes to essays, and in some of our questions "In Retrospect": that the essay is an egotistical form of writing. Flip through the collection, and among the essays you have read, see which ones make you aware of the author's presence and personality. See if you can find other essays that definitely do not strike you as being egotistical. (Incidentally, does an essayist have to use the pronoun *I* to make you aware of himself or herself?) Cite examples to back up your findings. How does the personality that comes through to you in an essay affect your response to the essay?

# *Why I Write*

## GEORGE ORWELL

You may have read George Orwell's essay "Politics and the English Language" in chapter 9 of this collection. Here you will read Orwell's essay "Why I Write"—primarily an autobiographical piece in which Orwell tells us how he was driven, from an early age, to put words down on paper. At first he wrote poems. Then he started to spin out stories. Then he became fascinated with the aesthetic pleasure of the mere sound of words. Later, he was motivated by a strong political purpose. In "Why I Write," he lists what he considers to be every author's "four great motives for writing." Each author, he says, will be driven more compellingly by one or another of these motives, but finally all four motives will serve every author, in some degree, as impulses to write. If you are hooked on writing, ask yourself whether you are driven to write by any or all of the motives Orwell discusses. If you are not yet hooked on writing, try to analyze *why* you do not feel the urge to record your words on paper or on a computer screen. One of your reasons may be that writing is extremely hard work. But remember, *everyone* finds writing to be hard work.

From a very early age, perhaps the age of five or six, I knew that when I grew up I should be a writer. Between the ages of about seventeen and twenty-four I tried to abandon this idea, but I did so with the consciousness that I was outraging my true nature and that sooner or later I should have to settle down and write books. 1

I was the middle child of three, but there was a gap of five years on either side, and I barely saw my father before I was eight. For this and other reasons I was somewhat lonely, and I soon developed disagreeable mannerisms which made me unpopular throughout my schooldays. I had the lonely child's habit of making up stories and holding conversations with imaginary persons, and I think from the very start my literary ambitions were mixed up with the feeling of being isolated and undervalued. I knew that I had a facility with words and a power of facing unpleasant facts, and I felt that this created a sort of private world in which I could get my own back for my failure in everyday life. Nevertheless the volume of serious—i.e., seriously intended—writing which I produced all through my childhood and boyhood would not amount to half a dozen pages. I wrote my first poem at the age of four or five, my mother taking it down to dictation. I cannot remember anything about it except that it was about a tiger and the tiger had "chair-like teeth"—a good enough phrase, but I fancy the poem was a plagiarism of Blake's "Tiger, Tiger." At eleven, when the war of 1914–18 broke out, I wrote a patriotic poem which was printed in the local newspaper, as was another, two years later, on the death of Kitchener. From time to time, when I was a bit older, I wrote bad and usually unfinished "nature poems" in the Georgian style. I also, about twice, attempted a short story which was a ghastly failure. That was the total of the would-be serious work that I actually set down on paper during all those years. 2

However, throughout this time I did in a sense engage in literary activities. To begin with there was the made-to-order stuff which I produced quickly, easily and without much pleasure to myself. Apart from school work, I wrote *vers d'occasion,* semi-comic poems which I could turn out at what now seems to me astonishing speed—at 3 fourteen I wrote a whole rhyming play, in imitation of Aristophanes, in about a week—and helped to edit school magazines, both printed and in manuscript. These magazines were the most pitiful burlesque stuff that you could imagine, and I took far less trouble with them than I now would with the cheapest journalism. But side by side with all this, for fifteen years or more, I was carrying out a literary exercise of a quite different kind: this was the making up of a continuous "story" about myself, a sort of diary existing only in the mind. I believe this is a common habit of children and adolescents. As a very small child I used to imagine that I was, say, Robin Hood, and picture myself as the hero of thrilling adventures, but quite soon my "story" ceased to be narcissistic in a crude way and became more and more a mere description of what I was doing and the things I saw. For minutes at a time this kind of thing would be running through my head: "He pushed the door open and entered the room. A yellow beam of sunlight, filtering through the muslin curtains, slanted on to the table, where a matchbox, half open, lay beside the inkpot. With his right hand in his pocket he moved across to the window. Down in the street a tortoiseshell cat was chasing a dead leaf," etc etc. This habit continued till I was about twenty-five, right through my non-literary years. Although I had to search, and did search, for the right words, I seemed to be making this descriptive effort almost against my will, under a kind of compulsion from outside. The "story" must, I suppose, have reflected the styles of the various writers I admired at different ages, but so far as I remember it always had the same meticulous descriptive quality.

When I was about sixteen I suddenly discovered the joy of mere words, i.e., the sounds and associations of words. The lines from *Paradise Lost,* 4

> So hee with difficulty and labour hard
> Moved on: with difficulty and labour hee.

which do not now seem to me so very wonderful, sent shivers down my backbone; and the spelling "hee" for "he" was an added pleasure. As for the need to describe things, I knew all about it already. So it is clear what kind of books I wanted to write, in so far as I could be said to want to write books at that time. I wanted to write enormous naturalistic novels with unhappy endings, full of detailed descriptions and arresting similes, and also full of purple passages in which words were used partly for the sake of their sound. And in fact my first completed novel, *Burmese Days,* which I wrote when I was thirty but projected much earlier, is rather that kind of book.

I give all this background information because I do not think one can assess a writer's motives without knowing something of his early development. His subject matter will be determined by the age he 5 lives in—at least this is true in tumultuous, revolutionary ages like our own—but before he ever begins to write he will have acquired an emotional attitude from which he will never completely escape. It is his job, no doubt, to discipline his temperament and avoid getting stuck at some immature stage, or in some perverse mood: but if he escapes from his early influences altogether, he will have killed his impulse to write. Putting aside the need to earn a living, I think there are four great motives for writing, at any rate for writing prose. They exist in different degrees in every writer, and in any one writer the proportions will vary from time to time, according to the atmosphere in which he is living. They are:

1. Sheer egoism. Desire to seem clever, to be talked about, to be 6
remembered after death, to get your own back on grown-ups who snubbed you in childhood, etc. etc. It is humbug to pretend that this is not a motive, a strong one. Writers share this characteristic with scientists, artists, politicians, lawyers, soldiers, successful business-men—in short, with the whole top crust of humanity. The great mass of human beings are not acutely selfish. After the age of about thirty they abandon individual ambition—in many cases, indeed, they almost abandon the sense of being individuals at all—and live chiefly for others, or are simply smothered under drudgery. But there is also the minority of gifted, wilful people who are determined to live their own lives to the end, and writers belong in this class. Serious writers, I should say, are on the whole more vain and self-centered than journalists, though less interested in money.

2. Aesthetic enthusiasm. Perception of beauty in the external 7
world, or, on the other hand, in words and their right arrangement. Pleasure in the impact of one sound on another, in the firmness of good prose or the rhythm of a good story. Desire to share an experience which one feels is valuable and ought not to be missed. The aesthetic motive is very feeble in a lot of writers, but even a pamphleteer or a writer of textbooks will have pet words and phrases which appeal to him for non-utilitarian reasons; or he may feel strongly about typography, width of margins, etc. Above the level of a railway guide, no book is quite free from aesthetic considerations.

3. Historical impulse. Desire to see things as they are, to find out 8
true facts and store them up for the use of posterity.

4. Political purpose—using the word "political" in the widest 9
possible sense. Desire to push the world in a certain direction, to alter other people's idea of the kind of society that they should strive after. Once again, no book is genuinely free from political bias. The opinion that art should have nothing to do with politics is itself a political attitude.

It can be seen how these various impulses must war against one 10
another, and how they must fluctuate from person to person and

from time to time. By nature—taking your "nature" to be the state you have attained when you are first adult—I am a person in whom the first three motives would outweigh the fourth. In a peaceful age I might have written ornate or merely descriptive books, and might have remained almost unaware of my political loyalties. As it is I have been forced into becoming a sort of pamphleteer. First I spent five years in an unsuitable profession (the Indian Imperial Police, in Burma), and then I underwent poverty and the sense of failure. This increased my natural hatred of authority and made me for the first time fully aware of the existence of the working classes, and the job in Burma had given me some understanding of the nature of imperialism: but these experiences were not enough to give me an accurate political orientation. Then came Hitler, the Spanish civil war, etc. By the end of 1935 I had still failed to reach a firm decision. I remember a little poem that I wrote at that date, expressing my dilemma:

A happy vicar I might have been
Two hundred years ago,
To preach upon eternal doom
And watch my walnuts grow;

But born, alas, in an evil time,
I missed that pleasant haven,
For the hair has grown on my upper lip
And the clergy are all clean-shaven.

And later still the times were good,
We were so easy to please,
We rocked our troubled thoughts to sleep
On the bosoms of the trees.

All ignorant we dared to own
The joys we now dissemble;
The greenfinch on the apple bough
Could make my enemies tremble.

But girls' bellies and apricots,
Roach in a shaded stream.
Horses, ducks in flight at dawn,
All these are a dream.

It is forbidden to dream again;
We maim our joys or hide them;
Horses are made of chromium steel
And little fat men shall ride them.

I am the worm who never turned,
The eunuch without a harem;
Between the priest and the commissar
I walk like Eugene Aram;

And the commissar is telling my fortune
While the radio plays,

But the priest has promised an Austin Seven.
For Duggie always pays.

I dreamed I dwelt in marble halls,
And woke to find it true;
I wasn't born for an age like this;
Was Smith? Was Jones? Were you?

The Spanish war and other events in 1936–37 turned the scale and thereafter I knew where I stood. Every line of serious work that I have written since 1936 has been written, directly or indirectly, *against* totalitarianism and *for* democratic Socialism, as I understand it. It seems to me nonsense, in a period like our own, to think that one can avoid writing of such subjects. Everyone writes of them in one guise or another. It is simply a question of which side one takes and what approach one follows. And the more one is conscious of one's political bias, the more chance one has of acting politically without sacrificing one's aesthetic and intellectual integrity.

What I have most wanted to do throughout the past ten years is 11
to make political writing into an art. My starting point is always a feeling of partisanship, a sense of injustice. When I sit down to write a book, I do not say to myself, "I am going to produce a work of art." I write it because there is some lie that I want to expose, some fact to which I want to draw attention, and my initial concern is to get a hearing. But I could not do the work of writing a book, or even a long magazine article, if it were not also an aesthetic experience. Anyone who cares to examine my work will see that even when it is downright propaganda it contains much that a full-time politician would consider irrelevant. I am not able, and I do not want, completely to abandon the world-view that I acquired in childhood. So long as I remain alive and well I shall continue to feel strongly about prose style, to love the surface of the earth, and to take pleasure in solid objects and scraps of useless information. It is no use trying to suppress that side of myself. The job is to reconcile my ingrained likes and dislikes with the essentially public, non-individual activities that this age forces on all of us.

It is not easy. It raises problems of construction and language, 12
and it raises in a new way the problem of truthfulness. Let me give just one example of the cruder kind of difficulty that arises. My book about the Spanish civil war, *Homage to Catalonia*, is, of course, a frankly political book, but in the main it is written with a certain detachment and regard for form. I did try very hard in it to tell the whole truth without violating my literary instincts. But among other things it contains a long chapter, full of newspaper quotations and the like, defending the Trotskyists who were accused of plotting with

Franco. Clearly such a chapter, which after a year or two would lose its interest for any ordinary reader, must ruin the book. A critic whom I respect read me a lecture about it. "Why did you put in all that stuff?" he said. "You've turned what might have been a good book into journalism." What he said was true, but I could not have done otherwise. I happened to know, what very few people in England have been allowed to know, that innocent men were being falsely accused. If I had not been angry about that I should never have written the book.

In one form or another this problem comes up again. The prob- 13
lem of language is subtler and would take too long to discuss. I will only say that of late years I have tried to write less picturesquely and more exactly. In any case I find that by the time you have perfected any style of writing, you have always outgrown it. *Animal Farm* was the first book in which I tried, with full consciousness of what I was doing, to fuse political purpose and artistic purpose into one whole. I have not written a novel for seven years, but I hope to write another fairly soon. It is bound to be a failure, every book is a failure, but I know with some clarity what kind of book I want to write.

Looking back through the last page or two, I see that I have made 14
it appear as though my motives in writing were wholly public-spirited. I don't want to leave that as the final impression. All writers are vain, selfish and lazy, and at the very bottom of their motives there lies a mystery. Writing a book is a horrible, exhausting struggle, like a long bout of some painful illness. One would never undertake such a thing if one were not driven on by some demon whom one can neither resist nor understand. For all one knows that demon is simply the same instinct that makes a baby squall for attention. And yet it is also true that one can write nothing readable unless one constantly struggles to efface one's own personality. Good prose is like a window pane. I cannot say with certainty which of my motives are the strongest, but I know which of them deserve to be followed. And looking back through my work, I see that it is invariably where I lacked a *political* purpose that I wrote lifeless books and was betrayed into purple passages, sentences without meaning, decorative adjectives and humbug generally.

## IN RETROSPECT

**1.** In paragraphs 6–9 Orwell lists what he considers to be every author's "four motives for writing." As the headnote to this essay suggests, consider whether you are moved to write by any or all of the motives Orwell lists. Are there some motives for you that Orwell does not list? If you are never or only rarely moved to write, try to analyze *why* you are not motivated to write.

**2.** In the last paragraph of the essay, where Orwell is struggling to articulate his basic reason for writing, he says, "And yet it is also true that one can write nothing readable unless one constantly struggles to efface one's personality." But both Montaigne and Woolf in their essays in this chapter insist that writing an essay is an act of egoism, implying that they could not write if they did not *assert* their personality. What do you make of the seeming contradiction in these three essays?

# *Why I Write*

## JOAN DIDION

Joan Didion (1934–     ) is represented in chapter 2 of this book by the essay "On Going Home." At the beginning of the essay reproduced here, Didion confesses that she appropriated the title of her essay from the essay by George Orwell that is also reprinted here. Didion says that she stole Orwell's title because it seemed to her to sum up what writing is all about. The most significant word in the title "Why I Write" is, she says, the first-person pronoun *I*. In a sense, every specimen of a writer's production is an assertion of that writer's ego. And, of course, in the kind of essays featured in this anthology, the *I*, the ego, is especially prominent. Didion goes on to tell us why she had so much trouble graduating from the University of California at Berkeley as an English major; she then proceeds to tell us about the genesis of two of the novels she wrote. When she starts talking about the genesis of these novels, Didion seems to have shifted from a discussion of *why* she writes to a discussion of *how* she writes. Maybe the reason for this shift is revealed in the intriguing final sentence of the essay: "Let me tell you one thing about why writers write: had I known the answer to any of these questions I would never have needed to write a novel." See if you can figure out why Didion writes.

Of course I stole the title for this talk, from George Orwell. One 1
reason I stole it was that I like the sound of the words: Why I Write. There you have three short unambiguous words that share a sound; and the sound they share is this:

*I* 2

*I* 3

*I* 4

In many ways writing is the act of saying *I*, of imposing oneself 5
upon other people, of saying *listen to me, see it my way, change your mind*. It's an aggressive, even a hostile act. You can disguise its aggressiveness all you want with veils of subordinate clauses and qualifiers and tentative subjectives, with ellipses and evasions—with

the whole manner of intimating rather than claiming, of alluding rather than stating—but there's no getting around the fact that setting words on paper is the tactic of a secret bully, an invasion, an imposition of the writer's sensibility on the reader's most private space.

I stole the title not only because the words sounded right but 6
because they seemed to sum up, in a no-nonsense way, all I have to tell you. Like many writers I have only this one "subject," this one "area": the act of writing. I can bring you no reports from any other front. I may have other interests: I am "interested," for example, in marine biology, but I don't flatter myself that you would come out to hear me talk about it. I am not a scholar. I am not in the least an intellectual, which is not to say that when I hear the word "intellectual" I reach for my gun, but only to say that I do not think in abstracts. During the years when I was an undergraduate at Berkeley I tried, with a kind of hopeless late-adolescent energy, to buy some temporary visa into the world of ideas, to forge for myself a mind that could deal with the abstract.

In short I tried to think. I failed. My attention veered inexorably 7
back to the specific, to the tangible, to what was generally considered, by everyone I knew then and for that matter have known since, the peripheral. I would try to contemplate the Hegelian dialectic and would find myself concentrating instead on a flowering pear tree outside my window and the particular way the petals fell on my floor. I would try to read linguistic theory and would find myself wondering instead if the lights were on in the bevatron up the hill. When I say that I was wondering if the lights were on in the bevatron you might immediately suspect, if you deal in ideas at all, that I was registering the bevatron as a political symbol, thinking in shorthand about the military-industrial complex and its role in the university community, but you would be wrong. I was only wondering if the lights were on in the bevatron, and how they looked. A physical fact.

I had trouble graduating from Berkeley, not because of this inabil- 8
ity to deal with ideas—I was majoring in English, and I could locate the house-and-garden imagery in *The Portrait of a Lady* as well as the next person, "imagery" being by definition the kind of specific that got my attention—but simply because I had neglected to take a course in Milton. For reasons which now sound baroque I needed a degree by the end of that summer, and the English department finally agreed, if I would come down from Sacramento every Friday and talk about the cosmology of *Paradise Lost,* to certify me proficient in Milton. I did this. Some Fridays I took the Greyhound bus, other Fridays I caught the Southern Pacific's City of San Francisco on the last leg of its transcontinental trip. I can no longer tell you whether Milton put the sun or the earth at the center of his universe in *Paradise Lost,* the

central question of at least one century and a topic about which I wrote ten thousand words that summer, but I can still recall the exact rancidity of the butter in the City of San Francisco's dining car, and the way the tinted windows on the Greyhound bus cast the oil refineries around Carquinez Straits into a grayed and obscurely sinister light. In short my attention was always on the periphery, on what I could see and taste and touch, on the butter, and the Greyhound bus. During those years I was traveling on what I knew to be a very shaky passport, forged papers: I knew that I was no legitimate resident in any world of ideas. I knew I couldn't think. All I knew then was what I couldn't do. All I knew then was what I wasn't, and it took me some years to discover what I was.

Which was a writer. 9

By which I mean not a "good" writer or a "bad" writer but simply 10
a writer, a person whose most absorbed and passionate hours are spent arranging words on pieces of paper. Had my credentials been in order I would never have become a writer. Had I been blessed with even limited access to my own mind there would have been no reason to write. I write entirely to find out what I'm thinking, what I'm looking at, what I see and what it means. What I want and what I fear. Why did the oil refineries around Carquinez Straits seem sinister to me in the summer of 1956? Why have the night lights in the bevatron burned in my mind for twenty years? *What is going on in these pictures in my mind?*

When I talk about pictures in my mind I am talking, quite specifi- 11
cally, about images that shimmer around the edges. There used to be an illustration in every elementary psychology book showing a cat drawn by a patient in varying stages of schizophrenia. This cat had a shimmer around it. You could see the molecular structure breaking down at the very edges of the cat: the cat became the background and the background the cat, everything interacting, exchanging ions. People on hallucinogens describe the same perception of objects. I'm not a schizophrenic, nor do I take hallucinogens, but certain images do shimmer for me. Look hard enough, and you can't miss the shimmer. It's there. You can't think too much about these pictures that shimmer. You just lie low and let them develop. You stay quiet. You don't talk to many people and you keep your nervous system from shorting out and you try to locate the cat in the shimmer, the grammar is the picture.

Just as I meant "shimmer" literally I mean "grammar" literally. 12
Grammar is a piano I play by ear, since I seem to have been out of school the year the rules were mentioned. All I know about grammar is its infinite power. To shift the structure of a sentence alters the meaning of that sentence, as definitely and inflexibly as the position

of a camera alters the meaning of the object photographed. Many people know about camera angles now, but not so many know about sentences. The arrangement of the words matters, and the arrangement you want can be found in the picture in your mind. The picture dictates the arrangement. The picture dictates whether this will be a sentence with or without clauses, a sentence that ends hard or a dying-fall sentence, long or short, active or passive. The picture tells you how to arrange the words and the arrangement of the words tells you, or tells me, what's going on in the picture. *Nota bene:*

It tells you. 13

You don't tell it. 14

Let me show you what I mean by pictures in the mind. I began 15
*Play It As It Lays* just as I have begun each of my novels, with no notion of "character" or "plot" or even "incident." I had only two pictures in my mind, more about which later, and a technical intention, which was to write a novel so elliptical and fast that it would be over before you noticed it, a novel so fast that it would scarcely exist on the page at all. About the pictures: the first was of white space. Empty space. This was clearly the picture that dictated the narrative intention of the book—a book in which anything that happened would happen off the page, a "white" book to which the reader would have to bring his or her own bad dreams—and yet this picture told me no "story," suggested no situation. The second picture did. This second picture was of something actually witnessed. A young woman with long hair and a short white halter dress walks through the casino at the Riviera in Las Vegas at one in the morning. She crosses the casino alone and picks up a house telephone. I watch her because I have heard her paged, and recognize her name: she is a minor actress I see around Los Angeles from time to time, in places like Jax and once in a gynecologist's office in the Beverly Hills Clinic, but have never met. I know nothing about her. Who is paging her? Why is she here to be paged? How exactly did she come to this? It was precisely this moment in Las Vegas that made *Play It As It Lays* begin to tell itself to me, but the moment appears in the novel only obliquely, in a chapter which begins: "Maria made a list of things she would never do. She would never: walk through the Sands or Caesar's alone after midnight. She would never: ball at a party, do S-M unless she wanted to, borrow furs from Abe Lipsey, deal. She would never: carry a Yorkshire in Beverly Hills.

That is the beginning of the chapter and that is also the end of the 16
chapter, which may suggest what I meant by "white space."

I recall having a number of pictures in my mind when I began the 17
novel I just finished, *A Book of Common Prayer.* As a matter of fact one of these pictures was of that bevatron I mentioned, although I would

be hard put to tell you a story in which nuclear energy figures. Another was a newspaper photograph of a hijacked 707 burning on the desert in the Middle East. Another was the night view from a room in which I once spent a week with paratyphoid, a hotel room on the Colombian coast. My husband and I seemed to be on the Colombian coast representing the United States of America at a film festival (I recall invoking the name "Jack Valenti" a lot, as if its reiteration could make me well), and it was a bad place to have fever, not only because my indisposition offended our hosts but because every night in this hotel the generator failed. The lights went out. The elevator stopped. My husband would go to the event of the evening and make excuses for me and I would stay alone in this hotel room, in the dark. I remember standing at the window trying to call Bogotá (the telephone seemed to work on the same principle as the generator) and watching the night wind come up and wondering what I was doing eleven degrees off the equator with a fever of 103. The view from that window definitely figures in *A Book of Common Prayer,* as does the burning 707, and yet none of these pictures told me the story I needed.

The picture that did, the picture that shimmered and made these 18
other images coalesce, was the Panama airport at 6 A.M. I was in this airport only once, on a plane to Bogotá that stopped for an hour to refuel, but the way it looked that morning remained superimposed on everything I saw until the day I finished *A Book of Common Prayer.* I lived in that airport for several years. I can still feel the hot air when I step off the plane, can see the heat already rising off the tarmac at 6 A.M. I can feel my skirt damp and wrinkled on my legs. I can feel the asphalt stick to my sandals. I remember the big tail of a Pan American plane floating motionless down at the end of the tarmac. I remember the sound of a slot machine in the waiting room. I could tell you that I remember a particular woman in the airport, an American woman, a *norteamericana,* a thin *norteamericana* about forty who wore a big square emerald in lieu of a wedding ring, but there was no such woman there.

I put this woman in the airport later. I made this woman up, just 19
as I later made up a country to put the airport in, and a family to run the country. This woman in the airport is neither catching a plane nor meeting one. She is ordering tea in the airport coffee shop. In fact she is not simply "ordering" tea but insisting that the water be boiled, in front of her, for twenty minutes. Why is this woman in this airport? Why is she going nowhere, where has she been? Where did she get that big emerald? What derangement, or disassociation, makes her believe that her will to see the water boiled can possibly prevail?

> She had been going to one airport or another for four months, one could see it, looking at the visas on her passport. All those airports where Charlotte Douglas's passport had been stamped would have looked alike. Sometimes the sign on the tower would say "Bienvenidos" and sometimes the sign on the tower would say "Bienvenue," some places were wet and hot and others dry and hot, but at each of these airports the pastel concrete walls would rust and stain and the swamp off the runway would be littered with the fuselages of cannibalized Fairchild F-227's and the water would need boiling.
>
> I knew why Charlotte went to the airport even if Victor did not.
> I knew about airports.

These lines appear about halfway through *A Book of Common Prayer,* but I wrote them during the second week I worked on the book, long before I had any idea where Charlotte Douglas had been or why she went to airports. Until I wrote these lines I had no character called "Victor" in mind: the necessity for mentioning a name, and the name "Victor," occurred to me as I wrote the sentence: *I knew why Charlotte went to the airport* sounded incomplete. *I knew why Charlotte went to the airport even if Victor did not* carried a little more narrative drive. Most important of all, until I wrote these lines I did not know who "I" was, who was telling the story. I had intended until that moment that the "I" be no more than the voice of the author, a nineteenth-century omniscient narrator. But there it was: 20

> I knew why Charlotte went to the airport even if Victor did not.
> I knew about airports.

This "I" was the voice of no author in my house. This "I" was someone who not only knew why Charlotte went to the airport but also knew someone called "Victor." Who was Victor? Who was this narrator? Why was this narrator telling me this story? Let me tell you one thing about why writers write: had I known the answer to any of these questions I would never have needed to write a novel. 21

**IN RETROSPECT**

**1.** Both Orwell and Didion in these back-to-back essays tell us why they write. If you asked most students why they write, they probably would answer, "Because somebody makes me write." Even if you are coerced to write, how might Orwell's and Didion's accounts of why they write help you to write more voluntarily and also help you to make your writing worthy of being read by others?

**2.** In paragraph 6, Didion says that she cannot think abstractly, that her temperament compels her to think and write concretely. Thinking abstractly and thinking concretely are different ways of thinking, but are they mutually exclusive ways? When you read other essayists in this or other chapters of this book, do you tend to classify them as either abstract thinkers or concrete thinkers—one or the other? Reviewing Didion's account of how she became a writer, see if you can find places where she is alternating between writing abstractly and writing concretely. For instance, look at the final sentence of her essay. Is she speaking abstractly or concretely there?

## *What I Think, What I Am*

**EDWARD HOAGLAND**

Edward Hoagland (1932– ) is represented in chapter 4 of this collection by the essay "The Courage of Turtles." Hoagland started out his literary career by writing short stories and novels. Soon, however, he became intrigued by the essay form and by 1988 had published five collections of essays. In the essay reprinted here from one of those collections, *The Tugman's Passage* (1982), Hoagland contrasts the essay with short stories and novels. He retains his allegiance both to the essay and to the fictional forms but reserves a special place in his heart for the essay. He speaks of the essay as being the output of "mind speaking to mind," and in the last sentence of this essay he says, "Because essays are directly concerned with the mind and the mind's idiosyncrasy, the very freedom the mind possesses is bestowed on this branch of literature that does honor to it, and the fascination of the mind is the fascination of the essay." The notion of one mind speaking to another is a fresh and enlightened way to conceive of the essay as a literary form.

Our loneliness makes us avid column readers these days. The 1
personalities in the San Francisco *Chronicle,* Chicago *Daily News,* New York *Post* constitute our neighbors now, some of them local characters but also the opinionated national stars. And movie reviewers thrive on our yearning for somebody emotional who is willing to pay attention to us and return week after week, year after year, through all the to-and-fro of other friends, to flatter us by pouring out his/her heart. They are essayists of a type, as Elizabeth Hardwick is, James Baldwin was.

We sometimes hear that essays are an old-fashioned form, that 2
so-and-so is the "last essayist," but the facts of the marketplace argue quite otherwise. Essays of nearly any kind are so much easier than short stories for a writer to sell, so many more see print, it's strange that though two fine anthologies remain that publish the year's best stories, no comparable collection exists for essays. Such changes in the reading public's taste aren't always to the good, needless to say.

The art of telling stories predated even cave painting, surely; and if we ever find ourselves living in caves again, it (with painting and drumming) will be the only art left, after movies, novels, photography, essays, biography, and all the rest have gone down the drain—the art to build from.

3 One has the sense with the short story as a form that while everything may have been done, nothing has been overdone; it has a permanence. Essays, if a comparison is to be made, although they go back four hundred years to Montaigne, seem a mercurial, newfangled, sometimes hokey affair that has lent itself to many of the excesses of the age, from spurious autobiography to spurious hallucination, as well as to the shabby careerism of traditional journalism. It's a greased pig. Essays are associated with the way young writers fashion a name—on plain, crowded newsprint in hybrid vehicles like the *Village Voice, Rolling Stone,* the *New York Review of Books,* instead of the thick paper stock and thin readership of *Partisan Review.*

4 Essays, however, hang somewhere on a line between two sturdy poles: this is what I think, and this is what I am. Autobiographies which aren't novels are generally extended essays, indeed. A personal essay is like the human voice talking, its order of the mind's natural flow, instead of a systematized outline of ideas. Though more wayward or informal than an article or treatise, somewhere it contains a point which is its real center, even if the point couldn't be uttered in fewer words than the essayist has used. Essays don't usually boil down to a summary, as articles do, and the style of the writer has a "nap" to it, a combination of personality and originality and energetic loose ends that stand up like the nap on a piece of wool and can't be brushed flat. Essays belong to the animal kingdom, with a surface that generates sparks, like a coat of fur, compared with the flat, conventional cotton of the magazine article writer, who works in the vegetable kingdom, instead. But essays, on the other hand, may have fewer "levels" than fiction, because we are not supposed to argue much about their meaning. In the old distinction between teaching and storytelling, the essayist, however cleverly he camouflages his intentions, is a bit of a teacher or reformer, and an essay is intended to convey the same point to each of us.

5 This emphasis upon mind speaking to mind is what makes essays less universal in their appeal than stories. They are addressed to an educated, perhaps a middle-class, reader, with certain presuppositions, a frame of reference, even a commitment to civility that is shared—not the grand and golden empathy inherent in every man or woman that a storyteller has a chance to tap.

6 Nevertheless, the artful "I" of an essay can be as chameleon as any narrator in fiction; and essays do tell a story quite as often as a short story stakes a claim to a particular viewpoint. Mark Twain's

piece called "Corn-pone Opinions," for example, which is about public opinion, begins with a vignette as vivid as any in *Huckleberry Finn*. Twain says that when he was a boy of fifteen, he used to hang out a back window and listen to the sermons preached by a neighbor's slave standing on top of a woodpile:

> He imitated the pulpit style of the several clergymen of the village, and did it well and with fine passion and energy. To me he was a wonder. I believed he was the greatest orator in the United States and would some day be heard from. But it did not happen; in the distribution of rewards he was overlooked. . . . He interrupted his preaching now and then to saw a stick of wood, but the sawing was a pretense—he did it with his mouth, exactly imitating the sound the bucksaw makes in shrieking its way through the wood. But it served its purpose, it kept his master from coming out to see how the work was getting along.

A novel would go on and tell us what happened next in the life of 7
the slave—and we miss that. But the extraordinary flexibility of essays is what has enabled them to ride out rough weather and hybridize into forms that suit the times. And just as one of the first things a fiction writer learns is that he needn't actually be writing fiction to write a short story—that he can tell his own history or anybody else's as exactly as he remembers it and it will be "fiction" if it remains primarily a story—an essayist soon discovers that he doesn't have to tell the whole truth and nothing but the truth; he can shape or shave his memories, as long as the purpose is served of elucidating a truthful point. A personal essay frequently is not autobiographical at all, but what it does keep in common with autobiography is that, through its tone and tumbling progression, it conveys the quality of the author's mind. Nothing gets in the way. Because essays are directly concerned with the mind and the mind's idosyncrasy, the very freedom the mind possesses is bestowed on this branch of literature that does honor to it, and the fascination of the mind is the fascination of the essay.

## IN RETROSPECT

**1.** Hoagland comes closer than any other writers in this book (including the editors of this book) to giving us a sharp definition of an essay—especially the familiar or personal essay. The key to his success can be found in the first sentence of paragraph 4: "Essays, however, hang somewhere on a line between two sturdy poles: this is what I think, and this is what I am." Using this sentence as a focus, see if you can piece together from Hoagland's discussion those features which differentiate the personal or familiar essay from other forms of fictional and nonfictional prose. Having read this essay, consider whether any other essays in this book do not, according to Hoagland's definition, qualify as familiar or personal essays. If you identify such pieces, name them and show why they do not conform to Hoagland's definition, as you have pieced that definition together.

**2.** In paragraph 5, Hoagland says, "This emphasis upon mind speaking to mind is what makes essays less universal in their appeal than stories. They are addressed to an educated, perhaps a middle-class, reader, with certain presuppositions, a frame of reference, even a commitment to civility that is shared—not the grand and golden empathy inherent in every man and woman that a storyteller has a chance to tap." What essays in this book have most appealed to you, and what role have your presuppositions, frame of reference, and shared commitments to civility played in this meeting of the minds?

# BIBLIOGRAPHY

## *A. Bibliographies of the Essay*

Many of the books and articles in section B and a few of the collections in section C carry a short bibliography of the essay.


Bateson, F. W., ed. *The Cambridge Bibliography of English Literature.* 4 vols. Cambridge, England: Cambridge University Press, 1941. See "Character Books and Essays," 1:721–26; "Essayists and Pamphletteers [of the seventeenth and eighteenth centuries]," 2:567–656; "The Periodical Essay," 2:660–68; "Collections of Essays [of the nineteenth century]," 3:7–12; and "The Nineteenth-Century Essayists," 3:629–757.

Conway, Adaline May. "Bibliography." In *The Essay in American Literature,* 85–127. New York: Faculty of the Graduate School of New York University, 1914. The most complete bibliography of the American essay.

Crane, R. S., and F. B. Kaye. *A Census of British Newspapers and Periodicals, 1620–1800.* Chapel Hill: University of North Carolina Press, 1927.

Sears, Minnie Earl, and Marian Shaw, eds. *Essay and General Literature Index, 1900–1933.* New York: H. W. Wilson, 1934. "An Index to about 40,000 essays and articles in 2144 volumes of collections of essays and miscellaneous works." Subsequent volumes of this author and subject index are cumulated every two years.

Spiller, Robert E., et al. "Literary Journalism and the Essay." In *Literary History of the United States: Bibliography,* 164–66. New York: Macmillan, 1963.

Weed, K. K., and R. P. Bond. *Studies in British Newspapers and Periodicals from Their Beginning to 1800: A Bibliography.* Chapel Hill: University of North Carolina Press, 1946.


## *B. Books and Articles on the History and/or the Art of the Essay*


Abrams, M. H. "Essay." In *A Glossary of Literary Terms,* 55–56. New York: Holt, Rinehart, and Winston, 1981.

Adorno, Theodor. "The Essay as Form." Translated by Bob Hullott-Kentor. *New German Critique* 32 (1984):151–71.

Anderson, Charles M. *Richard Selzer and the Rhetoric of Surgery*. Carbondale: Southern Illinois University Press, 1989.

Anderson, Chris, ed. *Literary Nonfiction: Theory, Criticism, Pedagogy*. Carbondale: Southern Illinois University Press, 1989.

______. *Style as Argument: Contemporary American Nonfiction*. Carbondale: Southern Illinois University Press, 1987.

Atkins, G. Douglas. "The Return of/to the Essay." *ADE Bulletin*, no. 96 (Fall 1990):11–18.

______. *Estranging the Familiar: Towards a Revitalized Critical Essay*. Athens: University of Georgia Press, forthcoming.

Belloc, Hilaire. "An Essay upon Essays upon Essays." In *One Thing and Another*, 11–14. London: Hollis and Carter, 1955.

Benson, Arthur Christopher. "The Art of the Essayist." In *Modern English Essays* (5 vols.), edited by Ernest Rhys, 4:50–63. London: Dent, 1922.

Bloom, Lynn Z. "What We Talk about When We Talk about Literary Nonfiction." *College English* 53 (December 1991):944–48.

Buell, Lawrence. "From Conversation to Essay." In *Literary Transcendatalism: Style and Vision in the American Renaissance*, 77–102. Ithaca, N.Y.: Cornell University Press, 1973.

Butrym, Alexander, ed. *Essays on the Essay: Redefining the Genre*. Athens: University of Georgia Press, 1989.

Chadbourne, Richard. "A Puzzling Literary Genre: Comparative Views of the Essay." *Comparative Literature Studies* 20 (1983):133–53.

Chesterton, G. K. "On Essays." In *Come to Think of It*, 1–5. London: Methuen, 1930.

Clark, Glenn. *Personality in Essay Writing*. New York: R. Long and R. R. Smith, 1932.

Connors, Robert J. "Personal Writing Assignments." *College Composition and Communication* 38 (1987):166–83.

Conway, Adaline May. *The Essay in American Literature*. New York: Faculty of the Graduate School of New York University, 1914.

Dawson, William J., and Coningsby W. Dawson. *The Great English Essayists* New York: Harper and Brothers, 1908.

Epstein, Joseph. "Writing Essays." *New Criterion*, June 1984, 26–34.

______. "Piece Work: Writing the Essay." In *Plausible Prejudice: Essays on American Writing*, 397–411. New York: W. W. Norton, 1985.

"Essay." *Encyclopaedia Britannica* (1973), 8:713–14.

Fort, Keith. "Form, Authority, and the Critical Essay." *College English* 32 (1971):629–39.

Gass, William H. "Emerson and the Essay." In *Habitations of the Word*, 9–50. New York: Simon and Schuster, 1985.

Good, Graham. *The Observing Self: Rediscovering the Essay*. London: Routledge, 1988.

Haefner, Joel. "Democracy, Pedagogy, and the Personal Essay." *College English* 54 (1992):127–37.

Hazlitt, William. "On the Periodical Essayists." In *The Complete Works of William Hazlitt*, 6:91–105. London: Dent, 1931.

Heath, Shirley Brice. "Women in Conversation: Covert Models in American Language and Ideology." In *Language, Society, and Thought*, edited by Robert Cooper and Bernard Spolsky, 203–22. Berlin: Walter de Gruyter, 1990.

______. "The Essay in English: Readers and Writers in Dialogue." In *Dialogue and Critical Discourse,* edited by Michael Macovski. New York: Oxford University Press, 1992.

Hesse, Douglas. "The Recent Rise of Literary Nonfiction: A Cautionary Assay." *Journal of Advanced Composition* 11 (1991):323–33.

Johnson, Burges, *Essaying the Essay.* Boston: Little, Brown, 1927.

Kazin, Alfred. "The Essay as Modern Form." In *The Open Form: Essays for Our Times,* vii–xi. New York: Harcourt, Brace, 1961.

Klaus, Carl H. "Essayists on the Essay." In *Literary Nonfiction: Theory, Criticism, Pedagogy,* edited by Chris Anderson, 155–75. Carbondale: Southern Illinois University Press, 1989.

Krutch, Joseph Wood. "No Essays, Please." *Saturday Review of Literature,* March 1951, 18–19, 35.

Lopate, Phillip. "The Essay Lives—in Disguise." *New York Times Book Review,* November 18, 1984, 1, 47–49.

Lukacs, Georg. "On the Nature and Form of the Essay." In *Soul and Form,* 1–18. Translated by Anna Benstock. Cambridge, Mass.: MIT Press, 1971.

Marius, Richard. "On Academic Discourse." *ADE Bulletin,* no. 96 (Fall 1990):4–7.

Newkirk, Thomas. *Critical Thinking and Writing: Reclaiming the Essay.* Urbana: National Council of Teachers of English, 1989.

O'Leary, Raphael D. *The Essay.* New York: Thomas Y. Crowell, 1928.

Rucker, Mary K. "The Literary Essay and the Modern Temper." *Publications in Language and Literature* 11 (1975):317–35.

Rygiel, Dennis. "On the Neglect of Twentieth-Century Nonfiction: A Writing Teacher's View." *College English* 47 (1984):392–400.

Sanders, Scott Russell. "The Singular First Person." *Sewanee Review* 96 (1988):658–72.

Spellmeyer, Kurt. "A Common Ground: The Essay in the Academy." *College English* 51 (1989):262–76. See Susan Miller's comment on this article in *College English* 52 (1992):330–34.

Stephen, Leslie. "The Essayists." In *Men, Books, and Manners,* 45–73. Minneapolis: University of Minnesota Press, 1956.

Thomas, Lewis. "Essays and Gaia." In *The Youngest Science,* 239–48. New York: Viking, 1983.

Tilley, A. A. "The Essay and the Beginning of Modern English Prose." In *Cambridge History of English Literature* (15 vols.), 6:4211–46. Cambridge, England: Cambridge University Press, 1912.

Torgovnick, Mariana. "Experimental Critical Writing." *ADE Bulletin,* no. 96 (Fall 1990):8–10.

Walker, Hugh. *The English Essay and the Essayists.* London: Dent, 1915. The fullest and most appreciative of the studies of British essayists.

Weber, Ronald. *The Literature of Fact: Literary Nonfiction in American Writing.* Athens: Ohio University Press, 1980.

Whitmore, Charles. "The Field of the Essay." *Publications of the Modern Language Association* 36 (1921):551–64. An attempt to classify the various kinds of essays.

Winchester, Otis, and Winston Weathers. *The Prevalent Forms of Prose.* Boston: Houghton Mifflin, 1968.

Winterowd, W. Ross. *The Rhetoric of the "Other" Literature.* Carbondale: Southern Illinois University Press, 1990.

———. "Rediscovering the Essay." *Journal of Advanced Composition* 8 (1988): 146–57.

Withington, Robert. "Essay." *Encyclopedia Americana* (1971), 10:508–11.

Wolfe, Thomas. "The New Journalism." In *The New Journalism,* edited by Thomas Wolfe and E. W. Johnson, 3–52. New York: Harper, 1973.

Zeiger, William. "The Exploratory Essay: Enfranchising the Spirit of Inquiry in College Composition." *College English* 47 (1985):454–66.

______. "The Circular Journey and the Natural Authority of Form." *Rhetoric Review* 8 (1990):208–19.

## C. General Collections of Essays

Collections of essays by a particular author are mentioned in headnotes and in source notes but are not listed here.

Alden, Raymond MacDonald, ed. *Essays English and American.* Glenview, Ill.: Scott, Foresman, 1920.

Allen, H. C., and C. P. Hill, eds. *British Essays in American History.* London: Edward Arnold, 1957.

Atwan, Robert, ed. *Ten on Ten: Major Essayists on Recurring Themes.* New York: Bedford Books, 1992.

Baudin, Maurice, Jr., and Karl G. Pfeiffer, eds. *Essays for Study.* New York: McGraw-Hill, 1960.

*The Best American Essays 1986.* Edited by Elizabeth Hardwick. New York: Ticknor and Fields, 1986. Robert Atwan is the general editor of this series. The editor of each book in the series provides an introduction to that volume.

*The Best American Essays 1987.* Edited by Gay Talese. New York: Ticknor and Fields, 1987.

*The Best American Essays 1988.* Edited by Annie Dillard. New York: Ticknor and Fields, 1988.

*The Best American Essays 1989.* Edited by Geoffrey Wolff. New York: Ticknor and Fields, 1989.

*The Best American Essays 1990.* Edited by Justin Kaplan. New York: Ticknor and Fields, 1990.

*The Best American Essays 1991.* Edited by Joyce Carol Oates. New York: Ticknor and Fields, 1991.

Brewer, David J., Edward A. Allen, and William Schuyler, eds. *The World's Best Essays.* 10 vols. St. Louis: F. P. Kaiser, 1899.

Bryan, William F., and R. S. Crane, eds. *The English Familiar Essay.* Boston: Ginn, 1916.

Carver, George, ed. *Periodical Essays of the Eighteenth Century.* Garden City, N.Y.: Doubleday, 1930.

Chalmers, Alexander, ed. *The British Essayists, with Prefaces Historical and Biographical.* 45 vols. London: Longman and Rees, 1802–1803.

Collins, V. H., ed. *Three Centuries of English Essays: From Francis Bacon to Max Beerbohm.* Freeport, N.Y.: Books for Libraries Press, 1931.

Daiches, David, ed. *A Century of the Essay, British and American.* New York: Harcourt Brace Jovanovich, 1951.

Drake, Nathan, ed. *Essays, Biographical, Critical, and Historical, Illustrative of the "Tatler," "Spectator," and "Guardian."* 3 vols. London: J. Sharpe, 1805.

Fakundiny, Lydia, ed. *The Art of the Essay.* Boston: Houghton Mifflin, 1991.

Ferguson, James, ed. *The British Essayists, to Which Are Prefixed Prefaces, Biographical, Historical and Critical.* 40 vols. London: Thomas Tegg, 1819.

Fiedler, Leslie, ed. *The Art of the Essay.* 2d ed. New York: Thomas Y. Crowell, 1969.

Gross, John. *The Oxford Book of Essays.* New York: Oxford University Press, 1991.

Hall, Donald, ed. *The Contemporary Essay.* 2d ed. New York: St. Martin's Press, 1989.

Howard, Maureen, ed. *The Penguin Book of Contemporary American Essays.* New York: Viking Penguin, 1984.

Humphreys, A. R., ed. *Steele, Addison, and Their Periodical Essays.* London: Longmans, Green and Company for the British Council, 1959.

Hunt, Douglas, ed. *The Dolphin Reader.* Boston: Houghton Mifflin, 1986.

Leary, Lewis, ed. *American Literary Essays.* New York: Thomas Y. Crowell, 1960.

Lynam, Robert, ed. *The British Essayists, with Prefaces Biographical, Historical, and Critical.* 40 vols. London: J. F. Dover, 1927.

Marr, George S., ed. *The Periodical Essayists of the Eighteenth Century.* London: J. Clarke, 1923.

Miles, Josephine, ed. *Classic Essays in English.* 2d ed. Boston: Little, Brown, 1965.

*The Modern British Essayists.* 8 vols. Philadelphia: Carey and Hart, 1848–1850.

Pritchard, Francis Henry, ed. *The World's Best Essays from Confucius to Mencken.* New York: Albert and Charles Boni, 1932.

Rhys, Ernest, ed. *Modern English Essays.* 5 vols. London: Dent, 1922.

———, and Lloyd Vaughan, eds. *A Century of English Essays.* London: Dent, 1913.

Robertson, Stuart, ed. *Familiar Essays.* Englewood Cliffs, N.J.: Prentice Hall, 1930.

Segar, M. G., ed. *Essays from Eighteenth-Century Periodicals.* London: Methuen, 1947. Contains essays from fifteen periodicals covering the period from 1709 to 1787.

Shugrue, Michael F., ed. *The Essay.* New York: Macmillan, 1981.

Silberstein, Suzanne, and Marian Seldin, eds. *Sense and Style: The Craft of the Essay.* New York: Random House, 1962.

Smithberger, Andrew T., ed. *Essays, British and American.* Boston: Houghton Mifflin, 1953.

Starkweather, Chauncey C., ed. *Essays of British Essayists.* Rev. ed. 2 vols. New York: Colonial Press, 1900.

Taylor, Warner, ed. *Times and Types in the Essay.* New York: Harper and Row, 1932.

Tinker, Harold L., ed. *Essays—Yesterday and Today.* New York: Macmillan, 1934.

Walter, Erich A., ed. *Essay Annual: A Yearly Collection of Significant Essays, Personal, Critical, Controversial, and Humorous.* 8 vols. Glenview, Ill.: Scott, Foresman, 1933–1941.

Wann, Louis, ed. *Century Readings in the English Essay.* New York: Century, 1926.

Warnock, John, ed. *Representing Reality: Readings in Literary Nonfiction.* New York: St. Martin's Press, 1989.

Winchester, C. T., ed. *A Group of English Essayists of the Early Nineteenth Century.* New York: Macmillan, 1910.

## *D. Collections of Essays from a Particular Periodical*

Bogorad, Samuel N., and Cary B. Graham, eds. *Atlantic Essays.* Lexington, Mass.: D. C. Heath, 1958.

Christman, Henry M., ed. *One Hundred Years of "The Nation": A Centennial Anthology, 1865–1965.* New York: Macmillan, 1965.

Connolly, Cyril, ed. *The Golden Horizon.* London: Weidenfeld and Nicolson, 1953.

Haydn, Hiram, and Betsy Saunders, eds. *The American Scholar Reader.* New York: Atheneum, 1960.

Knowles, Horace, ed. *Gentlemen, Scholars, and Scoundrels: A Treasury of the Best of Harper's Magazines.* New York: Harper and Row, 1959.

Lasky, Melvin J., ed. *Encounters: An Anthology from the First Ten Years of "Encounter" Magazine.* New York: Basic Books, 1963.

Leavis, F. R., ed. *A Selection from Scrutiny.* 2 vols. Cambridge, England: Cambridge University Press, 1968.

Luce, Robert B., ed. *The Faces of Five Decades: Selections from Fifty Years of the "New Republic," 1914–1964.* New York: Simon and Schuster, 1964.

Phillips, William, and Philip Rahv, eds. *The New Partisan Reader, 1945–1953.* New York: Harcourt Brace Jovanovich, 1953.

Podhoretz, Norman, ed. *The Commentary Reader.* New York: Atheneum, 1966.

Tanner, William Maddux, ed. *Essays and Essay-Writing Based on "Atlantic Monthly" Models.* Boston: Atlantic Monthly, 1917. A collection of familiar essays published anonymously in the "Contributors Club" section of the *Atlantic.*

Weeks, Edward, and Emily Flint, eds. *Jubilee: One Hundred Years of the "Atlantic."* Boston: Little, Brown, 1957.

# ACKNOWLEDGMENTS


Sherwood Anderson, "Discovery of a Father" from *The Memoirs of Sherwood Anderson.* Reprinted by permission of Harold Ober Associates Incorporated. Copyright 1939 by *The Reader's Digest.* Copyright renewed 1966 by Eleanor Copenhauer Anderson.

Hannah Arendt, "Power and Violence." Excerpts from "On Violence," © Copyright 1970 by Hannah Arendt, reprinted by permission of Harcourt Brace Jovanovich, Inc.

Russell Baker, "Little Red Riding Hood Revisited." Copyright © 1980 by The New York Times Company. Reprinted by permission.

Wendell Berry, "The Tyranny of Charity" from the September 27, 1965, issue of *The Nation.* This article is reprinted by permission of *The Nation* magazine/The Nation Company, Inc., © 1965.

Judy Brady, "I Want a Wife" from the December, 1971 issue of *MS.* magazine. Copyright 1970 by Judy Brady. Reprinted by permission of the author.

Brigid Brophy, "Women" from *Don't Never Forget: Collected Views and Reviews* (New York: Holt, Rinehart, and Winston), by Brigid Brophy. Copyright © 1966, 1967. Originally appeared in the *Saturday Evening Post.*

William F. Buckley, Jr. "Why Don't We Complain" from *Rumbles Left and Right* by William F. Buckley, Jr. Copyright © 1963 by William F. Buckley, Jr. Reprinted by permission of the Wallace Agency and William F. Buckley, Jr.

Elias Canetti, "The Tattletale" from *Earwitness: Fifty Characters* by Elias Canetti. English translation from *Der Ohrenzeuge: 50 Characktere* by Neugroschel. The Continuum Publishing Company, 1979. Reprinted by permission of The Continuum Publishing Company.

Joan Didion, "On Going Home" from *Slouching Towards Bethlehem* by Joan Didion. Copyright © 1966, 1967, 1968 by Joan Didion. Reprinted by permission of Farrar, Straus and Giroux, Inc.

Joan Didion, "Why I Write," Reprinted by permission of the Wallace Literary Agency, Inc. Copyright © 1976 by Joan Didion. First appeared in *The New York Times Book Review,* December 5, 1976.

Annie Dillard, "A Field of Silence" from *The Atlantic Monthly* magazine, February, 1978. Reprinted by permission of the author and her agent, Blanche C. Gregory, Inc. Copyright © 1978 by Annie Dillard.

Gerald Early, "Baseball: The Ineffable National Pastime" from "House of Ruth, House of Robinson: Some Observations on Baseball, Biography, and the American Myth" by Gerald Early. Copyright © 1990 by Gerald Early. Published in *Openings: Original Essays by Contemporary Soviet and American Writers,* edited by Robert Atwan and Valerie Valerivinokurov (Seattle, WA: University of Washington Press). Reprinted by permission of the author.

Gretel Ehrlich, "The Smooth Skull of Winter," from *The Solace of Open Spaces* by Gretel Ehrlich. Copyright © 1985 by Gretel Ehrlich. Used by permission of Viking Penquin, a division of Penquin Books USA Inc.

Doris Kearns Goodwin, "Fathers, Daughters, and the Magic of Baseball" from *Diamonds Are Forever: Artists and Writers on Baseball* by Doris Kearns Goodwin. Reprinted by permission of the author.

Stephen Jay Gould, "The Creation Myths of Cooperstown" is reprinted from *Bully for Brontosaurus: Reflections in Natural History,* by Stephen Jay Gould, by permission of the author and W. W. Norton & Company, Inc. Copyright © 1991 by Stephen Jay Gould.

Emily Hahn, "Clever Hans," excerpted from *Look Who's Talking* by Emily Hahn. Originally appeared as "Getting Through to Others" in *The New Yorker,* 1978. Copyright © 1978 by Emily Hahn. Reprinted by permission of Harper & Row, Publishers, Inc.

Edward Hoagland, "The Courage of Turtles" from *The Courage of Turtles* by Edward Hoagland. Copyright © 1970 by Edward Hoagland. Reprinted by permission of Random House, Inc.

Edward Hoagland, "What I Think, What I Am" from *The Tugman's Passage* by Edward Hoagland. Copyright © 1976, 1977, 1978, 1979, 1980, 1982 by Edward Hoagland. Reprinted by permission of Random House, Inc.

Langston Hughes, "That Word *Black*" from *Simple Takes a Wife.* Reprinted by permission of Harold Ober Associates Incorporated. Copyright 1953 by Langston Hughes. Copyright renewed 1982 by George Houston Bass.

Alfred Kazin, "The Block" from "The Block" (originally entitled "The Block and Beyond" in *A Walker in the City* by Alfred Kazin). Copyright © 1951, 1979 by Alfred Kazin. Reprinted by permission of Harcourt Brace Jovanovich, Inc.

Maxine Hong Kingston, "The Silence of a Chinese-American Schoolgirl" from *The Woman Warrior: Memoirs of a Childhood Among Ghosts.* Copyright © 1975, 1976 by Maxine Hong Kingston. Reprinted by permission of Alfred A. Knopf, Inc.

H. L. Mencken, "The Politician" from *A Mencken Chrestomathy* by H. L. Mencken. Copyright © 1949 by Alfred A. Knopf, Inc. Reprinted by permission of Alfred A. Knopf, Inc.

N. Scott Momaday, "The Way to Rainy Mountain." First published in *The Reporter,* 26 January 1967. Reprinted from *The Way to Rainy Mountain,* © 1969 by The University of New Mexico Press.

Michel de Montaigne, "Of Practice" and "Of Giving the Lie." Reprinted from *The Complete Works of Montaigne,* translated by Donald M. Frame, with the permission of the publishers, Stanford University Press. Copyright 1943 by Donald M. Frame, © 1948, 1957 by the Board of Trustees of the Leland Stanford Junior University.

George Orwell, "Politics and the English Language," copyright 1946 by Sonia Brownell Orwell and renewed 1974 by Sonia Orwell, reprinted from his volume *Shooting an Elephant and Other Essays* by permission of Harcourt Brace Jovanovich, Inc.

George Orwell, "Why I Write" from *Such, Such Were the Joys* by George Orwell, copyright 1953 by Sonia Brownell Orwell and renewed 1981 by Mrs. George Perutz, Mrs. Miriam Gross, Dr. Michael Dickson, Executors of the Estate of Sonia Brownell Orwell, reprinted by permission of Harcourt Brace Jovanovich, Inc., and the estate of the late Sonia Brownell Orwell and Martin Secker and Warburg Ltd.

Dorothy Parker, "Good Souls," copyright 1944 by Dorothy Parker, copyright © renewed 1972 by Lillian Hellman, from *The Portable Dorothy Parker* by Dorothy Parker, Introduction by Brendan Gill. Used by permission of Viking Penguin, a division of Penguin Books USA Inc.

Katherine Anne Porter, "The Necessary Enemy" from *The Collected Essays and Occasional Writings of Katherine Anne Porter.* Copyright © 1970 by Katherine Anne Porter. Reprinted by permission of Houghton Mifflin/Seymour Lawrence. All rights reserved.

Adrienne Rich, "On Taking Women Students Seriously" is reprinted from *On Lies, Secrets, and Silence: Selected Prose 1966–1978,* by Adrienne Rich, by permission of W. W. Norton & Company, Inc. Copyright © 1979 by W. W. Norton & Company, Inc.

Richard Rodriguez, "The Achievement of Desire." Copyright © 1981 by Richard Rodriguez. Reprinted by permission of Georges Borchardt, Inc. for the author.

Scott Russell Sanders, "The Men We Carry in Our Minds." Copyright © 1984 by Scott Russell Sanders; first appeared in *Milkweed Chronicle;* reprinted by permission of the author and the author's agent, Virginia Kidd.

Richard Selzer, "The Knife" from *Mortal Lessons.* Copyright © 1974, 1975, 1976 by Richard Selzer. Reprinted by permission of Simon & Schuster, Inc.

Wilfred Sheed, "Confessions of a Sports Nut" from *The Morning After: Selected Essays and Reviews.* Copyright © 1971. Reprinted by permission of Farrar, Straus and Giroux, Inc.

Shelby Steele, "On Being Black and Middle Class" from "On Being Black and Middle Class" by Shelby Steele. First published in *Commentary.* Copyright © 1988 by Shelby Steele. Reprinted by permission of the author.

Paul Theroux, "Subterranean Gothic" from "Subterranean Gothic" in *Sunrise with Seamonsters* by Paul Theroux. Copyright © 1985 by Cape Cod Scriveners. Reprinted by permission of Houghton Mifflin Co. All rights reserved.

Lewis Thomas, "The Long Habit," copyright © 1972 by the Massachusetts Medical Society, from *The Lives of a Cell* by Lewis Thomas. Used by permission of Viking Penquin, a division of Penguin Books USA Inc.

Dorothy Thompson, "Concerning Tolerance" from *The Courage to Be Happy* by Dorothy Thompson. Copyright © 1957. This essay and others in this collection originally appeared in monthly editions of *The Ladies Home Companion.*

James Thurber, "University Days." Copyright © 1933, 1961 James Thurber. From *My Life and Hard Times,* published by Harper and Row. Reprinted by permission of Rosemary A. Thurber.

John Updike, "Hub Fans Bid Kid Adieu" from *Assorted Prose* by John Updike. Copyright © 1960 by John Updike. This essay originally appeared in *The New Yorker.* Reprinted by permission of Alfred A. Knopf, Inc.

Alice Walker, "Brothers and Sisters" from *In Search of Our Mother's Gardens,* copyright © 1975 by Alice Walker, reprinted by permission of Harcourt Brace Jovanovich, Inc.

Eudora Welty, "The Little Store" from *The Eye of the Story* by Eudora Welty. Copyright © 1975 by Eudora Welty. Reprinted by permission of Random House, Inc.

E. B. White, "Once More to the Lake" from *Essays of E. B. White.* Copyright © 1941 by E. B. White. Reprinted by permission of HarperCollins Publishers.

E. B. White, "The Essayist and the Essay" from *The Essays of E. B. White.* Copyright © 1977 by E. B. White. Reprinted by permission of HarperCollins Publishers.

George F. Will, "The Hard Blue Glow." Reprinted with the permission of Macmillan Publishing Company from *Men at Work: The Craft of Baseball* by George F. Will. Copyright © 1989 by George F. Will.

Virginia Woolf, "The Death of the Moth" from *The Death of the Moth and Other Essays* by Virginia Woolf, copyright 1942 by Harcourt Brace Jovanovich, Inc. and renewed 1970 by Marjorie T. Parsons, Executrix. Reprinted by permission of the publisher, the Estate of Virginia Woolf, and The Hogarth Press.

Virginia Woolf, "The Modern Essay" from *The Common Reader* by Virginia Woolf, copyright 1925 by Harcourt Brace Jovanovich, Inc. and renewed 1953 by Leonard Woolf. Reprinted by permission of the publisher, the Estate of Virginia Woolf, and The Hogarth Press.

# Index of Authors and Titles


"Achievement of Desire, The," 171
Addison, Joseph, "Dissection of a Beau's Head, The," 350
Anderson, Sherwood, "Discovery of a Father," 48
Arendt, Hannah, "Power and Violence," 315

Bacon, Francis, "Of Studies," 146
Baker, Russell, "Little Red Riding Hood Revisited," 289
"Baseball: The Ineffable National Pastime," 241
Berry, Wendell, "Tyranny of Charity, The," 308
"Block, The," 131
Brady, Judy, "I Want a Wife," 359
Brophy, Brigid, "Women," 361
"Brothers and Sisters," 62
Buckley, William F. Jr., "Why Don't We Complain?" 341

Canetti, Elias, "Tattletale, The," 85
Chesterton, G. K., "Tommy and the Traditions," 305
"Clever Hans," 109
"Concerning Tolerance," 338
"Confessions of a Sports Nut," 229
"Corn-pone Opinions," 333
"Courage of Turtles, The," 99
Cowley, Abraham, "Of Myself," 2
"Creation Myths of Cooperstown, The," 218

"Day Language Came into My Life, The," 279
"Death of the Moth, The," 197
"Definition of a Gentleman, A," 72
Defoe, Daniel, "Undesirable Husbands," 348
Dickens, Charles, "Night Walks," 116
Didion, Joan, "On Going Home," 54; "Why I Write," 398
Dillard, Annie, "Field of Silence, A," 127
"Discovery of a Father," 48
"Dissection of a Beau's Head, The," 350
Douglass, Frederick, "Learning to Read and Write," 152
Du Bois, W. E. B., "Of the Passing of the First-Born," 43

Early, Gerald, "Baseball: The Ineffable National Pastime," 241
Ehrlich, Gretel, "Smooth Skull of Winter, The," 135
"Essayist and the Essay, The," 389

"Fathers, Daughters, and the Magic of Baseball," 238
"Field of Silence, A," 127
Franklin, Benjamin, "On Education," 148

Goldsmith, Oliver, "Of Eloquence, 260
"Good Souls," 79
Goodwin, Doris Kearns, "Fathers, Daughters, and the Magic of Baseball," 238
Gould, Stephen Jay, "Creation Myths of Cooperstown, The," 218

Hahn, Emily, "Clever Hans," 109
"Hard Blue Glow, The," 248
Hazlitt, William, "On the Feeling of Immortality in Youth," 190
"History of an Adventurer in Lotteries, The," 68
Hoagland, Edward, "Courage of Turtles, The," 99; "What I Think, What I Am," 404
"How It Feels to Be Colored Me," 14
"Hub Fans Bid Kid Adieu," 254
Hughes, Langston, "That Word *Black*," 282
Hurston, Zora Neale, "How It Feels to Be Colored Me," 14

"I Want a Wife," 359

Johnson, Samuel, "History of an Adventurer in Lotteries, The," 68

Kazin, Alfred, "Block, The," 131
Keller, Helen, "Day Language Came into My Life, The," 279
Kingston, Maxine Hong, "Silence of a Chinese-American Schoolgirl, The," 284
"Kitten, A," 211
"Knife, The," 211

"Learning to Read and Write," 152
"Little Red Riding Hood Revisited," 289
"Little Store, The," 18
London, Jack, "What Life Means to Me," 6
"Long Habit, The," 206
Lopez, Barry, "Wolf Notes," 106

"Men We Carry in Our Minds, The," 368
Mencken, H. L., "Politician, The," 75
Mill, John Stuart, "On the Liberty of Thought and Discussion," 326
"Modern Essay, The," 380
"Modest Proposal, A," 294
Momaday, N. Scott, "Way to Rainy Mountain, The," 57
Montaigne, Michel de, "Of Giving the Lie," 376; "Of Practice," 180

"Necessary Enemy, The," 354
Newman, John Henry, "Definition of a Gentleman, A," 72
"Night Walks," 116

"Of Eloquence," 260
"Of Giving the Lie," 376
"Of Myself," 2
"Of Practice," 180
"Of Studies," 146
"Of the Passing of the First-Born," 43
"On Being Black and Middle Class," 26
"On Education," 148
"On Going Home," 54
"On the English House-Martin," 88
"On the Feeling of Immortality in Youth," 190
"On the Liberty of Thought and Discussion," 326
"On Two Children in Black," 40

"Once More to the Lake," 200
Orwell, George, "Politics and the English Language," 267; "Why I Write," 391

Parker, Dorothy, "Good Souls," 79
"Plea to Women to Change Their Image, A," 302
"Politician, The," 75
"Politics and the English Language," 267
"Ponds, The," 124
Porter, Katherine Anne, "Necessary Enemy, The," 354
"Power and Violence," 315

Repplier, Agnes, "Kitten, A," 92
Rich, Adrienne, "Taking Women Students Seriously," 163
Rodriguez, Richard, "Achievement of Desire, The," 171

Sanders, Scott Russell, "Men We Carry in Our Minds, The," 368
Selzer, Richard, "Knife, The," 211
Sheed, Wilfred, "Confessions of a Sports Nut," 229
"Silence of a Chinese-American Schoolgirl, The," 284
"Smooth Skull of Winter, The," 135
Steele, Shelby, "On Being Black and Middle Class," 26
"Subterranean Gothic," 138
Swift, Jonathan, "Modest Proposal, A," 294

"Taking Women Students Seriously," 163
"Tattletale, The," 85
Thackeray, William Makepeace, "On Two Children in Black," 40
"That Word *Black*," 282
Theroux, Paul, "Subterranean Gothic," 138
Thomas, Lewis, "Long Habit, The," 206
Thompson, Dorothy, "Concerning Tolerance," 338
Thoreau, Henry David, "Ponds, The," 124
Thurber, James, "University Days," 157
"Tommy and the Traditions," 305
Twain, Mark, "Corn-pone Opinions," 333
"Tyranny of Charity, The," 308

"Undesirable Husbands," 348
"University Days," 157
Updike, John, "Hub Fans Bid Kid Adieu," 254

Walker, Alice, "Brothers and Sisters," 62
"Way to Rainy Mountain, The," 57
Welty, Eudora, "Little Store, The," 18
"What I Think, What I Am," 404
"What Life Means to Me," 6
White, E. B., "Essayist and the Essay, The," 389; "Once More to the Lake," 200
White, Gilbert, "On the English House-Martin," 88
"Why Don't We Complain?" 341
"Why I Write," 391
"Why I Write," 398
Will, George F., "Hard Blue Glow, The," 248
"Wolf Notes," 106
Wollstonecraft, Mary, "Plea to Women to Change Their Image, A," 302
"Women," 361
Woolf, Virginia, "Modern Essay, The," 380; "Death of the Moth, The," 197